HIDDEN FROM HISTORY

◆

RECLAIMING THE GAY AND LESBIAN PAST

HIDDEN FROM
HISTORY

◆

RECLAIMING THE
GAY AND
LESBIAN PAST

EDITED BY
Martin Bauml Duberman
Martha Vicinus
and George Chauncey, Jr.

NAL BOOKS

NEW AMERICAN LIBRARY

A DIVISION OF PENGUIN BOOKS USA INC., NEW YORK

PUBLISHED IN CANADA BY
PENGUIN BOOKS CANADA LIMITED, MARKHAM, ONTARIO

Acknowledgments

"Lesbian Sexuality in Medieval and Early Modern Europe" by Judith C. Brown. Reprinted from *Immodest Acts: The Life of a Lesbian Nun in Renaissance Italy,* copyright © 1985 by Judith C. Brown. Reprinted by permission of Oxford University Press.

"Lesbians in American Indian Cultures" by Paula Gunn Allen. Reprinted from *The Sacred Hoop,* copyright © 1986 by Paula Gunn Allen. Reprinted by permission of Beacon Press.

"Inverts, Perverts, and Mary-Annes: Male Prostitution and the Regulation of Homosexuality in England in the Nineteenth and Early Twentieth Centuries" by Jeffrey Weeks. Reprinted from *Historical Perspectives on Homosexuality,* eds. Salvatore J. Licata and Robert P. Peterson, copyright © 1981 by Jeffrey Weeks. Reprinted by permission of The Haworth Press, Inc.

"Discourses of Sexuality and Subjectivity: The New Woman 1870–1936" by Carroll Smith-Rosenberg. Reprinted from *Disorderly Conduct: Visions of Gender in Victorian America,* copyright © 1985 by Carroll Smith-Rosenberg. Reprinted by permission of Alfred A. Knopf, Inc.

NAL TRADEMARK REG. U.S. PAT. OFF. AND FOREIGN COUNTRIES
REGISTERED TRADEMARK—MARCA REGISTRADA
HECHO EN DRESDEN, TN, U.S.A.

SIGNET, SIGNET CLASSIC, MENTOR, ONYX, PLUME, MERIDIAN and NAL BOOKS are published *in the United States* by New American Library, a division of Penguin Books USA Inc., 1633 Broadway, New York, New York 10019, *in Canada* by Penguin Books Canada Limited, 2801 John Street, Markham, Ontario L3R 1B4

Designed by Leonard Telesca

Library of Congress Cataloging-in-Publication Data

Hidden from history : reclaiming the gay and lesbian past / edited by
    Martin Bauml Duberman, Martha Vicinus, and George Chauncey, Jr.
        p.   cm.
    Includes bibliographies.

    1. Homosexuality—History. 2. Gays—History. I. Duberman,
Martin B. II. Vicinus, Martha. III. Chauncey, George.
HQ76.25.H527   1989
306.76′6′09—dc20   89-9417
                                                            CIP

To all those we have lost to AIDS,
and to all those struggling against it

EDITORS' NOTE

This book has been four years in the making, and during that time the editors have shared on an equal basis both the creative responsibilities and the more mundane tasks associated with its preparation: We jointly authored the introduction and selected the essays, and each of us took primary responsibility for editing a third of them.

Contents

ix

x   CONTENTS

The Nineteenth Century

Early Twentieth Century

INTRODUCTION

◆

GEORGE CHAUNCEY, JR., MARTIN BAUML DUBERMAN, AND MARTHA VICINUS

For a century, research on the history of homosexuality has been constrained by the intolerance of governments and academics alike. John Addington Symonds, the nineteenth-century British classicist and arguably the first modern historian of homosexuality, in 1883 dared print only ten copies of his study of Greek homosexuality, *A Problem in Greek Ethics*. In 1897, four years after his death, his executor bought out the first edition of Havelock Ellis's *Sexual Inversion* because Symonds' essay had been appended, and forbade any reference to Symonds in the second edition (which the British government, in any case, promptly suppressed). In Berlin, Magnus Hirschfeld and other German homosexual intellectuals founded the Institute for Sex Research in 1919, only to see its research collection destroyed in 1933 in the first major book-burning organized by the Nazis (the photograph of the fire consuming the Institute's library is famous, but captions rarely indicate the subject matter of the burning books). In this country, the courageous men and women who launched the ONE Institute for Homophile Studies in Los Angeles in the mid-1950s were ignored by Cold War-era scholars. Even the prestigious Kinsey Institute for Sex Research lost most of its funding in 1954 when conservatives denounced its research findings, particularly regarding the high incidence of homosexual behavior in the United States, as a threat to the moral fiber of the country. As recently as 1982, foreign scholars attending an international gay history conference in Toronto had to misrepresent their purpose to Canadian immigration officials for fear of being refused admittance. Repression and marginalization have often been the lot of historians of homosexuality as well as of homosexuals themselves.

But two developments, one in the political arena and one in the world of history itself, have resulted in an unprecedented outpouring of scholarship in lesbian and gay history in the last decade. Most important has been the success of the lesbian and gay movement in creating a more tolerant climate in which such work could be undertaken and in challenging certain orthodoxies, particularly psychological theories of pathology,

1

which had hindered creative thinking about sexuality for decades. Indeed, much of the first wave of historical research was undertaken by people with backgrounds in the movement rather than the academy, most notably Jonathan Katz, whose pioneering collection of documents and commentaries, *Gay American History* (1976), signalled the new era of scholarship. Grass-roots gay archives and history projects sprang up in several American cities in the late 1970s, including New York's Lesbian Herstory Archives, founded by Joan Nestle, Judith Schwartz, and Deborah Edel, and San Francisco's Lesbian and Gay History Project, which has supported, among other studies, the work of Allan Bérubé on World War II, Estelle Freedman, Liz Stevens, and Allan Bérubé on cross-dressing women, and Eric Garber on the Harlem Renaissance (all three studies are represented in this volume).

Professional historians have generally been slower to take up the subject. Some have been reluctant to publish in the field due to fear of the possible consequences for their careers; sympathetic faculty still caution graduate students to avoid linking themselves to so "controversial" a topic. Many scholars still consider the history of homosexuality a marginal field, if not an embarrassing or distasteful subject of study. But the doors of the academy have begun to open. Gay and lesbian activists on campus have helped pry them ajar, but so too have changing ideas about what constitutes acceptable historical inquiry, particularly the recent ascendancy of social history within the discipline. The interest that gay and lesbian historians take in ordinary people, the structure of everyday life, and the "private" sphere is consistent with—and a logical extension of—the concerns of the new social historians. The dramatic growth of women's history, in particular, has played a groundbreaking role by sensitizing historians to issues of gender and sexuality and by providing institutional support for a variety of new perspectives. Some of the most widely discussed essays and books in women's history, such as Carroll Smith-Rosenberg's essay on "The Female World of Love and Ritual," have highlighted questions of concern to historians of lesbianism.[1] As historians have paid more attention to the questions addressed by women's history and social history, their openness to gay and lesbian history has grown.

This anthology brings together some of the most exciting recent work in this new field. It is intended to summarize the research done in the "first phase" of historical reclamation during the last decade and to point to some of the questions the next generation of historical scholarship must address. We have been unable to overcome entirely the considerable imbalance in the amount of work done on lesbian and gay male history in the last decade, but are pleased that a third of our essays focus on lesbianism and that another quarter of them consider both men's and women's historical experience. We have asked the authors of almost all of the previously published pieces to revise their articles in light of recent work, and we have commissioned nine completely new essays—a third of the volume—in an effort to fill some of the gaps in documentation and argument. This has been particularly necessary in order to include histories of homosexuality in third-world societies, about which little had been published in English before this anthology. As we hope this collection will demonstrate, such histories are critically important not only in their own right, but also because of the questions they raise about our understanding of the Western past.

To date, the subject matter and purposes of historians of the gay experience have varied widely. It has long been reassuring for gay people, raised in a society offering them no positive images of themselves, to claim gay heroes, ranging from Sappho, Julius Caesar, and Shakespeare to Willa Cather, Walt Whitman, and Gertrude Stein, and much of the earliest work by historians simply sought to establish in a more scholarly fashion the homosexuality attributed to certain respected historical figures. As in other new fields of social history, historians of homosexuality first considered the experience of the literate elite before grappling with the more elusive evidence about "ordinary" people. Moreover, such biographies have often taken the subject's homosexuality as a given, without assessing the meaning of such behavior either for the individual or for the culture in which it occurred. A. L. Rowse's *Homosexuals in History* (1977), to take only the best-known example, provides short sketches of figures ranging from Richard the Lion-Hearted to Oscar Wilde, without considering the enormously different social forms and meanings "homosexuality" took in their lives.

Some recent studies, such as Blanche Wiesen Cook's discussion of the private support networks of several women reformers and political activists of the Progressive Era and Andrew Hodges's biography of Alan Turing, the brilliant British mathematician who broke the Nazi submarine code during the war and whose own life was broken upon the discovery of his homosexuality, have taken care to examine the interplay between the subject's "private" and "public" lives.[2] But many biographies have failed to explain the *social* significance of the individual's homosexuality—how their homosexual loves, their fear of exposure and experience of marginalization, or their involvement in a gay subculture influenced their work and affected their careers. The group biographies in this volume by Shari Benstock and Eric Garber, like the work of Cook and Hodges, demonstrate that homosexuality is not merely a personal characteristic to be alternately ignored or celebrated, as some historians have assumed, but a significant influence on the lives of individuals and on patterns of cultural organization in ways historians need to explore.

A second major project of gay historians, beyond biographical reclamation, has been to document the history of homosexual repression and resistance, and in doing so historians have recovered a history suppressed almost as rigorously as gay people themselves. To give but one example, the Nazi persecution of homosexuals was quickly hidden by an action heavy with symbolism as well as tragic practical effect: The Allied powers decided to continue the imprisonment of the homosexuals they found in the concentration camps, and hence silence their testimony, because they considered their incarceration by the Nazis justifiable. Only recently have historians such as Richard Plant, James Steakley, Manfred Herzer, and Erwin Haeberle begun to recover that history, and even now their work is ignored in many accounts of the Holocaust.[3]

The determination of historians to document social hostility to homosexuality, though, has sometimes led them to obscure the richness of the gay culture suppressed; the popular myth that homosexual life in the United States—and elsewhere—before the 1969 Stonewall rebellion consisted of nothing but repression and isolation, opprobrium and closetry, is sometimes reproduced in scholarly works. They have also sometimes given undue significance to hostile medical and religious injunctions, as if such prescriptive literature were an irresistible influence on—or even coterminous with—actual behavior. Lillian Faderman's thesis, in her groundbreaking *Surpassing the Love of Men: Romantic Friendship and Love Between Women from the Renaissance to the Present* (1981), that doctors' warnings about the pathology of lesbianism at the turn of the twentieth century forced a generation of women either to sunder their close relationships with other women or to label themselves lesbians has, in particular, been criticized for attributing inordinate power to prescriptions and oversimplifying the complex dialectic between social conditions, ideology, and consciousness that produces sexual identities.

Supplementing—and sometimes revising—the histories of homosexual victimization has been a growing number of studies of homosexual resistance that begin to restore the historical agency of gay women and men themselves. The work of John D'Emilio, Toby Marotta, and Salvatore Licata, among others, has traced the development of homosexual civil rights organizations in the decades before Stonewall, and the explosive growth of lesbian feminism and the gay liberation movement after it.[4] Still to be explored, however, are the more subtle forms of individual and collective resistance to oppressive conditions so thoroughly examined in recent histories of slaves, workers, women, and other groups.

The newest—and still least developed—field of gay history, deeply influenced by sociological and anthropological theory, has sought to reconstruct the *social* history of homosexuality: the categories used by ordinary people to interpret sexual relations, and the patterns of homosexual behavior in everyday life. The oral history research of Liz Kennedy and Madeline Davis has provided a model for others who seek to recuperate the lives of those who left few written documents. The social organization of working class lesbian relationships and the roots of the gay liberation movement are both far better understood now, thanks to their interviews with self-identified lesbians who took part in the bar scene in Buffalo, New

York, during the 1940s and 1950s. Allan Bérubé and Dunbar Moodie have also made creative use of oral histories, while historians of earlier periods have had to rely on more fragmentary material. Robert K. Martin, Martha Vicinus, and Martin Bauml Duberman, for instance, have used unpublished letters and diaries, novels and memoirs, to try to reconstruct the varying understandings and expectations of friendship among nineteenth-century upper-class men and women.

How one should interpret such sources—and, indeed, what constitutes the proper subject of inquiry—has increasingly divided historians of homosexuality. John Boswell's erudite study, *Christianity, Social Tolerance and Homosexuality: Gay People in Western Europe from the Beginning of the Christian Era to the Fourteenth Century* (1980), has come to represent one school in the debate and has served as the lightning rod for much of it. His book offered a revolutionary interpretation of the Western tradition, arguing that the Roman Catholic Church had not condemned gay people throughout its history, but rather, at least until the twelfth century, had alternately evinced no special concern about homosexuality or actually celebrated love between men. But a number of critics challenge as "essentialist" one of the key premises of Boswell's inquiry: that a gay identity and gay people can be found throughout history. Rather than a history of changing attitudes toward an unchanging "gay people," they argue, a history of the changes in sexual categories themselves is needed: The people and phenomena about which the church pontificated in the twelfth century, they maintain, were not the same as those of Saint Paul's time or the modern era. These historians, influenced by Michel Foucault and led by Jeffrey Weeks and Jonathan Katz, are known as "social constructionists" because they argue that all such sexual categories and identities are socially constructed and historically specific. The "modern homosexual" (to use Kenneth Plummer's label), whose social identity was determined by his or her homosexuality and who based a whole way of life on that sexual preference, was, they suggest, a unique creation of late nineteenth-century Western societies.

David Halperin argues (in this volume), for instance, that Aristophanes's myth in Plato's *Symposium*, which Boswell takes as evidence for the existence of homosexuals, heterosexuals, and bisexuals in classical Greece, actually demonstrates just the opposite: that Plato, in common with most Greek men, could not conceive of "homosexual" men who could desire a sexual relationship with other adult men. In response to such criticism Boswell (also in this volume) has elaborated his own position, arguing that although the dominant sexual categories of Greek and medieval societies may have been different from our own, members of those societies still recognized the existence of people who our own culture would label "homosexual." We bring together these two divergent readings of the *Symposium* to illustrate the complexity of historical recuperation.

Historians of lesbianism have most often entered the debate between essentialism and social constructionism from the vantage point of women's history. Carroll Smith-Rosenberg, for example, is specifically concerned with how the "New Woman" of the early twentieth century combatted the growing dominance of a male medical discourse. Tracing competing (and continually changing) public discourses, she points to the increasing use of symbolic language to describe same-sex relations. She reminds us that however socially constructed language may be, "words are rooted in our earliest and most profound experiences of social location and of the distribution of power."

Carole Vance, in a lecture given at a 1987 international gay studies conference held in Amsterdam, "Homosexuality, Which Homosexuality?", points to the contribution of social constructionism in forcing us to reconsider our commonsense assumptions about the nature of sexuality, but warns against the oversimplified and undifferentiated use of the theory. She pinpoints the major difficulty faced by social constructionists:

> [T]o the extent that social construction theory grants that sexual acts, identities and even desire are mediated by cultural and historical factors, the object of study—sexuality—becomes evanescent and threatens to disappear. If sexuality is constructed differently at each time and place, can we use the term in a comparatively meaningful way? More to the point in lesbian and gay history, have constructionists undermined their own categories? Is there an "it" to study?

Many social constructionists would argue that this is precisely the point: that the constitution of "sexuality" and of identity itself must be the subject of inquiry. But most would also agree that even if our sexual identities are socially constructed they cannot be readily changed, nor, indeed, do they need to be, as right-wing religious and political groups have insisted. The strength of social construction theory, Vance argues, lies in its fluidity and ambiguity, which makes "the future less closed than we feared, but perhaps more open than we hoped."[5]

Historians of male homosexuality have tended to assume that certain acts have always been recognized as "homosexual," and to ask only when desire for such acts became the basis for a gay male identity. As a result, studies of sodomy laws and sodomite subcultures have abounded. But many historians of lesbianism have questioned the centrality given genital sexuality in defining the "erotic" content of women's relationships. Indeed, many of them have asked a question different from that posed by historians of men: When did desire for intimate bonds with other women—rather than for genital contact—become eroticized and a basis for lesbian identity?

Those interested in the lesbian past have faced the very practical problem of a relative absence of records concerning same-sex sexual activity by women as well as the political reluctance of many to define lesbianism exclusively, or even predominantly, in "sexual" terms. As a result, studies of women's friendships and support networks have been plentiful, but their relationship to lesbian history proper continues to be disputed. Lillian Faderman, for instance, whose study, *Surpassing the Love of Men*, has fueled much of this debate, minimizes the genital aspects of lesbianism and emphasizes the history of romantic friendship. Both Blanche Wiesen Cook and the poet Adrienne Rich have privileged the traditional bonds of support between women as the foundation of lesbian history. In an influential essay, Rich argues that a continuum of homoerotic feeling is the norm for women—that, in effect, all women are naturally homosexual, not heterosexual.[6]

This emphasis upon romantic friendship as the normative form of lesbianism has precipitated two quite different political and theoretical responses. One group of historians, as Leila Rupp shows in this volume, has tried to "save" women's relationships from the "taint" of lesbianism by insisting that evidence of genital contact is required before a relationship can be called lesbian. For quite different reasons, other historians charge Faderman, Cook, and Rich with denying the importance of sexual activity in lesbian women's lives. In 1981 the feminist art journal *Heresies* published its special "Sex Issue," insisting upon the centrality of genital activity in defining the lesbian. In her essay in that issue, "Butch-Fem Roles: Sexual Courage in the 1950s," Joan Nestle criticizes the idea that emotions alone characterize the modern lesbian and defends the polarized sexual role playing in the 1950s as an important political and sexual statement: "Butch-fem relationships, as I experienced them, were complex erotic statements, not phony heterosexual replicas. . . . Butch-fem was an erotic partnership, serving as a conspicuous flag of rebellion and as an intimate exploration of women's sexuality."[7]

The debate about the nature of lesbian history has occurred in the context of an extensive feminist theoretical discourse that has no real parallel among gay men. Yet it sometimes seems that both groups have regarded only the "acceptable" elements of contemporary lesbian and gay male culture as suitable for historical inquiry. Faderman's reluctance to discuss the specifically sexual character of lesbian relationships has been parallelled by the reluctance of most historians to discuss the role of effeminacy in gay male cultural history or of butch-fem role-playing in the history of lesbianism.

As even this brief review of the major debates within gay and lesbian historiography makes clear, gay history has necessarily engaged profound philosophical questions concerning the definition and constitution of the self; it has become an important vehicle for exploring issues concerning the origins and character of both individual and communal identity. Yet such exploration has been impeded by the lack of consensus concerning the essential characteristics even of contemporary gay or lesbian identity and culture. Those historians who reject the idea that a clearly identifiable (and self-identified) homosexual minority has existed throughout history have faced special difficulties in defining the proper subject of their study. Same-sex genital sexuality, love and friendship, gender non-conformity, and a certain aesthetic or political perspective are all considered to have some (often ambiguous and always contested) relationship to that complex of attributes we today designate as homosexuality. As we have seen, much historical research has been an effort to locate the antecedents of those characteristics a given historian believes are constitutive of contemporary gay identity, be they sodomitical acts, cross-dressing, or intimate friendships. To note the contingency of such research is not to denigrate it, but simply to reconfirm that historical research is inherently self-reflexive and inescapably influenced by present-day concerns.

In compiling this volume, we have not started from the assumption that there have been people who identified themselves as "homosexuals" in all cultures and historical periods—but neither have we rejected a priori the possibility that individuals did define themselves in such terms. We have deliberately assembled essays crossing national and temporal boundaries, as well as those of race and gender, in order to encourage the varying histories to speak to one another. This seems to us particularly important because much recent work has been weakened by unwarranted assumptions about other periods in the history of homosexuality. Moreover, the comparative issues that such a juxtaposition of essays raises are—although rarely posed—among the most intriguing in gay history and thus for gay theory in general: Why, for instance, did a mass-based gay movement flourish in Weimar Germany when nothing remotely comparable existed in Prohibition-era America, even though major American cities had well-developed gay institutions and social networks? Why have lesbian and gay male social networks taken such different forms, and what does this tell us about the differences between women's and men's history? How have the boundaries between homosociality and homosexuality changed over time and varied between men and women, between ethnic groups and classes, and between national cultures? Too little research has been done yet on the local and national levels to support the extensive comparative studies necessary to answer such questions, but they point to future directions for research and suggest the ways in which gay history may illuminate broader historical issues as well.

As the essays gathered here demonstrate, historians have grown more sophisticated in their understanding of sexual ideology and of the relationship between social roles and identity formation. The earliest studies by social constructionists argued that no one who engaged in homosexual behavior before the last century was labelled—or assumed a distinct identity—as a result of that behavior because it was considered a sin of which everyone was potentially capable. These studies disagreed primarily about the dating of the emergence of the "modern homosexual," a distinctive "type" of person defined on the basis of his or her sexual behavior and self-identification. Some historians, such as Randolph Trumbach and Alan Bray, dated the appearance of the "homosexual" from the early eighteenth century, with the appearance of the "molly houses" in London; others, such as Jeff Weeks, Lillian Faderman, and John D'Emilio, placed it at the end of the nineteenth, with the advent of medical inquiry and the further growth of cities.[8]

Most recent work argues that the homosexual role, as we currently think of it, developed only in the modern period, but it also establishes that the modern role is not the *only* homosexual role possible. Researchers have identified cultures in which no "homosexuals" such as those of the modern West can be found, but in which other roles and identities are associated with same-sex contacts. Homosexual behavior in those cultures and in the West before the modern period thus was not just a sin in which "normal" people randomly engaged, but was governed by definite conventions that sometimes involved the labeling of at least one participant as abnormal. As Randolph Trumbach argues in this volume, for instance, the men who dressed as women and had sexual contacts with other men in the eighteenth-century molly houses should not be seen as early versions of the modern homosexual but as evidence of a radically different sexual system, in which one's identity and role were based as much on effeminacy as on homosexual interest.

Indeed, the essays gathered here suggest that homosexual relations (among both women and men) are likely to be organized in one of three broad patterns: (1) between adults and youths, often in an initiatory context; (2) between persons who abide by their culture's gender conventions (i.e., "feminine" women and "masculine" men) and persons who assume the cultural status of the other sex or of an "intermediate" gender; and (3) between persons of equal age and status (as is conventional in our own society). Considerable evidence also exists of homosexual relations between men whose status is differentiated as superordinate and subordinate on the basis of class or race, rather than age or gender.

For the people engaged in such relations, a distinct identity and role are assumed in some societies but not in others. Pedophiles, men who characteristically prefer relations with youths, for instance, are considered to be a discrete category of men in our culture, but many other cultures consider age-asymmetrical relations to be a transient and natural stage in the lives of both adults and youths. As Paul Schalow's study of seventeenth-century Japan implies, such cultures are as unlikely to believe that only a particular "type" of man engages in such relations as we are to believe that the boy in such a relationship is constitutionally a "man-lover," rather than a victimized—or precocious—but otherwise "normal" boy.

Distinct identities have been even less common in women's age-asymmetrical relationships. The adolescent girl's crush on or passion for an admired older student, teacher, or counselor, has often been defined as a normative emotional experience that many girls pass through on their way to sexual "maturity." Nineteenth- and early twentieth-century female (and in some school settings, male) teachers were expected to nurture each generation of students, providing them with role models of the successful celibate; such conventions masked, to a varying degree, the homoerotic content sometimes present.

A distinct role and identity are more likely to be involved when same-sex relations are organized on the basis of an asserted gender difference between the partners. In such relationships the "cross-gender" party has usually been labeled the "queer" and taken on a distinct identity, whether it be Stephen Gordon in *The Well of Loneliness* or the "Mary Annes" of late nineteenth-century London. On the other hand, the gender-conforming partner, the femme who "passed" as a "normal" woman or the man who penetrated the "queer," was often not considered abnormal, as Esther Newton's essay on Radclyffe Hall and George Chauncey's study of homosexual patterns among World War I-era sailors show. But even such identities were not always permanent. Madeline Davis and Liz Kennedy's history of lesbian bar culture in Buffalo, New York, documents the belief in the lesbian community itself in the 1950s that only the butch partner was a "real" lesbian. But it also reveals the equally widespread belief that a woman could *change* her role (and in some sense, then, her basic character) over the years; "this year's [femme] lover," butch women used to observe, "is next year's competition." (The analog among men was: "Today's trade is tomorrow's competition.")

A distinct identity is most likely to be involved in the pattern with which contemporary Westerners are most familiar: coeval egalitarian relationships in which both partners are labeled as "abnormal" on the basis of their homosexual desire rather than their gender nonconformity. But, as even this brief review of the literature shows, this pattern, while familiar, is hardly universal.

The parochialism of our own sexual mores suggested by this anthology's historical essays is confirmed by a glance at the anthropological literature. Almost forty years ago Clellan S. Ford and Frank A. Beach revealed in *Patterns of Sexual Behavior* (1951) that roughly two-thirds of the societies for which evidence existed condoned homosexuality among men (the data for women are still far too sketchy to allow for even preliminary generalizations). Gilbert Herdt, in three studies about Melanesia written and edited from 1981 to 1984, found that a "normal" part of the maturation process for boys was male/male sexual contact.[9] Among the New Guinea Keraki, anal intercourse was mandated between an older man and a boy as a necessary ritual to ensure the boy's satisfactory growth. Among the Anga, the oral ingestion of semen was considered necessary. But, contrary to Western expectations, these boys married and had families upon becoming adults. Moreover, the decision to have sexual relations *only* with one's own sex would have been seen as a shirking of vital family duties. Ritualized *and* erotic same-sex acts did not preclude, and indeed, often preceded or accompanied, marriage. To study the history of the West is to understand that our own sexual expectations and behavior have varied through time. But to study the Keraki or the Anga of Melanesia is to understand that at every point in time both our values and theirs have been based on transient and local social dictates, rather than biological or religious imperatives.

Likewise, the gender-mixing of the North American *berdache* and the Polynesian *mahu* are unrecognizable in terms of our own categories. Though anatomically male, the *berdache* and the *mahu* act and dress in ways that are comparable, though not identical, to what is considered appropriate female behavior in their respective cultures. Walter Williams, in *The Spirit and the Flesh* (1986), reminds us that it is mistaken to view the *berdache* simply as an alternative female, providing sexual services for males, doing women's work, and performing social roles generally reserved for women. Not only is the *berdache* thought to be endowed with special shamanistic powers—and therefore held in special esteem—but his behavior also combines elements traditionally assigned to male and female genders, creating a "third" gender category. North American Indian tribes, in other words, legitimized, even exalted, those individuals who were gender nonconformists, rather than insisting (as we do in the West) that the nonconformists define themselves as one or the other of two preexisting gender categories—or to be cast to the margin as "sick."

In contrast to nonindustrial cultures, industrial societies do not usually employ a single moral system to judge or even explain the character of people involved in homosexual relations; indeed, one of the characteristics of a complex society may be its multiplicity of moral systems. In our own society the churches disagree among themselves about the morality of homosexual conduct and the character and possible salvation of "homosexuals," while collectively they also disagree with the views held by lesbians and gay men, legal authorities, the heterosexual lay public, and psychiatrists (each group itself internally divided many times over along lines of class, race, generation, and region). Moreover, in every society there are likely to be deviants from the norms of deviance: "mannish women" who want to take the femme's role in bed or men who like sex with boys in other than ritually acceptable contexts.

Lesbian and gay male historical research has played an unusually important role in the development of gay theory in the last decade. The gay and lesbian communities have increasingly recognized that some of the most important issues facing, agitating, and sometimes dividing them today, personally and collectively, are best addressed historically: What is the nature of gay or lesbian "identity"? To what extent do lesbians and gay men constitute a "community"—and what are its origins? What is the relationship or pedophilia (or sado-masochism) to homosexual culture and politics? What social conditions and political strategies have made the enormous progress of gay people in the last two decades possible—and how secure is that progress? Can the history of the treatment of homosexuals by the government and medical profession shed light on the current controversy about how the gay movement should deal with those entities during the AIDS crisis?

Because the history of homosexuality has been denied or ignored, omitted in formal historical instruction and given no place in the family-centered oral traditions available to other disenfranchised groups, gay people's hunger for knowledge of their past is strong. Having struggled to create a public presence for themselves in the world today, they seek to reclaim their historical presence. For many, gay history helps constitute the gay community by giving it a tradition, helps women and men validate and understand who they are by showing them who they have been.

As a result, gay history has generated unusual interest among people otherwise unconcerned about history (history lectures and slide shows are among the most widely attended events at gay conferences and community centers) and has generated intense controversy when—even in its most academic forms—it has seemed to challenge previously cherished concepts of gay identity and community. To reclaim the homosexuality of a widely respected historical figure such as Michaelangelo lends welcome support to the work of political activists seeking to counteract negative stereotypes of gay people. But to question whether Michaelangelo can properly be called a homosexual—or whether anyone in his time could be so characterized, because the social categories of sexuality are variable, rather than biologically fixed and immutable—may appear to the same activists to undermine the very foundations of their argument that homosexuals are a "minority" deserving equal rights rather than willful misfits deserving punishment or treatment. As a result, the relationship between gay historians and the gay community has sometimes been uneasy. Although this tension has usually been only implicit, some historians have intervened directly in current community debates *as historians:* When Joan Nestle pointed to the historical significance of butch-fem roles, for instance, she launched an attack that still reverberates on the lesbian-feminist critique popular in the 1970s of such roles.

Historians of women have identified three stages of work in women's history: filling in the gaps left by traditional historians with women's stories; developing periodizations and theories of women's historical experience; and, finally, forcing a reconsideration of the conceptual frameworks and schemas of periodization governing our understanding of history as a whole on the basis of the perspectives offered by women's experience. Gay history has already begun to exhibit a comparable process of development. The gaps are beginning to be filled: More new data have been brought to the attention of historians and important stories reclaimed. Preliminary efforts have been made to periodize the history of homosexuality, and this has resulted in a productive debate that has clarified the inquiry.

Moreover, the history of homosexuality has an importance that goes well beyond filling in missing gaps in our knowledge of the past. It has already demonstrated that personal sexual behavior is never simply a private matter, but is always shaped by *and* shapes the wider social and political milieux. Cultural historians would do well, for example, to consider the significance of gay and lesbian social networks to the infrastructure of European and American cultural history. The role of homosexual communities in shaping urban culture and social geography also needs to be recognized, and the interaction of such communities with other ethnic, occupational, and neighborhood groupings explored. Gay and lesbian history can also illuminate the history of families and gender roles, for the changes in the cultural definition of deviance that it traces clarify the changing parameters of the acceptable. And studying the recurrent appearance in Western politics of the homosexual specter—be it in the form of the supposed invidious influence of homosexuals on the Kaiser in Wilhelmine Germany or of the "child molestor" and "security risk" in Cold War America—can expand our understanding of political culture. Just as the lives of lesbians and gay men are enhanced by a knowledge of their history, so too will the field of history be enriched by a reclamation of the homosexual past.

The
◆
ANCIENT
WORLD

REVOLUTIONS, UNIVERSALS, AND SEXUAL CATEGORIES

◆

JOHN BOSWELL

John Boswell's book, *Christianity, Social Tolerance, and Homo-sexuality* (1980), quickly became the lightning rod for much of the debate in gay history between essentialists and social construction-ists: it was hailed by historians for its ground-breaking scholarship and argument but was also criticized by constructionists for making "essentialist" suppositions. In this essay (which originally appeared in 1982 and has been revised for this volume), Boswell offers his first major intervention in the controversy and an extended discus-sion of the issues it has raised. Placing the debate in a broader historiographical context, he compares its philosophical underpin-nings to the older and broader conflict between "realists" and "nominalists" over the nature and accuracy of abstractions. After outlining the weaknesses he sees in "absolutist" forms of both positions—including the position outlined by the social construction-ist Robert Padgug in his essay in this volume—he attempts to craft an intermediate position by exploring typologies of sexuality from other cultures and discussing the manner in which social structures and broader cultural concerns may affect such typologies. David Halperin offers a constructionist perspective on the same questions in the following essay.

One of the revolutions in the study of history in the twentieth century might be called "minority history": the effort to recover the histories of groups previously overlooked or excluded from mainstream historiography. Minority history has provoked predictable skepticism on the part of some traditional historians, partly because of its novelty—which will, of course, inevitably wear off—and partly because the attitudes that previously induced neglect or distortion of minority history still prevail in many quarters. The most reasonable criticism of minority history (aside from the objection that it is sometimes very poor scholarship, against which no discipline is proof) is that it lends itself to political use, which may distort scholarly integrity. As a point about minority history as a genre this is not cogent: Since the exclusion of minorities from much historiography prior to the twentieth century was related to or caused by concerns other than purely scholarly interest, their inclusion now, even for purely political ends, not only corrects a previous "political" distortion but also provides a more complete data base for judgments about the historical issues involved. Such truth as is yielded by historical analysis generally emerges from the broadest possible synthesis of the greatest number of viewpoints and vantages: The addition of minority history and viewpoints to twentieth-century historiography is a net gain for all concerned.

But at a more particular level political struggles can cause serious problems for scholars, and a curious debate now taking place among those interested in the history of gay people provides a relevant and timely example of a type of difficulty that could subvert minority history altogether if not addressed intelligently. To avoid contributing further to the undue political freight the issue has lately been forced to bear, I propose to approach it by way of another historical controversy, one that was—in its day—no less heated or urgent, but that is now sufficiently distant to be viewed with dispassion by all sides.

The conflict in question is as old as Plato and as modern as cladism, and although the most violent struggles over it took place in the twelfth and thirteenth centuries, the arguments of the ancients on the subject are still in use today. Stated as briefly and baldly as possible, the issues are these: Do categories exist because humans recognize real distinctions in the world around them, or are categories arbitrary conventions, simply names for things that have categorical force because humans agree to use them in certain ways? The two traditional sides in this controversy, which is called "the problem of universals," are "realists" and "nominalists." Realists consider categories to be the footprints of reality ("universals"): They exist because humans perceive a real order in the universe and name it. The order is present without human observation, according to realists; the human contribution is simply the naming and describing of it. Most scientists operate—tacitly—in a realist mode, on the assumption that they are discovering, not inventing, the relationships within the physical world. The scientific method is, in fact, predicated on realist attitudes. On the other hand, the philosophical structure of the modern West is closer to nominalism: the belief that categories are only the

---

Note: This essay originally appeared in somewhat different form in *Salmagundi*, No. 58-59, Fall 1982–Winter 1983, 89–113.

names (Latin: *nomina*) of things agreed upon by humans, and that the "order" people see is their creation rather than their perception. Most modern philosophy and language theory is essentially nominalist, and even the more theoretical sciences are nominalist to some degree: In biology, for example, taxonomists disagree strongly about whether they are discovering (realists) or inventing (nominalists) distinctions among phyla, genera, species, etc. (When, for example, a biologist announces that bats, being mammals, are "more closely related to" humans than to birds, is he expressing some real relationship, present in nature and detected by humans, or is he employing an arbitrary convention, something that helps humans organize and sort information but that bears no "truth" or significance beyond this utility?)

This seemingly arcane struggle now underlies an epistemological controversy raging among those studying the history of gay people. The "universals" in this case are categories of sexual preference or orientation (the difference is crucial). Nominalists ("social constructionists" in the current debate) in the matter aver that categories of sexual preference and behavior are created by humans and human societies. Whatever reality they have is the consequence of the power they exert in those societies and the socialization processes that make them seem real to persons influenced by them. People consider themselves "homosexual" or "heterosexual" because they are induced to believe that humans are either "homosexual" or "heterosexual." Left to their own devices, without such processes of socialization, people would simply be sexual. The category "heterosexuality," in other words, does not so much describe a pattern of behavior inherent in human beings as it creates and establishes it.

Realists ("essentialists") hold that this is not the case. Humans are, they insist, differentiated sexually. Many categories might be devised to characterize human sexual taxonomy, some more or less apt than others, but the accuracy of human perceptions does not affect reality. The heterosexual/homosexual dichotomy exists in speech and thought because it exists in reality: It was not invented by sexual taxonomists, but observed by them.[1]

Neither of these positions is usually held absolutely: Most nominalists would be willing to admit that some aspects of sexuality are present, and might be distinguished, without direction from society. And most realists are happy to admit that the same real phenomenon might be described by various systems of categorization, some more accurate and helpful than others. One might suppose that "moderate nominalists" and "moderate realists" could therefore engage in a useful dialogue on those areas where they agree and, by careful analysis of their differences, promote discussion and understanding of these issues.

Political ramifications hinder this. Realism has historically been viewed by the nominalist camp as conservative, if not reactionary, in its implicit recognition of the value and/or immutability of the status quo; and nominalism has generally been regarded by realists as an obscurantist radical ideology designed more to undercut and subvert human values than to clarify them. Precisely these political overtones can be seen to operate today in scholarly debate over issues of sexuality. The efforts of sociobiology to demonstrate an evolutionary etiology of homosexuality have been vehemently denounced by many who regard the enterprise as reactionary realism, an effort to persuade people that social categories are fixed and unchangeable, while on the other side, psychiatric "cures" of homosexuality are bitterly resented by many as the cynical folly of nominalist pseudoscience: Convince someone he shouldn't want to be a homosexual, persuade him to think of himself as a "heterosexual," and—presto!—he is a heterosexual. The category is the person.

Whether or not there are "homosexual" and "heterosexual" persons, as opposed to persons called "homosexual" or "heterosexual" by society, is obviously a matter of substantial import to the gay community, since it brings into question the nature and even the existence of such a community. It is, moreover, of substantial epistemological urgency to nearly all of society,[2] and the gravity and extent of this can be seen in the case of the problems it creates for history and historians.

The history of minorities poses ferocious difficulties: censorship and distortion, absence or destruction of records, the difficulty of writing about essentially personal and private aspects of human feelings and behavior, problems of definition, political dangers attendant on choosing certain subjects, etc. But if the nominalists are correct and the realists wrong, the problems in regard to the history of gay people are of an entirely different order: If the categories "homosexual/heterosexual" and "gay/straight" are the inventions of particular societies rather than real aspects of the human psyche, there is no gay history.[3] If "homosexuality" exists only when and where people are persuaded to believe in it, "homosexual" persons will have a "history" only in those particular societies and cultures.

In its most extreme form, this nominalist view has argued that only early modern and contemporary industrial societies have produced "homosexuality," and it is futile and misguided to look for "homosexuality" in earlier human history.

> What we call "homosexuality" (in the sense of the distinguishing traits of "homosexuals"), for example, was not considered a unified set of acts, much less a set of qualities defining particular persons, in pre-capitalist societies. . . . Heterosexuals and homosexuals are involved in social "roles" and attitudes which pertain to a particular society, modern capitalism.[4]

If this position is sustained, it will permanently alter, for better or worse, the nature and extent of minority history.

Clearly it has much to recommend it. No characteristics interact with the society around them uniformly through time. Perceptions of, reactions to, and social response regarding blackness, blindness, left-handedness, Jewishness, or any other distinguishing (or distinguished) aspect of persons or peoples must necessarily vary as widely as the social circumstances in which they occur, and for this reason alone it could be reasonably argued that being Jewish, black, blind, left-handed, etc., is essentially different from one age and place to another. In some cultures, for example, Jews are categorized chiefly as an ethnic minority; in others they are not or are not perceived to be ethnically distinct from the peoples around them, and are distinguished solely by their religious beliefs. Similarly, in some societies anyone darker than average is considered "black"; in others, a complex and highly technical system of racial categorization classes some persons as black even when they are lighter in color than many "whites." In both cases, moreover, the differences in attitudes held by the majority must affect profoundly the self-perception of the minority itself, and its patterns of life and behavior are in all probability notably different from those of "black" or "Jewish" people in other circumstances.

There can be no question that if minority history is to merit respect it must carefully weigh such fundamental subtleties of context: Merely cataloguing references to "Jews" or to "Blacks" may distort more than it reveals of human history if due attention is not paid to the meaning, in their historical setting, of such words and the concepts to which they apply. Do such reservations, on the other hand, uphold the claim that categories such as "Jew," "black," or "gay" are not diachronic and can not, even with apposite qualification, be applied to ages and times other than those in which the terms themselves were used in precisely their modern sense? Extreme realists, without posing the question, have assumed the answer was no; extreme nominalists seem to be saying yes.

The question can not be addressed intelligently without first noting three points. First, the positions are not in fact as clearly separable as this schema implies. It could be well argued, for example, that Padgug, Weeks, et al., are in fact extreme *realists* in assuming that *modern* homosexuality is not simply one of a series of conventions designated under the same rubric, but is instead a "real" phenomenon that has no "real" antecedent in human history. Demonstrate to us the "reality" of this homosexuality, their opponents might legitimately demand, and prove to us that it has a unity and cohesiveness that justifies your considering it a single, unparalleled entity rather than a loose congeries of behaviors. Modern scientific literature increasingly assumes that what is at issue is not "homosexuality" but "homosexualities"; if these disparate patterns of sexuality can be grouped together under a single heading in the present, why make such a fuss about a diachronic grouping?

Second, adherents of both schools fall prey to anachronism. Nearly all of the most prominent nominalists are historians of the modern U.S., modern Britain, or modern Europe, and it is difficult to eschew the suspicion that they are concentrating their search where the light is best rather than where the answers are to be found, and formulating a theoretical position to justify their approach. On the other hand, nominalist objections are in part a response to an extreme realist position that has been predicated on the unquestioned, unproven, and overwhelmingly unlikely assumption that exactly the same categories and patterns of sexuality have always existed, pure and unchanged by the systems of thought and behavior in which they were enmeshed.

Third, both extremes appear to be paralyzed by words. The nominalists are determined that the same word can not apply to a wide range of meaning and still be used productively in scholarly discourse: In order to have meaning, "gay," for example, must be applied only as the speaker would apply it, with all the precise ramifications he associates with it. This insistence follows understandably from the implicit assumption that the speaker is generating the category himself, or in concert with certain contemporaries, rather than receiving it from a human experience of great longevity and adjusting it to fit his own understanding. Realist extremists, conversely, assume that lexical equivalence betokens experiential equality, and that the occurrence of a word that "means" "homosexual" demonstrates the existence of "homosexuality," as the modern realist understands it, at the time the text was composed.

It is my aim to circumvent these difficulties as far as possible in the following remarks, and my hope that in so doing I may reduce the rhetorical struggle over "universals" in these matters and promote thereby more useful dialogue among the partisans. Let it be agreed at the outset that something can be discussed, by modern historians or ancient writers, without being named or defined. (Ten people in a room might argue endlessly about proper definitions of "blue" and "red," but could probably agree instantly whether a given object was one or the other [or a combination of both].) "Gravity" offers a useful historical example. A nominalist position would be that gravity did not exist before Newton invented it, and a nominalist historian might be able to mount a convincing case that there is no mention of gravity in any texts before Newton. "Nonsense," realists would object. "The Latin gravitas, which is common in Roman literature, describes the very properties of matter Newton called 'gravity.' Of course gravity existed before Newton discovered it."

Both, of course, are wrong. Lack of attention to something in historical sources can in no wise be taken as evidence of its nonexistence, and discovery can not be equated with creation or invention. But gravitas does not mean "gravity"; it means "heaviness," and the two are not at all the same thing. Noting that objects have heaviness is entirely different from understanding the nature and operations of gravity. For adherents of these two positions to understand each other each would have to abandon specific nomenclature, and agree instead on questions to be asked of the sources. If the proper questions were addressed, the nominalist could easily be persuaded that the sources prove that gravity existed before Newton, in the sense that the operations of the force now designated gravity are well chronicled in nearly all ancient literature. And the realist could be persuaded that despite this fact the nature of gravity was not clearly articulated—whether or not it was apprehended—before Newton.

The problem is rendered more difficult in the present case by the fact that the equivalent of gravity has not yet been discovered: There is still no essential agreement in the scientific community about the nature of human sexuality. Whether humans are "homosexual" or "heterosexual" or "bisexual" by birth, by training, by choice, or at all is still an open question.[5] Neither realists nor nominalists can, therefore, establish any clear correlation—positive or negative—between modern sexuality and its ancient counterparts. But it is still possible to discuss whether modern conceptualizations of sexuality are novel and completely socially relative, or correspond to constants of human epistemology which can be documented in the past.

To simplify discussion, three broad types of sexual taxonomy are abbreviated here as Types A, B, and C. According to Type A theories, all humans are polymorphously sexual, i.e., capable of erotic and sexual interaction with either gender. External accidents, such as social pressure, legal sanctions, religious beliefs, historical or personal circumstances determine the actual expression of each person's sexual feelings. Type B theories posit two or more sexual categories, usually but not always based on sexual object choice, to which all humans belong, though external pressures or circumstance may induce individuals in a given society to pretend (or even to believe) that they belong to a category other than their native one. The most common form of Type B taxonomy assumes that humans are heterosexual, homosexual, and bisexual, but that not all societies allow expression of all varieties of erotic disposition. Subsets or other versions of Type B categorize on the basis of other characteristics, e.g., a predilection for a particular role in intercourse. Type C theories consider one type of sexual response normal (or "natural" or "moral" or all three) and all other variants abnormal ("unnatural," "immoral").

It will be seen that Type A theories are nominalist to the extent that they regard categorizations like "homosexual" and "heterosexual" as arbitrary conventions applied to a sexual reality that is at bottom undifferentiated. Type B theories are conversely realist in predicating categories that underly human sexual experience even when obscured by social constraints or particular circumstances. Type C theories are essentially normative rather than epistemological, but borrow from both sides of the universals question in assuming, by and large, that people are born into the normal category but become members of a deviant grouping by an act of the will, although some Type C adherents regard "deviants" as inculpably belonging to an "abnormal" category through mental or physical illness or defect.

That no two social structures are identical should require no proof; and since sexual categories are inevitably conditioned by social structure, no two systems of sexual taxonomy should be expected to be identical. A slight chronological or geographical shift would render one Type A system quite different from another one. But to state this is not to demonstrate that there are no constants in human sexual epistemology. The frequency with which these theories or variations on them appear in Western history is striking.

The apparent gender blindness of the ancient world has often been adduced as proof that Type B theories were unknown before comparatively recent times. In Plutarch's *Dialogue on Love* it is asserted that

> the noble lover of beauty engages in love wherever he sees excellence and splendid natural endowment without regard for any difference in physiological detail. The lover of human beauty [will] be fairly and equally disposed toward both sexes, instead of supposing that males and females are as different in the matter of love as they are in their clothes.[6]

Such statements are commonplaces of ancient lore about love and eroticism, to the extent that one is inclined to believe that much of the ancient world was completely unaware of differentiation among humans in sexual object choice, as I have myself pointed out at length elsewhere.[7] But my statements and the evidence on which they rest can easily be misapprehended. Their purport is that ancient *societies* did not distinguish heterosexuality from homosexuality, not that all, or even most, individuals failed to make such a distinction.

A distinction can be present and generally recognized in a society without forming any part of its social structure. In some cultures skin color is a major determinant of social status; in others it is irrelevant. But it would be fatuous to assume that societies that did not "discriminate on the basis of" [i.e., make invidious distinctions concerning] skin color could not "discriminate" [distinguish] such differences. This same paranomastic subtlety must be understood in regard to ancient views of sexuality: City-states of the ancient world did not, for the most part, discriminate on the basis of sexual orientation, and, as societies, appear to have been blind to the issue of sexual object choice, but it is not clear that individuals were unaware of distinctions in the matter.

It should be obvious, for instance, that in the passage cited above Plutarch is arguing against precisely that notion that Padgug claims had not existed in precapitalist societies, i.e., Type B theories. Plutarch believes that a normal human being is susceptible to attraction to either gender, but his comments are manifestly directed against the contrary view. Which attitude was more common in his day is not apparent, but it is clearly inaccurate to use his comments as demonstration that there was only one view. The polemical tone of his remarks, in fact, seems good evidence that the position he opposes was of considerable importance. The whole genre of debates about the types of love of which this dialogue is a representative[8] cuts both ways on the issue: On the one hand, arguing about the matter and adducing reasons for preferring one gender to the other suggests a kind of polymorphous sexuality that is not predirected by heredity or experience toward one gender or the other. On the other, in each of the debates there are factions that are clearly on one side or the other of the dichotomy not supposed to have existed before modern times: Some disputants argue for attraction to males only; some for attraction to females only. Each side derogates the preference of the other side as distasteful. Sometimes bisexuality is admitted, but as a third preference, not as the general nature of human sexuality:

> Zeus came as an eagle to god-like Ganymede, as a swan came he to the fair-haired mother of Helen.
> So there is no comparison between the two things: one person likes one, another likes the other; I like both.[9]

This formulation of the range of human sexuality is almost identical to popular modern conceptions of Type B: Some people prefer their own gender; some the opposite; some both. Similar distinctions abound in ancient literature. The myth of Aristophanes in Plato's *Symposium* is perhaps the most familiar example: Its manifest and stated purpose is to explain why humans are divided into groups of predominantly homosexual or heterosexual interest. It is strongly implied that these interests are both exclusive and innate; that is stated outright by Longus, who describes a character as "homosexual by nature [*physei*]."[10]*

---

*Among many complex aspects of Aristophanes' speech in the *Symposium* as an indication of contemporary sexual constructs, two are especially notable. (1) Although it is the sole Attic reference to lesbianism as a concept, male homosexuality is of much greater concern as an erotic disposition in the discussion than either female homosexuality or heterosexuality. (2) It is this, in my view, which accounts for the additional subtlety of age distinctions in male-male relations, suggesting a general pattern of older *erastes* and younger *eromenonos*. Age differential was unquestionably a part of the construct of sexuality among elements of the population in Athens, but it can easily be given more weight than it deserves. "Romantic love" of any sort was thought to be provoked by and directed toward the young, as is clearly demonstrated in Agathon's speech a little further on, where he uses the greater beauty of young males and females interchangeably to prove that Love is a young god. In fact, most Athenian males married women considerably younger than themselves, but since marriage was not imagined to follow upon romantic attachment, this discrepancy does not appear in dialogues on *eros*.

David Halperin argues in "Sex Before Sexuality" (in this volume) that the speech does not indicate a taxonomy comparable to modern ones, chiefly because of the age differential, although in fact the creatures described by Aristophanes must have been seeking a partner of the same age, since, joined at birth, they were coeval. What is clear is that Aristophanes does not imagine a populace undifferentiated in experience or desire, responding circumstantially to individuals of either gender, but persons with lifelong preferences arising from innate character (or a mythic prehistory).

It is true that there were no terms in common use in Greece or Rome to describe categories of sexual preference, but it does not follow that such terms were wholly unknown: Plato, Athenaeus, and other writers who dealt with the subject at length developed terms to describe predominant or exclusive interest in the apposite gender.[11] Many writers, moreover, found it possible to characterize homosexuality as a distinct mode of erotic expression without naming it. Plautus, for example, characterized homosexual activity as the "mores of Marseilles," suggesting that he considered it a variant on ordinary human sexuality.[12] Martial found it possible to describe an exclusively heterosexual male, even though he had no terminology available to do so and was himself apparently interested in both genders.[13]

One even finds expressions of solidarity among adherents of one preference or another in ancient literature, as when Clodius Albinus, noted for his exclusively heterosexual interest, persecutes those involved in homosexual behavior,[14] or when a character who has spoken on behalf of love between men in one of the debates bursts out, "We are like strangers cut off in a foreign land . . . ; nevertheless, we shall not be overcome by fear and betray the truth,"[15] or when Propertius writes, "Let him who would be our enemy love girls; he who would be our friend enjoy boys."[16] That there is a jocular tone to some of these statements, especially the last, is certainly attributable to the fact that the distinctions involved in no way affected the well-being, happiness, or social status of the individuals, owing to the extreme sexual tolerance of ancient societies; but it does not cast doubt on the existence of the distinctions. Even when preferences are attributed ironically, as is likely the case in Plato's placing the myth of sexual etiology in the mouth of Aristophanes, the joke depends on the familiarity of the distinction.

Subtler indications of Type B taxonomies can also be found. In the *Ephesiaca*, a Hellenistic love novel by Xenophon of Ephesus, sexual categories are never discussed, and are clearly not absolute, but they do seem to be well understood and constitute an organizing principle of individual lives. Habrocomes is involved throughout only with women, and when, after his long separation from his true love Anthia, she desires to know if he has been faithful to her, she inquires only if he has slept with other women, although she knows that men have been interested in him, and it is clear that sex with a man would also constitute infidelity (as with Corymbus). It seems clear that Habrocomes is, in fact, heterosexual, at least in Anthia's opinion. Another character, Hippothoos, had been married to an older woman and attracted to Anthia, but is apparently mostly gay: The two great loves of his life are males (Hyperanthes and Habrocomes); he left all to follow each of these, and at the end of the story he erects a statue to the former and establishes his residence near that of the latter. The author tidies up all the couples at the end by reuniting Anthia and Habrocomes and introducing a new male lover

(Clisthenes) for Hippothoos. This entire scenario corresponds almost exactly to modern conceptualizations: Some people are heterosexual, some homosexual, some bisexual; the categories are not absolute, but they are important and make a substantial difference in people's lives.

Almost the very same constellation of opinions can be found in many other preindustrial societies. In medieval Islam one encounters an even more overwhelming emphasis on homosexual eroticism than in classical Greek or Roman writing. It is probably fair to say that most premodern Arabic poetry is ostensibly homosexual, and it is clear that this is more than a literary convention. When Saadia Gaon, a Jew living in Muslim society in the tenth century, discusses the desirability of "passionate love,"[17] he apparently refers only to homosexual passion. There is the sort of love men have for their wives, which is good but not passionate; and there is the sort of love men have for each other, which is passionate but not good. (And what of the wives' loves? We are not told.) That Saadia assumes the ubiquity of homosexual passion is the more striking because he is familiar with Plato's discussion of homosexual and heterosexual varieties of love in the *Symposium*.[18]

Does this mean that classical Islamic society uniformly entertained Type A theories of human sexuality and regarded eroticism as inherently pansexual? No. There is much evidence in Arabic literature for the very same Type B dichotomies known in other cultures. Saadia himself cites various theories about the determination of particular erotic interests (e.g., astrological lore),[19] and in the ninth century Jahiz wrote a debate involving partisans of homosexual and heterosexual desire, in which each disputant, like his Hellenistic counterpart, expresses distaste for the preference of the other.[20] Three debates of this sort occur in the *Thousand and One Nights*, a classic of Arabic popular literature.[21] "Homosexuals" are frequently (and neutrally) mentioned in classical Arabic writings as a distinct type of human being. That the "type" referred to involves predominant or exclusive preference is often suggested: In tale 142 of the *Nights*, for example, it is mentioned as noteworthy that a male homosexual does not dislike women; in Night 419 a woman observes a man staring longingly at some boys and remarks to him, "I perceive that you are among those who prefer men to women."

A ninth-century text of human psychology by Qustā ibn Luqā treats twenty areas in which humans may be distinguished psychologically.[22] One area is sexual object-choice: Some men, Qustā, explains, are "disposed towards" [*yamīlu ilā*] women, some toward other men, and some toward both.[23] Qustā has no terminology at hand for these categories; indeed, for the second category he employs the euphemism that such men are disposed toward "sexual partners other than women"[24]: obviously lack of terminology for the homosexual/heterosexual dichotomy should not be taken as a sign of ignorance of it. Qustā, in fact, believed that homosexuality was often inherited, as did ar-Razi and many other Muslim scientific writers.[25]

It has been claimed that "homosexuality" was viewed in medieval Europe "not as a particular attribute of a certain type of person but as a potential in all sinful creatures."[26] It is certainly true that some medieval writers evinced Type A attitudes of this sort: Patristic authors often address to their audiences warnings concerning homosexual attraction predicated on the assumption that any male might be attracted to another.[27] The Anglo-Saxon life of Saint Eufrasia[28] recounts the saint's efforts to live in a monastery disguised as a monk and the turmoil that ensued: The other monks were greatly attracted by Agapitus (the name she took as a monk), and reproached the abbot for bringing "so beautiful a man into their minster" ["forþam swa wlitigne man into heora mynstre gelædde," p. 344]. Although it is in fact a woman to whom the monks are drawn, the account evinces no surprise on anyone's part that the monks should experience intense sexual attraction toward a person ostensibly of their own gender.

Some theologians clearly regarded homosexual activity as a vice open to all rather than as the peculiar sexual outlet of a portion of the population, but this attitude was not universal and was often ambiguously or inconsistently held even by those who did most to promulgate it. Albertus Magnus and Thomas Aquinas both wrote of homosexual acts as sins that presumably anyone might commit, but both also recognized that it was somewhat more complex than this: Aquinas, following Aristotle, believed that some men were "naturally inclined" to desire sexual relations with other men—clearly a theory of Type B—and Albertus Magnus considered homosexual desire to be a manifestation of a contagious disease, particularly common among the wealthy, and curable through the application of medicine.[29] This attitude is highly reminiscent of psychiatric opinion in late Victorian times, and a far cry from categorizing homosexuality simply as a vice.

"Sodomy" was defined by many clerics as the improper emission of semen—the gender of the parties and their sexual appetites being irrelevant—but many others understood *sodomita* to apply specifically to men who preferred sexual contact with other men, generally or exclusively, and *sodomia* to apply only to the sexual acts performed in this context.[30]

Medieval literature abounds in suggestions that there is something special about homosexuality, that it is not simply an ordinary sin. Many writers view it as the special characteristic of certain peoples; others argue that it is completely unknown among their own kind. There are constant associations of homosexual preference with certain occupations or social positions, clearly indicating that it is linked in some way to personality or experience. The modern association of homosexuality with the arts had as its medieval counterpart a regular link with the religious life: When

Bernard of Clairvaux was asked to restore life to the dead son of a Marquess of Burgundy he had the boy taken to a private room and lay down upon him. No cure transpired; the boy remained lifeless. The chronicler, who had been present, nonetheless found humor in the incident and remarked, "That was the unhappiest monk of all. For I've never heard of any monk who lay down upon a boy that did not straightaway rise up after him. The abbot blushed and they went out as many laughed."[31]

Chaucer's pardoner, also a cleric, appears to be innately sexually atypical, and his association with the hare has led many to suppose that it is homosexuality that distinguishes him.[32] Even non-Christians linked the Christian clergy with homosexuality.[33]

Much of the literature of the High Middle Ages that deals with sexual-object choice assumes distinct dispositions, most often exclusive. A long passage in the *Roman d'Énéas* characterizes homosexual males as devoid of interest in women and notable in regard to dress, habits, decorum, and behavior.[34] Debates of the period characterize homosexual preference as innate or God-given, and in the well-known poem "Ganymede and Helen" it is made pellucidly clear that Ganymede is exclusively gay (before the intervention of the gods): It is Helen's frustration at his inability to respond properly to her advances that prompts the debate.[35] In a similar poem, "Ganymede and Hebe," homosexual relations are characterized as "decreed by fate," suggesting something quite different from an occasional vice.[36] Indeed, the mere existence of debates of this sort suggests very strongly a general conceptualization of sexuality as bifurcated into two camps distinguished by sexual object-choice. Popular terminology of the period corroborates this: as opposed to words like *sodomita*, which might designate indulgence in a specific activity by any human, writers of the High Middle Ages were inclined to use designations like "Ganymede," whose associations were exclusively homosexual, and to draw analogies with animals like the hare and the hyena, which were thought to be naturally inclined to sexual relations with their own gender.

Allain of Lille invokes precisely the taxonomy of sexual orientation used in the modern West in writing about sexuality among his twelfth-century contemporaries: "Of those men who employ the grammar of Venus there are some who embrace the masculine, others who embrace the feminine, and some who embrace both. . . ."[37]

Clearly all three types of taxonomy were known in Western Europe and the Middle East before the advent of modern capitalist societies. It is, on the other hand, equally clear that in different times and places one type of theory has often predominated over the others, and for long periods in many areas one or two of the three may have been quite rare. Does the prevalence of one theory over another in given times and places reveal something about human sexuality? Possibly, but many factors other than sexuality itself may influence, deform, alter, or transform conceptualizations of sexuality among peoples and individuals, and much attention must be devoted to analyzing such factors and their effects before it will be possible to use them effectively in analyzing the bedrock of sexuality beneath them.

Nearly all societies, for example, regulate sexual behavior in some way; most sophisticated cultures articulate rationalizations for their restrictions. The nature of such rationalizations will inevitably affect sexual taxonomy. If "the good" in matters sexual is equated with procreation, homosexual relations may be categorically distinguished from heterosexual ones as necessarily excluding the chief good of sexuality. Such a moral taxonomy might create a homosexual/heterosexual dichotomy in and of itself, independent of underlying personal attitudes. This appears, in fact, to have played some role in the Christian West. That some heterosexual relations also exclude procreation is less significant (though much heterosexual eroticism has been restricted in the West), because there is not an easily demonstrable *generic* incompatibility with procreative purpose. (Compare the association of chest hair with maleness: Not all men have hairy chests, but only men have chest hair; hence, chest hair is thought of as essentially masculine; though not all heterosexual couplings are procreative, only heterosexual acts could be procreative, so heterosexuality seems essentially procreative and homosexuality essentially not.)

In a society where pleasure or the enjoyment of beauty are recognized as legitimate aims of sexual activity, this dichotomy should seem less urgent. And in the Hellenistic and Islamic worlds, where sexuality has traditionally been restricted on the basis of standards of decorum and propriety[38] rather than procreative purpose, the homosexual/heterosexual dichotomy has been largely absent from public discourse. Just as the presence of the dichotomy might be traceable to aspects of social organization unrelated to sexual preference, however, its absence must likewise be seen as a moot datum: As has been shown, individual Greek and Muslim writers were often acutely conscious of such a taxonomy. The prevalence of either Type A or Type B concepts at the social level, in other words, may be related more to other social structures than to personal perceptions of or beliefs about the nature of sexuality.

Another factor, wholly overlooked in previous literature on this subject, is the triangular relationship of mediated desire, beauty, and sexual stereotypes. It seems safe enough to assume that most humans are influenced to some degree by the values of the society in which they live. Many desires are "mediated" by the valorization accorded things by surrounding society, rather than generated exclusively by the desiring individual. If one posits for the sake of argument two opposed sets of social values regarding beauty and sex roles, it is easy to see how conceptualizations of sexual desire might be transformed to fit "mediated desire" resulting from either pole. At one extreme, beauty is conceived as a male attribute: Standards and ideals of beauty are predicated on male models, art emphasizes male beauty, and males take pride in their own physical attractions. Greece and the Muslim world approach this extreme: Greek legend abounds in examples of males pursued for their beauty, standards of beauty are often predicated on male archetypes (Adonis, Apollo, Ganymede, Antinous), and beauty in males is considered a major good, for the individual and for his society. Likewise, in the Muslim world, archetypes of beauty are more often seen in masculine than in feminine terms, beauty is thought to be a great asset to a man, and the universal archetype of beauty, to which even beautiful women are compared, is Joseph.

This pole can be contrasted with societies in which "maleness" and beauty are thought unrelated or even contradictory, and beauty is generally predicated only of females. In such societies "maleness" is generally idealized in terms of social roles, as comprising, for example, forcefulness, strength, the exercise of power, aggression, etc. In the latter type of society, which the modern West approaches, "beauty" would generally seem inappropriate, perhaps even embarrassing in males, and males possessing it would be regarded as "effeminate" or sexually suspect to some degree.

In nearly all cultures some linkage is expressed between eroticism and beauty, and it should not therefore be surprising that in societies of the former type there will be greater emphasis on males as sex objects than in those of the latter type. Since beauty is conceptualized as a good, and since it is recognized to subsist on a large scale—perhaps even primarily— among men, men can be admired even by other men for their beauty, and this admiration is often indistinguishable (at the literary level, if not in reality) from erotic interest. In cultures of the latter type, however, men are not admired for their beauty; sexual interest is generally imagined to be applied by men (who are strong, forceful, powerful, etc., but not beautiful) to women, whose beauty may be considered their chief—or even sole—asset. In the latter case, expressions of admiration for male beauty will be rare, even among women, who will prize other attributes in men they desire.

These descriptions are deliberate oversimplifications to make a point: In fact, no society is exclusively one or the other, and elements of both are present in all Western cultures. But it would be easy to show that many societies tend more toward one extreme than the other, and it is not hard to see how this might affect the prominence of the homosexual/ heterosexual dichotomy: In a culture where male beauty was generally a source of admiration, the dividing line between what some taxonomies would define as homosexual and heterosexual interest would be considerably blurred by common usage and expression. Expressions of admiration and even attraction to male beauty would be so familiar that they would not provoke surprise or require designation as a peculiar category. Persons in such a society might be uninterested in genital interaction with persons of their own sex, might even disapprove of it, but they would tend not to see romantic interest in male beauty—by males or females—as bizarre or odd or as necessitating special categorization.

In cultures that deemphasize male beauty, however, expressions of interest in it by men or women might be suspect. In a society that has established no place for such interest in its esthetic structures, mere admiration for a man's physical attraction, without genital acts, could be sharply stigmatized, and a strict division between homosexual and heterosexual desire would be easy to promulgate and maintain.

Female roles would also be affected by such differences: If women are thought of as moved by beauty, even if it is chiefly male beauty, the adoption of the role of admirer by a woman will not seem odd or peculiar. If women are viewed, however, as the beautiful but passive objects of a sexual interest largely limited to men, their expressing sexual interest—in men or women—may be disapproved.[39] George Chauncey has documented precisely this sort of disapproval in Victorian medical literature on "homosexuality": At the outset sexual deviance is perceived only in women who violate the sex role expected of them by playing an active part in a female-female romantic relationship. The "passive" female, who does not violate expectations of sex role by receiving, as females are thought naturally to do, the attentions of her "husband," is not considered abnormal. Gradually, as attitudes and the needs of society to define more precisely the limits of approved sexuality change, attention is transferred from the role the female "husband" plays to the sexual object choice of both women, and both come to be categorized as "homosexual" on the basis of the gender to which they are attracted.[40]

Shifts of this sort, relating to conceptions of beauty, rationalization of sexual limitations, etc., are supported, affected, and overlaid by more specific elements of social organization. These include patterns of sexual interaction (between men and women, the old and young, the rich and the poor, etc.), specific sexual taboos, and what might be called "secondary" sexual behavior. Close attention must be devoted to such factors in their historical context in assessing sexual conceptualizations of any type.

Ancient "pederasty," for example, seems to many to constitute a form of sexual organization entirely unrelated to modern homosexuality. Possibly this is so, but the differences seem much less pronounced when one takes into account the sexual context in which "pederasty" occurs. The age differential idealized in descriptions of relations between the "lover" and the "beloved" is less than the disparity in age between heterosexual lovers as recommended, for example, by Aristotle (nineteen years). "Pederasty" may often represent no more than the homosexual side of a general pattern of cross-generation romance.[41] Issues of subordination and power likewise offer parallel structures that must be collated before any arguments about ancient "homosexuality" or "heterosexuality" can be mounted. Artemidorus Daldianus aptly encapsulates the conflation of sexual and social roles of his contemporaries in the second century A.D.

in his discussion of the significance of sexual dreams: "For a man to be penetrated [in a dream] by a richer and older man is good: for it is customary to receive from such men. To be penetrated by a younger and poorer is bad: for it is the custom to give to such persons. It signifies the same [i.e., is bad] if the penetrator is older and poor."[42] Note that these comments do not presuppose either Type A or Type B theories: They might be applied to persons who regard either gender as sexually apposite, or to persons who feel a predisposition to one or the other. But they do suggest the social matrix of a system of sexual distinctions that might override, alter, or disguise other taxonomies.

The special position of passive homosexual behavior, involving the most common premodern form of Type C theory, deserves a separate study, but it might be noted briefly that its effect on sexual taxonomies is related not only to status considerations about penetration, as indicated above, but also to specific sexual taboos that may be highly culturally variable. Among Romans, for instance, two roles were decorous for a free adult male, expressed by the verbs *irrumo*, to offer the penis for sucking, and *futuo*, to penetrate a female, or *pedico*, to penetrate a male.[43] Indecorous roles for citizen males, permissible for anyone else, were expressed in particular by the verbs *fello*, to fellate, and *ceveo*, not translatable into English.[44] The distinction between roles approved for male citizens and others appears to center on the giving of seed (as opposed to the receiving of it) rather than on the more familiar modern active/passive division. (American prison slang expresses a similar dichotomy with the terms "catchers" and "pitchers.") It will be seen that this division obviates to a large degree both the active/passive split—since both the *irrumator* and the *fellator* are conceptually active[45]—and the homosexual/heterosexual one, since individuals are categorized not according to the gender to which they are drawn but to the role they play in activities that could take place between persons of either gender. It is not clear that Romans had no interest in the gender of sexual partners, only that the division of labor, as it were, was a more pressing concern and attracted more analytical attention.

Artemidorus, on the other hand, considered both "active" and "passive" fellatio to be categorically distinct from other forms of sexuality. He divided his treatment of sexuality into three sections—the natural and legal, the illegal, and the unnatural—and he placed fellatio, in any form, among illegal activities, along with incest. In the ninth-century translation of his work by Hunain ibn Ishaq (the major transmitter of Aristotelian learning to the West), a further shift is evident: Hunain created a separate chapter for fellatio, which he called "that vileness of which it is not decent even to speak."[46]

In both the Greek and the Arabic versions of this work the fellatio that is objurgated is both homosexual and heterosexual, and in both, anal intercourse between men is spoken of with indifference or approval. Yet in the Christian West the most hostile legislation regarding sexual behavior has been directed specifically against homosexual anal intercourse: Fellatio has generally received milder treatment. Is this because fellatio is more widely practiced among heterosexuals in the West, and therefore seems less bizarre (i.e., less distinctly homosexual)? Or is it because passivity and the adoption of what seems a female role in anal intercourse is particularly objectionable in societies dominated by rigid ideals of "masculine" behavior? It may be revealing, in this context, that many modern languages, including English, have skewed the donor/recipient dichotomy by introducing a chiastic active/passive division: The recipient (i.e., of semen) in anal intercourse is "passive"; in oral intercourse he is "active." Could the blurring of the active/passive division in the case of fellatio render it less obnoxious to legislative sensibilities?

Beliefs about sexual categories in the modern West vary widely, from the notion that sexual behavior is entirely a matter of conscious choice to the conviction that all sexual behavior is determined by heredity or environment. The same individual may, in fact, entertain with apparent equanimity contradictory ideas on the subject. It is striking that many ardent proponents of Type C etiological theories who regard homosexual behavior as pathological and/or depraved nonetheless imply in their statements about the necessity for legal repression of homosexual behavior that it is potentially ubiquitous in the human population, and that if legal sanctions are not maintained everyone may suddenly become homosexual.

Humans of previous ages were probably not, as a whole, more logical or consistent than their modern descendants. To pretend that a single system of sexual categorization obtained at any previous moment in Western history is to maintain the unlikely in the face of substantial evidence to the contrary. Most of the current spectrum of belief appears to have been represented in previous societies. What that spectrum reveals about the inner nature of human sexuality remains, for the time being, moot and susceptible of many divergent interpretations. But if the revolution in modern historical writing—and the recovery of whatever past the "gay community" may be said to have—is not to be stillborn, the problem of universals must be sidestepped or at least approached with fewer doctrinaire assumptions. Both realists and nominalists must lower their voices. Reconstructing the monuments of the past from the rubble of the present requires quiet concentration.

Postscript

This essay was written five years ago, and several of the points it raises now require clarification or revision. I would no longer characterize the constructionist-essentialist controversy as a "debate" in any strict sense: One of its ironies is that no one involved in it actually identifies him- or herself as an "essentialist," although constructionists (of whom, in contrast, there are many)[47] sometimes so label other writers. Even when applied by its opponents the label seems to fit extremely few contemporary scholars.[48] This fact is revealing, and provides a basis for understanding the controversy more accurately not as a dialogue between two schools of thought, but as a revisionist (and largely one-sided) critique of assumptions believed to underlie traditional historiography. This understanding is not unrelated to my nominalist/realist analogy: One might describe constructionism (with some oversimplification) as a nominalist rejection of a tendency to "realism" in the traditional historiography of sexuality. The latter treated "homosexuality" as a diachronic, empirical entity (not quite a "universal," but "real" apart from social structures bearing on it); constructionists regard it as a culturally dependent phenomenon or, as some would have it, not a "real" phenomenon at all. It is not, nonetheless, a debate, since no current historians consciously defend an essentialist point of view.

Second, although it is probably still accurate to say that "most" constructionists are historians of the nineteenth and twentieth centuries, a number of classicists have now added their perspective to constructionist theory. This has broadened and deepened the discussion, although, strikingly, few if any historians of periods between Periclean Athens and the late nineteenth century articulate constructionist views.[49]

Third, my own position, perhaps never well understood, has changed. In my book *Christianity, Social Tolerance and Homosexuality* I defined "gay persons"[50] as those "conscious of erotic inclination toward their own gender as a distinguishing characteristic" (p. 44). It was the supposition of the book that such persons have been widely and identifiably present in Western society at least since Greco-Roman times, and this prompted many constructionists to label the work "essentialist." I would now define "gay persons" more simply as those whose erotic interest is predominantly directed toward their own gender (i.e., regardless of how conscious they are of this as a distinguishing characteristic). This is the sense in which, I believe, it is used by most American speakers, and although experts in a field may well wish to employ specialized language, when communicating with the public it seems to me counterproductive to use common words in senses different from or opposed to their ordinary meanings.

In this sense, I would still argue that there have been "gay persons" in most Western societies. It is not clear to me that this is an "essentialist" position. Even if societies formulate or create "sexualities" that are highly particular in some ways, it might happen that different societies would construct similar ones, as they often construct political or class structures similar enough to be subsumed under the same rubric (democracy, oligarchy, proletariat, aristocracy, etc.—all of which are both particular and general).[51]

Most constructionist arguments assume that essentialist positions necessarily entail a further supposition: that society does not create erotic feelings, but only acts on them. Some other force—genes, psychological forces, etc.—creates "sexuality," which is essentially independent of culture. This was not a working hypothesis of *Christianity, Social Tolerance and Homosexuality*. I was and remain agnostic about the origins and etiology of human sexuality.

March 1988

SEX BEFORE SEXUALITY: PEDERASTY, POLITICS, AND POWER IN CLASSICAL ATHENS

◆

David M. Halperin

The sexual practices and institutions of the classical Greeks, along with the enduring prestige that in modern times has traditionally surrounded their achievements, have long made them a kind of rallying point for lesbians and gay men of the educated classes, to whom they have seemed to offer an ideological weapon in the struggle for dignity and social acceptance. Recent scholarly attempts to bring the Greeks within the purview of the emerging "history of sexuality" have also focused on "Greek homosexuality." Against this background, David M. Halperin argues that in fact the Greek record confronts us with a radically unfamiliar set of values, behaviors, and social practices. These, Halperin further argues, expose the purely conventional character of our own social and sexual experiences, including, most notably, "sexuality," conceived as an autonomous dimension of human life, and "heterosexuality" and "homosexuality," understood as the fundamental organizing principles of sexual object-choice. According to Halperin, "heterosexuality" and "homosexuality" do not properly name eternal aspects of the human psyche but represent, instead, a distinctively modern cultural production alien to the experience of the ancient Greeks. The study of the cultural articulation of sexual desire in classical Athens therefore calls into question the stability of the concept of "sexuality" as a category of historical analysis.

I

In 1992, when the patriots among us will be celebrating the five hundredth anniversary of the discovery of America by Christopher Columbus, our cultural historians may wish to mark the centenary of an intellectual landfall of almost equal importance for the conceptual geography of the human sciences: the invention of homosexuality by Charles Gilbert Chaddock. Though he may never rank with Columbus in the annals of individual achievement, Chaddock would hardly seem to merit the obscurity that has surrounded him throughout the past hundred years. An early translator of Krafft-Ebing's *Psychopathia sexualis*, Chaddock is credited by the *Oxford English Dictionary*[1] with having introduced "homo-sexuality" into the English language in 1892, in order to render a German cognate twenty years its senior.[2] Homosexuality, for better or for worse, has been with us ever since.

Before 1892 there was no homosexuality, only sexual inversion. But, as George Chauncey, Jr., has demonstrated:

> Sexual inversion, the term used most commonly in the nineteenth century, did not denote the same conceptual phenomenon as homosexuality. "Sexual inversion" referred to a broad range of deviant gender behavior, of which homosexual desire was only a logical but indistinct aspect, while "homosexuality" focused on the narrower issue of sexual object choice. The differentiation of homosexual desire from "deviant" gender behavior at the turn of the century reflects a major reconceptualization of the nature of human sexuality, its relation to gender, and its role in one's social definition.[3]

Throughout the nineteenth century, in other words, sexual preference for a person of one's own sex was not clearly distinguished from other sorts of nonconformity to one's culturally defined sex role: Deviant object-choice was viewed as merely one of a number of pathological symptoms exhibited by those who reversed, or "inverted," their proper sex roles by adopting a masculine or a feminine style at variance with what was deemed natural and appropriate to their anatomical sex. Political aspirations in women and (at least according to one expert writing as late as 1920) a fondness for cats in men were manifestations of a pathological condition, a kind of psychological hermaphroditism tellingly but not essentially expressed by the preference for a "normal" member of one's own sex as a sexual partner.[4]

This outlook on the matter seems to have been shared by the scientists and by their unfortunate subjects alike: Inversion was not merely a

---

Note: Originally published, in different form, as "One Hundred Years of Homosexuality" in *The Mêtis of the Greeks*, ed. Milad Doueihi, *Diacritics*, 16, no. 2 (Summer 1986): 34–45.

medical rubric, then, but a category of lived experience. Karl Heinrich Ulrichs, for example, an outspoken advocate for the freedom of sexual choice and the founder, as early as 1862, of the cult of Uranism (based on Pausanias's praise of Uranian, or "heavenly," pederasty in Plato's *Symposium*), described his own condition as that of an *anima muliebris virili corpore inclusa*—a woman's soul confined by a man's body. That sexual object-choice might be wholly independent of such "secondary" characteristics as masculinity or femininity never seems to have occurred to anyone until Havelock Ellis waged a campaign to isolate object-choice from role-playing and, concurrently, Freud, in his classic analysis of a drive in the *Three Essays* (1905), clearly distinguished in the case of the libido between the sexual "object" and the sexual "aim."[5]

The conceptual isolation of sexuality per se from questions of masculinity and femininity made possible a new taxonomy of sexual behaviors and psychologies based entirely on the anatomical sex of the persons engaged in a sexual act (same sex vs. different sex); it thereby obliterated a number of distinctions that had traditionally operated within earlier discourses pertaining to same-sex sexual contacts and that had radically differentiated active from passive sexual partners, normal from abnormal (or conventional from unconventional) sexual roles, masculine from feminine styles, and pederasty from lesbianism: All such behaviors were now to be classed alike and placed under the same heading.[6] Sexual identity was thus polarized around a central opposition defined by the binary play of sameness and difference in the sexes of the sexual partners; people belonged henceforward to one or the other of two exclusive categories, and much ingenuity was lavished on the multiplication of techniques for deciphering what a person's sexual orientation "really" was—independent, that is, of beguiling appearances.[7] Founded on positive, ascertainable, and objective behavioral phenomena—on the facts of who had sex with whom—the new sexual taxonomy could lay claim to a descriptive, trans-historical validity. And so it crossed the "threshold of scientificity"[8] and was enshrined as a working concept in the social sciences.[9]

A scientific advance of such magnitude naturally demanded to be crowned by the creation of a new technical vocabulary, but, unfortunately, no objective, value-free words readily lent themselves to the enterprise. In 1891, just one year before the inauguration of "homosexuality," John Addington Symonds could still complain that "The accomplished languages of Europe in the nineteenth century supply no terms for this persistent feature of human psychology, without importing some implication of disgust, disgrace, vituperation."[10] A number of linguistic candidates were quickly put forward to make good this lack, and "homosexuality" (despite scattered protests over the years) gradually managed to fix its social-scientist signature upon the new conceptual dispensation. The word itself, as Havelock Ellis noted, is a barbarous neologism sprung from a monstrous mingling of Greek and Latin stock;[11] as such, it belongs to a rapidly growing lexical breed most prominently represented by the hybrid names given to other recent inventions—names whose mere enumeration suffices to conjure up the precise historical era responsible for producing them: e.g., "automobile," "television."

Unlike the language of technology, however, the new terminology for describing sexual behavior was slow to take root in the culture at large. In his posthumous autobiographical memoir, *My Father and Myself* (1968), J. R. Ackerley recalls how mystified he was when, about 1918, a Swiss friend asked him, "Are you homo or hetero?": "I had never heard either term before," he writes. Similarly, T. C. Worsley observes in his own memoir, *Flannelled Fool* (1966), that in 1929 "The word [homosexual], in any case, was not in general use, as it is now. Then it was still a technical term, the implications of which I was not entirely aware of."[12] These two memoirists, moreover, were not intellectually deficient men: At the respective times of their recorded bewilderment, Ackerley was shortly about to be, and Worsley already had been, educated at Cambridge. Nor was such innocence limited—in this one instance, at least—to the holders of university degrees: The British sociologist John Marshall, whose survey presumably draws on more popular sources, testifies that "a number of the elderly men I interviewed had never heard the term 'homosexual' until the 1950s."[13] The *Oxford English Dictionary*, originally published in 1933, is also ignorant of (if not willfully blind to) "homosexuality"; the word appears for the first time in the *OED*'s 1976 three-volume Supplement.[14]

It is not exactly my intention to argue that homosexuality, as we commonly understand it today, didn't exist before 1892. How, indeed, could it have failed to exist? The very word displays a most workmanlike and scientific indifference to cultural and environmental factors, looking only to the sexes of the persons engaged in the sexual act. Moreover, if homosexuality didn't exist before 1892, heterosexuality couldn't have existed either (it came into being, in fact, like Eve from Adam's rib, eight years later),[15] and without heterosexuality, where would all of us be right now?

The comparatively recent genesis of heterosexuality—strictly speaking, a twentieth-century affair—should provide a clue to the profundity of the cultural issues over which, hitherto, I have been so lightly skating. How is it possible that until the year 1900 there was not a precise, value-free, scientific term available to speakers of the English language for designating what we would now regard, in retrospect, as the mode of sexual behavior favored by the vast majority of people in our culture? Any answer to that question—which, in its broadest dimensions, I shall leave for the intellectual heirs of Michel Foucault to settle—must direct our attention to the inescapable historicity of even the most innocent, unassuming, and seemingly objective of cultural representations. Although a blandly descriptive, rigorously clinical term like "homosexuality" would appear to be unobjectionable as a taxonomic device, it carries with it a heavy complement of ideological baggage and has, in fact, proved a significant obstacle to understanding the distinctive features of sexual life in the ancient world.[16] It may well be that homosexuality properly speaking has no history of its own much before the beginning of our century. For, as John Boswell remarks, "If the categories 'homosexual/heterosexual' and 'gay/straight' are the inventions of particular societies rather than real aspects of the human psyche, there is no gay history."[17]

II

Of course, if we are to believe Foucault, there are basic historical and cultural factors that prohibit the easy application of the concept of homosexuality to persons living in premodern societies. For homosexuality presupposes sexuality: It implies the existence of a separate, sexual domain within the larger field of man's psychophysical nature and it requires the conceptual demarcation and isolation of that domain from other, more traditional, territories of personal and social life that cut across it, such as carnality, venery, libertinism, virility, passion, amorousness, eroticism, intimacy, love, affection, appetite, and desire—to name but a few. The invention of homosexuality therefore had to await, in the first place, the eighteenth-century discovery and definition of sexuality as the total ensemble of physiological and psychological mechanisms governing the individual's genital functions and the concomitant identification of that ensemble with a specially developed part of the brain and nervous system; it had also to await, in the second place, the early-nineteenth-century interpretation of sexuality as a singular "instinct" or "drive," a mute force that shapes our conscious life according to its own unassailable logic and thereby determines, at least in part, the character and personality of each one of us.[18]

Before the scientific construction of "sexuality" as a positive, distinct, and constitutive feature of individual human beings—an autonomous system within the physiological and psychological economy of the human organism—a person's sexual *acts* could be individually evaluated and categorized, but there was no conceptual apparatus available for identifying a person's fixed and determinate sexual *orientation*, much less for assessing and classifying it.[19] That human beings differ, often markedly, from one another in their sexual tastes in a great variety of ways (of which the liking for a sexual partner of a specific sex is only one, and not necessarily the most significant one) is an unexceptionable and, indeed, an ancient observation;[20] but it is not immediately evident that differences in sexual preference are by their very nature more revealing about the temperament of individual human beings, more significant determinants of personal identity, than, for example, differences in dietary preference.[21]

And yet, it would never occur to us to refer a person's dietary object-choice to some innate, characterological disposition or to see in his or her strongly expressed and even unvarying preference for the white meat of chicken the symptom of a profound psychophysical orientation, leading us to identify him or her in contexts quite removed from that of the eating of food as, say, a "pectoriphage" or a "stethovore" (to continue the practice of combining Greek and Latin roots); nor would we be likely to inquire further, making nicer discriminations according to whether an individual's predilection for chicken breasts expressed itself in a tendency to eat them quickly or slowly, seldom or often, alone or in company, under normal circumstances or only in periods of great stress, with a clear or a guilty conscience ("ego-dystonic pectoriphagia"), beginning in earliest childhood or originating with a gastronomic trauma suffered in adolescence.[22] If such questions did occur to us, moreover, I very much doubt whether we would turn to the academic disciplines of anatomy, neurology, clinical psychology, or genetics in the hope of obtaining a clear causal solution to them. That is because (1) we regard the liking for certain foods as a matter of taste; (2) we currently lack a theory of taste; and (3) in the absence of a theory we do not normally subject our behavior to intense scientific or etiological scrutiny.

In the same way, it never occurred to premodern cultures to ascribe a person's sexual tastes to some positive, structural, or constitutive feature of his or her personality. Just as we tend to assume that human beings are not individuated at the level of dietary preference and that we all, despite many pronounced and frankly acknowledged differences from one another in dietary habits, share the same fundamental set of alimentary appetites, and hence the same "dieticity" or "edility," so most premodern and non-Western cultures, despite an awareness of the range of possible variations in human sexual behavior, refuse to individuate human beings at the level of sexual preference and assume, instead, that we all share the same fundamental set of sexual appetites, the same "sexuality." For most of the world's inhabitants, in other words, "sexuality" is no more a fact of life than "dieticity." Far from being a necessary or intrinsic constituent of the eternal grammar of human subjectivity, "sexuality" seems to be a uniquely modern, Western, even bourgeois production—one of those cultural fictions that in every society give human beings access to themselves as meaningful actors in their world, and that are thereby objectivated.

At any rate, positivism dies hard, and sexual essentialism (the belief in fixed sexual essences) dies even harder. Not everyone will welcome a neohistoricist critique of "sexuality." John Boswell, for example, has argued reasonably enough that any debate over the existence of universals in human culture must distinguish between the respective modes of being proper to words, concepts, and experiences: According to this line of reasoning, the ancients experienced gravity even though they lacked both the term and the concept; similarly, Boswell claims that the "manifest and stated purpose" of Aristophanes' famous myth in Plato's *Symposium* "is to explain why humans are divided into groups of predominantly homosexual or heterosexual interest," and so this text, along with a number of others, vouches for the existence of homosexuality as an ancient (if not a universal) category of human experience—however newfangled the word for it may be.[23] Now the speech of Plato's Aristophanes would seem indeed to be a *locus classicus* for the differentiation of homo from heterosexuality, because Aristophanes' taxonomy of human beings features a distinction between those who desire a sexual partner of the same sex as themselves and those who desire a sexual partner of a different sex. The Platonic passage alone, then, would seem to offer sufficient warrant for positing an ancient concept, if not an ancient experience, of homosexuality. But closer examination reveals that Aristophanes stops short of deriving a distinction between homo- and heterosexuality from his own myth just when the logic of his analysis would seem to have driven him ineluctably to it. That omission is telling—and it is worth considering in greater detail.

According to Aristophanes, human beings were originally round, eight-limbed creatures, with two faces and two sets of genitals—both front and back—and three sexes (male, female, and androgyne). These ancestors of ours were powerful and ambitious; in order to put them in their place, Zeus had them cut in two, their skin stretched over the exposed flesh and tied at the navel, and their heads rotated so as to keep that physical reminder of their daring and its consequences constantly before their eyes. The severed halves of each former individual, once reunited, clung to one another so desperately and concerned themselves so little with their survival as separate entities that they began to perish for lack of sustenance; those who outlived their mates sought out persons belonging to the same sex as their lost complements and repeated their embraces in a foredoomed attempt to recover their original unity. Zeus at length took pity on them, moved their genitals to the side their bodies now faced, and invented sexual intercourse, so that the bereaved creatures might at least put a temporary terminus to their longing and devote their attention to other, more important (if less pressing) matters. Aristophanes extracts from this story a genetic explanation of observable differences among human beings with respect to sexual object-choice and preferred style of life: males who desire females are descended from an original androgyne (adulterers come from this species), whereas males descended from an original male "pursue their own kind, and would prefer to remain single and spend their entire lives with one another, since by nature they have no interest in marriage and procreation but are compelled to engage in them by social custom" (191e–192b, quoted selectively). Boswell, understandably, interprets this to mean that, according to Plato's Aristophanes, homosexual and heterosexual interests are "both exclusive and innate."[24]

But that, significantly, is not quite the way Aristophanes sees it. The conclusions that he draws from his own myth help to illustrate the lengths to which classical Athenians were willing to go in order to avoid conceptualizing sexual behaviors according to a binary opposition between different- and same-sex sexual contacts. First of all, Aristophanes' myth generates not two but at least three distinct "sexualities" (males attracted to males, females attracted to females, and—consigned alike to a single classification, evidently—males attracted to females as well as females attracted to males). Moreover, there is not the slightest suggestion in anything Aristophanes says that the sexual acts or preferences of persons descended from an original female are in any way similar to, let alone congruent or isomorphic with, the sexual acts or preferences of those descended from an original male;[25] hence, nothing in the text allows us to suspect the existence of even an implicit category to which males who desire males and females who desire females *both* belong in contradistinction to some *other* category containing males and females who desire one another.[26] On the contrary, one consequence of the myth is to make the sexual desire of every human being *formally identical* to that of every other: We are all looking for the same thing in a sexual partner, according to Plato's Aristophanes—namely, a symbolic substitute for an originary object once loved and subsequently lost in an archaic trauma. In that respect we all share the same "sexuality"—which is to say that, despite the differences in our personal preferences or tastes, we are not individuated at the level of our sexual being.

Second, and equally important, Aristophanes' account features a crucial distinction *within* the category of males who are attracted to males, an infrastructural detail missing from his description of each of the other two categories: "while they are still boys [i.e., pubescent or preadult],[27] they are fond of men, and enjoy lying down together with them and twining their limbs about them, . . . but when they become men they are lovers of boys. . . . Such a man is a pederast and philerast [i.e., fond of or responsive to adult male lovers]"[28] at *different stages of his life* (*Symposium* 191e–192b, quoted selectively). Contrary to the clear implications of the myth, in other words, and unlike the people comprehended by the first two categories, those descended from an original male are *not* attracted to one another *without qualification*; rather, they desire boys when they are men and they take a certain (nonsexual) pleasure in physical contact with men when they are boys.[29] Now since—as the foregoing passage suggests—the classical Athenians sharply distinguished the roles of pederast and philerast, relegating them not only to different age-classes but virtually to different "sexualities,"[30] what Aristophanes is describing here is not a single, homogeneous sexual orientation common to all those who descend from an original male but rather a set of distinct and incommensurable behaviors that such persons exhibit in different periods of their lives; although his genetic explanation of the diversity of sexual object-choice among human beings would seem to require that there be some adult males who are sexually attracted to other adult males, Aristophanes appears to be wholly unaware of such a possibility, and in any case he has left no room for it in his taxonomic scheme.[31] That omission is all the more unexpected because, as Boswell himself has pointed out (in response to the present argument), the archetypal pairs of lovers from whom all homoerotically inclined males are supposed to descend must themselves have been the same age as one another, inasmuch as they were originally halves of the same being.[32] No age-matched couples figure among their latter-day offspring, however: The social reality described by Aristophanes features an erotic asymmetry absent from the mythical paradigm used to generate it. In the world of contemporary Athenian actuality—at least, as Aristophanes portrays it—reciprocal erotic desire among males is unknown.[33] Those who descend from an original male are not defined as male homosexuals but as willing boys when they are young and as lovers of youths when they are old. Contrary to Boswell's reading of the passage, then, neither the concept nor the experience of "homosexuality" is known to Plato's Aristophanes.

A similar conclusion can be drawn from careful examination of the other document from antiquity that might seem to vouch for the existence both of homosexuality as an indigenous category and of homosexuals as a native species. Unlike the myth of Plato's Aristophanes, a famous and much-excerpted passage from a classic work of Greek prose, the document to which I refer is little known and almost entirely neglected by modern historians of "sexuality";[34] its date is late, its text is corrupt, and, far from being a self-conscious literary artifact, it forms part of a Roman technical treatise. But despite its distance from Plato in time, in style, in language, and in intent, it displays the same remarkable innocence of modern sexual categories, and I have chosen to discuss it here partly in order to show what can be learned about the ancient world from texts that lie outside the received canon of classical authors. Let us turn, then, to the ninth chapter in the Fourth Book of *De morbis chronicis*, a mid-fifth-century A.D. Latin translation and adaptation by the African writer Caelius Aurelianus of a now largely lost work on chronic diseases by the Greek physician Soranus, who practiced and taught in Rome during the early part of the second century A.D.

The topic of this chapter is *molles* (*malthakoi* in Greek)—that is, "soft" or unmasculine men who depart from the cultural norm of manliness insofar as they actively desire to be subjected by other men to a "feminine" (i.e., receptive) role in sexual intercourse. Caelius begins with an implicit defense of his own unimpeachable masculinity by noting how difficult it is to believe that such people actually exist;[35] he then goes on to observe that the cause of their affliction is not natural (that is, organic) but is rather their own excessive desire, which—in a desperate and foredoomed attempt to satisfy itself—drives out their sense of shame and forcibly converts parts of their bodies to sexual uses not intended by nature. These men willingly adopt the dress, gait, and other characteristics of women, thereby confirming that they suffer not from a bodily disease but from a mental (or moral) defect. After some further arguments in support of that point, Caelius draws an interesting comparison: "For just as the women called *tribades* [in Greek], because they practise both kinds of sex, are more eager to have sexual intercourse with women than with men and pursue women with an almost masculine jealousy . . . so they too [i.e., the *molles*] are afflicted by a mental disease" (132–133). The mental disease in question, which strikes both men and women alike and is defined as a perversion of sexual desire, would certainly seem to be nothing other than homosexuality as it is often understood today.

Several considerations combine to prohibit that interpretation, however. First of all, what Caelius treats as a pathological phenomenon is not the desire on the part of either men or women for sexual contact with a person of the same sex; quite the contrary: Elsewhere, in discussing the treatment of satyriasis (a state of abnormally elevated sexual desire accompanied by itching or tension in the genitals), he issues the following advice to people who suffer from it (*De morbis acutis*, 3.18.180–181).[36]

> Do not admit visitors and particularly young women and boys. For the attractiveness of such visitors would again kindle the feeling of desire in the patient. Indeed, *even healthy persons*, seeing them, would in many cases seek sexual gratification, stimulated by the tension produced in the parts [i.e., in their own genitals].[37]

There is nothing medically problematical, then, about a desire on the part of males to obtain sexual pleasure from contact with males; what is of concern to Caelius,[38] as well as to other ancient moralists,[39] is the male desire to be sexually penetrated by males, for such a desire represents the voluntary abandonment of a "masculine" identity in favor of a "feminine" one. It is sex-role reversal, or *gender deviance*, that is problematized here and that also furnishes part of the basis for Caelius's comparison of *molles* to *tribades*, who assume a "masculine" role in their relations with other women and actively "pursue women with an almost *masculine* jealousy." Indeed, the "soft"—that is, sexually submissive—man, possessed of a shocking and paradoxical desire to surrender his masculine autonomy and precedence, is monstrous precisely because he seems to have "a woman's soul confined by a man's body" and thus to violate the deeply felt and somewhat anxiously defended sense of congruence on the part of the ancients between gender, sexual practices, and social identity.[40]

Second, the ground of the similitude between Caelius's *molles* and *tribades* is not that they are both homosexual but rather that they are both *bi*sexual (in our terms). The *tribades* "are *more* eager to have sexual intercourse with women *than with men*" and "practise both kinds of sex"—that is, they have sex with both men and women.[41] As for the *molles*, Caelius's earlier remarks about their extraordinarily intense sexual desire implies that they turn to receptive sex because, although they try, they are not able to satisfy themselves by means of more conventionally masculine sorts of sexual activity, including insertive sex with women;[42] far from having desires that are structured differently from those of normal folk, these gender-deviants desire sexual pleasure just as most people do, but they have such strong and intense desires that they are driven to devise some unusual and disreputable (though ultimately futile) means of gratifying them. That diagnosis becomes explicit at the conclusion of the chapter when Caelius explains why the disease responsible for turning men into *molles* is the only chronic disease that becomes stronger as the body grows older (137).

> For in other years when the body is still strong and can perform the normal functions of love, the sexual desire [of these persons] assumes a dual aspect, in which the soul is excited sometimes while playing a passive and sometimes while playing an active role. But in the case of old men who have lost their virile powers, all their sexual desire is turned in the opposite direction and consequently exerts a stronger demand for the feminine role in love. In fact, many infer that this is the reason why boys too are victims of this affliction. For, like old men, they do not possess virile powers; that is, they have not yet attained those powers which have already deserted the aged.[43]

"Soft" or unmasculine men, far from being a fixed and determinate sexual species, are evidently either men who once experienced an orthodoxly masculine sexual desire in the past or who will eventually experience such a desire in the future. They may well be men with a constitutional tendency to gender-deviance, according to Caelius, but they are not homosexuals. Moreover, all the other ancient texts known to me that place in the same category both males who enjoy sexual contact with males and females who enjoy sexual contact with females display one or the other of the two taxonomic strategies employed by Caelius Aurelianus: If such men and women are classified alike, it is either because they are both held to *reverse* their proper sex roles and to adopt the sexual styles, postures, and modes of copulation conventionally associated with the opposite sex or because they are both held to *alternate* between the personal characteristics and sexual practices proper, respectively, to men and to women.[44] No category of homosexuality, defined in such a way as to contain men and women alike, is indigenous to the ancient world.

No scruple need prevent *us*, to be sure, from qualifying as "homosexual" any person who seeks sexual contact with another person of the same sex, whether male or female. But the issue before us isn't whether or not we can accurately apply our concept of homosexuality to the ancients—whether or not, that is, we can discover in the historical record

of classical antiquity evidence of behaviors or psychologies that are ame-
nable to classification in our own terms (obviously, we can, given the
supposedly descriptive and trans-historical nature of those terms); the
issue isn't even whether or not the ancients were able to express within
the terms provided by their own conceptual schemes an experience of
something approximating to homosexuality as we understand it today.[45]
The real issue confronting any cultural historian of antiquity, and any
critic of contemporary culture, is, first of all, how to recover the terms in
which the experiences of individuals belonging to past societies were
actually constituted and, second, how to measure and assess the differences between those terms and the ones we currently employ. For, as this
very controversy over the scope and applicability of sexual categories
illustrates, concepts in the human sciences—unlike in this respect, perhaps, concepts in the natural sciences (such as gravity)—do not merely
describe reality but, at least partly, constitute it.[46] What this implies about
the issue before us may sound paradoxical, but it is, I believe, profound—or,
at least, worth pondering: Although there have been, in many different
times and places (including classical Athens), persons who sought sexual
contact with other persons of the same sex as themselves, it is only within
the last hundred years or so that such persons (or some portion of them)
have been homosexuals.

Instead of attempting to trace the history of "homosexuality" as if it
were a *thing*, therefore, we might more profitably analyze how the significance of same-sex sexual contacts has been variously constructed over
time by members of human living groups. Such an analysis will probably
lead us into a plurality of only partly overlapping social and conceptual
territories, a series of cultural formations that vary as their constituents
change, combine in different sequences, or compose new patterns. In the
following paragraphs I shall attempt to draw a very crude outline of the
cultural formation underlying the classical Athenian institution of pederasty, an outline whose details will have to be filled in at some later point
if this aspect of ancient Greek social relations is ever to be understood
historically.

III

The attitudes and behaviors publicly displayed by the citizens of Athens
(to whom the surviving evidence for the classical period effectively re-
stricts our power to generalize) tend to portray sex not as a collective
enterprise in which two or more persons jointly engage but rather as an
action performed by one person upon another. The foregoing statement
does not purport to describe positively what the experience of sex was
"really" like for all members of Athenian society but to indicate how sex
is *represented* by those utterances and actions of free adult males that

were intended to be overheard and witnessed by other free adult males.[47] Sex, as it is constituted by this public, masculine discourse, is either act or impact: It is not knit up in a web of mutuality, not something one invariably has *with* someone. Even the verb *aphrodisiazein*, meaning "to have sex" or "to take active sexual pleasure," is carefully differentiated into an active and a passive form; the active form occurs, tellingly, in a late antique list (that we nonetheless have good reason to consider representative for ancient Mediterranean culture, rather than eccentric to it)[48] of acts that "do not regard one's neighbors but only the subjects themselves and are not done in regard to or through others: namely, speaking, singing, dancing, fist-fighting, competing, hanging oneself, dying, being crucified, diving, finding a treasure, having sex, vomiting, moving one's bowels, sleeping, laughing, crying, talking to the gods, and the like."[49] As John J. Winkler, in a commentary on this passage, observes, "It is not that second parties are not present at some of these events (speaking, boxing, competing, having sex, being crucified, flattering one's favorite divinity), but that their successful achievement does not depend on the cooperation, much less the benefit, of a second party."[50]

Not only is sex in classical Athens not intrinsically relational or collaborative in character; it is, further, a deeply polarizing experience: It serves to divide, to classify, and to distribute its participants into distinct and radically dissimilar categories. Sex possesses this valence, apparently, because it is conceived to center essentially on, and to define itself around, an asymmetrical gesture, that of the penetration of the body of one person by the body—and, specifically, by the phallus[51]—of another. Phallic penetration, moreover, is construed as sexual "activity"; even if a sexual act does not involve physical penetration, it still remains polarized by the distribution of phallic pleasure: The partner whose pleasure is promoted is considered "active," while the partner who puts his or her body *at the service* of another's pleasure is deemed "passive"—read "penetrated," in the culture's unself-conscious ideological shorthand. Sexual penetration, and sexual "activity" in general, are, in other words, thematized as domination: The relation between the "active" and the "passive" sexual partner is thought of as the same kind of relation as that obtaining between social superior and social inferior, between master and servant.[52] "Active" and "passive" sexual roles are therefore necessarily isomorphic with superordinate and subordinate social status; hence, an adult, male citizen of Athens can have legitimate sexual relations only with statutory minors (his inferiors not in age but in social and political status): The proper targets of his sexual desire include, specifically, women, boys, foreigners, and slaves—all of them persons who do not enjoy the same legal and political rights and privileges that he does.[53] Furthermore, what a citizen does in bed reflects the differential in status that distinguishes him from his sexual partner: The citizen's superior prestige and authority express themselves by his sexual precedence—by his power to initiate a sexual act, his right to obtain pleasure from it, and his assumption of an "active" sexual role. What Paul Veyne has said about the Romans can apply equally well to the classical Athenians: They were indeed puritans when it came to sex, but (unlike modern bourgeois Westerners) they were not puritans about conjugality and reproduction; rather, like many Mediterranean peoples, they were puritans about virility.[54]

The very enterprise of inquiring into ancient Greek "sexuality," then, necessarily obscures the nature of the phenomenon it is designed to elucidate because it effectively isolates sexual norms from social practices and thereby conceals the strict sociological correspondences between them. In classical Athens sex, as we have seen, was not simply a private quest for mutual pleasure that absorbed, if only temporarily, the social identities of its participants. Sex was a manifestation of public status, a declaration of social identity; it did not so much express an individual's unique "sexuality" as it served to position social actors in the places assigned to them (by virtue of their political standing) in the hierarchical structure of the Athenian polity. Instead of reflecting the peculiar sexual orientation of individual Athenians, the sexual protocols of classical Athens reflected a marked division in the social organization of the city-state between a superordinate group, composed of citizens, and a subordinate group, composed of noncitizens; sex between members of the first group was practically inconceivable, whereas sex between a member of the first group and a member of the second group mirrored in the minute details of its hierarchical arrangement the relation of structured inequality that governed their wider social interaction. Far from being interpreted as an expression of commonality, as a sign of some shared sexual status or orientation, sex between social superordinate and subordinate served, at least in part, to articulate the social distance between them. To assimilate both the senior and the junior partner in a pederastic relationship to the same "sexuality," for example, would therefore have struck a classical Athenian as no less bizarre than to classify a burglar as an "active criminal," his victim as a "passive criminal," and the two of them alike as partners in crime[55] (burglary—like sex, as the Greeks understood it—is, after all, a "nonrelational" act). The sexual identities of the ancient Greeks— their experiences of themselves as sexual actors and as desiring human beings—were hardly autonomous; quite the contrary: They were inseparable from, if not determined by, their social identities, their outward, public standing. Indeed, the classical Greek record strongly supports the conclusion drawn (from a quite different body of evidence) by the French anthropologist Maurice Godelier: "It is not sexuality which haunts society, but society which haunts the body's sexuality."[56]

In classical Athens, then, sexual partners came in two different kinds— not male and female but active and passive, dominant and submissive.[57] The relevant features of a sexual object were not so much determined by a physical typology of genders as by the social articulation of power. That is why the currently fashionable distinction between homosexuality and heterosexuality had no meaning for the classical Athenians: There were not, so far as they knew, two different kinds of "sexuality," two differently structured psychosexual states or modes of affective orientation, but a single form of sexual experience, which all free adult males shared— making due allowance for variations in individual tastes, as one might make for individual palates. Thus, in the Third Dithyramb by the classical poet Bacchylides, the Athenian hero Theseus, voyaging to Crete among the seven youths and seven maidens destined for the Minotaur and defending one of the maidens from the sexual advances of the libidinous Cretan commander, warns him vehemently against molesting *any one* of the Athenian youths (*tin' ēïtheôn:* 43)—that is, any girl *or boy.* Conversely, the antiquarian *littérateur* Athenaeus, writing six or seven hundred years later, is amazed that Polycrates, the tyrant of Samos in the sixth century B.C., did not send for any boys *or women* along with the other luxury articles he imported to Samos for his personal use during his reign, "despite his passion for relations with males" (12.540c–e).[58] Now *both* the notion that an act of heterosexual aggression in itself makes the aggressor suspect of homosexual tendencies *and* the mirror-opposite notion that a person with marked homosexual tendencies is bound to hanker after heterosexual contacts are nonsensical to us, associating as we do sexual object-choice with a determinate kind of "sexuality," a fixed sexual nature, but it would be a monumental task indeed to enumerate all the ancient documents in which the alternative "boy or woman" occurs with perfect nonchalance in an erotic context, as if the two were functionally interchangeable.[59] Scholars sometimes describe this cultural formation as a bisexuality of penetration[60] or as a heterosexuality indifferent to its object,[61] but I think it would be more accurate to describe it as a single, undifferentiated phallic "sexuality" of penetration and domination, a socio-sexual discourse whose basic terms are phallus and non-phallus.[62]

If there is a lesson that historians should draw from this picture of ancient sexual attitudes and behaviors, it is that we need to de-center *sexuality* from the focus of the interpretation of sexual experience. Just because modern bourgeois Westerners are so obsessed with sexuality, so convinced that it holds the key to the hermeneutics of the self (and hence to social psychology as an object of historical study), we ought not therefore to conclude that everyone has always considered sexuality a basic and irreducible element in, or a central feature of, human life. On the contrary, if the sketch I have offered is accurate, it seems that many ancients conceived of "sexuality" in nonsexual terms: What was fundamental to their experience of sex was not anything *we* would regard as essentially sexual; rather, it was something essentially social—namely, the modality of power relations that informed and structured the sexual act. Instead of viewing public and political life as a dramatization of individual sexual psychology, as we often tend to do, they saw sexual behavior as an expression of the dominant themes in contemporary social relations. When Artemidorus, a master dream analyst who lived and wrote in the second century A.D., came to address the meaning of sexual dreams, for example, he almost never presumed that such dreams were *really* about sex: They were about the rise and fall of the dreamer's public fortunes, the vicissitudes of his domestic economy.[63] If a man dreams of having sex with his mother, according to Artemidorus, his dream signifies nothing in particular about his own sexual psychology, his fantasy life, or the history of his relations with his parents; it may signify—depending on the family's circumstances at the time, the sexual postures of the partners in the dream, and the mode of penetration—that the dreamer will be successful in politics, that he will go into exile or return from exile, that he will win his lawsuit, obtain a rich harvest from his lands, or change professions, among many other things (1.79). Artemidorus' system of dream interpretation begs to be compared to the indigenous dream lore of certain Amazonian tribes, equally innocent of "sexuality," who (despite their quite different socio-sexual systems) also believe in the predictive value of dreams and similarly reverse what modern bourgeois Westerners take to be the natural flow of signification in dreams (i.e., from what is public and social to what is private and sexual): in both Kagwahiv and Mehinaku culture, for example, dreaming about the female genitalia portends a wound; dreamt wounds do not symbolize the female genitalia.[64]

To discover and to write the history of sexuality has long seemed to many a sufficiently radical undertaking in itself, inasmuch as its effect (if not the intention behind it) is to call into question the very naturalness of what we currently take to be essential to our individual natures. But in the course of implementing that ostensibly radical project many historians of sexuality seem to have reversed—perhaps unwittingly—its radical design: By preserving "sexuality" as a stable category of historical analysis not only have they not denaturalized it but, on the contrary, they have newly idealized it.[65] To the extent, in fact, that histories of "sexuality" succeed in concerning themselves with *sexuality*, to just that extent are they doomed to fail as *histories* (Foucault himself taught us that much), unless they also include as an integral part of their proper enterprise the task of demonstrating the historicity, conditions of emergence, modes of construction, and ideological contingencies of the very categories of analysis that undergird their own practice.[66] Instead of concentrating our attention specifically on the history of sexuality, then, we need to define and refine a new, and radical, historical sociology of psychology, an intellectual discipline designed to analyze the cultural poetics of desire, by which I mean the processes whereby sexual desires are constructed, mass-produced, and distributed among the various members of human living-groups.[67] We must train ourselves to recognize conventions of feeling as well as conventions of behavior and to interpret the intricate texture of personal life as an artefact, as the determinate outcome, of a complex and arbitrary constellation of cultural processes. We must, in short, be willing to admit that what seem to be our most inward, authentic, and private experiences are actually, in Adrienne Rich's admirable phrase, "shared, unnecessary/and political."[68]

SEXUAL MATTERS: RETHINKING SEXUALITY IN HISTORY

◆

ROBERT PADGUG

Denying that the categories of sexual behavior currently familiar to us (heterosexual, homosexual, etc.) are predetermined and universal, Padgug argues, *contra* Boswell, that our sexuality is neither a fixed essence nor even, necessarily, an individual's innermost reality. To the contrary, human sexuality, unlike animal sexuality, is never more than "a set of potentialities," rich and ever-varying, tied above all to whatever is currently viewed as *social* reality. Just as social reality changes radically through time, so do the sexual categories that reflect it.

Sexuality—the subject matter seems so obvious that it hardly appears to need comment. An immense and ever-increasing number of "discourses" has been devoted to its exploration and control during the last few centuries, and their very production has, as Foucault points out,[1] been a major characteristic of bourgeois society. Yet, ironically, as soon as we attempt to apply the concept to history, apparently insurmountable problems confront us.

To take a relatively simple example, relevant to one aspect of sexuality only, what are we to make of the ancient Greek historian Alexis' curious description of Polykrates, sixth-century B.C. ruler of Samos?[2] In the course of his account of the luxurious habits of Polykrates, Alexis stresses his numerous imports of foreign goods, and adds: "Because of all this

---

Note: Originally published, in different form, *Radical History Review* 20 (Spring/Summer 1979): 3–23.

there is good reason to marvel at the fact that the tyrant is not mentioned as having sent for women or boys from anywhere, despite his passion for liaisons with males. . . ." Now, that Polykrates did not "send for women" would seem to us to be a direct corollary of "his passion for liaisons with males." But to Alexis—and we know that his attitude was shared by all of Greek antiquity[3]—sexual passion in any form implied sexual passion in all forms. Sexual categories which seem so obvious to us, those which divide humanity into "heterosexuals" and "homosexuals," seem unknown to the ancient Greeks.

In any approach that takes as predetermined and universal the categories of sexuality, real history disappears. Sexual practice becomes a more or less sophisticated selection of curiosities, whose meaning and validity can be gauged by that truth—or rather truths, since there are many competitors—which we, in our enlightened age, have discovered. This procedure is reminiscent of the political economy of the period before, and all too often after, Marx, but it is not a purely bourgeois failing. Many of the chief sinners are Marxists.

A surprising lack of a properly historical approach to the subject of sexuality has allowed a fundamentally bourgeois view of sexuality and its subdivisions to deform twentieth-century Marxism. Marx and Engels themselves tended to neglect the subject and even Engels' *Origin of the Family, Private Property and the State* by no means succeeded in making it a concern central to historical materialism. The Marxism of the Second International, trapped to so great a degree within a narrow economism, mainly dismissed sexuality as merely superstructural. Most later Marxist thought and practice, with a few notable exceptions—Alexandra Kollontai, Wilhelm Reich, the Frankfurt School—has in one way or another accepted this judgment.

In recent years questions concerning the nature of sexuality have been re-placed on the Marxist agenda by the force of events and movements. The women's movement, and, to an increasing degree, the gay movement, have made it clear that a politics without sexuality is doomed to failure or deformation; the strong offensive of the American right-wing, which combines class and sexual politics, can only reenforce this view.[4] The feminist insistence that "the personal *is* political," itself a product of ongoing struggle, represents an immense step forward in the understanding of social reality, one which must be absorbed as a living part of Marxist attitudes toward sexuality. The important comprehension that sexuality, class, and politics cannot easily be disengaged from one another must serve as the basis of a materialist view of sexuality in historical perspective as well.

The most commonly held twentieth-century assumptions about sexuality imply that it is a separate category of existence (like "the economy," or "the state," other supposedly independent spheres of reality), almost identical with the sphere of private life. Such a view necessitates the location of sexuality within the individual as a fixed essence, leading to a classic division of individual and society and to a variety of psychological determinisms, and, often enough, to a full-blown biological determinism as well. These in turn involve the enshrinement of contemporary sexual categories as universal, static, and permanent, suitable for the analysis of all human beings and all societies. Finally, the consequences of this view are to restrict class struggle to nonsexual realms, since that which is private, sexual, and static is not a proper arena for public social action and change.

If we compare human sexuality with that of other species, we are immediately struck by its richness, its vast scope, and the degree to which its potentialities can seemingly be built upon endlessly, implicating the entire human world. Animal sexuality, by contrast, appears limited, constricted, and predefined in a narrow physical sphere.

This is not to deny that human sexuality, like animal sexuality, is deeply involved with physical reproduction and with intercourse and its pleasures. Biological sexuality is the necessary precondition for human sexuality. But biological sexuality is only a precondition, a set of potentialities, which is never unmediated by human reality, and which becomes transformed in qualitatively new ways in human society. The rich and ever-varying nature of such concepts and institutions as marriage, kinship, "love," "eroticism" in a variety of physical senses and as a component of fantasy and religious, social, and even economic reality, and the general human ability to extend the range of sexuality far beyond the physical body, all bear witness to this transformation.

Even this bare catalogue of examples demonstrates that sexuality is closely involved in *social* reality. Marshall Sahlins makes the point clearly, when he argues that sexual reproduction and intercourse must not be

> considered *a priori* as a biological fact, characterized as an urge of human nature independent of the relations between social persons . . . [and] acting *upon* society from without (or below). [Uniquely among human beings] the process of "conception" is always a double entendre, since no satisfaction can occur without the act and the partners as socially defined and contemplated, that is, according to a symbolic code of persons, practices and proprieties.[5]

Such an approach does not seek to eliminate biology from human life, but to absorb it into a unity with social reality. Biology as a set of potentialities and insuperable necessities[6] provides the material of social interpretations and extensions; it does not *cause* human behavior, but conditions and limits it. Biology is not a narrow set of absolute imperatives. That it is malleable and broad is as obvious for animals, whose nature is altered with changing environment, as for human beings.[7] The uniqueness of human beings lies in their ability to create the environment which alters their own—and indeed other animals'—biological nature.

It is clear, within certain limits, human beings have no fixed, inherited nature. We *become* human only in human society. Lucien Malson may overstate his case when he writes, "The idea that man has no nature is now beyond dispute. He has or rather is a history,"[8] but he is correct to focus on history and change in the creation of human culture and personality. Social reality cannot simply be "peeled off" to reveal "natural man" lurking beneath.[9]

This is true of sexuality in all its forms, from what seem to be the most purely "natural" acts of intercourse[10] or gender differentiation and hierarchy to the most elaborated forms of fantasy or kinship relations. Contrary to a common belief that sexuality is simply "natural" behavior, "nothing is more essentially transmitted by a social process of learning than sexual behavior," as Mary Douglas notes.[11]

There do exist certain sexual forms which, at least at a high level of generality, are common to all human societies: live, intercourse, kinship, can be understood universally on a very general level. But that both "saint and sinner" have erotic impulses, as George Bataille rightly claims,[12] or that Greece, Medieval Europe, and modern capitalist societies share general sexual forms, do not make the contents and meaning of these impulses and forms identical or undifferentiated. They must be carefully distinguished and separately understood, since their inner structures and social meanings and articulations are very different. The content and meaning of the eroticism of Christian mysticism is by no means reducible to that of Henry Miller, nor is the asceticism of the monk identical to that of the Irish peasants who delay their marriages to a relatively late age.[13]

The forms, content, and context of sexuality always differ. There is no abstract and universal category of "the erotic" or "the sexual" applicable without change to all societies. Any view which suggests otherwise is hopelessly mired in one or another form of biologism, and biologism is easily put forth as the basis of normative attitudes toward sexuality, which, if deviated from, may be seen as rendering the deviant behavior "unhealthy" and "abnormal." Such views are as unenlightening when dealing with Christian celibacy as when discussing Greek homosexual behavior.

Sexuality as Praxis (I)

When we look more directly at the social world itself, it becomes apparent that the general distinguishing mark of human sexuality, as of all social reality, is the unique role played in its construction by language, consciousness, symbolism, and labor, which, taken together—as they must be—are *praxis*, the production and reproduction of material life. Through *praxis* human beings produce an ever-changing human world within nature and give order and meaning to it, just as they come to know and give meaning to, and, to a degree, change, the realities of their own bodies, their physiology.[14] The content of sexuality is ultimately provided by human social relations, human productive activities, and human consciousness. The *history* of sexuality is therefore the history of a subject whose meaning and contents are in continual process of change. It is the history of social relations.

For sexuality, although part of material reality, is not itself an object or thing. It is rather a group of social relations, of human interactions. Marx writes in the *Grundrisse* that "Society does not consist of individuals, but expresses the sum of interrelations, the relations within which these individuals stand."[15] This seems to put the emphasis precisely where it should be: Individuals do exist as the constituent elements of society, but society is not the simple multiplication of isolated individuals. It is constituted only by the relationships between those individuals. On the other hand, society does not stand outside of and beyond the individuals who exist within it, but is the expression of their complex activity. The emphasis is on activity and relationships, which individuals ultimately create and through which, in turn, they are themselves created and modified. Particular individuals are both subjects and objects within the process, although in class societies the subjective aspect tends to be lost to sight and the processes tend to become reified as objective conditions working from outside.

Sexuality is relational.[16] It consists of activity and interactions—active social relations—and not simply "acts," as if sexuality were the enumeration and typology of an individual's orgasms (as it sometimes appears to be conceived of in, for example, the work of Kinsey and others), a position which puts the emphasis back within the individual alone. "It" does not do anything, combine with anything, appear anywhere; only people, acting within specific relationships create what we call sexuality. This is a significant aspect of what Marx means when he claims, in the famous Sixth Thesis on Feuerbach, that "the essence of man is no abstraction inherent in each single individual. In its reality it is the ensemble of the social relations."[17] Social relations, like the biological inheritance, at once create, condition, and limit the possibilities of individual activity and personality.

Praxis is fully meaningful only at the level of socio-historical reality. The particular interrelations and activities which exist at any moment in a specific society create sexual and other categories which, ultimately, determine the broad range of modes of behavior available to individuals who are born within that society. In turn, the social categories and interrelations are themselves altered over time by the activities and changing relationships of individuals. Sexual categories do not make manifest essences implicit within individuals, but are the expression of the active relationships of the members of entire groups and collectivities.

We can understand this most clearly by examining particular categories. We speak, for example, of homosexuals and heterosexuals as distinct categories of people, each with its sexual essence and personal behavioral characteristics. That these are not "natural" categories is evident. Freud, especially in the *Three Essays on the Theory of Sexuality*, and other psychologists have demonstrated that the boundaries between the two groups in our own society are fluid and difficult to define. And, as a result of everyday experience as well as the material collected in surveys like the Kinsey reports, we know that the categories of heterosexuality and homosexuality are by no means coextensive with the activities and personalities of heterosexuals and homosexuals. Individuals belonging to either group are capable of performing and, on more or less numerous occasions, do perform acts, and have behavioral characteristics and display social relationships thought specific to the other group.

The categories in fact take what are no more than a group of more or less closely related acts ("homosexual"/"heterosexual" behavior) and convert them into case studies of people ("homosexuals"/"heterosexuals"). This conversion of acts into roles/personalities, and ultimately into entire subcultures, cannot be said to have been accomplished before at least the seventeenth century, and, as a firm belief and more or less close approximation of reality, the late nineteenth century.[18] What we call "homosexuality" (in the sense of the distinguishing traits of "homosexuals"), for example, was not considered a unified set of acts, much less a set of qualities defining particular persons, in pre-capitalist societies. Jeffrey Weeks, in discussing the act of Henry VIII of 1533 which first brought sodomy within the purview of statute law, argues that

> the central point was that the law was directed against a series of sexual acts, not a particular type of person. There was no concept of the homosexual in law, and homosexuality was regarded not as a particular attribute of a certain type of person but as a potential in all sinful creatures.[19]

The Greeks of the classical period would have agreed with the general principle, if not with the moral attitude. Homosexuality and heterosexuality for them were indeed groups of not necessarily very closely related acts, each of which could be performed by any person, depending upon his or her gender, status, or class.[20] "Homosexuals" and "heterosexuals" in the modern sense did not exist in their world, and to speak, as is common, of the Greeks, as "bisexual" is illegitimate as well, since that merely adds a new, intermediate category, whereas it was precisely the categories themselves which had no meaning in antiquity.

Heterosexuals and homosexuals are involved in social "roles" and attitudes which pertain to a particular society, modern capitalism. These roles do have something in common with very different roles known in other societies—modern homosexuality and ancient pederasty, for example, share at least one feature: that the participants were of the same sex and that sexual intercourse is often involved—but the significant features are those that are not shared, including the entire range of symbolic, social, economic, and political meanings and functions each group of roles possesses.

"Homosexual" and "heterosexual" *behavior* may be universal; homosexual and heterosexual *identity and consciousness* are modern realities. These identities are not inherent in the individual. In order to be gay, for example, more than individual inclinations (however we might conceive of those) or homosexual activity is required; entire ranges of social attitudes and the construction of particular cultures, subcultures, and social relations are first necessary. To "commit" a homosexual act is one thing; to *be* a homosexual is something entirely different.

By the same token, of course, these are changeable and changing roles. The emergence of a gay movement (like that of the women's movement) has meant major alterations in homosexual and heterosexual realities and self-perceptions. Indeed, it is abundantly clear that there has always existed in the modern world a dialectical interplay between those social categories and activities which ascribe to certain people a homosexual identity and the activities of those who are so categorized. The result is the complex constitution of "the homosexual" as a social being within bourgeois society. The same is, of course, true of "the heterosexual," although the processes and details vary.[21]

The example of homosexuality/heterosexuality is particularly striking, since it involves a categorization which appears limited to modern societies. But even categories with an apparently more general application demonstrate the same social construction.

For example, as feminists have made abundantly clear, while every society does divide its members into "men" and "women," what is meant by these divisions and the roles played by those defined by these terms varies significantly from society to society and even within each society by class, estate, or social position. The same is true of kinship relations. All societies have some conception of kinship, and use it for a variety of purposes, but the conceptions differ widely and the institutions based on them are not necessarily directly comparable. Above all, the modern nuclear family, with its particular social and economic roles, does not appear to exist in other societies, which have no institution truly analogous to our own, either in conception, membership, or in articulation with other institutions and activities. Even within any single society, family/kinship patterns, perceptions, and activity vary considerably by class and gender.[22]

The point is clear: The members of each society create all of the sexual categories and roles within which they act and define themselves. The categories and the significance of the activity involved will vary as widely as do the societies within whose general social relations they occur, and categories appropriate to each society must be discovered by historians.

Not only must the categories of any single society or period not be hypostastized as universal, but even the categories which are appropriate to each society must be treated with care. Ultimately, they are only parameters within which sexual activity occurs or, indeed, against which it may be brought to bear. They tend to be normative—and ideological—in nature, that is, they are presented as the categories within which members of particular societies *ought* to act. The realities of any society only approximate the normative categories, as our homosexual/heterosexual example most clearly showed. It is both as norms, which determine the status of all sexual activity, and as approximations to actual social reality that they must be defined and explored.

Sexuality as Praxis (II)

Within this broad approach, the relationship between sexual activity and its categories and those that are nonsexual, especially those that are economic in nature, becomes of great importance.

Too many Marxists have tried to solve this problem by placing it within a simplified version of the "base/superstructure" model of society, in which the base is considered simply as "the economy," narrowly defined, while sexuality is relegated to the superstructure; that is, sexuality is seen as a "reflex" of an economic base.[23] Aside from the problems inherent in the base/superstructure model itself,[24] this approach not only reproduces the classic bourgeois division of society into private and public spheres, enshrining capitalist ideology as universal reality, but loses the basic insights inherent in viewing sexuality as social relations and activity.

Recently, many theorists, mainly working within a feminist perspective, began to develop a more sophisticated point of view, aiming, as Gayle Rubin put it in an important article,[25] "to introduce a distinction between 'economic' system and 'sexual' system, and to indicate that sexual systems have a certain autonomy and cannot always be explained in terms of economic forces." This view, which represented a great advance, nonetheless still partially accepted the contemporary distinction between a sphere of work and a sphere of sexuality.

The latest developments of socialist-feminist theory and practice have brought us still further, by demonstrating clearly that both sexuality in all its aspects and work/production are equally involved in the production and reproduction of *all* aspects of social reality, and cannot easily be separated out from one another.[26] Above all, elements of class and sexuality do not contradict one another or exist on different planes, but produce and reproduce each other's realities in complex ways, and both often take the form of activity carried out by the same persons working within the same institutions.

This means, among other things, that what we consider "sexuality" was, in the pre-bourgeois world, a group of acts and institutions not necessarily linked to one another, or, if they were linked, combined in ways very different from our own. Intercourse, kinship, and the family, and gender, did not form anything like a "field" of sexuality. Rather, each group of sexual acts was connected directly or indirectly—that is, formed a part of—institutions and thought patterns which we tend to view as political, economic, or social in nature, and the connections cut across our idea of sexuality as a thing, detachable from other things, and as a separate sphere of private existence.

The Greeks, for example, would not have known how, and would not have sought, to detach "sexuality" from the household (*oikos*), with its economic, political, and religious functions; from the state (especially as the reproduction of citizenship); from religion (as fertility cults or ancestor worship, for example); or from class and estate (as the determiner of the propriety of sexual acts, and the like). Nor would they have been able to distinguish a private realm of "sexuality"; the Greek *oikos* or household unit was as much or more a public institution as a private one.[27] This is even more true of so-called primitive societies, where sexuality (mediated through kinship, the dominant form of social relations) seems to permeate all aspects of life uniformly.

It was only with the development of capitalist societies that "sexuality" and "the economy" became separable from other spheres of society and could be counterposed to one another as realities of different sorts.[28] To be sure, the reality of that separation is, in the fullest sense of the word, ideological; that is, the spheres do have a certain reality as autonomous areas of activity and consciousness, but the links between them are innumerable, and both remain significant in the production and reproduction of social reality in the fullest sense. The actual connections between sexuality and the economy must be studied in greater detail, as must the specific relations between class, gender, family, and intercourse,[29] if the Marxist and sexual liberation movements are to work in a cooperative and fruitful, rather than antagonistic and harmful, manner.

A second major problem area stands in the way of a fuller understanding of sexuality as *praxis*. The approach to sexuality we have outlined does overcome the apparently insurmountable opposition between society and the individual which marks the ideological views with which we began our discussion. But it overcomes it at a general level, leaving many specific problems unsolved. The most important of these is the large and thorny problem of the determination of the specific ways in which specific individuals react to existing sexual categories and act within or against them. To deal with this vast subject fully, Marxists need to develop a psychology—or a set of psychologies—compatible with their social and economic analyses.[30]

Much the most common approach among western Marxists in the last fifty years toward creating a Marxist psychology has been an attempt, in one manner or another, to combine Marx and Freud. Whether in the sophisticated and dialectical versions of the Frankfurt School, Herbert Marcuse, or Wilhelm Reich, or in what Richard Lichtman has called "the popular view that Freud analyzed the individual while Marx uncovered the structure of social reality,"[31] these attempts arose out of the felt need for a more fully developed Marxist psychology in light of the failure of socialist revolutions in the West.

None of these attempts has, ultimately, been a success, and their failure seems to lie in real contradictions between Marxist and Freudian theory. Both present theories of the relationship between individual and society, theories which contradict each other at fundamental levels.

Freud does accept the importance of social relations for individual psychology. For him, sexuality has its roots in physiology, especially in the anatomical differences between the sexes, but these distinctions are not in themselves constitutive of our sexuality. Sexuality is indeed a process of development in which the unconscious takes account of biology as well as of society (mediated through the family) to produce an individual's sexuality.[32]

The problems begin here. Society, for Freud, is the medium in which the individual psyche grows and operates, but it is also in fundamental ways antipathetical to the individual, forcing him or her to repress instinctual desires. Freud's theory preserves the bourgeois division between society and the individual, and ultimately gives primacy to inborn drives within an essentially ahistorical individual over social reality. In a revealing passage, Freud argues:

> Human civilization rests upon two pillars, of which one is the control of natural forces and the other the restriction of our instincts. The ruler's throne rests upon fettered slaves. Among the instinctual components which are thus brought into service, the sexual instincts, in the narrow sense of the word, are conspicuous for their strength and savagery. Woe if they should be set loose! The throne would be overturned and the ruler trampled under foot.[33]

In spite of the fact that Freud does not view instincts as purely biological in nature,[34] he certainly sees sexuality as an internal, biologically based force, a thing inherent in the individual. This is a view which makes it difficult to use Freud alongside of Marx in the elucidation of the nature of sexuality. This is not to say that we need necessarily discard all of Freud. The general theory of the unconscious remains a powerful one. Zillah Eisenstein pointed in a useful direction when she wrote, "Whether there can be a meaningful synthesis of Marx and Freud depends on whether it is possible to understand how the unconscious is reproduced and maintained by the relations of the society."[35] But it is uncertain whether the Freudian theory of the unconscious can be stripped of so much of its specific content and remain useful for Marxist purposes. The work of Lacan, which attempts to "de-biologize" the Freudian uncon-scious by focusing on the role of language, and that of Deleuze and Guattari, in their *Anti-Oedipus*, which attempts to provide it with a more fully socio-historical content, are significant beginnings in this process.[36]

At the present time, however, Marxism still awaits a psychology fully adequate to its needs, although some recent developments are promising, such as the publication in English of the important non-Freudian work of the early Soviet psychologist L. S. Vygotsky.[37] But if psychology is to play a significant role in Marxist thought, as a science whose object is one of the dialectical poles of the individual/society unity, then it must have a finer grasp of the nature of that object. At this point, we can only agree with Lucien Seve that the object of psychology has not yet been ade-quately explored.[38]

PREINDUSTRIAL
◆
SOCIETIES

LESBIAN SEXUALITY IN MEDIEVAL AND EARLY MODERN EUROPE

◆

JUDITH C. BROWN

Although lesbian sexuality was recognized as a sin and a crime in medieval and early modern times, it did not receive the attention given to male homosexuality in legal codes and theological treatises. In this essay Judith Brown explores the reasons for this relative lack of concern and how it both contributed to and was in turn reinforced by conflicting male notions about lesbian sexuality. Brown also explores how the cases of lesbian sexuality that came before the courts were actually treated and concludes that the severity of punishment was related to concerns about women's gender behavior rather than sexual object-choice.

In premodern Europe, women were thought to be much more lustful than men and easily given to debauchery. Vast quantities of literature—medical, legal, and theological—going as far back as Aristotle and the Bible had demonstrated the point to the satisfaction of contemporary opinion.[1] Consequently, criminal accusations against women on the grounds of sexual misconduct were rather frequent.[2] Yet in virtually all cases the object of women's sexual desires was said to be men, for Europeans had long found it difficult to accept that women could actually be attracted to other women. Their view of human sexuality was phallocentric—women might be attracted to men and men might be attracted to men, but there was nothing a woman could do that would long satisfy the sexual desires of another woman. In law, in medicine, and in the public mind, lesbian

Note: From *Immodest Acts,* by Judith C. Brown (Oxford University Press, 1986). Reprinted by permission of Oxford University Press.

sexuality was therefore ignored. Among the hundreds if not thousands of cases of homosexuality tried by lay and ecclesiastical courts in medieval and early modern Europe, only a few involved sexual relations between women. Several prosecutions took place in Spain. Four sketchily known cases occurred in France, two in Germany, one in Switzerland, and one in Italy.[3]

This obliteration of a significant aspect of female sexuality from contemporary consciousness is all the more curious because at some level of knowledge, people were well aware that it existed. In his epistle to the Romans (1:26), Saint Paul, referring to pagans who rejected the one true God, had stated: ". . . God gave them up unto vile affections: for even their women did change the natural use into that which is against nature." Exactly what Paul had in mind is not clear, but from the earliest days of the Church, his words were interpreted by many as a reference to sexual relations between women. Explaining this passage in the fourth century, Saint Ambrose stated: "He testifies that, God being angry with the human race because of their idolatry, it came about that a woman would desire a woman for the use of foul lust."[4] To which Saint John Chrysostom (d. 407) added that "it is even more shameful that the women should seek this type of intercourse, since they ought to have more modesty than men."[5] Similar views could still be found centuries later in the works of Saint Anselm and Peter Abelard.[6]

Because sexual relations between women offended the laws of God and nature, a number of early medieval manuals of penance include them in the catalogue of sins which clergy might encounter among their parishioners. In the seventh century, Theodore of Tarsus told clergy what to do "if a woman practices vice with a woman." The Venerable Bede also mentions sexual relations between women, as do Pope Gregory III and Hrabanus Maurus.[7]

But without doubt the most widely influential book to guide Christian thought on the subject was Saint Thomas Aquinas' *Summa theologiae*, which subsumed four categories of vice against nature under the rubric of lust: masturbation, bestiality, coitus in an unnatural position, and "copulation with an undue sex, male with male and female with female."[8] Later theologians took their cue from Saint Thomas, often citing him in their own work, as did, for example, Francescus Sylvestris in his confessional manual and Jean Gerson, the fifteenth-century rector of the University of Paris, who included sex between women, along with "semination in a vessel not ordained for it" in his list of crimes against nature.[9] Similarly, the Archbishop of Florence, Saint Antoninus (1363–1451), included lesbian sexuality as the eighth of nine categories of lustful sins, although unlike most writers of his time, he differentiated it from lusts against nature, which he thought were lustful acts between a man and a woman "outside of the natural place where children are made." Finally, Saint Charles Borromeo (d. 1584), who accepted the Thomistic definition of sodomy as coitus against nature, on the other hand, imagined it only as a male vice. In his penitential, the acts of women came under the category of fornication, a sin of lust which was not unnatural, and which included adultery and rape.[10]

Awareness of lesbian sexuality among a few ecclesiastical leaders led to efforts to curb it in monastic communities. As early as 423, Saint Augustine had warned his sister, who had taken holy vows, that "The love which you bear one another ought not to be carnal, but spiritual: for those things which are practiced by immodest women, even with other females, in shameful jesting and playing, ought not to be done even by married women or by girls who are about to marry, much less by widows or chaste virgins dedicated by a holy vow to be handmaidens of Christ."[11] To remove temptation, the councils of Paris (1212) and Rouen (1214) prohibited nuns from sleeping together and required a lamp to burn all night in dormitories. From the thirteenth century on, monastic rules usually called for nuns to stay out of each other's cells, to leave their doors unlocked so that the abbess might check on them, and to avoid special ties of friendship within the convent. The reasons for the rules were never explicitly stated. No details were given of what practices the nuns might fall into if their cells were locked, although it is obvious from the evidence of a surviving poem sent by one nun to another that the subjects of the legislation did not lack imagination.[12]

In the secular world there were also occasional references to lesbian sexuality. A few jurists concerned with civil law, for example, discussed the issue. In the early fourteenth century, Cino da Pistoia erroneously believed that the *lex Foedissimam*, a Roman imperial edict of 287 A.D., referred to relations between women. According to Cino, "this law," which actually was meant to protect the rights of rape victims, "can be understood in two ways: first, when a woman suffers defilement by surrendering to a male; the other way is when a woman suffers defilement in surrendering to another woman. For there are certain women, inclined to foul wickedness, who exercise their lust on other women and pursue them like men." This interpretation was followed by Bartholomaeus de Saliceto (1400), whose glosses were widely used in the next few centuries.[13] Yet despite these writings, there appears to have been little civil legislation on the issue. Among the scant mentions of lesbian sexuality in secular laws are a provision in the Constitution of the Holy Roman Empire, promulgated by Charles V in 1532, and a statute adopted in Treviso in 1574. Most civil laws against same-sex relations, including the English act of 1533, which made buggery punishable by death, did not specifically mention women. Yet they were quite explicit about the acts committed by males and the penalties that should be imposed on them.[14]

In light of the knowledge that Europeans had about the possibility of lesbian sexuality, their neglect of the subject in law, theology, and literature suggests an almost active willingness to *dis*believe. A characteristic remark is the one attributed to Anastasius with reference to Romans 1:26: "Clearly, [the women] do not mount each other but, rather, offer themselves to the men."[15] Compared to the frequency with which male homosexuality is mentioned, in canon and civil law, in penitentials and confessional manuals, and in popular sermons and literature, especially after the thirteenth century, the handful of documents which cite the love of women for one another is truly scant.[16] In a period of roughly fifteen hundred years, they amount to no more than a dozen or so scattered references. Even Peter Damian's *Book of Gomorrah* (ca. 1051), a long and detailed diatribe against homosexual acts, confines itself to the misdeeds of men.[17] One looks in vain for the hell-fire and brimstone condemnations of the sort that popular preachers hurled against what they called "the clerical vice."[18] And a search of secular literature for the kinds of homosexual relations commonly attributed to men yields virtually nothing about women until mid-seventeenth century. In the Middle Ages, only the verses of Etienne de Fougeres make playful mention of lesbian sexuality.[19] Dante, who encounters most types of sinners in his journey through Hell and Purgatory, does not come across any female sodomites. Indeed, the male gender of the sodomites is implicit in the remarks he attributes to Brunetto Latino: "We all were clerks and men of youth, great men of letters, scholars of renown; all by the same crime defiled on earth."[20] Among Renaissance writers, Ariosto comes close to depicting erotic feelings between women, but even he ultimately dismisses the possibility.[21]

Why sexual relations between women were either ignored or dismissed in this way is amply clear from the few authors who did write about them. In Agnolo Firenzuola's *Ragionamenti amorosi* (1548), the female characters debate why it might not be better for a woman to love another woman since she would thus avoid risking her chastity. After much argument, the author concludes that this kind of love is not preferable because the beauty of men, by a decree of nature, inspires greater desire in a woman than does the beauty of other women. The same kind of attraction for the opposite sex holds true for men. As proof, he forwards the observation that no man can see a beautiful woman without feeling a natural desire to please her, and so it is with a woman at the sight of a beautiful man.[22]

More willing to admit the existence of erotic attractions between women, Brantôme, the late-sixteenth century commentator on the sexual antics of French courtiers, observed that lately, after "the fashion was brought from Italy by a lady of quality who I will not name," sexual relations between women have become very common. Some of these were young girls and widows who preferred to make love to each other than "to go to a man and thus become pregnant and lose their honor or their virginity . . ."[23] Others were women who used other women to enhance their lovemaking with men: "Because this little exercise, as I have heard say, is nothing but an apprenticeship to come to the greater [love] of men; because after they are heated up and well on their way with one another, their heat does not diminish unless they bathe in a livelier and more active current. . . . Because in the end, as I have heard many ladies tell, there is nothing like a man; and what they get from other women is nothing but enticements to go and satisfy themselves with men."[24]

In short, whether common or rare, sexual relations between women could have only one purpose: to enhance and glorify real sex, i.e., sex with a man. This is one of the reasons why some contemporaries may have felt they could safely ignore lesbian sexuality. "Let us excuse the young girls and widows," wrote Brantôme, "for loving these frivolous and vain pleasures."[25] For him, as for many other men of his time, the attraction of women for each other was not to be taken as a serious threat to their own access to women's sexual favors.

Another reason for ignoring lesbian sexuality was the belief that women, who were thought to be naturally inferior to men, were merely trying to emulate them: "It is better that a woman give herself over to a libidinous desire to do as a man, than that a man make himself effeminate; which makes him out to be less courageous and noble. The woman, accordingly, who thus imitates a man, can have a reputation for being more valiant and courageous than another . . ."[26] While such reasoning did not condone sex between women, it placed it within a long Western tradition in which women, like all other creatures, tried to ascend to a more perfect state of nature. Paradoxically, such relations tended to reaffirm, rather than subvert, the assumed biological hierarchy, in which "the body of a man is as superior to that of a woman as the soul is to the body."[27]

The findings of physicians and anatomists with regard to female reproductive organs also influenced attitudes toward lesbian sexuality. While it was commonly believed that women had semen-producing testes, their semen was thought to be less active and less important in human reproduction than that of men. Consequently the notion that they could pollute each other like men through the spilling of seed in the wrong vessel was generally dismissed. A society that had such imperfect knowledge of human biology, and that in the process of procreation valued the male sperm above all else, considered the waste of male seed a worse offense against the laws of God and nature than the misuse of female seed or female reproductive organs.[28]

Thus, for a number of reasons, most of the writers concerned with establishing penalties for lesbian acts tended to be more lenient toward them than toward male homosexuality. Theodore of Tarsus, for example, prescribed a penance of three years for a woman who "practices vice with a woman," the same as if "she practices solitary vice." In contrast, "fornication" between males was to be atoned through a penance of ten years.[29] Gregory III's penitential prescribed 160 days for women who had sex with other women and one year or more for male homosexuality.[30]

And Charles Borromeo's penitential meted out two years' penance if a woman "fornicated" with another woman or by herself, while giving men seven to fifteen years of penance, depending on their marital status, for engaging in coitus with another man.[31]

Yet, the tendency to view lesbian sexuality as a lesser offense was not unanimous. Some authorities viewed it on a par with male homosexuality, and therefore, punishable by death. What appears to be the earliest secular law to mention sexual relations between women, a statute in a late thirteenth-century French law code, states: "Those men who have been proved to be sodomites must lose their c_____[?]. And if anyone commits this offense a second time, he must lose a member. And if he does it a third time, he must be burned. A woman who does this shall lose a member each time, and on the third must be burned."[32] Bartholomaeus de Saliceto, in the fifteenth century, also recommended the death penalty.[33] But it was not until the sixteenth century, when the Catholic and Protestant reformations brought about a growing concern with legislating moral conduct and curbing heresy, an offense traditionally associated with homosexuality,[34] that such harsh views became common in the few laws and juridical commentaries that discussed the subject.[35] The two laws of the period that specifically mentioned women in connection with same-gender sex both provided the death sentence. Charles V's statute of 1532 stated: "If anyone commits impurity with a beast, or a man with a man, or a woman with a woman, they have forfeited their lives and shall, after the common custom, be sentenced to death by burning."[36] Treviso's law similarly noted that "If . . . a woman commits this vice or sin against nature, she shall be fastened naked to a stake in the Street of Locusts and shall remain there all day and night under a reliable guard, and the following day shall be burned outside the city."[37] In Spain, Gregorio Lopez's mid-sixteenth-century gloss on the country's basic law code, *Las Siete Partidas* (1256), reflected this hardening stance by extending the death penalty to women. Although the original code had not mentioned them, Lopez observed that "women sinning in this way are punished by burning according to the law of their Catholic Majesties which orders that this crime against nature be punished with such a penalty, especially since the said law is not restricted to men, but refers to any person of whatever condition who has unnatural intercourse."[38]

Even among those who believed in the death penalty for such acts, however, there were other disagreements. Whereas Lopez thought that the death penalty applied in all cases, his compatriot, Antonio Gomez (b. 1501), felt that burning should be mandatory only in cases in which "a woman has relations with another woman by means of any material instrument." If, on the other hand, "a woman has relations with any woman without an instrument," then a lighter penalty such as beating could be applied.[39] The distinctions were carried one step further by the Italian jurist Prospero Farinacci (1554–1618). Taken at its most general, if a woman "behaves like a man with another woman," according to Farinacci, "she will be in danger of the penalties for sodomy and death." But looking at the particulars, if a woman simply made overtures to another woman, she should only be denounced publicly. "If she behaves corruptly with another woman only by rubbing," she is to be subject to an unspecified "punishment," and "if she introduces some instrument into the belly of another," she should be put to death.[40]

Yet, despite these harsh pronouncements, there were often discrepancies between the letter of the law and its implementation. To be sure some women were put to death for having engaged in sodomy. But in most cases ending in a death sentence there were what the authorities perceived as aggravating circumstances. In some, as in the Spanish and one of the French cases, the women had "by illicit devices, supplied the defects of [their] sex," thus using "material instruments" to make their offenses the worst possible sodomitical acts. In other cases, one of the partners in the relationship had attempted to live and dress like a man. This was a more dangerous crime than ordinary sodomy, for transvestism struck at the very heart of European gender and power relations.[41] By dressing like men, such women were attempting to sever the bonds that held them to the female sphere of the social hierarchy. And, more important, they were attempting to usurp the functions of men. The result was that such "males," and not their female partners, tended to incur the greater wrath of the authorities. Their executions were thus necessary to protect the existing forms of social organization.[42] But ordinary lesbian sexuality did not usually result in such repressive measures. In Granada, for example, several women were flogged and sent to the galleys. Elsewhere women were "simply" banished.

These disagreements about how to deal with lesbian sexuality betray a fundamental ignorance about women's sexual practices and how they fit into established sexual categories and sexual crimes. For example, in defining as "unnatural and sinful those sexual acts in which intercourse did not take place in a vessel fit for procreation," Saint Augustine thought primarily of male homosexuality and anal intercourse among heterosexual couples. His only allusion to lesbian sexuality shows clearly that he thought of it as a different and lesser sin.[43] While Theodore of Tarsus and Gregory III followed Saint Augustine's lead, Albertus Magnus and Thomas Aquinas, on the other hand, viewed lesbian sexuality as part of sodomy, an act "against nature, male with male and female with female."[44] Still others, such as Vincent Filliucio, who agreed with the Thomistic definition of sodomy, added that it occurred only when there was ejaculation, thus making it primarily a male crime.[45]

The conceptual difficulties that contemporaries had with lesbian sexuality are reflected in the lack of an adequate terminology. *Lesbian* sexuality did not exist. For that matter, neither did *lesbians*. Although the word "lesbian" appears once in the sixteenth century in the work of Brantôme, it was not commonly used until the nineteenth, and even then was applied first to certain acts rather than a category of persons.[46] Lacking a precise vocabulary and precise concepts, a large array of words and circumlocutions came to be used to describe what women allegedly did: mutual masturbation, pollution, fornication, sodomy, buggery, mutual corruption, coitus, copulation, mutual vice, the defilement or impurity of women by one another. And those who did these terrible things, if called anything, were called fricatrices, that is women who rubbed each other, or Tribades, the Greek equivalent for the same action.[47]

The confusion on these issues was so great that in the early eighteenth century, a learned Italian cleric, Lodovico Maria Sinistrari, sought to clarify them by writing extensively on what he called female sodomy. The need to dispel widespread ignorance on the subject was critical, he felt, especially for clerics who had to know precisely from what sins to absolve the stray females in their flocks: "In practice, it is necessary for Confessors to be able to discern the case in which women by touching each other provoke themselves to voluntary pollution (*mollitiem*) and when they fall into the Sodomitical crime, in order to come to a judgment about the gravity of the sin." Another important reason for knowing was that in many Catholic areas, sodomy was considered a serious enough sin that it was reserved for the courts of bishops.

After consulting many theological, legal, and medical sources, Sinistrari defined sodomy as carnal intercourse in the wrong vessel. This included heterosexual anal intercourse and coitus between women, but not mutual masturbation with any other part of the body or the use of "material instruments." The "heart of the problem," however, was "how can one woman lie with another in such a way that their rubbing against each other can be called Sodomy?" Using the latest medical treatises, Sinistrari concluded that only those women who had an excessively large clitoris could engage in sodomy with each other. Likely candidates to have this condition were girls who masturbated as children and women who had an overabundance of heat and semen. But unlike Middle Eastern women, whose passions had to be curbed by surgical means, Western European women seldom found themselves in this predicament.[48]

This, of course, did not mean that female sodomy should be ignored. If charges were brought against a woman, she should be examined by competent midwives to determine if she was physiologically capable of committing the act. An enlarged clitoris was a presumption of guilt which should bring in its wake a sentence of death by hanging followed by burning at the stake. This was the punishment to be given to all sodomites, male or female.[49]

Harsh punishment was necessary both to avoid the wrath of God, who might otherwise destroy the world as he had Sodom and Gomorrah, and also for its deterrent effect. Sinistrari's recommendations for eliciting information from suspects points to the ancient fear that women, with their abundant capacity for lust and their limited capacity for reason, might develop ideas if they heard of such goings on. If a confessor suspected one of his parishioners, he should proceed with his questions "modestly and prudently," and only gradually, depending on the answers received, get to the specifics of the acts committed.[50]

Even more than male sodomy, sodomy between females was "the sin which cannot be named." In the sixteenth century, Gregorio Lopez had called it "the silent sin," *peccatum mutum*, and earlier Jean Gerson had called it a sin against nature in which "women have each other by detestable and horrible means which should not be named or written."[51] For this reason the famous jurist Germain Colladon (16th c.) advised the Genevan authorities, who had no prior experience with lesbian crimes, that the death sentence should be read publicly, as it normally was in cases of male homosexuality, but that the customary description of the crime committed should be left out. "A crime so horrible and against nature," he wrote, "is so detestable and because of the horror of it, it cannot be named."[52] The problem was not just that Colladon had a particular abhorrence for this kind of offense, but that because women were thought to have weaker natures, it was feared that they were more susceptible to suggestion. Consequently, while men found guilty of sodomy were to have their crimes read aloud in order to deter others, sexual relations between women were better left unmentioned.

Crimes that cannot be named, thus, literally had no name and left few traces in the historical record. The contradictory notions that Western Europeans had about women's sexuality made it impossible to discuss lesbian sexuality openly, if at all. Silence bred confusion and confusion bred fear. On these foundations Western society built an impenetrable barrier that has lasted for nearly two thousand years.[53]

HOMOSEXUALITY AND THE STATE
IN LATE IMPERIAL CHINA

◆

VIVIEN W. NG

In the seventeenth century, China experienced a burst of public interest in male homosexuality. Confucian scholars made references to it in their jottings, and novelists and playwrights celebrated it in their works. This open discussion of homosexuality led to a conservative backlash. Responding to the widespread perception that homosexuality had become "rampant" in China, the Qing government, in 1740, decreed that consensual sodomy between adults was a punishable offense. Ng's essay first establishes the social milieu of seventeenth-century China, then explores descriptions of homosexual love in literature and the relations of such descriptions to Confucian ideology, and, finally, analyzes the response of Chinese officialdom.

In 1740, the Manchu Qing government enacted its first male homosexual rape law.[1] This law addressed more than the issue of rape: one of its clauses spelled out, for the first time in Chinese history, punishment for sodomy between consenting adults. What was the impetus for this homophobic legislation? What led the ultraconservative government to believe that homosexuality was dangerous and therefore must be proscribed? What was the relation of homosexuality to orthodox Confucian ideology?

Male homosexuality has a long and documented history in China. The third-century B.C. text, *Chronicles of the Warring States*, for example, includes numerous biographies of major figures of the period that make

Note: "Late Imperial" covers the late Ming (ca. sixteenth to mid-seventeenth centuries) and Qing (1644–1912) periods.

plain their homosexuality. One of the expressions for male love, *longyang*, stems from the well-known homosexual relationship between Longyang Jun, a fourth-century B.C. minister, and the prince of Wei.[3] From the *Chronicles*, too, we know about the affection between Duke Ling of Wei and his minister, Ni Xia. Once, when the two men were taking a stroll in an orchard, Ni picked a peach off one of the trees and took a bite off it. The fruit was so delicious that he offered the rest of it to the duke; a common euphemism for male homosexual love, *fen tao zhi ai* (literally, "the love of shared peach"), is derived from this account.[4] Later official histories, too, did not hide the fact of the homosexual orientation of key historical personages. Thus we learn from *The History of the Former Han* that the last emperor of the Former Han dynasty, Aidi (r. 6–1 B.C.), had a number of male lovers, and that he was especially fond of one of them, a certain Dong Xian. One day, as the two men were napping together on a couch, with Dong's head resting on the emperor's sleeve, the latter was called away to grant an audience. He cut off the sleeve rather than to awaken his beloved. From this episode is derived another common literary term for male homosexual love, *duanxiu*, literally, "the cut sleeve."[5]

It appears that male homosexuality was tolerated as long as it was not an exclusive sexual expression and the men fulfilled their procreative duties. On the other hand, tolerance meant, at best, a neutral attitude. Biographies of the period do not celebrate homosexual relationships in any way. It was not until the seventeenth century that homoerotic literature came into its own and flourished in China.

Indeed the seventeenth century holds the key to our understanding of subsequent Qing homophobia. During this period, there was a discursive explosion regarding male homosexuality. Confucian scholars made references to it in their jottings, and novelists and playwrights celebrated it in their works. Several critical issues need to be explored: (1) the social milieu of seventeenth-century China that fueled the discursive explosion; (2) descriptions of homosexual love in scholarly jottings and in homoerotic literature; (3) the relation of such descriptions to the larger question of the ideology of sexuality; (4) the response of the Qing government to the perception that homosexuality had become "rampant" in China.

The Milieu

In the eyes of many Confucian scholars living in the seventeenth century, the moral fiber of China began to disintegrate some time during the latter part of the sixteenth century. The center and symbol of the Chinese moral order, the Ming emperor Wanli (r. 1573–1620), came to the throne when he was only nine. During the first decades of his reign, when real power was in the hands of his prime minister, Zhang Juzheng, the government functioned with smooth efficiency. The fiscal health of the state was basically sound, the borders secure, commerce and industry were flourishing. But after the death of Zhang, the Wanli emperor became increasingly derelict and arbitrary in his exercise of power, and the dynasty began its slow decline. The emperor did not seem to care. He led a life of such self-indulgence that toward its close, he became too obese to carry his own weight.[6]

The sumptuous lifestyle of the Wanli emperor set the tone for the rich and powerful in late Ming society. In the words of one seventeenth-century commentator: "During the late Ming period, it was commonplace for a scholar, once he had passed the metropolitan examination [and thus secured a place in government,] to immediately acquire a concubine. And, as soon as it was feasible, he would build an enormous and luxuriously-appointed mansion for himself. The number of these mansions was truly mind-boggling."[7] Other commentators descried a similar pattern of conspicuous consumption. Banquets usually required several days of preparation, and it was considered the height of vulgarity to invite guests to dinner unless the menu was extensive and included "products from land and sea." In the realm of fashion, men increasingly favored brocade over cloth, and muted colors gave way to light shades of red.[8] The disregard for propriety went beyond mere flouting of sumptuary rules. What was more disturbing—as far as the moralists were concerned— were blatant violations of mourning ritual: "[M]en going to a funeral would bring with them women of dubious character and they would sing and dance to the funeral music. They did not even blush to induce mourners in mourning clothes to drink toasts with them. Others would get married even immediately after their father or mother had died."[9] Such a cavalier attitude toward fundamental filial obligations could signify only one thing—the moral fabric of China had become unravelled.

Nor did Confucian moralists have to look hard to find evidence of "moral decay." In the Jiangnan region—the heartland of literati culture— courtesans and prostitutes enjoyed a thriving business. Their patrons were government officials, wealthy landlords, rich merchants, scholars, writers, artists and the like. Male prostitutes, too, flourished during the Ming period. According to the late Ming writer Shen Defu (1578–1642), government officials began to turn to boys and young men for sexual entertainment after 1429, when the Xuande emperor ordered them to desist from cavorting with courtesans.[10] These male prostitutes came to be known as *xiaochang* (literally, "little singer"), and by the seventeenth century, they had become as much a part of the brothel scene as their female counterparts. The attempt of the Xuande emperor to gather his officials into the moral fold, in effect, produced the opposite result.

The "hedonism" so denounced by conservative critics was, in a way, an inevitable extension of the preoccupation with the self that so characterized late Ming discourse. The subjective approach to moral cultivation propounded by the influential Ming philosopher Wang Yangming (1472–1528), literally opened up unlimited possibilities for individual development and self-expression, and his followers took it as their mission to explore these opportunities fully.[11] According to the formulations of one adherent of the Wang Yangming school, He Xinyin (1517–1579), emotional desires and sensual appetites are rooted in human nature; to repress them is to dwindle human beings to nothingness; to give free rein to desires and appetites is to give full expression to human nature.[12] Scholars in the Qing period liked to blame the Wang Yangming school for the collapse of the Ming dynasty in 1644.

Such was the milieu that fueled an explosion in social commentary in the seventeenth century. The most graphic depictions of the decadence of late Ming China could be found in literature written in the vernacular language, particularly those with blatantly sexual themes.

Homosexuality in Vernacular Literature

The writers of erotic and pornographic literature of the seventeenth century were members of the literati. This means that they had received a traditional education and were well versed in Classical Chinese, a written language that had been developed almost two thousand years before and had since become stylized and removed from the spoken language, the vernacular. Most scholarly works were written in Classical Chinese, whereas the vernacular was confined to the novel and story—contributing to the low esteem with which the Chinese literati regarded those media.[13]

Writers of vernacular stories and novels were not all iconoclasts who sought to unravel the fabric of Chinese society; some of them, in fact, were serious scholars who used the popular genre to become more effective social critics. There were, however, radical vernacular writers who no longer subscribed to orthodox morality. To be sure, we still find references to conventional virtues in their works, but a close reading suggests that they only paid lip service to these virtues. One notable iconoclast was Li Yu (1611–1680), author of the notorious novel *The Carnal Prayer Mat*. Li begins his story with a long homily on sexual ethics. He tells his readers that sex is indeed good for a person, but only if it is enjoyed in moderation and in the confines of the home. Sex with prostitutes can be harmful, and illicit liaisons with married women invite catastrophes. Readers must not be misled, Li warns, by the fact that his novel is fun to read, and that it is full of sizzling erotic details, because it has a very serious purpose—to urge people to restrain their lusts rather than to indulge them.[14]

Having thus registered his serious, moralistic intent, Li Yu then proceeds in his novel to describe his protagonist's sexual quest in all its glorious (and gory) detail. The celebration of sexuality is moderated only much later, toward the end of the novel, when the protagonist discovers that all the men whose wives he seduced have also slept with his own. Thus shamed and enlightened, he ends his misguided quest by cutting off his "enemy" (read penis).

The contradictory tone in *The Carnal Prayer Mat* reflects Chinese society's ambivalence toward sexuality in general. An ancient and well-known aphorism declared: "The desire for good food and the desire for sexual pleasure are two aspects of human nature." Obviously, it was perfectly natural for a person to indulge in sex. On the other hand, the cardinal virtue of filial piety required Chinese men (and women) to engage in sex only for the purpose of procreation. Promiscuity was regarded as unfilial, because sexual excesses could lead to dissipation of sexual potency and reproductive powers. In order to mediate between these two conflicting attitudes—and to forestall sexual paralysis for men—Chinese sexologists offered this advice: Men must engage in heterosexual activity, because they needed to absorb the regenerative qualities of the female "juices" to compensate for the loss of male essence through ejaculation. And they must try to conserve their seminal fluids as much as possible.

The virtue of filial piety, together with the consequent condemnation of promiscuity, was part and parcel of the straitlaced Confucian ideology embraced by the founder of the Ming dynasty. With full support from the state, Confucian moralists in the Ming period also created a cult out of the virtue of female chastity. Women were indoctrinated to be faithful to their spouses and to deny their sexuality after their husband's death. Widow remarriage was taboo. The identification of female chastity with Confucian ideology, especially its repressive attitudes toward sexuality, inspired some seventeenth-century iconoclasts to attack Confucian mores by trivializing the cult of chastity. Li Yu, for example, did so in a story about male homosexual marriage, "Male Mother of Mencius" (Silent Opera Number 6).[15] Given the fact that Confucian moralists frowned upon all expressions of nonprocreative sexuality, it seems likely that Li chose the homosexual theme to make his criticism more pointed.

In the story, Li Yu informs his readers that male homosexuality is commonly known as *nanfeng* (literally, "the southern persuasion") and that it is especially rampant in the southern province of Fujian. Even the banyan trees in the region seem to display "homosexual" tendencies, for the main trunks tend to bend over the lower trunks and the vines from both become so intertwined that neither saws nor axes can separate them. In fact, the local nickname for the banyan tree is, appropriately, "*nanfeng* tree." One of the protagonists in Li's story is a scholar by the name of Xu Jifang. During his youth, Xu displays no inclination whatsoever for study or any other productive enterprise; instead, he spends his time indulging his homosexual proclivities (*longyang*). At around the age of twenty, he suddenly enrolls himself in a school and manages to master enough of the requisite curriculum to obtain a degree. His surrender to the social pressure to become an academician eventually leads to another concession to convention. In spite of his inborn disdain for the female sex, Xu finally marries a woman in order to fulfill his filial duty to procreate. Yet it soon becomes obvious that he harbors no affection for his wife, for he spends no more than a few requisite nights a month with her. After a couple of years of semi-cohabitation, his wife conceives and gives birth to a son, conveniently dying of complications from childbirth. Xu therefore finds himself living in the best of all possible worlds—he has a son and heir, and he is no longer encumbered by a wife. He makes up his mind to remarry, but this time to a suitable man. However, because his standards are very high, several years have to pass before he finally manages to find his ideal mate.

It is a match made in heaven, or rather, *by* heaven. Just to the east of town is a famous resort called Meizhou Island. Every spring, people from all over the county flock to the island to spend several nights at a temple. On one such night, the patron goddess of the temple appears in the dream of the local magistrate and tells him that a drought will soon hit most parts of China, but because of her intercession on the county's behalf, the local area will suffer only a modest decline in food production. After the fall harvest, the magistrate announces to the populace that a major thanksgiving celebration will be held on the feast day of the patron goddess. He also makes clear that only men will be allowed to go to the island and participate in the festivities.

Practically every male resident of the county can be found on the resort island on the appointed day. Those with *nanfeng* tendencies also arrive in droves. Many of them are elaborately dressed in shades of red or purple and they vie with one another for the attention of the choice few. Some connoisseurs come armed with notebooks, so that they can jot down their impressions and evaluations of all the beautiful youths that cross their path. One of these youths is a fair-skinned charmer by the name of You Ruilang, who has come to the island with four or five companions. He is all the more conspicuous because, unlike the others, he is dressed in a plain, dark-colored cloth garment. Instantly, he becomes the center of attention. "What is all this?" he says to himself, "I have come to see the show, but instead I have become a spectacle!" Unmoved by the numerous offers of tea and other delicacies, he chooses instead to explore the island with his friends.

Presently, Ruilang realizes that a handsome man, about twenty-odd years old, has been following him quietly for some time. Just as he is about to question the intentions of this stranger, he loses his footing on one of the moss-covered stone steps. He is saved from disaster by the stranger, who reaches out and manages to arrest his fall. During that instant of physical contact, Ruilang feels a slight caressing pressure on his palm, and he blushes uncontrollably. The "stranger," not surprisingly, turns out to be none other than Xu Jifang. It is truly love at first touch. That night, Xu Jifang makes up his mind to marry Ruilang—it is not enough just to be friends, because friendship cannot guarantee absolute fidelity; only marriage can ensure Ruilang's eternal affection and loyalty. A few days later, he pays Ruilang's father a visit, using as a pretext his offer to accept the youth as a student. The old man is no fool. He gathers from the way the two look at each other that the visit has another purpose.

The following day, the old man returns the visit, and he allows Ruilang to accompany him. At this point, Li Yu injects himself into the story as the narrator:

[Readers], you must be saying to yourself how it is that [the boy's father] can be so spineless. He knows that someone wants to take advantage of his son, yet he does nothing to stop it. Not only does he open his home to the thief, but he personally leads his son to the thief! What kind of sense does this make?

Well, you have to realize that in that part of the country, this lifestyle is rampant. Those who practice it do not consider it shameful. Moreover, [the old man] has heavy debts to repay and he has yet to raise enough money to bury his two deceased wives. He knows full well that his son can fetch a high price. This is why he does not turn down suitors. . . .

[You may ask] if this is the case, then why doesn't he give Ruilang free rein and allow him to do as he pleases? Why then, on the feast day of the goddess, just before the boy left for the island, did he warn him to avoid isolated places and not to talk with strangers? You have got to know that in Fujian, virginity is very important for homosexuals, just as much as it is for women. There is a distinction between first marriage and remarriage. If [the youth] is a virgin, people will pay a heavy betrothal price for him, and all the proper wedding rituals are observed. But if a parent's vigilance is lax, and the youth has already been deflowered, he will be regarded as "rotten willow and withered flower." Even though he may not be considered trash, and may still find someone willing to pay for him, his parent no longer has any say about the price. . . . This is why the old man dared not relax his vigilance over his son.[16]

Eventually, a suitable bride's price is arranged for Ruilang. Xu Jifang and You Ruilang begin to live together as man and wife. The relationship between the two mirrors that of a heterosexual marriage, with the younger man showing total devotion to his "husband," so much so that he castrates himself to preserve his delicate features and to allay the fear of the older man about his growing masculinity. He also begins to dress in drag. After the death—from natural causes—of Jifang, Ruilang remains chaste for the rest of his life. He brings up Jifang's son by his first marriage, just as any virtuous widow would. The son eventually becomes a successful scholar and official.

Li Yu's blatant disregard for orthodox morality, his undisguised enjoyment in sensual pleasures, and his refusal to condemn unconventional lifestyles marked him as persona non grata among the literate elite. It is impossible to say with any great certainty what Li's personal views on homosexuality were, but reading "Male Mother of Mencius," as well as his other two known works on the theme, "The Antique Shop" (the sixth of his *Twelve Towers* or *Shi'er lou*) and "Pitying the Fragrant Companion" (*Lian xiang ban*), suggests that he was basically neutral. As can be seen in "The Antique Shop," Li's homosexual characters are capable of doing evil as well as good, and his homosexual villains are no more (or less) evil than heterosexuals in his other stories.[17]

The two major characters in "The Antique Shop" are Quan Ruixiu, a young and fair skinned antique shop clerk (he owns a small share of the business), and the evil Yan Donglou, the son of a high-ranking official. Donglou is notorious for his indiscriminate indulgence in his homosexual proclivities. No one is off-limits to him—he has tried every known male prostitute and entertainer—and he is constantly on the lookout for potential prey. He learns from the grapevine about this beautiful young man who works in an antique shop and decides to take a firsthand look. He makes an appointment with the shop owners, Ruixiu's good friends and lovers. They are well aware of Donglou's unscrupulous ways and decide that Ruixiu must not be present at the shop on the day of the appointment.

On the agreed-upon day, Yan Donglou arrives with his entourage. He is naturally disappointed that the object of his curiosity is not there, but he makes a great show of browsing and picks out a number of very expensive items, which he arranges to pay for at a later date. But when the owners subsequently present him with the bill, he refuses to pay it. He insists that he will not pay anyone but Ruixiu, and that the latter must come to his residence to collect the money. Ruixiu has no choice but to present himself at Donglou's home, but he steadfastly rejects Donglou's sexual overtures. After three futile nights, Donglou gives up and releases Ruixiu.

But the story does not end here. Yan Donglou later conspires with the eunuch Sha, who lures Ruixiu to his palace, drugs him, and castrates him. When Sha dies a short while later, Ruixiu is handed over to Donglou. He pretends to let bygones be bygones and makes every effort to satisfy Donglou's whims. His real intention, however, is to learn the ins and outs of the Yan household. His knowledge later serves him well. Subsequently, during one of the many factional strifes that plague the Ming court, Yan Donglou is condemned to temporary banishment. All his retainers must be accounted for, either to be returned to their original owners, or to be dispersed elsewhere. When Ruixiu's name is called, he announces himself a eunuch and asks to be returned to the palace to live among the eunuchs. Some time later, when he is asked to explain how he became a eunuch, he answers that he has a long story to tell but he dares not tell anyone but the emperor. It is thus that Yan Donglou's various offenses come to light. He is beheaded, and his skull is later acquired by Ruixiu, who uses it as a urinal.

To find more positive descriptions of homosexual love, one has to turn to the more explicitly homoerotic literature of the seventeenth century. Because of the censorship efforts of the subsequent Qing dynasty, only a few are extant today.[18] One of these rare works is *Bian er chai*, or "Hairpins Beneath His Cap." It is a collection of four stories, all based on the theme that sexual relationship between two men can be emotionally as well as sexually fulfilling. All four stories contain graphic descriptions—celebrations, actually—of the sex act.

The first of the four stories, "A Chronicle of True Love," relates the seduction of a young student by an academician. At the beginning of the story, we are told how the boy, who has very delicate and attractive features, has steadfastly resisted the sexual overtures of his fellow classmates. He goes so far as to transfer to another school in order to escape the unwanted attention of the other schoolboys. One day, however, the academician catches a glimpse of the boy and falls instantly in love; the remainder of the story recounts his gradual seduction of the boy.

The academician schemes to enroll in the same school under an assumed name, and secures a room directly across from that of the boy. He reminds himself constantly to be patient, for he is well aware of the boy's high moral standards and does not want to frighten him. In the meantime, the academician uses his servant boy to satisfy his sexual urges. Ultimately, he manages to seduce the boy, and when the youngster expresses confusion, consoles him with these words: "If we go by the logic of Reason, then what we have done today is wrong; but if we use the logic of Love, then we are right. For a man can become a woman and a woman can become a man. It is possible to go from life to death as well as from death into life. I have often said, 'The sea may become dry, the mountains may erode, but love alone cannot surrender to reason!' "[19] But love without sex cannot be entirely fulfilling, and sex cannot be pleasurable unless one can become totally uninhibited. After a while, under the expert coaching of the academician, the boy finally realizes the ecstasy of sexual abandonment. The story ends abruptly with the unfortunate separation of the pair, but they—and their respective families—remain lifelong friends.

The anonymous author of *Bian er chai* displays very intimate knowledge of the mechanics and sensations of the sex act. His graphic descriptions of men in the throes of sex place *Bian er chai* in the same genre as *The Carnal Prayer Mat*, which celebrates unbridled heterosexuality But the author's literary skills are well below those of Li Yu; instead of being art, *Bian er chai* straddles the fine line that distinguishes erotic from pornographic literature. Since publishing was a money-making enterprise in Ming China, *Bian er chai* would have been printed only if there was a lucrative market for it. Literally hundreds of thousands of presses sprung into operation during the Ming period, though most of them were rather short-lived. Book publishing was also a very competitive business, and in order to stay afloat, publishers could afford to print only titles able to guarantee a profitable return on the investment. The hedonistic, anything-goes attitude that pervaded the seventeenth century allowed and fostered the boom in erotic and pornographic literature.

Homoerotic literature of the seventeenth century celebrated only male-male relations. This was not surprising given the fact that the writers were all men and the market for literature in general was predominantly male. Very few women in Ming-Qing China were literate, and among those who were proficient in the literary and musical arts, many were courtesans. In fact, the close association of female literary accomplishment and the courtesan's life gave rise to the aphorism, "She who is unskilled in arts and literature is a virtuous woman." Thus, in China, as elsewhere, the female experience was not given written expression.

There was one notable literary exception—Li Yu's play, *Lian xiang ban* or "Pitying the Fragrant Companion." It is a story about two women (one of them married) who love each other so much that they perform a wedding ceremony for themselves. The married woman conspires successfully to have her husband accept her lover as a concubine and the two women live together happily ever after. That the play later became closely identified with the lesbian experience is unmistakable; for example, in the autobiographical work of Shen Fu (1763–?), *Six Chapters of a Floating Life*, we find him teasing his wife about her infatuation with a singsong girl, "Are you trying to imitate Li-weng's 'Pitying the Fragrant Companion'?"[20]

Homosexuality in Scholarly "Jottings"

Descriptions of male homosexual affection were not confined to erotic and pornographic literature. References to homosexuality can also be found in scholarly jottings[21] of the seventeenth century. One example is *Wanli ye huo pian*, a miscellany compiled by Shen Defu (1578–1642). We (and no doubt his contemporaries as well as later writers such as Li Yu) learn from this work that male homosexuality was commonplace in the province of Fujian:

> The Fujianese especially favor male homosexuality. This preference is not limited to any particular social or economic class, but the rich tend to cavort with the rich, and the poor with the poor. They call each other bond brothers. The older partner is called *qixiong* (bond elder brother); the younger is called *qidi* (bond younger brother). When the elder brother enters the home of the younger brother, he is welcomed and loved by the parents as one would a son-in-law. The younger

brother's livelihood, including expenses incurred when he later marries a wife, is provided for by the elder brother.[22]

Since the coastal regions of Fujian were infested with sea rovers, and pirate leaders were often called *qixiong* by their subordinates, Shen ingeniously concluded that the prevalence of homosexual practices in Fujian was a result of the influence of pirate culture. According to his theory, homosexuality was rampant among pirates because they had a particular superstition against bringing women on board their ships, believing them to be bad luck. In order to satisfy their sexual urges, they had no recourse but to turn to each other for release. Although Shen did not pass any moral judgment on homosexuality, he appeared to deny the possibility that it could be a natural condition; rather, he viewed it as acquired behavior resulting from heterosexual deprivation.

Shen Defu also included several biographical accounts revealing male homosexual activity in his miscellany. One example is his sketch of the scholar Zhou Yongzhai: When Zhou was an aspiring degree candidate, he boarded at the home of an old man named Dong. One day, Zhou told Dong that he wanted to quit school in order to return to his native place. Dong knew that the young man was lonely rather than homesick, but he kept the insight to himself. He did, however, mention in a deliberately offhanded way the story about Longyang Jun (the fourth-century B.C. homosexual). Zhou immediately flew into a rage, castigating homosexuality as bestiality. At one point, he declared, "I have never understood how men could be sexually attracted to other men!" Old man Dong did not immediately respond to Zhou's tirade, but later that evening, he sent a servant boy, experienced in the ways of male love, to Zhou's bed.

Taking advantage of Zhou's drunken stupor, the boy proceeded to perform oral sex on him. Zhou was startled into wakefulness, but the boy worked furiously on, transporting Zhou to a state of undescribable bliss. When he found out about Dong's complicity in the affair, he was beside himself in his gratitude for the old man's insight. News about his homosexual initiation leaked far and wide, making him the butt of numerous unkind jokes, but he remained unremorseful. Indeed, Shen noted, Zhou's indulgence in male love grew to the point where he welcomed all varieties of partners—old or young, ugly or beautiful.[23]

Shen Defu, as in the case with many of his seventeenth-century contemporaries, appears to take a neutral stance toward male homosexuality, as is clearly reflected in the tone of their writings. Later in the Qing period, however, a more negative attitude begins to emerge. For example, we find in the Qing collection, *Guobao wenjian lu* (Anthology of Retributive Tales), the following story:

On the grounds of Tianning temple in Ningbo was a deserted shrine where a statue of the deity Guandi was housed. One day, two young men, taking advantage of the secluded location, committed a homosexual act directly in front of the statue. This immediately brought forth a ferocious response from Guandi. "How dare you defile this temple!" he roared. "You shall die for this!"

The frightened youths were able to pull up their pants, but the shock was so great that they began to scream uncontrollably, attracting a huge crowd to the usually deserted shrine. After a short while, the parents of the two youths caught wind of the incident and hurried to the shrine to offer a pledge to Guandi that they would arrange for a play to be performed as an atonement for their sons' sin. Guandi's anger subsided, and the screaming fit finally came to an end. However, the two youths remained in a daze for another month.[24]

The suggestion that homosexuality was a sin or the result of demonic possession can also be found in other Qing collections, for example, in Ji Yun's *Yue wei zao tang biji* ("Jottings of Yue wei zao tang").

Another common device employed by critics to disparage same-gender sexuality was to include in their jottings unsavory aspects of the behavior of known homosexuals. A stereotype began to emerge: Homosexuals cannot control themselves; they prey on young men; they employ any means to attain their goals; they care nothing about public opinion; they are desperate men. An example of this is Liang Caoren's *Liang ban qiu yu an xu bi* ("Jottings of Liang ban qiu yu an"). It is likely that the change in attitude—from neutrality to disparagement—was a product of the homophobic efforts of the Qing state.

Homosexuality and the Qing State

When the alien Manchus entered the city of Beijing in the summer of 1644 and declared the birth of a new dynasty—the Qing—in China, they knew that they faced a formidable task of reconstruction. In order to consolidate their rule, the Manchus had to face up to some serious problems: First, order and stability had to be restored to an empire that had been torn apart, terrorized by peasant rebellions and widespread banditry. A cowed and demoralized populace had to have its confidence restored, or it would be unable to contribute to the great enterprise of rebuilding the empire. Equally important, the literati must be won over, for without their support, the restructuring of the bureaucratic state would be difficult.

The Manchus were not uneducated barbarians. Before their ultimate success in 1644, they had been preparing themselves diligently for the eventual challenge of governing China. By 1644, they had learnt much about Chinese history and culture, and especially the principles of Confucianism. One of the basic premises of Confucianism is the principle called "rectification of names." For a society to exist in harmony, each member must know his/her role and perform it accordingly. Thus, a ruler is expected to fulfill all the obligations of a ruler, a father all the responsibilities of fatherhood, and so on. Chaos ensues when people no longer behave according to their prescribed roles. Confucianists once believed that education and moral suasion were sufficient to ensure proper behavior, but eventually, they conceded that punishments had to be employed as well. The process known as "Confucianization of Law" was an outcome of this new attitude. If law (and punishment) must be used by the state, then it should be used to promote Confucian values as well as, more generally, to maintain order. Very early on, the Qing government recognized in the law codes a powerful symbol of the moral authority of the state as well as a potent tool for social engineering. One prominent example of such awareness is the statute of 1646, which imposed stringent evidential requirements for rape charges. The intent of this law was to promote the cult of chastity—that is, to embrace and, further, to sponsor a revival of Ming Confucian ideology in order to win the cooperation of conservative Chinese scholars.[25]

By the end of the seventeenth century, the Qing government had successfully restored peace and stability to China, and its various attempts to bring Confucian scholars into the fold had also been successful. But the Qing rulers knew that they had only managed to set down their roots in Chinese soil; for the Qing state to thrive, these roots had to be nourished carefully and protected from future harm. The Qing rulers laid down an ambitious program of propaganda and indoctrination. They believed in social engineering, and they used both education and the penal code to help the state to shape and control behavior. Subscribing to the Confucian conviction that "rectification of names" ensured harmony and stability, they insisted that men must become husbands and fathers, and women must become good wives and wise mothers; deviation from these prescribed roles would not be tolerated. Seen in this light, homosexuality was a violation of the principle of "rectification of names."

Perhaps if the Qing rulers had believed that homosexuality was limited only to a very small percentage of the population, they might not have taken any action against it. But they were convinced otherwise. The boom in homoerotic literature in the seventeenth century, along with the frequent references to homosexual behavior in scholarly jottings, heightened their awareness of the extent of homosexuality, transforming it, in their minds, into a "problem." The 1740 law that felonized consensual sodomy between adults was a product of the overall effort on the part of the Qing state to bolster traditional gender roles. Sexual behavior that threatened to undermine these roles was rendered punishable offenses. It is unclear from criminal records how effective the homophobic law was in regulating male sexuality, but clearly, it served notice to the public that homosexuality was no longer considered a private matter.

A survey of trial cases reveals one final point: that the Qing government was less forgiving of male homosexuals than of women found guilty of unsavory sexual conduct, suggesting that the state regarded male homosexuality as a worse evil than unchaste female behavior—probably because only males could carry on the family name and it was considered imperative that they fulfill their filial duty to sire sons. Seen in this light, male homosexuality (that is, nonprocreative sexual activity) was viewed as a direct challenge to the requirements of filial piety. Unchaste women, on the other hand, did not threaten the continuation of family name; they could be replaced and their reproductive function taken over by other women.

HOMOSEXUALITY IN THE RENAISSANCE: BEHAVIOR, IDENTITY, AND ARTISTIC EXPRESSION

◆

JAMES M. SASLOW

The Renaissance and Baroque periods (ca. 1400–1650) mark the first era in Western culture when we can relate themes and images to the biographies of individual artists; that relationship reveals early attempts to express homosexual interests in visual arts and literature. Patterns of homosexuality in the early modern period constitute a transition from the social systems and philosophical constructs of the classical and medieval world toward the modern models that would begin to emerge after about 1700. Male homosexual behavior can be more fully recovered from the historical record than can lesbianism; both are documented across the spectrum of classes and occupations, though first-person testimony is relatively rare, which poses problems in interpreting self-image.

The emergence of homosexuality as a widely observable and documented social phenomenon coincides with that splendid and critical period in Western culture known as the Renaissance. Although the era between the late fourteenth and late seventeenth centuries only gradually altered the religious and social organization of the Middle Ages, it was marked off by a revival of classical learning that stimulated a creative upsurge in the arts, sciences, and philosophy; by the development of urbanization, mercantile capitalism, and world-exploring national states; and by the prolonged doctrinal warfare of the Reformation and Counter-Reformation. The central energizing tension of the period was the attempt to reconcile Catholic faith with the knowledge and values represented by pagan antiquity and the emerging empirical sciences—an ultimately impossible task that profoundly influenced every sphere of human action, from theology to politics to sexuality.

Officially, homosexuality was subject to severe condemnation, both religious and civil; this general attitude, however, varied considerably between different genders, cultures, and time periods. Far fewer women than men were prosecuted, and rates of male prosecution ranged from several hundred a year in fifteenth-century Florence to less than one in Calvinist Geneva; within one society, periods of relative neglect could alternate with phases of intensified repression. Early gay-studies scholars glorified High Renaissance Italy, where the legacy of the Greco-Roman past sanctioned some expression of "Greek love," but this movement probably had little impact outside the educated classes. By the time the Council of Trent (1545–1563) codified a broad moral house-cleaning in response to Protestant critiques of Rome, the scope of sexual and other heterodoxy was sharply curtailed. Many factors have been put forth as explanations for these fluctuations of tolerance: demographic (concern about declining birth rates or family stability); medical (periodic outbreaks of the plague); sociological (new forms of social breakdown and control due to urbanization); and religious (upswings of pietistic activism).[1]

This essay seeks to outline what we now know, and what we are still trying to fathom, about homosexual experience in the Renaissance: the prevalence and variety of homosexual behavior, the psychological meanings and identities assigned to such acts, and the construction and expression of these psychosocial patterns in imaginative art and literature.

Behavior

Evidence about sexual practices and attitudes in the Renaissance varies greatly depending on the age, sex, class, and power of the participants. As with most social life, we are better informed about men than women, and know more about the private feelings of the literate classes—artistocracy, clergy, and educated humanists—than about the generally illiterate lower classes. While enough material has been assembled to permit reconstruction of the broad outlines of sexual behavior, the available data present both lacunae and inherent limitations that leave us with several unresolved questions.

Three principal generalizations can be made about the sexual preferences and prerogatives of adult men. First, for many individuals homosexual relations were only one element of what we would call bisexuality. Second, homosexual activity occurred mainly, though not exclusively, between adult men and boys or adolescents. And third, the surviving evidence about these relations is incomplete and biased because of the gravity of the crime and the nature of the sources.

Few noblemen were exclusively homosexual; most fulfilled their class and gender obligation to marry in order to cement alliances and produce dynastic heirs. Scholars uncomfortable with homosexuality long tended to discount the male "favorites" of such monarchs as France's Henri III or Britain's James I as political or social rather than physical intimates. Contemporaries, however, clearly read them as sexual liaisons: one of Henri's courtiers, the Sieur de Caylus, was called "Culus," a pun on the French for rectum. Many clergymen, from Pope Julius III to Carlo Cardinal Carafa, though theoretically celibate, were also open to the gamut of bisexual pleasure, while the Florentine poet Antonio Beccadelli reassured questioners that his ode to sodomy, *L'ermafrodito* (The Hermaphrodite, 1425), did not preclude his love for his mistresses.[2]

The prevalence and character of male bisexuality reflect two important determinants of sexuality in this period: It was often associated with a generalized permissiveness, even license, and it is consistent with adult men's position at the pinnacle of a social system that privileged patriarchy, age, and power. Sigismondo Malatesta, lord of Rimini, had a reputation for sexual atrocities involving both boys and women; his French contemporary Gilles de Rais ("Bluebeard," 1403–1440) was executed after sexually abusing and murdering one hundred children of both sexes. Though less violent, a similarly catholic hedonism was found in Stuart England: The Earl of Castlehaven was prosecuted in 1631 for raping his wife and sodomizing two male attendants, and during the bawdy Restoration the Earl of Rochester wrote blithely that "missing my whore, I bugger my page." In an atmosphere of indiscriminate pleasure-seeking, boys were considered interchangeable with women because of the still-"feminine" physical characteristics of beardless, high-voiced, smooth-skinned adolescents.[3]

Rochester's implied equality of women and boys also suggests how the powerful tended to prefer their sexual objects subordinated by gender, age, and/or socioeconomic status. Many adult noblemen were known to have sexual relations with their pages, young men who served them as an apprenticeship in courtly skills; others found sexual partners among actors, stableboys, craftworkers, and other commoners. The criminal archives of Venice recount the group sodomy arrest of fifteen nobles and eighteen non-nobles in 1406, while Maurel de Volonne, a courtier of Louis XIV's homosexual brother Philippe, duc d'Orléans, reportedly "sold boys like horses and would go shopping in the pit of the Opéra."[4]

Similar intergenerational patterns prevailed among the clergy and educated humanists. Charges against Popes Paul II and Julius II centered around their seduction of much younger men; Cellini's autobiography records a beautiful and talented youth, Luigi Pulci, who made a career out of service to Roman bishops, from one of whom he contracted syphilis. Perhaps the most colorful and frankly sexual among scholars was Angelo Poliziano (1454–1494), whose Greek epistles beg kisses and caresses from specific young men and who reportedly died from getting out of his sickbed to serenade a youth he'd been smitten by.[5]

The intimate living arrangements of the all-male clerical world and the opportunities that educational and religious duties afforded for privacy and emotional intimacy, while not themselves "causes" of homosexuality, may have contributed circumstantially to its expression. Priests in fifteenth-century Venice and Stuart Sussex were convicted of sex with young parishioners; unpublished records of church trials in Loreto, Italy, in the 1570s detail the sexual activities of a choirboy, Luigi dalla Balla, who slept successively with various older monks, canons, and musicians, and record other youths' accusations against their superiors. Similarly, Nicholas Udall, headmaster of Eton, was convicted of sodomizing two students and a servant, as was a headmaster in Essex in 1594. Antonio, a thirteen-year-old Venetian caught in a long-term sexual affair with a public herald, saw their relation as a "friendship" because Benedicto was "teaching him like a master"; city authorities, more concerned about the fact of seduction than the feelings it evoked, issued regulations in 1444 and 1477 to curb "this abominable vice" in schools of music, gymnastics, fencing, and mathematics.[6]

Sodomy was practiced across the entire spectrum of middle- and lower-class occupations: London merchants and actors, Venetian barber-surgeons and *gondolieri*, Genevan printers, laborers, and servants, and the navy. The apprenticeship system, under which boys from age twelve or thirteen lived with craftworkers as student-assistants, replicated the intimate master-servant and pedagogic patterns of the upper classes. Donatello (1386–1466) was only the first of many Italian artists believed to choose their disciples more for beauty than talent; most notorious was the Sienese Gianantonio Bazzi, whose train of foppish *garzoni* earned him the nickname "Il Sodoma." The Flemish sculptor Jérôme Duquesnoy the Younger (1602–1654) was executed for committing sodomy with an acolyte in a church where Duquesnoy was working.[7]

While adult-youth sex clearly predominated, recent research calls for reexamination of the older assertion that it was the exclusive model, sanctified by Greek precedent. In 1418, a Venetian priest seduced both a noble whom he served as chaplain and the noble's son, and when the Anglican bishop John Atherton was hanged in 1640 for the libertine combination of adultery, incest, and sodomy, an illustrated pamphlet about his case showed Atherton and his lover, John Childe, both wearing full beards. At the opposite end of the age spectrum, five "beastly Sodomiticall boyes" caught with one another during an Atlantic crossing in 1629 were sent back to England for punishment. It is suggestive that there are more recorded incidents of sex between working-class men of roughly the same age, usually adolescents or young adults. It remains to be investigated whether those already toward the bottom of the status ladder had less to lose by not remaining socially "on top" in age and/or had fewer resources with which to attract someone of even lower standing.[8]

Whatever the relative proportion of sex between men or boys of the same age, the adult-youth model remained a dominant paradigm. In colonial Virginia in 1625, ship's master Richard Cornish was executed for sex with one of his stewards. His passive partner, William Crouse, was referred to as a "rascally boy" though he was twenty-nine years old, suggesting that the pederastic construct was applied even where chronologically tenuous.[9]

The evidence for this behavior is selective and sporadic, posing several obstacles to interpretation. Not surprisingly for an illegal activity, little first-person testimony was committed to paper or survived. Most of our knowledge thus derives from hostile outside sources: for the lower classes, from police and court records; for the clergy and aristocracy, from individuals whose opinions may have been colored by personal or political motives. Royal brides provide an indispensable testimony for their spouses' private activities, but hardly an objective one: Princess Elizabeth Charlotte, wife of Philippe d'Orléans, deeply resented her husband's neglect and was disinclined to interpret his extramarital relations as anything more than a frivolous disgrace.[10] In the political realm, broadsides against Henri III complained that his extravagance toward his *mignons* was bankrupting the government. And, sodomy being particularly embarrassing within the very institution responsible for upholding the moral taboo against it, Protestants denounced Rome as a "cistern full of sodomy," while Catholics tried to discredit Calvin's successor, Théodore de Bèze, by dredging up his early poems to young men. It is often difficult to establish independently which such charges had merit and which were exaggerated propaganda.

In those few instances where we have firsthand accounts, the same behavior is depicted as a more complex and emotionally profound experience. Like the sexually frank and affectionate correspondence between the composer Orlando di Lasso (1532–1594) and his patron, the crown prince of Bavaria, King James's letters to his favorite, the Duke of Buckingham, bear witness to great feeling and commitment. The usually gruff Cellini records his youthful affection for another adolescent close to his own age in a way that, if not explicitly sexual, is physically intimate and tender, while letters between a seventeenth-century musician and cleric, preserved by the Portuguese Inquisition, hint at a loving relationship of some years' duration. Archives of the secular courts occasionally yield a tantalizing, "microhistorical" glimpse of real individuals: Two Venetian boatmen arrested in 1357 had remained together willingly for several years, shared a business, and when interrogated separately each lied hoping to protect the other.[11]

The primary question raised by the extensive trial records of Venice, Florence, and other large cities is collective and sociological: to what extent did such repeated incidents imply embryonic urban subcultures in the modern sense? The fragmentary evidence suggests that the growth of continuous sexual subcultures required a critical mass of urbanized population for both contact and anonymity. Such sociological networks have been posited for relatively small communities in twelfth- and fourteenth-century France, but substantial documentation is first found for cosmopolitan Venice, where sodomy arrests in the fifteenth century shifted toward groups rather than isolated pairs, and male prostitution was recorded about 1500. Besides schools, in 1450 the authorities there expressed suspicions about intergenerational dinners in private homes, suggesting that contact networks included social and intellectual as well as purely sexual interchange. Subcultural meeting places and activities were apparently common knowledge: To judge from ribald popular songs of the 1570s, the mass of Londoners were well aware of the "Sodome and Gomorra" in their midst, and Donne and Marston inveighed against tavern-brothels there in the 1590s. An unsolved problem in this area is the wide variation of tolerance for open violations of official taboo. Montaigne reported several "marriages" between Portuguese men celebrated in a Roman church in 1578; the couples lived together for some time before being arrested and burned.[12]

Lesbianism in the Renaissance is documented far less often than male homosexuality, for three reasons. Fewer women were literate, and no female voices describe erotic experience firsthand. Since women above the laboring classes were generally sequestered within the household sphere, they had few opportunities to form wider social networks, except in convents. Finally, female deviance, like most aspects of women's behavior, was of less concern to male authorities: The total number of known prosecutions ranges from four in sixteenth-century France to two in Germany and one each in Spain, Italy, Geneva, and the Netherlands.

The record suggests that lesbians, like their male counterparts, cut across the spectrum of classes. There are reliable seventeenth-century accounts of Queen Christina of Sweden, who abdicated in order not to marry; of a Miss Hobart, lady-in-waiting to the Duchess of York; and of a French actress, Mademoiselle de Maupin. In colonial Plymouth, two housewives were accused of "lewd behavior each with the other upon a bed." Surprisingly, considering that the passions of nuns were a literary commonplace, only two cases of convent relationships have come down to us, most richly the prosecution of Sister Benedetta Carlini in Pescia, sentenced to life imprisonment in 1619–1623 for claiming to have had visions that required her cell-mate to masturbate her.

The fact that Carlini was condemned not for lesbianism, but for blasphemy, raises a series of questions about how the perception of female sexual deviance was conflated with other forms of unorthodoxy, gender and doctrinal. Sodomy and heresy had been conceptually linked throughout the late Middle Ages; while the atrocities attributed to women in the witchcraft persecutions of the fifteenth to seventeenth centuries were largely heterosexual, lesbian acts remained one element in the ecclesiastical demonology. We cannot yet determine with certainty whether sex between women was the primary phenomenon, and the religious interpretation of it an epiphenomenon reflecting male inquisitors' greater concern with threats to their authority; or, conversely, whether heresy was often a true charge, and imputations of lesbianism were simply stereotypical assumptions about the character of nonbelievers.

A similar ambiguity surrounds the "passing woman," or female transvestite: Did women choose this risky option as a strategy for sexual and emotional expression, or was lesbianism as such less of a motive than a general desire for the greater economic and political freedom of men? Evidence is inconclusive about the sexuality of the outlaw Moll Cutpurse and her "Roaring Girls" in Jacobean London; nor can we be sure whether sexuality or usurpation of male privilege was the primary issue in the case of a woman burned at Fontaines, France, about 1535 when authorities discovered that she had been passing as a man in order to marry another woman and "counterfeit the office of a husband." It does seem clear that male authorities viewed lesbianism itself as more grave the more it laid claim to active male prerogatives: In Spain, two women were merely whipped and sent to the galleys for sex "without an instrument," but the penalty for penetration with a dildo was burning, suffered by two fifteenth-century nuns.[13]

Identity

As historians have made great strides in documenting sexual behavior, our second order of questions—the psychological constructs and dynamics that underlie these visible actions—has become more controversial. The issue is Identity: How was homosexuality perceived and understood by both practitioners and "outsiders"? To what extent did it imply a discrete category of individuals with shared personality traits? And, most problematically, can we speak of any consciousness among these individuals of their common desires and emotions, or of their problematic relation as a group to the dominant society?

The prevailing opinion holds that, prior to the modern period, homosexuality was conceived only as a range of acts hypothetically available to all individuals, and that the notion implicit in today's sense of "gay"—a total psychic identity unique to a distinctive minority—did not emerge until the rise of extensive urban subcultures in the eighteenth century and of medical psychiatry, which coined the term "homosexual" in 1869. This social-constructionist model assumes a universal bisexual potential that is channeled into changing behavioral paradigms by cultural forces, while the opposing "essentialist" school looks for evidence of a distinct, historically constant homosexual personality.[14] The scarcity and diversity of surviving sources make an essentialist model difficult to apply to our period. Moreover, support for the profound influence of formalized social constructs on understanding and behavior is found in a central dichotomy in Renaissance philosophy that, while still imperfectly understood, constitutes perhaps the most problematic discontinuity with modern conceptualizations of same-sex relationships: the separation of sexuality from emotional intimacy.

At the same time, the constructionist model has thus far failed to account fully for three provocative aspects of Renaissance culture that suggest we should "push back" the temporal frontier of an emerging modern consciousness, at least in embryonic form, well into the early modern period. Notwithstanding the official division of love from sex, some writers allude to the mixing of the two: Renaissance terms for homosexuality imply a nexus of ideas amounting to a rudimentary psychological theory; and scattered individuals expressed resentment over their stigmatization and skepticism toward dominant cultural values.

Our post-Freudian taxonomy of sexual orientation embraces as inseparable all forms of real or fantasied intimacy between persons of the same sex, grading them along a continuum from "homosocial" to "homoerotic" to genital. In contrast, Renaissance humanists and theologians maintained a sharp conceptual divide between acts and feelings. Canon law outlawed as sodomy certain physical acts, ambiguously embracing all forms of nonprocreative sexuality, while passionate but chaste male emotional intimacy, modeled on classical notions of *amicitia*, was held up as the highest earthly happiness. To the extent that Christian writers troubled themselves about motivation, they subsumed it under such broader categories as demonic influence (heresy, possession); lustful example set by others (it was frequently asserted that a "fashion" for sodomy was imported into England and France by Italians); and the sin of gluttony, embracing all physical indulgence: Marlowe was reported to have claimed that "they who loved not tobacco and boys were fools."[15]

The institutions of Greco-Roman antiquity, notably Plato's writings on love, venerated by the Neoplatonist philosophers, provided eloquent justification for a passionate but purely spiritual love between two men. Montaigne and Erasmus echoed Ficino's commentary on Plato's *Symposium*, which had declared that "Some men . . . are better equipped for offspring of the soul than for those of the body. . . . [They] therefore, naturally love men more than women, because [men] are much stronger in mental keenness . . . essential to knowledge." These idealized unions were often the emotional equivalent of a marriage: The Florentine intellectuals Giovanni Pico della Mirandola and Girolamo Benivieni were buried in the same tomb, like husband and wife.[16]

The modern notion of "romance," as a fusion of sexual and emotional attraction, is not articulated in such writings: The language of "masculine love" is applied only to chaste relationships, and sexual desire is not justified by the same terms. There is, however, some evidence to suggest that the boundaries between chaste theory and erotic practice were fluid and ambiguous. Classical sources also familiarized Renaissance readers with *paiderastia*, the sexualized pedagogic relationship between men and youths, which offered a precedent for genital expression of an emotional bond. Some theorists were aware that their passionate ideal could thus be easily read as justifying sodomy: In his *Libro d'amore* (1525), the Mantuan Mario Equicola pointedly insisted that "not a word of this work is to be understood as the love of boys or sexual acts against nature."

He was reacting to a common perception: In the same year, Ariosto's *Satires* asserted that "few humanists are without that vice" and reported that "the vulgar laugh when they hear of someone who possesses a vein of poetry, and then they say, 'It is a great peril to turn your back if you sleep next to him.' " Popular wisdom was not without basis: Francis Bacon (1561–1626), who wrote a proper essay on friendship, obviously grasped the wider implications of Greek love, since even his mother knew that he slept with his servants. Conversely, relationships that struck authorities as primarily sexual, like Benedicto and his herald-apprentice, were seen by the participants as involving a strong emotional component as well: The canon Luigi Fontino justified his sexual interest in Luigi dalla Balla on the grounds that "I thought to have a disciple who could take care of me if I became ill in my final years."

In their care to avoid jumping to anachronistic conclusions about such statements, some scholars interpret even the most heated avowal of passion as conventional Neoplatonic rhetoric; at the opposite extreme, Joseph Pequigney's psychoanalytic reading of Shakespeare's Sonnets takes every sexual metaphor, however tenuous or allegorized, as an allusion to physical behavior. The question remains open whether some individuals viewed homosexuality as a more nearly unitary phenomenon than formal theory allowed, or whether they dealt with the contradiction by, in Bray's phrase, perpetuating "a cleavage . . . between an individual's behavior and his awareness of its significance."[17]

Another conceptual dichotomy that seems to have enabled many men to avoid identification (or self-identification) as "homosexual" is evident in the vocabulary for describing homosexual acts and their perpetrators: Sexual acts were categorized not only by the gender of one's object-choice, but also by the role one performed. As part of a broader effort to demarcate male and female social roles and appropriate gender constructs, contemporary theory drew a sharp distinction between active (masculine) and passive (feminine) sexual roles. Italian verbs, like classical Greek, differentiated between active and passive roles by the corresponding grammatical voice: The formula for the former was *soddomitare*, "to sodomize," for the latter *farsi soddomitare*, "to let oneself be sodomized."

As a result, adult bisexual men who consistently played the active role could engage in homosexual acts without being considered to deviate from the norms of their gender role. Even here, however, there are faint hints that they possessed a variant personality. In a bawdy tale by Matteo Bandello, the poet Porcellio, upbraided by his confessor for denying sex with young men, replies, "To divert myself with boys is more natural to me than eating and drinking, and you asked me if I sinned against nature!"—the joke turning on his inversion of Aquinas' sense of "natural" order.

By contrast, many nouns existed for passive homosexual partners, implying a person as much as an act. Their mocking tone indicates that habitual passivity was considered a fundamental deficiency, and they reveal a complex (and misogynistic) theory imputing a distinct psychological nature to such individuals. *Ganymede* and *cinaedus, androgyne* and *hermaphrodite*, all borrowed from antiquity, conflate effeminacy, youthful androgyny, transvestism, and homosexuality into one constellation of gender transgressions; by implication, passive men were a psychic hybrid amounting to a third gender. One Florentine usage for a passive partner was *si tiene come donna*, "he regards himself as a woman"; in Venice, such a person could be punished by cutting off his nose, a penalty otherwise reserved for women. Conversely, to the extent that male observers noted females' active pursuit of other women, some granted it a grudging respect: the sixteenth-century Frenchman de Brantôme wrote, " 'Tis much better for a woman to be masculine and a very Amazon and lewd in this fashion, than for a man to be feminine."[18]

The final psychological question is about self-consciousness: to what extent "sodomites" may have reacted to their stigmatized position by articulating some nascent sense of what we would term "oppression" and "alienation." As in most societies, the majority probably accepted and internalized prevailing norms; Seymour Kleinberg's study of *The Merchant of Venice* presents Antonio as the first self-loathing homosexual in literature.[19] More subversive private opinions, if they existed, were even less likely to be written down or preserved than declarations of individual affection. Even so, a few tantalizing biographical fragments suggest that some homosexually oriented men were aware that their deviation made their relationship to society problematic, and that they developed various rationales in self-defense.

Commenting on a depiction of Christ as an androgynous youth, Leonardo alluded bitterly to his earlier sodomy accusation: "When I painted Our Lord as a boy, you put me in jail; if I were now to paint him as a grown man, you would do worse to me." Michelangelo's Neoplatonic passion for several young men was widely known through his poems and drawings; although he insisted angrily on his pious celibacy, Aretino took advantage of popular rumors to threaten blackmail. The similar temperament of both artists—reclusive, suspicious, sublimating through work—

suggests one pattern of response to the anxieties of sexual nonconformity. By contrast, after his horse won a race in Siena, their more flamboyant colleague Bazzi defiantly threw back in his fellow citizens' faces their mocking nickname for him, insisting on being announced as "Il Sodoma," the sodomite—arguably the first "coming-out" statement in Western history.[20]

For those seeking to resolve cognitive dissonance—an awareness of conflict between their subjective desire and external authority—three strategies can be discerned. Some justified homosexuality by appeal to the alternative morality of classical example. When Cellini's rival Bandinelli publicly called him a "dirty sodomite," he retorted, "I wish to God I did know how to indulge in such a noble practice; after all, we read that Jove enjoyed it with Ganymede in paradise." Others similarly "appropriated" aspects of the Christian mythos, such as Marlowe's claim that Christ and Saint John, "the beloved disciple," were physical lovers. The most daring position denied Christianity's moral authority: The seventeenth-century French libertine poet Chauvigny flaunted his paired desires to be "an unbeliever and a sodomite," and William Plaine was executed in Connecticut in 1646 not only for corrupting town youths but because "to some who questioned the lawfulness of such filthy practice, he did insinuate seeds of atheism, questioning whether there was a God."[21] Perhaps the Church's ancient linkage of sodomy and heresy, though overdrawn, intuited a more subtle reality: Some of those who are defined as deviant will, to retain a measure of self-respect, become "conceptual traitors" capable of deconstructing the official symbols and values that deny their worth and wholeness.

The Arts

The third general question of Renaissance homosexuality encompasses the construction and transmission of these desires and values through culture, in the specifically artistic sense. How, by whom, and for what audiences were the psychosocial realities of homosexuality imaginatively integrated and given concrete form in prose literature, poetry, drama, painting, and sculpture? The stimuli of the classical revival and vernacular literature, coupled with the richness of biographical data inspired by the new cult of the creative individual, produced the earliest conditions under which artists and patrons could leave behind both homosexual imagery and the evidence to relate it to their own lives. This art was divided into two very different genres, with contrasting expressive strategies, by a crucial dichotomy in point of view: between "insiders," who had some firsthand knowledge of or sympathy toward this form of love, and "outsiders," to whom it was alien and distasteful.

Those seeking to explore homosexual sensibilities with understanding acceptance drew their subject matter from three cultural sources: pagan antiquity, Judeo-Christian tradition, and everyday life. The richest of these was the classical heritage, beginning with Beccadelli's *L'ermafrodito*, inspired by Catullus, and reaching an early summit in Poliziano's *L'Orfeo* (1480), in which Orpheus misogynistically extols the love of "the better sex." Marlowe imagined sweetly comic scenes between Jupiter and Ganymede (*Dido, Queen of Carthage*) and Neptune and Leander, while the pastoral tradition of Virgil inspired Marlowe's poem "Come live with me and be my love" and Richard Barnfield's more poignantly post-Christian "Affectionate Shepherd," who declares, "If it be sin to love a lovely lad, O then sin I."[22]

These and other classical archetypes of male love—Apollo, Narcissus, Cupid, and Bacchus—were illustrated by sympathetic artists from Donatello to Caravaggio. Ganymede alone appears in several hundred artworks: The story of the beautiful shepherd boy borne heavenward by the infatuated bisexual king of the gods was ideally suited to embody the principal patterns of homosexuality at the time. In the versions by Michelangelo and Cellini, we possess enough biographical background to understand the personal significance they attached to the myth.

Michelangelo's Ganymede (1532) is one in a series of drawings through which he expressed to the young Roman nobleman, Tommaso de' Cavalieri, the range of his feelings in this most passionate relationship of his life. The youth's ecstatic ascent to the heavens in the pinions of the eagle/ Jupiter symbolizes the "transport" of Neoplatonic friendship, but Michelangelo was also aware of the myth's erotic connotations from his teacher Poliziano. As his poems and other drawings make clear, he was deeply torn between chaste Christian ideals and the temptations of the flesh; calling himself "prisoner of an armed cavalier" (Cavalieri), he lamented that "my senses and their own fire have bereft/all peace from my heart." Less introspective, Cellini was deprived of peace more by external pressures: It was his proposal to restore an antique fragment as Ganymede that occasioned Bandinelli's accusation. It is tempting to read his "Apollo and Hyacinthus," carved immediately after that altercation, as an ironically defiant visual retort; certainly the image had deep personal meaning, since Cellini kept it in his studio all his life.[23]

Beginning with Freud, the personal testimony of such artists has been mined for psychoanalytic explanations of their creativity, which basically view it as sublimation of erotic drives unacceptable to the societal or individual super-ego. Psychoanalytic approaches to historical figures are inherently unverifiable, since the subject is no longer available for analytic exchange, and are often out of touch with newer theories of sexuality; but such studies as Robert Liebert's on Michelangelo offer provocative personality portraits for the earliest individuals whose inner homoerotic feelings are known to us in any depth. Their model of intrapsychic conflict illuminates the change in esthetic strategy that both Michelangelo and Cellini underwent in later life: Succumbing to the ascetic Counter-Reformation, each turned from the erotic pagan subjects forbidden by the Council of Trent toward exclusively religious imagery.[24]

Although Judeo-Christian myth officially offered less material for homosexual identification, many artists' treatment of religious heroes suggests a veiled or half-conscious sensitivity toward male beauty and emotions. Donatello's nude "David" fused the Old Testament hero with a sleek classical ephebe; like Caravaggio, who later painted his own features into Goliath, Donatello emphasized the erotic decapitation of the giant, who has symbolically "lost his head" over the handsome youth. Leonardo and Botticelli, both charged with sodomy, imbued their adolescent angels and martyrs with a seductive androgynous grace; Sodoma's Saint Sebastian, bound to a tree and pierced with arrows, writhes in ostensibly religious ecstasy open to multiple personalized interpretations, from the epitome of sado-masochism to the artist's comment on his own public "martyrdom."[25]

In the sixteenth century, writers and artists turned their attention from ideal divinities to realistic portrayal of the world around them. Marlowe, like Shakespeare, borrowed plots from secular history, significantly the lives of two bisexual kings, England's *Edward II* and Henri III of France (*The Massacre at Paris*). Theatrical satire often focused on the foibles of the day: Aretino's *The Stablemaster* poked fun at a boy-lover well known to his Mantuan audience, while Rochester's *Sodom, or the Quintessence of Debauchery* burlesques the gross pansexuality of the Stuart court. The practice of transvestite boy actors, necessitated by women's banishment from the stage, was exploited for comic effects that must have resonated provocatively among the older, bisexual spectators of this eroticized demimonde.

The great innovator of naturalistic painting was Caravaggio, whose portrayal of ordinary life drew on his own model-catamites and his wealthy patrons' boy entertainers and banquetmates. His young Romans disguised as Bacchus stretch classical justification to its breaking point, while his androgynous, sultry "Musicians" dispense with mythological allusion altogether. The unprecedented frankness of these pictures results from a landmark in patronage: Cardinal Francesco del Monte is the first known client with homosexual interests who hired an artist to represent scenes with a common emotional subtext for both parties. Caravaggio was also the first such artist to consciously borrow erotically relevant motifs from an earlier artist of similar tastes: His "Victorious Cupid," based on Michelangelo's sculpture of a youth triumphing over an older man, may represent the beginning of a rudimentary sense of homoerotic visual tradition.[26]

At the opposite pole, works produced with the patronage and viewpoint of nonhomosexuals were concerned to construct and disseminate strongly negative attitudes. Three strategies can be discerned: moral invective, documentary accounts of punishment, and censorship. Sermons, religious tracts, and scathing satire were directed against male sodomy from the Italian monk Savonarola (d. 1498) to Thomas Artus's *Island of the Hermaphrodites* (1605), an illustrated parody of Henri III's court. Lustful male couples were inserted in Quattrocento paintings as a moral foil to the main scene of religious virtue; in the seventeenth century, the Jesuit missionary Matteo Ricci introduced Western homophobia to Asia, commissioning an engraving of the destruction of Sodom to illustrate his Mandarin essay on "Depraved Sensuality."[27]

Women, as usual, were generally ignored: Although Sappho's poetry was rediscovered in the sixteenth century, most commentators refused to credit her lesbian feelings. The paucity of women as artists and patrons left imaging of lesbians to men, who, viewing them as object from the standpoint of a male subject, usually chose to illustrate myths like Diana and Callisto, with its titillating transvestite-heterosexual hero, or Diana and Actaeon, primarily a vehicle for male fears of women's unknown life together. Similarly, Hans Baldung Grien's "Witches' Orgy" drawings conflate female bacchanales with occult heresy.[28]

When authorities suppressed homosexual behavior, they occasionally recorded the event visually. Ironically, this negative propaganda now provides such uniquely informative records as a 1482 manuscript illustration of two men burned at the stake in Zurich and the Atherton pamphlet in England, with its revealing woodcut portraits. An engraving in the chronicle of Balboa's invasion of Central America graphically depicts the Europeans setting their dogs on homosexual *berdaches* in the New World.[29]

As part of a wider campaign to control nonconformity, censorship of offending texts and images was institutionalized under church and state auspices. A set of engravings depicting mostly heterosexual intercourse, with captions by Aretino, was burned in 1524 by papal authorities, who later established the *Index of Prohibited Books*. Conquistador accounts attest to similar hostile responses by the Spaniards to the positive erotic art discovered in the Americas: Gonzalo de Oviedo y Valdes boasted of destroying a Colombian gold relief depicting "a man mounted upon another in that diabolic and nefarious act of Sodom."[30]

The chilling effect of official disapproval is clear from Cellini's *Vita*, which omits or denies his known homosexual exploits even as he brags about his female conquests. In the 1600s, pagan subjects were gradually sanitized: Rubens's copy of Titian's "Venus Worship" changed the embracing *putti* from male to heterosexual couples, and Monteverdi's opera *Orfeo* omitted Poliziano's episodes recounting life after Eurydice. Homosexual behavior and imagery were explicitly expelled from the public realm in the theatrical masque *Coelum britannicum* (1634), in which

Charles II dissociated himself from his father James I with the declaration that "Ganymede is forbidden the bedchamber."[31]

Conclusion

Much is now known about homosexual practice and theory in the Renaissance and Baroque centuries, but crucial questions remain, including such behavioral variables as age and social class. While psychological identity was not as bifurcated into "homosexual" and "heterosexual" categories as in modern times, some awareness existed of distinctive personality types, and some individuals articulated the personal effect of being marked as deviant. Same-sex relations were explored in the arts, but we are not yet sure where the prevailing terminology implied genital expression, or to what extent practice corresponded to theory; nor have we fully explored the contrasting assumptions and strategies underlying sympathetic versus hostile patronage.

Whether further evidence will surface to flesh out the hints that homosexuality was becoming a discrete phenomenon, or whether they constitute merely inchoate and scattered anomalies, remains to be seen. The recent work of discourse theorists, notably Foucault, suggests caution: However prescient of modern attitudes these utterances may seem, they were embedded in an epistemology that could not fully articulate their implications. The Renaissance, like the Middle Ages before it, operated mentally by means of Platonic poetic or metaphoric analogy: Individual human actions were conceptualized and judged by their adherence to eternal, transcendent paradigms. But the twin cosmologies of the time, classical and Christian, could not accommodate the realities of homosexuality any more than the telescope or the factory.

With Kepler, Descartes, and Newton, an alternative new mode of more Aristotelian discourse, variously termed analytic, experimental, and empiricist, supplanted supernatural cosmology with a new faith in individual reason and in science. The resultant transformation of Western thought in this period was particularly crucial for the history of sexuality and gender: Christianity's fearful linkage of sinful "deviance" with divine plague was about to succumb to bacteriology and psychology, while Greek values, though more accepting, had never anticipated the mass industrial metropolis or the (relative) equality of women.[32]

The decline of the old discourse was implicit in the very beginning of the Renaissance, when the revival of antiquity exposed the relativity of Christian culture. When the tension between these two worldviews led to their mutual breakdown, the way was clear for a reconceptualization of all sexuality by the new paradigms of medicine and social science. The outward forms of what we now term the Ancien Régime persisted well into the eighteenth century and beyond; but the Renaissance planted the first seeds of a new identity and social status for homosexuality, and of a new self-awareness and self-expression on the part of those who found themselves marked off by this role.

LESBIANS IN AMERICAN INDIAN CULTURES

PAULA GUNN ALLEN

This essay addresses the question of how we can recover the lost tradition of women's same-sex relationships in American Indian culture since information about women-oriented-women is scanty and well hidden in white-generated documentation of native social systems. Gunn Allen argues that we must explore lesbianism by examining the social organization of women's relationships within a larger social and spiritual tribal context. Women were members of clans and bands or villages, but their daily lives and experiences were shared with other women rather than men. She examines the possibility of distinguishing between those women who formed erotic bonds with other women within this milieu, and those whose relationships with women were understood to derive from Spirit-direction. Such women, called *Koskalaka* among the Lakota, possessed special, sacred powers which are now devalued in modern, patriarchal societies. Gunn Allen's approach suggests a way of interpreting fragmentary traditions and radically altered customs.

The lesbian is to the American Indian what the Indian is to the American—invisible. According to ethnographers' accounts, among the tribes there were women warriors, women leaders, women shamans, women husbands, but whether any of these were lesbians is seldom mentioned. On the few occasions lesbianism is referred to, it is with regard to a specific individual who is noted because she is a lesbian. This fosters the impression of uniform heterosexuality among Indian women except for a very few who deviate from that norm. It is an impression that is false.

In all the hundreds, perhaps thousands, of books and articles about American Indians that I have read while pursuing my studies or preparing for the variety of courses in American Indian studies that I have taught, I have encountered no reference to lesbians except one.[1] That one was contained in a novel by Fred Manfred, *The Manly-Hearted Woman*,[2] and though its protagonist dresses as a man and rejects her feminine role and though she marries a woman, the writer is very explicit: She and her wife do not share sexual intimacies, a possibility that seems beyond the writer's ability to envision. Indeed, the protagonist eventually falls in love with a rather strange young warrior who possesses enormous sexual prowess (given him by spirit power and a curious genetic circumstance). After the warrior's death the manly hearted woman divorces her wife and returns to woman's garb and occupation, discarding the spirit stone that has determined her life to that point. It seems that heterosexual love conquers all—even ritual tradition, custom, and spirit command.

Direct references to lesbians or lesbianism among American Indians are even more sparse than those about homosexual men (usually called hermaphrodites or *berdache* or, less often, transvestites), occurring almost outside the body of information about tribal life or included in ways that underscore white attitudes about tribes, Indians, and homosexuality. Consequently, much of my discussion of lesbians is necessarily conjectural, based on secure knowledge of American Indian social systems and customs that I have gathered from formal study, personal experience, and personally communicated information from other Indians as well as from my own knowledge of lesbian culture and practice.

My idea in this essay is to explore lesbianism within a larger social and spiritual tribal context as contrasted with its occurrence as an individual aberration that might show up on occasion but that has nothing to do with tribal life in general. Because tribal civilizations (like all others) function in entire gestalts and because they are based on the life-enhancing interconnectedness of all things, it is my contention that gayness, whether female or male, traditionally functions positively within tribal groups.

Certainly, the chances that aboriginal American women formed affectional alliances are enormous. Many tribes had a marked tendency to encourage virginity or some version of chastity among pubescent women; this tendency rarely affected the sexual habits of married women, however, and it referred to intercourse with males. Nothing is said, to my knowledge, about sexual liaisons between women, except indirectly. It is equally likely that such relationships were practiced with social sanction, though no one is presently talking about this. The history of Native America is selective; and those matters pertaining to women that might contradict a Western patriarchal worldview are carefully selected out.

Some suggestions about how things were in "time immemorial," as the old folks refer to pre-contact times, have managed to find their way into contemporary literature about American Indians. Many tribes have recorded stories concerning daughters born to spirit women who were dwelling alone on earth. These daughters then would become the mothers of entire tribes. In one such tale, First Mother was "born of the dew of the leaf of the beautiful plant."[3] Such tales point to a time prior to the advent of patriarchy. While historical and archeological evidence suggests that this time predated European contact in some regions of the Western Hemisphere, the change in cultural orientation was still proceeding. The tribes became more male-oriented and more male-dominated as acculturation accelerated. As this process continued, less and less was likely to be said by American Indians about lesbians among them. Indeed, less and less about women in any position other than that sanctioned by missionaries was likely to be recorded.

There are a number of understandings about the entire issue that will be important in my discussion of American Indian women, heterosexual or lesbian. It is my contention and belief that those two groups were not nearly as separate as modern lesbian and straight women are. My belief is based on my understanding of the cultures and social systems in which women lived. These societies were tribal, and tribal consciousness, with its attendant social structures, differs enormously from that of the contemporary Western world.

This difference requires new understanding of a number of concepts. The concept of family, the concept of community, the concept of women, the concept of bonding and belonging, and the concept of power were all distinctly understood in a tribal matrix; and those concepts were/are very different from those current in modern America.

Women and Family in Tribal Societies

Among American Indians, Spirit-related persons are perceived as more closely linked than blood-related persons. Understanding this primary difference between American Indian values and modern Euro-Anglo-American Judeo-Christian values is critical to understanding Indian familial structures and the context in which lesbians functioned. For American Indian people, the primary value was relationship to the Spirit world. All else was determined by the essential nature of this understanding. Spirits, gods and goddesses, metaphysical/occult forces, and the right means of relating to them determined the tribes' every institution, every custom, every endeavor and pastime. This was not peculiar to inhabitants of the Western Hemisphere, incidentally; it was at one time the primary value of all tribal people on earth.

Relationship to the Spirit world has been of primary value to tribal people, but not to those who have studied them. Folklorists and ethnographers have other values that permeate their work and their under-standings, so that most of what they have recorded or concluded about American Indians is simply wrong. Countless examples could illustrate this basic misunderstanding, but let me share just one, culled from the work of one of the most influential anthropologists, Bronislaw Malinow-ski. His massive study of the Keres Pueblo Acoma presumably qualified him as an authority on mother-right society in North America. In *Sex, Culture, and Myth* Malinowski wrote: "Patrilocal households are 'united households,' while 'split households' are the exclusive phenomena of matrilocal mother-right cultures."[4] While acknowledging that economic considerations alone do not determine the structure of marriage patterns, Malinowski fails to recognize marriage as a construct founded on laws derived from conversations with Spirits. The primary unit for a tribe is not, as he suggests, the household; even the term is misleading, because a tribal "household" includes a number of individuals who are clan rather than blood relatives. For nontribal people, "household" typically means a unit composed of a father, mother, and offspring—though contemporary living arrangements often deviate from that stereotyped conception. A tribal household might encompass assorted blood-kin, medicine society "kin," adoptees, servants, and visitors who have a clan or supernatural claim on membership although they are biologically unrelated to the rest of the household.

While there can be little question about the fact that most women married, perhaps several times, it is important to remember that tribal marriages often bore little resemblance to Western concepts of that institution. Much that has been written about marriage as practiced among American Indians is wrong.

Among many tribes divorce was an easy matter for both women and men, and movement of individuals from one household to another was fluid and essentially unconstrained. There are many exceptions to this, for the tribes were distinct social groups; but many had patterns that did not use sexual constraint as a means of social control. Within such systems, individual action was believed to be directed by Spirits (through dreams, visions, direct encounter, or possession of power objects such as stones, shells, masks, or fetishes). In this context it is quite possible that lesbianism was practiced rather commonly, as long as the individuals cooperated with the larger social customs. Women were generally con-strained to have children, but in many tribes, childbearing meant empow-erment. It was the passport to maturity and inclusion in woman-culture. An important point is that women who did not have children because of constitutional, personal, or Spirit-directed disinclination had other ways to experience Spirit instruction and stabilization, to exercise power, and to be mothers.

"Family" did not mean what is usually meant by that term in the modern Western world. One's family might have been defined in biological terms as those to whom one was blood kin. More often it was defined by other considerations; spiritual kinship was at least as important a factor as "blood." Membership in a certain clan related one to many people in very close ways, though the biological connection might be so distant as to be practically nonexistent. This facet of familial ordering has been much obscured by the presence of white Christian influence and its New Testament insistence that the term "family" refers to mother, father, and children, and those others who are directly related to mother and father. In this construct, all persons who can point to common direct-line ancestors are in some sense related, though the individual's distance from that ancestor will determine the "degree" of relationship to other descendants of that ancestor.

Among many American Indians, family is a matter of clan membership. If clan membership is determined by your mother, and if your father has a number of wives, you are not related to the children of his other wives unless they themselves happen to be related to your mother. So half-siblings in the white way might be unrelated in an Indian way. Or in some tribes, the children of your mother's sister might be considered siblings, while those of your father's brother would be the equivalent of cousins. These distinctions should demonstrate that the concept of family can mean something very different to an Indian than it does to a non-Indian.

In gynecentric systems, a unified household is one in which the relationships among women and their descendants and sisters are ordered; a split household is one in which this is not the case. A community, then, is an ordering of sister relationships that determine who can depend on whom for what. Male relationships are ordered in accordance with the maternal principle; a male's spiritual and economic placement and the attendant responsibilities are determined by his membership in the community of sisterhood. A new acquaintance in town might be asked, "Who is your mother?" The answer identifies the person and determines the ensuing relationship between the questioner and the newcomer.

Again, community in the non-Indian modern world tends to mean people who occupy a definable geographical area or who share a culture (lifestyle) or occupation. It can extend to include people who share an important common interest—political, avocational, or spiritual. But "community" in the American Indian world can mean those who are of a similar clan and Spirit; those who are encompassed by a particular Spirit-being are members of a community. In fact, this was the meaning most often given to the concept in traditional tribal cultures. So it was not impossible that members of a community could have been a number of women who "belonged" to a given medicine society or who were alike in that they shared consciousness of a certain Spirit.

Women and Power

Any discussion of the status of women in general and of lesbians in particular cannot hope for accuracy if one misunderstands women's power in tribal societies. Indeed, in a recent random sampling of general ethnographies of several groups, I have noted that all matters of female life in the group under discussion can be found under the heading "Woman." This heading is divided into marriage, childbearing, childrearing, housekeeping, and, perhaps, menstruation. The discussions are neatly ordered according to middle-class white views about where women fit into social schemes, but they contain a number of false implications, not the least of which is that men don't marry, have children, or participate in childrearing.

It is clear, I think, that the ground we are exploring here is obscure: Women in general have not been taken seriously by ethnographers or folklorists, and explorations that have been done have largely been distorted by the preconceptions engendered by a patriarchal world-view, in which lesbians are said not to exist and women are perceived as oppressed, burdened, powerless, and peripheral to interesting accounts of human affairs except in that they have babies.

Power among tribal people is not perceived as political or economic, though status and material possessions can and often do derive from it. Power is conceived of as being supernatural and paranormal. It is a matter of spirit involvement and destiny. Woman's power comes automatically, by virtue of her femaleness, her natural and necessary fecundity, and her personal acquaintance with blood. The Arapaho felt that dying in war and dying in childbirth were of the same level of spiritual accomplishment. In fact, there are suggestions in the literature on ritualism and tribal ceremony that warriors and male initiates into medicine societies gain their supernatural powers by imitating ritually the processes that women undergo naturally.

The power of women can be controlled and directed only by other women who possess power that is equal in magnitude but that is focused and under their control. A woman who is older is more cognizant of what that power entails, the kinds of destruction it can cause, and the ways in which it can be directed and used for good. Thus pubescent women are placed under the care of older women and are trained in manners and customs of modesty so that their powers will not result in harm to themselves or the larger community. Usually, a woman who has borne a child becomes an initiate into the mysteries of womanhood, and if she develops virtues and abilities beyond those automatically conferred on her by nature, she becomes a medicine woman. Often, the medicine woman knows of her destiny in early childhood; such children are watched very carefully so that they will be able to develop in the way ordained for them by the Spirits. Often these children as identified by excessive "sickliness," which leads them to be more reflective than other children and which often necessitates the added vigilance of adults around them.

Eventually, these people will enter into their true profession. How and when they do so will vary from tribe to tribe, but they will probably be well into their maturity before they will be able to practice. The Spirit or Spirits who teach and guide them in their medicine work will not appear for them until they have stabilized. Their health will usually improve, and their hormone-enzyme fluctuations will be regularized. Very often this stabilization will occur in the process of childbearing and nursing; this is one reason why women usually are not fully accepted as part of the woman's community until after the birth of a first child. Maternity was a concept that went far beyond the simple biological sense of the word. It was the prepotent power, the basic right to control and distribute goods, because it was the primary means of producing them. And it was the perfect sign of right spirit-human relationship. Among some modern American Indians this principle is still accepted. The Keres, for example, still recognize the Deity as female, and She is known as Thought Woman, for it is understood that the primary creative force is Thought.

Lesbians and Tribal Life

Simple reason dictates that lesbians did exist widely in tribal cultures, for they exist now. Because they were tribal people, the terms on which they existed must have been suited to the terms of tribal existence. The concepts of tribal cultures and of modern, Western cultures are so dissimilar as to make ludicrous attempts to relate the long-ago women who dealt exclusively with women on sexual-emotional and spiritual bases to modern women who have in common an erotic attraction for other women.

This is not to make light of the modern lesbian but rather to convey some sense of the enormity of the cultural gulf that we must come to terms with when examining any phenomenon related to the American Indian. The modern lesbian sees herself as distinct from "society." She may be prone to believe herself somehow out of sync with "normal" women and often suffers great anguish at perceived differences. And while many modern lesbians have come to see themselves as singular but not sick, many of us are not that secure in our self-assessment. Certainly, however we come to terms with our sexuality, we are not in the position of our American Indian foresister who could find safety and security in her bond with another woman because it was perceived to be destined and nurtured by nonhuman entities, as were all Indian pursuits, and was therefore acceptable and respectable (albeit occasionally terrifying) to others in her tribe.

Spheres of influence and activity in American Indian cultures were largely divided between the sexes: There were women—goddesses, spirit-women, mothers, sisters, grandmothers, aunties, shamans, healers, proph-ets, and daughters; and there were men—gods, fathers, uncles, shamans, healers, diviners, brothers, and sons. What went on in one group was often unknown to the other.

There were points of confluence, of course, such as in matters pertain-ing to mundane survival. Family-band-clan groups interacted in living arrangements, in the procural or production of food, weaponry, clothing, and living space, and in political function. Men and women came together at certain times to perform social and ceremonial rituals or to undertake massive tasks such as hunts, harvests, or wars. They performed certain reciprocal tasks for one another. But in terms of any real sense of community, there were women and there were men.

Yet women who shared their lives with women did follow the usual custom of marrying. The duration of marriage and the bonding style of marriage differed among tribes. Many people practiced serial monogamy; others acknowledged the marriage bond but engaged in sexual activities outside of it. Women's adultery was not viewed with any particular alarm in most tribes, although some tribes did severely punish a woman who "transgressed" the marriage bonds, at least after they had some contact with Christian religious concepts.

But overall women spent a great deal of time together, outside the company of men. They had a whole array of women's rituals, only some of which were related to menstruation or childbearing. Together they spent weeks in menstrual huts; together women tilled their fields, har-vested wild foods and herbs, ground grains, prepared skins, smoked or dried foodstuffs, and just visited. Women spent long periods together in their homes and lodges while the men stayed in men's houses or in the woods or were out on hunting or fishing expeditions. Young women were often separated from the larger groups for periods of months or years, as were young men. In such circumstances, lesbianism and homosexuality were probably commonplace. Indeed, same-sex relationships may have been the norm for primary pair-bonding. Families did not consist of nuclear units in any sense. There were clans and bands or villages, but the primary personal unit tended to include members of one's own sex rather than members of the opposite sex. It is questionable whether these practices would be identified as lesbian by the politically radical lesbian community of today; for while sex between women probably occurred regularly, women also regularly married and raised children, often adopt-ing children if they did not have any.

We should not see relationships among Indian women as being moti-vated primarily by opportunity. Lesbianism must be viewed in the context of the spiritual orientation of tribal life. It may be possible to distinguish between those women who took advantage of the abundant opportunities to form erotic bonds with other women and those women whose relationships with women were as much a matter of Spirit-direction as of personal preference (though the two were one in some senses).

It might be that some American Indian women could be seen as "dykes," while some could be seen as "lesbians," if one thinks of "dyke" as one who bonds with women to further some Spirit and supernatural directive and "lesbian" as a woman who is emotionally and physically intimate with other women. (The two groups would not have been mutually exclusive.)

The dyke (we might also call her a "ceremonial lesbian") was likely to have been a medicine woman in a special sense. She probably was a participant in the Spirit (intelligence, force field) of an Entity or Deity who was particularly close to earth during the Goddess period (though that Deity is still present in the lives of some American Indian women who practice Her ceremonies and participate actively and knowingly in Her reality). Signs of this Deity remain scattered all over the continent: Snake Mound in Ohio is probably one. La Virgin de Guadalupe is another. There are all sorts of petroglyphs, edifices, and stories concerning some aspect of Her, and Her signs are preserved in much of the lore and literature of many tribes.

Essentially a woman's spiritual way is dependent on the kind of power she possesses, the kind of Spirit to whom she is attached, and the tribe to which she belongs. She is required to follow the lead of Spirits and to carry out the tasks they assign her. For a description of one such rite, Fr. Bernard Haile's translation and notes on the Navajo Beautyway/Night chant is instructive. Such stories abound in the lore and literature of the American Indian people.[5] They all point to a serious event that results in the death of the protagonist, her visit to the Spirit realms from which she finally returns, transformed and powerful. After such events, she no longer belongs to her tribe or family, but to the Spirit teacher who instructed her. This makes her seem "strange" to many of her folk, and, indeed, she may be accused of witchcraft, though that is more likely to be charged at present than it was in the past. A dyke's initiation takes the same course as a male's: She is required to pass grueling physical tests, to lose her mundane persona, and to transform her soul and mind into other forms. (I might note here that among American Indians men are often accused of the same thing. Tales of evil sorcerers abound; in fact, in my reading, they seriously outnumber the tales about sorceresses.)

The Lakota have a word for some of these women, *koskalaka*, which is translated as "young man" or "woman who doesn't want to marry," in our terms, "dyke." These women are said to be the daughters (the followers/practitioners) of a Spirit/Divinity who links two women together making them one in Her power. They do a dance in which a rope is twined between them and coiled to form a "rope baby." The exact purpose or result of this dance is not mentioned, but its significance is clear. In a culture that values children and women because they bear them, two women who don't want to marry (a man) become united by the power of the Deity and their union is validated by the creation of a rope baby. That is, the rope baby signifies the potency of their union in terms that are comprehensible to their society, which therefore legitimizes it.

It is clear that the *koskalaka* are perceived as powerful, as are their presumed male counterparts, the *winkte*. But their power does not constitute the right "to determine [their] own and others' actions."[6] Rather, it consists of the ability to manipulate physical and nonphysical reality toward certain ends. When this power is used to determine others' actions, it at least borders on black magic or sorcery.

To clarify the nature of the power I am talking about, we can consider what Lame Deer says about the *winkte*. Lame Deer is inclined to speak rather directly and tends not to romanticize either the concept of power as it is understood and practiced by his people or the *winkte* as a person who has certain abilities that make him special.

He says that a *winkte* is a person who is a half-man and half-woman, perhaps even a hermaphrodite with both male and female organs. In the old days, *winktes* dressed like women and lived as women. Lame Deer admits that though the Lakotas thought people are what nature, or dreams, make them, still men weren't happy to see their sons running around with *winktes*. Still, he says that there are good men among the *winktes* and that they have special powers. He took Richard Erdoes (who was transcribing his conversation for their book *Lame Deer: Seeker of Visions*) with him to a bar to interview a *winkte*. He asked the man to tell him all about *winktes*, and the *winkte* told Lame Deer that "a *winkte* has a gift of prophecy and that he himself could predict the weather." The Lakota go to a *winkte* for a secret name, and such names carry great power, though they are often off-color. "You don't let a stranger know [the secret name]," the *winkte* told them. "He would kid you about it."[7] A *winkte*'s power to name often wins the *winkte* great fame and usually a fine gift as well.

The power referred to here is magical, mysterious, and sacred. That does not mean that its possessors are to be regarded as a priestly pious people, for this is hardly the case. But it does mean that those who possess "medicine power," women and men, are to be treated with a certain cautious respect.

It is interesting to note that the story—one of the few reliable accounts of persons whose sexual orientation differs from the heterosexual—concerns a male, a *winkte*. The stories about *koskalaka* are yet to be told. It seems to me that this suppression is a result of a series of coincidental factors: the historical events connected with the conquest of Native America; the influence of Christianity and the attendant brutal suppression of medicine people and medicine practices; the patriarchal suppression of all references to power held by women; Christian notions of proper sexual behavior; and, recently, an attempt on the part of a number of American Indian men to suppress knowledge among their own people (and among Europeans and Americans) of the traditional place of women as powerful medicine people and leaders in their own right, accompanied by a dismissal of women as central to tribal ritual life.[8]

Under the reign of the patriarchy, the medicine-dyke has become anathema; her presence has been hidden under the power-destroying blanket of complete silence. We must not allow this silence to prevent us from discovering and reclaiming who we have been and who we are. We must not forget the true Source of our being, nor her powerfulness, and we must not allow ourselves to be deluded by patriarchal perceptions of power that rob us of our true power, regardless of how many feathers those perceptions are cloaked in. As Indian women, as lesbians, we must make the effort to understand clearly what is at stake, and this means that we must reject all beliefs that work against ourselves, however much we have come to cherish them as we have lived among the patriarchs.

Womanculture is unregulated by males and is misperceived by ethnographers. Perhaps this is so because it is felt—at least among ethnographers' tribal informants—that it is wise to let "sleeping dogs lie." There may also be fear of what power might be unleashed if the facts about American Indian lesbianism were discussed directly. A story that has recently come to my attention might best clarify this statement.

Two white lesbians, feminists and social activists, were determined to expand their activities beyond the lesbian and feminist communities and to this end became involved in an ecological movement that centered on American Indian concerns. In pursuit of this course, they invited a Sioux medicine man to join them and arranged to pick him up from the small rural town he was visiting. When he saw them, he accused them of being lesbians and became very angry. He abused them verbally, in serious and obscene terms. They left him where he was and returned home, angry and confused.

A certain amount of their confusion was a result of their misperception of Indians and of this particular medicine man. I have friends in the primarily white lesbian community who seem to think that Indian men, particularly medicine men, are a breed apart who are "naturally just." Like other Americans, Indians are inclined to act in ways that are consistent with their picture of the world, and, in this particular Indian's picture, the world was not big enough for lesbians. The women didn't announce their sexual preference to him, by the way; but he knew a *koskalaka* when he saw one and reacted accordingly.

A friend who knew the women involved asked me about this encounter. She couldn't understand why the medicine man acted the way he had. I suspect that he was afraid of the lesbians' power, and I told her that. Another American Indian woman to whom I recounted the story had the same reaction. *Koskalaka* have singular power, and this medicine man was undoubtedly aware of it. The power of the *koskalaka* can (potentially, at least) override that of men, even very powerful medicine men such as the one in my story. I know this particular man, and he is quite powerful as a medicine man.

Not so long ago, the American Indians were clearly aware of the power that women possessed. Even now there are those among traditionals who know the medicine power of women. This is why a clear understanding of the supernatural forces and their potential in our lives is necessary. More than an interesting tour through primitive exotica is to be gained.

Before we worry about collecting more material from aborigines, before we join forces with those who are in a position to destroy us, and before we decide that belief in ancient matriarchal civilization is an irrational concept born of conjecture and wish, let us adjust our perspective to match that of our foresisters. Then, when we search the memories and lore of tribal peoples, we might be able to see what eons and all kinds of institutions have conspired to hide from our eyes.

The evidence is all around us. It remains for us to *dis*cover what it means.

MALE LOVE IN EARLY MODERN JAPAN: A LITERARY DEPICTION OF THE "YOUTH"

◆

PAUL GORDON SCHALOW

The history of Western scholarship on Japanese homosexuality is illustrative of the fortunes of all Western gay scholarship in the last century. The example of same-sex male love in Japanese culture, like that of classical Greece, was an inspiration to turn-of-the-century European sex reformers, because it seemed to prove that homosexual relations could be a healthy, "manly" force in human culture. As a result, German researchers described it in detail and Edward Carpenter devoted a chapter to it in his pioneering study, *Intermediate Types Among Primitive Folk* (1911). But the rise of fascism brought an end to such research, along with the gay movement itself, and only very recently, in the wake of the new gay movement, have Western scholars begun to examine the phenomenon again.

In this paper, Paul Schalow makes explicit what most Japanese scholars have recognized but chosen to leave only implicit: that in seventeenth-century Japanese culture men were *expected* sexually to desire both women and boys; the two "kinds" of love were thought to differ and to play distinct roles in a man's life. Schalow's paper provides rich evidence for the "essentialist-constructionist" debate by describing—and then complicating his portrayal of—a sexual system radically different from that of the modern West. For, as Schalow shows, "male love" took different forms in different classes, and the conventions governing such relationships were regularly flaunted—even at the cost of social ridicule.

In 1687, a collection of forty short stories depicting homosexual relations between men and youths was published in Japan. It was titled *The Great Mirror of Male Love* (Nanshoku ōkagami)[1] and written by Japan's first commercial author, Ihara Saikaku (1642–1693).[2] Male love between Buddhist priests and their *chigo* lovers[3] and between samurai men and youths had been depicted in literature since the thirteenth century, and relations between male kabuki actor-prostitutes and their merchant patrons were the subject of more recent works, but *The Great Mirror of Male Love* was the first to combine the world of priest, samurai, and merchant on the basis of a single shared concern: their love of youths. The book was an immediate success. It was the first of Saikaku's works to receive wide distribution outside his native Osaka, due (it is thought) to the popularity of male love in Edo, where large numbers of samurai men with an appreciation of handsome youths served the Tokugawa shōgun and other regional lords.[4] Although *The Great Mirror of Male Love* was imitated by other writers and publishers anxious to capitalize on its success, neither its scope nor impact was ever equalled, and it still holds its place in Tokugawa literature as the definitive literary expression of the social construct called *wakashudō*, or "the way [of loving] youths."[5]

To readers three centuries later, *The Great Mirror of Male Love* provides a unique glimpse into the way male homosexuality was conceptualized in early modern Japan. Evidence from the narratives suggests that male homosexual relations were accepted as a normal component of male sexuality and followed established social conventions, though the conventions differed when prostitution was involved, and that the roles assumed in man-youth relations sometimes superseded literal definitions of "man" and "youth." The present paper identifies the salient features of early modern Japanese male homosexuality by examining evidence from *The Great Mirror of Male Love*. It begins with a description of the social conventions governing sexual relations in general and man-youth love relations in particular. Next, it contrasts the way sexual relations were practiced between men and male prostitutes in the kabuki theater with those between men and regular youths. Finally, the issue of "role" is discussed with particular attention to Saikaku's literary depiction of sexual role-play in his narratives.

Society and Sexuality in Early Modern Japan

In early modern Japanese sexuality, both the love of women (*joshoku,* or "female love") and the love of men (*nanshoku*, or "male love") were considered normal components of sexual love and represented the two varieties of sexual activity open to adult males.[6] Male homosexual relations occurred almost exclusively within a context of bisexuality, the assumption being that sex with youths did not preclude sex with women, and vice versa.[7] Those who pursued sexual relations exclusively with women or exclusively with youths were in a minority and were considered mildly eccentric for limiting their pleasurable options. Because homosexual relations were not marked as aberrant, men with an exclusive preference for youths were identified not in terms of their preference for youths but as *onnagirai*, or "woman-haters." This should be understood not as misogyny or hatred of women in the normal sense, but in terms of the failure of such men to love women sexually. *The Great Mirror of Male Love*'s "woman-hater" ethos suggests that an exclusively homosexual social role and identity existed in early modern Japan.[8]

The sexual act seems to have been conceived of strictly in terms of vaginal penetration of a woman (*onna*) or anal penetration of a preadult youth (*wakashu*) by an adult male (*yarō*). At some level, adult men distinguished preadult youths from themselves as occupying a different social category: not women, but not yet men either. That is to say, both *wakashu* and *yarō* were of the male sex (*otoko*), but there was a clear distinction made between the two based on age and/or sexual role.[9] The anomalous position of the *wakashu* as male (*otoko*) but not adult man (*yarō*) is vividly apparent in a few surviving erotic woodblock prints and scroll paintings of the period in which three figures are portrayed in sexual embrace: A youth simultaneously penetrates the vagina of a woman while being penetrated from behind by a man.[10]

According to the depiction in *The Great Mirror of Male Love*, the *wakashu* was defined primarily by chronological age, with certain modifications we will look at later. The stages from childhood to adulthood were marked by ceremonies symbolizing the male child's gradual recognition as a full-fledged adult.[11] The first of these ceremonies occurred at or slightly before the time of puberty, when the child underwent the initial shaving of the top of his head. The natural hairline (*marubitai*) and forelocks on either side (*maegami*) were left uncut to distinguish the youth from the adult male. In his mid-teens, a youth would shave the natural hairline of the forehead so that it angled back at the temples. This was called "putting in corners" (*kado wo ireru*) and symbolized that the youth was halfway to adulthood.[12] A youth sporting such a hairstyle was frequently identified as a *sumi-maegami*, or "corner-forelocks," just as a younger youth might be called a *maegami*, or "forelocks." The final step into adulthood was celebrated at approximately age nineteen with *gembuku*, the full coming-of-age ceremony, at which point the youth's forelocks were shaved, leaving the pate of his head completely bald in the manner of an adult male. In addition, the youth exchanged his long-sleeved robe with open vents under the sleeves (*nagasode*) for the ventless, short-sleeved robe (*marusode*) of an adult to further symbolize the assumption of adult male social status and responsibilities.[13] Once a youth had achieved adult status, he was no longer available for the sexual role of "youth" and was instead expected to take on the adult male role in a new relationship.

One of the primary goals of Japan's seventeenth-century Tokugawa government was to establish Confucian-inspired hierarchies within and between the social classes.[14] These class hierarchies defined to a large extent with whom one could have sexual relations. Townsmen were allowed to patronize courtesans and kabuki boy actors for prostitution because the pleasure quarters and kabuki theaters were their own creation, but for samurai to frequent those places for the same purpose was frowned upon because of the status boundary crossing it entailed. Within class-based confines, all youths between puberty and adulthood were potential sexual partners for adult males, just as all women potentially were. As one would expect, the depictions in *The Great Mirror of Male Love* indicate that there were many types of relations between men and youths, ranging from informal, secret affairs to publicly acknowledged bonds resembling marriages, which were preceded by sometimes lengthy courtship procedures and formalized with spoken vows, written contracts, or both.[15] Some were brief, others long-term, though all man-youth relationships normally terminated with the youth's coming of age.[16] Most were entered into with mutual agreement, though a few were forced on the youth. The case of Nagasaka Korin in "Though Bearing An Umbrella, He Was Rained Upon" (II:2), for example, was not a mutual affair. He boldly told the lord who took him as his page and lover, "Forcing me to yield to your authority is not true love. My heart remains my own, and if one day someone should tell me he loves me, I would risk my life for him. As a memento of this floating world, I want a lover on whom I can lavish my affection." When Korin acted on his threat and took a common samurai for his secret lover, the lord severed the boy's arms and decapitated him as an example to others. Stories like Korin's, in which the samurai convention of duty to one's lord was violated, provided ample opportunity for Saikaku to develop the tragic theme of conflict between social obligation and human desire which so fascinated Tokugawa readers and theater audiences.[17]

Although violations of ethical and class-based social conventions were treated in *The Great Mirror of Male Love* (and in society generally) as a serious matter, usually resulting in severe punishment at the hands of the Tokugawa authorities, violations of the other major conventions of male homosexual relations—that they be between a man and youth and terminate with the youth's coming of age—provided humor in the narrative and generally met with little more than amusement or, possibly, accusations of "eccentricity." This indicates that sexual variation was not invested with the aura of social heresy it acquired in the West, and in general was accepted with tolerance and equanimity.

The Image of the Wakashu

The Great Mirror of Male Love consists of eight sections (I–VIII) of five stories each (1–5) totaling forty narratives. All are fictional or fictionalized historical accounts of noteworthy cases of male love, and the central person in each is a specific exemplary *wakashu*.[18] Most of the liaisons depict a mutual emotional exchange between man and youth which embodies *ikiji*, or "shared masculine pride," an element naturally lacking in male-female relations. A youth was deemed worthy of male love, and his story worthy of inclusion in *The Great Mirror of Male Love*, if he possessed *nasake*, a form of "empathy" or "love" involving emotional sensitivity to the suffering of a potential lover, and a desire to alleviate that suffering.[19]

The idea that money might alter the nature of the relationship between man and youth, turning it from an emotional to a financial transaction, was of great enough significance to Saikaku that he structured his book around it. Saikaku divided the forty individual stories into two groups of twenty on the basis of what type of youth was involved: *ji-wakashu*, or "regular youths," are described in the first twenty stories, and kabuki *wakashu*, who acted on the kabuki stage while working as male prostitutes, are described in the second group of twenty.[20] The narratives on kabuki youths often focused on the youth's transcendence of the financial transaction and his entry into the emotional realm of *ikiji*, "shared masculine pride." This shift usually required that he abandon prostitution, but as far as the narrative organization was concerned the initial emotional or sexual encounter as male prostitute placed the story in the second group of stories. In Saikaku's depiction, *ikiji* frequently represented the ennobling potential of the samurai ethic on the townsman's world of kabuki, but a few narratives showed noncommercial relations based on shared masculine pride developing between merchant or priest and kabuki youth.[21]

While *ikiji* seems to have been incompatible with prostitution, the ideal of *nasake* remained potent for kabuki youths and did not require that they abandon prostitution. In the kabuki theater *nasake* was simply proven differently, not by alleviating the love-pangs of one suitor and remaining faithful to him, but by generously giving oneself to all patrons. Saikaku explored the irony of the kabuki version of *nasake* in "Loved By A Man In A Box" (VIII:3).

> Professional *wakashu* are the finest. Other youths make vows of love from mutual feelings of affection and give their lives to their lovers in return for support in a crisis, but these kabuki *wakashu* have no such pleasures. They must make themselves available to their patrons from the very first meeting before they have even had time to get acquainted. Such love [*nasake*] far surpasses the affection of other youths.

The majority of narratives in the first half of *The Great Mirror of Male Love* depict relationships between samurai men and youths. The adult male (called a *nenja*) is depicted as providing social backing and a model of manliness for the youth. In exchange, the youth is expected to be worthy of his lover by being a good student of samurai manhood. This meant vowing to be loyal, steadfast, and honorable in one's actions. Not infrequently, the sincerity of the vow was proved by self-mutilation such as cutting and piercing the flesh on the arms or legs or severing parts of fingers.[22] One of the strangest examples of self-mutilation in *The Great Mirror of Male Love* appears in "Nightingale in the Snow" (II:5), when a samurai named Shimamura Tōnai pledges himself to two youths.[23] " 'From now on, you will be the only ones I love,' he vowed. Then he bit off the last joint of each of his little fingers and gave one to each of the youths. In this way their destinies were joined. In the annals of boy love, this surely ranks as one of the most unusual troths.''

The ultimate proof of devotion between man and youth was found in self-sacrifice, particularly the willingness to die for the sake of the other to uphold his honor. Many of Saikaku's narratives in *The Great Mirror of Male Love* conclude with a paean to a youth who was made this ultimate sacrifice. The story of Nozaki Senjūrō, in "The Boy Who Sacrificed His Life In The Robes Of His Lover" (IV:2), is a good example. Senjūrō is caught in a love triangle caused by the unwelcome advances of a samurai suitor and decides to resolve the situation by a complicated plot in which Senjūrō dies to protect his lover. The suitor is so moved by Senjūrō's display of loyalty and love that he too sacrifices his life. In the face of such selfless examples, Senjūrō's lover decides he cannot go on living and commits *seppuku* (ritual suicide). The account concludes, "Those who recounted the story wept as they told it; those who heard it wept as they listened. Not only people of sensitivity but even unfeeling peasants and horse drivers reverently avoided walking on the spot where Senjūrō spilled his lifeblood, a lingering testimony to the way of boy love. Were one to walk all the provinces in sandals of iron, one would not be likely to find another such example.''

The second half of *The Great Mirror of Male Love* (Sections V–VIII) is a depiction of man-youth love in the kabuki theater. In "Tears in a Paper Shop" (V:1), Saikaku describes the historical process whereby male prostitution became popular in the kabuki theater.

After the prohibition of Grand Kabuki, Murayama Matabei opened a mime and dance show for which he gathered together a large troupe of handsome young actors.[24] Until that time it was uncommon even in the capital for men to take pleasure with boy actors. Each went for the same sum, one *bu* of gold, and took on customers the way street-boys do nowadays. At some point, it became the custom to celebrate a boy's promotion as a full-fledged actor of female roles by inviting the entire cast to Higashiyama for a tremendous feast. After that, his fee increased to five *ryō* of silver. . . .

Then one year wealthy priests assembled in the capital from all over the country to commemorate the three hundred fiftieth anniversary of the death of Zen master Kanzan, first rector of Myōshin-ji.[25] After the religious services were over, they went sight-seeing at the pleasure quarters on the dry riverbed. They fell in love with the handsome youths there, the likes of which they had never seen in the countryside, and began buying them up indiscriminately without a thought for their priestly duties. Any boy with forelocks who had two eyes and a nose on his face was guaranteed to be busy all day. Since that time, boy actors have continued to sell themselves in two shifts, daytime and nighttime. The fee for a boy who was appearing on stage rose to one piece of silver. The priests did not care about the cost, for they had only a short time to amuse themselves in the capital. But their extravagance continues to cause untold hardship for the pleasure-seekers of our day.

The majority of the kabuki youths featured in the second half of *The Great Mirror of Male Love* have been identified as historical persons from records maintained by kabuki theaters or from contemporary accounts such as the evaluation booklets on actors, called *yakusha hyōbanki*.[26] The preceding passage indicates that kabuki youths originally served in the theaters of Osaka, Kyoto, and Edo primarily as actors who might on occasion entertain patrons at night. As the seventeenth century progressed, however, kabuki youths were increasingly kept purely for prostitution and many never set foot on stage. Their situation by the late seventeenth century was not unlike that of the female prostitutes in the pleasure quarters: They were indentured to their proprietors until they paid their debts or were ransomed by a wealthy patron.[27]

The Wakashu Role

By and large, the youth in the first half of *The Great Mirror of Male Love* was defined in literal terms: He was between the ages of eleven and nineteen; he sported forelocks, dictated by society as the hairstyle of a youth, which would be shaved off when he reached adulthood; and he wore the long-sleeved robes of a youth with open vents under the arms. Thus, the youth was associated with chronological features of youthful appearance and manner that made him immediately recognizable to Japanese people of the period. There is nevertheless in Saikaku's depiction a definite awareness of the "youth" as an idea divorced from any chronologically defined reality of youthfulness.

Saikaku developed the idea of "youth" as an abstract role in the very first story of *The Great Mirror of Male Love*, "The ABCs of Boy Love"

(I:2).[28] Two nine-year-old children are depicted playing as lovers not unlike the way children in many societies play "house" as a way of internalizing their future social roles. The roles they play are seventeenth-century Japanese stereotypes of man-youth love: Daikichi, the "man" in the relationship, is the active, protective partner. His body bears the marks of their pact of love, which he in turn bears manfully. On the other hand, the "youth" Shinnosuke is helpless and vain, preferring to tidy his hair while Daikichi does the physical work assigned them. The narrative describes their preparations for evening calligraphy lessons.

> On the way [to class], they had come to a shaky bridge which Daikichi thought too dangerous to cross at dusk, so he hitched up the hem of his robe and solicitously carried Shinnosuke across the river on his back. Once at school, Daikichi insisted on carrying water from spigot to teahouse all by himself. Alone, he built a fire of dry leaves and braved the billowing smoke. He even swept the classroom himself, not allowing his partner to lift a finger. Shinnosuke merely scrutinized his face in a pocket mirror and smoothed a few stray hairs of his forelocks. The way he primped was strangely sophisticated. . . .
> Shinnosuke took Daikichi's hand in his. "Is that spot still painful?" he asked.
> Daikichi scoffed. "A little thing like this?"
> He pulled back his robe and bared his shoulder for Shinnosuke to see. A welt, symbol of their pact of boy love, stood purple and swollen where he had pierced and cut himself.
> "And to think that you did it for my sake," Shinnosuke said tearfully.

Observing the children in their role-playing is Ichidō, their penmanship instructor. The narrative states, "Since he was himself such a devotee of this way of love, Ichido thought perhaps his young charges had unconsciously learned it from him. That would explain the show of affection between the two boys. Afterwards, he took careful notice of them and discovered that, indeed, they were always side by side, inseparable as two trees grafted together or a pair of one-winged birds."[29] The story suggests that, though they are both actually mere children, the two boys acted like lovers in a way normally observed only between a man and youth.

The emphasis on role in samurai man-youth relations is explored in "Two Old Cherry Trees Still in Bloom" (IV:4). This narrative describes two elderly samurai lovers named Tamashima Mondo and Toyoda Han'emon living in seclusion in the environs of Edo. They became lovers when Mondo was a youth of sixteen and Han'emon a young man (having already undergone the coming-of-age ceremony) of nineteen. The handsome youth Mondo was approached by a persistent suitor who was subsequently killed by Han'emon in a duel. As a result, the two lovers were obliged to flee their native province and live incognito in Edo, where they settled in a merchant-class section of town. They had preserved their roles as "man" and "youth" long after any reality of Mondo's youthfulness had disappeared.

Mondo was now sixty-three and Han'emon sixty-six. Their love for each other had not changed since the days of their youth; neither of them had ever gazed at a woman's face in his life. Having lived together all these years, they truly deserved to be emulated as models of the way of love for all who love boys.

Han'emon still thought of Mondo as a boy of sixteen. Though his hair was thinning and had turned completely white, Mondo sprinkled it with "Blossom Dew" hair oil and bound it up in a double-folded topknot anyway. (A strange sight, indeed!) There was no sign that he had ever shaved his temples; he still had the rounded hairline he was born with. He followed the daily rituals of his youth, polishing his teeth with a tufted toothpick and carefully plucking his whiskers. Someone unaware of Mondo's reasons for this could hardly have imagined the truth.

The depiction of "youth" as an idealized role not contingent on the reality of youthfulness is developed further in the latter half of *The Great Mirror of Male Love*, for it was in the kabuki theater that the forms of youth were stylized and turned into a masquerade. Saikaku points out the gap between the role and reality of youth in this kabuki section largely for humorous effect, but the additional effect is to create an interplay between surface (the way things seem to be) and substance (the way things are) that lends the second half of *The Great Mirror of Male Love* an intriguing texture lacking in the first half.

In "Bamboo Clappers Strike the Hateful Number" (VII:4), the narrative begins with the statement, "When being entertained by a kabuki youth, one must be careful never to ask his age." The narrative goes on to develop this notion with the following fanciful passage. A group of kabuki actors and their patrons are on an outing in the hills of Fushimi, near Kyoto, and have paid a visit to a young monk.

Among them was one "youth" who, judging from the time when he worked the streets, must have been quite old. In the course of the conversation, someone asked him his age.

"I don't remember," he said, causing quite some amusement among the men.

Then the monk who lived in the cottage spoke up.

"By good fortune, I have here a bamboo clapper that has the ability to tell exactly how old you are."

He gave the clapper to the "youth" and had him stand there while the monk himself reverently folded his hands in prayer. Shortly, the bamboo clappers began to sound. Everyone counted along with each strike.

At first, the actor stood there innocently as it struck seventeen, eighteen, nineteen, but beyond that he started to feel embarrassed. He tried with all his strength to separate his right hand from his left and stop the clappers from striking but, strangely, they kept right on going. Only after striking thirty-eight did the bamboo clappers separate. The face of the "youth" was red with embarrassment.

"These bamboo clappers lie!" he said, throwing them down.

The monk was outraged.

"The Buddhas will attest that there is no deceit in them. If you still have doubts, try it again as many times as you like."

The other actors in the room were all afraid of being exposed, so no one was willing to try them out.

Saikaku's purpose in this passage was to generate some humor by pointing out the gap between what the kabuki "youths" represented (youth) and what they actually were (middle-aged). This gap resulted largely from the government order banning boy actors from the kabuki stage in 1651 and from the greater desirability of youthfulness that made it necessary for older actors to attempt to pass as youths in order to attract customers.[30] Saikaku describes the government ban in "Votive Picture of Kichiya Riding a Horse" (V:5).

One year there was a riot among samurai guards at a theater in Naniwa [Osaka] over a certain actor's affections. As a result, kabuki came under legal restriction. All boy actors were required to shave off their forelocks in the manner of adult men. It was like seeing unopened blossoms being torn from the branch. Theater proprietors and the boys' managers alike were upset at the effect it might have on business, but looking back on it now the law was probably the best thing that ever happened to them. It used to be that no matter how splendid the boy, it was impossible for him to keep his forelocks and take on patrons beyond the age of nineteen. Now, since everyone wore the hairstyle of adult men, it was still possible at age thirty-four or thirty-five for youthful-looking actors to get under a man's robe. How strange are the ways of love!

In order to be allowed to reopen, kabuki theater proprietors in Kyoto, Osaka, and Edo made an agreement with the authorities that youths live offstage as adult men.[31] The government reasoned that if the allure represented by forelocks and long-sleeved robes were eliminated from the kabuki theater, then youths would no longer attract the attention of the samurai and social hierarchies would be preserved. Unfortunately for the authorities, far from eliminating the kabuki youth's allure, the agreement had the effect of removing him from the normal constraints and definitions of youth and turning his sexual appeal into an abstract theatrical role. The literal equation of youth = "youth" on stage was shattered; from then on "youth" was a role, and actors learned to act the part of the "youth" both on stage and off. Theater proprietors exploited this new state of affairs for their own advantage, as did the actors themselves. Almost incidentally, the kabuki theater profited as a dramatic art form by being forced to invent, rather than simply present, stage personas for its actors.[32]

Conclusion

In early modern Japan we find a society in which male homosexuality was integrated into normal sexual life by means of social conventions governing relations between men and youths in much the same way that male-female relations were regulated. In Ihara Saikaku's *The Great Mirror of Male Love* we have a depiction of male homosexuality that suggests the tremendous range of sexual behaviors that existed within, and sometimes on the borders of, these socially ascribed constraints. The fact that Saikaku explored the extended sense of "youth" as an abstract role beyond its literal definitions is highly significant to our understanding of the way sexuality was conceptualized and enacted in early modern Japan. It means that the conventions of male homosexual love were not just dictating the way men and youths related to each other, but that individual personalities were manipulating those conventions to express their inner sexual and emotional needs. Saikaku recognized the subtle, personal manipulation of socio-sexual convention and wove his insights into the text for the readers of his day, and ours, to enjoy.

THE BIRTH OF THE QUEEN: SODOMY AND THE EMERGENCE OF GENDER EQUALITY IN MODERN CULTURE, 1660–1750

◆

RANDOLPH TRUMBACH

Randolph Trumbach argues in this essay that a major shift occurred in the conventions governing male homosexual relations in Europe's large cities around 1700. Whereas before then many citizens of cities such as London accepted the existence of adult male "rakes" who had sex with both women and boys, after 1700 they were increasingly likely to think of homosexual behavior as the forbidden activity of a deviant, effeminate minority of adult males. Groups of such men actually appeared about then, and were best known because of raids on the "molly houses" where they gathered. Trumbach argues that their emergence should be understood in the context of a growing gender equality between men and women.

In probably all human societies other than those under the influence of the Christian religion, it has been legitimate for two males to have sexual relations with each other. There have been only two restrictions: that the adult men who had sexual relations with males also marry women and produce families; that the adult male in the sexual act always take the active or penetrator's role. The second point was guaranteed in one of two ways. In the first pattern (as in Japan, China, New Guinea, Australia, some tribal African societies, in Islam, and in the classical Mediterranean world), the adult male had sexual relations with an adolescent boy who might be his wife, his concubine, his lover, or his whore. In the second pattern (to be found in southern Asia from Polynesia to Madagascar, among the North American Indians, and among some African tribes), the adult male had sexual relations with a small minority of adult males who had permanently adopted many (but not all) of the characteristics of women in speech, gesture, clothes, and work. Christian Europe, by contrast, had since the twelfth century made illicit all sexual relations between two persons of the same gender. Such sexual relations nonetheless occurred. And when they did so they were enacted within the framework of the two worldwide human patterns.

In traditional European societies, men who did not restrict their sexual experience to marriage usually had sex with both adolescent boys and female whores. But as modern Western societies emerged in the late seventeenth century this pattern began to change. By 1700 there were appearing in the cities of northern Europe, especially in those like London, Paris, and Amsterdam, which had populations of half a million, a minority of markedly effeminate men whose most outstanding characteristic was that they desired to have sex only with other males. These men either seduced males from the majority who were not effeminate and thereby ran the risks of arrest and punishment, or of blackmail; or they safely had relations with each other inside a protective subculture. It looks as though Europe was switching from one world pattern to another— from men having sex with boys to men having sex with transvestite adult males. But it was not quite that, for at the same moment it began to be felt that it was impossible for the average, normal male to feel any sexual desire for another male of any age or condition. To be masculine was to experience sexual desire only for women. Europe was switching from adult male libertines who had sex with boys and with women to a world divided between a majority of men and women who desired only the opposite gender, and a minority of men and women who desired only the same gender. It is the purpose of this essay to show this change happening in a single European society between 1660 and 1750, in England, and especially in London. The conclusion of the essay will consider why this great change occurred.[1]

Part I: The Sodomite as Rake

The behavior of the relatively small circle of aristocratic libertines in the 1660s and 1670s provides the best, if fragmentary, evidence of bisexual libertinism. These libertines can be found in three kinds of material: in letters and diaries; in the trials for sodomy; and in the imaginative literature of the stage and of the new pornographic genre. In this world the love of boys certainly did not exclude the love of women; but the love of boys was seen as the most extreme act of sexual libertinism; and it was often associated, as well, with religious skepticism, and even republican politics. It is as though sodomy were so extreme a denial of the Christian expectation that all sexual acts ought to occur in marriage and have the potential of procreation, that those who indulged in it were likely also to break through all other conventions in politics and religion. The unconventionality of that minority of rakes who were sodomitical was therefore frightening to society at large; but they were not held in contempt. It was, instead, that they were secretly held in awe for the extremity of their masculine self-assertion, since they triumphed over male and female alike. Most men who did not keep within the bounds of matrimony indulged in a more quotidian fornication. But in the *Wandering Whore* (1660), the anonymous author explained that there were men who "will not be contented with doing the business." One man, for instance, wanted to be under a table snarling as if he would bite off the "whibbbobs" of the half-dozen girls who stood around him; another "will needs shite in one of our wenches mouth's"; a third "will needs be whipt to raise lechery and cause a standing P——." But it was the fourth who would "fayn be buggering some of our wenches, if the Matron could get their consent, but had rather be dealing with smooth-fac'd prentices." Anal intercourse was the most extreme of sexual acts, and the libertine desired to perform it either with a woman or with an adolescent boy whose beard had not begun to grow.[2]

It was in this libertine world that the twenty-four-year-old Sir Charles Sedley stood naked on the balcony of an inn and in full daylight, "showed his nakedness," "acting all the postures of lust and buggery that could be imagined," abused the Scriptures, and preached that he had such a powder to sell "as should make all the cunts in town run after him." He was punished by the magistrate. But when Pepys discussed the story in 1663, what stood out was the buggery—two of Pepys' acquaintances declaring that "buggery is now almost grown as common among our gallants as in Italy, and that the very pages of the town begin to complain of their masters for it." The supposed Italian origins of this act long continued to be a familiar way for Englishmen to distance themselves from it. Pepys' alarm at this aristocratic vice made him piously conclude that "blessed be God, I do not to this day know what is the meaning of this sin, nor which is the agent nor which the patient." But all the Restoration sources (except Pepys) took for granted that the boy was passive.[3]

This was the presumption that Lord Rochester made when he sang to his mistress:

> Nor shall our love-fits, Chloris, be forgot,
>   When each the well-looked link boy strove t'enjoy,
> And the best kiss was the deciding lot
>   Whether the boy fucked you, or I the boy.

But both Rochester and the boy were interested in Chloris as well as in each other. Rochester's letters to Henry Savile confirm that this and the other references in his poems were genuine reflections of Rochester's taste. Once he sent Savile a young Frenchman, his valet, of whom he said, "The greatest and gravest of this court of both sexes have tasted his beauties." It is possible that the valet later tried to blackmail his master. For despite the public bravado of the libertine's statements, the law could exact a harsh price if an actual act could be proven.[4]

The lawyer John Hoyle, for instance, was arrested and indicted for buggering William Bristow, a poulterer. Hoyle is one of the clearest examples of the bisexual libertine, but not surprisingly, it has been very difficult for this to be seen by twentieth-century readers who are committed to the presumption of mutually exclusive conditions of homosexuality and heterosexuality. Hoyle moved in libertine circles. Sir Charles Sedley described his republican conversation in a tavern, and his lover Aphra Behn wrote of his fondness for Lucretius. Whitelocke Bulstrode went further and called him an "atheist, a sodomite professed, a corrupter of youth, and a blasphemer of Christ." Hoyle had a number of women lovers in addition to Mrs. Behn; but Behn also gave the name of at least one of his male lovers. Behn's twentieth-century biographers, however, simply label Hoyle "a homosexual" and take this as the cause of the failure of his affair with Behn. They presume that a man who had sex with males must be *really* interested only in men, even though he also had affairs with women. There is no room in their philosophy for the bisexual libertine. But Hoyle escapes their net, as he escaped the charge before the grand jury. He died, instead, in a drunken brawl that he had begun by "railing against all government."[5]

Other libertine rakes did not escape the law as easily as Hoyle, as the case of Lord Castlehaven illustrates. In 1631 Castlehaven was found guilty and executed for promoting a rape on his wife and for sodomy with his young male pages. He took the boys to bed with his wife, and after he had watched them entering her, he sodomized them by coming between their thighs. He was also fully capable of relations with a woman, having had several children by a first wife. In libertine fashion, he was a skeptic in religion.[6]

The life of the rake sometimes made it into the plays of the Restoration stage—even if less often than is sometimes thought—and mainly in the 1670s. But the bisexual libertine made it there even less often.[7]

Aphra Behn (1671), Thomas Otway (1680), and Nathaniel Lee (1680) did each write a play in which it was indicated that one of their rakes (who was shown mainly in hot pursuit of women) was also interested in boys. Behn's Lorenzo looks at a woman who in her disguise he thinks a male page, and says "this stripling may chance to mar my market of women now—'tis a fine lad, how plump and white he is; would I could meet him somewhere i' th' dark, I'd have a fling at him, and try whether I were right Florentine." He later asks the "smooth-fac'd boy" how long he has "been set up for thy self" (as a prostitute), and advises him to leave women alone, as wenching will "spoil a good face and mar your better market of the two." Otway's Sir Jolly Jumble tickles Beaugard's legs and calls him "my Ganimede"; he calls Courtine a pretty fellow and tries to kiss him; but he then moves on to romp with his three (female) whores. Lee's Nemour similarly calls Bellamore his "sweet-fac'd pimp" and later "thou dear soft rogue, my spouse, my Hephestion, my Ganymed"; but Bellamore is as interested as his master in women and guarantees where Nemours will be able to meet the Duchess of Cleves by saying that he has it from "one of her women whom I have debauched."[8]

What is missing in all this material is the adult, effeminate, exclusively homosexual male who seeks an adult male partner. I have found only one possible reference to such men in the *Wandering Whore*: "There are likewise hermaphrodites, effeminate men, men given to much luxury, idleness, and wanton pleasures, and to that abominable sin of sodomy, wherein they are both active and passive in it, whose vicious actions are onely to be whispered amongst us." These men were deviant, however, not so much because of their sodomy, but because they were adult males who sometimes played the passive role. But hermaphrodites were also actual people who possessed sexually ambiguous genitalia—a child, for instance, on whom Robert Wittie reported to the Royal Society in 1672: assigned to the female gender at birth by the midwives but thought by Wittie to be a boy. Canonical tradition had required such persons to permanently choose one gender or another and had held them guilty of sodomy if they alternated in their sexual behavior. For this reason, perhaps, "hermaphrodite" could be used to refer to adult men who switched from active to passive without being biological hermaphrodites. But such men were presumably interested in taking the active role with women. There is also no suggestion that they engaged in cross-dressing. We must therefore distinguish their effeminacy from the predominating effeminacy of the adult male fop.[9]

Part II: Fops and Beaus: Effeminacy and Sodomy

The fop is often misinterpreted by the twentieth-century reader of Restoration plays to be a "homosexual." But in an important essay, Susan Staves has pointed out that fops, while effeminate in manner from their contemporaries' point of view, were also presumed to be sexually interested in women. That interest, however, was differently expressed from the rake's. Maiden in Thomas Baker's *Tunbridge-Walks* (1703) confides that "I never keep company with lewd rakes that go to nasty taverns, talk smuttily, and get fuddl'd; but visit the ladies, and drink tea, and chocolate." In the three generations between 1660 and 1750, public attitudes toward the fop changed dramatically by generation. Between 1660 and 1690, Restoration drama firmly rejected the fop in favor of the rake. After 1690, however, the rake himself fell to the power of romantic marriage on the stage, and the fop's domesticated interests came to be more highly valued. But between 1720 and 1750 the fop's effeminacy came under a new kind of criticism (and this is the point at which Staves does not fully see the significance of her evidence), which by the late eighteenth century made the fop a character appropriate only to low farce and exiled him from high comedy.[10]

After 1720 the fop's effeminacy, in real life and on the stage, came to be identified with the effeminacy of the then emerging role of the exclusive adult sodomite—known in the ordinary language of his day as a *molly*, and later as a *queen*. The meaning of the word *effeminate* consequently changed. In the seventeenth century it had been used to describe one of two types: the smooth-faced Ganymedes who might even be transvestite to attract their adult male partners; or the adult male obsessed with women—"thou call'st me effeminate," wrote Donne, "for I love women's joys."[11] But by the early eighteenth century, the second of these two meanings had disappeared; by then an adult effeminate male was likely to be taken to be an exclusive sodomite. Consequently when Garrick in 1747 wrote the role of Fribble in *Miss in Her Teens*, a critic could see that he was attempting "to laugh out of countenance that *mollifying elegance* which manifests itself with such bewitching grace in the *refined* youths of this *cultivated age*." And to be mollified was to adopt the manners of the molly.[12]

The transformation of the fop into the molly can clearly be seen in the way in which Smollett in his novel *Roderick Random* (1748) treated his source for the figure of Captain Whiffle. The character was based on the "finical sea fop" in Charles Shadwell's *The Fair Quaker of Deal* (1710), about whom there is no hint of sodomitical desires. But Whiffle comes on board in the most extravagant garb with a "crowd of attendants, all of whom . . . seemed to be of their patron's disposition"; and the ship's gossip soon accuses him of "maintaining a correspondence with his surgeon, not fit to be named." When, therefore, the late eighteenth century developed a male gender role that eschewed the violence of the rake for the domesticity of the faithful husband, who avoided smut, drunkenness, and violence, it was a role that had also put aside those extravagances of the fop that were now associated with the molly.[13]

Among those extravagances were elaborate clothes and enthusiastic forms of greeting. Consequently men's clothes were simplified. And they gave up kissing each other. By 1749 it could be said that when males kissed each other in greeting, it was the "first inlet to the detestable sin of sodomy"; and that the same thing was true of extravagant male dress. But kissing was, of "all the customs effeminacy has produced," the most "hateful, predominant, and pernicious." It was a custom brought over, of course, "from Italy (the mother and nurse of sodomy); where the master is oftener intriguing with his page, than a fair lady." It was better to shake hands—"more manly; more friendly, and more decent." A society of men was formed who vowed never to kiss any man, and they kept their rule "many times at the expense of a quarrel." Even brothers ceased to kiss: "I saw myself two brothers take a very solemn leave of each other without one kiss, though not without tears." By contrast two men in a private room in a tavern in 1727 were identified by the waiter as sodomites because "he heard them kissing each other." At the end of the eighteenth century, Continental visitors had to be warned that kissing between men had unacceptable connotations: Only handshaking or a civil bow were allowed.[14]

It should now be clear that the effeminacy of the fop was not associated before the 1690s with the practice of adult male sodomy. Such reckless sexual practices as sodomy were the province instead of the abandoned rake. In the mid-1680s, however, the new role of the beau emerged; he mediated between the fop and the rake and he made it possible for foppish effeminacy by the end of the 1690s to become associated with sodomy. *Fop* had been a derogatory epithet applied by others. *Beau* was used by some men as a term of self-description for the overdressed man who had taken on some of the splash of the old-style rake. And part of that splash was sodomy with boys.[15]

This is the context that gives meaning to the trial for sodomy in 1698 of Captain Rigby, and it helps to explain why the case was so much discussed. Rigby was a beau who attempted to seduce a boy he had met in the park. One of his critics blamed his actions on his "effeminate madness" as a fop, though the critic presumed that as a fop he was still interested in women as well, since he "manages his whore." This is one of the very earliest attempts to tie effeminacy to sodomy, and it was clearly inspired by the elaborate way Rigby dressed. Rigby himself gave a quite different motive for his actions. When the boy had complained that "a woman only was fit" to raise a man's lust to the highest degree (as Rigby said the boy had done for him), Rigby replied that the women were all diseased: "D—mn 'em, they are all pox'd, I'll have nothing to do with them." Other men according to John Dunton in 1710, followed a similar course: Prostitutes had "burnt so many beaus, that now he-whores are coming in use." These men were to him, however, "a new society . . . call'd S—d——ites; men worse than goats, who dressed themselves in petticoats." But Rigby was a beau whose elaborate male clothes were still quite different from those of a woman.[16]

Part III: The Sodomite as He-Whore

It is almost certainly the case that the effeminate manner of a beau like Rigby was seen in 1699 as the cause of his sodomy, only because there had begun to appear a new kind of sodomite who was identified principally by his effeminate manner. Consequently, by the 1720s a complete lack of interest in women, and male transvestism, had become in the public mind the accompaniments of sexual desire between two adult males. But it is very hard to find this new sodomite in the sources prior to 1707. There are only hints. There were arrests of groups of sodomites (as opposed to the usual single individual) at London and at Windsor in 1699. In 1704 John Norton took hold of the privates of John Coyney, "putting them into his mouth and sucking them." Now, the mouth is an ambiguous sexual organ when it comes to the question of who is in control, but it is probably safe to see Norton's action as evincing a desire on the part of one adult man to be sexually submissive to another.[17] But it was dangerous to attempt to seduce men who did not share such tastes. Such relations could be more safely pursued in a subculture of the like-minded where men who could be both active and passive sought each other. This begins to appear clearly three years later, in 1707, with the arrests of sodomites in a number of known meeting places, which could not suddenly have come into existence in that year. The further arrests and commentary in 1709 reinforce this and document groups of effeminate adult males who were interested in men or in boys, but not at all in women; these men had sexual relations with each other, and sometimes with males who were not effeminate sodomites.

In 1707 the Societies for the Reformation of Manners sent its agents into the recognized meeting places on London-bridge and around the arcades of the Royal Exchange. Two of the younger men who made passes at the agents had been seduced previously for money by older men. But William Huggins, who was a porter and had been married for a year to a young wife who was pregnant, confessed when apprehended that "he had heard there were such sort of persons in the world, and he had a mind to try." The boghouses, or public latrines, of London provided a third meeting place where old and new sodomites intermingled. An apothecary in the Strand picked up Thomas Vaughan in the piazzas of Covent Garden—another arcade (like that of the Exchange) that was ideal for sauntering—and took Vaughan to the boghouse in the Savoy and asked him "to bugger him." Vaughan also forced a confession out of another man, William Guilham, "a person that frequently committed frigging" (i.e., masturbation—the word sodomy is deliberately crossed out in the deposition). Guilham had made an attempt on a boy in the Temple boghouse. The question for us, though, is whether the apothecary who wanted to be buggered by an adult man belonged to the same world as the one who masturbated boys. It may be that in the boghouses the old rakish sodomites intermingled with the new, more passive kind.

The popular literature that the trials produced certainly presumed that the passive adult male was something new. A broadside ballad called "The Women-hater's Lamentation" was published on the occasion of the suicide in jail of three of the arrested men. It claimed that nearly a hundred more were "accused for unnatural deprising the fair sex, and intriguing with one another." It sported three woodcuts with a picture of two adult men embracing in the middle, and the three suicides on either side. The ballad called them a "club" and a "gang." Lady Cowper noted in her diary that one of the suicides left a note claiming his innocence, and that this indicated to many that there existed an extensive trade in the blackmailing of timid men who could not manage their defense, even if innocent of the charge. She was very likely right, since throughout the rest of the century the odium attached to the new role of the effeminate sodomite, and the difficulty of disproving the charge, led to a great many blackmail cases.[18]

The material from 1709 makes it even clearer that contemporaries were beginning to see a kind of sodomite different from the men who frigged and sodomized boys and advised them to try lewd women. The new sodomites met as clubs in taverns, and they called themselves (according to Ned Ward) *mollies*. It is a word probably related to *molly*, which meant a female prostitute; it starts a long tradition in English language usage whereby the slang terms for prostitutes in one generation subsequently are appropriated for sodomites (e.g., queen, punk, gay, faggot, fairy, and fruit). It makes clear that the sodomite viewed himself, and was seen by others, no longer as a rake but as a species of outcast woman. One sodomite could later say to another, "Where have you been, you saucy Queen?" (When queen still meant prostitute.) "If I catch you strolling and caterwauling I'll beat the milk out of your breasts, I will so." Dunton called them "he-whores." Jonathan Wild recalled that William Hitchen, the London Under-Marshal and himself a sodomite, had offered to "introduce him to a company of he-whores." When Wild, "not apprehending rightly his meaning, asked if they were hermaphrodites," Hitchen replied, "No ye fool . . . they are sodomites, such as deal with their own sex instead of females." Dunton added that "some doat on men, and some on boys."[19]

Inside the tavern or molly-house, as the sources from 1709 to 1730 testify, the mollies enacted the rituals of their new identity. (There are four principal sources: Ned Ward in 1709; Wild in 1718 describing an event in 1714; the trials of 1726; and James Dalton in 1728.)[20] In the safety of their clubs, which (as Dalton noted) lessened the likelihood of blackmail, they greeted each other as Madam and Your Ladyship, as Wild discovered when he entered with Hitchen: "calling one another my dear, hugging and kissing, tickling and feeling each other, as if they were a mixture of wanton males and females; and assuming effeminate voices, female airs"; with some mollies evidently taking the active role and some the passive. There were ceremonies mocking the connection of sex to marriage and childbearing; these might be seen as suggestions of religious skepticism, but their principal purpose is more likely to have been the imitation of the lives of women. Dalton was present at a wedding between a man called "Moll Irons and another Molly" who was a butcher; two other butchers stood as bridesmaids. One of them was the Princess Seraphina, who by a trial four years later is confirmed as a real enough person. There were mock deliveries of children, complete with the groaning mother, the midwife, and a baby in the form of a wooden doll, which both Ward and Dalton described. The actual sexual encounters in the molly-houses in 1725 and 1726 occurred in this same context of mock marriage. In Mother Clap's house in Field Lane in Holborn, after "kissing, hugging, and making love (as they called it)," they went into another room where there were beds, "which, in their dialect, they called *Marrying*." Edward Courtney claimed (though the jury did not believe him) that George Whitle's alehouse had a room with a bed for couples who had a mind to be married and that it was called the chapel.

Dalton was taken to molly-houses by a man whom he always called Sukey or Susanna Haws, who specialized in blackmailing his fellow sodomites. Dalton noted the female names that most mollies used in the houses were taken to conceal their true identities, but these names probably also allowed them to take on a second effeminate identity. There was Garter Mary, "a man who sells garters about the streets"; and Nurse Ashcroft and Fish Hannah, who were both fishmongers; and Aunt Mug, who kept a molly-house. The trials of 1726 yield a rich crop of pseudonyms. York Horner was Pru, John Towleton was Mary Magdalen, Thomas Mugg was Judith, and Samuel Roper (who was married to a woman) was Plump Nelly. All of these kept molly-houses. Samuel Gadiger alias Miss Rose, Thomas Wareham alias Miss Wareham, William Gent alias Mademoiselle Gent, John Whale alias Margaret or Peggy Whale, and Martin McIntosh alias Orange Dib, were all charged with sodomy.[21]

Occasionally a group of mollies went dancing, with many of them dressed as women. Wild recalled that Hitchen, the sodomitical Under-Marshal, had arrested (in revenge for being ignored by some young men) a group of mollies as they returned home from a ball in Holborn. Some had "gowns, petticoats, headcloths, fine laced shoes, furbelow scarves, masks and complete dresses for women; others had riding hoods; some were dressed like shepherdesses; others like milkmaids with fine green hats, waistcoats, and petticoats; and others had their faces painted and patched and very extensive whoop petticoats which were then very lately introduced."

There were men who when on their own dressed as women, like the lone footman arrested late at night in the street in 1727. More revealingly, there were cases of men like Dalton's acquaintances Sukey Haws and the Princess Seraphina, who seem to have spent most of their time in women's clothes and to have been referred to by their ordinary acquaintances almost entirely as *she* and *her*. John Cooper was the Princess Seraphina. Margaret Holder described him as a Mollycull, "one of the runners that carries messages between gentlemen . . . going of sodomitical errands."

Mary Poplet said she had "never heard she [sic] had any other name than the Princess Seraphina"; she had "seen him [sic] several times in women's clothes, she [sic] commonly used to wear a white gown and a scarlet cloak with her hair frizzled and curled all around her forehead; and then she would so flutter her fan and make such fine curtsies that you would not have known her from a woman: she takes great delight in balls and masquerades." Even the Princess, however, sometimes dressed as a man, as the evidence comes from a case in which she had charged Thomas Gordon with forcing her to undress in Chelsea Fields in order to exchange her fine male clothes for his. But Gordon insisted that the clothes had been given in the expectation that he would allow Seraphina to bugger him.[22]

Seraphina establishes the extent to which effeminacy could be taken. Even his identity was not entirely feminine, however, but a combination of both genders: He sometimes dressed as a male, and he had proposed to take the active or penetrator's role with Gordon. On the other hand, even the men who were married to women adopted female names once inside the molly-house. It had become the case that after 1700 most adult sodomites were both active and passive, whereas before 1700 only a minority of sodomites had been so. But in a parallel way, there existed after 1700 a minority of adult sodomites (like sailors in the navy) who would refer to a boy as "cunt," and were presumably exclusively active.[23] In other words, every predominant system produces its variant.

Those sailors at sea, and the married men in the molly-houses, would, however, have caused great difficulty for the common belief that the majority of men could feel no interest at all in other men. Because of this belief many men accused of sodomy attempted to disprove the charge by showing that they were either married or had "loved a girl too well to be concerned in other affairs"; and sometimes they succeeded. The sodomites who picked up boys therefore faced a new level of hostility both from the boys and their friends, since it was no longer possible, as it had been in the seventeenth century, for a boy to pass from the passive to the active role at manhood. All males now needed to be active at every stage of life in order to establish masculine status.[24]

It was not yet the case, however, that women were obliged to disavow all sexual interest in women to establish feminine status. There was as yet no lesbian role to be avoided, though men were aware that some women desired women. Women's gender role revolved, instead, around the avoidance of the prostitute's identity. The differences between male and female identity can be seen in the attitude toward male and female cross-dressing in the theater. Until 1660, all female roles on the English stage were played by cross-dressing boys, with many suggestions made as to their sexual passivity with the older actors. (It partly accounts for the libertine behavior of Marlowe and Shakespeare.) At the Restoration, actresses began to share the female roles with boy actors, and probably by the end of the century had replaced them. But there then grew up instead a convention by which actresses played male roles in male attire; this continued in popularity throughout the eighteenth century. There were limits to this public female transvestism. Charlotte Charke made a reputation playing these "breeches parts," as her father Colley Cibber had made his reputation playing fops. But when Charke took to dressing as a man in the London streets, and toured the provinces with an actress who passed as her wife, it caused a break with her family. On the other hand, she published an account of her behavior and was never arrested for it.[25]

The final task is to ask why the great transition should have occurred. In most other cultures that produce an adult male transvestite group—whether the North American *berdache*, the Polynesian *mahu*, or the Omani *xanith*—this role usually serves as bridge between the male and female roles in societies where those roles are not radically differentiated.[26] The appearance of the English molly and his European counterparts would therefore indicate that male and female roles had begun to grow more nearly equal. This is confirmed by the development at that time of the companionate marriage and the domesticated family.[27] But the older European tradition that all sexual acts must be procreative—which had partly produced the older system of illicit relations between men and boys—now guaranteed that the molly could not find licit partners among the majority of adult males. The molly was therefore a wall of separation between the genders rather than a bridge. But he was a wall that perhaps made possible an unprecedented development of equality between the other two genders, since it was now the case that there would remain a radical separation of male and female experience, no matter how far equality might go in other ways. Men would never know what it was like to desire men: Only women knew that. And the molly's outcast status was the demonstration of what awaited a man who tried to cross the boundary between sexual desire in the two legitimated genders.

SODOMY IN THE DUTCH REPUBLIC DURING THE EIGHTEENTH CENTURY

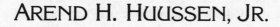

Arend H. Huussen, Jr.

Providing an overview on the emerging literature on homosexuality in the eighteenth century, this essay utilizes Dutch criminal-law records in order to cast new light on several much-debated issues in that literature. Whereas most historians of the United States have placed the appearance of a self-conscious homosexual identity and a visible homosexual subculture in the mid-nineteenth century, Huussen's evidence suggests that, for the Dutch Republic at any rate, both phenomena can be glimpsed at least a hundred years earlier. The evidence, Huussen acknowledges, is still too fragmentary to allow for definite conclusions, but it merits close attention in what is a developing debate.

The introduction of Calvinism in the emerging Dutch Republic seems to have had little effect on conceptions of morality. Legislation against sex crimes, for example, was little changed. The Reformed ministers were struggling for stricter observance of Calvinist norms of behavior; but in a society in which the Reformed church was not the state religion, the clergy's influence was necessarily less formal and less direct than in England or France. Synods asked for stricter legislation against such vices as inebriety, dancing, theater, luxury, and other intemperances; but public authorities did not yield to these puritan tendencies. The Calvinist church, though privileged, had to rely on its own methods to induce changes in attitude and behavior among its members. This was effected by

Note: Originally published Robert P. Maccubkin ed., *Unauthorized Sexual Behavior during The Enlightenment* (William & Mary: 1985) pp. 169–178.

means of the discipline (*censura morum*) exercised by the local consistories and regional synods.[1]

Legislation on moral issues was gradually adapted to Calvinist norms, but this does not necessarily imply that it was stiffened or puritanized. In conformity with Reformed ecclesiastical dogma regarding the nonsacramental character of marriage, divorce was introduced, and civil marriage for dissenters was made a legal option in Holland after 1580. However, divorce was neither advertised nor otherwise promoted. Marriage for life remained the ideal alliance between man and woman.[2]

New "reformed" secular legislation was introduced; but no special attention to sex crimes can be traced. Adultery, prostitution, incest, sodomy, and bestiality continued to be considered particularly heinous crimes; it appears, however, that during the seventeenth century they were not singled out for punishment that was exceptionally severe by the standards of the day, which frequently imposed corporal and capital punishment.

If we are to single out the position and treatment of homosexuals for the purposes of this essay, one caveat must be stressed: As far as we know, the Calvinists did not develop a new vision of the phenomenon of sodomy. Calvinists considered it a sin and a crime, *contra naturam*, as did the Roman Catholic theologians and criminalists before them.[3] As "natural," or as ordained by God, heterosexual intercourse was normally to be confined to marriage, where its end was procreation. Sodomy's origins as a grave sin are found in the traditional interpretation of the biblical events at Sodom and Gomorrah and the destruction of those cities by the wrath of God. Secular interference with the sin/crime of sodomy could be justified in a society in which the active, revenging hand of God was still expected and feared. Indeed, belief in magic and Satan still informed the average *outillage mental* of Dutch people, although witch trials were virtually nonexistent in Holland after 1600.[4]

People of the "world we have lost" avoided discourse about sodomy as either sin or crime. This avoidance makes it even more difficult for us to form an image of the real status of sodomy and homosexuality. The "unspeakable" crime (*crimen nefandum*) has left, by definition, little trace of itself. Nevertheless, historians, progressive or not, are looking for answers to such questions as: Did homosexuality exist in this period? If so, how prevalent was it, and in what social groups? May we speak of a homosexual subculture during the seventeenth and eighteenth centuries? What did people mean by "sodomy," and what kinds of reactions did they have to homosexual and, especially, sodomitic, behavior?

An inquiry into Dutch criminal law reveals a certain degree of indistinctness in interpreting the concept of sodomy and therefore in using the term. The famous German *Peinlich Gerichtsordnung* (penal code) or Constitutio Criminalis Carolina of 1532, promulgated by Emperor Charles V—a criminal statute that gained authority among criminalists in the republic—assigned to the category of crimes against nature (article 116) intercourse between men, between women, and between humans and animals.[5] The Dutch laws on military discipline mandated capital punishment for "unnatural misuses"; and, in defining *sodomia*, commentators Petrus Pappus van Tratzberg and Gerhard Feltman alleged *expressis verbis* the German Carolina, though this statute did not use the term "sodomy."[6]

The same picture emerges from local and regional customary laws and statutes that contained provisions against the crime of sodomy. In fact, many laws do not contain any regulations on this topic at all. Death by burning was the usual prescription for sodomy: a practice confirmed without much comment by such prominent criminalists and commentators on Roman and common law as Joos de Damhouder (1507–1581) and Antonius Matthaeus II (1601–1654).[7]

From these sources alone it would be virtually impossible to answer our questions. Where "theory" fails, it seems appropriate to consult practice. Before the beginning of the nineteenth century criminal jurisdiction in the Dutch Republic was fragmented into hundreds of local and regional courts. Quantitative research into the incidence of a specific crime would be an enormous task, even supposing the series of criminal sentences to be complete and uninterrupted.[8] Moreover, as has been rightly stressed by Robert Oaks, court records must be handled with care when seeking information about sexual activities:[9] The historian is dependent upon the governmental and judicial policy of the moment in uncovering certain crimes; he or she will read, more often than not, a description of the prosecuted offenses as viewed by the judge or clerk; and so-called "confessions" may have been obtained by torture or other means.[10] In the case of trials against sodomites it even seems that some were burned along with their files. Even conceding the methodological problems that have to be solved by the historian's usual critical devices, criminal records can be a source of great importance. By studying them serially over a long period we can develop insight into the changing attitudes of peoples and governments toward deviant or abnormal behavior.

Modern serial research in Dutch criminal records before the eighteenth century is scarce, yet it seems justified to contend that sodomy was not unknown and was not unrecognized. Judicial proceedings were rarely instituted, however. What does this mean? Was sodomy rare or merely not manifest? From contemporary reactions and literature about the notorious mass persecutions of sodomites and homosexuals in general in Holland and Utrecht in 1730 and 1731, we know that perplexed spectators perceived sodomy as a completely new evil never before seen among them. Explanations given for this "new" phenomenon varied widely but stressed effeminate French cultural influences and general relaxation of morality. Panic spread, both among sodomites, who fled to escape death, and among Calvinist ministers and the judges themselves, who feared the wrath of God. We now know that accepting these perceptions would be to misinterpret the facts. First, before 1700 there were several capital sentences against sodomites: in 1629 in the town of Breda, Province of Brabant, against the painter Carel (or Daniel) de Lasco; in 1676 in Utrecht against a cooper's workman; and in 1686 in Amsterdam against a ship-boy. Serial research of the criminal records of the university town of Leiden has revealed five sentences for sodomy out of five thousand sentences during the years 1533–1700.[11]

Second, we find that courts or judges often ignored unambiguous evidence. In November 1702 the Court of Holland was confronted with a delinquent who made remarkable statements indeed. The suspect, twenty-five or -six years old, born at The Hague, had just arrived in the town, probably on leave from his military regiment. He told the judges that several persons, whom he named, had propositioned him at the Vijverberg to commit sodomy. Was he at this area of rendezvous for homosexuals by chance or on purpose? Was extortion his malicious intent? It seems that the suspect, Gabriel de Berger, assaulted and robbed three persons, of whom one was rescued by a strong coachman who delivered the suspect to the police and who gave evidence of the disorder of the victim's clothes at the time of rescue. The court, which had jurisdiction over the "Binnenhof" (now the House of Parliament) and over the neighboring Vijverberg, thus became involved.

From the files of this case it is evident that at first the court was alarmed by the accusations of de Berger against the sodomites he named. Although de Berger revoked his charges at some point during the preliminary examination, on 12 December, the court ordered a special interrogation, during which, on 10 January 1703, he gave information on the special signs by which sodomites could be recognized and on the places where they met in The Hague, and he confessed to having walked in female dress two days before his arrest.

The interesting point is that although the Court of Holland condemned de Berger to death, it did not condemn him for attempted sodomy or travesty. Capital punishment was imposed on 22 January for multiple assault and falsely accusing people of propositioning him to commit sodomy. In this case the attention of the authorities was drawn to a subculture of sodomitic behavior; that they did not pursue it indicates a lack of concern about sodomy in the beginning of the eighteenth century.

From the many trials that occurred throughout the republic during the eighteenth century it is evident that there existed a kind of sodomitic or homosexual subculture, especially in the great cities, where networks of friends and clubs of men met regularly, presumably to seek sexual partners, apply their own rules of behavior, and play their specific roles. Many interesting features of this subculture have been brought to light by recent research into, in particular, the waves of persecution of 1730, 1764, and 1776.[12]

In 1730 the Court of Frisia was puzzled by the fact that homosexuals often seemed to give each other girls' names. The court informed the authorities of the neighboring province of Groningen of this custom. In 1764 the authorities in Amsterdam became aware of special places in the city where sodomites or homosexuals gathered, recognizing each other by specific signs. Arcades of the town hall, dark parts of the churches, and public urinals were all favorite meeting places. By the middle of the century there existed houses or taverns, so-called *lolhuysen*, where homosexuals met. Contacts were also sought in parks or in the theater. Transient contacts were contrasted with intense love affairs and the lasting engagements of men who sealed "marriage" contracts with blood. A traveling Don Juan such as Zacharias Wilsma, who must have been paid for his services during the 1720s, seems as atypical as the couple who wrote ardent love letters to each other in the 1770s, for many of the prosecuted sodomites were married and had children. The social positions of those accused of sodomy varied widely; they formed a range of social statuses and occupations, from distinguished gentlemen to simple manservants.

Serial research of criminal court records in the republic during the eighteenth century provides evidence that before 1730 sodomy was only sporadically prosecuted, although it certainly was not an unknown phenomenon. After 1730 several waves of persecution occurred; isolated trials became more frequent until 1811. Three points should be noted: the definition of the crime of sodomy, the seemingly arbitrary penalties, and the scarcity of condemnations of women.

After prosecution of sodomites began in Utrecht in the spring of 1730, the town of Groningen and the provincial state of Holland proclaimed special statutes against sodomy. Apparently, the purpose of these new laws was to make it possible to prosecute those who had made themselves suspects by fleeing the country. The courts could condemn these suspects by default—an unusual procedure for that time. From the records it is evident that the crime of sodomy was defined narrowly. Capital punishment was to be applied only in cases in which the suspect had confessed to anal contact and to *ejaculatio in ano* with another man. This seems in accord with legal practice in England and France during the period.[13]

Capital punishment was imposed in only about 10 percent of the sentences. Prison terms of up to thirty or fifty years or banishment, sometimes in combination with corporal punishment, were the prescribed sentences for the large majority of cases. Fugitives were usually punished with "eternal" banishment. The death penalty and banishment for life were, until 1732, combined with the confiscation of the condemned man's personal property. Some suspects committed suicide while being held in detention.[14] (See table, "Criminal Sentences.")

We know of very few cases in which women were prosecuted for lesbianism or tribadism: three women at Leiden in the seventeenth century and some twelve women at Amsterdam during the years 1792–1798. (Indeed, romantic stories of brave young women who fought as soldiers or went aboard ship as sailors tickled public imagination.) Perhaps the fact that physical contact between women is more accepted in Western culture explains why women remained largely outside the scope of criminal justice in these instances. Moreover, lesbians could not be implicated in the crime of sodomy as it was usually defined, which perhaps also explains the relatively light penalties conviction for lesbianism incurred; punishments were often due in part to other offenses of which they were also accused.[15]

The last known imposition of the death penalty against sodomites was in 1803 in the little town of Schiedam, near Rotterdam. Six years later the first national criminal code, the *Crimineel Wetboek voor het Koningrijk Holland*, fixed life imprisonment as the most severe penalty for sodomy. Two years later, after the annexation of the Kingdom of Holland by Emperor Napoleon in 1810, the French penal code was introduced. The *Code pénal* did not fix penalties for the traditional sodomitic acts. A new chapter had begun.

Most contemporaries defined sodomy literally in terms of a sexual *act*. No other approach seemed justified as long as one wished to see in sodomy only the unmentionable sin or crime. Yet one finds traces of other opinions in some trial records after 1730. Particularly interesting in this regard is Rev. Andreas Klink, on whom the Court of Holland on 13 November 1759 imposed "eternal" banishment from the provinces of Holland, Zeeland, and Utrecht for sodomy. Klink, a Calvinist minister, had defended himself, saying in substance that his attraction to young men was proper by nature ("hem van natuure eijgen was"), because while his mother was pregnant she had a very strong desire for his absent father, a desire which he inherited in the womb from her. The lawyer Pieter Loens, who wrote a tract about the case, seems not to have been convinced by this explanation.[16] Yet one may venture to suppose that some of Klink's contemporaries empathized with him, interpreting their homosexual or homoerotic attraction to men as an inborn disposition.

Twenty years later we find a plea for tolerance toward sodomites in a tract written as a consequence of the wave of homosexual persecution in 1776. Anonymous, but attributed to Abraham Perrenot, the tract considered sodomites or homosexuals as infected by a disease that did little harm to society at large. Influenced by the enlightened ideas of the self-styled *philosophe* and criminalist Cesare Beccaria, Perrenot was of the opinion that the act of sodomy was a crime only if perpetrated with a boy under age. Perrenot rejected capital punishment, preferring a long prison term for convicted sodomites.[17]

During the seventeenth and eighteenth centuries sodomites were not persecuted in the Dutch Republic on the same scale and intensity as were heretics and witches elsewhere. Persecutions found a place, indeed, at a time when one would expect more tolerance, and they ended during a period when "Victorian" prudery announced itself.[18] But while the introduction of the French penal code in 1811 may account for the ending of the persecution of sodomy as a crime, the persecutions from 1730 on are more complicated and difficult to explain.

It seems an established fact that the frequent demands for stricter observance of norms and prescriptions of morality were already put into practice in the 1720s (for example, prosecution of prostitution or adultery). By 1730 there seems to have emerged a stricter moral climate, voiced by "spectatorial," theological, and other writers, in which a radical new view on sodomites and on the sin/crime of sodomy was promulgated.[19]

The much-debated issues of the existence of a homosexual identity and of homosexual subcultures before the new medical observations of the nineteenth century cannot as yet be verified.[20] However, research in Dutch criminal records has brought to light some evidence both on contemporary self-perceptions, which point to a kind of homosexual awareness, and on groups that formed a kind of subculture: There were special meeting places in the open air and indoors; and homosexuals used peculiar mimicry, specific signs, love names, and a network of friends and contacts. A true sexual market existed all over the republic.

A final point emerges from the court records: The amount of physical distance between men seems, in this period, to have been less than in later periods. Guest and host, master and servant, and manservants among themselves often slept in one bed. It was undoubtedly the same group of people who both stressed the importance of maintaining a stricter moral code and who tried to impose their own notion of "privacy" and of physical distance on the lower strata of society. Certain intimate customs of sleeping together were increasingly perceived as uncivilized. From the end of the eighteenth century, the bourgeoisie worried about immoral situations in the houses of the working class and in the dormitories of prisons and workhouses. The cell, symbol of the smallest individual entity and space, seemed the best guarantee for disciplining—to refer to Foucault—body and soul.

CRIMINAL SENTENCES (269) IN SODOMY CASES, 1701–1811

	1	2	3	4	5	6	7	8	9	10	11	12	13
1730	8	12	—	—	—	—	—	—	1	21	—	—	12
1731	—	40	—	—	—	—	—	—	—	—	—	1	1
1732	—	—	—	—	—	—	—	—	—	—	—	—	1
1733	—	1	—	—	—	—	—	—	—	—	—	—	—
1734	2	—	—	—	—	—	—	—	—	—	—	—	—
1739/40	—	—	—	—	—	—	—	—	—	—	—	—	1

	1	2	3	4	5	6	7	8	9	10	11	12	13
1741	—	—	—	—	—	—	—	—	—	—	—	—	3
1743	—	—	—	—	—	—	—	—	—	—	—	—	2
1746	—	—	—	—	—	—	—	—	—	—	—	—	3
1749	—	—	—	—	—	—	—	2	—	—	—	—	1
1750	—	—	—	—	—	—	—	—	—	—	—	—	2
1755	—	—	1	—	—	—	—	—	—	—	—	—	—
1757	1	—	—	—	—	—	—	—	—	—	—	—	—
1758	—	—	—	—	—	—	—	—	—	4	—	—	—
1759	1	1	—	—	—	—	—	—	—	—	—	—	—
1760	—	—	—	—	—	—	—	—	—	—	—	—	1
1761	—	—	—	—	—	—	—	—	—	—	—	—	1
1762	—	—	—	—	—	—	—	—	—	—	—	—	1
1763	—	—	—	—	—	—	—	—	—	—	—	—	3
1764	—	—	—	—	—	—	—	—	—	2	—	—	10
1765	—	—	—	—	—	—	—	—	—	2	—	—	4
1766	3	—	—	—	—	—	—	—	—	—	—	—	—
1768	1	—	—	—	—	—	—	—	—	—	—	—	—
1772	—	—	—	—	—	—	—	—	—	1	—	—	—
1774	1	—	—	—	—	—	—	—	—	—	—	—	—
1775	3	—	—	—	—	—	—	—	—	—	—	1	—
1776	—	1	—	—	—	—	—	—	—	2	—	3	4
1777	—	—	—	—	—	—	—	—	—	2	—	—	—
1778	—	—	—	—	—	—	—	—	—	—	—	1	—
1779	—	6	—	—	—	—	—	—	—	—	—	2	—
1781	—	—	—	—	—	—	—	2	—	—	—	—	—
1784	—	—	—	—	—	—	—	—	—	—	—	1	—
1789	—	—	—	—	—	—	—	1	—	3	—	—	—
1790	—	—	1	—	—	—	—	—	—	—	—	—	—
1791	—	—	—	—	—	—	—	—	—	1	—	—	2
1792	—	—	—	—	—	—	—	—	—	—	—	—	2
1793	—	—	—	—	—	—	—	—	—	1	—	—	—
1794	—	—	—	—	—	—	—	—	—	—	—	—	2
1795	—	—	—	—	—	—	—	—	—	—	—	—	3
1796	—	—	—	—	—	—	—	—	—	—	—	—	12
1797	1	—	—	—	—	—	—	—	—	—	—	2	5
1798	1	—	—	—	—	—	—	—	—	—	1	1	19
1799	—	—	—	—	—	—	—	—	—	—	—	—	3
1801	—	—	—	—	—	—	—	—	—	—	—	2	2
1802	—	—	—	—	—	—	—	—	—	—	—	—	1
1803	—	—	—	—	—	—	—	—	—	2	1	—	1
1804	—	—	—	—	—	—	—	—	—	—	—	1	1
1805	—	—	—	—	—	—	—	—	—	1	—	—	—
1806	—	—	—	—	—	—	—	—	—	—	—	—	1
1808	2	—	—	—	—	—	—	—	—	—	—	—	2

	1	2	3	4	5	6	7	8	9	10	11	12	13
1809	1	—	—	—	—	—	—	—	—	—	1	—	6
1810	—	—	—	—	—	—	—	—	—	—	—	—	3
	25	61	2	—	—	—	—	5	1	42	3	15	115

Total 269

Legend

1) Provincial Court of Frisia 2) Provincial Court of Holland 3) District Court of Waterland 4) District Court of Wassenaar & Zuidwijk 5) Town Court of Brielle 6) District Court of Twente 7) District Court of Heerlen 8) Town Court of Zierikzee 9) Town Court of Vlaardingen 10) Town Court of Leiden 11) Town Court of Breda 12) Town Court of The Hague 13) Town Court of Amsterdam
NOTE: The total of 269 sentences includes cases of default; the Amsterdam numbers do not include the cases in which no definite sentence is recorded (1730–32, 33 cases; 1764–65, 61; and 1776, 16).

Sources

1) A. H. Huussen Jr., "Gerechtelijke vervolging van 'sodomie' gedurende de 18e eeuw in de Republiek, in het bijzonder in Friesland" ["Judicial Persecutions of 'Sodomy' during the 18th Century in the Republic, Especially in Friesland"] *Groniek, Gronings Historisch Tijdschrift* 66 (Jan. 1980): 18–33; 2–7) unpub. material collected by H. A. Diederiks, S. Faber, A. H. Huussen Jr., et al.; 8–9) unpub. material kindly put at our disposal by Dr. H. A. Diederiks; 10) D. J. Noordam, "Homosexualiteit en sodomie in Leiden, 1533–1811" ["Homosexuality and Sodomy at Leiden, 1533–1811"] *Leids Jaarboekje* 75 (1983): 72–105; 11) J. van Haastert, "Beschouwingen bij de criminele vonnissen van de schepenbank van de stad Breda uit de jaren 1626 tot 1795" ["Considerations on the Criminal Sentences of the Town Court of Breda during the Years 1626 till 1795"] and "Beschouwingen bij de criminele vonnissen van Bredase rechtbanken in de periode 1796–1811 ["Considerations on the Criminal Sentences of the Courts of Breda during the Period 1796–1811"] *Jaarboek van de Geschieden Oudheidkundige Kring van Stad en Land van Breda "De Oranjeboom"* 29 (1976): 56–106 and 35 (1982): 62–119, with unpub. material kindly put at our disposal by the author; 12) A. J. van Weel "De strafvonnissen van de Haagse Vierschaar in de periode 1700–1811" ["The Criminal Sentences of the Court of The Hague in the Period 1700–1811"] in *Die Haghe* (1984), pp. 134–189; 13) Theo van der Meer, *De wesentlijke sonde van sodomie en andere vuyligheeden. Sodomietenvervolgingen in Amsterdam, 1730–1811 [The Real Sin of Sodomy and other Lewdness. Persecutions of Sodomites in Amsterdam 1730–1811]* (Amsterdam, 1984).

The
NINETEENTH
CENTURY

"WRITHING BEDFELLOWS" IN ANTEBELLUM SOUTH CAROLINA: HISTORICAL INTERPRETATION AND THE POLITICS OF EVIDENCE

◆

MARTIN BAUML DUBERMAN

James H. Hammond and Thomas J. Withers were two of the "great men" of the antebellum South; Hammond, especially, held high office and was widely regarded as a pillar of traditional morality. As twenty-year-olds, however, the two turn out to have been far less staid and conventional than their textbook images have long suggested. Recently discovered letters in the Hammond Family Papers reveal an antic, wanton—and homoerotic—side that stands in sharp contrast to their later reputations. The importance of the letters goes beyond the new light they shed on two individuals. Their contents reveal a dimension of life in antebellum America previously unexplored, as well as possible new approaches to historical interpretation of the period. The controversy surrounding the author's decision to publish the letters, moreover, reveals issues about archival research, the nature of the academic enterprise, and the politics of controlling interpretations of the past which have wide-ranging repercussions for all researchers into sexuality.

The two manuscript letters that form this article's centerpiece have been concealed from public view for 150 years. No portion of them has been previously published, nor even obliquely paraphrased. Yet as will be seen

Note: Originally published, in somewhat different form, in *Journal of Homosexuality*, Vol. 6, Nos. 1/2, pp. 85–102, Fall/Winter 1980–81.

at a glance, the content of the letters is startling, and opens up suggestive new avenues for historical exploration. The importance of the letters requires that they be introduced on several levels.

To start with the simplest, we need to identify the sender ("Jeff") and the recipient ("Jim"). In 1826, when the letters were written, Jeff and Jim were inconsequential young men—yet both destined for distinguished careers, Jim (James H. Hammond) eventually achieving national renown. Jeff (Thomas Jefferson Withers) was also to cut a considerable, if lesser swath—as journalist, lawyer, "nullifier," and judge of the South Carolina Court of Appeals.

In 1826, twenty-two-year-old Jeff Withers was studying law at South Carolina College—discontentedly. "An useful man," he wrote Jim Hammond, "must, at last, be self-educated." In Jeff's view, it was "behind the state of society" to concentrate on the "dead languages" of Greek and Latin; it was time "murdered," preparing a student poorly for "the duties of life." By 1826 Jeff Withers had reached some basic decisions about his future. Henceforce, he wrote Jim, he would "sacrifice" his previous "Northern mania" and devote himself to what he now realized was his "appropriate sphere of action"—the southern states. Though in general he did not have "strenuous opinions upon political matters," he did feel strongly about the intensifying controversy between "strict" and "broad" constructionists—over the kind and amount of power the Constitution had given to the federal government. Withers stood with the strict constructionists. South Carolina Senator William Smith, probably the country's fiercest defender in the early 1820s of the sovereign and "inviolable" rights of the individual states against the threatening encroachments of national power, had become his hero.[1]

To activate his newfound convictions, Jeff Withers in 1828 became editor of the Columbia Telescope, *an organ of the powerful nullification movement that had arisen in South Carolina to protest and defy the recent federal tariff. For several years thereafter he gave full energies to the struggle, delaying the completion of his law studies until 1833 (the same year he married Elizabeth Boykin, whose niece, Mary Boykin Chestnut, later won enduring fame for her Civil War journals, published as* Diary from Dixie). *Elected a common-law judge soon after, Withers later moved up to the state Court of Appeals, where he served until his death in 1866. His moment of greatest public prominence came in 1861, when he was chosen to be one of fifty delegates sent by the seven seceded states of the lower South to meet in Montgomery, Alabama, there to draw up a provisional government for the pending new Confederacy.[2] Except for a few additional details, little more is known about Withers' public career.*

Still less is known about his private life. He seems to have been generally viewed as an "irritable" man, quick-tempered and sarcastic, though we have the testimony of at least one close friend that Withers was "a very kind-hearted gentleman and most indulgent and affectionate in all relations of life."[3] It's tempting—given the contents of the letters printed below—to read innuendos into that description; but since such phraseology was then commonplace, the temptation is better resisted.

We know a great deal more about "Jim." James H. Hammond became one of the antebellum South's "great men," his career ranging from politics to agricultural reform to pro-slavery polemics. At various times he was governor, congressman, and senator from South Carolina, a leading exponent of southern economic diversification, and a highly influential "moralist" whose theories in defense of slavery became cornerstones of the South's "Pro-Slavery Argument." Hammond's name may not be well known today, but in the antebellum period he was likened in importance to John C. Calhoun—and considered his likely heir.[4]

For the limited purpose of elucidating two letters from 1826, a detailed description of Hammond's subsequent public career would be gratuitous—especially since it has been ably recounted many times.[5] Still, certain aspects of Hammond's public life, plus what little is known of his private life, are indeed vital to our attempt at interpreting young Jim's erotic activities, as described in the 1826 letters—and for tracing continuities in Hammond's behavior and temperament over time.

We need to begin by getting acquainted with young Jim himself—the lusty roisterer revealed for the first time in these 1826 letters.

The Documents

The following letter was written by Withers to Hammond, May 15, 1826, Columbia, South Carolina.[6]

Dear Jim:

   I got your Letter this morning about 8 o'clock, from the hands of the Bearer . . . I was sick as the Devil, when the Gentleman entered the Room, and have been so during most of the day. About 1 o'clock I swallowed a huge mass of Epsom Salts—and it will not be hard to imagine that I have been at dirty work since. I feel partially relieved—enough to write a hasty dull letter.

   I feel some inclination to learn whether you yet sleep in your Shirt-tail, and whether you yet have the extravagant delight of poking and punching a writhing Bedfellow with your long fleshen pole—the exquisite touches of which I have often had the honor of feeling? Let me say unto thee that unless thou changest former habits in this particular, thou wilt be represented by every future Chum as a nuisance. And, I pronounce it, with good reason too. Sir, you roughen the downy Slumbers of your Bedfellow—by such hostile—furious lunges as you are in the habit of making at him—when he is least prepared for defence against the crushing force of a Battering Ram. Without reformation my imagination depicts some

awful results for which you will be held accountable—and therefore
it is, that I earnestly recommend it. Indeed it is encouraging an
assault and battery propensity, which needs correction—& uncor-
rected threatens devastation, horror & bloodshed, etc. . . .

*The remaining two pages of the letter deal with unrelated matters of no
special interest. But the way the letter signs off is:*

With great respect I am the old
Stud,
Jeff.

Withers' second letter to Hammond is dated September 24, 1826:

My dear Friend,
   . . . Your excellent Letter of 13 June arrived . . . a few weeks
since[7] . . . Here, where anything like a systematic course of thought,
or of reading, is quite out of the question—such system leaves no
vacant, idle moments of painful vacuity, which invites a whole
Kennel of treacherous passions to prey upon one's vitals . . . the
renovation of spirit which follows the appearance of a *friend's* Letter—
the diagram of his soul—is like a grateful shower from the cooling
fountains of Heaven to reanimate drooping Nature. Whilst your
letters are Transcripts of real—existing feeling, and are on that
account peculiarly welcome—they at the same time betray too much
honesty of purpose not to strike an harmonious chord in my mind. I
have only to regret that, honesty of intention and even assiduity in
excition [execution?] are far from being the uniform agents of our
destiny [sic] here—However it must, at best, be only an a priori
argument for us to settle the condemnation of the world, before we
come in actual contact with it. This task is peculiarly appropriate to
the acrimony of old age—and perhaps we had as well defer it, under
the hope that we may reach a point, when 'twill be all that we can
do—
   I fancy, Jim, that your *elongated protruberance*—your fleshen
pole—your [two Latin words; indecipherable]—has captured complete mastery over you—and I really believe, that you are charging
over the pine barrens of your locality, braying, like an ass, at every
she-male you can discover. I am afraid that you are thus prostituting
the "image of God" and suggest that if you thus blasphemously
essay to put on the form of a Jack—in this stead of that noble
image—you will share the fate of Nebuchadnazzer of old, I should
lament to hear of you feeding upon the dross of the pasture and
alarming the country with your vociferations. The day of miracles
may not be past, and the flaming excess of your lustful appetite may
drag down the vengeance of supernal power.—And you'll "be damn-d
if you don't marry"?—and felt a disposition to set down and gravely
detail me the reasons of early marriage. But two favourable ones

strike me now—the first is, that Time may grasp love so furiously as totally[?] to disfigure his Phiz. The second is, that, like George McDuffie,[8] he may have the hap-hazzard of a broken backbone befal him, which will relieve him from the performance of affectual family-duty—& throw over the brow of his wife, should he chance to get one, a most foreboding gloom—As to the first, you will find many a modest good girl subject to the same inconvenience—and as to the second, it will only superinduce such domestic whirlwinds, as will call into frequent exercise rhetorical displays of impassioned Eloquence, accompanied by appropriate and perfect specimens of those gestures which Nature and feeling suggest. To get children, it is true, fulfills a department of social & natural duty—but to let them starve, or subject them to the alarming hazard of it, violates another of a most important character. This is the dilemma to which I reduce you—choose this day which you will do.

Commentary

The portrait of young Hammond that emerges from these 1826 letters is in startling contrast with the standard view of the adult Hammond. Nineteen-year-old Jim's "flaming excess" and "lustful appetite" bear no resemblance to James H. Hammond of the history books—conservative moralist, staid traditionalist pillar of the traditional Old South. In an effort to reconcile this gross disparity in Hammond's image, some additional biographical details are needed.

By birth, Hammond was a "commoner"—his father a native New Englander who had gone south to teach school, his mother a native South Carolinian of undistinguished ancestry. Through his own talent and drive (Hammond graduated near the top of his college class) and then through what is called a "fortunate" marriage, Hammond entered the ranks of the southern planter aristocracy. His wedding to the Charleston heiress Catherine Fitzsimmons was critically important: Overnight Hammond became owner of Silver Bluff, a 10,000-acre plantation on the Savannah River worked by 220 slaves—thereby instantly rising into the ranks of the ruling elite.[9]

He used his opportunities well. Always the apt pupil, Hammond quickly acquired the cultivated externals—manners, rituals, and social preoccupations—of the master class. Just as quickly, he internalized its values. By the mid-1830s, Hammond had already won high regard as a "brilliant" advocate of "states' rights," a zealous defender of slavery, and a "superb" manager of his landed estates. (He had also acquired a reputation for willingness to use the lash and to send his slaves to cut fodder in malaria-infested swamps.)[10] A number of Hammond's contemporaries thought his temperament more enigmatic than his social values, often describing him as mercurial and impetuous, as well as aloof, vain, willful and proud as well, though to be described as having such traits was not for that region, class, and time, necessarily to be derided.

That Hammond the adult was sometimes considered "impetuous" does suggest that the tumultuous young Jim of 1826 had never been wholly superceded in later life by the Statesman and Seer. We have few details about the nature of his adult "impetuousness," but of those we do, none suggest it ever took the form it had in his youth—of "furious lunges" at male bed partners, lusty "charges over the pine barrens" to seek out "she-males." If those youthful penchants and impulses did continue to exert some hold over him in adulthood (given how pronounced they had been in his youth, it's hard to believe they totally disappeared), if homoerotic images did maintain some subterranean sway on his fantasies, there is no scintilla of evidence he acted them out.

But there is considerable evidence that Hammond's lusty appetite in general—however much its loci may have shifted—continued to be strong throughout his life, his public image notwithstanding. As an adult, Hammond had the reputation for stern rectitude, and was at pains to reinforce it. For example, he haughtily denounced as "grossly and atrociously exaggerated" the abolitionists' charge that racial mixing was common on southern plantations; the actual incidence of miscegenation, he insisted, was "infinitely small" in contrast to the "illicit sexual intercourse" known to be widespread among the factory populations of England and the North. As a plantation owner, he sternly enforced puritanical sexual mores among his slaves. He allowed the slaves on his plantation to marry but not to divorce unless a slave couple could manage to convince him that "sufficient cause" existed; even then he subjected both members of the couple to a hundred lashes and forbid both the right to remarry for three years.[11]

Hammond's entrenched reputation as the guardian and exemplar of traditional morality got a sudden, nasty jolt in 1846. In that year, George McDuffie resigned his seat in the U.S. Senate, and the state legislature seemed on the verge of choosing Hammond to succeed him. Hammond's brother-in-law, Wade Hampton, thwarted that result. He warned Hammond that he would publicly reveal an incident that took place three years earlier unless Hammond immediately removed his name from contention for the Senate seat. The nature of that incident was finally revealed twenty years ago, when the historian Clement Eaton discovered and published excerpts from Hammond's secret diary. That diary reveals that Hammond had attempted to seduce Wade Hampton's teenage daughters.[12]

Hardly a peccadillo, one might think. Yet Hammond himself apparently viewed it as no more than that. He agreed to withdraw his candidacy for the Senate; rumors of the sexual scandal had already circulated and Hammond could hardly afford to let Hampton confirm them. Hammond also gave up his family mansion in Columbia and retired to manage his estates—a retirement which lasted fourteen years. But he did none of this in a spirit marked by contrition or chagrin. The dominant tone he adopted (in diary entries and in letters to friends) was aggrieved petulance— *he* was the wounded party! Merely for "a little dalliance with the other sex," for an incident marked by "impulse, not design," he wrote, he had been forced into political retirement, whereas numerous other public figures, past and present, had indulged "amorous & conjugal infidelity" without incurring censure or retribution of any kind.[13]

Hammond's unapologetic tone, astonishing in itself, reveals much about his actual (as opposed to his rhetorical) sexual morality. The casual view he took of "dalliance" suggests that he had far more personal experience with it than we can currently document (indeed, aside from the 1846 run-in with Hampton we have no documentation). But his attitude towards "dalliance" is the least of it. His truculent defense of seducing teenage girls—relatives through marriage, no less—as an event of neither great import nor cause for remorse makes it hard to imagine what if any erotic expression he considered beyond the pale.

The "two" Hammonds—the youthful sexual adventurer of 1826 and the staid eminence of 1846—no longer seem unrelated. Hammond's range of sexual tastes as an older man may have narrowed (*may;* that impression could be due to the paucity of extant evidence), but his sex drive apparently remained strong, impulsive, self-justifying, defiant of the conventional mores of the day. The external circumstances of Hammond's life changed radically from youth to middle age, but his inner life apparently underwent less of a sea change.

As both a young and a middle-aged man, his lust—whether aroused by male college friends or by teenage female relatives—continued strong, arrogantly assertive, ungoverned. Hammond never seems to have struggled very hard to control it. Certainly not as a young man. Nothing in the 1826 letters suggests that Jim Hammond expended much energy, or saw any reason to restrain his impulses and curtail his pleasures. He may have made more of an effort as an older man, if only to maintain his public image for rectitude and to safeguard his privileges. Even that is conjecture; conjecture based, moreover, on our assumptions about what constitutes "logical" behavior for a man of Hammond's position. Judging from his actual behavior in the 1840s, and his indignant reaction to discovery and threatened exposure, our logic and values don't seem to coincide at all closely with Hammond's own.

Which deepens the enigma. How might we understand this uncategorizable man? Looked at from the angle of 1826, Hammond seems (by my mores) admirably playful, exploratory and freewheeling, uninhibited and attractively unapologetic. Looked at from the angle of 1846, he seems merely repulsive: grossly insensitive and irresponsible, perhaps pathologically willful. But possibly the change in perspective is at bottom a function of a shift in *our* angle of vision (and the moral assumptions which underlie it), not in Hammond himself; the shift in context between the 1826 and 1846 episodes encouraging us to adopt radically different judgments of what were in fact unwavering traits in his personality.

The discomforting fact is that we understand very little—whether about Hammond the man, or the alien social climate which made possible the 1826 Withers letters. Having exhausted the scanty historical data available for trying to construct a plausible context in which to read the erotic meaning of those letters, we can only fall back on conjecture. The tone of Withers' letters—consistently ironic and playful—strongly suggests that his erotic involvement with Hammond carried no "romantic" overtones. Not that we can be sure. Irony, as we know, is a common device for concealing emotion. Besides, an occasional phrase in the letter—such as Withers' reference to the "exquisite touch" of Hammond's "long fleshen pole"—could be read as more than "playful." Unfortunately, no other correspondence from the period of remotely comparable content exists to which we might turn in an attempt to draw parallels, clarify attitudes, consolidate or amplify tentative "conclusions."

Given our impoverished results in trying to pin down what the two letters mean, it might be thought foolish to move beyond the Withers/Hammond relationship itself and try posing broader questions still: "foolish," because to do so invites additional futility and frustration. Yet broader questions are implicit in the material—they seem to suggest themselves—and posing them may alone be of value, though answers prove elusive.

The critical question, historically, is whether the same-gender erotic experiences suggested in the two letters should be regarded as "anomalous" or "representative." Was Withers' and Hammond's behavior unique, or does it reveal and illustrate a wider pattern of male-male relationships—till now unsuspected and undocumented, yet in some sense "typical" of their time, region, race, and class? The question, on its face, is an enigma wrapped in a mystery. At best, we can approach, not resolve it. Let the reader be forewarned: What follows is hypothesis nearly pure, to be taken with generous grains of salt.

The best clues are provided by the internal evidence of the letters themselves, and especially their tone. It has a consistent ring: offhanded, flip. Jeff's bantering call to repentance is transparently mocking, his "warnings of retribution" uniformly irreverent—"campy," in the modern vernacular. The letters are *so* devoid of any serious moral entreaty or fervor, of any genuine attempt to inspire shame or reformation, as to take on negative significance. The values and vocabulary of evangelical piety had not yet, in the 1820s, come to permeate American consciousness and discourse. Even when those values carried most influence—roughly 1830–1870—they seem to have held sway in the South to a lesser extent than elsewhere in the country.[14]

So the geographical locale and time period in which Jeff and Jim grew up may be important factors in explaining their freewheeling attitudes. The American South of the latter part of the eighteenth and early part of the nineteenth centuries was (for privileged, young, white males) one of those rare "liberal interregnums" in our history when the body could be treated as a natural source of pleasure and "wanton" sexuality viewed as the natural prerogative—the exemplification even—of "manliness."

In this sense, Jeff and Jim's relaxed attitude toward sex in general, far from being anomalous, may have been close to mainstream mores. Whether that also holds for their high-spirited, unself-conscious attitude about same-gender sexuality is more problematic. At the least, Jeff's light-hearted comedic descriptions of male bedfellows "poking and punching" each other with their "fleshen poles" seems so devoid of furtiveness or shame that it is possible to believe male-male sexual contact was nowhere nearly stigmatized to the degree long assumed. Withers and Hammond, after all, were ambitious aspirants to positions of leadership and power. Could Hammond have indulged so freely (and Withers described so casually) behavior widely deemed disgraceful and abhorrent, outside the range of "permissible" experience? If homoeroticism had been utterly taboo, wouldn't one expect Withers' tone to betray some evidence of guilt and unease? Instead, it is breezy and nonchalant, raising the possibility that sexual contact between males (of a certain class, region, time, and place), if not commonplace, was not wholly proscribed either. Should that surmise be even marginally correct, our standard view of the history of male homosexuality in this country as an unrelieved tale of concealment and woe needs revision.[15]

The surmise, of course, is shaky, lacking any corroborating evidence, any additional documentation from the period recounting attitudes and experiences comparable to those of Jeff and Jim. That much is undeniable, but perhaps not in itself sufficient proof that same-gender sexuality never (or rarely) happened. Other corroborating records may still survive, and are only waiting to be retrieved. After all, to date we have accumulated only a tiny collection of historical materials that record the existence of *heterosexual* behavior in the past. Yet no one claims that that minuscule amount of evidence is an accurate measure of the actual amount of heterosexual activity which took place.

Just so with Jeff and Jim. What now appears unique and anomalous behavior may one day come to be seen as unexceptional—casually tolerated, if not actively encouraged or institutionalized. This will only happen if the new generation of scholars continues to press for access to previously suppressed materials and if the new generation of archivists continues to cultivate its sympathy toward such scholarship, declassifying "sensitive" data at an accelerated pace. I myself believe that additional source material, possibly a great deal of it, relating to the history of homosexuality has survived and awaits recovery from well-guarded vaults. I base this belief on my own research experiences over the past decade.

The two Withers/Hammond letters presented here are a case in point. Until they turned up, few if any scholars (myself included) would have credited the notion that "carefree" male-male eroticism ever existed in this country (let alone in the 1820s)—or that offhanded, unemphatic descriptions of it could ever be found.

In that vein, it may be worth providing some additional details about how the Withers/Hammond letters were discovered. The tale might encourage other scholars to persevere in the search for long-suppressed material; might suggest tactics for extracting it; might alert them to some of the obstacles and ploys custodial guardians will use to deflect the search—and might suggest how these can be neutralized or counteracted.

Recovering the Withers/Hammond Letters

In offering this cautionary tale, the chief purpose is not to establish the villainy of archivists. As a group, they are no more the enemy of innovative scholarship nor the defenders of traditional morality than are historians as a group—most of whom scornfully dismiss the study of sexual ideology and behavior as a non-subject. During my research travels to manuscript libraries, several individual archivists have been enormously supportive: people like Stephen T. Riley of the Massachusetts Historical Society, Sandra Taylor of the Lilly Library in Indiana, and Richard J. Wolfe of the Countway Library of Medicine in Boston. Such people (I could name others) acted from the conviction that research into the "history of intimacy" was overdue and held great potential importance for better understanding our national experience and character.

Their attitude is still a minority one within the archival profession as a whole (in the historical profession, too). Many of those who stand guard over the nation's major manuscript collections see their function as protective and preservative—of traditional moral values in general and of a given family's "good name" in particular. They tend to equate—as is true everywhere in academia, and perhaps to a greater degree than in the population at large—the libidinous with the salacious, and to be profoundly distrustful of both. Given this discomfort, some archivists invent obstacles to put in the researcher's path or claim to be hamstrung (and, in truth, even sympathetic curators sometimes *are*) by certain access restrictions which the donor of a given manuscript collection originally appended to the deed of gift.

The six-month tangle I had over the Withers/Hammond letters illustrates all this. The trail began (confining myself to the main outlines) with Catherine Clinton, then a doctoral student in history at Princeton. She first brought the letters to my attention, and although she has modestly asked that her efforts not be detailed, I did at least want to acknowledge her pivotal role.[16] Once having seen the letters and realized their importance, I started in motion the standard procedures for acquiring permission to publish manuscript materials. On March 6, 1979, I sent a formal request to that effect to the South Caroliniana Library (henceforth, SCL), where the original letters are housed.

That move, according to one of the several legal experts I later consulted, was my first, and worst, mistake. By formally requesting permission, I was (to quote the expert) being "super-dutiful" and, in the process, making life infinitely more difficult for *all* parties concerned. Technically, I had done the "correct" thing—I had gone through proper channels, adhered to the terms most manuscript libraries require regarding permission to publish manuscript material. But in real life, my chiding expert added, what is technically correct can prove functionally awkward. In practice, it seems (and after twenty years of archival research, this came as a surprise to me), some scholars publish manuscript material without making any formal request to do so. And libraries, it seems, prefer it that way. A formal request, after all, requires a formal reply. The given library is pressured to make a clear-cut decision, one that can place it (sometimes unwillingly and unfairly) in a no-win situation: Should the library grant permission, it risks the wrath of a donor or family descendant, charges of dereliction, possible loss of future acquisitions; should the library deny permission, it risks accusations of censorship from an outraged scholar. Let others take note: Though archivists will not or cannot say so openly, they may well prefer to be handed a *fait accompli*, and will feel silently grateful to researchers who adopt what might be called the Macbeth ploy: "Do what ye need to do, but tell me not of it till after 'tis done" (roughly paraphrased).

Lacking such wisdom at the time, I instead sent off a formal letter requesting permission to publish. This left SCL with two choices: to act on my request (which, given the contents of the 1826 letters, almost certainly assured a negative response), or to do nothing. They opted for the latter, letting my letter go unanswered. If SCL had thereby meant to signal me to proceed (quietly) without insisting on their formal acquiescence, I misread the signal. Instead of quietly retreating, I noisily persisted. On April 15 I sent them a second letter, a near duplicate of the first. That, too, went unacknowledged. I got angry (blame it on the Zodiac: Leos can't stand being ignored). In early June, after thirteen weeks without a response, I sent—no, shot off by certified mail—a third letter, this one longer and decidedly more testy than its predecessors. SCL's obdurate silence, I wrote, could be interpreted either as "silence giving consent" or as a subtly calculated attempt at censorship. Should I opt for the first interpretation (my letter went on), I would simply publish the letters without further ado—and on the assumption I had tacit approval. Should I instead opt for the second interpretation—their disapproval—I would then feel an obligation to other scholars to report the incident to the prestigious Joint Committee of Historians and Archivists, a group empowered to deal with matters of censorship. While deciding between the two courses of action, my letter concluded, "I would be glad to receive any information which might have a bearing on my pending decision." (Leos get snotty when pushed.)

Within the week, I got a reply—proving once more, I suppose, that threats may not bring out the best in people, but they do bring out something. The reply came from SCL's director (Dr. Archer, I'll call him). He began by expressing regret that I had "found it necessary to write such a sharp letter"—although he acknowledged that the delayed response to my previous letters might have contributed to my ill temper. Nonetheless, he went on, I could surely understand that he had had to put my letters aside while "awaiting a convenient opportunity" to seek advice "on the status of the restrictions" attached to the Hammond Papers. Such an opportunity had finally presented itself; he was now able to report that the original donor of the Hammond Papers had "asked" (the choice of word, subsequently pointed out by several of my legal consultants, is significant, implying as it does a request from the donor, not a binding stipulation) that none of the manuscripts be used in a way that might "result in embarrassment to descendants." The donor was dead, but Dr. Archer considered the "restriction" to be "still in force." He was also of the view that the two Withers letters were unquestionably "embarrassing." Therefore, he had decided to deny my request to publish them.

In a curious concluding paragraph, Archer suggested he might reconsider my request if I could provide "full assurances" that the letters would be published in such a way as to disguise their provenance and prevent their identification with Hammond or Withers—if I would agree, in short, to strip the letters of all historical context, a context integral to their meaning and importance, and treat them as floating objects unanchored in time or space. That suggestion struck me as comparable to insisting a Haydn string quartet be performed solely with tambourines and vibraharp. I declined the suggestion.

I embarked instead on a double course: drafting a reply to Dr. Archer and starting up a round of consultations with various scholars, friends, and legal experts about what to include in my reply. My advisors diverged on this or that particular, but concurred on the main one: Legally and morally, I was justified in proceeding straightaway to publication. In support of that conclusion, they cited several arguments but put special stress on the legal doctrine of "fair usage"; an author's right to quote (without permission) an appropriate amount of copyrighted material. The body of law defining what does or does not constitute a "fair" amount of unauthorized quotation has shifted over time, but in recent years (most significantly in *Nizer* v. *Rosenberg*) the courts have leaned consistently toward a permissive view.*

---

*In the years since the publication of this article, the courts have dramatically curtailed "fair usage."

One of the experts I consulted in copyright law felt "absolutely confident" that I was entitled to publish the two Withers letters *in full*, if I wished—though I ultimately decided to use only the erotic portions as relevant to my purpose. In that expert's opinion, SCL "had already fatally weakened its copyright claim to the Hammond Papers, however unintentionally." The library's long-standing practice of allowing scholars access to the papers (instead of sealing them off) was tantamount to admitting that the original deed of gift had not been encumbered by any substantive, detailed restrictions—and that aside from some vague admonitory advice, the donor had apparently left final discretionary power to the library itself. The fact that SCL had, in addition, catalogued the two Withers letters and provided photocopies of them on request had further weakened their position in the view of the copyright lawyers—indeed, had made my legal right to publish "unassailable." All this I dutifully incorporated in the ongoing draft of my letter to Dr. Archer. In the upshot, I never sent it. My Council of Experts finally persuaded me that I had nothing further to gain and might needlessly stir quiet waters. As one consultant put it, "If you formally notify SCL of your intention to publish, the library might feel obligated to bring suit, though they'd much prefer not to, given their shaky legal case and the additional publicity any litigation would give to the contents of the letters. Do yourself and them a favor: Say and write nothing further; simply proceed to publication."

Which is what I did. Not, I should add, without misgivings. I felt a direct challenge to SCL, though it would likely have involved time-consuming, expensive litigation, might have yielded an important precedent useful to future scholars. I also regretted that Dr. Archer had never gotten the chance to read my unmailed final letter, especially the part in which I had asked him to spell out his specific reasons for deciding that publication of the Withers manuscripts would prove an "embarrassment." "For two men like Hammond and Withers," I had written Archer (hot tongue in hard cheek), "who have gone down in history as among the country's staunchest defenders of human slavery, I should think their reputations could only be enhanced by the playful, raucous—the humanizing —revelations contained in the two letters." Yes, I was being patently disingenuous; and yes, it was unlikely I could force from Dr. Archer an explicit avowal of homophobia. Still, it would have done my soul good to try (it's doing it some good just quoting the unsent letter here).

Certain ethical considerations implicit in my decision to publish the Withers letters without authorization leave me the most uncomfortable: that familiar array of moral conundrums (in however diminutive a form) long associated with acts of "civil disobedience." To explain why I proceeded nonetheless, I have to step back a bit and approach the matter indirectly through some general observations.

There is a long-standing and long-sanctified notion that academia consists of a "community of scholars"—in the ideal sense of a disinterested collectivity of truth-seekers. This is an exalted, but to me, illusory conceit. In practice, as I see it, the notion has served as a useful device for codifying professional behavior and a convenient rationale for denying credentials to those who might challenge the academy's entrenched values—women, gays, ethnic minorities. The conceit of a community of scholars, in short, has characteristically been a blind for parochialism and discrimination.

Yet the *ideal* of such a community remains attractive (as does the related notion that a genuinely unharnessed scholarship could provide needed data for challenging the status quo and nurturing alternative visions of the good society). In my view, a scholar's prime allegiance and responsibility should be to the ideal itself, not to those academic guilds which claim to represent it (even as they enforce standards for membership and employ definitions of "legitimate" inquiry that straightjacket and subvert it). Most of the scholarship emanating from universities functions primarily, if "unintentionally," to rationalize existing arrangements of power; and the academic guilds, in excluding or ostracizing mavericks, play an important role in perpetuating such arrangements.

What may seem obvious on an abstract level becomes less so when reduced to a personal one; then the whole question of "responsibility" becomes much stickier. As someone who chose to join the academic community and to remain in it (with attendant profit, such as a secure salary), it could be argued that I, and others like me, are obligated either to abide by academe's conventions or—if convinced we cannot—to resign. In response to that argument, I would say that a scholar owes *primary* allegiance to what academe might be—to its promise, not its practice—and would add the specific observation that academe's own official standards about what constitutes "acceptable" professorial behavior and proper scholarly inquiry are muddled and slippery. To give one example, there is no agreement among university-affiliated historians about what constitutes "correct" (or even preferred) research procedures, modes of analysis or styles of presentation: Cliometricians battle impressionists, generalists disparage specialists, literary stylists war with statistical analysts.

Adding to the confusion is academe's contradictory record in its treatment of dissenters. It is not a record of monolithic repression. Many principled and innovative academicians have indeed suffered grievously for their political, personal, and professional nonconformity (as well as for belonging to a particular sex, class, and race). But it is also true that academe has sometimes honored its eccentrics and insurgents, if often belatedly; the political radical William Appleman Williams was elected president of the Organization of American Historians. While the academy is assuredly not the free-swinging arena of open inquiry its champions claim, neither is it as tightly sealed against novelty or as unvaryingly hostile to fractious upstarts, as its detractors insist.

Academe's ambiguous traditions help persuade many intellectuals who by temperament, conviction, or lifestyle are "deviant"—i.e. outside mainstream orthodoxy—to establish and maintain university affiliations. Some of these intellectuals would claim ("lull themselves into believing," left-wing skeptics might say) that academe is one of the few arenas in which innovative inquiry remains possible, and that the "long march through the institutions" at present seems the only promising tactic available for creating substantive social change. But others among the group of "deviant" intellectuals do worry that by retaining their ties to academic disciplines and educational institutions which function essentially as "conservators"—preservers and transmitters of conventional knowledge and norms—that they are putting their own values at risk. The danger of co-optation is always present; unorthodoxy and personal integrity can be gradually, sometimes undiscernibly, sapped. The best one can do to guard against that prospect is to try to stay vigilant—in touch with the different drummer within, resistant to the efforts to muffle it. But vows of vigilance, as we know, are more easily made than kept.

Anyway, that's about as close as I can come to delineating (and possibly idealizing) the relationship I've tried to maintain within the academic world, and also to conveying, however circuitous the route, some of the ingredients that went into my inner debate about publishing the Withers/Hammond letters. By finally deciding to publish them against the wishes of their official custodian, my own personal discomfort played a considerable role—discomfort at the prospect of yielding to the prevailing (and to my mind dangerously narrow) view of what is acceptable historical inquiry and, by implication, "permissible" norms of behavior. I also concluded, on more general grounds, that the public *does* have the "right to know"—and in regard to the Withers letters specifically, the gay public has a desperate *need* to know.

That last consideration proved decisive. I felt it was essential to challenge the tradition of suppressing information which might prove useful to gay people in better understanding the historical dimensions of our experience, the shifting strategies we have adopted over time to cope with oppression, and the varied styles we have developed to express our special sensibilities. If the "lawless" tactics I've resorted to seem extreme to some, well, so is our need; more orthodox tactics (like polite letters of inquiry), have done little to meet it. The heterosexist world has long held a monopoly on defining legal and ethical propriety, has long imposed its definitions on the rest of us, using them as weapons for keeping us in line by denying us access to knowledge of our own antecedents. Let heterosexism take the blame then if, having finally despaired of gaining that knowledge by humble petition through proper channels, we now turn, by default and in anger at the continuing impasse, to "improper" tactics. It seems better to stand accused of impropriety than to go on accepting someone else's right to control access to *our* heritage.

Power has created that "right" in the past. In the future, other claims to right must be pressed—like the right of a people to a knowledge of its own history (to *memory*), an indispensable prerequisite for establishing collective identity and for enjoying the solace of knowing that we too have "come through," are bearers of a diverse, rich, unique heritage. To press those claims, it may be necessary to defy entrenched conventions and to risk the attendant consequences, professional and legal, of doing so, which is not the sort of thing one welcomes. Yet the alternative is still less palatable: to continue to accept and abide by anachronistic definitions of what constitutes "sensitive material" and "acceptable" areas of historical inquiry. To go that route is to collaborate in sustaining "things as they are"—to be complicitous, in sum, in our own oppression.

KNIGHTS-ERRANT AND GOTHIC SEDUCERS: THE REPRESENTATION OF MALE FRIENDSHIP IN MID-NINETEENTH-CENTURY AMERICA

◆

ROBERT K. MARTIN

A variety of popular fictions of mid-nineteenth-century America include frequent depictions of male friendships in ways that indicate the troubled status of those relationships. By analyzing the nearly forgotten novels of Theodore Winthrop, this essay reveals two dramatically different images of male friendship: the chivalric knight-errant who is sworn to fraternal loyalty with his fellow warrior, and the Gothic seducer who threatens rape as the consequence of an exploration of the unknown. Such provocative images coincided in nineteenth-century fiction with the better-known pastoral figures of Whitman's *Calamus* or the cross-racial love of Ishmael and Queequeg in *Moby-Dick*.

Rather than seeing a gulf between the normal and the abnormal, we [should] view sexual and emotional impulses as part of a continuum or spectrum of affect gradations strongly affected by cultural norms and arrangements.[1]

Despite Michel Foucault's brilliant explosion of the "repressive hypothesis,"[2] we are all still all too likely to imagine sexual rebels such as Walt Whitman standing alone against their time. If it is true that no one else in the America of the mid-nineteenth century gave quite the inflection to male love that Whitman did, the subject was far from absent elsewhere.

In popular novels with readerships hundreds, even thousands, of times those of Whitman, in letters and in diaries, American men at mid-century loved each other, sought verbal and physical forms for the expression of that love, located it in a tradition, and worried about its place in a social order.

An amusing example of the ways in which nineteenth-century male friendship has been denied may be seen in a critical study of Bayard Taylor, the most outspoken advocate of "the other love" in mid-century America. Writing in 1936, Richard Croom Beatty provided several pages of evidence for Taylor's homosexuality, but presented them in an ironic tone of voice, as the "distort[ions]" of "Freudians." Beatty's evidence includes Taylor's "fervent love" for George Henry Boker as well as literary texts such as "Twin Love" (1871) about two boys (called David and Jonathan!) who, when living apart, are "as unhappy as separated lovers," or the more famous *Joseph and His Friend* (1870), from which he quotes a passage in celebration of a "manly love, rarer, alas! but as tender and true as the love of woman." Beatty's denial of the very evidence he assembles is offered in the name of historical accuracy: "The truth is that Taylor was quite healthy, quite safe, and for his day quite normal" (288–90). Beatty's statement raises some important questions about social and cultural shifts in the definition of the boundaries of normality. By the 1930s Taylor's close friendships had become evidence for accusations of "abnormality," against which Beatty felt the need to defend him. While we may be amused by Beatty's attempt to make Taylor "safe," we must acknowledge that he was perceived as "normal" in his time (that is, his personal friendships and his spirited defense of the right to intense male friendship opposed to heterosexual love were openly acknowledged by his family and his biographer and were no impediment to his obtaining high public office)[3] and felt no need to suppress the evidence of his intense male friendships and their physical expression in kisses and embraces. A modern insistence on Taylor's "homosexuality" may be as blunt and culturally blind as Beatty's insistence on "normality," a term that can only be understood in a social context. It remains to be learned what was "normal" "for [Taylor's] day."[4]

The biography of Taylor published a year after his death by Russell Conwell makes it clear that Taylor's friendships were, at least to a degree, part of the permissible discourse of the time. Conwell calls Taylor's friendship for the German with whom he travelled to Egypt "a second love" (160), and asserts that he "felt a love for him like that of Jonathan for David" (170). Taylor himself, encouraged perhaps by the example of Goethe's *Westostlicher Divan*, published such poems as "To a Persian Boy" (1851): "I beheld thine eyes,/ And felt the wonder of thy beauty grow/ Within my brain" (*Poetical Works*, 63), or "Hylas" (1850), with its frank celebration of adolescent beauty:

Dewy and sleek his dimpled shoulders rounded
To the white arms and whiter breast between them.
Downward, the supple lines had less of softness;
His back was like a god's; his loins were moulded
As if some pulse of power began to waken. (73)

He wrote with enthusiasm to Whitman after reading *Leaves of Grass*,
praising "that tender and noble love of man for man which once certainly
existed, but now seems to have gone out of the experience of the race" (2
December 1866; Traubel, 153). What made such frank celebration of
male love and male beauty possible? How and when did it disappear, or
go underground? Putting it in somewhat different terms, and shifting our
focus to England, what made *In Memoriam* (1850) possible as a work in
celebration of male friendship ("the comrade of my choice . . . /The
human-hearted man I loved") by the poet laureate of England? The
debate has too often been between those who argue that the friendship of
such a text means nothing and those who argue that it means exactly what
we now mean by homosexuality. The truth perhaps lies between, in a
way that can only be understood as the product of a relationship between
desire and social formations, one that allows such a friendship to be at
once "normal" and sexual. We may make a start toward answering
questions about the social meanings of such texts by examining the nature
of male friendship as it was celebrated in popular literary works of the
mid-nineteenth century.

In the 1830s and 1840s American male writers seem to have located
their erotic fantasies in the South Seas, in a pattern that would find later
echoes in writers such as Stevenson, Loti, Brooke, and Maugham, as well
as artists such as Gauguin. The "noble savages" of these exotic lands
provided both sexual excitement and cultural difference. Travel accounts
both depended upon and undercut the colonial systems that provided the
first encounters between north and south and that could draw upon the
earlier European stereotype of the appeal of the south, and its association
with forbidden love. The South Seas thus assumed for many artists the
role that had been played by Greece and Italy.[5] Love for the young men
of the South Seas was thus not only personal affection, but a political
response as well to a (Western) culture increasingly put into question.
Richard Henry Dana's account of his friendships in *Two Years Before the
Mast* (1840) may be taken as a paradigmatic text, since it served as at
least a partial model for later works including Melville's *Typee* (1846)
and Charles Warren Stoddard's *South Sea Idyls* (1873). Dana's presentation of friendship is clearly demarcated along racial lines. Bill Jackson, a
"fine specimen of manly beauty" (90–91), is given the attributes of
classical beauty and strength. He is not far from the sailors in the
romantic friendships of Captain Marryat's novels. Hope, the young Hawaiian who is Dana's special friend or *aikane*, serves to demonstrate, by

contrast, the failures of Western civilization. Dana learns to respect the "affection" he feels for Hope, despite his race which renders him simply "a d——d Kanaka" (255) for the captain. He is thus the model for the morally superior Queequeg who must teach Ishmael the lessons of love as a means to overturning a capitalist order of power.[6] Apparently such lessons could only be learned outside the boundaries, and hence the moral limits, of nineteenth-century America.

Two very popular works of mid-century by Theodore Winthrop, set in America, offer an illustration of the range and possibility of male friendship in works without the excuse, or camouflage, of exoticism. Son of a distinguished family, descendant of Governor John Winthrop and of Jonathan Edwards, Winthrop never found a firm place for himself in the rapidly changing world of mid-century America. He saw himself as curiously dislocated in the world of work, remarking in his diary, "I am afraid that I have lived too much among women" (22 September 1848, quoted Propst, 8). He was unable to publish any of his novels during his lifetime. After his death in the first days of the Civil War, Winthrop became a popular and widely read author. Five volumes of his work were published from 1861 to 1863 by the famous Boston publishers Ticknor and Fields (Hawthorne's publishers), and one hundred editions had appeared by 1900.

Winthrop's novel *John Brent*, based on his experiences in the American West, went through twenty-eight editions following its first publication in 1862. Although there are elements of a conventional heterosexual love story, particularly at the end of the novel, most of the book is devoted to the adventures of Richard Wade, the narrator, and his friend John Brent.[7] The first three chapters consist of an ecstatic account of the relationship between Wade and his black stallion, Don Fulano, of whom he reports, "I loved that horse as I have loved nothing else yet" (50). Wade's relationship to the horse is consistently presented in terms of (male) friendship and sexuality. When he first sees the stallion, "He pranced and curvetted as if he were the pretty plaything of a girl"; later the horse "put his head upon my shoulder, [and] suffered me to put my arm around his neck" (39). Wade rides the horse only through an act of sympathetic joining: "He did not obey, but consented. I exercised no control. We were of one mind. We became a Centaur"(50). These terms are nothing compared to the ardor lavished on the book's "real hero," John Brent.

When Wade first sees Brent, he takes him for an Indian, and specifically one linked to the tradition of the handsome Indian created by James Fenimore Cooper's novels:

"The Adonis of the copperskins!" I said to myself. . . . "A beautiful youth! O Fenimore, why are you dead! There are a dozen romances in one look of that young brave. . . . What a poem the fellow is! I wish I was an Indian myself for such a companion; or, better, a squaw, to be made love to by him."(52)

Wade's response is fascinating in its indication of the extent to which Cooper had already been identified, within a few years of his death, with the creation of the erotic male Indian.[8] Wade's initial phrase for the young man, "Adonis of the copperskins," testifies to the ways in which two cultural myths, one European and one American, were being con-flated. The beautiful Greek youth killed by Aphrodite and serving as a figure of doomed male beauty was reborn in the figure of the handsome Indian, his copper skin at once precious and natural. The American West was still seen in part as a recaptured Arcadia, and thus its appeal could be associated with the Romantic revival of interest in Greek mythology as a source of cultural renewal and personal fulfillment. The quests of Ameri-can poets and novelists of this period are thus direct counterparts to the Byronic image of Greece: a place where personal liberty, political liberty, and erotic attraction were joined.[9] (It may well be that the image of the berdache as recorded by early travellers and artists and given particular prominence in the 1830s by George Catlin's drawings of Indian ceremoni-als colored the erotic perception of the American Indian, especially when, as in the passage from John Brent, it could be joined to the idea of Greek homosexuality.) The white representative of a culture largely judg-ing itself effete is sexually drawn to a figure of potency that is at once personal and cultural: The appeal of the North American Indian is the appeal of a newly "masculinized" culture for the highly "European" hero. Wade's concluding line situates for us the precariousness of the position being staked out in such texts: It is but a tiny step from being the companion to being the "squaw." What remains striking is that such a wish can be expressed openly, even if not directly fulfilled, in a text that is so thoroughly conventional. Winthrop's readers were apparently undis-turbed by such a wish, perhaps because it was expressed in a way that posed no challenge to the gender economy. As men, they can be compan-ions; but in order to "be made love to," Wade would have to be a squaw. Their love can be celebrated in a system in which genital expression is unthinkable, precisely because it would require such an act of transforma-tion. Within the framework of a conventional male-female love, posited as a future goal and located safely distant, all degrees of male friendship can be explored.

It turns out that the "brave" is actually an old college friend. His new masculinity is the result of "ten years of experience [that] have taken all the girl out of" him. When the two boys first knew each other, Brent "was a delicate, beautiful, dreamy boy" (53) who complemented Wade's more prosaic nature. Time has rendered him less feminine, but also brought him more into harmony with the natural world (as Wade's first mistaking him for an Indian suggests). He seems to Wade a magician who can make the ordinary marvelous, with enthusiasm for everything he encounters. These qualities permit Wade to rediscover his adolescent love: "I learned to love the man John Brent, as I had loved the boy; but as mature man loves man. I have known no more perfect union than that one friendship. Nothing so tender in any of my transitory loves for women" (63). The contrast is explicit: the love of the two men provides a "more perfect union" than any marriage; it lasts through changes, while the love of women is merely "transitory." It is clear that such a relationship, although including some acknowledgment of femininity at its origins, in the appeal of the "delicate" boy, is based upon the idea of a masculine world that is linked culturally and textually to the rediscovery of the primitive. Put another way, this love is in part the expression of a flight from civilization, from the encumbrances of a social world where it can have no place. The homoerotic cowboy romance, which lingered on in popular culture well into the twentieth century (and was so well known that it could be parodied in *Lonesome Cowboys*), was not simply a result of the relative absence of women; the West served as a place that was an increasingly threatened refuge for the "masculine." The disparate locales of the text, from the American West of the men's adventure to the London of reunion and marriage, make it clear that woman's domain is the city and the home, while man's is the college and the open sky.

The terms under which the two men can affirm their friendship are those of fraternity, the sense of shared responsibility for an inadequate and endangered woman. By choosing their fraternal affections, these friends become more than mere brothers, and rise to the level of "completed brotherhood," or "knight-errantry" (136–37). This concept, which is based on the idea of an exclusive world of male privilege, runs through much of the history of male friendship, with origins in the "sacred band" of Theban warriors, who pledged love to each other and fought together,[10] and literary repercussions from classical epics to modern popular culture. It would gain particular prominence in the theoretical writings of proto-Nazism (such as those of Blüher) and the fictions of D. H. Lawrence. It lacks the socialist and feminist concerns of the other, egalitarian strain of nineteenth-century male friendship, to which Whitman gave rise, and helps to explain why so many of the figures under consideration, such as Taylor or Winthrop, could be at once fervent advocates of male friendship and defenders of an aristocratic, masculinist culture. Wade and Brent gallop "side by side" in furious flight from an increasingly feminine world in which they fear they will have no place; their search is ultimately for an imagined past before the civilizing entry of women.

The connections between intense male friendship and certain forms of heterosexuality are suggested by Winthrop. The two young men "in brotherhood had trained each other to high thoughts of courtesy and love" (163). Their friendship serves thus as a kind of apprenticeship to a later relationship of service, or courtesy (it is striking that "love" follows "courtesy" in Wade's account). In fact it even allows for the possibility that it may never achieve this second stage, since "it might be that the wounded knight would never know his lady." What is crucial to recognize is that the patterns of male relationship outlined in Winthrop's text do not stand in opposition to heterosexuality.[11] It is assumed that one leads to, and is in service to, the other. At the same time, the structuring of the narrative so that Ellen, the presumed object of desire, is offstage for most of the novel, first captured by hostile Indians and then with her father in England, allows for the full exploration of male friendship and the virtual silencing of heterosexuality (and, not incidentally, of women). Thoughts of the worthlessness of the beloved he will ultimately renounce for his friend's sake fill Wade as he and the wounded Brent travel East. The terms in which they are expressed give some indication of the stresses underlying this triangular romance:

> Did she love him? Ah! that is the ancient riddle. Only the Sphinx herself can answer. Those fair faces of women, with their tender smiles, their quick blushes, their starting tears, still wear a mask until the moment comes for unmasking. If she did not love him—this man of all men most lovable, this feminine soul in the body of a hero, this man who had spilled his blood for her, . . . if she did not love him, she must be, I thought, some bloodless creature of a type other than human, an angel and no woman, a creature not yet truly embodied into the body of love we seemed to behold. (173)

The legend of Oedipus evoked here, through the references to the riddle and the Sphinx, suggests the ancient association of heterosexuality with incest and animality. Woman is seen as the devouring Sphinx, a challenging reminder of the bestial. All of women's femininity may thus be unmasked as mere lust, the horrifying animal genitals beneath the "higher," angelic self. The two dominant nineteenth-century images of woman—the demon and the angel—are here both negative, with the implication that only the self-sacrificing Wade is worthy of Brent's love, not the woman who must always be either too much body or not enough. The strong misogynistic accents of this passage are joined to the elevation of the feminine, in what is only an apparent paradox: for both the hatred of women and the elevation of women act as means of prohibiting relations between men and women other than those of property. While the beloved is fantasized as a vampire, the dying knight is seen in terms (the "feminine soul in the body of a hero") that strikingly anticipate late-nineteenth-century definitions of homosexuality, first formulated a few years after Winthrop's novel was published: the "feminine soul in the [male] body."[12] Brent's love gives him a feminine soul, just as the woman's presumed indifference unmasks her as the beast beneath the smile. At the same time we have a better view of Wade's attraction to Brent; Brent brings together the fetishized male body and the "feminine soul," what Wade has earlier called the "delicate, beautiful, [and] dreamy." Thus the "feminine" itself is divided and dispersed, its higher qualities attributed to men, its lower qualities reserved for women. In such a construction, male friendship accomplishes its elevation of the feminine without the female.

Another novel of Winthrop's, *Cecil Dreeme*, gives further evidence of the insistence with which close male friendship was inscribed in the popular culture of mid-century America. Totally urban in setting, this novel cannot draw upon the tradition of Indian beauty for its model of masculinity; it is thus at once more classical in its references and, in its use of transvestism, more daring in its exploration of gender. It is a major text of what Eve Kosofsky Sedgwick has called "homosexual panic."[13] The hero finds himself between two forms of male love, one sinister, the other gentle, and ultimately chooses the "good" man, but only through an extraordinary turn of the plot in which he is revealed to be a woman, and thus all obstacles to their love dissolve. Much of the tension of the novel derives from the hero's simultaneous attraction/repulsion, as much of its humor is based on deep anxiety about male friendship and gender definition. By moving male relationships indoors, Winthrop has lost the ability to see his heroes as knights of the Western prairies, and must now face the delicate problem of placing them in a social context.

The villain, Densdeth, is introduced in terms that immediately suggest the sexual context as well as Winthrop's persistent racism. Speaking to his old friend Stillfleet, Robert Byng identifies Densdeth as "the cleverest man I have ever met" and describes him as "handsome as Alcibaides, or perhaps I should say Absalom, as he is Hebrewish" (23). The reference can hardly be casual. On the one hand, it embodies a form of the Hellenic/Hebraic distinction so crucial to nineteenth-century thought, and soon to be given definitive expression by Matthew Arnold in *Culture and Anarchy* (1869). Arnold's contrast between the freedom and self-expression of Hellenism and the narrow moralism of Hebraism would become a central text in the process of recovery of Greek culture and its reclamation for a homosexual ethos, in writers such as Pater and Wilde. To draw upon the figure of Alcibaides, however, was also to make a direct reference to the central text of male love, *The Symposium*, one that had only recently been provided intact for English readers.[14] By shifting from Alcibaides to Absalom, Winthrop sets up his central contrast between two forms of male love: one Greek and presumably pure, the other Hebrew and impure. One leads to philosophy, the other to death. Byng and Stillfleet are also imagined in terms drawn from the Greeks. When Byng agrees to take over Stillfleet's apartment, he wonders if Stillfleet can trust him, to which his friends replies, "Haven't we been brats together, lads together, men together? . . . Haven't we been the historic friends, Demon and Pythagoras,—no, Damon and Pythias?" (32–33). The allusion is treated in an interestingly ambivalent manner. The reference to the "historic friends" suggests the role that a Greek model of heroic friendship played for Winthrop and his time.[15] Damon and Pythias offered the example of a culturally authorized story of self-sacrificial fraternal love. But there is an immediate attempt to undercut, or ironize, that model by the play on the names, particularly when it involves a play on the demonic. There can be no doubt about the troubled status of such verbal structures; they give voice to the difficulties Winthrop faced as he tried to resituate collegiate friendships in a world of adult sexuality.

Densdeth is a fascinating embodiment of the anxiety produced by male love. He anticipates in striking ways a figure such as Lord Henry in Wilde's *The Picture of Dorian Gray*, "the tall, graceful young man . . . [with a] romantic olive-coloured face and worn expression." Like Wilde's portrait of the seducer, Densdeth is attractive, worldly, exotic, and slightly feminine. He is accompanied, in a pattern that would later recur in such figures as Mandrake and Lothar or the Lone Ranger and Tonto, by a black servant, presented in racist terms as "black, ugly, and brutal as the real Mumbo Jumbo" (64). The male couple here serves as a physical confirmation of what can only be suggested in the text, as the realization of male sexuality in a union with the dark and forbidden. To be a male homosexual is thus to couple with the devil, to embrace the primitive, for it was these figures that the African represented metonymically in the popular culture of the mid-nineteenth century.[16] In the American context, the *locus classicus* is Poe's *Arthur Gordon Pym* (1838), particularly the couple Pym and the "dusky, fiendish" Dirk Peters (whose phallicism could hardly be underlined more than by his name), but it often overlaps with the association of the Indian (Peters himself is an Indian although his head is said by Pym to look like that of "most Negroes") with witchcraft and devil-worship and, hence, anality (as in *The Scarlet Letter* [1850]). At the same time the African serves as a reminder of Densdeth's "real" or hidden self, like the portrait in *Dorian Gray* or Mr. Hyde in Stevenson's novel. Winthrop makes this reading explicit when Byng remarks, "At the moments when I mistrusted Densdeth, I felt that the Afreet's repulsive appearance more fitly interpreted his master's soul than the body by which it acted" (64).

Densdeth's power over Byng is extraordinary, joining the sexual and the economic with the magical. He is a kind of sorcerer whose eyes are agents of possession. As Byng imagines his thoughts, they are astonishing in their frankness: "I saw on the steamer that you were worth buying, worth perverting. I have spent more civility than usual on you already. How much more have I to pay? Are you a cheap commodity? Or must I give time and pains and study to make you mine?" What Byng ascribes to Densdeth is the power and the maliciousness of the Gothic villain, in a manner that shifts the focus of the victim from the female to the male: Densdeth is the dark seducer, here revealing to Byng his own darkest, most hidden self. For Byng finds himself here feminized, that is, read as the woman to be purchased and corrupted; but the presence of the concept of "perverting" makes it clear that this feminization is precisely what is feared in homosexual panic: the loss of male autonomy and power.

To accept the embrace of Densdeth is to succumb to Densdeth's other self, the dark African, to accept, symbolically at least, anal penetration (entry into the darkness within), and thus to make oneself over as female, a commodity to be exchanged. These "horrors" are evidently not without their attractions, however, since Byng fears that Densdeth may "master my will" through his "potency" (65). To repel him he must resort to "desperate evasion," a "feeble dodge." Once again the imagery of rape is dominant, and is accompanied by the fear of loss of self or will. It is the fear of a masculinity that has been projected outward, the male imagery that, exiled by Victorian proprieties, returned with a vengeance in such fantasies of possession and destruction. The power of such male figures (the hidden self, the vampire, the seducer, the mesmerist) for Victorian culture derived in part precisely from their removal from the sphere of culture; the fear was always in large part the fear of the return of the repressed self.

The power of such a male derived in part from his external concealing of his maleness, his projection of it as it were onto the African (a drama that was of course not only acted out in Victorian England and America but in the colonial empire as well, the destruction of native peoples and the imposition of white rule being a battle against a male self that had no place in a "feminized" culture). His external self was suave and civilized, indeed almost feminine (thus signalling his gender transgressions by a kind of inversion). Densdeth is marked by all the conventional signs of femininity. He is inscribed as the Oriental (he has a "marked Orientalism of face," and we have already observed his dangerous Hebraism) in a culture for which the Oriental figured the physical and sensual.[17] He "spoke with a delicate lisp, or rather Spanish softness" (74). This femininity is only superficial, for, like the emblem of the Sphinx, "there was a claw curled under the velvet." Densdeth's representation of evil derives in part from his *false* femininity. His evil is signalled by his assumption of a gender code to which he is not entitled, by his transgression of gender expectations. He is "too carefully dressed" and reveals himself by the presence of such signifiers as "a diamond stud, or an elaborate chain" (75).

Opposed to Densdeth, as the negative incarnation of the male love object, is Cecil Dreeme. The painter is recognized by Byng as the model for Cordelia in his painting of Lear and his Daughters, and in fact the play serves as a clue to the mystery of Cecil's identity. Cecil displays qualities of "tenderness, pity, undying love" (141). Because of them Byng feels a special love for him, one that is clearly marked off from the love of women: "His friendship I deemed more precious than the love of women"

(235) and "him I love with a love passing the love of women" (275). In both formulations, an echo of David's love for Jonathan is consciously evoked. Not only was that love authorized by its presentation in a sacred text, but the particular way in which it was formulated served the development of a concept of two loves. According to the Platonic definition, given such a central place in Victorian culture and used as a justification by many early homosexual apologists, the love for Cecil is thus a higher, more spiritual love, while the attraction is a lower, more bestial one.[18] And yet the terms have been reversed, for Densdeth has taken on the part reserved by Diotima's theory (in *The Symposium*) for woman's love, while Cecil, the disguised female, takes on the part reserved for the love of a young man. Byng's love for Cecil thus accomplishes a double strategy: It expresses the need for a refusal of physical love, and it makes Greek love "safe," by rereading it in heterosexual terms.

At the same time the conclusion is strikingly ambivalent. Although Cecil is revealed to be a woman, and thus the love can be consummated in a polite novel, the entire action of the novel has been based on the assumption that he is a man. Byng has fallen in love with a man, albeit a feminine man, and it is with him that he remains at the end. In fact he is less than enthusiastic about the revelation of gender: "Every moment it came to me more distinctly that Cecil Dreeme and I could never be Damon and Pythias again. Ignorantly I had loved my friend as one loves a woman only. This was love,—unforced, self-created, undoubting, complete. And now that the friend proved a woman, a great gulf opened between us" (347–48). Romantic love offers no equivalent to the totality and frankness of male comradeship. Thus the novel's happy ending is a distinctly mixed one. The thrust of its inner text is not toward the revelation of Cecil as a woman, but to the contrast of two forms of male love, toward the search for a male love that will not be sullied by the flesh. Paradoxically, that can only be achieved in the love of a woman disguised as a man.

Winthrop apparently modelled Cecil Dreeme on William Henry Hurlbut, a native of South Carolina and a beloved friend of Thomas Wentworth Higginson when the two were at Harvard in the 1840s.[19] Higginson wrote, in answer to a question about any intimate friends, "I never loved but one male friend with passion—and for him my love had no bounds—all that my natural fastidiousness and cautious reserve kept from others I poured on him; to say that I would have died for him was nothing. I lived for him . . ." (M. T. Higginson, 126). Higginson's second wife said of this intense friendship, "Their letters were more like those between man and woman than between two men" (125). The sense of transgression was evidently not troubling,[20] however, since the remark could be made in a memorial biography. Higginson himself described Hurlbut as being "so handsome in his dark beauty that he seemed like a picturesque Oriental; slender, keen-eyed, raven-haired, he arrested the eye and the heart like some fascinating girl" (*Yesterdays,* 107). Although Higginson says that Hurlbut was the "hero" of *Cecil Dreeme,* one may wonder, after reading this description, if a lot of him did not go into Densdeth as well. Higginson's allusion to Hurlbut's "moral deterioration" and to "social scandals" also seem to link him to the evil and alluring figure of Densdeth rather than the idealized Dreeme, although it may well be that Hurlbut's androgynous beauty provided the idea for a female character passing as a man. For our purposes, what is striking is the extent to which such a friendship could be an integral part of the life, and of the public record of the life, of a very distinguished public figure.

It is obvious that the boundaries between permissible and impermissible forms of expression of male friendship were drawn very differently in mid-nineteenth-century America than they are now. It is possible that a strict interdiction against full genital sexuality, which gave rise to the deep anxieties of Winthrop's novels, at the same time allowed for a much fuller expression of male friendship, since that in no way threatened to spill over into genitality. It also seems likely that the American world of the nineteenth century (particularly in such all-male domains as the West or the college) was closer to the social organization we now associate with Mediterranean cultures, with the relative seclusion of women and an enlarged (in our terms) repertory of male relationships. Friendships such as Higginson's did not challenge gender boundaries and were thus unthreatening; what they meant for the objects of such love (for those read as female) is less certain—certainly a dark fate awaited Hurlbut. Even within Higginson's lifetime the boundaries may have been shifting.

It is instructive to compare Higginson's enthusiasm for his friend Hurlbut with his attack on Whitman and Wilde, published in the feminist *Woman's Journal* in 1882 when he was almost sixty. It may be partly the influence of the audience Higginson had in mind that this piece is almost obsessively concerned with what could be heard by women. Higginson, like many of the post–Civil War feminists, identified the women's movement with a social purity movement: For him women are "recognized as the guardians of the public purity." Higginson seems to have had little doubt about the dangers inherent in Wilde's work: He is outraged that women receive Wilde socially while none of them would remain in the room if "Charmides" were to be read aloud. He refers with apparent approval to the social ostracism of Byron and the censoring of Thomas Moore's poems. And he denies the "Greek" quality to Wilde's poems, claiming they "do not suggest the sacred whiteness of an antique statue." Higginson thus writes not out of ignorance, but out of knowledge. He knows what the poems mean, and he will judge them unfit for women. His linking of Byron and Moore, and his association of Whitman and Wilde (although slightly qualified), as well as the reference to Greece, seem to indicate that Higginson was aware of a homosexual context that he deliberately wanted to suppress, or at least restrict. By the 1880s, in other words, homosexuality seems to have emerged sufficiently so that it has a public profile (certain authors, certain poems, certain subjects), while in the 1840s it was indistinguishable from other forms of male friendship. Winthrop seems to be located at an interesting junction: He could draw his model from the friendship of two Harvard divinity students, and locate his friendships within a romantic frame, but he clearly saw the implications of the sexuality he sought to handle and control. He looks both back to the Gothic novels of the end of a previous century and forward to the *fin-de-siècle* horrors of an unleashed sexuality.

Winthrop's dilemma appears to have arisen from his attempt to work within a realistic novel tradition that could hardly absorb the energies that he evoked as he worked out the possible terms of male relationships. His novels were far from the aestheticising of the young male body by his friend George William Curtis, who, like Bayard Taylor, used travel writing as a means toward the celebration of the exotic, classicized ephebe. The figure of such a boy was not located, as it had been in Melville's *Typee*, in a social landscape as a means toward the questioning of political power and sexuality, but served rather as a frozen image of a desire most likely unrealized. Curtis's *The Howadji in Syria* (1856), for instance, includes an ecstatic account of the baths in Damascus and concludes with the figure of a handsome boy standing as the representation of a reunion of art and nature: "The pensive grace of his posture, the dark beauty of his face, and the suppleness of his limbs, arrest the artist's eye. He sketches him, and a figure more graceful than the Apollino has justified art and asserted nature upon the twilight plain of Baalbec, whose columns glimmer and fade in the distance and the dark" (344–45). What sets Taylor off from this world of aestheticized male beauty, especially in his works of the 1870s, is the move from the aesthetic to the personal,[21] a move that entails a political self-awareness. *Joseph and His Friend* seems to be located at a point where homosexual panic gives way to a self-conscious awareness of a sexual identity and a defense of its rights. If the fictions of homosexual panic are marked by a strong swerve away from an endangering homosexuality, this novel locates its energies at the moment of a swerve from heterosexuality. It is on Joseph's return from Philadelphia where he is engaged to Julia that he first sees Philip Held (German for hero): Philip "felt his gaze, and turning slowly in his seat, answered it. Joseph dropped his eyes in some confusion, but not until he had caught the full, warm, intense expression of those that met them" (91). The scene is remarkably "modern" in its depiction of a kind of cruising, confirming the sort of eye contact that Whitman had recorded a few years earlier in *Calamus* ("frequent and swift flash of eyes offering me love"). Its location in the narrative clearly situates a sense of crisis, the need to turn away from marriage, a dilemma that is represented rather melodramatically by the train crash that also lands Joseph in Philip's arms. Although there is no direct representation of genital love in the novel,

Taylor draws upon the assumption of two kinds of love ("a man's perfect friendship is rarer than a woman's love"[112]), and upon the physical expression of that love in a kiss. Joseph recognizes the transgressive nature of his love: It is a "cry of passion" against a "whisper" of "conscience" (217). And he sees in the situation of Joseph and Philip a form of social and legal injustice:

> There must be a loftier faith, and a juster law, for the men—and the women—who cannot shape themselves according to the common-place pattern of society,—who were born with instincts, needs, knowledge, and rights—ay, rights!—of their own! (214)

We are now, although only ten years later, a long distance from the world of Winthrop, or for that matter from the anxieties of the older Higginson ten years in the future. What this suggests in part is the impossibility of drawing clear chronological lines in the nineteenth century between conceptions of male friendship: From the 1840s to the 1880s a range of possibilities existed that could run from boyhood "chums" to an idealized comradeship of "knights-errant" to an anguished and guilt-ridden projection of the self onto figures of Gothic evil. The very range of these possibilities may suggest the extent to which the categories that we now take for granted, such as an absolute split between homo- and heterosexual based on genital behavior, were nascent and fluid. Their emergence provided a sense of greater identity for some, but simultaneously meant a loss of possibility for others.

   The existence of such a continuum of male relationships means that it is not possible to distinguish between a Winthrop and a Whitman on the basis of the "homosexuality" of one and the "heterosexuality" of the other. Winthrop and Whitman are different, and their differences do point, in part, to the emergence of a self-conscious homosexuality in the later nineteenth century. But their differences are primarily ways of seeing themselves and ways of regulating their relationships with other men. What sets Whitman off, and defines his achievement, is his politics and its textual location. It is not simply that Whitman sees the possibility of male love: Such a vision was common enough in his time, even if often (for him as well) fraught with terror. It is that for Whitman such a love has consequences for the organization of society; it challenges the very order of male power. Whitman's sexuality is unlike that of many of his male contemporaries (Melville excepted), which could be comfortably located within the parameters of a patriarchal order. In its verbal structures as in its social force, it was a reordering of affective arrangements that could no longer be contained. Taking its origin in the discourses of male power, it nonetheless sought to explode them. For most of the men of his world, male friendship, no matter how fully celebrated or in what form, was but another permutation of a familiar set of relations of power and exchange.

"SHE EVEN CHEWED TOBACCO": A PICTORIAL NARRATIVE OF PASSING WOMEN IN AMERICA

◆

THE SAN FRANCISCO LESBIAN AND GAY HISTORY PROJECT

This essay is an edited version of the slide-tape show, "She Even Chewed Tobacco." It represents the efforts of local history projects to popularize gay and lesbian history through media presentations: The slide-tape show has been shown to community groups throughout the country since 1979 and has been used in women's studies and history classes as well. In addition to providing images of women in nontraditional roles, it raises questions about the relationship of women who passed as men in the nineteenth century and the emergence of lesbian identity in the twentieth century. Since so many of these women came from the working class, it suggests important continuities in working-class lesbian history.

Over the past fifteen years, feminist research has done much to dispel the stereotypes of life in Victorian America. One contribution to this revision is the study of women who dressed as men, worked for men's wages, courted and married women they loved, and even voted. "Passing women" succeeded in hiding their female identities from most of the world and

Note: "She Even Chewed Tobacco" is primarily a visual history. We urge readers of this book to see the slide-tape from which this excerpt is drawn (available for rental from Women Make Movies, 225 Lafayette Street, New York, NY 10012). For primary sources and historical analysis, see works listed in the list of sources. The slide-tape was produced by Estelle Freedman and Liz Stevens, based on primary research by Allen Bérubé. We are grateful to Martha Vicinus for editorial help with this version.

claimed economic and political privilege enjoyed by men. As Jonathan Katz has written, they not only cross-dressed, but also cross-worked and cross-spoke. American newspapers headlined their stories—"Poses, Undetected, 60 years as a Man," "A Gay Deceiver of the Feminine Gender," and "Death Proves 'Married Man' a Woman"—announcing to readers the shocking discovery of these women's deceptions. These reports, which appeared more frequently after 1850, provide our most visible evidence of a larger social phenomena in which many American women chose to abandon constraining feminine roles and to pass as men. To call these women "lesbians" is historically inaccurate, but many actively pursued—and won—the women they loved.

Since Biblical times some women have attempted to pass as men, and they have been severely punished if they were discovered. And yet they took the risks, for reasons we can as yet only guess. Pictures and ballads show that women dressed as soldiers and sailors to fight in wars, to join a lover, or to see the world. Mary Read and Anne Bonney, who were convicted of piracy in 1720, dressed as men (Illus. 1). Dr. James Barry, the most famous British woman to go to war, rose to become Inspector-General of army hospitals (Illus. 2). Deborah Sampson fought with the Fourth Massachusetts Regiment during the American Revolution, and hundreds of other women soldiers have been identified in later wars.

In a fund-raising autobiography, written in 1855, Lucy Ann Lobdell, of rural New York State, explained her decision to pass as one of economic necessity: "I made up my mind to dress in men's attire to seek labor, as I was used to men's work and only got a dollar per week, and I was capable

Illustration 1. "Ann Bonney and Mary Read, Who Were Convicted of Piracy in 1720."

SOURCE: C. J. S. Thompson, *The Mysteries of Sex: Women Who Posed As Men and Men Who Impersonated Them.* New York: Causeway Books, 1974, opp. 72.

Illustration 2. Dr. James Barry.
SOURCE: Thompson, *The Mysteries of Sex.* opp. 101.

of doing men's work and getting men's wages. I resolved to try to get work away, among strangers." The courageous women who could pass not only earned more money for the same work; they could also open bank accounts, write checks, own houses and property, and vote in local and national elections. In New York City, Murray Hall, a woman who passed as a man for twenty-five years, became an influential politician in the Tammany Hall Democratic machine during the 1880s and 1890s. She married other women twice; both marriages broke up because Hall was "too attentive to other women." Hall kept her identity a secret. Even though she had breast cancer, she refused to see a doctor for fear he would expose her, and eventually one did. Indeed, we know of many passing women because they were exposed to the press by doctors.

Whatever their motives for passing—to earn a decent wage, to marry women, or to enjoy political rights—all passing women were in constant danger of exposure, arrest, and incarceration in a jail or insane asylum. At the very least they risked fines or imprisonment (and consequent loss of work) for wearing male attire. To avoid exposure, passing women had to be physically strong, confident in the streets, and know how to flirt with women! A newspaper account of "Bill," a Missouri laborer who became the local secretary of the International Brotherhood of Boilermakers, typified a successful passing woman: "She drank, she swore, she courted

Illustration 3. Cora Anderson.
SOURCE: Jonathan Katz, *Gay American History: Lesbians and Gay Men in the U. S. A.*
New York: Thomas Y. Crowell, 1976, p. 254.

girls, she worked as hard as her fellows, she fished and camped, she even chewed tobacco.''

The women who passed often had a clear sense of the political implications of their decision. An American Indian woman, Cora Anderson, passed as Ralph Kerwinnieo for thirteen years (Illus. 3). When she was arrested in Milwaukee in 1914 for ''disorderly conduct,'' she defended herself,

> Do you blame me for wanting to be a man, free to live life in a man-made world? . . . In the future centuries, it is probable that woman will be the owner of her own body and the custodian of her own soul. [But] the well-cared for woman [now] is a parasite, and the woman who must work is a slave. . . . Do you blame me for hating to again resume a woman's clothing and just belong? Is it any wonder that I determined to become a member of the privileged sex, if possible?

Throughout the United States, nineteenth-century newspapers reported on women who passed as men, but the history of the San Francisco Bay area includes several especially well-documented cases. The city's rapid growth after the Gold Rush (from three hundred inhabitants in 1847 to thirty thousand in 1850) brought opportunities for many single men—and women. The free and easy atmosphere of the city seems to have encouraged many women to wear men's clothing. In the 1850s the well-known Lillie Hitchcock Coit visited night spots dressed in male attire, but she avoided arrest because she was wealthy (Illus. 4). Charlie Parkhurst, a famous Wells Fargo stagecoach driver, worked as a man for over twenty years, and voted as well. A San Francisco newspaper called another passing woman a "freak of fancy," and recognized the political significance of her act by editorializing, "Our municipal laws have affixed a penalty to this manner of deceiving the opposite sex. Our city laws have but little regard for the Bill of Rights adopted by the Women's Convention in the Atlantic States." The stories of Jeanne Bonnet, Luisa Matson, and Babe Bean illustrate these "deceptions."

The most notorious passing woman in San Francisco was Jeanne Bonnet. Born in Paris in 1849, she moved to San Francisco with her family as part of the French Theatrical Troupe. Soon Jeanne was in trouble, possibly for petty thievery. She was committed to the Industrial School, San

Illustration 4. Lillie Hitchcock Coit.
SOURCE: Unidentified original source. Reprinted from Lucius Beebe and Charles Clegg, *San Francisco's Golden Era.* Berkeley: Howell-North, 1960, p. 236.

Francisco's first reformatory. Newspaper reporters condemned her un-feminine behavior:

> By the time she was 15, Jeanne Bonnet evinced a disposition to go it alone, spurning the advice of relatives and friends and hastening down the broad road to moral destruction. She became imbued with the spirit of heroism and cursed the day she was born a female instead of a male.

Upon release from the reformatory Jeanne organized a gang of boy thieves. Her illegal acts, the newspapers claimed, were "seldom equalled by even the more daring men of her class for their boldness of execution." One reporter described her as a "man-hater" with "short cropped hair, an unwomanly voice, and a masculine face which harmonized excellently with her customary suit of boys' clothes, including a jaunty hat which she wore with all the grace of an experienced hoodlum." Although arrested over twenty times for "wearing male attire," Jeanne Bonnet refused to pay her fine and often went to jail, declaring, "The police might arrest me as often as they wish—I will never discard male attire as long as I live."

In 1875, when Jeanne was twenty-six, she began visiting San Francisco brothels. She organized an all-woman gang with members from the brothels. These women swore off prostitution, had nothing to do with men, and supported themselves by petty thievery and shoplifting. Jeanne's special friend, and probably her lover, was gang member Blanche Buneau. Blanche had arrived in San Francisco from Paris in 1875 with a man named Arthur Deneve, who had been living off her earnings as a prostitute. Jeanne persuaded Blanche to leave him. She had resolved to "step in between as many women of Blanche's character and men of Deneve's stripe as she possibly could and cause a separation." Jeanne's life was threatened and she was physically attacked many times by pimps, who were furious at her for stealing away the prostitutes they considered their own property. Jeanne's life came to an abrupt end at the San Miguel Saloon, some four miles outside San Francisco. She had gone there on September 14, 1876, to spend the night with Blanche. Lying in bed, waiting for Blanche, she was shot through the window and killed. The murder was never solved.

In 1895 the police near San Jose, California, arrested businessman Milton Matson for passing bad checks. Discovered to be, in reality, Luisa Matson, she insisted, "I have no reason whatever for wearing this garb except monetary matters" (Illus. 5). Yet, reporters learned, Matson was engaged to a San Francisco schoolteacher, Helen Fairweather. After her release from jail, Matson secretly moved to San Francisco and became S. B. Matson, a man who worked in the San Francisco Public Library. Eleven years later, in 1906, Matson lost her job and home in the fire

Illustration 5. Milton B. Matson [sic.]
SOURCE: Drawing from the San Francisco *Call*, January 27, 1895.

following the earthquake. She moved to a permanent refugee settlement called Point Lobos, and was rediscovered when she died of a stroke. Letters from "Helen" revealed that Helen Fairweather was still part of Matson's life, although Fairweather denied continuing their friendship.

In August 1897, the police in Stockton, California, briefly held a twenty-year-old woman for masquerading in men's clothing. She claimed to have lost her speech in an accident, but she wrote out her story for police and reporters, explaining that although her neighbors called her Jack, her real name was Babe Bean (Illus. 6). Bean lived on a houseboat, or ark, on McLeod's Lake, near Stockton. She wore a blue suit, white silk shirt, large shoes, and a hat pulled over her eyes. "I have been wearing men's clothing off and on for five years," she wrote, "for as a man, I can travel freely, feel protected and find work." She refused to reveal her family origins, but, she claimed, they were one of the best in the land:

> I loved my mother with all my heart, but I feared even to talk to her at times, lest my rough manner might offend her. From a tomboy full of ambitions, I was made into a sad and thoughtful woman. I commenced to be rebellious. My mother feared for my future, and thought that nothing but a convent would save me, and there I remained. How I yearned for that freedom I dreamed of and how often I wished I could enjoy the liberty that the world sees fit to allow a boy.

Illustration 6. Babe Bean.
SOURCE: Drawing from the Stockton *Evening Mail*, October 9, 1897.

At fifteen she decided to marry her brother's best friend in order to escape the convent and to see the world. Within a few months she divorced her husband and set out on her own, passing as a man. She lived for four years in the mountains, on city streets, and in hobo camps.

The people of Stockton became fascinated with Babe Bean, the ark dweller in a man's attire, and they began to treat her with affectionate curiosity. For months her every movement made front-page news in the Stockton papers, and stories of the "Trousered Puzzle" reached San Francisco and Boston papers (Illus. 7). The Stockton Bachelor's Club made Babe Bean an honorary member and the guest of honor at a dinner. She was hired by the Stockton *Evening Mail* as a reporter and assigned to cover the Baby Show at the San Joaquin County Fair.

But all was not well. The "Girls of Stockton" spitefully wrote to the newspaper:

What puzzles us girls is why Babe Bean should be allowed to dress in that way, while if any of the rest of us wanted to walk out in that kind of costume for a change, we would be arrested quicker than quick. There used to be a law against females dressing like the male human being, but it seems not to apply to Babe Bean. If Babe Bean is a girl,

Illustration 7. "The Neat and Tasty Interior of Babe Bean's Ark."
SOURCE: Stockton *Evening Mail*, October 9, 1897.

and continues to dress in boys' clothing, the rest of us ought to have the same privilege, and we are going to do it. Some fine evening, there are going to be about twenty-five young women on the streets of Stockton, all dressed in men's clothing and we're going to go to the ark and get Babe Bean and duck her in McLeod's Lake till she cries, "Nuff." Then she can talk if she wants to.

Babe Bean replied to this attack with characteristic aplomb, "It is your privilege to dress as you see fit, whether it is after the fashion of Venus or after the fashion of Babe Bean. I wish to state that boys' clothes are still selling in Stockton at reduced prices. You are quite welcome to that information." She also added that she was quite capable of defending herself. Another more supportive letter appeared, declaring, "I do not know Babe Bean, but she is a woman, and I do not think it is a woman's place to try to injure a sister because she does not happen to live just as we do; and if she wants to wear men's clothes and have sixteen pockets, it is none of our business."

In 1898 war was declared between the United States and Spain, and front-page articles about Babe Bean were replaced by accounts of Stockton's recruits leaving for Cuba or the Philippines. Babe Bean disappeared from Stockton, but a small man named Jack Garland served as a lieutenant during the Spanish-American War. He later moved to San Francisco, where in 1906, he served as a male nurse during the earthquake and fire, and provided emergency medical care for the homeless. For the next thirty years Jack Garland lived in San Francisco rooming houses and acted as a kind of free-lance social worker, aiding homeless and hungry people. He was affectionately known as "Uncle Jack" by those who knew and loved him. On September 18, 1936, this "little man with the big heart" collapsed and was taken to a hospital, where attendants did not at first realize that he was really a woman. His death revealed not only his true sex, but also his true identity. The sixty-six-year-old "Uncle Jack," alias Babe Bean, had once been Elvira Virginia Mugarrieta, the daughter of José Marcos Mugarrieta, who had founded the Mexican consulate in San Francisco; her mother, Eliza Alice Garland, was said to be the daughter of a Louisiana Supreme Court Justice.

By the time Jack Garland/Babe Bean died, the world had changed enormously for women. The vote had been won; educational opportunities had increased; the professions had admitted a few determined women; and women were visible in a wide variety of new jobs. Nonetheless, early-twentieth-century newspapers continued to report stories of passing women. In 1903, a group of at least ten women passed as men and worked for the New York Central Railway in Buffalo, New York. They were porters (most likely black women), train agents, "switchmen," and cooks. A reporter claimed that these women "often met together and made themselves not a little merry over the success of their transference from one class of humanity to another." During the Depression of the 1930s, women hoboes sometimes passed as men. In the meantime, passing women sought companionship with other women, and even married them. In 1925, for example, the marriage of "Peter" Stratford and Elizabeth Rowland made headlines.

After 1920 women who occasionally wore men's clothing and those who passed as men began to socialize more openly in cafés and night clubs. In Chicago two night clubs, the Roselle Club, run by Eleanor Shelly, and the Twelve-thirty Club, run by Becky Blumfield, were closed by the police during the 1930s because "women in male attire were nightly patrons of the places." Many of the couples who frequented these clubs had been married to each other by a black minister on Chicago's South Side. In San Francisco, lesbians met at Mona's, where, it was said, "Girls will be boys" (Illus. 8). This growing subculture marked a change from the earlier passing woman, who seems to have been a loner, wary of doctors, police, and reporters.

Public attitudes toward passing women also changed in the early twentieth century, imposing stricter penalties on cross-dressing. In addition to the older, legal sanctions against passing, new medical and psychiatric theories labelled these women as "sexual deviants." Some doctors described passing women as typical of all lesbians. "The female invert," wrote an American doctor in 1915, "likes to . . . dress herself entirely in

Illustration 8. Mona's. Advertisement from 1940s theater program.

men's attire and disguise her identity. She further prefers the occupations of men." Psychologists labelled these new passing women as inverts, tribadists, sapphists, men-women, he-shes, gyanders, femino-sexuals, uraniads, delusional masculinity, and women who suffered from viraginous disorders.

Illustration 9. Mabel Jane Taylor, friend of Mabel Hampton, ca. 1930.
SOURCE: Courtesy Lesbian Herstory Archives/L.H.E.F., Inc., New York.

But passing women had already developed a more positive language to describe their own emerging lesbian identities. In the 1870s the word "dike" referred to a man who was all dressed up, or "diked out," perhaps for a night on the town. By 1900 the word "bulldyker" had come into use in the red-light district of Philadelphia to mean lesbian lovers. And, in 1935, black blues singer Bessie Jackson recorded a song titled "B-D Woman," meaning "Bulldagger Woman," which described lesbians who adopted a masculine style (Illus. 9). It describes the oppression and celebrates the economic independence and rebellious spirit shared by generations of women who passed as men:

> Comin a time, B-D women ain't gonna need no men.
> The way they treat us is a low down and dirty shame.
>
> B-D women, they can lay their claim,
> They can lay that jive just like a natural man.
>
> B-D women, you know they sure is rough,
> They all drink up plenty whiskey and they sure can strut their stuff.
>
> B-D women, you know they work and make their dough,
> And when they get ready to spend it they know just where to go.*

The tradition of passing women, begun in the nineteenth century, lives on today, a small but important part of lesbian and women's history.

---

*AC/DC Blues: Gay Jazz Re-issues, Vol I., Stash Records, 1977, ST-106.

INVERTS, PERVERTS, AND MARY-ANNES: MALE PROSTITUTION AND THE REGULATION OF HOMOSEXUALITY IN ENGLAND IN THE NINETEENTH AND EARLY TWENTIETH CENTURIES

◆

JEFFREY WEEKS

This essay examines male prostitution within the context of the changing perceptions and regulation of homosexual behavior in the late nineteenth and early twentieth centuries. It explores the ways in which patterns of legal and ideological control dictated a close relationship between male homosexual subcultures and male prostitution. The public definition of homosexuality as a stigmatized category led to a variety of both self-definitions and behaviors between client and contact. Many young working-class men received gifts and cash from wealthier men for their sexual favors without considering themselves either prostitutes or homosexuals. As a result, unlike female prostitution, no subculture developed among male prostitutes.

Note: Originally published in *Journal of Homosexuality,* Vol 6, nos.1/2 (Fall/Winter 1980/81). This paper was first written for a conference in 1979 and subsequently revised for publication in 1980. A small amount of material has been deleted from this version, but otherwise it remains as originally published. A good deal of work on homosexuality in history has been written since 1979, but none of it, I believe, fundamentally changes the arguments advanced here.

The Problem

It is significant that writings on male prostitution began to emerge simultaneously with the notion of "homosexuals" being an identifiable breed of persons with special needs, passions, and lusts. The early studies of male prostitution by F. Carlier, head of the morals police in Paris in the 1860s, were also the first major quantitative studies of homosexuality.[1] Havelock Ellis, Iwan Bloch, Magnus Hirschfeld, and Sigmund Freud also commented on the prevalence of homosexual prostitution. "Xavier Mayne," who wrote on the homosexual subculture in the early part of this century, suggested that male was no less frequent than female prostitution in major European cities. In 1948, Alfred Kinsey noted that male prostitutes were not far inferior in number to females. In the 1960s, D. J. West suggested that homosexual males' "inclination to such an outlet with prostitutes" was greater than that of heterosexual males, who usually were married and consequently had less pressing sexual urges as well as less time or opportunity to consort with prostitutes.[2]

But, although the existence of male prostitution is mentioned frequently, it has been studied less often. Most of our information is anecdotal and impressionistic.[3] As late as the mid-1960s, a writer on the subject could complain that the literature on boy prostitutes was scant when compared with studies of female prostitution.[4] This neglect is unfortunate. The subject should not be regarded as marginal. A study of homosexual prostitution could illuminate the changing images of homosexuality and its legal and social regulation, as well as the variability of sexual identities in our social history and their relationship to wider social structures.

Iwan Bloch, writing in 1909, suggested that a discussion of male prostitution in E. A. Duchesne's *De La Prostitution dans la Ville d'Alger depuis la Conquête,* published in Paris in 1853, was ". . . an expansion of the idea of prostitution which is, as far as my knowledge goes, found here for the first time. Naturally, in earlier works we find allusions to men who practice pederasty for money, but the idea of "prostitution" had hitherto been strictly limited to the class of purchasable women."[5] Bloch pinpoints the need to locate studies of prostitution within their specific social conditions and discriminates between promiscuity in earlier cultures and modern forms of prostitution, for the social meanings ascribed to the two behaviors are usually quite different.

Much recent work has stressed the vital importance of distinguishing among behavior, role, and identity in any sociological or historical approach to the subject of homosexuality.[6] Cross-cultural studies, as well as studies of schoolboy sex play, prison homosexuality, and sex in public places, show that homosexual behavior does not give rise automatically, or even necessarily, to a homosexual identity. Homosexual roles and identities are historically constructed.[7] Even if the homosexual "orientation" were given in a fixed minority of the population, as some recent writers suggest,[8] the social definitions and the subjective meaning given to the orientation can vary enormously. The mass of typologies and categorizations in the works of Krafft-Ebing, Albert Moll, Havelock Ellis, Magnus Hirschfeld, and others at the beginning of the century was an early attempt to grapple with this fact. Historians and social scientists alike have failed to fit everyone who behaves in a homosexual manner within a definition of "the homosexual" as a unitary type. Even those categorized as "homosexuals" often have had great difficulty in accepting the label.

If this is the case for the clients of male prostitutes (the "steamers" or "punters," "swells" or "swanks"), how much more true is it for the prostitute himself who must confront two stigmatized identities—that of the homosexual and that of the prostitute? There is no legitimizing ideology for homosexual prostitution similar to that which condones heterosexual prostitution even when condemning the female prostitute. A number of studies have suggested that many males who prostitute themselves regard themselves as heterosexual and devise complex strategies to neutralize the significance of their behavior.[9] Our knowledge of this phenomenon is speculative, however, limited to particular classes of people, such as "delinquents," and we do not know how attitudes change historically or in a particular lifetime. More generally, there is the problem of what constitutes an act of prostitution. One of Oscar Wilde's pickups in the 1890s, Charlie Parker, who eventually gave evidence against him, commented: "I don't suppose boys are different to girls in taking presents from them who are fond of them."[10] On a superficial level this is true, but the association with a stigmatized sexual activity has shaped profoundly the contours of male prostitution. These deserve serious examination.

This essay does not pretend to be an exhaustive study of the patterns of male prostitution. The necessary detailed empirical research still has to be done. Rather, the intention is to examine some of the practical and theoretical problems attendant upon this research and to make specific reference to evidence from the late nineteenth and early twentieth centuries. There are three broad areas of concern. First, we must pay closer attention than hitherto to the specific social circumstances that shaped concepts of, and attitudes toward, homosexuality. Second, the close, indeed symbiotic, relationship between forms of prostitution and the homosexual subcultures has to be recognized and analyzed. Third, the nature of the prostitution itself, the self-concepts it led to, the "way of life" it projected, and its differences from female prostitution must be articulated and theorized.

The Social and Legal Context

Certain types of subcultural formations associated with homosexual activity have existed in Britain for centuries, at the courts of certain monarchs (where the royal "favorite" can be seen as analogous to the "courtesan"), in the theatrical profession from the sixteenth century, or in developing urban centers, such as London and Bristol, from the seventeenth century.[11] Forms of prostitution undoubtedly existed within these subcultures and became more complex as the subculture expanded in the nineteenth century. Well into the present century the lineaments of the subcultures were much less well defined in Britain, even in London, than in such places as Paris and Berlin, and as a result the evidence of prostitution is less concrete.[12] Different legal practices and moral traditions have had highly significant effects. In Britain, in contrast to France, homosexual behavior per se (not just prostitution) was regarded as a major social problem. Contemporary foreign observers had no doubt that male prostitution was as rife in England as elsewhere,[13] but its visibility was minimal. Much of our evidence for British prostitution is consequently sporadic, often the result of zealous public morality drives or of spectacular scandals.

Police, legal, and medical attitudes were manifestly confused. When the two "men in women's clothes," Ernest Boulton and Frederick Park, were arrested in 1870 for indecent behavior (for cross-dressing in public), they were immediately and without authorization examined for evidence of sodomy and eventually charged with conspiracy to commit such acts. The police, who had been observing the two men for over a year, often in notorious haunts of female prostitution, were of the opinion that Boulton and Park were male prostitutes. Indeed, some of the letters exchanged between Boulton, Park, and other defendants mentioned money. It is obvious, however, from the transcripts of the trial (before the Lord Chief Justice, in Westminster Hall) that neither the police nor the court were familiar with either male homosexuality or prostitution.[14] It is not even clear whether the men were charged with *male* prostitution. The opening remarks by the Attorney General hinted that it was their transvestism and their soliciting men *as women* that were the core of the crime.[15] A Dr. Paul, who examined them for sodomy upon their arrest, had never encountered a similar case in his whole career. His only knowledge came from a half-remembered case history in Dr. Alfred Swaine Taylor's *Medical Jurisprudence*.[16] The unclaimed body of one Eliza Edwards in 1833 had turned out on inspection to be the body of a twenty-four-year-old male: "The state of the rectum left no doubt of the abominable practices to which this individual had been addicted."[17] The implication was that sodomy might itself be an indication of prostitution, but even Dr. Taylor, who also gave evidence in the case, had had no other previous experience, and the other doctors called in could not agree on what the signs of sodomitical activity were. The Attorney General observed that "it must be a matter of rare occurrence in this country at least for any person to be discovered who has any propensity for the practices which are imputed to them."[18] The only "scientific" literature to which the court had recourse was French. Dr. Paul had not heard of the work of Tardieu, who had investigated over two hundred cases of sodomy for purposes of legal proof, until an anonymous letter informed him of its existence.[19] The Attorney General suggested that it was fortunate that there was "very little learning or knowledge upon this subject in this country."[20] One of the defense counsellors was more bitter, attacking Dr. Paul for relying on "the newfound treasures of French literature upon the subject—which thank God is still foreign to the libraries of British surgeons."[21]

It is striking that as late as 1871 concepts of both homosexuality and male prostitution were extremely undeveloped in the Metropolitan Police and in high medical and legal circles. Neither was there any comprehensive law relating to male homosexuality before 1885. Prior to that date, the only relevant law was that concerning buggery, dating from the 1530s, and notionally carrying the maximum of a death sentence until 1861. Other male homosexual acts generally were subsumed under the heading of conspiracy to commit the major offense.[22] Proof was notoriously difficult to obtain, however, and it was ostensibly to make proof, and therefore conviction, easier that Henry Labouchère introduced his famous amendment to the Criminal Law Amendment Act of 1885. Labouchère claimed, though the substantiating evidence for this appears no longer to exist, that it was a communication from W. T. Stead about homosexual prostitution in London that prompted him to act.[23] The amendment defined "acts of gross indecency" between two men whether in *public* or *private* as "misdemeanors," punishable by up to two years of hard labor. This in effect made all male homosexual acts and all homosexual "procuring" illegal.

The 1898 Vagrancy Act further affected homosexual activities by enacting that any male person who knowingly lived wholly or in part on the earnings of female prostitutes, or who solicited or importuned for immoral purposes, was to be deemed a rogue and a vagabond under the terms of the Vagrancy Acts. The latter clauses were applied almost invariably to homosexual offenses. By a further Criminal Law Amendment Act ("The White Slave Trade Act") in 1912, the sentence was set at six months' imprisonment, with flogging for a second offense, *on summary jurisdiction* (that is, without a jury trial), a clause which, as G. B. Shaw put it, "is the final triumph of the vice it pretends to repress."[24] It is not entirely clear why the soliciting clauses were in practice confined exclusively to men meeting each other for homosexual purposes. The Royal Commission on the Duties of the Metropolitan Police noted in 1908 that there was nothing in the Act to prevent the clauses being applied to men soliciting women for immoral purposes,[25] but in fact they never were, nor have the activities of men who solicit women for acts of prostitution ever been illegal. The 1928 Street Offences Committee recommended that no change take place in these provisions.[26]

Although obviously less severe than a death sentence or life imprisonment for buggery, the new clauses were all-embracing and more effectively applied. They had specific effects on the relationship between male prostitution and homosexuality. *All* male homosexual activities were illegal between 1885 and 1967, and this fact largely shaped the nature of the homosexual underworld in the period "between the Acts." In particular it shaped the relationship between those who defined themselves as "homosexual" and those who prostituted themselves; for instance, it increased the likelihood of blackmail and violence. It also affected the nature of the prostitution itself, certainly making it less public and less sharply defined. As observers noted at the time, the male prostitute had the professional disadvantage of being obliged to avoid the open publicity of solicitation available to female prostitutes. This had important consequences.

In terms of social obloquy, all homosexual males as a class were equated with female prostitutes. It is striking that all the major enactments concerning male homosexuality were drawn from Acts designed to control female prostitution (1885, 1898, 1912). The juncture of the two concerns was maintained as late as the 1950s, when a Departmental Committee (the "Wolfenden Committee") was established to investigate both.[27]

After the repeal of the Contagious Diseases Acts in the 1880s, female prostitution was subject to a peculiar "compromise" that sought neither outright repression nor formal state regulation.[28] Prostitution was frowned upon, and the female prostitute was an outcast increasingly defined as a member of a separate caste of women,[29] but prostitution was "tolerated" as fulfilling a necessary social need. Beyond this was the distinction, which social purity campaigns sought to emphasize, between the sphere of public decency and that of private behavior. There were periods, particularly in the early decade of the twentieth century, when the advocates of social purity did reach toward straightforward repression, but by and large the compromise held.

On a formal level, the compromise never applied to male homosexuality. Even the sodomy provisions were applied to private as well as public behavior,[30] and after 1885 the situation was even more explicit. In practice, of course, enforcement varied between different police areas, depending on local police chiefs, the power of watch committees, and, over time, on the general social climate and the effectiveness of social-purity campaigns. There were also difficulties in the legal situation. Juries often refused to convict under the 1885 Act, and police often preferred not to prosecute if "public decency" were reasonably maintained.[31] Even after 1885, the government's legal officers preferred caution. In 1889, the

Director of Public Prosecutions noted "the expediency of not giving unnecessary publicity" to cases of gross indecency. At the same time, he felt that much could be said for allowing "private persons—being full grown men—to indulge their unnatural tastes in private."[32]

When the law was applied, however, it was applied with rigor, particularly against males who importuned. Figures are difficult to come by, for until 1954 statistics for prosecution of male solicitation were always published with those for men living off immoral earnings, but one observer has suggested that the law was the cause of even greater misery than the 1885 Act.[33] It was enforced through summary jurisdiction, and, compared to the forty-shilling fine imposed on female prostitutes before 1959, the maximum sentence of six months' imprisonment and the associated stigmatization ground hard on homosexual males.

Given the social restrictions on forms of sexual contact, the demand for special services, and, in the case of homosexuality, the continuing difficulties of leading an openly homosexual life, there is undoubtedly at all times a market for prostitution. Given the legal situation since the end of the nineteenth century and the simultaneous refinement of hostile social norms, homosexual activity was potentially very dangerous for both partners and carried with it not only public disgrace but the possibility of a prison sentence. This also fed into the market for prostitution and dictated much of the furtiveness, guilt, and anxiety that was a characteristic of the homosexual way of life.

In the diaries of Roger Casement, the Irish patriot executed in 1916, notes on his work for the colonial service lie cheek by jowl with descriptions of pickups, the price he paid for them, the size of their organs, and the occasional cry of despair. When he heard of the suicide of (the homosexual) Sir Hector Macdonald, Casement called for "saner methods of curing a terrible disease,"[34] but the surrounding entries joyfully extol his own recent adventures:

December 6, 1903
Very busy on report with typer. Did 6,000 words today and revised a lot. Dined at Comedy Restaurant alone. First time there in life. Porter good, excellent dinner, French chef, then walked. Dusky depradator huge, saw 7 in. in all. Two beauties.

December 7, 1903
. . . Awful mistake. Dine with Cui B and Mrs. C., jolly dinner, strolled. Dick, West End, biggest and cleanest, mui mua ami.

December 8, 1903
Busy all day and then to Robertson's at 30, Hemstall Road. Home by Marble Arch. D. W. 14. C.R.£1. Drizzle, home tired and to bed. Bertie walked part of way.[35]

The frequency of encounters varied from thirty-nine in the 1903 diary to several hundred in 1911.[36] These adventures were completely hidden from friends and colleagues but evidently were a central part of his life, entering into his regular financial accountancy. The 1911 ledger, for instance, contains brief accounts of all activities and financial transactions, including payments for boys. Casement was exceptional in recording such (ultimately damning) details, but his life cannot have been unique. Indeed, there are striking parallels with the anonymous author of the Victorian sexual chronicle, *My Secret Life,* who also wrote of having a secret homosexual life, hidden from respectable friends and colleagues: "Have all men had the strange letches which late in life have enraptured me?"[37] Casement might well have asked the same question, for he seems to have had no sustained contact with a subculture or with other homosexual men except through casual prostitution.

The Homosexual Subculture

A sexual subculture can fulfill a number of complementary functions: alleviating isolation and guilt, schooling members in manners and mores, teaching and affirming identities.[38] The most basic purpose of the homosexual subculture in the nineteenth and early twentieth centuries, however, was to provide ways to meet sexual partners. Until comparatively recently, very few people found it either possible or desirable to incorporate sexual mores, social activities, and public identity into a full-time homosexual "way of life." Perhaps the only people who lived wholly in the subculture were the relatively few "professionals," the chief links between the world of aristocratic homosexuality and the metropolitan subculture of Molly houses, pubs, fields, walks, squares, and lavatories.

As early as the 1720s, these meeting places had been known as "markets," corresponding to the contemporaneous heterosexual use of the term "marriage market."[39] This does not differ much from Evelyn Hooker's description of the modern American gay bar scene as free markets in which the buyer's right to enter is determined solely by having the right attributes and the ability to pay.[40] By the 1870s, any sort of homosexual transaction, whether or not money was involved, was described as "trade." One defendant in the Boulton and Park scandal wrote to the other, "I will confess that I give you reason to think that I care for nothing but trade and I think you care too little for it as far as I am concerned."[41] In this world of sexual barter, particularly given the furtiveness, the need for caution, and the great disparities of wealth and social position among the participants, the cash nexus inevitably dominated.

Despite the wide social range of the subculture, from pauper to peer, it was the ideology of the upper classes that seems to have dominated, probably because there was a much more clearly defined homosexual identity amongst men of the middle and upper middle class and because these men had a greater opportunity, through money and mobility, to make frequent homosexual contacts.[42] A related phenomenon was the widely recognized upper-middle-class fascination with crossing the class divide, a fascination that shows a direct continuity between male heterosexual and male homosexual mores.[43] J. A. Symonds might have disapproved of some of his friends' compulsive chasing after working-class contacts,[44] but it was undoubtedly an important component of the subculture. The Post Office messenger boys of the Cleveland Street scandal and the stable lads, newspaper sellers, and bookmakers' clerks in the Wilde trial illustrate a few of the many sections of the working class involved.

The moving of class barriers, the search for "rough trade," or Wilde's "feasting with panthers" could become the defining tone. Lasting partnerships did develop, but in a world of relatively easy sex, promiscuity was a temptation, despite the dangers. Middle-class men generally had nonsexual relationships with friends, sex with casual pickups. One respondent of mine who found it difficult to have sex with friends of his own class had a fascination with the Guards and "suffered," as he put it, from "scarlet fever": "I have never cared for trading with homosexuals . . . I always wanted to trade with men. But of course, mine's always been prostitution . . . I don't say I never went with homosexuals because I did. But I would say that as a rule I wanted men."[45]

The desire for a relationship across class lines (the product, perhaps, of a feeling that sex could not be spontaneous or "natural" within the framework of one's own class) interacted with a desire for a relationship with a "man," a real man, a heterosexual. E. M. Forster wanted "to love a strong young man of the lower classes and be loved by him" and finally developed an ambiguous relationship with a policeman. Edward Carpenter proclaimed his love for the poor and uneducated in obviously erotic tones: "The thick-thighed, hot, coarse-fleshed young bricklayer with the strip around his waist." J. R. Ackerley sometimes felt that "the Ideal friend . . . should have been an animal man . . . the perfect human male body always at one's service through the devotion of a faithful and uncritical beast."[46]

There are very complex patterns recurring here. On the one hand was a form of sexual colonialism, a view of the lower classes as a source of "trade." On the other were an often sentimental rejection of one's own class values and a belief in reconciliation through sexual contact. As J. A. Symonds put it, "The blending of Social Strata in masculine love seems to me one of its most pronounced and socially hopeful features."[47] With this went a common belief that the working class and the Guardsmen (notorious from the eighteenth century and throughout Europe for their easy prostitution) were indifferent to homosexual behavior.[48] One regular customer of the Guardsmen observed: "Young, they were normal, they were working class, they were drilled to obedience."[49] They also were widely available: "The skeptic has only to walk around London, around any English garrison centre, to stroll around Portsmouth, Aldershot, Southampton, Woolwich, large cities of North Britain or Ireland to find the soldier prostitute in almost open self-marketing."[50] With the guards, the money transaction was explicit. In the rarefied atmosphere of the "Uranian" poets, money would change hands but ideology minimized its significance. The Uranians worshipped youth, spoke of the transience of boyhood, and delighted in breaking class barriers.[51]

These class and gender interactions ("working class" equals "masculine" equals "closeness to nature") were to play important roles in the rituals of prostitution, affecting, for instance, the stance adopted by the "prostitute" and the behaviors he was expected to tolerate.[52]

The Nature of Prostitution

The exchange of money could create a host of different symbolic meanings for both parties, while the uncertainty of both could make the transaction itself very ambiguous. It was not always easy, for instance, to distinguish among extortion, blackmail, and a begging letter. The giving of gifts could have the same complex inflection. Oscar Wilde's gift to his contacts of a dinner at Kettner's and a silver cigarette box (varying in cost from £1 to £5) could be interpreted either as payment for services about to be rendered or as tokens of friendship. A working-class man like George Merrill, Edward Carpenter's long-time companion, was able to recount quite unself-consciously his liaison in the 1880s with an Italian count who gave him presents, flowers, neckties, handkerchiefs, and money, which Merrill usually sent home to his mother.[53] In this sort of situation, the significance attached to the transaction could be quite complex, with the money and gifts often playing a quite secondary role.

Even when the commercial element was quite unambiguous, complex mechanisms could be adopted to mask the exchange. A client easily could adopt a self-saving attitude: "I seemed always to be pretending . . . that the quid that usually passed between us at once (the boys were always short of cash) was not a *quid pro quo* but a gift."[54] Joe Ackerley has told of his nightly search for an ideal comrade and of his numberless pickups (Guardsmen and policemen). He writes, however: "The taint of prostitution in these proceedings nevertheless displeased me and must, I thought, be disagreeable to the boys themselves . . . I therefore developed mutually self-saving techniques to avoid it, such as standing drinks and giving cash at once, without any suggestive conversation, leading the boy free to return home with me if he wished, out of sexual desire or gratitude, for he was pretty sure to know what I was after."[55]

Payment could also be a necessary ritual to alleviate guilt:

There's a famous place behind a pub—in Camberwell, which was very interesting. And there was a—Army Captain there, who showed interest in me, and I in him. And he said, oh well, there are a lot of ditched houses over there, let's go round there. Which we did. And afterwards he pressed a ten shilling note into my hand. I said, I don't want this money. I don't take money, I enjoyed your company and so on. I said, I will not have it. He said, but you've got to have it. I said, I won't have it. And he went on and on. And eventually pressed it on—into my hand and ran. Now I think he got a thrill out of paying people. Most extraordinary.[56]

In a historical survey it is often very difficult to determine which actions are purely instrumental and which are affective. It is easier to describe the motivations and fantasies of the clients than to delineate the experiences and beliefs of those who prostituted themselves. Late-nineteenth-century theorists of the etiology of homosexuality looked to masturbation, bad parentage, congenital degeneracy, or corruption. A consensus developed among sexologists that, whatever one's moral views of homosexual behavior, there were essentially two types to distinguish: those who were inherently, perhaps congenitally, homosexual, "the inverts"; and those who behaved in a homosexual way from lust, "the perverts." Thoinot noted that "male prostitution finds as clients, on the one hand, *true uranists,* or the *passionates* as they are called in the language of the French police, and, on the other hand, libertines, old or young, disgusted with normal relations and impotent towards women."[57] This was an important distinction because it colored a great deal of public reaction. The Director of Public Prosecutions, reflecting on the affair of the Cleveland Street brothel in 1889, wrote that it was a duty "to enforce the law and protect the children of respectable parents taken into the service of the public . . . from being made the victims of the unnatural lusts of full-grown men."[58] The notion of the upper class corrupting the working class into vice is repeated in Labouchère's description of the boys named in the Cleveland Street affair as being "more sinned against than sinning." The constable in charge of the boys came to the conclusion that "they were ignorant of the crimes they committed with other persons."[59] The merging of homosexuality with the class question was recurrent in the press during the Cleveland Street scandal and continued through the 1950s.[60]

Alongside this view, and to some extent contradicting it, was the theory that the prostitute exhibited a characteristic predisposition toward corruption and sexual degeneracy, a characteristic sign of which was effeminacy. It is true that throughout Europe, from the eighteenth century on, those who prostituted themselves often displayed stereotyped "effeminate" characteristics and adopted female names,[61] but it is wrong to assume that male prostitutes were drawn from any particular type of person predisposed toward prostitution. Effeminate behavior can be as much an adopted role as inherent, and, as we have seen, the homosexual subculture stressed the desire for "manly" men. In fact, a variety of factors drew people into prostitution.

Writing of Berlin in the 1920s, Werner Picton mentions two prostitute populations: an "outer ring" that fluctuated in numbers and composition and was caused by unemployment and want: and "the inner and more stable nucleus of this variable and non-coherent body . . . less driven by want or unemployment than by other circumstances, such as psychopathy, hysteria, mental instability, sexual curiosity, love of adventure and longing for luxuries."[62] Some of these categories ("psychopathy," "hysteria," "mental instability") conform to the view that prostitutes were "degenerate" or had been pushed into prostitution by emotional inadequacy or sex-role confusion. The other categories, however, suggest what appears to have been commonly the case: that the men had experienced a general and characteristic "drift into deviancy" (described as a "sliding down"[63]) that had varying, and certainly not predetermined, effects on their self-concepts and identities.

"Drift" has been identified as characteristic for both female and male prostitution, with "situational and cognitive" processes tending to be the dominant influences.[64] Whereas with female prostitution frequent sexual relations with men can lead to a woman's decision that her future transactions will be for money, the pattern is significantly different for male prostitutes. Here the dominant pattern seems to be one of chance contacts, accidental learning, or association with a subculture (such as that of the Guards) with a tradition of casual prostitution.

Youthful sex play frequently led to casual prostitution. Thickbroom, a boy messenger for the Post Office who was involved in the Cleveland Street affair, told how mutual masturbation in a water closet with Newlove, another messenger, had been followed by Newlove asking him, in Thickbroom's words, "if I would go to be with a man. I said no. He then said: you'll get four shillings for a time and persuaded me."[65] The messenger boys did not prostitute themselves frequently, and, were it not for the subsequent scandal, their involvement probably would have had minor impact on their lives. Sometimes, however, the decision could be more calculating. Charlie Parker recounted how he became involved with Alfred Taylor and Oscar Wilde. Taylor approached him, "passed the compliments of the day, and asked us to have a drink. We got into conversation with him. He spoke about men. Taylor said, 'you could get money in a certain way easily enough if you cared to.' I understood to what Taylor alluded and made a coarse reply . . . I said that if any old gentleman with money took a fancy to me, I was agreeable. I was agreeable. I was terribly hard up."[66] These initial purposeful contacts could slide easily into a transitional career of blackmail and threat, but this was not a necessary development.

A third route to prostitution was through a world symbiotic with homosexuality, such as the Guards. A working-class recruit would soon learn how extra money could be made with little effort and with no risk of stigma by his fellows. Indeed, tradition and perennial shortage of funds among the Guards sanctioned these activities.[67] Subcultural support from peers was likely to militate against a Guardsman becoming a "professional." Sometimes a propensity for leading an explicitly homosexual life, a particular skill for learning the ways of the subculture, support from other prostitutes or homosexual men, or the willingness to recognize himself as a prostitute would turn a man to "professionalization," but "professionals" were very much in a minority among Guardsmen and nonmilitary youths alike.

The records of professional prostitutes are rare, which gives a particular interest to *The Sins of the Cities of the Plain* (1881),[68] the life story of Jack Saul (a historical character who later—in 1890—gave evidence in the Euston libel case as part of the Cleveland Street brothel scandal). A choice piece of homosexual pornography, the book is purportedly Saul's autobiography and, despite its presumably fictionalized account, gives vivid insights into male prostitution. In the libel trial, Saul asserted proudly that he was still a "professional Maryanne": "I have lost my character and cannot get on otherwise. I occasionally do odd jobs for different gay people."[69] These odd jobs, as he made clear in his cross-examination, were house cleaning for women on the beat, suggesting a commitment to a career as a professional, the ghettoization that could result from this choice of career, and its vagaries as age diminished charm. The life was by no means completely harsh, however, as this dialogue shows:

And were you hunted by the police?
No, they have never interfered. They have always been kind to me.
Do you mean they have deliberately shut their eyes to your infamous practices?
They have had to shut their eyes to more than me.[70]

The likes of Saul were few, however. His purported memoirs note that "We do not know of many professional male sodomites in London."[71]

The Life

The professional organization that has been characteristic of female prostitution never arose within homosexual prostitution. Even in the larger European cities, such as Berlin and Paris, the "boy-houses" were rare, though numerous places of rendezvous existed under the guise of literary clubs and athletic societies.[72] In England, the Criminal Law Amendment Act of 1885 had been directed partly against brothels but was ambiguous in its application to homosexual haunts. The Director of Public Prosecutions complained to the Home Secretary in 1889 that he was "quite aware that although it is a legal offence to keep a bawdy house—it is not a legal offence to keep or frequent a house kept for the accommodation of sodomites."[73] Labouchère claimed in 1889 to have in his possession "a short list of houses, some in fashionable parts of the city, which are every inch as bad; if not worse,"[74] but nothing seems to have followed from his threat to reveal them.

Such establishments had dozens of clients. Soldiers, MPs, peers, members of the National Liberal Club, a tailor, and a banker all frequented 19 Cleveland Street, for example. The boys were paid "sometimes a sovereign, sometimes half a sovereign; 4/- was kept by themselves and the rest given to Hammond or kept by Newlove."[75] Jack Saul lived with Hammond for a while, and both earned their livelihood as "sodomites:" "I used to give him all the money I earned, oftentimes as much as £8 or £9 a week."[76]

Hammond lived a fully professional life as a "madame," married a French prostitute, Madame Carolino, and lived with her thereafter. He also had a "spooney-boy," one Frank Hewitt, who used to "go with him" and procure boys for the establishment.

Even within this twilight world there were subtle distinctions. Saul complained to Hammond of his allowing boys "in good position in the Post Office to be in the house while I had to walk the streets for what is in my face and what is shame."[77] Professional Mary-Annes with neatly printed calling cards like gentlemen's visiting cards[78] were scarcely the norm. More common contact would be the likes of Mrs. Truman, who received orders for Guardsmen at her tobacconist shop near the Albany Street barracks in Regents Park.[79] The Guards themselves also might take up an informal pimping role. One customer tells how he met one Guard several times: ". . . and then he said, well do you want anybody else . . . I can bring them along . . . So I said . . . have you got one with ginger hair . . . And then of course (he) procured me—oh—dozens. Dozens of them."

There were also widespread informal coteries.[80] Oscar Wilde made many of his contacts through his friend, Alfred Taylor, who lived in exotically furnished rooms in Little College Street near Westminster Abbey. The son of a wealthy cocoa manufacturer, Taylor became notorious for introducing young men to older men and as the center of a "sort of secret society."[81] Others, like John Watson Preston, who lived at 46 Fitzroy Street (near Cleveland Street), held openly transvestite parties, one of which was raided by the police. One such raid precipitated Taylor's first arrest.[82]

Similar arrangements continued into the 1930s: "I was introduced to somebody called Tommy . . . he had a flat. . . . And he used to have 'friends' who used to call on him for tea, and he would invite his 'friends' and pair them off. And—presents used to change hands . . . his clients were MPs, doctors, lawyers and professional gentlemen. . . . They paid him. . . . He paid the boy . . ."

In London, however, most contacts would be made in the normal picking-up places and at "watering holes" (public lavatories), the occasional "mixed" pubs, the rare private clubs, the public walks, and parks. Some places, such as Piccadilly Circus, were notorious, and here the more "obvious" or blatant young prostitutes might gather. Some of the more obviously effeminate prostitutes wore women's clothing and powder,[83] but most young men were more discreet. Discretion was indeed the hallmark of homosexual prostitution.

Definitions of Homosexuality

Picton's survey of 154 Berlin prostitutes revealed that approximately two-thirds spent between one and five years on the game, having started between the ages of seventeen and twenty-five. This admittedly very rough survey suggests that most men had quit the trade by their mid-twenties.[84] The routes out were numerous, from becoming a "kept boy" (either in a long-term relationship or in successive relationships), to integration into the homosexual world, or to a return to heterosexual family life. At least two of the boys involved in the Cleveland Street affair founded "modest but upwardly mobile family dynasties"[85] and lost all contact with the world of prostitution. The participants' self-concepts, as homosexual and as prostitute, were likely to determine how long a man remained a "Mary-Anne." Historically specific definitions are all-important here.

A human identity is not a given in any particular historical situation but is the product of different social interactions, of the play of power, and sometimes of random choices. The homosexual orientation may be strong, but its significance depends on a host of factors that change over time.

For example in the 1890s Jack Saul regarded himself as a "sodomite," a term not necessarily coextensive with "homosexual." In his memoirs he reports that one of his clients was "not an actual sodomite. He likes to play with you and then 'spend' on your belly."[86] The distinction would be strange to the present century, but in 1890 the term "sodomite" was related to an act; "homosexual" implied a type of person, a member of a "species."[87]

An individual who could identify as "a homosexual" was more likely to be absorbed into the homosexual subcultures, to develop friendship networks and relationships (whether as "kept boy" or as partner), and to use his homosexuality as a way to rise in the world. One respondent, who took pride in having been "passed from hand to mouth" in the 1930s, moved from a poor working-class background in the North of England to the center of the metropolitan subculture as the companion of a gregari-ous member of the London intelligentsia: "I was never kept in the background . . . he wore me like a badge." The respondent was fully prepared to adapt himself to his new ambience, adopting a new accent and learning to "entertain": "You weren't just taken . . . out because you were pretty . . . you weren't taken out the second time because you were just a pretty face." Such a person is more likely to be able to cope with a wider range of sexual demands than one who is anxious to preserve a male and heterosexual self-image. (A Guardsman, for example, might charge extra for taking an "active" role in anal intercourse ["taking a real liberty"] but would baulk at taking a "passive" role.[88]) Reiss's classic study of delinquent youth has shown the sort of norms that may govern casual transactions. First, because the boy must make it clear to his partner and to himself that the relationship is solely a way to make money, the boy must not actively pursue his own sexual gratification. Secondly, the sexual transaction must be limited to specific sexual acts (for example, no buggery) or sexual roles ("active"). Thirdly, the partici-pants must remain emotionally neutral for fear of endangering the basis for the contract. Violence can be avoided as long as these rules are maintained but could erupt if they were threatened.[89]

A variety of self-definitions is possible: as homosexual, as homosexual prostitute, as a prostitute but not homosexual, or as neither homosexual nor prostitute. One respondent, who admitted to having been maintained by a friend, was highly indignant at having been described in a book as a "well-known male prostitute." Another interviewee, who as a Guards-man had had a large number of homosexual experiences and had fol-lowed these by a lifelong friendship with a homosexual man, was careful to explain that he was neither homosexual nor bisexual, but a "real" man who did it for the money.

The general impression that emerges from the nineteenth and early twentieth century is that the more casual the prostitution, the less likely was the individual to identify himself as homosexual or as a prostitute in the absence of any firm public categorization. Conversely, the longer the person stayed in the homosexual subculture the more likely he was to accept its values and to identify himself as primarily homosexual. In each case the important factor was not inherent propensity but the degree to which the man's activities and self-concepts were supported by the subcul-ture. Prostitution flourished among the Guardsmen and among the mes-senger boys of Cleveland Street precisely because the ideology operating in both networks acted to sustain the men's existing self-images as hetero-sexual "trade."

Conclusion

It is difficult to define homosexual prostitution, dependent as it is on changing definitions of homosexuality and shifts in the homosexual subculture. Clearly, there was a vast difference between the casual act of prostitution in a public lavatory for a small amount of money and the conscious adaptation of homosexuality as a "way of life." The experiences are related, however, not so much by the fact of the sexual acts as by the experience of homosexuality as a stigmatized category. This opprobrium demanded strategies of adaptation and techniques of avoidance. In this regard, male prostitution was strikingly different from the experience of female prostitution, for once the barrier to the initial act of prostitution has been crossed, the female prostitute could enter a world of values that served to support the choices she made and to reinforce the identity she was adopting. There was no comparable subculture of homosexual prostitution. For the young man who prostituted himself, the choices were effectively between retaining a conventional self-concept (and hence adopting neutralizing techniques to explain his behavior to himself and to others) or accepting a homosexual identity with all its attendant dangers in a hostile society.

Once the choice had been made, however, full integration into the nonprofessional homosexual subculture could take place. In this there were advantages unavailable to the female prostitute. The asymmetry of relationship between the female prostitute and client was permanent, and the stigma of prostitution was lasting. In the homosexual world the patterns and relationships were inevitably more ambiguous. The "deviance" of prostitution was supplementary to the "deviance" of homosexuality.

DISTANCE AND DESIRE: ENGLISH BOARDING SCHOOL FRIENDSHIPS, 1870–1920

◆

MARTHA VICINUS

This essay discusses the relationship between the schoolgirl crush and new, public roles for women at the end of the nineteenth century. It argues that the strong emphasis upon self-control and public duty was incorporated into the love of a schoolgirl for an admired teacher or older student, so that self-discipline became a manifestation of love. The essay concludes with an analysis of the competing public discourses of the sexologists and women educators; while the latter continued to adhere to a model of self-control and friendships channeled into school spirit, the sexologists provided a language, if imperfect, for explaining the extreme feelings individuals had. The essay argues that the process whereby women's friendships were publicly labelled deviant is more complex and uneven than previous historians have declared, and calls for more detailed studies of the period 1890–1930.

Recovering lost lesbians of the past and establishing bases for self-definition have been to this point the chief concerns of lesbian historiography.[1] The vexed question of when and why single-sex genital contact became labeled deviant has absorbed much energy. Scholars have concentrated, for example, on such issues as whether the famous sexologists of the late nineteenth and early twentieth centuries were detrimental or helpful to

Note: Originally published, in somewhat different form, in *Signs: Journal of Women in Culture and Society*, vol. 9 (1984), no. 4.

women's single-sex friendships.[2] Some, following the lead of the British historian Jeffrey Weeks, have argued that labelling has enabled women to identify themselves, to seek out companions, and to form conscious subcultures, such as those created in Paris and Berlin between the wars.[3] Others, however, have seen the work of sexologists such as Richard von Krafft-Ebing, Havelock Ellis, and Cesare Lombroso as effecting a blight on romantic friendships, leading to their "morbidification." According to these critics, the medical world's labelling of women's friendships as deviant had a wholly pernicious effect on women.[4] A major difficulty these historians have faced is that of dating: Exactly when did the theories of the medical men become well known among the general public? What impact did this knowledge have? When precisely did public disapproval of women's friendships begin? These questions have led to premature and exaggerated claims for several different time frames. They have, moreover, left lesbian history overly concerned with external labelling, rather than with the consideration of what homoerotic friendships were like and how they were a part of and apart from general social attitudes toward women as private and public beings.

In this essay I examine one aspect of the most widely known of women's friendships, the adolescent crush, during the late nineteenth and early twentieth centuries. I am concerned with its social origins, its various phases, and its impact on both the younger woman and the older recipient of her love. Neither the ingredients that make up an intense friendship nor its impact on the participants may have changed over time, but I believe that beginning in the late nineteenth century we find a different conjunction of public demands and private needs; these will be explored here. Boarding-school life during a period when women were pioneering new public roles and professional occupations especially encouraged an idealized love for an older, publicly successful woman. I cannot from my evidence answer the question of precisely how sexually aware the participants were in these "new" crushes, but surely some were, while others were not. Although a religious vocabulary effectively masked personal desires, a woman who loved another girl or woman always spoke of this love in terms that replicated heterosexual love. The strong emphasis on the power of the emotions suggests an understanding of what we would now label as sexual desire; commentators would probably not have argued so forcefully for the control of these emotions if they had not recognized their sexual source. Indeed, self-control became a key means of expressing love within the boarding-school world, and herein lies the core of my analysis.

Women's homoerotic friendships require specific preconditions to flourish. As Lillian Faderman has documented, women need to be minimally freed from the constraints of family and kinship (although friendships between cousins were common).[5] Familial responsibilities and economic dependence meant that few women before 1870 in Europe or America could hope to live with a beloved woman. Many might have wished to flee the world with a special friend, following the example of Sarah Ponsonby and Eleanor Butler, who eloped in 1778. The "Ladies of Llangollen" lived on a small stipend from their families, but they were a rare exception at that time. Far more common were lifetime friendships formed during the school years, in which neither woman ever lived with her beloved. By the late eighteenth century, with the expansion of boarding schools, increasing numbers of middle- and upper-class girls in England and the United States had opportunities to form close ties with someone of their own sex, which were encouraged by both families and schools. As one nineteenth-century guide explained, "Perhaps not even her acceptance of a lover is a more important era in the life of a young girl than her first serious choice of a friend."[6] Yet these same advisors also repeatedly warned parents about the excessive affections of girls. From the very beginning a tension surfaced between the desirability of forming close friendships and fears of their superseding family duties. In the words of Elizabeth Sewell, "When romantic friendship puts itself forward as having a claim above those ties which God has formed by nature, it becomes the source of untold misery to all who are connected with it."[7] Friendships, therefore, frequently became the arena in which a young woman fought for independence from her family.

These early relationships were necessarily conducted under the eye of one's family, although they often originated at boarding school or at a relative's home, or even at a church function. During the second half of the nineteenth century, however, the course of such friendships changed as the experiences of adolescent girls in boarding schools changed. The small, family-style schools where middle-class girls had been sent for a few years to learn social skills and a little French and music gradually gave way to schools of two hundred or more girls, with graded learning, organized sports, regular examinations, and trained teachers.[8] These reforms, begun in the 1850s, accelerated rapidly during the last thirty years of the century, so that by 1900 such schools and colleges became the model for middle- and upper-class girls' education in England and America.

The founding of large girls' boarding schools and colleges that were attuned to the needs of an expanding industrial and imperialist economy created a new set of psychological demands for the adolescent. These new institutions changed an emphasis on private duty and renunciation into a more publicly oriented ethic of service and discipline. Students were trained to enter the public worlds of teaching, medicine, philanthropy, and community service and to relate to others on the basis of shared professional concerns or principles rather than personal feelings. The enclosed, private world of women's domestic space, replicated in the old-fashioned boarding schools, was changed into a more public domain, where greater autonomy and individualism were encouraged. A girl was expected to take responsibility for her actions and to recognize their consequences for others. She was to become an autonomous and controlled being within the larger public world of the school, in preparation for the atomized world of industrial capitalism. At the same time, this new individuality was supposed to find expression through the corporate life and values of the school. Her self-development was redefined as part of a public ethos instead of being circumscribed by her family.

The effect of this increased emphasis on self-control and public life was twofold. On the one hand, girls had a greater sense of freedom and independence. On the other hand, the desire for closeness, for a special, cherished friend, was enhanced. If one's daily life demanded a public mask, a carefully cultivated sense of duty toward the group, then one found refuge—and an assertion of selfhood—through personal friendships. Under these circumstances friendships between girls and young women of roughly the same age continued to flourish. But corporate life encouraged the intense and erotically charged crush on an older and more experienced student or teacher as a girl's most significant emotional experience. Although similarly strong and complex emotions may have been felt by those involved, both the psychic and public structures of this relationship differed from the well-established model of adolescent friendship between girls of the same age. Questions of public power, authority, and control were central to relationships between women of differing ages, just as they were central to the new schools' ideology.

The adolescent crush was so common in the late nineteenth and early twentieth centuries that it was known by many different slang words besides "crush": "rave," "spoon," "pash" (for passion), "smash," "gonage" (for gone on), or "flame." But the particular form it took and general social attitudes toward it were rooted in a specific historical period and social class. The phenomenon of "smashing" in the new women's colleges of New England was identical in its nature to the English schoolgirls' raves. In both cases middle- and upper-class young women and adolescent girls were placed in single-sex communities with a strong reforming ethos. Women leaders were pioneering new roles for their students and were under great external pressure to demonstrate the viability of their institutions. At the same time, the students were eager to prove themselves worthy of the new institutions. A rave simultaneously satisfied the desire for intimacy and individuality, independence and loyalty.

The control of one's personal feelings meant self-respect and power for Victorian women, who had for so long been considered incapable of reason. Bodily self-control became a means of knowing oneself; self-realization subsumed the fulfillment of physical desire. Love itself was not displaced, but focused on a distant object, while nonfulfillment—sacrifice—became the source of personal satisfaction.[9] The emotions were concentrated on a distant, inaccessible, but admired student or teacher; differences in age and authority encouraged and intensified desire. The loved one became the object of a desire that found its expression through symbolic acts rather than actual physical closeness or even friendship in an ordinary sense of daily contact and conversation. Distance was a means of deepening a pleasure, which was experienced as the more fulfilling because nonsexual. Indeed, genital sexual fulfillment would have meant a failure of self-discipline and, therefore, of self-identity.

Although the ravee might not have been aware of the sexual roots of her passion, the older rave usually recognized some aspects of it; she described love, however, in emotional rather than sexual terms, emphasizing the idealistic feelings it aroused. For her the satisfactions of self-control came from knowing one could channel one's almost overpowering emotions into a higher cause, whether religion, the school, or the general betterment of women. The New Woman disliked uncontrolled emotions as much as did conservative advisers. She consecrated love on the altar of public duty. Soon after she had opened the doors of her new college in 1882, Constance Maynard happily recorded her pleasure at the admiration of an attractive student who intended to become a missionary. She sought to establish the ideal balance of personal love and higher duty with her:

> I told her how the capacity for loving always meant the capacity for suffering, & how I should expect the utmost self-control from her; I should expect it continuously, I said, & never say Thank you, for I belonged to the cause, the object, not to the individual, & all Students must be alike to me. And then, coming closer yet, I told her that self-control was not needed for the sake of appearances only, but for our own two selves, for real love, "the best thing in all the world" could be a terribly weakening power . . . suppose when she was sad or in perplexity she only came to me for help, instead of going *there* beside her little white bed, would that not be a step downward? . . . In spite of the glow that seemed to fill her, she seemed fully to see how the cause must come before the single individual, & we both agreed that a denial such as this enforced upon one part of our nature, was a sort of genuine satisfaction to another part, to the love of order, of justice, of doing something great & public.[10]

Maynard's advice catches exactly the combination of loving through self-discipline, of satisfaction through the suppression of desire, that characterized the late nineteenth- and early twentieth-century rave.

Almost inevitably the adolescent girl was brought into collision with her mother and her family because she found at school a whole new set of older women to admire and love at a time when she was necessarily loosening her ties with her family. The system of fostering friendships between girls of different ages and of encouraging school loyalties led to an increase in family tensions. The more astute headmistresses attempted to link the new values they were encouraging, as well as the new emotions, to family relations. Lucy Soulsby warned her students to "see how natural and loving [your Mother's] jealousy is, and spare it by constant tact—instead of being a martyr, feel that it is *she,* and not *you,* who is ill-used." Desire was to be transformed into "discipline and self-denial, so as to develop all the possibilities of nobleness. . . ." Nonfulfillment was a key to improving one's passionate attachment, for, as Soulsby cautioned, "outside, self-chosen affections burn all the stronger for repression and self-restraint; while home ones burn stronger for each act of attention to them and expression of them."[11] She suggested that love for both family and friend could be strengthened if a girl postponed visiting her friend in order to spend time with her family. Opposites—family duty and personal pleasure—could be brought together through iron discipline, which would yield a double reward. One did not give up love, but used it to further self-knowledge and self-control. The proper use of friendship could actually enhance the development of personal autonomy—so important for the New Woman—without loss of family ties.

Raves thrived on two apparently contradictory elements—public affirmation and secrecy. Public affirmation came through the continual discussion in school of favorite students and teachers. But secrecy helped to confirm and heighten private pleasure. Fantasies of service and sacrifice were fostered by the very emotional distance between the lover and the loved one. For most young girls emotions focused on either the head girl or the games captain or a favorite young teacher—all remote, yet familiar and publicly admired figures. These persons could be seen daily, yet rarely in private, and even more rarely in any kind of intimate setting. Such situations encouraged a life lived largely through symbolic acts and symbolic conversations.

The thrills of being "gone on" someone could be discussed endlessly among peers, adding delicious excitement to the routine of the school. Boarding school encouraged a kind of public voyeurism, with admiring girls dissecting the clothes, conversation, and appearance of a favorite. Theodora Benson remembered, "What endless discussions of tactics and strategy we used to hold after supper!" Unaffected herself, she enjoyed passing out advice to her "afflicted friends," even though they rarely took it.[12] Girls made public their most private desires not only because of group encouragement, but also because through talking they could make real impossible fantasies. Moreover, even the most trivial act of homage—helping the loved one put on her coat or cleaning the blackboard—could gain emotional significance through later conversations with other girls. Self-fulfillment came through the endless articulation of each newly aroused feeling, each action, each hope, before an admiring audience.

But secrecy was far more important, for it reinforced self-control. Every girl had her special, secret acts of homage, special ways of betraying her own desires to herself and her rave. Within the limited and confined world of the boarding school, certain acts took on important symbolic significance. The most common form of devotion was to make the be-loved's bed or buy her flowers or candy.[13] Every act became freighted with a sense of self-abnegation. At Cheltenham a ravee indignantly claimed that she could fill her rave's hot-water bottle better than her rival could.[14] These acts of service never involved physical contact but were a means of penetrating the private space of the loved one, of entering her room and secretly making it more attractive. One's presence was then felt by one's absence. Every ravee hoped that her good offices might be noticed, even as she did her work in secret.

An essential pleasure for those who loved a remote figure was the very distance itself, which gave room, paradoxically, for an enriched con-sciousness of self. Without gratification, countless fantasies could be constructed, a seemingly continuous web of self-examination, self-inspection, self-fulfillment. In the autobiographical tale by Dorothy Strachey Bussy, *Olivia*, the main character felt "a curious repugnance, a terror of getting *too* near" her beloved French teacher at Les Avons, lest mundane facts interrupt the rich emotional life she enjoyed within herself. She especially savored the moment before she entered Mlle. Julie's room: "It seemed an almost superhuman effort to open it. It wasn't exactly fear that stopped me. No, but a kind of religious awe. The next step was too grave, too portentous to be taken without preparation—the step which was to abol-ish absence. All one's fortitude, all one's powers, must be summoned and concentrated to enable one to endure that overwhelming change. She is behind that door. The door will open and I shall be in her presence."[15] A love such as Olivia's was passionately self-involved, for it opened a wide range of emotions to be experienced in solitude, especially nights when she listened to Mlle. Julie's footsteps in the corridor, hoping she would stop and give her a good-night kiss.

After a ravee had received some sign from her rave that feelings might be reciprocated, moments of greater intimacy were sought, though not necessarily in private, for secrecy could be created in the public domain of the school. The two lovers found means of speaking silently to each other, of sharing words and thoughts that could not be, and would not be, talked about in the general strategy sessions among peers. The secret sharing of a private world in a public place became a major source of pleasure; it affirmed the love, while never removing it from the realm of self-discipline. Indeed, self-control itself was heightened and embraced as a source of pleasure by the very creation of private understandings. Olivia felt certain of Mlle. Julie's love after hearing her read a poem to the class: "It was to me she was reading. I knew it. Yes, I understood, but no one else did. Once more the sense of profound intimacy, that communion beyond the power of words or caresses to bestow, gathered me to her heart. I was with her, beside her, for ever close to her, in that infinitely lovely, infinitely distant star, which shed its mingled rays of sorrow, affection and renouncement on the dark world below."[16] The distance between the lover and the loved one was bridged not through consummation but rather through a unity of sorrow and self-sacrifice.

The rave flourished on a paradox of fulfillment through unrequited love. Had Olivia and Mlle. Julie come too close, they might have found the tensions of love unsupportable. So much of the emotional life of a ravee centered on a world of fantasy, out of time and place, on some "infinitely lovely, infinitely distant star." Only there could the love remain safe and unchanged. And yet the very act of falling in love precipitated a crisis of identity in which the ravee moved inexorably toward an increased self-awareness. This new stage, however, involved a kind of reentry into the temporal world, where love had to face the reality of daily life and its buffetings. Later critics emphasized the very temporary nature of the adolescent crush and claimed that it was a preamble to heterosexual love which educated the girl emotionally.

The adolescent crush should instead be seen as a love based on a temporary condition of isolation, seeming powerlessness, and a willingness to devote oneself entirely to so new and overwhelming an experience. Only rarely did the older woman begin a rave. Even as a ravee felt she might be Echo to her great love, in reality, much of her love was self-created. By her adoration she initiated a response; the distance between herself and her rave then gave her an opportunity, through fantasy, to echo her own love, to examine and reexamine its different facets. Many women, including Bussy (speaking in the voice of Olivia), appear to have found a more complete love as an adolescent than they were ever to find with a man, possibly because they found that the male ego continually demanded that a woman be Echo to its needs and desires, whereas a woman permitted the full range of self-expression, enabling the youthful lover to be both Narcissus and Echo, creator and respondent.

However much a ravee might sustain her love on slight indications of favor and her own imagination, she still hoped that her homage might be repaid by another symbolic act, a vital reward that temporarily bridged the distance between the girl and her beloved. An admired teacher or prefect was ordinarily given social permission to kiss all the younger students. Every night Penelope Lawrence, head of Roedean, kissed each girl in her house good night; Saturdays she kissed the whole school. She might have used this moment to check each child, but the hurried, physically active, and overfull days of the students hardly suggest such sensitivity on the part of school administrators. More probably she was incorporating an aspect of family life into the residential houses in order to encourage a family atmosphere.[17] Olive Willis, when she started Downe House in the early twentieth century, shed the innumerable regulations she had hated as a student at Roedean, but she kept the symbolic good-night kiss.[18] Such a gesture was so drained of its meaning that it actually acted to remind girls of how far they were from home. Yet for the couple involved, on special occasions the kiss was reinvested with meaning, carrying overtones of transitory fulfillment. A virtually mean-ingless social gesture regained its original meaning and became a private, yet public, expression of love. The mother-daughter moment became a special act of kindness by the loved one, promising untold, unrealizable, future happiness.[19]

Raves existed at boarding schools in a delicate balance between privacy and publicity, self-discipline and uncontrolled feeling, timelessness and the school calendar. Mockery or jealousy could momentarily tip a ravee into the depths of depression and yet also leave her feeling more loyal and trustful of her love. At Roedean during Rachel Davis's time, school raves so dominated that the head, Penelope Lawrence, decided to have the games captain speak before the entire school on the subject. Her short lecture condemning such "sickening *nonsense*" left the students temporarily chastened, but her admirers loved her even more for her courage. Davis shrewdly diagnosed why gonages dominated at Roedean: "It can hardly be called a disease unless it reaches a feverish and inflamed condition. Unfortunately this is nearly always brought about by the clumsy fingers of the unloving, which, in school, as well as outside, must always interfere with what they do not understand. In truth the world has always been afraid of love, and until it can be made to realise that here is the one thing that is right and beautiful in all its shapes, persecution followed by distortion is bound to carry on its work."[20] On the fateful night when the games captain spoke, Davis herself was caught in the "clumsy fingers of the unloving." Those in authority were never alone in their desire to control the uncontrollable. A particularly nasty housemate held up to ridicule Davis's own rave for an older girl. By puncturing the idealism of others she could win attention. Yet the very vulnerability implicit in being gone on someone increased the deliciousness of the feelings. To be mocked for love was another means of self-sacrifice, of demonstrating one's love. To suffer both inwardly and publicly gave both the young girl and her rave greater importance—and fulfillment. And Davis was re-warded on that dreadful night by a special good-night kiss from her beloved prefect.

Our understanding of raves is incomplete without an examination of the recipients of so much admiration. Since most of the attention not only of the sexologists but also of memoirs and autobiographies has focused on the ravee, it is difficult to find the same kind of detailed descriptions about the feelings and responses of the older teacher or student. What evidence we have suggests that they reacted in a variety of ways, some-times trying to downplay the emotions that they had fanned, sometimes using them to enhance their own self-image publicly and privately, and sometimes channeling them into school loyalty. Students were often fickle and always transient; a teacher or older student who reciprocated with love had to recognize the temporary nature of the relation. Nevertheless, the rave was defined as an opportunity for mutual spiritual growth under the leadership of the older woman. In the 1870s and 1880s this often meant an evangelical awakening to God's love through a shared earthly love. For a later generation of teachers specific religious commitment had gradually become a generalized sense of duty, public and vaguely Christian.[21]

A rave also offered many concrete advantages, in addition to the more commonly emphasized spiritual benefits. Teachers were in a position to help with the careers of their protégées. Many older women urged young girls to seize the new opportunities opening up for women and to enter new occupations. M. Carey Thomas's favorite teacher, Miss Slocum, for example, took her aside and told her that she had particular talents as a scholar: "Minnie, I wish I had the chance you girls have—it is too late for me to begin to study now—all I can do is to give you what thoughts I have and help you all I can and then send you out to do what I might have done."[22] Miss Slocum helped Thomas to convince her parents to let her go on to Cornell to study and generally advised her during her early career. This support—a combination of practical information, moral advice, and personal affection—was extremely common. Grace Hadow was given permission to return to school as a pupil-teacher because she so loved her headmistress; with the head's help she went on to university and a distinguished career as an educational reformer.[23] Similar examples are recorded in numerous autobiographies and biographies of famous women.[24]

Many teachers felt an almost awesome sense of responsibility for their protégées, watching over their spiritual well-being with greater care than many mothers. In the late 1870s, for example, Maynard fell in love with a series of admiring students at St. Leonards School. Concerned about balancing the public, academic standards of the new school with her own high sense of Christian mission, she sought a resolution by concentrating on the moral welfare of her favorites. Erotic and maternal love were subsumed under religious duty. Thus, she could write in her diary, "Looking at Katherine, all the mother in me wakes & I think how tender I would be of letting any evil in on a mind such as that, so quick of apprehension yet at present so lovely so sensitive so pure."[25] The student was caught in a particular moment of adolescence, in an innocence that by definition must pass, negating Maynard's efforts at protection. The potential for disappointment and failure rested not simply in the possible changes on the part of the student but also in Maynard's own attitude toward her.

Reading aloud, exchanges of letters, and private talks took on the same symbolic importance for the older woman that bed-making and flower-giving had for the ravees. Some of Mlle. Julie's happiest moments were reading French classics with her favorite students. Private talks, of course, offered intimacy without the loss of distance, for the teacher retained her privileged position of moral instructor. Minor sins, school infractions, and spiritual struggles could be discussed at great length, encouraging a self-examination that became grounds for further intimacies, confessions, and avowals to do better. Maynard, for example, made it a habit to pray with her current favorite as often as possible. Passion was transferred to a spiritual realm, which made it more acceptable, more manageable, and yet also more satisfying.

Letters were an especially important means of communication, as they helped to bridge the distance between the rave and ravee. Shy students who feared to speak directly with someone they loved could pour out their affection in letters. In turn, teachers who were anxious about their public, professional role could break their silence through letters of advice, consolation, and love. Letter-writing, however, also reveals the ways in which school life differed from home life for the ravee. Many girls begged their raves to write to them during the holidays, to give them advice while they were away from school and in the midst of what they saw as "worldly" temptations. School seemed to make possible a loftier ideal of living, which included both love for a teacher and service to a wider community, whereas at home a young girl often felt confined by the husband-hunting social round and the petty duties of stepping and fetching for various members of the family. Constance Maynard became deeply involved in the spiritual life of another student, Mary Tait, after Katherine left St. Leonards. The adolescent Mary found her home life to be "distasteful or a bore" and hated her family obligations. Maynard wrote to her exhorting her to greater self-discipline. Maynard noted in her diary that, just before the end of the Christmas holidays, Mary wrote, "You can't think how delicious it is to know you are pleased. It is awfully severe sometimes to do what is right, but I always think of you & it becomes quite easy to do it."[26] Maynard, in turn, prayed for Mary, carrying her letters with her "as a secret unaccountable source of gladness of heart."[27] The discipline Constance imposed on Mary was one of obedience to her family as well as to her teachers, so that at least temporarily the rave improved her general attitude toward her elders, as all the authorities hoped it would.

But after the holidays Mary began to wilt under the pressures exerted by Constance. When she was reprimanded for a poor effort on her Drawing exam, Mary wrote back, "I was not aware that Drawing was a subject of such extreme importance. . . . I *am* indifferent to everything, except that you should not take everything I do so much to heart." Constance was heartbroken, interpreting her rejection not as stemming from the fickleness of an admittedly spoiled girl but, instead, as involving the loss of a soul. She wrote in her diary, "Oh, Mary, Mary, I loved you, *loved*—do you know what that means? . . . Oh my child my child, are you lost to me indeed? and I was the link through which you were dimly feeling after a higher life—are you lost to that too?"[28] Mary had sought to overturn the discipline of her family life, but she was then unwilling to embrace another new discipline, which Constance's love demanded of her. She escaped into her circle of adolescent friends, leaving Constance as forlorn as any rejected mother—or lover. Idealized self-control and spiritual seeking did not satisfy Mary, but Constance based much of her emotional life on this combination.[29]

Maynard's misery and confusion over Mary's rejection raises the issue of the power differential in school friendships and their transitory nature. Maynard, an inexperienced and unhappy teacher, hoped through her love of individual students to overcome her discipline problems and to find emotional fulfillment. But she failed to consider an inevitable teacher-student dilemma: The teacher is static, remaining in one spot, growing older but not altering in her or his role, while the student is in flux, bound to leave at a certain time, and is expected to flower and grow in the larger world. At school Mary Tait was experimenting and testing new emotions, ideas, and needs before she "came out" in society, while Maynard was learning to reconcile herself to a new, possibly permanent occupation and residence. The very temporary nature of her relationship with Mary gave it an urgency, if not desperation, that the girl sensed and rejected.[30]

Although the older woman had the greater power initially over the younger, she also had the most to lose in admitting her love. She gained most by keeping the relationship distant, by fostering self-control within herself and the ravee. When she bridged the inequality between them, she risked not only rejection but also the loss of spiritual leadership. Many teachers, like Maynard, found themselves brought under the sway of a younger student by their love for her.[31] Indeed, the emotional center of the relationship almost inevitably shifted to the ravee as soon as the attraction between the two women had been acknowledged because so much emphasis was placed on her spiritual growth. The older woman was in a position of self-sacrifice, giving moral guidance and personal love. But her sexuality could undermine the authority lent by distance, leading to a closeness that revealed the young girl's power over her. The implications were frightening, for they brought to the surface conflicting needs for power, autonomy, sexual expression, and spirituality. The ravee might prefer to retreat back to her former distance, her untouched fantasies, or she might use the love she had aroused to extend her emotional power and to explore her sexuality. The relationship could then only go forward to further intimacy.

Constance Maynard's friendship with Mary Tait was typical in many ways of those experienced by the new generation of professional single women who sought careers in the reformed girls' schools of the last thirty years of the nineteenth century. A devout Evangelical, Constance interpreted earthly love as a sign of God's love—and of a privileged duty. Not only was she involved with a favorite student at St. Leonards, but she was herself in a similar unequal, adoring relationship with her headmistress, Louisa Lumsden. The private and public inequality of power within the school made it easy for Constance to see her relationships in terms of the traditional family. She and Louisa both referred to their life together as a "marriage," in which Constance was expected to play the role of the submissive wife. Louisa was head and "husband" of the school, while Constance "mothered" the students. In this context Mary Tait was their wayward daughter, to be disciplined through love. Louisa had intervened for Constance, forcing Mary Tait to apologize for rudely rebuffing Constance; the incident strengthened her love for her vulnerable "wife." The transference of sexual tensions into the language of the family (and sexual love into the language of religion) left Constance, and many like her, without an appropriate vocabulary to describe and analyze their emotions. Indeed, these metaphors helped to conceal the physical basis of so much of their love. Although Constance could admit her loves to herself, she always saw them in emotional rather than physical terms.[32]

Passion such as Constance felt for so many of her students could not always be kept on the spiritual level; its very expression was rooted in earthly acts of love, however mediated by a spiritual vocabulary. In 1883, when Maynard was in charge of her own college, she was confronted by a hysterical student who could no longer hold back "the hopeless, perfectly self-controlled love which had evidently brought her into this state." On the doctor's advice, Maynard coaxed the deranged student into her room and away from the other students. She then had to lie down with her on her bed, which gave the girl the opportunity to grasp her tightly and to declare that they were now married. In "solemn tones" she insisted, "We are two no longer. I am part of you & you are part of me. I know all your thoughts by instinct. We can never be separated. Two souls for one forever."[33] The next day the girl was quickly taken away and returned to her family for care, and Maynard lost sight of her. Suddenly freed from parental restraints, the girl appears to have become unbalanced, although her expressions of passionate love never went beyond a parody of love making. However much a rave depended on the imagination of the ravee, virtually every girl wished for some sign that she had been singled out for special attention. As Maynard's preference for another student became obvious, the girl may have lost hope. Hysteria became a way of breaking through to her beloved teacher; when mad she could relinquish self-control and permit herself to act out the full expression of her love. Maynard, however, never felt that her declarations of love were anything more than the product of insanity, bearing no relation to the "sweet converse" she enjoyed with her favorite.

To judge from one fictionalized account, students were not always alone in their inability or unwillingness to place limits on their homoerotic love. In *Olivia* Mlle. Julie's "marriage" to Mlle. Cara could not tolerate the strains of adolescent adoration, and so the school was broken up. In the midst of this messy "divorce," Mlle. Cara died by what appeared to be suicide. Olivia's deeply idealistic love for Mlle. Julie provided meager comfort in the days that followed. Mlle. Julie's farewell to her beloved Olivia, just before going into exile, warned against and praised lesbian love:

> "It has been a struggle all my life—but I have always been victorious—I was proud of my victory." And then her voice changed, broke, deepened, softened, became a murmur: "I wonder now whether defeat wouldn't have been better for us all—as well as sweeter." Another long pause. She turned now and looked at me, and smiled. "You, Olivia, will never be victorious, but if you are defeated—" how she looked at me! "when you are defeated—" she looked at me in a way that made my heart stand still and the blood rush to my face, to my forehead, till I seemed wrapped in flame.[34]

Mlle. Julie, Olivia, and the others involved in the tragedy of Les Avons school recognized and gloried in the sexual roots of their spiritual love, even though they also insisted on containing it through self-control.

But *Olivia* is a fictionalized autobiography. Writing fifty years after the events, in the mid-1930s, Bussy portrayed her love for Mlle. Souvestre as wholly spiritual, even though she admitted its sexual undercurrent, and assumed her teacher's greater self-awareness. What Bussy remembered and what she knew or felt at the time must remain two different things. Moreover, she appears to have added the tragic finale, for no published evidence exists that Marie Souvestre's lover committed suicide; Mlle. Souvestre did not close her school but transferred it to Allenswood, near London, where Bussy was hired to teach Shakespeare. Perhaps Bussy revenged herself on the past by such a reordering of events, although she thereby continued the stereotype of the doomed lesbian relationship established by Radclyffe Hall's *Well of Loneliness* (1928). Bussy never thought of her love as deviant, but she interpreted victory as suppression, not expression. Yet her book—dedicated to the memory of Virginia Woolf—is a poignant tribute to an enduring love that was never replicated with the same strength, beauty, or power.

Olivia's year of love was a time when she found that "I first became conscious of myself, of love and pleasure, of death and pain, and when every reaction to them was as unexpected, as amazing, as *involuntary* as the experience itself."[35] Ravee, rave—and headmistress—all agreed that raves were in part involuntary and therefore especially difficult to banish. By the end of the nineteenth century those in authority, like previous generations, focused efforts on channeling them into areas they could more easily control. No attention was given to the rave, who was expected to control herself and the ravee; later she became the target of attack by those who publicly denounced women's friendships. Sara Burstall, an early head of the Manchester High School for Girls, explained in a textbook on English girls' schools that romantic friendship "should be recognised, allowed for, regulated, controlled, and made a help and not a hindrance to moral development. . . . A woman's life is, moreover, largely concerned with emotion; to suppress this will be injurious, to allow it to develop slowly and harmlessly, in respect or even reverence for someone who is older and presumably wiser than the girl herself, is not injurious and may be helpful."[36] Burstall defined homoerotic friendships in terms of woman's traditional sphere, as the familiar preamble to marriage. Lilian Faithfull, a second-generation headmistress, emphasized subordinating raves to the needs of the school. During the early years of the twentieth century, she advised her students to cure their raves by sharing their friend with everyone they knew. Girls were advised that, if their emotional attachment did not improve their work, play, and "general power of helping others," it should be "root[ed] out with unhesitating courage and unwavering will."[37] She even admitted to having cured herself in this manner. Olive Willis, headmistress of Downe House, had a teacher write a satirical play about raves when she found them too popular for her taste. Her comic rendition of the love-sick admirer is supposed to have shamed her students into recognizing what she saw as their immaturity.[38]

In all these cases the headmistress saw raves as a phase many adolescent girls underwent, which was unfortunately contagious in the confined world of a school and which could be contained, if not driven away, by hearty exposure to adult discipline. Well into the twentieth century educational texts and etiquette books focus on how best to control the girls' emotions so as to make their raves part of their moral development. Belief in the asexuality of girls persisted in schools, along with other traditional notions about women's innate nature; common sense and clearly articulated values, it was assumed, would cure virtually every problem. But this attitude left the authorities with little understanding of the profoundly disruptive nature of raves. By the middle of the nineteenth century male educators appear to have become fixated by fears of masturbation among their boys, minimizing the strong spiritual element in male raves.[39] Women, however, did the opposite, exaggerating the spiritual characteristics and neglecting the sexual. This failure to deal adequately with the sexual and emotional underpinnings of the rave left women teachers especially vulnerable to alternative analyses of what they interpreted as a controllable phase.

Women educators, etiquette-book writers, and other advice givers for over a century spoke the same language when discussing romantic friendships. This single discourse held as long as appropriate female roles were clearly defined both within the world of women and in the larger middle- and upper-class society.[40] But one of the natural results of the new educators' emphasis on careers for women, public responsibilities, and professional behavior was a blurring of the clear distinctions between the domestic, female world and the male, public world. As women gained a voice in the public sphere, their single-sex institutions came under attack. Their schools, settlement houses, and political organizations were often the home bases of reforming women and so were obvious targets for those who feared change. Friendships between teachers were stigmatized as abnormal, and raves were attacked as permanently distorting. At the height of the militant suffrage campaign a conservative journalist, Ethel Colquhoun, "regretted that the influence of mothers has been so largely superseded nowadays by the female celibate pedagogue."[41]

The attack by journalists in the popular media appears to have remained intermittent and closely linked to the public visibility of women. But a second alternative discourse began as early as the mid-1880s, when pioneering sexologists began to publish their elaborate taxonomies of sexual behavior in medical journals and other publications with a very limited distribution.[42] Rather than the emotional love that concerned women educators, this medical discourse described seemingly involuntary (and uncontrollable) sexual behavior that conflicted with approved social roles. Early definitions of lesbians all included descriptions of women engaged in so-called male behavior. When women appeared to be stepping outside their preconceived social role, they were pigeonholed as sexually variant, a label that was easy for journalists to use during periods of feminist militancy. But the sexologists were also concerned about the psychological roots of sexual behavior and were convinced that the powerful emotions felt by Olivia could be defined as either congenital, temporary (due to her youth), or acquired (by living in a single-sex institution). Thus, Havelock Ellis could explain,

> While there is an unquestionable sexual element in the "flame" relationship, this cannot be regarded as an absolute expression of real congenital perversion of the sex-instinct. The frequency of the phenomena, as well as the fact that, on leaving college to enter social life, the girl usually ceases to feel these emotions, are sufficient to show the absence of congenital abnormality. . . . We find here, in solution together, the physiological element of incipient sexuality, the psychical element of the tenderness natural to this age and sex, the element of occasion offered by the environment, and the social element with its nascent altruism.[43]

Ellis described in "scientific" language exactly the same elements that educators had found in the raves. But unlike them, he did not issue calls to personal duty, nor did he worry about the future moral development of girls. The medical men saw themselves as neutral, scientific recorders of existing and past sexual behavior. Ellis, in particular, prided himself on his efforts to remove sexuality from the realm of moral and social judgments. The route between Ellis, at least, and the labeling of schoolgirl friendships as deviant was extremely circuitous.

Raves, not surprisingly, did not significantly change after they had been labeled by the sexologists. Since more and more girls were going to secondary schools and joining such organizations as the Girl Guides, opportunities to know and love older women actually increased during the first thirty years of the twentieth century. These years were the heyday of the schoolgirl story, when millions of copies of Angela Brazil's novels were sold, not to mention those of her countless imitators. In many of her stories same-age girls become fast friends, share secrets and sweets, and love an admired older student or teacher. Inspired by loyalty to her and to their school, they learn to discipline their natural high spirits and are able to serve their school in an unexpected emergency.[44] Raves were a familiar part of the schoolgirl story. Adult fiction set in a school or college also frequently included a rave as an accepted, but minor, episode.[45] Although writers such as D. H. Lawrence and Clemence Dane portrayed raves negatively as early as World War I, they were by no means the majority among writers. Meanwhile, passionately admiring friendships appear to have continued through the 1940s and 1950s in single-sex institutions and organizations.[46]

For many years at least two separate discourses continued side by side, touching only occasionally through, for example, the private correspondence of the Bloomsbury intelligentsia, or novels such as Dane's *Regiment of Women* (1917), or in response to a specific scandal or feminist (unfeminine) public behavior.[47] The years leading up to and following World War I need to be studied in far greater depth if we are to understand the process whereby women's friendships, and specifically adolescent crushes, came to be seen as dangerous. Certainly by the time Radclyffe Hall published *Well of Loneliness* in 1928, many educators, journalists, politicians, and writers were actively discussing and reinterpreting women's sexuality, including their homosexuality. In 1921, for example, an attempt to amend the Criminal Law Amendment Act to make lesbianism (like male homosexuality) illegal was defeated on the grounds that women might learn something they knew nothing about.[48] The public discourse on sexuality had clearly altered by the 1920s, but we have yet to unravel the complex historical elements that brought about these changes.

The question is not whether the sexologists were pernicious or beneficial to women's romantic friendships and raves but, rather, when and why these two discourses came first to impinge on each other and then one discourse to replace the other.[49] The answers to these questions must remain tentative at this stage, especially given our limited sources and knowledge. A major contribution of the sexologists, and perhaps one reason why they came to be accepted, was their vocabulary, which made it possible to describe the complex connections among spirituality, sexuality, and personal emotions. Those who, like M. Carey Thomas and Constance Maynard (both of whom lived into the 1930s), were without a language of sexuality remained insulated from the medical discourse. But the lack of an appropriate language, or even an inappropriate one, could be as debilitating, as silencing, as any external labeling. Dorothy Strachey Bussy, looking back over fifty years, could see clearly the sexual nature of her love for Mlle. Souvestre, but at the time she may have had no means of understanding her passion. Only in the 1930s did she have the language to describe the emotions that had whirled through her during that fateful year. She could then crystallize the delicate balance of distance and desire, sacrifice and fulfillment, that made a rave so intoxicating: "Love has always been the chief business of my life . . . But at that time I was innocent, with the innocence of ignorance. I didn't know what was happening to me. I didn't know what had happened to anybody. I was without consciousness, that is to say, more utterly absorbed than was ever possible again. For after that first time there was always part of me standing aside, comparing, analyzing, objecting: 'Is this real? Is this sincere?' "[50]

EARLY

◆

TWENTIETH

◆

CENTURY

ICONOGRAPHY OF A SCANDAL; POLITICAL CARTOONS AND THE EULENBURG AFFAIR IN WILHELMIN GERMANY[1]

◆

JAMES D. STEAKLEY

From 1907 to 1909, Imperial Germany was rocked by a series of courts-martial concerned with homosexual conduct in the army as well as five courtroom trials that turned on the homosexuality of prominent members of Kaiser Wilhelm II's entourage and cabinet. National honor was palpably at stake in the Eulenburg Affair, as it has come to be known. While it was unfolding, the scandal led to an unprecedentedly detailed discussion of homosexual practices in the German and even foreign press, including a wealth of (anti-) gay images in political cartoons. These representations provide vivid insights into the nation's values, anxieties, and cultural norms, revealing that homophobia was yoked with anti-Semitism and antifeminism as part of a broader antimodernist backlash that ultimately led to Germany's entry into World War I. Yet at the same time, increased public awareness of homosexuality undoubtedly caused some individuals to reconceptualize their sexual activities and thus contributed to the making of modern homosexuals.

From 1907 to 1909, Imperial Germany was by turns amused and mortified by a series of journalistic exposés, libel trials, and Reichstag speeches, all

Note: Originally published, in somewhat different form, in *Studies in Visual Communication* 9, no. 2 (Spring 1983). Revised.

233

of which turned upon the alleged homosexuality of the chancellor and of two distinguished members of the entourage of Kaiser Wilhelm II. Taken together, these discourses constituted the most stunning scandal on the level of domestic politics in the history of the Second Reich (1871–1918). National honor was palpably at stake, and the German people were willing and even eager to judge the kaiser not by the company he kept but by the robustly paternal image he sought to project. It was defensively asserted from the rostrum of the Reichstag that "no one can doubt the moral earnestness of our kaiser and his consort, whose family life provides the entire country with a fine model."[2] Yet Philipp Prince zu Eulenburg-Hertefeld—the central figure in the scandal, which thus became known as the Eulenburg Affair—was to all appearances a happily married man too, and for a time the nation was brought uncomfortably close to having to consider the disturbing implications of the kaiser's penchant for frequent hunting trips and the annual holiday cruise on the royal yacht in exclusively male company. The implications were abundantly clear to the initiator of the attacks on Eulenburg, Maximilian Harden, for he possessed documentary evidence that might well have sufficed to expose and depose the kaiser.[3] He chose never to make use of it.

National attention shifted to yet another grave scandal late in 1908, this time affecting the Reich's foreign diplomacy rather than its domestic politics. The kaiser had given a bombastic interview to the *Daily Telegraph* of London in which, typically, he offered unwanted advice and rashly expounded on his peaceable vision of future relations between Germany and its archrival on the seas, Great Britain. Its publication unleashed a storm of outrage in the Reichstag, both from implacable foes of Anglo-German détente and from those who simply expected the kaiser to exercise reasonable discretion when discussing German strategy. Shaken by his obvious blunder and the ensuing furor, Wilhelm was all too happy to flee his duties for the regular November hunt at the Black Forest estate of an aristocratic confidant. It was here that the chief of the Military Secretariat, Dietrich Count von Hülsen-Häseler, donned a ballerina's tutu and was performing a *pas seul* as the after-dinner entertainment when he suddenly dropped to the floor, dead of a heart attack. "The incident with all that it implied was hushed up,"[4] but the combination of events proved too much for Wilhelm, who shortly suffered a nervous breakdown. One dinner-party guest who witnessed these events wrote: "In Wilhelm II I saw a man who, for the first time in his life, with horror-stricken eyes, looked upon the world as it really was."[5]

Like the bizarre death of Hülsen-Häseler, the entire Eulenburg Affair has been discreetly hushed up in all but the most recent historiography. Bound by disciplinary restraints, diplomatic historians have given due attention to the international controversy but have imposed what amounts to a scholarly blackout on its domestic counterpart—a disparity all the more striking in light of Maximilian Harden's astute observation that the Eulenburg scandal was "the underlying cause" of the *Daily Telegraph* affair.[6] This embarrassed silence has been even more obvious among German than among non-German historians, manifesting an understandable reluctance to wash the nation's dirty linen in public.

It is in the nature of scandal, however, to catapult sexual conduct out of the private sphere into the public arena, thus generating discussions on sexual politics that have the potential to alter actual attitudes and actions. In the specific instance of the Eulenburg Affair, the long-range consequences were so severe that the scandal defies dismissal as a mere episode. French, British, and American historians have linked the events of 1907–1909 to a far-reaching shift in German policy that heightened military aggressiveness and ultimately contributed to the outbreak of World War I.[7] Such insights were by no means unknown to earlier observers. Writing in 1933, for example, Magnus Hirschfeld argued that the outcome of the entire regrettable affair was "no more and no less than a victory for the tendency that ultimately issued in the events of the World War."[8] And in a bitterly racist vein, Wilhelm himself fulminated in 1927 that the scandal had been started by "international Jewry" and marked "the first step" of a conspiracy that led in 1918 to German defeat and his abdication.[9]

Yet these assessments of the long-range effects of the Eulenburg Affair, however apt or grotesque they may be, overlook the vital dimension of the scandal's more immediate, short-term impact on the manners and morals of the German nation. While hindsight can link the scandal with momentous events that occurred years later, such retrospective interpretations were obviously unavailable to contemporary observers struggling to draw their own set of conclusions. In many respects, the Eulenburg Affair represented for Wilhelmine Germany the same sort of "ritual of public condemnation" that the Oscar Wilde trial had been for Victorian England in 1895.[10] Both scandals were labeling events that dramatically accelerated the emergence of the modern homosexual identity by stimulating and structuring public perceptions of sexual normalcy and abnormalcy.

As the most tumultuous *cause célèbre* of its era, the Eulenburg Affair provoked a flood of press coverage, ranging from lengthy articles and editorials in daily papers to pocket digests of courtroom testimony. Political pamphlets and broadsides appeared, and virtually every facet of the shocking revelations was minutely depicted in political cartoons as the courtroom drama unfolded.[11] The cartoons selected for inclusion here provide a unique access point for a sociohistorical analysis of the Eulenburg Affair by illuminating many of the values, anxieties, and cultural norms of Wilhelmine society. Apart from the anti-Semitic interpretation of events advanced in reactionary nationalistic circles and adopted by Wilhelm, the pictorial handling of the scandal reveals a remarkable degree of uniformity. A handful of images appears repeatedly, a phenomenon that cannot adequately be attributed to the possibility of artistic borrowing or the favored use of certain motifs such as the cuirassiers' uniform (see Figures 3, 4, and 5). Among the cartoons' recurrent themes are the threats to national honor and security posed by the spread of decadence among the ruling class, the corruption of military discipline, and the inversion of traditional sex roles. The common denominator of these concerns was a profound sense of cultural pessimism that transcended party divisions and was only superficially belied by the humor of the caricatures.

Background Events

The starting point of the Eulenburg Affair can ultimately be traced back to the rupture between the political visions and programs of Chancellor Otto von Bismarck and Kaiser Wilhelm II. The "Iron Chancellor" had single-mindedly—some would say brilliantly—shaped Germany's destiny by founding the Second Reich and for almost two decades guiding the nation to great-power status under Wilhelm I, who was content to serve as a mere figurehead. Shortly after succeeding to the throne in 1888, Wilhelm II dismissed Bismarck and energetically instituted "personal rule," reclaiming for the crown constitutional powers that had heretofore devolved upon the chancellor. The young kaiser saw himself as the embodiment of the Reich's historical mission, but he struck seasoned political observers as brash and incompetent, and insiders were alarmed by his precarious mental balance—impressions that were only deepened by the passage of time. In a display of compensatory bravado, Wilhelm dismantled Bismarck's *Realpolitik*, based on a dense network of treaties designed to guarantee the European balance of power, and replaced it with a confrontational *Weltpolitik*, which promised to gain the Reich its rightful "place in the sun" by mounting a naval fleet and aggressively pursuing overseas expansion. But Bismarck's sophisticated statesmanship was actually supplanted by vacillatory bluster, for Wilhelm surrounded himself with a mixed retinue of military and civilian advisors whose outlooks diverged widely; tugged in competing directions, he proved incapable of synthesizing a consistent stance on foreign affairs.

The preeminent figure in Wilhelm's civilian entourage during the 1890s was Eulenburg, a member of the diplomatic corps whose anti-imperialist outlook and willingness to seek an accommodation with the "hereditary enemy," France, earned him the undying enmity of hawkish Gallophobes in the upper echelons of both the military and the Foreign Office. He seemed unassailable, however, for it was rumored in court circles "that His Majesty loves Philipp Eulenburg more than any other living being,"[12] and Wilhelm swiftly promoted his "bosom friend"[13] to an ambassadorship. Even prior to his dismissal, Bismarck's assessment of the relationship between the two was such that it could "not be confided to paper"; therefore, he explained in a letter to his son, "I will not *write* much that I intend to tell you."[14] In 1892, after his retirement, Bismarck also disclosed his suspicions to Maximilian Harden and elaborated on his concern in acidulous terms: "There are supposed to have been some quite good generals among the *cinaedi* [a pejorative Greek term for homosexuals], but I have yet to encounter any good diplomats of the sort."[15] Fourteen years would elapse before Harden's public disclosure of Eulenburg's homosexuality, but the motive was unaltered and widely shared: breaking his "mesmeric power" over the kaiser's heart and mind.[16] And indeed, his removal from the entourage signalled a decisive and fateful shift from competing civilian and military influences on German foreign policy to the outright dominance of "preventive war" advocates.

Were one to restrict the investigation of the Eulenburg Affair to the cartoons it inspired, it would be easy to arrive at the erroneous conclusion that Eulenburg came under fire solely because of his homosexuality and to lose sight entirely of the political dimension of Franco-German relations. Of some 350 cartoons examined by this writer, only one sets the scandal in the context of German foreign policy. The rarity of this explicit linkage of homosexuality and anti-imperialism is perhaps less surprising when one considers that all the other cartoons originally appeared in journals that dealt simultaneously with a broad range of foreign and domestic affairs. A survey of the political cartoons in their context would enable one to discern certain ramifications of the Eulenburg Affair that remain largely invisible when they are examined in isolation. Because political cartoons generally comment on or embellish news reports, they document rather than analyze history. They are useful indicators of the public response to new information that is still being digested (a process they stimulate), but their full operational effectiveness relies on a set of cultural and historical assumptions implicit but not necessarily explicit in their imagery. In the case of the Eulenburg Affair, the element left unspoken and unportrayed resides in the quest for power by his adversaries; they mobilized homophobia not as an end in itself, but in the pursuit of a higher goal. Indeed, the Eulenburg Affair was prompted neither by Eulenburg's homosexuality nor even by his political outlook. As his loyal and courageous wife remarked to Hirschfeld during a court recess, "They are striking at my husband, but their target is the kaiser."[17] The All-Highest Personage rarely appeared in any of the German cartoons (and in none selected for inclusion here), yet he figured prominently in numerous foreign cartoons—trying more or less successfully to distance himself from the stench of scandal.

Although Eulenburg had a formidable number of aristocratic opponents, including the kaiser's sister, these figures preferred to intrigue behind the scenes and to leave the public vendetta to a bourgeois individual, Maximilian Harden. At the height of the scandal, one homosexual nobleman asked indignantly (and with no little trepidation): "Does this Jew actually rule in Prussia, deposing generals and ambassadors?"[18] Harden was perhaps the most accomplished and, to use his word, "effective" political commentator in an era when German Jews were more strongly represented in journalism than in any other profession.[19] After meeting him, Bismarck blithely remarked that Harden "was not at all like a Jew" and thereby alluded to a current stereotype: at that time the word Jew was synonymous with hack journalist.[20] Harden edited and largely wrote by himself *Die Zukunft*, a fiercely independent Berlin weekly in which he called for progressive domestic reforms and for a coherent foreign policy combining Bismarckian diplomacy and expansionistic *Weltpolitik*. A relentless gadfly of Wilhelm's personal rule, Harden was repeatedly jailed and fined for *lèse majesté*; but he always returned to the thick of the fray.

Harden was equally vitriolic in his published attacks on Eulenburg, which began appearing in 1893 and continued intermittently throughout the decade. He refrained from sexual innuendo because he upheld the classic distinction between public and private spheres, a patrimony of bourgeois liberalism to which he was devoted as a beneficiary of Jewish emancipation. But his patience was wearing thin by 1902, and he quietly issued what amounted to an ultimatum: If Eulenburg did not resign from public life, his secret life would be exposed. Eulenburg capitulated to this blackmail at once, for retirement seemed not too dear a price to pay to avoid disgrace: suffering ill health, mourning the death of his mother, and disheartened by a cooling in his relationship with Wilhelm (who may have feared exposure himself), the fifty-five-year-old prince proved quite willing to yield his ambassadorship in Vienna and to retire to Liebenberg, his country estate in the tradition-steeped Mark Brandenburg, where he would spend the next years as a virtual recluse. Personally vindicated and genuinely relieved that exposing Eulenburg had not been necessary, Harden shared with his aristocratic allies the fond hope that a new and better day was dawning for the Reich.

It was therefore a rude jolt when, in late 1905 and 1906, Eulenburg ventured to resume contacts with foreign diplomats and the kaiser, whom he invited to shoot at Liebenberg. Moreover, Eulenburg's cautious rehabilitation coincided with a major foreign policy fiasco, Germany's yielding hegemony over Morocco to France at the Algeciras Conference, which it was all too easy to pin on Eulenburg's rising star. Finally, rumors began circulating that Eulenburg coveted the post of chancellor, and Harden renewed his attack in stronger language than ever: Two articles published in November of 1906 linked Eulenburg, "this unhealthy late-romantic visionary,"[21] with General Kuno Count von Moltke, military commandant of Berlin. They in fact had a long-standing friendship, and this was by no means Harden's first attack on Moltke, who had suffered the ignominy of having his nickname, Tütü, revealed in *Die Zukunft* five years earlier. In the second of the articles, ominously entitled "Dies

Irae," the pair was identified only as "the Harpist" (Eulenburg was a widely performed amateur composer) and as "Sweetie" (due to Moltke's weakness for chocolates; "sweet" was moreover a vernacular term for homosexual).[22] These encoded figures engaged in a brief dialogue in which they wondered agitatedly whether Harden would dare to reveal "even more" and agonized over the reaction of "Darling" (the kaiser) to their exposure.[23] Eulenburg beat a hasty retreat, withdrawing to Switzerland and dispatching an intermediary to mollify Harden and to avert further revelations.

And there matters remained for the moment. Journalists sensed that an important story was breaking, and newspapers throughout the country reported on Harden's second article or even reprinted it in full. But Harden's warning was initially cryptic to all but those immediately involved, and another six months would elapse before the identities of Sweetie and the Harpist became public knowledge and they could appear as heraldic figures in a "New Prussian Coat of Arms" (Figure 1), bedecked in floral garlands in an allusion to Eulenburg's most famous composition, the "Rosenlieder." With pursed lips, doe-eyed gaze, limp wrists, broad hips, and legs coyly pressed together, the pair presents a stereotype of male effeminacy that vividly violates the proud German escutcheon; the Harpist even threatens to topple the crown with his compromising gesture.

Harden's decision to expose Moltke and Eulenburg was an agonizing one and was reached due to an ensemble of factors. First, various aristocratic intriguers continued to egg him on. Second, military circles were embarrassed by a flurry of lesser scandals. They cumulatively convinced Harden that homosexuality was becoming rampant, and he hoped a death-blow to Eulenburg would halt its spread. The figures were indeed alarming: Within the preceding three years, courts-martial had convicted some twenty officers of homosexual conduct, and 1906–1907 witnessed six suicides by homosexual officers ruined by blackmail.[24] One officer stationed with the elite Garde du Corps regiment in Potsdam, Major Johannes Count von Lynar, was charged with molesting his aide-de-camp, while a second officer charged with homosexuality, Lieutenant General Wilhelm Count von Hohenau (see Figure 4), was not only commander of the Garde du Corps but also a blood relative of the kaiser. The final factor prompting Harden was Eulenburg's foolhardy decision to return from Switzerland to be initiated into the High Order of the Black Eagle. This honor appeared all the more inappropriate when, one month later, Friedrich Heinrich, Prince of Prussia, regretfully declined investiture as Grand Master of the Order of the Knights of St. John with the shocking explanation that his homosexual proclivities made him unsuited for the prestigious post. Convinced that the body politic was under assault, Harden denounced Eulenburg as a pervert on April 27, 1907, noting acidly that since his "vita sexualis [was] no healthier" than Friedrich Heinrich's, he should have the decency to follow the prince into exile.[25]

As anxious speculation about the homosexual camarilla scheming against the national interest began to fill the German press, the royal suite realized it would finally have to act. The kaiser was no reader, and it had been easy for his cabinet and entourage to keep him in blissful ignorance of the growing scandal. Now, however, the twenty-five-year-old crown prince—an officer in the Garde du Corps—was selected to break the news to his father. On May 2, he marched in to the appointment armed with back issues of *Die Zukunft*. He later reported that an expression of utter horror and despair had spread across his father's features, and charitably attributed this to disgust at the mention of homosexuality.[26] After regaining his composure, Wilhelm hastily conferred with Hülsen-Häseler and the minister of police affairs, who presented him with a carefully edited list of approximately fifteen prominent aristocrats adjudged homosexual by the Berlin vice squad; it had been pared down from several hundred to spare the kaiser's feelings.[27] Apparently finding their names on the list, the kaiser commanded Hohenau, Lynar, and Moltke to resign their commissions, while Eulenburg was told to either exculpate himself or go into exile. Pleased that the kaiser had acted so decisively, the nation hoped that the camarilla was eliminated and hailed Harden as a modern Wilhelm Tell, the liberator of his fatherland.

The Trials

Moltke and Eulenburg retained lawyers who pursued different tacks. Moltke's attempt to file a suit for criminal libel against Harden was rebuffed by the state prosecutor, who instead advised him to file for civil libel, thus placing him at a considerable procedural disadvantage. Eulenburg's strategy was more clever and avoided direct confrontation with Harden: After denying his culpability, he presented the local district attorney of his home area with a self-accusation of violating Paragraph 175 of the penal code, which punished "unnatural vice" between men with prison sentences of anywhere from one day to five years. By late July, the district attorney had completed his investigation and, predictably, cleared Eulenburg.

Harden meanwhile set about preparing his defense for the upcoming civil libel suit brought by Moltke, and Berlin was further shaken by accusations of homosexuality leveled against the manager of the Royal Theater, Georg von Hülsen, and the crown prince's equerry, von Stückradt. Finally, the imperial chancellor, Bernhard Prince von Bülow, was linked romantically with his secretary (described as his "better half"), Privy Councillor Scheefer, by two different publicists; against one of them, Adolf Brand, Bülow pressed criminal libel charges.

The first of these cases to go to court, *Moltke* v. *Harden*, opened on

October 23, 1907. The lackluster performance of Moltke's lawyer contrasted sharply with Harden's brilliant defense. Three chief witnesses took the stand: Moltke's former wife, who had divorced him nine years earlier; Dr. Magnus Hirschfeld, a forensic expert on homosexuality; and an enlisted man named Bollhardt (see Figure 4). Lili von Elbe testified that in two years of marriage, conjugal relations had occurred only on the first two nights; on the few other nights they had shared a bed, Moltke had sometimes placed a pan of water between them to discourage her advances. She reported that her husband had once espied a handkerchief left behind by Eulenburg (see Figure 1) and had warmly pressed it to his lips, murmuring "Phili, my Phili!" Moltke had variously addressed Eulenburg as "my soulmate, my old boy, my one and only cuddly bear" (the motto in Figure 1), and the two had referred to Wilhelm as their "darling." They had behaved in such a blatant fashion that her ten-year-old son (by a previous marriage) had taken to imitating their "revolting" mannerisms with the servants. Eulenburg had always vehemently opposed their marriage, she added, and her husband had spent more time with him than with her—including Christmas Eve; but she had not suspected the worst, since the very existence of homosexuality had been unknown to her at the time (*Prozesse*, pp. 16–36).[28]

As the trial entered its second day, an "enormous crowd" gathered before the courthouse and police reinforcements had to be summoned to maintain public order. The crowd grew larger day by day, and an "army" of German and foreign reporters encamped at the scene. The soldier Bollhardt offered the shocking testimony that in Potsdam regiments, sexual relations between officers and enlisted men were common knowledge (see Figure 4). He went on to describe at length his own participation in champagne orgies at Lynar's villa (see Figure 10), stating that he had seen both Hohenau and Moltke there. The hushed courtroom was fascinated by Bollhardt's report on the powerful sex appeal of the white pants and knee-high boots of the cuirassiers' uniform: Any guardsman who ventured to wear it in public was virtually certain to be approached by men soliciting homosexual intercourse (see Figure 3). "But that's forbidden now, you know," he remarked, unwittingly provoking an outburst of hilarity. After the mirth had subsided, he explained his meaning: Due to importunities, wearing the uniform while off duty had recently been banned (*Prozesse*, p. 44).

The final witness to take the stand was Hirschfeld, whose very appearance—immediately captured in numerous cartoons (e.g., Figure 2) —seemed to exemplify a Jewish stereotype. He had served for the past ten years as chair of the Scientific-Humanitarian Committee, an organization that campaigned for the repeal of Paragraph 175, and his courtroom appearance on Harden's behalf tended to strengthen the association between Jews and the unprecedented publicity being given to homosexuality. (In the following days, handbills publicizing anti-Semitic lectures were distributed in front of his apartment.[29]) Basing his remarks on Lili von Elbe's testimony and on his observation of Moltke in the courtroom, Hirschfeld asserted that the plaintiff had a "feminine side" that "deviated from the norm; i.e., from the feelings of the majority." In particular, his treatment of his wife, his devotion to Eulenburg, his "sensitivity" for the arts, and his use of makeup (apparently visible in the courtroom) permitted the deduction that Moltke's "unconscious orientation" could "objectively" be labeled "homosexual," even if he had never committed sodomy (*Prozesse*, pp. 65–68).

In his closing argument, Harden stressed that he, too, had never charged Moltke with violating the law but only with suffering from a "mawkish, unmanly, sickly condition" and that he had revealed Moltke's orientation not to profit from sensationalism (sales of his journal were up dramatically[30]) but for political ends (*Prozesse*, pp. 96–105). No such claim could be made by the political cartoonists, who were shamelessly exploiting the sensational side of the courtroom testimony. The champagne-drinking bluebloods and military men foregathered in their exclusive Berlin setting (Figure 10) are depicted as bug-eyed, wasp-waisted aliens, at once ominous and pathetically puny.

On October 29, the court handed down its verdict: Moltke's homosexuality had been confirmed and Harden was therefore acquitted of libel, court costs falling to Moltke. According to Hirschfeld, "a storm of moral outrage" swept through the country, but it was curiously two-pronged, directed both at the decadent "upper classes" and at the Jewish bearers of bad tidings.[31] A cloud of suspicion settled more firmly than ever over Eulenburg, and Moltke's disgrace seemed irremediable, when an unexpected development took place. The trial was voided due to faulty procedure, and in a reversal of its earlier standpoint, the state prosecutor called for a retrial against Harden, this time on grounds of criminal libel. This announcement came just a few days before the opening of the second major trial, which was to pit Chancellor Bülow against Adolf Brand. It appears that the German judiciary now regarded Harden's acquittal as a serious blunder that tended to undermine public confidence in the regime. In its determination to restore respectability to the ruling class, the justice system was henceforth far from impartial.

The *Bülow* v. *Brand* case was handled quickly, the entire trial and sentencing occurring on one day, November 6. Once again the courtroom was packed while throngs gathered outside. The first to testify was Brand, whose extensive history of prior convictions was read into the record. This remarkable publicist had founded *Der Eigene*, the first homosexual periodical in the world, in 1896, and had twice seen its distribution halted by obscenity charges. In 1902, he had founded an organization that, like Hirschfeld's group, aimed at repealing Paragraph 175. Brand was charged with authoring and distributing a libelous leaflet in which he stated that

Bülow had been blackmailed because of his homosexuality, alleged that Bülow had embraced and kissed Scheefer at all-male gatherings hosted by Eulenburg, and argued that the chancellor was morally obligated as a homosexual to use his influence for the repeal of Paragraph 175.

On the stand, Brand maintained the truth of the leaflet and stated that he had by no means intended to insult Bülow by calling him a homosexual, since he had a positive view of those who shared his own sexual orientation. He had exposed Bülow with the political goal of hastening the repeal of Paragraph 175, for he had come to believe that this could only be achieved by creating martyrs—the strategy of "the path over corpses." Finally, borrowing an argument from Harden's defense, he claimed that he had only labelled Bülow's orientation, not accused him of law-breaking.[32] Bülow took the stand next, airily dismissing Brand's imputations and demanding an exemplary punishment. He made the gratuitous observation that, while his private life was beyond reproach, the same could not be said of Eulenburg, about whom he had heard unsavory rumors.

The next witness was Eulenburg, who passed over Bülow's slur in silence and merely asserted that he had never hosted parties such as those described by Brand; he simultaneously used the opportunity to swear, as had Bülow, that he had never violated Paragraph 175. He appealed to public sympathy by arguing that Hirschfeld's sophistic system of sexual "nuances" could turn any innocent friendship into a source of calumny. Brand spoke again, expressing his esteem for Eulenburg's vision of ideal friendship and inserting a jarring political note: The campaign of vilification against Eulenburg could ultimately be traced to Bülow, who saw in him a rival for the post of chancellor. When Eulenburg was asked whether he gave any credence to Brand's analysis, the question was instantly ruled out of order by the judge, who claimed to be "determined to keep politics out of this case."[33] The proceedings took another unexpected turn when the head of the Berlin vice squad testified that Bülow may indeed have been a blackmail victim, but the prosecution hurriedly dropped this line of inquiry.[34] The judge withdrew briefly and returned with a conviction and an eighteen-month prison sentence for libel.

The *Brand* v. *Bülow* trial made a mockery of justice, but the nation was gratified by its outcome and little inclined to scrutinize the procedure. Brand had been railroaded, and he later pointed out that he was the sole individual actually imprisoned as a result of the scandal. His guilty verdict suggests that public opinion was beginning to rally around the established order and to turn against those Jewish and homosexual publicists who were increasingly perceived not as saviors but as rumor-mongers and purveyors of filth.

The *Harden* v. *Moltke* retrial opened on December 18 and lasted for two weeks, casting a pall over the holiday season. Lili von Elbe was placed back on the stand, and the state prosecutor destroyed the credibility of her earlier testimony by summoning expert medical witnesses who disqualified her as a classical hysteric. Both Moltke and Eulenburg spoke in defense of the spirit of male friendship and attacked the distinction Harden and Hirschfeld had drawn between homosexual orientation and practices as mere chicanery. Intimidated by the about-face in public opinion and the obvious direction of the proceedings, Hirschfeld was reduced to a national laughingstock (see Figure 2) when he formally retracted his initial forensic opinion, feebly asserting that it had been predicated on the assumed truth of Elbe's testimony. Even Harden's claim to have acted from political motives was now discounted as a red herring, and the verdict handed down on January 4, 1908, became a foregone conclusion: Moltke's reputation was cleared, while Harden was convicted of libel and sentenced to four months in prison.

Delighted by this turn of events, the kaiser envisioned a complete rehabilitation of Moltke and Eulenburg, planning for them a greater role than ever in his entourage. After six months of revelations and two months of trials, most observers prematurely concluded that the Eulenburg Affair was over. To be sure, the scandal had taken its toll: In the winter of 1908, all of the major parties involved—Moltke, Lili von Elbe, Eulenburg, Harden, Hirschfeld, Brand—suffered illness brought on by sheer exhaustion, while the kaiser was near a nervous breakdown.[35] But the public underestimated the resourcefulness of Harden, who was motivated not just by opposition to the rehabilitated camarilla but now, as well, by vengefulness.

By testifying under oath in the second and third trials that he had never violated Paragraph 175, Eulenburg had perjured himself.[36] Harden faced the challenge of producing incontrovertible evidence so as to force the state prosecutor into action. In an elaborate legal ruse, Harden colluded with an ally, the Bavarian editor Anton Städele, who published a fraudulent article alleging that Harden had received a million marks in hush money from Eulenburg to desist in his attacks. Harden then sued Städele for libel and turned the court proceedings into a forum for presenting his evidence on Eulenburg. Arranging for a trial outside of Berlin, in anti-Prussian Munich, was also part of the devious strategy.

With little advance fanfare in the press, the Harden-Städele trial was convened and completed on April 21, 1908. Harden had subpoenaed Georg Riedel, a Munich milkman, and Jakob Ernst, a Starnberg farmer and sometime fisherman on the Bavarian lakes where Eulenburg had vacationed in earlier years. Since the statute of limitations had expired, Riedel freely admitted that in 1881, while serving in the military, he had once engaged in sexual relations with Eulenburg, who later made him gifts of money and also introduced him to Moltke. The second witness, Ernst, had more on his conscience and initially denied any wrongdoing. But persuaded by the judge that swearing a false oath would lead to punishments in this world and the hereafter, he haltingly confessed that in 1883, as a nineteen-year-old, he had likewise been seduced by Eulenburg. Ernst later revealed that this incident initiated a long-term relationship with the prince that had continued until quite recently. During these years, Ernst had led a double but apparently charmed life as a respectable family man in Starnberg and as Eulenburg's intimate companion in Liebenberg, Munich, Berlin, and on princely vacations in Garmisch, Meran, Zurich, Rome, the Riviera, and Egypt.[37] The court's verdict was anticlimactic: Städele was convicted of libel and sentenced to a hundred-mark fine (which was covertly reimbursed by Harden).

Harden's real victory became evident in the stunned public reaction to the Munich trial. Gradually, a welter of opinions began to emerge. To some, Eulenburg seemed disgraced beyond repair; one close friend forthrightly suggested that he commit suicide.[38] Others gave credence to Eulenburg's claim that Riedel and Ernst must have been paid by unknown enemies to give false testimony; Harden was suspect to many. With considerable reluctance, the state prosecutor moved into action: Eulenburg was arraigned on perjury charges on May 7, 1908, and two weeks later the Imperial Supreme Court overturned Harden's libel conviction in the Moltke case on procedural and substantive grounds and called for a second retrial.

The fifth major trial of the scandal was convened in Berlin on June 29, after Eulenburg had unsuccessfully sought a postponement due to ill health. The state prosecutor introduced as evidence incriminating books and correspondence confiscated at Liebenberg Castle, including one letter to Ernst written by Eulenburg prior to the Munich trial, urging him to reveal nothing. Ernst was, in fact, the prosecution's star witness, turning at one point to Eulenburg and uttering in Bavarian dialect: "By God Almighty, Your Excellency, you can't deny that we two did it. . . . Excellency, it's true. We two haven't got a chance in the world."[39] So enfeebled that he had to be carried into the court on a litter, Eulenburg continued to protest his innocence even when confronted with ten witnesses summoned by the prosecution—including three police officers, two former stewards on the royal yacht *Hohenzollern*, and a court servant who testified to having observed Eulenburg through a keyhole in 1887.[40] The prosecution planned to call another thirty witnesses, but the defendant collapsed during a recess and was declared dangerously ill by medical attendants. Determined to press to a close, the judge resumed the trial on July 17 in Eulenburg's hospital. When the defendant passed out during the hearing, the judge relented and postponed further hearings until Eulenburg's health improved. Two months later he was provisionally released from the court's custody on posting a bond of one hundred marks and returned to his Liebenberg estate, where he was warmly received by his loyal tenants and gave interviews protesting his innocence.

Eulenburg's ill health enabled a broad sector of the German public to accept the fact that the trial was repeatedly postponed—and ultimately never concluded. While they were convinced that his illness was feigned, even the socialists were not entirely displeased, since the Eulenburg case could serve as an object lesson in class justice only as long as he was not convicted. When he was audacious enough to vacation at a foreign spa, press grumbling led the judge to reconvene the trial on July 7, 1909, almost a year after its postponement. But when Eulenburg fainted one hour into the proceedings, he was given a conditional postponement: He was to undergo a medical examination at six-month intervals to determine whether he was fit to stand trial. This charade continued for a decade, when the trial was indefinitely postponed. He died in 1921.

The final trial of the scandal—the third between Moltke and Harden—received far less media attention than the earlier ones. It was originally scheduled for November of 1908 (the time of the *Daily Telegraph* affair) but was delayed until the following April. Harden was again convicted of libel and sentenced to pay a fine of six hundred marks plus court costs, which now amounted to forty thousand marks. Unlike Eulenburg, Moltke was thus rehabilitated, and Harden continued to fret over the homosexual influence of Moltke and "the many other affiliates of the same caliber, who are *still* up there."[41] As litigious as ever, he fully intended to appeal the verdict but allowed himself to be talked out of it by Chancellor Bülow, who argued that they had both achieved their goal by eliminating Eulenburg and that further trials dealing with homosexuality would be detrimental to the national interest. Harden was finally satisfied with a formal acknowledgment that he had acted out of "patriotic considerations" and a full reimbursement for his fines, secretly paid by the Imperial Chancellery. Fifteen years later, Harden admitted to Magnus Hirschfeld that initiating the Eulenburg Affair had been the greatest political mistake of his career.[42] He regretfully came to realize that Eulenburg had exercised a moderating influence on the kaiser and that his elimination had set Germany on a war course. And although he never said so, Hirschfeld may well have regarded his involvement in the libel trials as the gravest misstep of his career too.

Effects on the German Image

Just a few days after the opening of the first trial in the three-year scandal, a leading Berlin daily described it as a "forensic drama claiming universal attention at home and abroad."[43] A month later, one Reichstag delegate asserted that the courtroom revelations quite properly filled "the entire German people with revulsion and loathing" but noted with concern that "these matters, naturally blown up, are entering the foreign press and there producing extremely odd views about German morality

and the future of Germany."[44] The Eulenburg Affair was thus a double
crisis, damaging both national self-image and the international image of
Germany; but while the former was subject to a certain amount of
control, the latter seemed exasperatingly beyond control. This concern
was captured in one cartoon, "The Effect Abroad." Here two English
tourists in Venice are struck by the appearance of a group of German
women, and one concludes that their egregious homeliness is what drives
German men to homosexuality. The thinly veiled misogyny of this cartoon points simultaneously to the thoroughgoing exclusion of women
from the discourses of the scandal (the courtroom silencing of Lili von
Elbe being the *locus classicus*) and to the attempt to find a scapegoat (be
it Jews, homosexuals, or women) for the nation's image problem.

While a comprehensive survey of the international coverage of the
scandal is beyond the scope of this essay, the reactions in France and
England deserve brief mention. France's national interest was at stake in
the affair because Raymond Lecomte, a friend of Eulenburg and councillor at the French Embassy in Berlin, was directly implicated in the
scandal by Harden. He claimed that as a result of a meeting between
Lecomte and the kaiser at a Liebenberg shoot in 1906, the French went to
the Algeciras Conference with the inside knowledge that Germany would
not go to war with France over hegemony in Morocco. When Harden
published his accusation, Lecomte—dubbed "king of the pederasts"[45]—was
hastily recalled to Paris, but only to be rewarded with a post in another
embassy.

In light of ingrained Franco-Prussian hostility, it is scarcely surprising
that the French press gloated over Germany's embarrassment; homosexuality was in any case already termed *"le vice allemand."*[46] Paris cartoonists
took special pleasure in lampooning the perverse esprit of the army
beyond the Rhine (see Figure 5). Beneath the obvious *Schadenfreude*
lurked the gleam of hope that the foe could be vanquished in the next war
and, on a deeper level, the pervasive fear that France itself was suffering
from decadence.[47] Overall, the Eulenburg Affair was of such consuming
interest to France that it remains the only country to have produced
monographs on the subject.[48]

The British response was initially quite restrained and even tactful, if
only due to prudishness; but as enmity between the countries grew,
various English publicists demonstrated that the scandal was by no means
forgotten. In the final year of World War I, the English "libel case of the
century" began with the remarkable assertion that Germany was ruled by
a homosexual clique whose secret agents had debauched thousands of
English men and women who now obeyed orders from Potsdam.[49] The
Eulenburg Affair was recalled during the war not just in Britain: Cartoonists in both France and Italy revived motifs from the era of the
scandal, portraying the German army as perversely effeminate and thus

easily defeated.[50] Yet the memory persisted longer at home than abroad: In the early 1930s, antifascist German cartoonists once again used the selfsame images to attack Ernst Röhm's SA, and both Hirschfeld and Hitler himself remarked on the historical parallel.[51] Fascists tended to perpetuate the anti-Semitic interpretation of the Eulenburg Affair and held up Harden and Hirschfeld as prime examples of the Jewish conspiracy against German morals.

Hitler's recollection of the scandal is indicative of the abiding damage it inflicted to the German self-image. Harden's voice was only one in a chorus that harped on the theme of "national disgrace,"[52] an outlook that also found frequent pictorial expression. Cartoonists employed a variety of symbolic figures to invoke the nation. The sole female representative was Germania, tellingly portrayed doing women's work—sweeping and washing—to cleanse the homeland. The nation's other avatars were all men and included the German Michel in his sleeping cap, the hero Siegfried, Germany's legendary dragon-slayer, and the medieval Kaiser Barbarossa, of whom legend said that he had not died but instead slept in a mountain fastness where he would awaken to do battle in the hour of Germany's greatest need. In addition to these mythical and allegorical figures, cartoonists also invoked historical figures to represent the nation. An amusing example is the statue of Goethe and Schiller in Weimar (see Figure 2). A statue of Hermann, the German leader whose warriors defeated three Roman legions in the year 9, figures similarly in another cartoon. In both cases Hirschfeld is shown questioning the normalcy of these historical giants; and indeed, articles published by Hirschfeld did explore the homosexual aspect of the writings of Goethe and Schiller.[53]

The most striking feature shared by these male national symbols is their apparent ineffectualness in the face of a moral transformation they can scarcely begin to comprehend. Germania alone rolls up her sleeves and resolutely sets about cleaning up the mess, whereas the men all embody one variant or another or powerlessness. Be it the German Michel timorously examining a dragon that may not be dead, the dragon-slayer Siegfried who belongs to an heroic past now irretrievably lost, Barbarossa still recumbent in his cavern, or Goethe and Schiller frozen in their statuesque but compromising embrace: These national symbols evoke a proud cultural heritage now perceived as crumbling under the onslaught of modernity. Not just in Germany but also in France and England, contemporaries experienced the era of the turn of the century as under assault by the accelerating tempo of change, and the rush of time brought in its wake new diseases of civilization: bad nerves, homosexuality, and degeneracy of all sorts.[54] One Viennese cartoon occasioned by the Eulenburg Affair (Figure 6) features an urban gathering place significantly named "Café Moderne" whose habitués are taken aback by the arrival of a heterosexual couple; the elongated head of the seated figure in the center of the cartoon is akin to the alien physiognomy of the Berlin aristocrats in Figure 10.

In an article entitled "Who Is to Blame?" Hirschfeld argued that the sensational publicity surrounding the Eulenburg Affair had given rise to three related but distinct misconceptions. First, he rejected the notion that "degeneration, a process of decay" was more advanced in Germany than elsewhere.[55] This welcome assurance was widely echoed, often in a stridently xenophobic tone, by newspaper editorialists, Reichstag speakers, and the like.[56] Second, he described as mistaken the impression that homosexuality was more prevalent among the aristocracy than among commoners. While upper- and middle-class apologists for the status quo accepted and repeated the assertion, it did not find universal acceptance. Some members of the educated middle class suggested that centuries of intermarriage among German bluebloods had resulted in hereditary degeneracy, of which homosexuality was one manifestation,[57] while others— including various middle- and working-class cartoonists—saw it simply as the latest variation on an age-old theme: the aristocracy's sexual license, at once despised and envied. And third, Hirschfeld claimed that contrary to popular belief, homosexuality was no more widespread at present than it had been in the past. With this thesis he stood virtually alone.

A disturbing increase in the occurrence of "unnatural crimes" had been noted by cultural critics as early as the 1880s,[58] and by 1908 one alarmed editorialist asserted that the continued spread of homosexuality threatened the German race with extinction.[59] The Eulenburg Affair prompted Adolf Stöcker, court chaplain under Kaiser Wilhelm I and the foremost anti-Semitic politician in the Reichstag, to argue that the growth of homosexuality was of a piece with the rise of the women's emancipation movement (see Figure 12) and the spread of pornography.[60] This outlook found expression in cartoons hearkening back to a healthier past with a "Then and Now" schema. In a remarkable number of instances, General Kuno von Moltke was derisively contrasted with military heroes of the nation's glorious past: Siegfried; Field Marshal G. L. von Blücher, who had vanquished Napoleon; and his namesake, General Helmuth von Moltke, the victorious commander in the Franco-Prussian War of 1870.

The overwhelming prevalence of military themes in the cartoons mirrors both the imperial preoccupations of the era and the concern that the army was extremely susceptible to corruption. Officers quite routinely subjected enlisted men to extreme abuse of various sorts. Extended into the sexual sphere, however, abuse not only undermined the status of rank but also sexualized the military, thus violating a major taboo (see Figures 4 and 10). Soldiers functioned as a particular variant of the national symbol, and although their uniforms were actually designed with aesthetic criteria in mind—and thus fostered fetishization as disembodied male power—the stereotype of the soldier was supposed to transcend sexuality by submitting aggressiveness to discipline, reshaping it to serve the national interest.[61] In this respect soldiers were not unlike criminals, and the army and the prison were perhaps the two paramount institutions for controlling and regulating the lives of the lower class.[62]

The years immediately prior to the Eulenburg Affair had witnessed a proliferation of discourses—journalistic exposés, novels, plays, autobiographies—suggesting that decay of the officer's code of honor and demoralization of troop discipline were undermining military preparedness.[63] Still, none of this had adequately prepared the nation for Harden's assertion that "entire cavalry regiments [were] infested with homosexuality" (*Prozesse*, p. 104). Various Reichstag speakers rose to defend the spirit of Potsdam, but their confidence in the army was badly shaken by Harden's disclosure that uniformed soldiers were flagrantly prostituting themselves in certain promenades of Berlin (*ibid.*), including the prestigious Victory Boulevard (clearly visible in Figure 3). The magnitude of the problem became apparent only after Harden revealed that the minister of police himself had been accosted while taking an evening stroll (see Figure 7).

The barrage of charges reached such intensity that the minister of war, General Karl von Einem, was compelled to deliver a rambling report to the Reichstag in which he variously asserted that there was no problem, that a problem did exist but was entirely attributable to civilian "rascals," and that the problem would be resolved by heightening disciplinary control of the soldiers. Any officer guilty of homosexual conduct, he argued, dishonored himself and thereby forfeited the respect of his troops; the resulting contempt for one's superior undermined the authority of the officer corps: "That cannot and must not be. If such a man with such feelings should be lurking in the army, I command him: Resign your commission, get out, for you do not belong in our ranks! (Bravo!) If, however, he should be caught, then, gentlemen, regardless of who he may be, regardless of his post, he must be destroyed. (Bravo!)"[64]

The trials of the Eulenburg Affair were indeed conducted against a somber tattoo of resignations, suicides, and courts-martial. Ironically, as Hirschfeld noted,[65] the publicity given these cases may have done more to erode than to restore the honor code and discipline for which the officer corps had traditionally been respected—and feared. Caught up in their own polemic against modernity, outraged conservatives ignored the extent to which soldier prostitution was a practice with considerable history: A Viennese cartoon dated as early as 1869 shows a stroller fleeing pell-mell from a soldier's solicitation (Figure 8). To be sure, the soldier-prostitute of 1907 (Figure 7) is portrayed as a simpering, purse-carrying surrogate for a female, whereas his predecessor from 1869 had been a full male. Creeping feminization of the army and social emasculation are the central concerns of Wilhelmine conservatives; the butt of the humor in 1869 had been the sanctimonious bourgeois who protested too much.

Sexual Practices and Identities

Just what sort of men did the minister of war want removed from the officer corps? The answer was not nearly so straightforward as it might at first seem, for a satisfactory definition of sexual normalcy and abnormalcy was still evolving.[66] Harden might thunder in court, "Let us draw a clear line between men like Eulenburg, Hohenau, Moltke, and the men of Germany!" but the precise border seemed elusive to many.[67] The scandal contributed significantly to publicizing and legitimating the embryonic discipline of sexology, which accounts for the grudging respect accorded Dr. Hirschfeld; not coincidentally, he founded the *Journal of Sexology (Zeitschrift für Sexualwissenschaft)* in 1908. As he noted, the very word "homosexuality" was either lacking in standard dictionaries or was hastily included in the latest editions; it had been coined in 1869 and, until the Eulenburg Affair, belonged exclusively to the parlance of forensic medicine. Throughout the trials, he complained, the term was continually confused with "pederasty" (which entailed two taboos, same-sex practices with minors), "unnatural vice" (the specific practices criminalized by Paragraph 175), and a host of pungent colloquialisms.[68]

In the first trial of the scandal, it will be recalled, Hirschfeld had argued—and the court had agreed—that Moltke was neither a pederast nor a felon but instead a homosexual, i.e., an effeminate man, a person who confounded sex-role stereotypes by virtue of his emotionality, passivity, artistic temperament, emotional attachment to men, and so on. By demonstrating the existence of a psychological deviance that did not necessarily find expression in sexual behavior, Hirschfeld naively hoped to advance the cause of enlightened tolerance, but the court's verdict had precisely the opposite effect. In an era that was obsessed with the imperialist projection of such masculine traits as strength, courage, hardness, and military aggressiveness, the violation or nonviolation of Paragraph 175 became a secondary concern while homosexuality—understood as male effeminacy—became a potent metaphor in political discourse.[69] This, of course, is why Harden had been able to exploit the issue in the first place, and why he produced evidence of Eulenburg's misconduct only when his hand was forced. Harden's final revelations rendered moot the distinction, so painstakingly constructed by Hirschfeld, between sexual orientation and conduct.

The dispassionate discourse of a sexological expert was drowned out by the saber-rattling rhetoric of sexual politics on a grander scale than Hirschfeld had imagined possible, but this does not mean that his standpoint was flawed or illogical—simply that more was at stake than an academic question. In the rather abstruse sense intended by Hirschfeld, Moltke and Eulenburg undoubtedly were homosexual and would have been so even if they had been totally sexually abstinent. In private correspondence, Eulenburg described himself as combining "feminine feeling with masculine activity"; he was proud, perhaps inordinately so, of his artistic "sensibility and finer organization," precisely the traits that appealed to Kaiser Wilhelm.[70] Moltke, too, was characterized by a close friend as deficient in the "dash," "masculinity," and "toughness" of the Kaiser's other military advisors,[71] but neither he nor Eulenburg thought of himself as a homosexual. In a remarkably candid and revealing letter to Moltke written prior to the first trial, Eulenburg struggled to defend his admittedly old-fashioned conception of their affinity against the new-fangled label:[72]

> At the moment when the freshest example of the modern age, a Harden, criticized our nature, stripped our ideal friendship, laid bare the form of our thinking and feeling which we had justifiably regarded all our lives as something obvious and natural, in that moment, the modern age, laughing cold-bloodedly, broke our necks. . . . The new concepts of sensuality and love stamp our nature as weak, even unhealthily weak. And yet we were also sensual, not any less than the moderns. But this area lay strictly segregated; it did not impose itself as an end in itself. Family, art, friendship, and all our ideals were completely divorced from sensuality and from that which we regarded only as dirt, even if it might have ruled us here or there in those unconscious reciprocal effects which characterize "mankind."

It would be all too pat to interpret the terms "ideal friendship" or "art" as mere euphemisms for homosexuality; in fact, the code word here is "dirt." This letter suggests that these two aristocrats—and others of their estate—made a clean break between homosexual and what might be termed homosocial relations, strictly confining the former to contacts with social inferiors and cultivating the latter with like-minded peers. They did not identify themselves as homosexuals because their occasional sexual escapades played at most a subordinate role in their lives.

When Eulenburg, trained as a lawyer, knowingly perjured himself by swearing that he had never violated Paragraph 175, he may have assuaged his conscience by reasoning that only relations in high society were at issue, and here he was no more and no less than a devoted father, husband, and friend. He was not dissembling when he swore in court:[73]

> In my youth I was an enthusiastic friend. I am proud of having had good friends. . . . The best thing we Germans have is friendship, and loyal friendship has always stood in high regard. I have had enthusiastic friendships, I have written letters that overflow with enthusiastic feelings, and I don't reproach myself for it at all. Surely we know the letters of great heroes, Goethe and so on, which are effusive. I have written such letters too, but there was never anything wicked, evil, filthy in them.

When Hirschfeld remarked that the language of Goethe's era was no longer appropriate "in our technological and military age,"[74] Eulenburg once again defended his ideal vision of friendship against sexual inferences in emphatic terms: "This is a slam at German friendship, it's a poison that's being trickled into friendship, no one is safe, this is a betrayal of Germany!"[75] And indeed, Hirschfeld may have underestimated the extent to which forms of expression regarded as outmoded by the middle class were perpetuated by the aristocracy, whose very station in life derived from and was legitimated by tradition.

If class distinctions were so central in Eulenburg's life that they allowed him to trivialize his felonies as mere peccadilloes and to resist the homosexual label, they likewise allowed Jakob Ernst to regard his extramarital intimacies as a separate sphere that did not impinge on his identity as a God-fearing Bavarian family man—blessed with good fortune, thanks to the generous prince. Harden's researches revealed that Ernst's liaison with Eulenburg was common knowledge in the village of Starnberg. Ernst had long been so proud of his association with the prince that he bragged of it to his neighbors, who appear to have been more awed than outraged: No one had ever brought the affair to the attention of the district attorney. Ernst's court confession was highly revealing:[76]

> If I have to say it: What people say is true. What it's called I don't know. He taught it to me. Having fun. Fooling around. I don't know of no real name for it. When we went rowing we just did it in the boat. He started it. How would I have ever dared! And I didn't know anything about it. First he asked me if I had a girlfriend. Then it went on from there.

It proved easier to extract a confession from Ernst than from Eulenburg, for the simple farmer was eager to oblige the court—just as he had proved willing to oblige "a fine gentleman." And unlike the prince, he had never cultivated a secret life.

Homosexual relations with the lower orders may have been regarded by the noblemen involved as an "obvious and natural" prerogative, but this outlook was anathema to the middle class, which—as Foucault noted— supplanted the aristocratic focus on blood with the bourgeois focus on sex (in German, one type of *Geschlecht* with another type of *Geschlecht*), genealogy with morality.[77] The German bourgeoisie had touted its moral superiority to the frivolity and cavalier licentiousness of the aristocracy beginning in the eighteenth century, and during the nineteenth it extended its condemnation to the moral turpitude of the proletariat. By exposing sexual liaisons between officers and enlisted men, a prince and a farmer, middle-class journalists suggested that two of the three pillars of society were shot through with moral rot and could precipitate national collapse. One liberal, middle-class delegate to the Reichstag proclaimed the scandal a portent of a relapse into barbarism; homosexuality was a contagion that could attain epidemic proportions and wipe out culture.[78] His relatively enlightened standpoint was evident in his use of the medical model, describing homosexuality as a sickness rather than a sin.

If homosexuality came to be regarded as perilous because it crossed class lines, it also came to be seen as traitorous because it crossed national frontiers. Eulenburg's French connection confirmed for Harden Bismarck's dire warning that the *cinaedi* constituted an international association in much the same way as the socialists—those "fellows without a fatherland." The homosexuals' secret "lodge," Harden asserted, was stronger than freemasonry and leaped over "the walls of creed, nation, and class" to create a "fraternity" that sneeringly regarded "normals as a lower form of life. . . . It is a different world than ours, with a different moral code, a different set of values." Since homosexuals regarded heterosexuals as the "common enemy" and were seeking "gradually [to] emasculate our courageous master race before the nation notices what is happening," Harden called for a "fight to the death" with this "powerful group." Eulenburg seemed to personify the danger: he was "the *amoureuse* who has toyed with scepters and thrashed in lustful ecstasy on the sweaty sheets of his coachman."[79]

Harden's mordant attacks on Eulenburg are particularly noteworthy because they signalled a complete about-face. In 1898, Harden had become the first German editor to support the campaign for homosexual emancipation led by Hirschfeld. Articles by Harden, Hirschfeld, and others in *Die Zukunft* had called for the repeal of Paragraph 175 and for greater tolerance toward these "martyrs of a misguided sexual drive" who deserved "neither punishment nor contempt."[80] He claimed that the flood of hate mail he received during the Eulenburg Affair from homosexuals in all walks of life convinced him that this tolerance was entirely misplaced, and his change of outlook matched a broader shift in middle-class attitudes toward homosexuality and sexuality in general. At the beginning of the scandal, Hirschfeld noted with dismay that the most vehement spokesmen of "the antihomosexual movement" came precisely from "the educated middle class,"[81] and he thanked the German working class and the socialist delegates in the Reichstag for their continued support of the campaign to repeal Paragraph 175. By the scandal's end, however, the "psychic epidemic" of homophobia had spread even to the far left.[82] It remained for the right-wing fanatic Dr. Wilhelm Hentschel to proclaim that the Eulenburg Affair had been beneficial if it had driven homosexuals to poverty and to suicide, and to describe the extermination of all homosexuals as a desideratum of German society.[83] The scandal not only scuttled the campaign to repeal Paragraph 175 but led to far harsher enforcement of the law and efforts to strengthen and extend it.[84] Whereas the existing statute punished homosexual acts only between men, a motion introduced by the Catholic-oriented Center Party sought to align

Paragraph 175 with the corresponding Austrian law, which included lesbians (see Figure 9).[85] With the imprisonment of Adolf Brand and the discrediting of Hirschfeld as a "monomaniac" who was lucky "not to be tarred and feathered,"[86] the homosexual emancipation movement entered a period of enforced quiescence from which it would not recover until after the kaiser's abdication in 1918. The women's movement was also profoundly affected by the moral-purity campaign advanced with evangelical fervor in the wake of the Eulenburg Affair. In 1908, a change of leadership in the League of German Women's Organizations replaced its progressive program of sexual self-determination with a racist and nationalist interpretation of women's sexuality that sought to increase the German birthrate.[87] Those few homosexuals and feminists who continued to agitate for sexual emancipation were regarded as threats to the social order (see Figure 12).

Repugnance at the inversion of traditional sex roles was particularly evident in the frequent use of animal and excremental metaphors for homosexuality in both the discourses and the cartoons occasioned by the scandal. This radically dehumanizing rhetoric reached a high point when one liberal Reichstag delegate, Dr. Siegfried Heckscher, declared that "homosexuality is dog morality," a slogan that was universally quoted and elaborated upon in the German press.[88] Eulenburg himself added ammunition to the antihomosexual arsenal when he swore that he had never engaged in "swinish" or "filthy" conduct,[89] but the impetus had actually been given on the first day of the first trial, when Lili von Elbe offered the shocking testimony that her ex-husband had called women "toilets" and termed marriage "a swinish institution" (*Schweinerei*) (*Prozesse*, pp. 29–30). Outraged, the virtually universal defenders of womanhood and family life responded in kind, and even the restrained *Vossische Zeitung*, the Berlin newspaper of record, rose to the occasion by coining the epithet *"cloaca maxima"* for Hirschfeld, slyly parodying the sexologist's Latinate neologisms.[90] Dozens of cartoons employed dogs, pigs, and excrement, and one from France featured a pig-faced man, effectively completing the transformation of human into subhuman. While well known in the history of racism, this phenomenon has an additional dimension in connection with homosexuality: The term "sodomy" has comprised both bestiality and homosexuality throughout the history of Christian Europe. During the Middle Ages and Renaissance, sodomy was further so closely linked with heresy and witchcraft that at times the terms were virtually synonymous; by equating homosexuality with treason, Harden was merely updating this legacy. These animal images are invested with a profoundly atavistic quality that may disclose a psychological fear of magical destruction of the body image; if so, such anxieties could only have been aggravated by Harden's revelation that Eulenburg dabbled in the occult.[91]

By representing homosexuality as unnatural, subhuman, animalistic—in short, as the radical Other—defenders of the status quo were striving to counteract the scandal's deleterious effects, not merely on the national image, but also on the sexual awareness and potential conduct of the German people. Commentators repeatedly lamented the loss of innocence precipitated by unprecedented discussions of sexual matters. The cartoons themselves offered something qualitatively new: the first depictions in public circulation of homosexuals.[92] Lili von Elbe spoke for many when she testified that she had not suspected her then husband of homosexuality because its very existence had been unknown to her, and one editorialist contrasted the small "circle of *cognoscenti*" with "the vast majority of people who heretofore knew nothing of all this."[93] Even Ernst confessed that he knew "no real name" for "it." With the courtroom extraction of sexual truths and the virtually unimpeded flow of journalistic reportage, newspapers began to take on a pornographic quality. Smut had been defined by a Reichstag commission in 1904 as a psychic danger to the community certain to confuse the hearts and minds of young people and thus lead to a loss of idealism and to moral decay.[94] When a Reichstag delegate complained that one could no longer leave a newspaper lying where it could be found by children, one paper protested that it was, sadly, compelled to print the news and helpfully suggested that family fathers simply remove the offending pages.[95]

It is fair to say that for at least a few months, the Eulenburg Affair brought homosexuality to the forefront of national discussion, prompting individuals to reflect on themselves and others in light of new knowledge. In one of his numerous case studies, Hirschfeld reported on a woman who correctly surmised her husband's homosexual orientation after reading about Moltke's marriage,[96] and this sort of family crisis also found its way into cartoons. Attitudes and forms of behavior that had heretofore been quite acceptable now became suspect, and parents were reluctant to allow their sons to enter the military or even to move from the country to the city (see Figure 11).[97] One Reichstag delegate expressed the most deep-seated fear when he argued: "There can be no doubt that many hundreds and thousands of people who earlier hadn't the foggiest notion of the things now being discussed in public will, after having been enlightened about these things, be tempted to try them out with their own bodies."[98] With rare directness, this politician's remark points to what Foucault described as the nub of sexual politics: "the fact that sex is located at the point of intersection of the discipline of the body and the control of the population."[99]

The biopolitical aim of the cartoons—as of the discourses that linked homosexuality with treason and the heightened enforcement of Paragraph 175—was the total suppression of homosexuality. But paradoxically, these images, discourses, and practices may well have incited many individuals to follow through on desires they had heretofore ignored or suppressed; indeed, desire itself may have been generated. And for others who had led double lives up to this point, the scandal led to a new possibility for conceptualizing their secret vices and arriving at a fundamentally new identity. If this be true, then Hirschfeld was simply wrong when he claimed that homosexuality was no more widespread in the present than in the past. Thus the effect of the Eulenburg Affair was not exclusively repressive: Despite its role in the outbreak of World War I, despite the campaign for moral rearmament, the anti-Semitic undertones, the heightening of military discipline, the concern about decadence, and the exhortations to middle-class morality, a subtle dialectic was at work tending to proliferate sexual practices and identities.

Figure 1.
New Prussian Coat of Arms (Liebenberg Design). (The motto on the scroll reads: My soulmate, my old boy, my one and only cuddly bear.)

SOURCE: *Jugend* (Munich), vol. 11, no. 45 (October 28, 1907), p. 1028.

Figure 2.
Panic in Weimar
"Wolfgang, let go of my hand! Dr. Magnus Hirschfeld is coming!"

SOURCE: *Jugend* (Munich), vol. 11, no. 48 (November 19, 1907), p. 1089.

Figure 3.
Hero-Worship

SOURCE: *Die Muskete*
(Vienna), vol. 5, no. 111
(November 14, 1907), p. 49.

Figure 4.
**Military Innovations
(From Bollhardt's
Recollections)**
"Since when is an about-
face order given for
inspections?"
"At your service,
Captain—reporting that
the division is being
inspected by Count
Hohenau today."

SOURCE: *Der wahre Jacob*
(Stuttgart), no. 447
(November 26, 1907), p. 5621.

Figure 5.
Byzantium in Germany

SOURCE: *Fantasio* (Paris), vol.
2 (November 15, 1907).

Figure 6.
**Sensation in the Cafe
Moderne**
"A married couple is
coming!"

SOURCE: *Wiener Caricaturen*
(Vienna), vol. 27, no. 44
(November 3, 1907), p. 4.

Figure 7.
Nightlife in Potsdam
"Say, big fellow, want to come along?"

SOURCE: *Der wahre Jacob* (Stuttgart), no. 557 (November 26, 1907), p. 5616.

Figure 8.
The New Egyptian Joseph in the City Park
COCKADOODLEDOO: "Why are you running so, dear sir?"
THE NEW EGYPTIAN JOSEPH: "The artillery man there wanted to conduct an immoral discourse with me, and I simply can't put up with it! This is the second time it's happened to me here."
COCKADOODLEDOO: "But if you already know that there are supposed to be such speakers here in the city park, why do keep coming back here all the time?"

SOURCE: *Kikeriki!* (Vienna), vol. 9, no. 10 (March 11, 1869), p. 1.

Figure 9.
Spring Excursion of a Berlin Ladies' Club
"Never, my sweet, will a man break up our love."
"Never, dearheart!—Unless it's a policeman."

SOURCE: *Simplicissimus* (Munich), vol. 14, no. 7 (May 17, 1909), p. 1.

Figure 10.
On the Harden Trial (in an Exclusive Berlin Restaurant)
"Well, what do you want, old Diogenes?"
"I'm searching for normal people."
"Oh no, my good man, that's pointless, for what you might call gentlemen of distinction are all perverse."

SOURCE: *Figaro* (Vienna), vol. 51, no. 44 (November 2, 1907), pp. 660–661.

Figure 11.
In the Country
Mother (weeping): "Farewell, Leni, nothing can happen to you, just be well. But you, Franz, watch out that you withstand temptation in the big city."

SOURCE: *Der Floh* (Vienna), undated special issue on Paragraph 175 (ca. November 1907), p. 8.

Figure 12.
New Goals in the Women's Movement
"Ladies! We can struggle effectively and successfully against the emancipation of men in one way only: by simply gunning the bastards down."

SOURCE: *Simplicissimus* (Munich), vol. 15, no. 46 (February 3, 1911), p. 765.

DISCOURSES OF SEXUALITY AND SUBJECTIVITY: THE NEW WOMAN, 1870–1936[1]

◆

CARROLL SMITH-ROSENBERG

This essay traces the medical, feminist, and literary discourses surrounding two generations of "new women." The first generation of educated, economically independent women from the middle class were novel and threatening in their independence from men, public visibility, and political demands. Medical men defined them as "inverts" who aped masculine ways. The second generation of "new women," dating from the early twentieth century, rejected many of the asexual characteristics of the first and attempted to fashion their own discourse of independent sexuality. Their use of the male medical language, including especially Krafft-Ebing and Havelock Ellis, however, led to their failure. Their efforts, however, are most powerfully evoked in the androgynous heroines of Virginia Woolf and Djuna Barnes, as well as Radclyffe Hall and other lesbian writers of this generation.

Who was the New Woman? Initially, Henry James's literary conceit. Affluent, educated, and intelligent, she boldly asserted her right to share in America's heritage of individualism and self-reliance. Heedless of social conventions and social consequences, she announced herself captain of her own destiny. She was Daisy Miller; she was Isabelle Archer. I

Note: Originally published, in different form, *Disorderly Conduct: Visions of Gender in Victorian America,* by Carroll Smith-Rosenberg (New York: Alfred A. Knopf, 1985).

have appropriated the term to refer to a cohort of middle- and upper-middle-class American women born between the late 1850s and the early 1900s, who were educated, ambitious, and, most frequently, single. By the early twentieth century, they had established places for themselves within the new professions and within government and reform agencies. Asserting their right to a public voice and visible power, they demanded rights and privileges customarily accorded only to white middle-class men. Their emergence within middle-class rhetoric signaled the symbolic death of that earlier female subject, the refined and confined Victorian lady.

For half a century, middle-class American women and men bitterly debated the social and sexual legitimacy of the New Woman. Through her, they argued about the "naturalness" of gender and the legitimacy of the bourgeois social order. They agreed on only one point: The New Woman challenged existing gender relations and the distribution of power. By defining her as physiologically "unnatural," the symptom of a diseased society, those whom she threatened reaffirmed the legitimacy and the "naturalness" of the bourgeois order. By insisting on their own social and sexual legitimacy in words formed out of a century of women's reform rhetoric, the New Women repudiated that order.

Suddenly, however, in the years immediately following the First World War, a new generation of New Women dramatically shifted these discursive strategies. Abandoning traditional feminist representations of self and sexual assumptions, New Women of the 1920s adopted the sexual rhetoric of male physicians, sex reformers, politicians, and novelists. This rhetoric represented the New Women as social and sexual hermaphrodites, as an "intermediate sex" that existed between and thus outside of the biological and social order. They did so with political intent. Investing male images with feminist meanings, they sought to use male myths to repudiate male power—to turn the male world upside down. They failed. By the 1930s, women and men alike had disowned the New Woman's brave vision. The New Woman herself, shorn of her connection to older feminists, of her political power, rhetoric, and influence, became a subject of misunderstanding and ridicule.

The New Women's discursive strategy raises significant questions for feminist scholars. It is easy to hypothesize why they might have adopted it. On the simplest level, for the marginal or powerless to challenge the dominant discourse, they must frame their challenge in a language meaningful within the hegemonical discourse. Moreover, to speak always in the language of the marginal frustrates those who wish to exercise power. But problems arise. Symbols and metaphors emerge out of and assume specific meanings within the relational and political world of their speakers. That being the case, could male-constructed metaphors (no matter how transposed) fully express women's perceptions and desires? By adopting male imagery had the New Women of the 1920s both curtailed their own expressive powers and relinquished a critical source of identity and political strength—the power to create language? Can embattled social and political groups survive if shorn of that power? The New Woman is critically important to new feminist scholars. In her twin incarnations—as a social and political actor and as the condensed symbol of disorder and rebellion—she forces us to examine the ways language forms and re-forms sexual and political identities and in so doing repositions power.

In her own mind and the minds of her contemporaries, education constituted the New Woman's most salient characteristic—and her first self-conscious demand.[2] Bitterly resenting any restrictions on women's options, the New Women saw in higher education an opportunity for intellectual self-fulfillment and for an autonomous role outside the patri-archal family.[3] Yet to place a woman outside of a domestic setting, to train a woman to think and feel "as a man," to encourage her to succeed at a career, indeed to place a career before marriage, violated virtually every late-Victorian norm. It took the New Woman outside of conventional structures and social arrangements. It made her a peer of men—and a social outcast. College women were liminal figures locked together in a novel ritual and a novel place. Conscious of being scrutinized by a dubious world, they reached out to one another, forming the intense bonds of shared identity that characterized the liminal experience.[4] Col-lege completed, facing traditional institutions and roles ill designed to fulfill their ambitions and desires, the more adventurous and determined of these educated women continued to experiment with alternative life-styles and institutions. Some chose to remain at the women's colleges as faculty.

The settlement house constituted a second favored institution.[5] Sororal intensity, the keystone of the earlier world of female love and ritual, marked the inner dynamics of both. College women and settlement-house residents called one another "sister." Teachers and settlement-house founders were loved as "mothers." Like countless women before them, many of these women teachers and settlement-house residents formed passionate relationships with one another. Unlike those earlier women, many of these New Women, eschewing men, felt they had married each other for life.[6]

Thus while rejecting the patriarchal family and their mothers' domestic lives, the first generation of New Women did not repudiate the traditional world of female love.[7] It was the male-dominated, not the female-bonded, family that restricted women's full development, they insisted. Educated women could develop alternative, single-sex familial institutions which would foster women's autonomy and creative productivity at the same time as they met her emotional and erotic needs. In radical new environ-ments, on the brink of developing a host of new roles for women, the first generation of New Women wove their mothers' intensely loving, often passionate friendships into the fabric of their brave new world. Indeed, the more politically radical of the New Women used the loving world of

female bonding to forge a network of women reformers and social inno-
vators into a singularly effective political machine responsible for many of
the social reforms we associate with the Progressive Era.

Alarmed by the real and the philosophical implications of equal education for women and men and of the increasingly public female leaders the
new education spawned, Victorian educators and physicians launched an
attack upon women's education that combined some of the most ancient
principles of medicine with the nineteenth-century's increasingly deter-
ministic vision. In this battle, the old female body and the New Woman's
mind became the contested loci of female subjectivity.

The human body, late Victorian male physicians insisted and male
educators readily concurred, was both hierarchical and fragile, its delicate
balances easily destroyed by external forces. A closed energy system, the
body allocated scarce energy resources governed by rigid, biologically
determined and gender-linked priorities. Within the male body, the higher
organs—the brain and heart—dominated. Predictably, the reproductive
organs dominated the female's body. The woman who favored her mind
at the expense of her ovaries—especially the woman who spent her
adolescence and early adulthood in college and professional school—would
disorder a delicate physiological balance. Physicians and asylum directors,
college regents and male professors stridently and repeatedly warned
young women and their mothers, the educated woman's brain would be
overstimulated. She would become morbidly introspective. Neurasthenia,
hysteria, insanity would follow. Her ovaries, robbed of energy rightfully
theirs, would atrophy, her menses become irregular, sterility and cancer
ensue. No longer reproductive, she would begin to look like a man. Her
breasts would shrivel, facial hair develop. Many such women, one highly
influential and well-published physician reported, began to wear heavy
boots. (It is important to note, however, that within the late Victorian
male medical discourse such women did not flirt with homosexuality—
only with hermaphroditism. These physicians talked of women's socio-
sexual deviance exclusively in terms of the rejection of motherhood—not
of men.)[8]

The New Women, bold in their claims to a place in the public arena
and a voice in public debates, were unaffected by these impotent warnings. Rather they constructed a uniquely female discourse and an alternative mythic female figure and identity. Interweaving the Enlightenment's
belief in the individual's right to self-fulfillment and a Victorian insistence
on women's higher morality and sexual purity, they infused these two
divergent discourses with a third—the new optimistic, nondeterministic
science of the Progressive Era. An amalgam of the familiar and the
respectable made modern, their female warrior for social justice, brim-
ming with energy and health, defending exploited child laborers, challenging corrupt politicians and callous capitalists, triumphed easily over
the male physicians' neurasthenic and sterile educated woman. Within a

bourgeois social structure, where both the birth rate and the marriage rate were steadily declining and the new urban values had triumphed, the New Woman, product and espouser of both, easily won this first "scientific" debate.[9]

Male physicians did not remain vanquished for long. They had already begun to construct a second mythic figure in order to condemn the politically disruptive New Woman as sexually dangerous to her class and race. By 1900 male physicians, sex reformers and educators had unveiled their new construction. The New Woman who, while standing outside of conventional institutions and socially acceptable roles, had proudly boasted of her sexual purity had lied. She was a secretly and dangerously sexualized figure. Her social liminality was rooted in sexual inversion. She belonged to an "intermediate sex." She embodied the unnatural and the monstrous. She was a "Mannish Lesbian."

While male homosexuality had been recognized throughout Western history, few discussions of lesbianism predate the late nineteenth century.[10] Until then, it is true, British and American physicians had described behavior we would now define as lesbian: young women, often schoolgirls or college women, in bed together enjoying genital stimulation, avowing passionate emotional attachment. Although physicians carefully labeled comparable behavior when engaged in by boys and college men as homosexual and perverted, they categorized the women as masturbators and female homosexuality as a rare and exotic phenomenon.[11] While medical and pornographic literature on the Continent contained graphic descriptions of lesbian behavior, few bourgeois American women (and apparently few American physicians) were familiar with those descriptions. Neither these women nor their families and their physicians perceived passion between women as either disturbing or deviant.[12]

By mid-nineteenth century, medical and scientific discussions of male homosexuality had begun to increase in number, forming one facet of the overall explosion of sexual and scientific discourse that marked the late nineteenth century.[13] This was the golden age of scientific determinism, of Social Darwinism and of eugenics. Taxonomy assumed unquestioned scientific centrality as Victorian men traced the precise evolution of their social as well as their natural world. Grammar and political institutions, man, birds, and fish were all placed within a grand evolutionary schema of progressive development or degenerative decay. The sexologists' fascination with human sexual variations exemplifies this pattern. Now specific sexual acts, fantasies, fetishes, sensations, became the subject of taxonomical scrutiny. Genus and species were assigned. Degrees of abnormality and perversion were carefully charted in much the same spirit as that with which the evolution of the horse and of the dative case were traced.

And with the same goal: the reassertion of order in a conflicting and changing world. This—not the control of literal sexual behavior—obsessed the sexologists. Within the sexologists' categorical elaborations, perverted behavior did not have to cease. A proxy, it existed to be railed against and thus to give the sexologists a sense of power and reaffirm their faith in their ability to restore order. Just as the male Victorian imagination fused the social and the sexual, it fused the emotive and the political. The object of the discourse was power—the regulation and control of the New Woman. By constituting her a sexual subject, they made her subject to the political regulation of the state.

While early medical students of the perverse had focused almost exclusively upon male homosexuality, by the mid-1880s (and the emergence of the New Woman in America and England) the lesbian became a critical figure within the new scientific representation of sexuality. Richard von Krafft-Ebing, in his canonical text, *Psychopathia Sexualis*, divided lesbianism into four categories or degrees of homosexual deviance. Each category fused sexual, physiological, and social characteristics. In his first category he included women who "did not betray their anomaly by external appearance or by mental (masculine) sexual characteristics." They were, however, responsive to the approaches of more masculine-appearing and -behaving women. The second classification of lesbians included women with a "strong preference for male garments." These women were the female analogy of effeminate men. By the third state, "inversion is fully developed, the woman so acting assumes a definitely masculine role." The fourth stage, or "gynandry," represented "the extreme grade of degenerative homosexuality." Krafft-Ebing explained in 1889:

> The woman of this type possesses of the feminine qualities only the genital organs; thought, sentiment, action, even external appearance are those of a man. Often enough does one come across in life such characters whose frame, pelvis, gait, appearance, coarse masculine features, rough, deep voice, etc., betrayed rather the man than the woman.[14]

Krafft-Ebing did not focus on the sexual behavior of the women he categorized as lesbian but rather on their social behavior and physical appearance. In every case study, Krafft-Ebing linked lesbianism to the rejection of conventional female roles, to cross-dressing, and to "masculine" physiological traits. The following statement exemplifies his approach:

> Uranism may nearly always be suspected in females wearing their hair short, or who dress in the fashion of men, or pursue the sports and pastimes of their male acquaintances; also in opera singers and actresses who appear in male attire on the stage by preference. . . . The female urning may chiefly be found in the haunt of boys. She is the rival of their play, preferring the rocking-horse, playing at soldiers, etc., to dolls and other girlish occupations. The toilet is neglected, and rough

boyish manners affected. Love for art finds a substitute in the pursuits of the sciences. . . . Perfumes and sweetmeats are disdained. The consciousness of being a woman and thus to be deprived of the gay college life, or to be barred from the military career, produces painful reflections. The masculine soul, heaving in the female bosom, finds pleasure in the pursuit of manly sports, and in manifestations of courage and bravado.[15]

Krafft-Ebing's lesbians seemed to desire male privileges and power as ardently as, perhaps more ardently than, they sexually desired women.

Krafft-Ebing made gender inversion physiologically manifest. Atavistic throwbacks, the women who "aped" men's roles looked like men. But even more, having rooted social gender in biological sexuality, Krafft-Ebing proceeded to make dress analogous to gender. Only the abnormal woman would challenge conventional gender distinctions—and by her dress you would know her. "She was quite conscious of her pathological condition," Krafft-Ebing reported of one woman. "Masculine features, deep voice, manly gait, without beard, small breasts; cropped her hair short and gave the impression of a man in women's clothes."[16] In this way Krafft-Ebing, through the creation of a new medico-sexual subject, the Mannish Lesbian, linked women's rejection of traditional gender roles and their demands for social and economic equality to cross-dressing, sexual perversion, and borderline hermaphroditism. This new sexual subject assumed a critical role in the grand Edwardian social drama, which used physical disease to enact social disorder.

The male sexologist who most directly broke into this female world of love and intimacy, defining it as both actively sexual and as sexually perverted, was Havelock Ellis. Ellis is a complex figure and his position on lesbianism ambivalent in the extreme. On the one hand, as an enemy of Victorian repression and hypocrisy, he holds a place of honor in our pantheon of sexual liberators. On the other hand, more clearly than any writer before Freud, Ellis insisted that a woman's love for other women was both sexual and degenerate.[17] Tearing away the New Women's cloak of respectability, Ellis argued that genteel, educated women, thoroughly feminine in appearance, thought, and behavior might well be active lesbians.[18]

Inversion, Ellis argued, was biological, hereditary, and irreversible. The "invert" was powerless to change her inclination. Had lesbianism been limited to the "congenital invert," women born to the "intermediate sex," Ellis advised, society would have no grounds for alarm. Genetic anomalies, these women constituted a small percentage of the population. Although aberrant, they should be tolerated and allowed to live out their sexual impulses. But, Ellis argued, many women, though not genetically inverted, possessed a genetic predisposition, a weakness, for the advances of other women. For such women homosexuality was an acquired characteristic, preventable and curable. Placed in an unwholesome environment—a woman's boarding school or college, a settlement house, a women's club, or a political organization—the homosexual woman could succumb to the blandishments of the "congenital invert" who sought her as a partner. Kept within a heterosexual world, she would overcome her predisposition and grow up to be a "normal" woman.[19]

By dichotomizing lesbians into "true inverts" and potential heterosexuals, Ellis depicted the female invert not as a genetic anomaly and a helpless victim but as a woman on the make, sexually and racially dangerous. Seeking a more feminine partner, she sexually rivaled men. Education, feminist ideology, the new women's colleges and settlement houses, all freed the "female invert" from the restraints of family, permitting her to reach out to young girls, drawing them into lesbianism. Ellis insisted that the numbers of lesbians had steadily increased since the expansion of women's roles and institutions. The connections Ellis drew between what he believed was a rising incidence of middle-class lesbianism and feminist political and educational advances reveal a man troubled by changes he could not in principle oppose. Feminism, lesbianism, equality for women, all emerge in Ellis's writings as problematic phenomena. All were unnatural, related in disturbing and unclear ways to increased female criminality, insanity, and "hereditary neurosis." Ellis continued:

> The modern movement of emancipation—the movement to obtain the same rights and duties, the same freedom and responsibility, the same education and the same work, must be regarded as on the whole a wholesome and inevitable movement. But it carries with it certain disadvantages. It has involved an increase in feminine criminality and in feminine insanity, which are being elevated towards the masculine standard. In connection with these, we can scarcely be surprised to find an increase in homosexuality which has always been regarded as belonging to an allied, if not the same, group of phenomena. . . . I do not say that these unquestionable influences of modern movements can directly cause sexual inversion, though they may indirectly, in so far as they promote hereditary neurosis; but they develop the germs of it. . . . This . . . is due to the fact that the congenital anomaly occurs with special frequency in women of high intelligence who, voluntarily or involuntarily, influence others.[20]

Citing Ellis as an unimpeachable scientific expert, American physicians and educators launched a political campaign against the New Woman, the institutions that nurtured her, and her feminist and reform programs. "Female boarding schools and colleges are the great breeding grounds of artificial [acquired] homosexuality," R. W. Shufeldt wrote in the *Pacific Medical Journal* in 1902.[21] William Lee Howard, in the respectable *New York Medical Journal* of 1900, commented acidly:

The female possessed of masculine ideas of independence, the virago who would sit in the public highways and lift up her pseudo-virile voice, proclaiming her sole right to decide questions of war or religion or the value of celibacy and the curse of woman's impurity, and that disgusting antisocial being, the female sexual pervert, are simply different degrees of the same class—degenerates.[22]

As Progressive women reformers increased their political power in the years immediately preceding the First World War, and as the suffrage movement reached a crescendo of public visibility (parades, arrests, forced-feedings) and of political power (the passage of the Twentieth Amendment), articles complaining of lesbianism in women's colleges, clubs, prisons, and reformatories—wherever women gathered—became common. While feminist leaders were not directly attacked as lesbians, the political climate began to change. College administrators, wary of changing professional and public attitudes, adopted restrictive dormitory policies. Warning young women of the dangers inherent in intense female friendships, they prohibited women from spending the night in one another's rooms.[23] Physicians as well as educators began to counsel women they now defined as "latent homosexuals." Forcefully drawing the young women's attention to their dangerous predisposition for "inversion," doctors pressed them to marry quickly and have children.[24] By the 1920s, charges of lesbianism had become a common way to discredit women professionals, reformers, and educators—and the feminist political, reform, and educational institutions they had founded.

Male companionate-marriage sex reformers and psychoanalysts popularized the "scientific" underpinning of this campaign, portraying the lesbian in two ways, as a "Mannish Lesbian," the ruthless, perverted competitor of the male suitor, or as the aging Lady in Lavender, who taught young girls to reject men and repress their own sexuality. The New Men, by redefining the issue of female autonomy in sexual terms, were able to portray the New Woman as the enemy of liberated women. Divorcing women's rights from their political and economic context, they made the daughter's quest for heterosexual pleasures, not the mother's demand for political power, personify female freedom. Linking orgasms to chic fashion and planned motherhood, male sex reformers, psychologists, and physicians promised a future of emotional support and sexual delights to women who accepted heterosexual marriage—and male economic hegemony. Offered such an alternative, only the "unnatural" woman, they argued, would continue to struggle with men for economic independence and political power.[25]

How did women respond to this new male discourse? The first generation of New Women, who had so effectively repudiated the attacks of the Victorian physicians, seemed unable to respond to Krafft-Ebing's and Havelock Ellis's redefinition of their loving relations as sexually perverted, the result of their unnatural desire for political equality and public power. Nor did they attempt to counter the alternative image of themselves as repressed old maids. Historians, long puzzled by their silence, have concluded that their inability to respond to the male use of sexuality as a political attack was rooted in a discursive disjuncture. The older New Women had come to sexual and intellectual maturity within a Victorian culture in which sex in the absence of men was inconceivable. Not only were men essential to women's primary sexual act, the generation of babies, they were essential to the generation of female sexual desire. As a result, having eschewed men sexually, they had no language in which to conceive of their erotic relations with other women as sexual; they could not construct themselves as sexual subjects.[26]

The New Women of the First World War period and the 1920s, our argument continues, grew up in a far different discursive world—a world that sexualized subjectivity and openly avowed its eroticism. For these later New Women, sexual autonomy no longer meant freedom from material oppression, but, rather, the right to sexual experimentation and self-expression. Radical New Women who, a generation earlier, had joined women's settlement houses, now flocked to Margaret Sanger's sex-education lectures.[27] Edna St. Vincent Millay's famous "First Fig" epitomized their flamboyant rejection of sexual conventions earlier New Women had simply not questioned.

> *My candle burns at both ends:*
> *It will not last the night;*
> *But ah, my foes, and oh, my friends—*
> *It gives a lovely light!*[28]

While the new, male-gendered sexual discourse attracted heterosexually adventuresome New Women, it posed significant problems for those who loved women. Resenting the older generation's failure to provide them with the sexual vocabulary or subjectivity their generation demanded, many of these women felt they had no alternative but to accept the sexual discourse pressed upon them by male sexologists, companionate marriage advocates, and psychoanalysts—even though that discourse categorized them as perverted and degenerate. British feminist Frances Wilder provides us with a case in point. She wrote British sexologist Edward Carpenter in the early 1920s thanking him for having provided an overtly sexual discourse within which to place her sexual desires. Wilder told Carpenter that since adolescence she had loved other women (yearned to "caress" and "fondle" them) yet she had never defined her feelings as sexual and consequently had not acted upon them. After reading Carpenter's discussion of "sexual inversion" she "realize[d] that I was more closely related to the intermediate sex than I had hitherto imagined. . . ." Now, she reported, she could admit her sexual feelings and reach beyond a loneliness rooted in sexual repression. Accepting a medical definition of herself as sexually abnormal, however, did not mean that Wilder, a feminist, accepted a definition of herself as politically deviant or disempowered. She ended her letter with a bitter attack upon the enslavement of women in heterosexual marriage.[29]

Wilder's poignant statement, Millay's flamboyant verse, underscore the irreconcilable divisions that rent the ranks of the New Women. They do not explain why the older women had not constructed themselves as sexual subjects. The answer to this, as to so many other questions about sexuality, lies not in sexual but in political factors. To understand the problem fully we must stop looking for answers in the events and words of the 1920s but move back in time to the eighteenth century and the beginnings of a new American identity.

Americans, struggling to distinguish themselves from decadent Europeans and savage Indians, had imagined themselves as virtuous citizens, helmsmen of an ideal Republic. In doing so, they drew upon a century of British political rhetoric that constructed civic virtue in aggressively virile terms, invoking images of Spartan asceticism and early Roman courage. The converse of civic virtue, political corruption, assumed a sexual aura as well, that of female sexuality. Corruption was rooted in passion and unruly desires, bedded down in luxury, was nonproductive—effeminate. And so Americans made civic virtue manly, the political and the public subject interchangeable with the Common and the Self-Made Man, female sexuality politically corrupting.[30]

Nineteenth-century women reformers rejected this male sexualization and gendering of the political and the public. Claiming the public sphere for God and sexually pure women, they insisted that *male* not female desires fostered political corruption and civic vice. This battle of the sexes raged throughout the nineteenth century as feminists fought to legitimate women as public and political subjects. It shaped the political consciousness of the first generation of New Women and the arguments that won suffrage for all women.[31]

Powerful and empowering, these arguments had their Achilles Heel. Nineteenth-century women reformers had turned to millennial Christianity, not to the egalitarian (even radical) components of Republican rhetoric and of liberal humanism, to legitimate women's political subjectivity. In doing so, however, they renounced women's claim to be active, self-conscious sexual subjects. They renounced as well any language or conceptual system in which to respond to the sexologists' attack—or to later New Women's demands for an active sexual subjectivity. The New Women of the 1920s, raised in a far more sexualized discursive universe, misunderstood and resented the older women's silence. They felt impelled to repudiate them as repressive and anachronistic. How better to do so than to seize the sexologists' discourse, with all its implicit and explicit condemnations of traditional feminism, and transform it into their own unique language? In that way they could simultaneously challenge the authority of their Edwardian mothers and their aggressive modernist brothers.

The New Women and the New Men of the 1920s spoke to each other and to the older feminists about sex and power, pleasures and independence in words that echoed with meanings accumulated over centuries, formed and re-formed during half forgotten political battles, rich with repressed significance. These words, gaining power from their unacknowledged histories, formed and re-formed their speakers in their turn, leading those speakers in baffling and often self-defeating ways, dividing sex from pleasure, independence from power. To understand the speakers we must understand the words. Political, scientific, even sexual texts will not help us, for they insist on the transparency of language and the "naturalness" of their messages. The novel does not. Rather, it catches the resonances of forgotten histories, plays with discursive inconsistencies, calls forth the repressed. To understand the New Women of the 1920s and 1930s, we cannot simply read their sexual and political statements. For fuller, richer stories about themselves and their world, we must reexamine their novels, Virginia Woolf's *Orlando*, for example, or Djuna Barnes's *Nightwood*, reading them as fragments meaningful only as part of a more elaborate and far older discourse.[32]

To do this, let us return for a moment to the critical phrases the new women of literature took from the new men of science. "The intermediate sex," "sexual inversion," "a male soul trapped in a female body," "the Mannish Lesbian," do not describe literal sexual acts. They are spatial and hierarchical images, concerned with issues of order, structure and difference. "Inversion" turns predictable and ordered hierarchies upside down. The "intermediate sex," stands between and thus outside of categories; liminal and disorderly, it embodies the New Women's demand for a role beyond gender conventions. The image of a male soul trapped in a female body, "the Mannish Lesbian" makes graphic the male/mind-female/body polarity inherent in all the other metaphors. Yet it remains a highly ambiguous political image. On one level, the "Mannish Lesbian" fused, and thus denied, that polarity. On the other, it held those immiscible essences in an eternal tension of difference.

Male commentators, from the sexologists of the 1880s to the companionate-marriage reformers and modernist writers of the 1920s, had deliberately used the "Mannish Lesbian," the "Sexual Invert," the "Intermediate Sex" to stand for freaks of nature, logical impossibilities. These "New Men," far more than their Victorian predecessors, sexualized their biological determinism and social conservatism. They rooted gender distinctions in genital differences. The genitals were biologically observable, unchangeable, incontestable—and above all "natural." To protest gender, therefore, was to deny the genitals, to war with nature. The woman who would be a man, the man who assumed the female role (homosexuals, transvestites, hermaphrodites) symbolized social chaos and decay. Sandra Gilbert argues in her brilliant essay "Costumes of the Mind" that the male modernists used the male transvestite and the hermaphrodite to symbolize the emasculation of both man's sexual and social powers, for society had fused the two. A sport of nature, he represented cognitive and social disarray.[33]

Women writers of the 1920s and 1930s deliberately transposed the male sexual metaphors into a feminist language. They insisted that women's assertion of "Male" power and ambition was "natural." Gender distinctions were artificial, man-made constructions. Gender, not the New Woman, was "unnatural." Gender distinctions twisted the *human* spirit, deforming men as well as women. Gender conventions lay at the heart of the confining traditions they, as modernists, fought against. Androgyny was their ideal. Feminist modernists turned to dress and to body imagery to repudiate gender and to assert a new order. Susan Gubar argues that women writers and artists in the 1910s and 1920s adopted male dress as a self-conscious political statement. She points to Stein's creation of an "intermediate" and unconventional costume; to the expatriate Paris lesbians' adoption of male fashion; and, much earlier, to American physician and feminist Alice Walker's use of Victorian male clothing to protest the oppression of the conventional female role.[34]

Not content with fabricating gender and costume into a personal statement of self, feminist modernists wove them into the heart of their creative and political imagery. In *Orlando*, Woolf created a mad surrealistic *Bildungsroman*, a female novel of initiation.[35] Orlando seeks identity and fulfillment first through the guidance of corrupt male literary advisers, next through an exotic romance set in a frozen carnival, and, finally, through public service in foreign lands. Each experience increases his alienation and confusion until, suddenly, Orlando awakes from a dream female. Thereafter gender becomes amorphous and time irrelevant. Centuries pass like days. A shimmering creature, Orlando as woman maintains the characteristics she displayed when a man, to which she simply adds, as if she were donning another layer of clothing, her sensitivity of being female and the ironic distance that experience gives her. Indeed, throughout *Orlando*, clothes, not genitals or personality, symbolize gender change. The body remains amorphous, Orlando's character beyond gender. Her husband, Marmaduke Bonthorp Shelmerdine, Sandra Gilbert points out, proves to be "as strange and subtle as a woman." Both glory in androgyny, the confusion of categories, the options that extend beyond social proprieties. Tying gender to dress rather than dress to gender, Woolf inverts Krafft-Ebing's dark vision of the "Mannish Lesbian." Her joyous androgyne ridicules his decadent hermaphrodite.

Orlando lampoons the sexologists' obsessive linking of cross-dressing and biological determinism. The self-conscious political imagery feminist modernists developed had even broader implications. It inverted the very process of bourgeois myth formation. Through metaphor and symbol, bourgeois myth invests the sociologically contingent with the characteristics of the biologically inevitable and unquestionable. What is bourgeois becomes "natural," all else "unnatural." Male modernists, by fusing gender and genitals, by insisting that to repudiate gender conventions was to war against nature, had joined with sexologists in constructing a classic bourgeois myth. They had clothed gender distinctions specific to late-nineteenth-century industrial countries in the unchangeability of human biology. Feminist modernists, by rejecting the "naturalness" of gender, insisted that society's most fundamental organizational category, gender, was artificial, hence "unnatural," as changeable as dress. From this first principle, it then followed that nothing social or political was "natural." Institutional structures, values, behavior, all were artifact, all relative, all reflective not of nature but of power.

Repudiating the "natural," feminist modernists set their novels in "unnatural" worlds and unstructured situations, beyond the threshold of conventional order. Their plots violate the conventions of time (*Orlando*), of day and night (*Nightwood*), of traditional literary forms (Gertrude Stein's novels), of national loyalties (*The Well of Loneliness*). In surrealistic and expatriate worlds, New Women float between genders and violate divisions between appearance and reality. We have already examined Orlando, whose life encompassed four centuries, two genders, and a number of countries. Stephen Gordon, Radclyffe Hall's classic "Mannish Lesbian," though she has none of Orlando's surrealism, ends the novel as a romantic figure in a darkened house, an expatriate in an alien land. Having discovered the intermediate nature of her sexuality, Stephen must flee the structured security of Morton, her family home, the conventions of the English gentry, and England itself to live a creative life in the no man's land of lesbian Paris in the 1920s. Djuna Barnes also chose the unstructured world of transvestite Paris for her novel.[36] Barnes's title, *Nightwood*, tells all, for a wood at night is a world without structure, a haunted place, invested with primitive magic. Her characters embody social, geographic, and gender disorder. Everyone in *Nightwood* is homeless, afloat between expatriate Paris and Berlin and a dreamlike America. Not one can claim a certain identity, few a clear gender. Their existence denies the inevitability of structure and categories. They are liminal.

Long before the 1920s, the human imagination had already created a character who specifically embodied the disorder and the creative power we associate with liminality, a creature who exists to break taboos, violate categories and defy structure. I refer, of course, to the Trickster, that disorderly figure, libidinous, scatological, of indeterminate sex and changeable gender.[37] Tricksters ritually violate taboos, dress as women (the Winnebago Trickster even becomes female for a time and bears children, only to remember suddenly that he is also a man and to move on).[38] They demonstrate the contingency of order, the fragility of social custom.

Youthful heroes on a journey of discovery, they float within a structure-less world. Their lives, as their stories, are episodic, for they live outside the home and the family, unconfined by social categories or real communities. Disorder defines the Trickster, but so does power. The Trickster continually alters her/his body, creates and re-creates a personality. A creative force at war with convention, beyond gender, the Trickster personifies unfettered human potential.[39] She/he constitutes the ideal feminist hero of the New Women artists.

Certainly, Orlando is a trickster par excellence. She floats across time, through unbelievable settings. Creating her/himself out of fancy, farce, and finery, she tricks us into abandoning all that we know: that sex is unchangeable, gender distinctions "natural," time confining, and patriarchy invincible. For a brief moment, as Orlando frees us, we revel in the headiness of what might be.

Barnes's *Nightwood* is filled with tricksters who have draped their lives in borrowed fancies and wear the whole cloth of illusion. Take Frau Mann, for instance: Her name is an oxymoron that calls forth both the androgyne and Krafft-Ebing's "Mannish Lesbian." A trapeze artist, Frau Mann escapes the confines of earth (society). The single, autonomous woman, she violates all social categories and gender restraints. Yet to do so she must live in a world beyond the "natural" order of the day, gender and propriety. Indeed, Frau Mann's very body denies the distinction between reality and illusion. She seemed, Barnes tells us, "to have a skin that was the pattern of her costume. . . . The stuff of the tights was no longer a covering, it was herself." Illusion frees her from gender re-straints. At the same time it robs her of her sexuality. "The span of the tightly stitched crotch was so much her own flesh that she was as unsexed as a doll. The needle that had made one the property of the child made the other the property of no man."[40]

Sexuality was the critical issue for this generation of New Women. They linked it with identity and with freedom. Yet Barnes's imagery is ambiguous. Has the defiance of gender restrictions made Frau Mann (and thus all women who define themselves as beyond conventional gender) "as unsexed as a doll"—that is, in a Freudian era, without a true identity? Or is Barnes's implication far more positive: that the woman beyond gender is beyond being owned? Frau Mann embodies one of the critical dilemmas of modern feminism: In rejecting gender as an artificial con-struction, does one lose one's identity as a woman? Beyond gender, what is one? Frau Mann remains enigmatic.[41]

Classically, the Trickster is a comic character, a joke who *momentarily* turns the world upside down. But a joke is not serious; its inversion of order is transitory, rather than suggestive of an alternative order. Woolf uses Orlando to expose the absurdity of rigid gender rules and the pomposity of the male literary canon. But Orlando changes neither England nor literature.

Not all tricksters are comic. The tragic tricksters who inhabit *Nightwood* exist to comment not only upon absurd social arrangements, as Orlando does, but also to war against social convention and to live out the consequences of their actions. Sadly, in defeat, they retreat into a mad night wood of inversion and of pain. They speak to a critical new aspect of the New Women's experience—the price paid by those who literally used their bodies and their emotions to invert received order.[42] The New Women of the 1920s and 1930s—Barnes and Hall especially—were among the first to challenge publicly the new sexual taboos against female love. They belonged to the first generation to bear the full brunt of social ostracism and legal censorship. The pain of Stephen in *Well of Loneliness* and Nora in *Nightwood* are the reverse side of the coin of Orlando's fantastic escape from gender.

Metaphor by metaphor, feminist modernists of the 1920s and 1930s had inverted men's language. By imbuing male imagery with feminist meaning, they transformed the sexologists' symbolic system. Boldly they asserted their right to participate in male discourse, to function in a public, male arena, and to act as men did—both in and out of bed. Female images of women beyond gender, however, did not simply affirm the individual's transcendence of social constructions. As the debate between the New Women and the New Men wore on without a feminist victory, their symbols acquired a second, darker message. *The Well of Loneliness,* and even more starkly, *Nightwood*, bespoke the pain that accompanied public condemnation, social ostracism, and legal censorship. The fate of their heroines was the coin levied by society as payment for attempting to live the life of the androgyne.

These authors' deliberate adaptation of male symbols in order to engage in political debate raises many philosophical and political questions. I have based my analysis on the premise that words are rooted in experience. If this is so, can male symbols accurately represent female experiences? Or, rather, by enveloping women's experiences in male forms, do we distort—indeed, deny—those experiences? Clothes are cultural artifacts, lightly donned or doffed, but words are rooted in our earliest and most profound experiences of social location and of the distribution of power. In stripping their discourse of female-originated metaphors and images, did the feminist modernists come dangerously close to denuding themselves of a female identity? And of female authority? Images and metaphors are the tools of authorship—a power to create that Gilbert and Gubar have persuasively argued is intimately linked to authority.

The issue of subjectivity frames the dilemma. The feminist modernists rejected an older Victorian and Edwardian female subjectivity, tied as it was to sexual purity and sacrifice. Unlike the earlier generation of New Women, they did not wish to be the Housekeepers of America, or to justify their political activities as Home Protection (a device used by Frances Willard and the Women's Christian Temperance Union). They wished to free themselves completely from considerations of gender, to be autonomous, powerful, and fully sexed subjects, to enter the world as if they were men. Hence they spoke with men's metaphors and images. (Yet, we must never forget, they simultaneously invested these images and metaphors with a denial of gender and demands for equality quite alien, even threatening, to the male originators of the discourse.)

Their words echoed their experiences. Both words and experiences defied traditional gender categories. The educated bourgeois women who came to political and creative maturity in the 1910s and 1920s had grown up in a uniquely androgynous world. They *assumed* their right to exist outside of gender, in the public arena. The victories won by earlier cohorts of New Women in professional and educational areas made their androgynous world possible. Yet, ironically, this greater freedom did not bond women across the generations. It alienated them. The New Women of the 1920s were unique—and isolated. They could speak meaningfully only to other women so uniquely situated. Neither the earlier generations, who had lived and fought in a far more separatist world, nor later women less advantageously situated than they in terms of access to professional advancement and economic autonomy shared their perspective, or their language. The political solidarity of the successive generations of New Women slipped away as their discourses became more disjointed and conflicted. In the process, the generation of the 1920s lost much of its political power and many of its economic and institutional gains.

The brave and unique generation of the 1920s confronted a profound dilemma. They shed their primary identity as women before the world they inhabited accepted the legitimacy of androgyny. Despite their brilliant inversions of male metaphors, men refused to share power with them. In fact, the public world was increasingly closed to the New Women. Divested of their primary alliance with the older feminists, they had few resources with which to challenge this reassertion of male power. And so the androgynous language through which they sought to affirm their legitimacy and centrality only confirmed their increasing marginality—to the world of women as well as that of men. Like Nora Flood of Barnes's masterpiece, they wandered, baffled, in a night wood of broken promises and thwarted expectations.

THE MYTHIC MANNISH LESBIAN: RADCLYFFE HALL AND THE NEW WOMAN

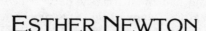

ESTHER NEWTON

The Well of Loneliness has long been regarded as the touchstone novel in discussions of lesbian history. Esther Newton argues that it deserves to hold this central place, for seen in the context of its own day, the book is a daring articulation of lesbian identity. Hall's image of the mannish or butch woman was and remains an important symbol of rebellion against male hegemony and, in Newton's view, of one significant pattern in lesbian sexuality and gender identification.

I hate games! I hate role-playing! It's so ludicrous that certain lesbians, who despise men, become the exact replicas of them! [Anonymous interview in The Gay Report, *ed. Karla Jay and Allan Young]*

Thinking, acting, or looking like a man contradicts lesbian feminism's first principle: The lesbian is a "woman-identified woman."[1] What to do, then, with that figure referred to, in various times and circumstances, as the "mannish lesbian," the "true invert," the "bull dagger," or the "butch"? You see her in old photographs or paintings with legs solidly planted, wearing a top hat and a man's jacket, staring defiantly out of the frame, her hair slicked back or clipped over her ears; or you meet her on the street in t-shirt and boots, squiring a brassily elegant woman.

Note: Originally published, in somewhat different form, in *Signs: Journal of Women in Culture and Society* 9, no. 4 (Summer 1984): 557–575.

Out of sight, out of mind! "Butch and femme are gone," declares one lesbian author, with more hope than truth.[2] And what about those old photographs? Was the mannish lesbian a myth created by "the [male] pornographic mind"[3] or by male sexologists intent on labelling nineteenth-century feminists as deviant? Maybe the old photographs portray a few misguided souls—or perhaps those "premovement" women thought men's neckties were pretty and practical.

In the nineteenth century and before, individual women passed as men by dressing and acting like them for a variety of economic, sexual, and adventure-seeking reasons. Many of these women were from the working class.[4] Public, *partial* cross-dressing among bourgeois women was a late-nineteenth-century development. Earlier isolated instances of partial cross-dressing seem to have been associated with explicit feminism (e.g., French writer George Sand and American physician Mary Walker), although most nineteenth-century feminists wore traditional women's clothing. From the last years of the century, cross-dressing was increasingly associated with "sexual inversion" by the medical profession. Did the doctors invent or merely describe the mannish lesbian? Either way, what did this mythic figure signify, and to whom?

At the center of this problem is British author Radclyffe Hall (1880–1943).[5] Without question, the most infamous mannish lesbian, Stephen Gordon, protagonist of *The Well of Loneliness* (1928), was created not by a male pornographer, sexologist, legislator, or novelist, but by Hall, herself an "out" and tie-wearing lesbian. And *The Well*, at least until 1970, was *the* lesbian novel.[6] Why is it that *The Well* rather than all the other lesbian novels became famous?

Embarrassed by Radclyffe Hall but unable to wish her away, sometimes even hoping to reclaim her, our feminist scholars have lectured, excused, or patronized her.[7] Radclyffe Hall, they declare, was an unwitting dupe of the misogynist doctors' attack on feminist romantic friendships. Or, cursed with a pessimistic temperament and brainwashed by Catholicism, Hall parroted society's condemnation of lesbians. The "real" Radclyffe Hall lesbian novel, the argument frequently continues, the one that *ought* to have been famous, is her first, *The Unlit Lamp* (1924). Better yet, Virginia Woolf's *Orlando* (1928) *should* have been the definitive lesbian novel. Or Natalie Barney's work. Or anything but *The Well*.[8]

Heterosexual conservatives condemn *The Well* for defending the lesbian's right to exist. Lesbian feminists condemn it for presenting lesbians as different from women in general. But *The Well* has continued to have meaning to lesbians because it confronts the stigma of lesbianism—as most lesbians have had to live it. Maybe Natalie Barney, with her fortune and her cast-iron ego, or married Virginia Woolf, were able to transcend the patriarchy, but most lesbians have had to face being called, or at least feeling like, freaks. As the Bowery bum represents all that is most feared and despised about drunkenness, the mannish lesbian, of whom Stephen

Gordon is the most famous prototype, has symbolized the stigma of lesbianism (just as the effeminate man is the stigma-bearer for gay men) and so continues to move a broad range of lesbians.[9] A second reason for *The Well*'s continuing impact, which I will explore briefly at the close of this essay, is that Stephen Gordon articulated a gender orientation with which an important minority of lesbians still actively identify, and toward which another minority is erotically attracted.

By "mannish lesbian" (a term I use because it, rather than the contemporary "butch," belongs to the time period in question) I mean a figure who is defined as lesbian because her behavior or dress (and usually both) manifest elements designated as exclusively masculine. From about 1900 on, this cross-gender figure became the public symbol of the new social/sexual category "lesbian." Some of our feminist historians deplore the emergence of the mannish lesbian, citing her association with the medical model of pathology. For them, the nineteenth century becomes a kind of lesbian Golden Age, replete with loving, innocent feminist couples.[10] From the perspective of Radclyffe Hall's generation, however, nineteenth-century models may have seemed more confining than liberating. I will argue that Hall and many other feminists like her embraced, sometimes with ambivalence, the image of the mannish lesbian and the discourse of the sexologists about inversion primarily because they desperately wanted to break out of the asexual model of romantic friendship. Two questions emerge from this statement of the problem. First, why did twentieth-century women whose primary social and intimate interest was other women wish their relationships to become explicitly sexual? Second, why did the figure of the mannish lesbian play the central role in this development?

The structure and ideology of the bourgeois woman's gender-segregated world in the nineteenth century have been convincingly described.[11] As British and American women gained access to higher education and the professions, they did so in all-female institutions and in relationships with one another that were intense, passionate, and committed. These romantic friendships characterized the first generation of "New Women"—such as Jane Addams, Charlotte Perkins Gilman, and Mary Wooley—who were born in the 1850s and 1860s, educated in the 1870s and 1880s, and flourished from the 1890s through the First World War. They sought personal and economic independence by rejecting their mothers' domestic roles. The goal of the battle to be autonomous was to stay single *and* to separate from the family sphere. They turned to romantic friendships as the alternative, and replicated the female world of love and commitment in the new institutional settings of colleges and settlement houses.

Whether or not these women touched each other's genitals or had orgasms together, two things seem clear: Their relationships were a quasi-legitimate alternative to heterosexual marriage, and the participants did not describe them in the acknowledged sexual language—medical, religious, or pornographic—of the nineteenth century. Letters between romantic friends exhibit no shame, in an era when lust was considered dirty and gross. On the contrary, the first generation had nothing to hide because their passionate outpourings were seen by others, and apparently by themselves, as pure and ennobling.

The bourgeois woman's sexuality proper was confined to its reproductive function; the uterus was its organ. But as for lust, "The major current in Victorian sexual ideology declared that women were passionless and asexual, the passive objects of male sexual desire."[12] Most bourgeois women and men believed that only males and déclassé women were sexual. Sex was seen as phallic, by which I mean that, conceptually, sex could only occur in the presence of an imperial and imperious penis. The low status of working women and women of color, as well as their participation in the public sphere, deprived them of the feminine purity that protected bourgeois women from males and from deriving sexual pleasure. But what "pure" women did with each other, no matter how good it felt, could not be conceived as sexual within the terms of the dominant nineteenth-century romantic paradigm. Insofar as first-generation feminists were called sexual deviants, it was because they used their minds at the expense of their reproductive organs.

The second generation of New Women were born in the 1870s and 1880s and came of age during the opening decades of the twentieth century. This was an extraordinarily distinguished group. Among them we count critics of the family and political radicals Margaret Sanger and Crystal Eastman; women drawn to new artistic fields, such as Berenice Abbot and Isadora Duncan; and lesbian writers such as Gertrude Stein, Willa Cather, Margaret Anderson, Natalie Barney, and Radclyffe Hall. For them, autonomy from family was, if not a given, emphatically a right. Hall's first novel, *The Unlit Lamp* (1924; hereafter called *The Lamp*), is a sympathetic analysis of the first generation from the perspective of the second. The novel portrays a devouring mother using the kinship claims of the female world to crush her daughter's legitimate bid for autonomy.[13]

Hall uses the family in *The Lamp* to symbolize society, the imposition of traditional gender divisions, and the subjugation of female fulfillment to traditional bourgeois norms. The family stands for bourgeois proprieties: proper dress, stifling garden parties, provincial gossip. Fearful of alternatives, uncreative and unimaginative, the mother seeks to bind her daughter to an equally banal and confining life. Conversely, Hall uses a masculinized body and a strong, active mind to symbolize women's rejection of traditional gender divisions and bourgeois values. Joan Ogden, the protagonist, wants to be a doctor. Her mind is swift, intelligent, her body large, strong, healthy. Although Hall does not strongly develop male body and clothing imagery in *The Lamp*, in a momentous confrontation near the novel's conclusion, masculine clothing is unambiguously used to symbolize assertiveness and modernity. Second-generation women are described as "not at all self-conscious in their tailor-made clothes, not ashamed of their cropped hair; women who did things well, important things . . . smart, neatly put together women, *looking like well bred young men* [emphasis mine]." When two such women see Joan, now faded and failed, they ridicule her old-fashioned appearance: " 'Have you seen that funny old thing with the short gray hair?' . . . 'Wasn't she killing? Why moire ribbon instead of a proper necktie?' . . . 'I believe she's what they used to call a New Woman,' said the girl in breeches, with a low laugh. 'Honey, she's a forerunner, a kind of pioneer that's got left behind. I believe she's the beginning of things like me.' "[14]

There is no explicit discussion of sexuality. Joan tells a male suitor, "I've never been what you'd call in love with a man in my life" (p. 302), without a trace of embarrassment. Joan's passionate relationship with another woman is described in the traditional language of sentiment, never in a language of lust.

For many women of Radclyffe Hall's generation, sexuality—for itself and as a symbol of female autonomy—became a preoccupation. These women were, after all, the "sisters" of D. H. Lawrence and James Joyce. For male novelists, sexologists, and artists rebelling against Victorian values, sexual freedom became the cutting edge of modernism. Bourgeois women like Hall had a different relation to modernist sexual freedom, for in the Victorian terms of the first generation, they had no sexual identity to express. Women of the second generation who wished to join the modernist discourse and be twentieth-century adults had to radically reconceive themselves.

That most New Women of the first generation resented and feared such a development, I do not doubt. But many women of the second welcomed it, cautiously or with naive enthusiasm. (One has only to think of Virginia Woolf's thrilled participation in Bloomsbury to see what I mean.) They wanted not simply male professions but access to the broader world of male opportunity. They drank, they smoked, they rejected traditional feminine clothing, lived as expatriates, and freely entered heterosexual liaisons, sometimes with such disastrous results as alcoholism, mental illness, and suicide. Modernism and the new sex ideas entailed serious contradictions for women,[15] who, no matter what their hopes, could not behave like men on equal terms; unwanted pregnancy and "bad" reputations were only two of the hazards from which men were exempt. Yet many women eagerly took up the challenge. This was what first-generation women had won for the second—the tenuous right to try out the new ideas such as psychoanalysis and sexual freedom and participate in the great social movements of the day.

It was in the first two decades of the twentieth century in Britain, with perhaps a ten-year lag in the United States, that, due to external attack and internal fission, the old feminist movement began to split along the heterosexual/homosexual divide that is ancestral to our own. If women were to develop a lustful sexuality, with whom and in what social context were they to express it? The male establishment, of course, wanted women to be lusty with men. A basic tenet of sexual modernism was that "normal" women had at least reactive heterosexual desire.[16] The sex reformers attacked Victorian gender segregation and promoted the new idea of companionate marriage in which both women's and men's heterosexual desires were to be satisfied.[17] Easier association with men quickly sexualized the middle-class woman, and by the 1920s the flapper style reflected the sexual ambience of working-class bars and dance halls. The flapper flirted with being "cheap" and "fast," words that had clear sexual reference.

But what of the women who did not become heterosexual, who remained stubbornly committed to intragender intimacy? A poignant example is furnished by Frances Wilder, an obscure second-generation feminist.[18] Wilder had inherited the orthodox first-generation views. In a 1912 letter to the radical *Freewoman*, she advocated self-restraint, denouncing the new morality for encouraging the "same degrading laxity in sex matters which is indulged in by most of the lower animals including man." She herself, aged twenty-seven, had "always practised abstinence" with no adverse effects. But just three years later she was writing desperately to homosexual radical Edward Carpenter: "I have recently read with much interest your book entitled The Intermediate Sex & it has lately dawned on me that I myself belong to that class & I write to ask if there is any way of getting in touch with others of the same temperament" (p. 930). Wilder was aware of the price tag on the new ideas. "The world would say that a physical relationship between two of the same sex is an unspeakable crime," she admits, but gamely reasons that, because of the "economic slavery" of women, *"normal sex"* is *"more* degrading."

The New Woman's social field was opening up, becoming more complex, and potentially lonelier. Thus, along with their desire to be modern, our bourgeois lesbian ancestors had another powerful reason to embrace change. Before they could find one another in the twentieth-century urban landscape, they had to become visible, at least to each other. They needed a new vocabulary built on the radical idea that women apart from men could have autonomous sexual feeling.

"I just concluded that I had . . . a dash of the masculine (I have been told more than once that I have a masculine mind . . .)," Frances Wilder had confessed to Carpenter in 1915, explaining her "strong desire to caress & fondle" a female friend.[19] Like most important historical developments, the symbolic fusion of gender reversal and homosexuality was overdetermined. God Himself had ordained gender hierarchy and heterosexuality at the Creation. The idea that men who had sex with other men were like women was not new. But in the second half of the nineteenth century, the emerging medical profession gave scientific sanction to tradition; homosexual behavior, the doctors agreed, was both symptom and cause of male effeminacy. The masculine female invert was perhaps an analogous afterthought. Yet the mannish lesbian proved a potent persona to both the second generation of New Women and their antifeminist enemies. Her image came to dominate the discourse about female homosexuality, particularly in England and America, for two reasons. First, because sexual desire was not considered inherent in women, the lesbian was endowed with a trapped male soul that phallicized her, giving her active lust. Second, gender reversal became a powerful symbol of feminist aspirations, positive for many female modernists, negative for males, both conservative and modernist.[20]

It was Richard von Krafft-Ebing who articulated the fusion of masculinity, feminist aspirations, and lesbianism that became, and largely remains, an article of faith in Anglo-American culture.[21] Krafft-Ebing categorized lesbians into four increasingly deviant and masculine types.[22] The first category of lesbians included women who "did not betray their anomaly by external appearance or by mental [masculine] sexual characteristics." They were, however, responsive to the approaches of women who appeared or acted more masculine. The second classification included women with a "strong preference for male garments." By the third stage "inversion" was "fully developed, the woman [assuming] a definitely masculine role." The fourth state represented "the extreme grade of degenerative homosexuality. The woman of this type," Krafft-Ebing explained, "possesses of the feminine qualities only the genital organs; thought, sentiment, action, even external appearance are those of the man."[23] Not only was the most degenerate lesbian the most masculine, but any gender-crossing or aspiration to male privilege was probably a symptom of lesbianism. In these pathological souls, "The consciousness of being a woman and thus to be deprived of the gay college life, or to be barred out from the military career, produces painful reflections."[24] In fact, lesbianism is a congenital form of lust caused by and manifested in gender reversal, as Krafft-Ebing makes clear in discussing one "case": "Even in her earliest childhood she preferred playing at soldiers and other boys' games; she was bold and tom-boyish and tried even to excel her little companions of the other sex . . . [After puberty] her dreams were of a lascivious nature, only about females, with herself in the role of the man . . . She was quite conscious of her pathological conditions. Masculine features, deep voice, manly gait, without beard, small breasts; cropped her hair short and made the impression of a man in woman's clothes."[25] Krafft-Ebing was so convinced of his thesis that the woman's most feminine feature—"without beard"—is lined up with the masculine traits as if they all prove the same point.

Havelock Ellis simplified Krafft-Ebing's four-part typology,[26] but retained an ascending scale of inversion, beginning with women involved in "passionate friendships" in which "no congenital inversion is usually involved" and ending with the "actively inverted woman." Ellis's discussion of the former was devastating; it turned the value that first-generation feminists had placed on passionate friendships upside down. A "sexual enthusiast,"[27] he saw these "rudimentary sexual relationships" as more symptomatic of female sexual ignorance and repression than of spiritual values. At the same time, his inclusion of such friendships in a discussion of inversion inevitably marked them with the stigma of "abnormality."

When Ellis got to the hard-core inverts, he was confounded by his contradictory beliefs. He wanted to construct the lesbian couple on the heterosexual model, as a "man" and a woman invert. But his antifeminism and reluctance to see active lust in women committed him to fusing inversion and masculinity. What to do with the feminine invert? His solution was an awkward compromise:

> A class of women to be first mentioned . . . is formed by the women to whom the actively inverted woman is most attracted. These women differ in the first place from the normal or average woman in that they are not repelled or disgusted by lover-like advances from persons of their own sex . . . Their faces may be plain or ill-made but not seldom they possess good figures, a point which is apt to carry more weight with the inverted woman than beauty of face . . . they are of strongly affectionate nature . . . and *they are always womanly* [emphasis mine]. One may perhaps say that they are the pick of the women whom the average man would pass by. No doubt this is often the reason why they are open to homosexual advances, but I do not think it is the sole reason. So far as they may be said to constitute a class they seem to possess a genuine, though not precisely sexual, preference for women over men.[28]

This extraordinary mix of fantasy, conjecture, and insight clashes with Ellis's insistence that "the chief characteristic of the sexually inverted woman is a certain degree of masculinity."[29] No mention is made of "congenital" factors in regard to this "womanly" invert, and like most examples that do not fit pet paradigms, she is dropped. Gender reversal is not always homosexual, Ellis contends, exempting certain "mannish women" who wear men's clothes out of pragmatic motives, but the "actively inverted woman" always has "a more or less distinct trace of masculinity" as "part of an organic instinct."[30] Because of her firm muscles, athletic ability, dislike of feminine occupations, and predilection for male garments "because the wearer feels more at home in them," the sexually inverted woman, people feel, "ought to have been a man."[31]

Thus the true invert was a being between categories, neither man nor woman, a "third sex" or "trapped soul." Krafft-Ebing, Ellis, and Freud all associated this figure with female lust and with feminist revolt against traditional roles, toward which they were at best ambivalent, at worst horrified.[32] But some second-generation feminists, such as Frances Wilder, Gertrude Stein, and Vita Sackville-West, identified with important aspects of the "third sex" persona. None did so as unconditionally and—this must be said—as bravely as Radclyffe Hall did by making the despised mannish lesbian the hero of *The Well of Loneliness*, which she defended publicly against the British government. Hall's creation, Stephen Gordon, is a double symbol, standing for the New Woman's painful position between traditional political and social categories and for the lesbian struggle to define and assert an identity.

Even newborn, Stephen's body achieves a biologically impossible masculinity: "Narrow-hipped and wide shouldered" (p. 13).[33] She grows and her body becomes "splendid," "supple," "quick"; she can "fence like a man"; she discovers "her body for a thing to be cherished . . . since its strength could rejoice her" (p. 58). But as she matures, her delight degenerates into angst. She is denied male privilege, of course, in spite of her masculine body. But her physical self is also fleshly symbol of the femininity Stephen categorically rejects. Her body is not and cannot be male; yet it is not traditionally female. Between genders and thus illegitimate, it represents Every New Woman, stifled after World War I by a changed political climate and reinforced gender stereotypes. But Hall also uses a body between genders to symbolize the "inverted" sexuality Stephen can neither disavow nor satisfy. Finding herself "no match" for a male rival, the adolescent Stephen begins to hate herself. In one of Hall's most moving passages Stephen expresses this hatred as alienation from her body:

> That night she stared at herself in the glass; and even as she did so, she hated her body with its muscular shoulders, its small compact breasts, and its slender flanks of an athlete. All her life she must drag this body of hers like a monstrous fetter imposed on her spirit. This strangely ardent yet sterile body . . . She longed to maim it, for it made her feel cruel . . . her eyes filled with tears and her hate turned to pity. She began to grieve over it, touching her breasts with pitiful fingers . . . [p. 187]

Stephen's difference, her overt sexuality, is also represented by cross-dressing. But if male writers used cross-dressing to symbolize and castigate a world upside down, while Virginia Woolf and other female modernists used it to express "gleeful skepticism" toward gender categories,[34] Stephen's cross-dressing asserts a series of agonizing estrangements. She is alienated from her mother, as the New Woman often was, and as the lesbian was, increasingly, from heterosexual women.

Unlike Orlando, Stephen is trapped in history; she cannot declare gender an irrelevant game. She, like many young women then and now, alternately rebels against her mother's vision of womanhood and blames herself for failing to live up to it. Preferring suits from her father's tailor, she sometimes gives in to her mother's demand that she wear "delicate dresses," which she puts on "all wrong." Her mother confirms Stephen's sense of freakishness: "It's my face," Stephen announces, "something's wrong with my face." "Nonsense!" her mother replies, "turning away quickly to hide her expression" [p. 73]. Cross-dressing for Hall is not a masquerade. It stands for the New Woman's rebellion against the male order and, at the same time, for the lesbian's desperate struggle to be and express her true self.

Hall, like the sexologists, uses cross-dressing and gender reversal to symbolize lesbian sexuality. Unlike the sexologists, however, Hall makes Stephen the subject and takes her point of view against a hostile world. Though men resent Stephen's "unconscious presumption," Hall defends Stephen's claim to what is, in her fictional universe, the ultimate male privilege: the enjoyment of women's erotic love. The mythic mannish lesbian proposes to usurp the son's place in the Oedipal triangle.[35]

Hall had begun to describe what I take to be a central component of lesbian orientation, mother/daughter eroticism,[36] several years earlier in *The Unlit Lamp*, where presumably the nonsexual framework of the novel as a whole had made it safe.[37] I write "eroticism" because sexual desire is distinct from either "identification" or "bonding." A woman can be close to her mother ("bond," "identify") in many ways and yet eroticize only men. Conversely, one can hate one's mother and have little in common with her, as did Radclyffe Hall, and yet desire her fiercely in the image of other women. In my view, feminist psychology has not yet solved the riddle of sexual orientation.

As bold as Hall was, she could not treat mother/daughter eroticism directly in *The Well*; instead, she turned it inside out. Stephen is strangely uncomfortable with all women, especially her mother. For her part, Stephen's mother gives her daughter only a quick good-night peck on the forehead "so that the girl should not wake and kiss back" (p. 83).

Instead, the Oedipal drama is played out with the maid standing in for the mother. At seven, Stephen's intense eroticism is awakened by Collins (who, as working-class sex object, never gets a first name), in an episode infused with sexual meaning. Collins is "florid, full-lipped and full-bosomed" (p. 16), which might remind informed readers of Ellis's dictum that the good figure counts more with the "congenital invert" than does a pretty face. Thinking of Collins makes Stephen "go hot down her spine," and when Collins kisses her on impulse, Stephen is dumbfounded by something "vast, that the mind of seven years found no name for" (p. 18). This "vast" thing makes Stephen say that "I must be a boy, 'cause I feel exactly like one" (p. 20). In case the 1928 reader hasn't gotten the message, Hall shows Stephen's father reading sexologist Karl Heinrich Ulrichs and making notes in the margins. Later Stephen reads Krafft-Ebing in her dead father's library and recognizes herself as "flawed in the making."

A high price to pay for claiming a sexual identity, yes. But of those who condemn Hall for assuming the sexologists' model of lesbianism I ask, Just how was Hall to make the woman-loving New Woman a sexual being? Despite Hall's use of words like "lover" and "passion" and her references to "inversion," her lawyer actually defended *The Well* against state censorship by trying to convince the court that "the relationship between women described in the book represented a normal friendship." Hall "attacked him furiously for taking this line, which appeared to her to undermine the strength of the convictions with which she had defended the case. His plea seemed to her . . . 'the unkindest cut of all' and at their luncheon together she was unable to restrain 'tears of heartbroken anguish.' "[38]

How could the New Woman lay claim to her full sexuality? For bourgeois women, there was no developed female sexual discourse; there were only male discourses—pornographic, literary, and medical—about female sexuality. To become avowedly sexual, the New Woman had to enter the male world, either as a heterosexual on male terms (like Emma Goldman and eventually the flapper) or as a lesbian in male body drag (the mannish lesbian/congenital invert). Feminine women like Alice B. Toklas and Hall's lover Una Troubridge could become *recognizable* lesbians by association with their masculine partners.

Ideas, metaphors, and symbols can be used for either radical or conservative purposes.[39] By endowing a biological female with a masculine self, Hall both questions the inevitability of traditional gender categories *and* assents to it. The mannish lesbian should not exist if gender is natural. Yet Hall makes her the hero—not the villain or clown—of her novel. Stephen survives social condemnation and even argues her own case. But she sacrifices her legitimacy as a woman and as an aristocrat. The interpersonal cost is high, too: Stephen loses her mother and her lover, Mary. *The Well* explores the self-hatred and doubt inherent in defining oneself as a "sexual deviant." For in doing so, the lesbian accepts an invidious distinction between herself and heterosexual women.

Heterosexual men have used this distinction to condemn lesbians and intimidate straight women. The fear and antagonism between us has certainly weakened the modern feminist movement. And that is why lesbian feminists (abetted by some straight feminists) are fanatical about redefining lesbianism as "woman-identification," a model that, not incidentally, puts heterosexual feminists at a disadvantage.[40] Hall's vision of lesbianism as sexual difference and as masculinity is inimical to lesbian feminist ideology.

*   *   *

Like Hall, I see lesbianism as sexual difference. But her equation of lesbianism with masculinity needs not condemnation, but expansion. To begin with, we need to accept that whatever their ideological purposes, Hall and the sexologists were describing something real. Some people, then and now, experience "gender dysphoria," a strong feeling that one's assigned gender as a man or a woman does not agree with one's sense of self.[41] This is not precisely the same thing as wanting power and male privilege—a well-paid job, abortion on demand, athletic prowess—even though the masculine woman continues to be a symbol of feminist aspirations to the majority outside the movement. Masculinity and femininity are like two dialects of the same language. Though we all understand both, most of us "speak" only one.[42] Many lesbians, like Stephen Gordon, are biological females who grow up thinking in and "speaking" the "wrong" gender dialect.

Obviously, the more narrow and rigid gender categories are, the more easily one can feel "out of role." And if there were no more gender categories, gender dysphoria would disappear (as would feminism). However, feminist critiques of traditional gender categories do not yet resolve gender dysphoria if only because we have made so little impact on child-rearing practices; it appears that individual gender identity is established in early childhood. Although gender dysphoria exists in some simple societies,[43] it may be amplified by the same socio-historical processes—radical changes in the economy, in family structure and function, and in socialization—that have given rise to feminism. Why should we as feminists deplore or deny the existence of masculine women or effeminate men? Are we not against assigning specific psychological or behavioral traits to a particular biology? And should we not support those among us, butches and queens, who still bear the brunt of homophobia?

Hall's association of lesbianism and masculinity needs to be challenged, not because it doesn't exist, but because it is not the only possibility. Gender identity and sexual orientation are, in fact, two related but separate systems; witness the profusion of gender variations (which are deeply embedded in race, class, and ethnic experience) to be found today in the lesbian community. Many lesbians *are* masculine; most have composite styles; many are emphatically feminine. Stephen Gordon's success eclipsed more esoteric, continental, or feminine images of the lesbian, such as Renee Vivien's *decadent*, Colette's bisexual, or Natalie Barney's *Amazone*. The notion of a feminine lesbian contradicted the congenital theory that many homosexuals in Hall's era espoused to counter demands that they undergo punishing "therapies." Though Stephen's lovers in *The Well* are feminine and though Mary, in effect, seduces Stephen, Hall calls her "normal," that is, heterosexual. Even Havelock Ellis gave the "womanly" lesbian more dignity and definition. As a character, Mary is forgettable and inconsistent, weakening the novel and saddling Hall with an implausible ending in which Stephen "nobly" turns Mary over to a man. In real life, Hall's lover Una Troubridge did not go back to heterosexuality even when Hall, late in her life, took a second lover.

Despite knowing Una, Natalie Barney and others like them, Hall was unable to publicly articulate—perhaps to believe in—the persona of a *real* lesbian who did not feel somehow male. If sexual desire is masculine, and if the feminine woman only wants to attract men, then the womanly lesbian cannot logically exist. Mary's real story has yet to be told.[44]

CHRISTIAN BROTHERHOOD OR SEXUAL PERVERSION? HOMOSEXUAL IDENTITIES AND THE CONSTRUCTION OF SEXUAL BOUNDARIES IN THE WORLD WAR I ERA[1]

◆

GEORGE CHAUNCEY, JR.

Using the unusually rich evidence generated by a navy investigation of homosexuality at the Newport Naval Training Station in 1919–1920, George Chauncey, Jr., reconstructs the social organization and self-understanding of homosexually active sailors. Newport's sexual culture was surprisingly different from our own, and Chauncey shows how large numbers of sailors were able to have sex with men identified as "queers" without its affecting their image of themselves as "normal" men. Also striking is his analysis of the relative insignificance of medical discourse in shaping homosexual identities, the class differences in sexual ideology, and the diversity of sexual cultures—only inadvertently brought into conflict by the investigation —which coexisted in this small community.

In the spring of 1919, officers at the Newport (Rhode Island) Naval Training Station dispatched a squad of young enlisted men into the community to investigate the "immoral conditions" obtaining there. The

Note: Originally published in *Journal of Social History* 19 (1985): 189–212. Used with permission.

decoys sought out and associated with suspected "sexual perverts," had sex with them, and learned all they could about homosexual activity in Newport. On the basis of the evidence they gathered, naval and munici- pal authorities arrested more than twenty sailors in April and sixteen civilians in July, and the decoys testified against them at a naval court of inquiry and several civilian trials. The entire investigation received little attention before the navy accused a prominent Episcopal clergyman who worked at the Y.M.C.A. of soliciting homosexual contacts there. But when civilian and then naval officials took the minister to trial on charges of being a "lewd and wanton person," a major controversy developed. Protests by the Newport Ministerial Union and the Episcopal Bishop of Rhode Island and a vigorous editorial campaign by the *Providence Jour- nal* forced the navy to conduct a second inquiry in 1920 into the methods used in the first investigation. When that inquiry criticized the methods but essentially exonerated the senior naval officials who had instituted them, the ministers asked the Republican-controlled Senate Naval Affairs Committee to conduct its own investigation. The Committee agreed and issued a report in 1921 that vindicated the ministers' original charges and condemned the conduct of the highest naval officials involved, including Franklin D. Roosevelt, President Wilson's Assistant Secretary of the Navy and the 1920 Democratic vice-presidential candidate.[2]

The legacy of this controversy is a rich collection of evidence about the organization and phenomenology of homosexual relations among white working-class and middle-class men and about the changing nature of sexual discourse in the World War I era.[3] On the basis of the thirty-five hundred pages of testimony produced by the investigations it is possible to reconstruct the organization of a homosexual subculture during this period, how its participants understood their behavior, and how they were viewed by the larger community, thus providing a benchmark for generalizations about the historical development of homosexual identities and communities. The evidence also enables us to reassess current hypoth- eses concerning the relative significance of medical discourse, religious doctrine, and folk tradition in the shaping of popular understandings of sexual behavior and character. Most importantly, analysis of the testi- mony of the government's witnesses and the accused churchmen and sailors offers new insights into the relationship between homosexual be- havior and identity in the cultural construction of sexuality. Even when witnesses agreed that two men had engaged in homosexual relations with each other, they disagreed about whether both men or only the one playing the "woman's part" should be labelled as "queer." More pro- foundly, they disagreed about how to distinguish between a "sexual" and a "nonsexual" relationship; the navy defined certain relationships as homosexual and perverted which the ministers claimed were merely broth- erly and Christian. Because disagreement over the boundary between homosexuality and homosociality lay at the heart of the Newport controversy, its records allow us to explore the cultural construction of sexual categories in unusual depth.

The Social Organization of Homosexual Relations

The investigation found evidence of a highly developed and varied gay subculture in this small seaport community, and a strong sense of collective identity on the part of many of its participants. Cruising areas, where gay men and "straight" sailors[4] alike knew that sexual encounters were to be had, included the beach during the summer and the fashionable Bellevue Avenue close to it, the area along Cliff Walk, a cemetery, and a bridge. Many men's homosexual experiences consisted entirely (and irregularly) of visits to such areas for anonymous sexual encounters, but some men organized a group life with others who shared their inclinations. The navy's witnesses mentioned groups of servants who worked in the exclusive "cottages" on Bellevue Avenue and of civilians who met at places such as Jim's Restaurant on Long Wharf.[5] But they focused on a tightly-knit group of sailors who referred to themselves as "the gang,"[6] and it is this group whose social organization the first section of this paper will analyze.

The best-known rendezvous of gang members and of other gay sailors was neither dark nor secret: "The Army and Navy Y.M.C.A. was the headquarters of all cocksuckers [in] the early part of the evening," commented one investigator, and, added another, "everybody who sat around there in the evening . . . knew it."[7] The Y.M.C.A. was one of the central institutions of gay male life; some gay sailors lived there, others occasionally rented its rooms for the evening so that they would have a place to entertain men, and the black elevator operators were said to direct interested sailors to the gay men's rooms.[8] Moreover, the Y.M.C.A. was a social center, where gay men often had dinner together before moving to the lobby to continue conversation and meet the sailors visiting the Y.M.C.A. in the evening.[9] The ties which they maintained through such daily interactions were reinforced by a dizzying array of parties; within the space of three weeks, investigators were invited to four "fagott part[ies]" and heard of others.[10]

Moreover, the men who had developed a collective life in Newport recognized themselves as part of a subculture extending beyond a single town; they knew of places in New York and other cities "where the 'queens' hung out," made frequent visits to New York, Providence, and Fall River, and were visited by gay men from those cities. An apprentice machinist working in Providence, for instance, spent "week-ends in Newport for the purpose of associating with his 'dear friends,' the 'girls,' " and a third of the civilians arrested during the raids conducted in the summer were New York City residents working as servants in the grand houses of Newport. Only two of the arrested civilians were local residents.[11]

Within and sustained by this community, a complex system of personal identities and structured relationships took shape, in which homosexual behavior per se did not play a determining part. Relatively few of the men who engaged in homosexual activity, whether as casual participants in anonymous encounters or as partners in ongoing relationships, identified themselves or were labelled by others as sexually different from other men on that basis alone. The determining criterion in labelling a man as "straight" (their term) or "queer" was not the extent of his homosexual activity, but the gender role he assumed. The only men who sharply differentiated themselves from other men, labelling themselves as "queer," were those who assumed the sexual and other cultural roles ascribed to women; they might have been termed "inverts" in the early twentieth-century medical literature, because they not only expressed homosexual desire but "inverted" (or reversed) their gender role.[12]

The most prominent queers in Newport were effeminate men who sometimes donned women's clothes—when not in uniform—including some who became locally famous female impersonators. Sometimes referred to as "queens," these men dominated the social activities of the gang and frequently organized parties at their off-base apartments to which gay and "straight" sailors alike were invited. At these "drags" gang members could relax, be openly gay, and entertain straight sailors from the base with their theatrics and their sexual favors. One gay man described a party held in honor of some men from the USS *Baltimore* in the following terms:

> I went in and they were singing and playing. Some were coked up that wasn't drunk. And there was two of the fellows, 'Beckie' Goldstein and Richard that was in drags, they call it, in costume. They had on some kind of ball gowns, dancing costumes. They had on some ladies' underwear and ladies' drawers and everything and wigs. . . . I saw them playing and singing and dancing and somebody was playing the piano. . . . Every once in a while 'Beckie' (Goldstein) would go out of the room with a fellow and . . . some would come back buttoning up their pants.[13]

Female impersonation was an unexceptional part of navy culture during the World War I years, sufficiently legitimate—if curious—for the *Providence Journal* and the navy's own magazine, *Newport Recruit*, to run lengthy stories and photo essays about the many theatrical productions at the navy base in which men took the female roles.[14] The ubiquity of such drag shows and the fact that numerous "straight"-identified men took part in them sometimes served to protect gay female impersonators from suspicion. The landlord of one of the gay men arrested by the navy cited the sailor's stage roles in order to explain why he hadn't regarded the man's wearing women's clothes as "peculiar," and presumably the wife of the training station's commandant, who loaned the man "corsets, stockings, shirt waists, [and] women's pumps" for his use in *H.M.S. Pinafore,* did not realize that he also wore them at private parties.[15]

But if in some circles the men's stage roles served to legitimate their wearing drag, for most sailors such roles only confirmed the impersonators' identities as queer. Many sailors, after all, had seen or heard of the queens' appearing in drag at parties where its homosexual significance was inescapable. According to the navy's investigators, for instance, numerous sailors in uniform and "three prize fighters in civilian clothes" attended one "fagott party" given in honor of a female impersonator visiting Newport to perform at the Opera House. Not only were some of the men at the party—and presumably the guest of honor—in drag, but two men made out on a bed in full view of the others, who "remarked about their affection for each other."[16] Moreover, while sailors commonly gave each other nicknames indicating ethnic origin (e.g., "Wop" Bianchia and "Frenchman" La Favor) or other personal characteristics (e.g., "Lucky" and "Pick-axe"), many of them knew the most prominent queers *only* by their "ladies' names," camp nicknames they had adopted from the opera and cinema such as "Salome," "Theda Bara," and "Galli Curci."[17]

Several of the navy's witnesses described other signs of effeminacy one might look for in a queer. A straight investigator explained that "it was common knowledge that if a man was walking along the street in an effeminate manner, with his lips rouged, his face powdered, and his eye-brows pencilled, that in the majority of cases you could form a pretty good opinion of what kind of a man he was . . . a 'fairy.' "[18] One gay man, when pressed by the court to explain how he identified someone as "queer," pointed to more subtle indicators: "He acted sort of peculiar; walking around with his hands on his hips. . . . [H]is manner was not masculine. . . . The expression with the eyes and the gestures. . . . If a man was walking around and did not act real masculine, I would think he was a cocksucker."[19] A sailor, who later agreed to be a decoy, recalled that upon noticing "a number of fellows . . . of effeminate character" shortly after his arrival at Newport, he decided to look "into the crowd to see what kind of fellows they were and found they were perverts."[20] Effeminacy had been the first sign of a deeper perversion.

The inverts grouped themselves together as "queers" on the basis of their effeminate gender behavior,[21] and they all played roles culturally defined as feminine in sexual contacts. But they distinguished among themselves on the basis of the "feminine" sexual behavior they preferred, categorizing themselves as "fairies" (also called "cocksuckers"), "pogues" (men who liked to be "browned," or anally penetrated), and "two-way artists" (who enjoyed both). The ubiquity of these distinctions and their importance to personal self-identification cannot be overemphasized. Witnesses at the naval inquiries explicitly drew the distinctions as a matter of course and incorporated them into their descriptions of the gay subculture. One "pogue" who cooperated with the investigation, for instance, used such categories to label his friends in the gang with no prompting from the court: "Hughes said he was a pogue; Richard said he was a cocksucker; Fred Hoage said he was a two-way artist . . ." While there were some men about whom he "had to draw my own conclusions; they never said directly what they was or wasn't," his remarks made it clear he was sure they fit into one category or another.[22]

A second group of sailors who engaged in homosexual relations and participated in the group life of the gang occupied a more ambiguous sexual category because they, unlike the queers, conformed to masculine gender norms. Some of them were heterosexually married. None of them behaved effeminately or took the "woman's part" in sexual relations, they took no feminine nicknames, and they did not label themselves—nor were they labelled by others—as queer. Instead, gang members, who reproduced the highly gendered sexual relations of their culture, described the second group of men as playing the "husbands" to the "ladies" of the "inverted set." Some husbands entered into steady, loving relationships with individual men known as queer; witnesses spoke of couples who took trips together and maintained monogamous relationships.[23] The husbands' sexual—and sometimes explicitly romantic—interest in men distinguished them from other men: one gay man explained to the court that he believed the rumor about one man being the husband of another must have "some truth in it because [the first man] seems to be very fond of him, more so than the average man would be for a boy."[24] But the ambiguity of the sexual category such men occupied was reflected in the difficulty observers found in labelling them. The navy, which sometimes grouped such men with the queers as "perverts," found it could only satisfactorily identify them by describing what they *did*, rather than naming what they *were*. One investigator, for instance, provided the navy with a list of suspects in which he carefully labelled some men as "pogues" and others as "fairies," but he could only identify one man by noting that he "went out with all the above named men at various times and had himself sucked off or screwed them through the rectum."[25] Even the queers' terms for such men—"friends" and "husbands"—identified the men only *in relation to* the queers, rather than according them an autonomous sexual identity. Despite the uncertain definition of their sexual identity, however, most observers recognized these men as regular—if relatively marginal—members of the gang.

The social organization of the gang was deeply embedded in that of the larger culture; as we have seen, its members reproduced many of the social forms of gendered heterosexuality, with some men playing "the woman's part" in relationships with conventionally masculine "husbands." But the gang also helped men depart from the social roles ascribed to them as biological males by that larger culture. Many of the "queers" interrogated by the navy recalled having felt effeminate or otherwise "different" most of their lives. But it was the existence of sexual subcultures—of which the gang was one—that provided them a means of structuring their vague feelings of sexual and gender difference into distinctive personal identities. Such groups facilitated people's exploration and organization of their homosexuality by offering them support in the face of social opprobrium and providing them with guidelines for how to organize their feelings of difference into a particular social form of homosexuality, a coherent identity and way of life. The gang offered men a means of assuming social roles which they perceived to be more congruent with their inner natures than those prescribed by the dominant culture, and sometimes gave them remarkable strength to publicly defy social convention.

At the same time, the weight of social disapprobation led people within the gang to insist on a form of solidarity which required conformity to its own standards. To be accepted by the gang, for instance, one had to assume the role of pogue, fairy, two-way artist, or husband, and present oneself publicly in a manner consistent with that labelling. But some men appear to have maintained a critical perspective on the significance of the role for their personal identities. Even while assuming one role for the purpose of interaction in the gang, at least some continued to explore their sexual interests when the full range of those interests was not expressed in the norms for that role. Frederick Hoage, for instance, was known as a "brilliant woman" and a "French artist" (or "fairy"), but he was also reported surreptitiously to have tried to "brown" another member of the gang—behavior inappropriate to a "queer" as defined by the gang.[26]

Gang members, who believed they could identify men as pogues or fairies even if the men themselves had not yet recognized their true natures, sometimes intervened to accelerate the process of self-discovery. The gang scrutinized newly arrived recruits at the Y.M.C.A. for likely sexual partners and "queers," and at least one case is recorded of their approaching an effeminate but "straight"-identified man named Rogers in order to bring him out as a pogue. While he recalled always having been somewhat effeminate, after he joined the gang Rogers began using makeup "because the others did," assumed the name "Kitty Gordon," and developed a steady relationship with another man (his "husband").[27] What is striking to the contemporary reader is not only that gang members were so confident of their ability to detect Rogers's homosexual interests that they were willing to intervene in the normal pattern of his life, but that they believed they could identify him so precisely as a "latent" (not their word) pogue.

Many witnesses indicated that they had at least heard of "fairies" before joining the service, but military mobilization, by removing men like Rogers from family and neighborhood supervision and placing them in a single-sex environment, increased the chances that they would encounter gay-identified men and be able to explore new sexual possibilities. Both the opportunities offered by military mobilization and the constraints of hometown family supervision were poignantly reflected in Rogers's plea to the court of inquiry after his arrest. After claiming that he had met gay men and had homosexual experiences only after joining the navy, he added:

> I got in their company. I don't know why; but I used to go out with them. I would like to say here that these people were doing this all their lives. I never met one until I came in the Navy. . . . I would like to add that I would not care for my folks to learn anything about this; that I would suffer everything, because I want them to know me as they think I am. This is something that I never did until I came in the Navy.[28]

Straight witnesses at the naval inquiry demonstrated remarkable familiarity with homosexual activity in Newport; like gay men, they believed that "queers" constituted a distinct group of people, "a certain class of people called 'fairies.' "[29] Almost all of them agreed that one could identify certain men as queer by their mannerisms and carriage. At the second court of inquiry, a naval official ridiculed the Bishop of Rhode Island's assertions that it was impossible to recognize "fairies" and that he had never even heard of the term as if claiming such naïveté were preposterous:

> Then you don't know whether or not it is common to hear in any hotel lobby the remark, when a certain man will go by, and somebody will say, 'There goes a fairy.' You have *never* heard that expression used in that way?[30]

Most people also knew that such men had organized a collective life, even if they were unfamiliar with its details. As we have seen, many sailors at the naval training station knew that the Y.M.C.A. was a "headquarters" for such people, and Newport's mayor recalled that "it was information that was common . . . in times gone by, summer after summer," that men called "floaters" who appeared in town "had followed the fleet up from Norfolk."[31] In a comment that reveals more about straight perceptions than gay realities, a navy officer described gay men to the Newport Chief of Police as "a gang who were stronger than the Masons . . . [and who] had signals and a lot of other stuff . . . [T]hey were perverts and well organized."[32]

"Straight" people's familiarity with the homosexual subculture resulted from the openness with which some gay men rejected the cultural norms of heterosexuality. Several servicemen, for instance, mentioned having encountered openly homosexual men at the naval hospital, where they saw patients and staff wear makeup and publicly discuss their romances and homosexual experiences.[33] The story of two gang members assigned to the Melville coaling station near Newport indicates the extent to which individual "queers," with the support of the gang, were willing to make their presence known by defying social convention, even at the cost of hostile reactions. "From the time that they arrived at the station they were both the topic of conversation because of their effeminate habits," testified several sailors stationed at Melville. They suffered constant harassment; many sailors refused to associate with them or abused them physically and verbally, while their officers assigned them especially heavy work loads and ordered their subordinates to "try to get [one of them] with the goods."[34] Straight sailors reacted with such vigor because the gay men flaunted their difference rather than trying to conceal it, addressing each other with "feminine names," witnesses complained, and "publish[ing] the fact that they were prostitutes and such stuff as that."[35] At times they were deliberately provocative; one astounded sailor reported that he had "seen Richard lying in his bunk take one leg and, putting it up in the air, ask everyone within range of his voice and within range of this place how they would like to take it in this position."[36]

Even before the naval inquiry began, Newport's servicemen and civilians alike were well aware of the queers in their midst. They tolerated them in many settings and brutalized them in others, but they thought they knew what they were dealing with: perverts were men who behaved like women. But as the inquiry progressed, it inadvertently brought the neat boundaries separating queers from the rest of men into question.

Disputing the Boundaries of the "Sexual"

The testimony generated by the navy investigation provided unusually detailed information about the social organization of men who identified themselves as "queer." But it also revealed that many more men than the queers were regularly engaging in some form of homosexual activity. Initially the navy expressed little concern about such men's behavior, for it did not believe that straight sailors' occasional liaisons with queers raised any questions about their sexual character. But the authorities' decision to prosecute men not normally labelled as queer ignited a controversy which ultimately forced the navy and its opponents to define more precisely what they believed constituted a homosexual act and to defend the basis upon which they categorized people participating in such acts. Because the controversy brought so many groups of people—working- and middle-class gay- and straight-identified enlisted men, middle-class naval officers, ministers, and town officials—into conflict, it revealed how differently those groups interpreted sexuality. A multiplicity of sexual discourses co-existed at a single moment in the civilian and naval seaport communities.

The gang itself loosely described the male population beyond its borders as "straight," but its members further divided the straight population into two different groups: those who would reject their sexual advances, and those who would accept them. A man was "trade," according to one fairy, if he "would stand to have 'queer' persons fool around [with] him in any way, shape or manner."[37] Even among "trade," gay men realized that some men would participate more actively than others in sexual encounters. Most gay men were said to prefer men who were strictly "straight and [would] not reciprocate in any way," but at least one fairy, as a decoy recorded, "wanted to kiss me and love me [and] . . . insisted and begged for it."[38] Whatever its origins the term "trade" accurately described a common pattern of interaction between gay men and their straight sexual partners. In Newport, a gay man might take a sailor to a show or to dinner, offer him small gifts, or provide him with a place to stay when he was on overnight leave; in exchange, the sailor allowed his host to have sex with him that night, within whatever limits the sailor cared to set. The exchange was not always so elaborate: The navy's detectives reported several instances of gay men meeting and sexually servicing numerous sailors at the Y.M.C.A. in a single evening. Men who were "trade" normally did not expect or demand direct payment for their services, although gay men did sometimes lend their partners small amounts of money without expecting it to be returned, and they used "trade" to refer to some civilians who, in contrast to the sailors, paid *them* for sexual services. "Trade" normally referred to straight-identified men who played the "masculine" role in sexual encounters solicited by "queers."[39]

The boundary separating trade from the rest of men was easy to cross. There were locations in Newport where straight men knew they could present themselves in order to be solicited. One decoy testified that to infiltrate the gang he merely sat with its members in the Y.M.C.A. lobby one evening. As the decoy had already been in Newport for some time, presumably without expressing any interest in the gang, a gang member named Kreisberg said

> he was surprised to see me in such company. I finally told him that I belonged to the gang and very soon after that Kreisberg . . . said 'So we can consider you trade?' I replied that he could. Very soon Kreisberg requested that I remove my gloves as he, Kreisberg, wanted to hold my hands. Kreisberg acknowledged that he was abnormal and wanted to spend the night with me.[40]

Almost all straight sailors agreed that the effeminate members of the gang should be labelled "queer," but they disagreed about the sexual character of a straight man who accepted the sexual advances of a queer. Many straight men assumed that young recruits would accept the sexual solicitations of the perverts. "It was a shame to let these kids come in and run in to that kind of stuff," remarked one decoy; but his remarks indicate he did not think a boy was "queer" just because he let a queer have sex with him.[41] Most pogues defined themselves as "men who like to be browned," but straight men casually defined pogues as "[people] *that you can 'brown'* " and as men who "offered themselves in the same manner which women do."[42] Both remarks imply that "normal" men could take advantage of the pogues' availability without questioning their own identities as "straight"; the fact that the sailors made such potentially incriminating statements before the naval court indicates that this was an assumption they fully expected the court to share (as in fact it did). That lonesome men could unreservedly take advantage of a fairy's availability is perhaps also the implication, no matter how veiled in humor, of the remark made by a sailor stationed at the Melville coaling station: "It was common talk around that the Navy Department was getting good. They were sending a couple of 'fairies' up there for the 'sailors in Siberia.' As we used to call ourselves . . . meaning that we were all alone."[43] The strongest evidence of the social acceptability of trade was that the enlisted men who served as decoys volunteered to take on the role of trade for the purpose of infiltrating the gang, but were never even asked to consider assuming the role of queer. Becoming trade, unlike becoming a queer, posed no threat to the decoys' self-image or social status.

While many straight men took the sexual advances of gay men in stride, most engaged in certain ritual behavior designed to reinforce the distinction between themselves and the "queers." Most importantly, they played only the "masculine" sex role in their encounters with gay men—or at least claimed that they did—and observed the norms of masculinity in their own demeanor. They also ridiculed gay men and sometimes beat them up after sexual encounters. Other men, who feared it brought their manhood into question simply to be approached by a "pervert," were even more likely to attack gay men. Gang members recognized that they had to be careful about whom they approached. They all knew friends who had received severe beatings upon approaching the wrong man.[44] The more militant of the queers even played on straight men's fears. One of the queers at the Melville coaling station "made a remark that 'half the world is queer and the other half trade,' " recalled a straight sailor, who then described the harassment the queer suffered in retribution.[45]

It is now impossible to determine how many straight sailors had such sexual experiences with the queers, although Alfred Kinsey's research suggests the number might have been large. Kinsey found that 37 percent of the men he interviewed in the 1930s and 1940s had engaged in some homosexual activity, and that a quarter of them had had "more than incidental homosexual experience or reactions" for at least three years between the ages sixteen and fifty-five, even though only 4 percent were exclusively homosexual throughout their lives.[46] Whatever the precise figures at Newport, naval officials and queers alike believed that very many men were involved. Members of the court of inquiry never challenged the veracity of the numerous reports given them of straight sailors having sex with the queers; their chief investigator informed them on the first day of testimony that one suspected pervert had fellated "something like fifteen or twenty young recruits from the Naval Training Station" in a single night. As the investigation progressed, however, even the court of inquiry became concerned about the extent of homosexual activity uncovered. The chief investigator later claimed that the chairman of the first court had ordered him to curtail the investigation because " 'If your men [the decoys] do not knock off, they will hang the whole state of Rhode Island.' "[47]

Naval officials never considered prosecuting the many sailors who they fully realized were being serviced by the fairies each year, because they did not believe that the sailors' willingness to allow such acts "to be performed upon them" in any way implicated their sexual character as homosexual. Instead, they chose to prosecute only those men who were intimately involved in the gang, or otherwise demonstrated (as the navy tried to prove in court) that homosexual desire was a persistent, constituent element of their personalities, whether or not it manifested itself in effeminate behavior. The fact that naval and civilian authorities could prosecute men only for the commission of specific acts of sodomy should not be construed to mean that they viewed homosexuality simply as an act rather than as a condition characteristic of certain individuals; the whole organization of their investigation suggests otherwise. At the January 1920 trial of Rev. Samuel Kent the prosecution contended that

> we may offer evidence of other occurrences similar to the ones the indictment is based on for the purpose of proving the disposition on the part of this man. I submit that it is a well known principle of evidence that in a crime of this nature where disposition, inclination, is an element, that we are not confined to the specific conduct which we have complained of in the indictment, that the other incidents are gone into for their corroborative value as to intent, as to disposition, inclination.[48]

As the investigation and trials proceeded, however, the men prosecuted by the navy made it increasingly difficult for the navy to maintain standards which categorized certain men as "straight" even though they had engaged in homosexual acts with the defendants. This was doubtless particularly troubling to the navy because, while its opponents focused their questions on the character of the decoys in particular, by doing so

they implicitly questioned the character of *any* man who had sex with a
"pervert." The decoys testified that they had submitted to the queers'
sexual advances only in order to rid the navy of their presence, and the
navy, initially at least, guaranteed their legal immunity. But the defendants readily charged that the decoys themselves were tainted by homosexual interest and had taken abnormal pleasure in their work. Rev.
Kent's lawyers were particularly forceful in questioning the character of
any man who would volunteer to work as a decoy. As one decoy after
another helplessly answered each question with a quiescent "Yes, sir,"
the lawyers pressed them:

> Q.   You volunteered for this work?
> A.   Yes, sir.
> Q.   You knew what kind of work it was before you volunteered,
>   didn't you?
> A.   Yes, sir.
> Q.   You knew it involved sucking and that sort of thing, didn't you?
> A.   I knew that we had to deal with that, yes, sir.
> Q.   You knew it included sodomy and that sort of thing, didn't you?
> A.   Yes, sir.
> Q.   And you were quite willing to get into that sort of work?
> A.   I was willing to do it, yes, sir.
> Q.   And so willing that you volunteered for it, is that right?
> A.   Yes, sir. I volunteered for it, yes, sir.
> Q.   You knew it included buggering fellows, didn't you?[49]

Such questions about the decoys' character were reinforced when members of the gang claimed that the decoys had sometimes taken the initiative in sexual encounters.

The defendants thus raised questions about the character of any man
capable of responding to the advances of a pervert, forcing the navy to
reexamine its standards for distinguishing "straight" from "perverted"
sexuality. At the second naval court of inquiry, even the navy's judge
advocate asked the men about how much sexual pleasure they had experienced during their contacts with the suspects. As the boundaries distinguishing acceptable from perverted sexual response began to crumble, the
decoys recognized their vulnerability and tried to protect themselves. Some
simply refused to answer any further questions about the sexual encounters
they had described in graphic detail to the first court. One decoy protested
that he had never responded to a pervert's advances: "I am a man . . . The
thing was so horrible in my sight that naturally I could not become passionate
and there was no erection," but was immediately asked, "Weren't [the
other decoys] men, too?" Another, less fortunate decoy had to plead:

> Of course, a great deal of that was involuntary inasmuch as a man
> placing his hand on my penis would cause an erection and subsequent
> emission. That was uncontrollable on my part . . .

Probably I would have had it [the emission] when I got back in bed anyway . . . It is a physiological fact.[50]

But if a decoy could be suspected of perversion simply because he had a certain physiological response to a pervert's sexual advances, then the character of countless other sailors came under question. Many more men than the inner circle of queers and husbands would have to be investigated. In 1920, the navy was unprepared to take that step. The decision of the Dunn Inquiry to condemn the original investigation and the navy's decision to offer clemency to some of the men imprisoned as a result of it may be interpreted, in part, as a quiet retreat from that prospect.

Christian Brotherhood under Suspicion

The navy investigation raised fundamental questions concerning the definition of a "sexual relationship" itself when it reached beyond the largely working-class milieu of the military to label a prominent local Episcopal clergyman, Samuel Kent, and a Y.M.C.A. volunteer and churchman, Arthur Leslie Green, as homosexual. When Kent fled the city, the navy tracked him down and brought him to trial on sodomy charges. Two courts acquitted him despite the fact that five decoys claimed to have had sex with him, because the denials of the respected minister and of the numerous clergymen and educators who defended him seemed more credible. Soon after Kent's second acquittal in early 1920, the Bishop of Rhode Island and the Newport Ministerial Union went on the offensive against the navy. The clergymen charged that the navy had used immoral methods in its investigation, by instructing young enlisted men "in details of a nameless vice" and sending them into the community to entrap innocent citizens. They wrote letters of protest to the Secretary of the Navy and the President, condemned the investigation in the press, and forced the navy to convene a second court of inquiry into the methods used in the first inquiry. When it exculpated senior naval officials and failed to endorse all of the ministers' criticisms, the ministers persuaded the Republican-controlled Senate Naval Affairs Committee to undertake its own investigation, which eventually endorsed all of the ministers' charges.[51]

The simple fact that one of their own had been attacked did not provoke the fervor of the ministers' response to the navy investigation, nor did they oppose the investigation simply because of its "immoral" methods. Close examination of the navy's allegations and of the ministers' countercharges suggests that the ministers feared that the navy's charges against the two churchmen threatened to implicate them all. Both Green and Kent were highly regarded local churchmen; Kent had been asked to preach weekly during Lent, had received praise for his work at the Naval Hospital during the influenza epidemic, and at the time of the investigation was expected to be named Superintendent of a planned Seaman's Church Institute.[52] Their behavior had not differed markedly from that of the many other men who ministered to the needs of the thousands of boys brought to Newport by the war. When the navy charged that Kent's and Green's behavior and motives were perverted, many ministers feared that they could also be accused of perversion, and, more broadly, that the inquiry had questioned the ideology of nonsexual Christian brotherhood that had heretofore explained their devotion to other men. The confrontation between the two groups fundamentally represented a dispute over the norms for masculine gender behavior and over the boundaries between homosociality and homosexuality in the relations of men.

The investigation threatened Newport's ministers precisely because it repudiated those conventions that had justified and institutionalized a mode of behavior for men of the cloth or of the upper class that would have been perceived as effeminate in other men. The ministers' perception of this threat is reflected in their repeated criticism of the navy operatives' claim that they could detect perverts by their "looks and actions."[53] Almost all sailors and townspeople, as we have seen, endorsed this claim, but it put the ministers as a group in an extremely awkward position, for the major sign of a man's perversion according to most sailors was his being effeminate. As the ministers' consternation indicated, there was no single norm for masculine behavior at Newport; many forms of behavior considered effeminate on the part of working-class men were regarded as appropriate to the status of upper-class men or to the ministerial duties of the clergy. Perhaps if the navy had accused only working-class sailors, among whom "effeminacy" was more clearly deviant from group norms, of perversion, the ministers might have been content to let this claim stand. But when the naval inquiry also identified churchmen associated with such an upper-class institution as the Episcopal Church of Newport as perverted because of their perceived effeminacy, it challenged the norms which had heretofore shielded men of their background from such suspicions.

One witness tried to defend Kent's "peculiar" behavior on the basis of the conventional norms when he contended that "I don't know whether you would call it abnormal. He was a minister."[54] But the navy refused to accept this as a defense, and witnesses repeatedly described Kent and Green to the court as "peculiar," "sissyfied," and "effeminate." During his daily visits to patients at the hospital, according to a witness named Brunelle, Green held the patients' hands and "didn't talk like a man—he talk[ed] like a woman to me."[55] Since there is no evidence that Green had a high-pitched or otherwise "effeminate" *voice*, Brunelle probably meant Green addressed men with greater affection than he expected of a man. But all ministers visited with patients and spoke quiet, healing words to them; their position as ministers had permitted them to engage in such conventionally "feminine" behavior. When the navy and ordinary sailors labelled this behavior "effeminate" in the case of Green and Kent, and further claimed that such effeminacy was a sign of sexual perversion, they challenged the legitimacy of many Christian social workers' behavior.

During the war, Newport's clergymen had done all they could to minister to the needs of the thousands of boys brought to the Naval Training Station. They believed they had acted in the spirit of Christian brotherhood, but the naval inquiry seemed to suggest that less lofty motives were at work. Ministers had loaned sailors money, but during the inquiry they heard Green accused of buying sex. They had visited boys in the hospital and now heard witnesses insinuate that this was abnormal: "I don't know what [Kent's] duties were, but he was always talking to some boys. It seems though he would have special boys to talk to. He would go to certain fellows [patients] and probably spend the afternoon with them."[56] They had given boys drives and taken them out to dinner and to the theater, and now heard Kent accused of lavishing such favors on young men in order to further his salacious purposes. They had opened their homes to the young enlisted men, but now heard Kent accused of inviting boys home in order to seduce them.[57] When one witness at the first court of inquiry tried to argue that Green's work at the Y.M.C.A. was inspired by purely "charitable" motives, the court repudiated his interpretation and questioned the motives of *any* man who engaged in such work:

> Do you think a normal active man would peddle stamps and paper around a Hospital and at the Y.M.C.A.? . . .
> Do you think that a man who had no interest in young boys would voluntarily offer his services and work in the Y.M.C.A. where he is constantly associated with young boys?[58]

The ministers sought to defend Kent—and themselves—from the navy's insinuations by reaffirming the cultural interpretation of ministerial behavior as Christian and praiseworthy. While they denied the navy's charge that Kent had had genital contact with sailors, they did not deny his devotion to young men, for to have done so would have implicitly conceded the navy's interpretation of such behavior as salacious—and thus have left all ministers who had demonstrated similar devotion open to suspicion. Rev. John H. Deming of the Ministerial Union reported that numerous ministers shared the fear of one man who was "frantic after all he had done for the Navy":

> When this thing [the investigation] occurred, it threw some of my personal friends into a panic. For they knew that in the course of their work they had had relations with boys in various ways; they had been alone with them in some cases. As one boy [a friend] said, frequently boys had slept in the room with him. But he had never

thought of the impropriety of sleeping alone with a navy boy. He thought probably he would be accused.[59]

Rather than deny the government's claim that Kent had sought intimate relationships with sailors and devoted unusual attention to them, therefore, Kent and his supporters depicted such behavior as an honorable part of the man's ministry. Indeed, demonstrating just how much attention Kent had lavished on boys became as central to the strategy of the ministers as it was to that of the government, but the ministers offered a radically different interpretation of it. Their preoccupation with validating ministerial behavior turned Kent's trial and the second naval inquiry into an implicit public debate over the cultural definition of the boundaries between homosociality and homosexuality in the relations of men. The navy had defined Kent's behavior as sexual and perverted; the ministers sought to reaffirm that it was brotherly and Christian.

Kent himself interpreted his relations with sailors as "[t]rying to be friends with them, urging them to come to my quarters and see me if they wanted to, telling them—I think, perhaps, I can best express it by saying 'Big Brotherhood.' " He quoted a letter from another minister commending his "brotherly assistance" during the influenza epidemic, and he pointed out that the Episcopal War Commission provided him with funds with which to take servicemen to the theater "at least once a week" and to maintain his automobile in order to give boys drives "and get acquainted with them."[60] He described in detail his efforts to minister to the men who had testified against him, explaining that he had offered them counsel, a place to sleep, and other services just as he had to hundreds of other enlisted men. But he denied that any genital contact had taken place, and in some cases claimed he had broken off the relationships when he realized that the *decoys* wanted sexual contact.

Kent's lawyers produced a succession of defense witnesses—respected clergymen, educators, and businesspeople who had known Kent at every stage of his career—to testify to his obvious affection for boys, even though by emphasizing this aspect of his character they risked substantiating the navy's case. The main point of their testimony was that Kent was devoted to boys and young men and had demonstrated such talent in working with them that they had encouraged him to focus his ministry on them. Kent's lawyers prompted a former employer from Kent's hometown of Lynn, Massachusetts, to recall that Kent, a "friend of [his] family, and especially [his] sons and sons' associates," had "[taken] charge of twelve or fourteen boys [from Lynn] and [taken] them down to Sebago Lake," where they camped for several weeks "under his charge." The Bishop of Pennsylvania recalled that, as Kent's teacher at the Episcopal Theological School in Cambridge in 1908, he had asked Kent to help him develop a ministry to Harvard men, "because [Kent] seemed peculiarly fitted for it in temperament and in experience, and in general knowledge of how to

approach young men and influence them for good." The sentiments of
Kent's character witnesses were perhaps best summarized by a judge who
sat on the Episcopal War Commission which employed Kent. The judge
assured the court that Kent's reputation was "excellent; I think he was
looked upon as an earnest Christian man [who] was much interested in
young men."[61]

The extent to which Kent's supporters were willing to interpret his
intimacy with young men as brotherly rather than sexual is perhaps best
illustrated by the effort of Kent's defense lawyer to show how Kent's
inviting a decoy named Charles Zipf to sleep with him was only another
aspect of his ministering to the boy's needs. Hadn't the decoy told Kent
he was "lonesome" and had no place to sleep that night, the defense
attorney pressed Zipf in cross-examination, before Kent invited him to
spend the night in his parish house? And after Kent had set up a cot for
Zipf in the living room, hadn't Zipf told Kent that he was "cold" before
Kent pulled back the covers and invited him to join him in his bed?[62] The
attorney counted on the presumption of Christian brotherhood to protect
the minister's behavior from the suspicion of homosexual perversion,
even though the same evidence would have seemed irrefutably incriminating in the case of another man.

Kent's defense strategy worked. Arguments based on assumptions about
ministerial conduct persuaded the jury to acquit Kent of the government's
charges. But Newport's ministers launched their campaign against the
navy probe as soon as Kent was acquitted because they recognized that it
had succeeded in putting their devotion to men under suspicion. It had
raised questions about the cultural boundaries distinguishing homosexuality from homosociality that the ministers were determined to lay to rest.

But while it is evident that Newport's ministers feared the consequences
of the investigation for their public reputations, two of their charges
against the navy suggest that they may also have feared that its allegations
contained some element of truth. The charges reflect the difference
between the ministers' and the navy's understanding of sexuality and
human sinfulness, but the very difference may have made the navy's
accusations seem plausible in a way that the navy could not have foreseen.
First, the ministers condemned the navy for having instructed young
enlisted men—the decoys—"in the details of a nameless vice," and having ordered them to use that knowledge. The naval authorities had been
willing to let their agents engage in sexual acts with the "queers" because
they were primarily concerned about people manifesting a homosexual
disposition rather than those engaging occasionally in homosexual acts.
The navy asserted that the decoys' investigative purpose rendered them
immune from criminal prosecution even though they had committed
illegal sexual acts. But the ministers viewed the decoys' culpability as "a
moral question . . . not a technical question at all"; when the decoys
had sex with other men, they had "scars placed on their souls," because,

inescapably, "having immoral relations with men is an immoral act."[63] The sin was in the act, not the motive or the disposition. In addition, the ministers charged that the navy had directed the decoys to entrap designated individuals and that no one, no matter how innocent, could avoid entrapment by a skillful decoy. According to Bishop Perry, the decoys operated by putting men "into compromising positions, where they might be suspected of guilt, [even though they were] guiltless persons." Anyone could be entrapped because an "innocent advance might be made by the person operated upon and he might be ensnared against his will."[64] Implicitly, any clergyman could have done what Kent was accused of doing. Anyone's defenses could fall.

The ministers' preoccupation with the moral significance of genital sexual activity and their fear that anyone could be entrapped may reflect the continued saliency for them of the Christian precept that *all* people, including the clergy, were sinners subject to a variety of sexual temptations, including those of homosexual desire.[65] According to this tradition, Christians had to resist homosexual temptations, as they resisted others, but simply to desire a homosexual liaison was neither a singular failing nor an indication of perverted character. The fact that the ministers never clearly elucidated this perspective and were forced increasingly to use the navy's own terms while contesting the navy's conclusions may reflect both the ministers' uncertainty and their recognition that such a perspective was no longer shared by the public.

In any case, making the commission of specified physical acts the distinguishing characteristic of a moral pervert made it definitionally impossible to interpret the ministers' relationships with sailors—no matter how intimate and emotionally moving—as having a "sexual" element, so long as they involved no such acts. Defining the sexual element in men's relationships in this narrow manner enabled the ministers to develop a bipartite defense of Kent which simultaneously denied he had had sexual relationships with other men and yet celebrated his profound emotional devotion to them. It legitimized (nonphysical) intimacy between men by precluding the possibility that such intimacy could be defined as sexual. Reaffirming the boundaries between Christian brotherhood and perverted sexuality was a central objective of the ministers' very public debate with the navy. But it may also have been of private significance to churchmen forced by the navy investigation to reflect on the nature of their brotherhood with other men.

Conclusion

The richly textured evidence provided by the Newport controversy makes it possible to reexamine certain tenets of recent work in the history of sexuality, especially the history of homosexuality. Much of that work, drawing on sociological models of symbolic interactionism and the labelling theory of deviance, has argued that the end of the nineteenth century witnessed a major reconceptualization of homosexuality. Before the last century, according to this thesis, North American and European cultures had no concept of the homosexual-as-person; they regarded homosexuality as simply another form of sinful behavior in which anyone might choose to engage. The turn of the century witnessed the "invention of the homosexual," that is, the new determination that homosexual desire was limited to certain identifiable individuals for whom it was an involuntary sexual orientation of some biological or psychological origin. The most prominent advocates of this thesis have argued that the medical discourse on homosexuality that emerged in the late nineteenth century played a determining role in this process, by creating and popularizing this new model of homosexual behavior (which they have termed the "medical model" of homosexuality). It was on the basis of the new medical models, they argue, that homosexually active individuals came to be labelled in popular culture—and to assume an identity—as sexual deviants different in nature from other people, rather than as sinners whose sinful nature was the common lot of humanity.[66]

The Newport evidence suggests how we might begin to refine and correct our analysis of the relationship between medical discourse, homosexual behavior, and identity. First, and most clearly, the Newport evidence indicates that medical discourse still played little or no role in the shaping of working-class homosexual identities and categories by World War I, more than thirty years after the discourse had begun. There would be no logical reason to expect that discussions carried on in elite journals whose distribution was limited to members of the medical and legal professions would have had any immediate effect on the larger culture, particularly the working class. In the Newport evidence, only one fairy even mentioned the favored medical term "invert," using it as a synonym for the already existing and widely recognized popular term "queer." Moreover, while "invert" was commonly used in the medical literature there is no reason to assume that it originated there, and the Newport witness specified that he had first heard it in theater circles and not through reading any "literature." The culture of the sexual underground, always in a complex relationship with the dominant culture, played a more important role in the shaping and sustaining of sexual identities.

More remarkably, medical discourse appears to have had as little influence on the military hierarchy as on the people of Newport.[67] Throughout the two years of navy investigations related to Newport, which involved the highest naval officials, not a single medical expert was invited to present the medical perspective on the issues at stake. The only member of the original board of inquiry who even alluded to the published literature (and this on only one occasion during the Foster hearings, and once more at the second inquiry) was Dr. E. M. Hudson, the welfare officer at the naval hospital and one of the decoys' supervisors. Hudson played a prominent role in the original investigation not because of his medical expertise, but because it was the flagrantly displayed (and normally tolerated) effeminacy and homosexuality of hospital staff and patients that first made naval officials consider undertaking an investigation. As the decoys' supervisor, Hudson drew on his training in fingerprinting and detective work considerably more than his medical background. Only after he became concerned that the decoys might be held legally culpable for their homosexual activity did he "read several medical books on the subject and read everything that I could find out as to what legal decisions there were on these cases."[68] But he never became very familiar with the medical discourse on sexual nonconformity; after his reading he still thought that the term "invert," which had first appeared in U.S. medical journals almost forty years earlier, was "practically a new term," less than two years old.[69]

Moreover, Hudson only accepted those aspects of the medical analysis of homosexuality that confirmed popular perceptions. Thus he accepted as authoritative the distinction that medical writers drew between "congenital perverts" (called "queers" in common parlance) and "normal people submitting to acts of perversion, as a great many normal people do, [who] do not become perverts themselves," such as men isolated from women at a military base. He accepted this "scientific" distinction because it only confirmed what he and other naval officials already believed: that many sailors had sex with the queers without being "queer" themselves. But when the medical literature differed from the assumptions he shared with most navy men, he ignored it. Rather than adopting the medical viewpoint that homosexuals were biological anomalies who should be treated medically rather than willful criminals who should be deterred from homosexuality by severe legal penalties, for instance, he agreed with his colleagues that "these conditions existed and should be eradicated and the men guilty of offenses should be rounded up and punished."[70] In the course of 109 days of hearings, Dr. Hudson referred to medical authorities only twice, and then only when they confirmed the assumptions of popular culture.

It thus appears more plausible to describe the medical discourse as a "reverse discourse," to use Michel Foucault's term, rather than as the central force in the creation of new sexual categories around which individuals shaped their personal identities. Rather than creating such categories as "the invert" and "the homosexual," the turn-of-the-century medical investigators whom Hudson read were trying to describe, classify, and explain a preexisting sexual underground whose outlines they only vaguely perceived. Their scientific categories largely reproduced those of popular culture, with "queers" becoming "inverts" in medical parlance but retaining the characteristic cross-gender behavior already attributed to them in popular culture. Doctors developed generalizations about homosexuals based on their idiosyncratic observations of particular individuals and admitted from the beginning that they were responding to the existence of communities of such people whose mysterious behavior and social organization they wished to explore. As one of the first American medical commentators observed in 1889, in explaining the need to study sexual perversion, "[t]here is in every community of any size a colony of male sexual perverts; they are usually known to each other, and are likely to congregate together."[71] By the time of the Newport investigation, medical researchers had developed an elaborate system of sexual classification and numerous explanations for individual cases of homosexuality, but they still had little comprehension of the complex social and cultural structure of gay life.

The Newport evidence helps put the significance of the medical discourse in perspective; it also offers new insights into the relationship between homosexual behavior and identity. Recent studies which have established the need to distinguish between homosexual behavior (presumably a transhistorically evident phenomenon) and the historically specific concept of homosexual identity have tended to focus on the evolution of people whose *primary* personal and political "ethnic" identification is as gay, and who have organized a multidimensional way of life on the basis of their homosexuality. The high visibility of such people in contemporary Western societies and their growing political significance make analysis of the historical development of their community of particular scholarly interest and importance.[72] But the Newport evidence indicates that we need to begin paying more attention to *other* social forms of homosexuality—other ways in which homosexual relations have been organized and understood, differentiated, named, and left deliberately unnamed. We need to specify the *particularity* of various modes of homosexual behavior and the relationships between those modes and particular configurations of sexual identity.

For even when we find evidence that a culture has labelled people who were homosexually active as sexually deviant, we should not assume a priori that their homosexual activity was the determinative criterion in the labelling process. As in Newport, where many men engaged in certain kinds of homosexual behavior yet continued to be regarded as "normal," the assumption of particular sexual roles and deviance from gender norms may have been more important than the coincidence of male or female sexual partners in the classification of sexual character. "Fairies," "pogues," "husbands," and "trade" might all be labelled "homosexuals" in our own time, but they were labelled—and understood themselves—as fundamentally different kinds of people in World War I-era Newport. They all engaged in what we would define as homosexual behavior, but they and the people who observed them were more careful than we to draw distinctions between different modes of such behavior. To classify their behavior and character using the simple polarities of "homosexual" and "heterosexual" would be to misunderstand the complexity of their sexual system. Indeed, the very terms "homosexual behavior" and "identity," because of their tendency to conflate phenomena that other cultures may have regarded as quite distinct, appear to be insufficiently precise to denote the variety of social forms of sexuality we wish to analyze.[73]

The problems that arise when different forms of homosexual activity and identity are conflated are evidenced in the current debate over the consequences of the development of a medical model of homosexuality. Recent studies, especially in lesbian history, have argued that the creation and stigmatization of the public image of the homosexual at the turn of the century served to restrict the possibilities for intimacy between all women and all men, by making it possible to associate such intimacy with the despised social category of the homosexual. This thesis rightly observes that the definition of deviance serves to establish behavioral norms for everyone, not just for the deviant. But it overlooks the corollary of this observation, that the definition of deviance serves to legitimize some social relations even as it stigmatizes others; and it assumes that the turn-of-the-century definition of "sexual inversion" codified the same configuration of sexual and gender phenomena which "homosexuality" does today. But many early twentieth-century romantic friendships between women, for instance, appear to have been unaffected by the development of a public lesbian persona, in part because that image characterized the lesbian primarily as a "mannish woman," which had the effect of excluding from its stigmatizing purview all conventionally feminine women, no matter how intimate their friendships.[74]

The stigmatized image of the queer also helped to legitimate the behavior of men in Newport. Most observers did not label as queer either the ministers who were intimate with their Christian brothers or the sailors who had sex with effeminate men, because neither group conformed to the dominant image of what a queer should be like. Significantly, though, in their own minds the two groups of men legitimized their behavior in radically different ways: The ministers' conception of the boundary between acceptable and unacceptable male behavior was almost precisely the opposite of that obtaining among the sailors. The ministers made it impossible to define their relationships with sailors as "sexual" by making the commission of specified physical acts the distinguishing characteristic of a moral pervert. But even as the ministers argued that their relatively feminine character and deep emotional intimacy with other men were acceptable so long as they engaged in no physical contact with them, the sailors believed that their physical sexual contact with the queers remained acceptable so long as they avoided effeminate behavior and developed no emotional ties with their sexual partners.

At the heart of the controversy provoked and revealed by the Newport investigation was a confrontation between several such definitional systems, a series of disputes over the boundaries between homosociality and homosexuality in the relations of men and over the standards by which their masculinity would be judged. The investigation became controversial when it verged on suggesting that the homosocial world of the navy and the relationships between sailors and their Christian brothers in the Newport ministry were permeated by homosexual desire. Newport's ministers and leading citizens, the Senate Naval Affairs Committee, and to some extent even the navy itself repudiated the Newport inquiry because they found such a suggestion intolerable. Although numerous cultural interpretations of sexuality were allowed to confront each other at the inquiry, ultimately certain cultural boundaries had to be reaffirmed in order to protect certain relations as "nonsexual," even as the sexual nature of others was declared and condemned. The Newport evidence reveals much about the social organization and self-understanding of men who identified themselves as "queer." But it also provides a remarkable illustration of the extent to which the boundaries established between "sexual" and "nonsexual" relations are culturally determined, and it reminds us that struggles over the demarcation of those boundaries are a central aspect of the history of sexuality.

A SPECTACLE IN COLOR:
THE LESBIAN AND GAY SUBCULTURE
OF JAZZ AGE HARLEM

◆

ERIC GARBER

The Harlem Renaissance has long been recognized as a seminal
moment in Afro-American history. Eric Garber's work shows that it
was also a significant moment in the history of gay Americans, and
that black lesbians and gay men—and the interracial gay social
networks they created—played a crucial role in the literary renaissance, in the blues, and in the clubs which made Harlem famous in
the 1920s. In this essay he documents those contributions and paints
a colorful portrait of the speakeasies, private parties, and drag balls
Harlem's homosexuals claimed as their own. He also considers the
effect of the intersection of racial and sexual oppressions in creating
a distinctive black gay subculture, and the sometimes uneasy relationship between black gays and the white homosexuals who flocked
uptown.

At the beginning of the twentieth century, a homosexual subculture,
uniquely Afro-American in substance, began to take shape in New York's
Harlem. Throughout the so-called Harlem Renaissance period, roughly
1920 to 1935, black lesbians and gay men were meeting each other on
street corners, socializing in cabarets and rent parties, and worshiping in
church on Sundays, creating a language, a social structure, and a complex
network of institutions. Some were discreet about their sexual identities;
others openly expressed their personal feelings. The community they built
attracted white homosexuals as well as black, creating friendships between people of disparate ethnic and economic backgrounds and building

318

alliances for progressive social change. But the prosperity of the 1920s was short-lived, and the Harlem gay subculture quickly declined following the Stock Market crash of 1929 and the repeal of Prohibition, soon becoming only a shadow of its earlier self. Nevertheless, the traditions and institutions created by Harlem lesbians and gay men during the Jazz Age continue to this day.

The key historical factor in the development of the lesbian and gay subculture in Harlem was the massive migration of thousands of Afro-Americans to northern urban areas after the turn of the century. Since the beginning of American slavery, the vast majority of blacks had lived in rural southern states. American participation in World War I led to an increase in northern industrial production and brought an end to immigration, which resulted in thousands of openings in northern factories becoming available to blacks. Within two decades, large communities of black Americans had developed in most northern urban areas. So significant was this shift in population that it is now referred to as the "Great Migration." Black communities developed in Chicago, Detroit, and Buffalo, but the largest and most spectacular was Harlem, which became the mecca for Afro-Americans from all over the world. Nowhere else could you find a geographic area so large, so concentrated, really a city within a city, populated entirely by blacks. There were black schoolteachers, black entrepreneurs, black police officers, and even black millionaires. A spirit was in the air—of hope, progress, and possibilities—which proved particularly alluring to the young and unmarried. Harlem's streets soon filled with their music, their voices, and their laughter.

They called themselves "New Negroes," Harlem was their capital, and they manifested a new militancy and pride. Black servicemen had been treated with a degree of respect and given a taste of near-equality while in Europe during the World War; their experiences influenced their expectations when they returned home. Participation in the war effort had given the entire black community a sense of involvement in the American process and led them to demand their place in the mainstream of American life. Marcus Garvey, the charismatic West Indian orator, had thousands of followers in his enormous black nationalist "Back to Africa" movement. W. E. B. DuBois and his National Association for the Advancement of Colored People (NAACP), with its radical integrationist position, generally appealed to a more educated, middle-class following, as did Charles W. Johnson's National Urban League, but were just as militant in their call for racial justice. A variety of individuals and organizations generated Afro-American pride and solidarity.

The New Negro movement created a new kind of art. Harlem, as the New Negro Capital, became a worldwide center for Afro-American jazz, literature, and the fine arts. Many black musicians, artists, writers, and entertainers were drawn to the vibrant black uptown neighborhood. Duke Ellington, Fletcher Henderson, Fats Waller, Cab Calloway, Bessie Smith, and Ethel Waters played in Harlem nightclubs. Langston Hughes, Zora Hurston, and Countee Cullen published in the local newspapers. Art galleries displayed the work of Aaron Douglas and Richmond Barthé. These creative talents incorporated the emerging black urban social consciousness into their art. The resulting explosion of self-consciously Afro-American creativity, now known as the "Harlem Renaissance," had a profound impact on the subsequent development of American arts.[1]

The social and sexual attitudes of Harlem's new immigrants were best reflected in the blues, a distinctly Afro-American folk music that had developed in rural southern black communities following the Civil War. Structurally simple, yet open to countless subtleties, the blues were immensely popular within American black communities throughout the 1920s. They told of loneliness, homesickness, and poverty, of love and good luck, and they provided a window into the difficult, often brutal, world of the New Negro immigrant.

Homosexuality was clearly part of this world. "There's two things got me puzzled, there's two things I don't understand," moaned blues great Bessie Smith, "that's a mannish-acting woman and a lisping, swishing, womanish-acting man."[2] In "Sissy Blues," Ma Rainey complained of her husband's infidelity with a homosexual named "Miss Kate."[3] Lucille Bogan, in her "B.D. Women Blues," warned that "B.D. [bulldagger] women sure is rough; they drink up many a whiskey and they sure can strut their stuff."[4] The "sissies" and "bulldaggers" mentioned in the blues were ridiculed for their cross-gender behavior, but neither shunned nor hated. "Boy in the Boat" for example, recorded in 1930 by George Hanna, counseled "When you see two women walking hand in hand, just shake your head and try to understand."[5] In fact, the casualness toward sexuality, so common in the blues, sometimes extended to homosexual behavior. In "Sissy Man Blues," a traditional tune recorded by numerous male blues singers over the years, the singer demanded "if you can't bring me a woman, bring me a sissy man."[6] George Hanna's "Freakish Blues," recorded in 1931, is even more explicit about potential sexual fludity.[7] The blues reflected a culture that accepted sexuality, including homosexual behavior and identities, as a natural part of life.

Despite the relatively tolerant attitude shown toward homosexuality by Afro-American culture, black lesbians and gay men still had a difficult time. Like other black migrants, they soon learned that racism crossed the Mason-Dixon line. Economic problems, unemployment, and segregation plagued black communities across the North. High rents and housing shortages made privacy a luxury for Harlem's newcomers. Moreover, black homosexuals, like their white counterparts, were continually under attack from the police and judicial systems. In 1920, young lesbian Mabel Hampton, recently arrived in Harlem from Winston-Salem, North Carolina, was arrested on trumped-up prostitution charges and spent two years in Bedford Hills Reformatory.[8] Augustus Granville Dill, distinguished business editor of the NAACP's *Crisis* and personal protégé of DuBois, had his political career destroyed when he was arrested for soliciting sex in a public restroom.[9] Black gay people were also under attack from the developing psychiatric institutions; Jonathan Katz cites a tragic case in which a young black gay man was incarcerated for most of the 1920s at the Worcester (Massachusetts) State Hospital.[10] But in spite of racial oppression, economic hardship, and homophobic persecution, black lesbians and gay men were able to build a thriving community of their own within existing Afro-American institutions and traditions.

Private parties were the best place for Harlem lesbians and gay men to socialize, providing safety and privacy. "We used to go to parties every other night. . . . The girls all had the parties," remembered Mabel Hampton.[11] Harlem parties were extremely varied; the most common kind was the "rent party." Like the blues, rent parties had been brought north in the Great Migration. Few of Harlem's new residents had much money, and sometimes rent was hard to come by. To raise funds, they sometimes threw enormous parties, inviting the public and charging admission. There would be dancing and jazz, and bootleg liquor for sale in the kitchen. It is about just such a party that Bessie Smith sang her famous "Gimme a Pigfoot and a Bottle of Beer." On any given Saturday night there were scores of these parties throughout Harlem, often with those in attendance not knowing their hosts. The dancing and merriment would continue until dawn, and by morning the landlord could be paid. Lesbians and gay men were active participants in rent parties. The *New York Age*, one of Harlem's newspapers, complained in 1926:

> One of these rent parties a few weeks ago was the scene of a tragic crime in which one jealous woman cut the throat of another, because the two were rivals for the affections of a third woman. The whole situation was on a par with the recent Broadway play [about lesbianism, *The Captive*], imported from Paris, although the underworld tragedy took place in this locality. In the meantime, the combination of bad gin, jealous women, a carving knife, and a rent party is dangerous to the health of all concerned.[12]

At another Harlem rent party, satirically depicted in Wallace Thurman's 1932 Harlem Renaissance novel *Infants of the Spring*, a flamboyantly bisexual Harlem artist proudly displayed his new protégé, a handsome bootblack, to the "fanciful aggregation of Greenwich Village uranians" he had invited.[13]

Gay men could always be found at the literary gatherings of Alexander Gumby. Gumby, who had arrived in Harlem near the turn of the century, immediately became entranced with the theatrical set and decided to open a salon to attract them. He worked as a postal clerk and acquired a white patron, eventually renting a large studio on Fifth Avenue between

131st and 132nd streets. Known as Gumby's Bookstore because of the hundreds of books that lined the walls, the salon drew many theatrical and artistic luminaries. White author Samuel Steward remembers being taken to Gumby's one evening by a lesbian friend and enjoying a delightful evening of "reefer," bathtub gin, a game of truth, and homosexual exploits.[14]

Certainly the most opulent parties in Harlem were thrown by the heiress A'Lelia Walker. Walker was a striking, tall, dark-skinned woman who was rarely seen without her riding crop and her imposing, jeweled turban. She was the only daughter of Madame C. J. Walker, a former washerwoman who had made millions marketing her own hair-straightening process. When she died, Madame Walker left virtually her entire fortune to A'Lelia. Whereas Madame Walker had been civic-minded, donating thousands of dollars to charity, A'Lelia used most of her inheritance to throw lavish parties in her palatial Hudson River estate, Villa Lewaro, and at her Manhattan dwelling on 136th Street. Because A'Lelia adored the company of lesbians and gay men, her parties had a distinctly gay ambience. Elegant homosexuals such as Edward Perry, Edna Thomas, Harold Jackman, and Caska Bonds were her closest friends. So were scores of white celebrities. Novelist Marjorie Worthington would later remember:

> We went several times that winter to Madame Allelia [sic] Walker's Thursday "at-homes" on a beautiful street in Harlem known as "Sugar Hill. . . ." [Madame Walker's] lavishly furnished house was a gathering place not only for artists and authors and theatrical stars of her own race, but for celebrities from all over the world. Drinks and food were served, and there was always music, generously performed and enthusiastically received.[15]

Everyone from chorus girls to artists to socialites to visiting royalty would come at least once to enjoy her hospitality.

Another Afro-American institution that tolerated, and frequently encouraged, homosexual patronage was the "buffet flat." "Buffet flats were after-hours spots that were usually in someone's apartment," explained celebrated entertainer Bricktop, "the type of place where gin was poured out of milk pitchers."[16] Essentially private apartments where rooms could be rented by the night, buffet flats had sprung up during the late 1800s to provide overnight accommodations to black travelers refused service in white-owned hotels. By the 1920s, buffet flats developed a wilder reputation. Some were raucous establishments where illegal activities such as drinking, gambling, and prostitution were available. Others offered a variety of sexual pleasures cafeteria-style. A Detroit buffet flat of the latter sort, which Ruby Smith remembered visiting with her aunt, Bessie Smith, catered to all variety of sexual tastes. It was "an open house, everything goes on in that house":

> They had a faggot there that was so great that people used to come there just to watch him make love to another man. He was that great. He'd give a tongue bath and everything. By the time he got to the front of that guy he was shaking like a leaf. People used to pay good just to go in there and see him do his act. . . . That same house had a woman that used to . . . take a cigarette, light it, and puff it with her pussy. A real educated pussy.[17]

In Harlem, Hazel Valentine ran a similar sex circus on 140th Street. Called "The Daisy Chain" or the "101 Ranch," it catered to all varieties of sexual tastes, and featured entertainers such as "Sewing Machine Bertha" and an enormous transvestite named "Clarenz." The Daisy Chain became so notorious that both Fats Waller and Count Basie composed tunes commemorating it.[18]

There were also buffet flats that particularly welcomed gay men. On Saturday nights pianist David Fontaine would regularly throw stylish flat parties for his many gay friends. Other noted hosts of gay male revelry were A'Lelia Walker's friend Caska Bonds, Eddie Manchester and the older Harlem couple, Jap and Saul.[19] The most notorious such flat was run by Clinton Moore. Moore was an elegant, light-skinned homosexual, once described as an "American version of the original . . . Proust's Jupien."[20] Moore had a fondness for celebrities, and his parties allegedly attracted luminaries like Cole Porter, Cary Grant, and society page columnist Maury Paul. Moore's entertainments were often low-down and dirty. According to Helen Lawrenson,

> Clinton Moore's . . . boasted a young black entertainer named Joey, who played the piano and sang but whose *specialité* was to remove his clothes and extinguish a lighted candle by sitting on it until it disappeared. I never saw this feat but everyone else seemed to have and I was told that he was often hired to perform at soirees of the elite. 'He sat on lighted candles at one of the Vanderbilts',' my informant said.[21]

Somewhat more public—and therefore less abandoned—were Harlem's speakeasies, where gays were usually forced to hide their preferences and to blend in with the heterosexual patrons. Several Harlem speakeasies, though, some little more than dives, catered specifically to the "pansy" trade. One such place, an "open" speakeasy since there was no doorman to keep the uninvited away, was located on the northwest corner of 126th Street and Seventh Avenue. It was a large, dimly lit place where gay men could go to pick up "rough trade." Artist Bruce Nugent, who occasionally visited the place, remembered it catering to "rough queers . . . the kind that fought better than truck drivers and swished better than Mae West."[22] Ethel Waters remembered loaning her gowns to the transvestites who frequented Edmond's Cellar, a low-life saloon at 132nd Street and Fifth Avenue. Lulu Belle's on Lenox Avenue was another hangout for female impersonators, named after the famous Broadway melodrama of 1926 starring Leonore Ulric. A more sophisticated crowd of black gay men gathered nightly at the Hot Cha, at 132nd Street and Seventh Avenue, to listen to Jimmy Daniels sing and Garland Wilson play piano.[23]

Perhaps the most famous gay-oriented club of the era was Harry Hansberry's Clam House, a narrow, smoky speakeasy on 133rd Street. The Clam House featured Gladys Bentley, a 250-pound, masculine, dark-skinned lesbian, who performed all night long in a white tuxedo and top hat.[24] Bentley, a talented pianist with a magnificent, growling voice, was celebrated for inventing obscene lyrics to popular contemporary melodies. Langston Hughes called her "an amazing exhibition of musical energy."[25] Eslanda Robeson, wife of actor Paul Robeson, gushed to a friend, "Gladys Bentley is grand. I've heard her three nights, and will never be the same!"[26] Schoolteacher Harold Jackman wrote to his friend Countee Cullen, "When Gladys sings 'St. James Infirmary,' it makes you weep your heart out."[27]

A glimpse into a speakeasy, based in part on the Clam House, is provided in Blair Niles' 1931 gay novel *Strange Brother*. The Lobster Pot is a smoky room in Harlem, simply furnished with a couple of tables, a piano, and a kitchen, where white heterosexual journalist June Westwood, *Strange Brother*'s female protagonist, is first introduced to Manhattan's gay subculture. The Lobster Pot features a predominantly gay male clientel and an openly lesbian entertainer named Sybil. "What rhythm!" June comments to her companions. "And the way she's dressed!" Westbrook finds the atmosphere intoxicating, but abruptly ends her visit when she steps outside and witnesses the entrapment of an effeminate young black gay man by the police.[28]

Decidedly safer were the frequent Harlem costume balls, where both men and women could dress as they pleased and dance with whom they wished. Called "spectacles in color" by poet Langston Hughes, they were attended by thousands. Several cities hosted similar functions, but the Harlem balls were anticipated with particular excitement. "This dance has been going on a long time," observed Hughes, "and . . . is very famous among the male masqueraders of the eastern seaboard, who come from Boston and Philadelphia, Pittsburgh and Atlantic City to attend."[29] Taylor Gordon, a noted concert singer, wrote in 1929:

> The last big ball I attended where these men got the most of the prizes for acting and looking more like ladies than the ladies did themselves, was at the Savoy in Harlem. . . . The show that was put on that night for a dollar admission, including the privilege to

dance, would have made a twenty-five dollar George White's *Scandals* opening look like a side show in a circus.[30]

The largest balls were the annual events held by the Hamilton Lodge at the regal Rockland Palace, which could accommodate up to six thousand people. Only slightly smaller were the balls given irregularly at the dazzling Savoy Ballroom, with its crystal chandeliers and elegant marble staircase. The organizers would obtain a police permit making the ball, and its participants, legal for the evening. The highlight of the event was the beauty contest, in which the fashionably dressed drags would vie for the title of Queen of the Ball.

Charles Henri Ford and Parker Tyler's classic 1933 gay novel *The Young and Evil* suggests that these balls were just as popular with white gays as with black. Julian, the white protagonist, dons a little makeup (just enough to be "considered in costume and so get in for a dollar less"), leaves his Greenwich Village apartment, and sets off to a Harlem ball.[31] Once there he greets his friends, dances to the jazz music, gets exceedingly drunk, flirts with the band leader, and eventually exchanges phone numbers with a handsome stranger.

But drag balls lacked the primary allure of the buffet flat: privacy. These cross-dressing celebrations were enormous events and many of those who attended were spectators, there to observe rather than participate. It was not unusual to see the cream of Harlem society, as well as much of the white avant-garde, in the ballroom's balconies, straining their necks to view the contestants.

The costume balls, parties, speakeasies and buffet flats of Harlem provided an arena for homosexual interaction, but not for the development of homosocial networks. One area where black lesbians and gay men found particular bonds of friendship was within Harlem's predominantly heterosexual entertainment world. While some entertainers, like popular composer Porter Grainger and choir leader Hall Johnson, kept their homosexual activities private, others were open with their audiences. Female impersonator Phil Black, entertainer Frankie "Half Pint" Jaxon, and singer George Hanna used elements of homosexuality in their professional acts and were still highly respected within the entertainment community. Both Black and Jaxon wore women's clothing while on stage and Hanna even recorded his "Freakish Blues" without fear of censure.[32]

For black lesbians, whose social options were more limited than those of their male counterparts, the support offered by the black entertainment world for nontraditional lifestyles was especially important. After leaving her family home in North Carolina, Mabel Hampton worked with her lover as a dancer in a Coney Island show before landing a position at Harlem's famed Lafayette Theatre. By entering the show business life, Hampton was able to earn a good income, limit her social contact with men, and move within a predominantly female social world. Many bisexual and lesbian black women, including Bessie Smith, Gladys Bentley, Jackie "Moms" Mabley, Alberta Hunter, Gertrude "Ma" Rainey, Josephine Baker and Ethel Waters found similar advantages in the show business life.[33]

Nearly all these women adopted a heterosexual public persona, most favoring a "red hot mama" style, and kept their love affairs with women a secret, but a few acknowledged their sexuality openly. Gladys Bentley, of course, was one exception. Another was Ma Rainey. Rainey was a short, squat, dark-skinned woman with a deep, earthy voice and a warm, friendly smile. She was the first vaudeville entertainer to incorporate the blues into her performance and has justifiably become known as the "Mother of the Blues." Though married, the flamboyant entertainer was known to take women as lovers. Her extraordinary song, "Prove It on Me Blues," speaks directly to the issue of lesbianism. In it she admits to her preference for male attire and female companionship, yet dares her audience to "prove it" on her. Rainey's defense of her lesbian life was quite remarkable in its day, and has lost little of its immediacy through the years.

Just as the black entertainment world served as a refuge for sexual nonconformists, so too did black artistic and intellectual circles. For the first time, widespread education of middle-class blacks had created an Afro-American intelligentsia. Many of the writers, intellectuals, and artists of what is now referred to as the Harlem Renaissance were homosexual, bisexual, or otherwise sexually unorthodox. Two of the central figures within Harlem artistic circles were Langston Hughes and Wallace Thurman. Langston Hughes was a gifted young poet from the Midwest who splashed onto the literary scene in 1926 with the publication by Knopf of his first poetry collection, *The Weary Blues*. His subsequent career would span forty years and establish Hughes as one of the premiere Afro-American writers of the twentieth century. Handsome and shy, Hughes was exceedingly cagy and evasive about his emotional involvements, even with his closest friends; as a result, though most of Hughes' biographers concede that the poet was at least sporadically homosexual, the exact nature of his sexuality remains uncertain.[35] Wallace Thurman was a brilliant, well-read, and prolific writer, the author of two best-selling novels and a successful Broadway play. Small, dark-skinned, and somewhat effeminate, Thurman had a difficult personality: bitter, cynical and confused. He lived openly with a white homosexual lover, yet despaired of his sexual orientation. "[He] liked to drink gin, but *didn't* like to drink gin; . . . liked being a Negro, but felt it a great handicap; . . . adored bohemianism, but thought it wrong to be a bohemian."[36] He was alcoholic, and could be suicidal.

Extreme opposites and good friends, Thurman and Hughes provided new role models for an exciting group of young artists and writers, most newly arrived in Harlem. Richmond Barthé, a Chicago-trained sculptor, had been born in Louisiana; painter Aaron Douglas was from Kansas.

Writer Arna Bontemps had come from Los Angeles. Zora Neale Hurston, an anthropology student at Columbia and a brilliant storyteller, hailed from Eatonville, Florida. Before he left home to dabble in painting, drawing, poetry, and acting, Richard Bruce Nugent had been raised in a proper Washington, D. C., family. Countee Cullen, author of the critically acclaimed poetry collection *Color*, was one of the few Harlem Renaissance artists who actually had been raised in Harlem. These young artists voiced an independent, self-consciously Afro-American cultural vision. Their use of folk material and their insistence on self-expression occasionally brought them in conflict with their elders, but their youthful revolt was tolerated. Established politicians like DuBois and Johnson considered the young artists part of the "Talented Tenth," the Afro-American vanguard of hope. The NAACP and the National Urban League sponsored literary contests, art shows, and awards dinners for the young artists. Zora Neale Hurston, always irreverent, wryly christened the bohemians "The Niggerati."

While some of these artists, like Bontemps and Douglas, were decidedly heterosexual, others were as sexually ambiguous as Hughes and Thurman. Cullen was homosexual and maintained a lifelong relationship with Harlem schoolteacher Harold Jackman. Bontemps later described the couple as the "Jonathan and David of the Harlem Renaissance."[37] Claude McKay, a writer associated with the Harlem Renaissance though he spent most of the 1920s in Europe, was active in Parisian gay circles and pursued relationships with both sexes. Richmond Barthé had followed an attractive actor to Harlem in 1928. But the most bohemian of them all was Bruce Nugent, who delighted in shocking the prudish with his erotic drawings and his openly homosexual promiscuity.[38] Apparently, the Niggerati's eccentricities were tactfully ignored by most. One elderly Sugar Hill resident remembered, "Of course they had not come out of the closet back then. They didn't have to. We all knew they were homosexuals. We admired them for their intelligence and work during a very difficult time."[39]

Alain Locke was one of these young artists' most important supporters. A small, dapper, fair-skinned professor from Howard University, Locke edited the important 1926 anthology, *The New Negro*, which focussed international attention on Harlem's emerging cultural renaissance. He channelled white patronage to Afro-American artists and provided essential intellectual and critical support. His influence was immense, but his young charges often found there were strings attached to his assistance. Locke was homosexual and was known to aggressively pursue his favorites. Zora Hurston once referred to him as "a malicious little snit,"[40] and Thurman bitterly caricatured him as "Dr. A. L. Parkes," a pompous intellectual, in *Infants of the Spring*.[41]

Support for fledgling writers and artists was also provided by a large network of white sympathizers, dubbed "Negrotarians" by Hurston, many of whom were homosexual. These white gays gave support and encouragement to Afro-American artists, channelled funds and publicity in their direction, and provided access to the international artistic and literary communities. Poet Witter Bynner judged the annual Urban League literary contest. Elizabeth Marbury, the elderly politician, theatrical producer, and enormous lesbian, acted as agent for manuscripts of Zora Neale Hurston and Wallace Thurman.

The Negrotarian journalist and novelist most visible in Harlem during the Renaissance was the tall, blond, Iowa-born author Carl Van Vechten. Van Vechten was the quintessential sophisticated Manhattan dilettante: witty, charming, talented, and homosexual. He had written for years as a music critic before achieving acclaim as an author during the 1920s. There was hardly an avant-garde intellectual movement or artistic form that Van Vechten did not keep abreast of. He introduced Gertrude Stein and Ronald Firbank to American audiences and rediscovered Herman Melville. Throughout the 1920s he produced a series of novels that were sparkling, frothy, and exceedingly camp, including *Peter Whiffle, The Tattooed Countess, The Blind Bow Boy*, and *Parties*. Though rarely overtly homosexual, Van Vechten's novels became popular with the gay set, who sensed a kindred spirit in his preciousness. In 1924 Van Vechten turned his attention to the Afro-American community. He quickly began visiting nightclubs and buffet flats, attending parties at A'Lelia Walker's, hobnobbing with Harlem's political and social elite, and even judging contestants at a Rockland Palace drag contest. He established close friendships with Harlem luminaries such as Langston Hughes, James Weldon Johnson, and Ethel Waters. He worked tirelessly to promote his new friends, publicizing their efforts, writing introductions to their books, and introducing them to his literary friends.[42]

Yet despite these accomplishments, Van Vechten was most notorious for his naively titled 1926 novel, *Nigger Heaven*. *Nigger Heaven* told the story of the tragic love between a young black writer and his Harlem girlfriend. The title was intended to be ironic; the novel intended to impart a sympathetic understanding of Harlem and its people. Many of Van Vechten's black friends appreciated it, but the majority of Harlem was outraged. The few who could get beyond the title were put off by the author's affectation, which had become a Van Vechten trademark. But the white reading public had the opposite reaction, and the novel quickly became a best-seller. After reading the novel, many whites hurried to Harlem to see the real thing.

Nigger Heaven's success was due, in part, to what Langston Hughes later called the "vogue" for the Negro.[43] Across the country, whites started listening to the jazz of Duke Ellington, Fletcher Henderson, and Fats Waller. The Charleston and the Black Bottom, dances previously limited to black jazz halls, became national crazes. *Shuffle Along*, an all-black musical, was a smash success on Broadway and rocketed Florence Mills to stardom. White authors and playwrights started using race and racial prejudice as serious literary material. Harlem nightclubs and speakeasies attracted a large white clientele. The center of "Hot Harlem" was "Jungle Alley," the nightclub area around 133rd Street—also a notorious center for organized crime and vice. Opulent Jungle Alley clubs, such as the Cotton Club, Connie's Inn, and Pod and Jerry's, were packed nightly with white tourists from downtown, drinking bootleg liquor and watching talented black entertainers. Rain James, in his "intimate" guide to New York, raved, "Harlem is a great place, a real place, an honest place, and a place that no visitor should ever even think of missing."[44] The potential for exploitation was obvious; many of the fanciest clubs were segregated and refused black patronage. Some blacks complained that Harlem had been "invaded."

White lesbians and gay men were among those "invading" Harlem. Forty years later lesbian socialite Mercedes de Acosta remembered, "Everyone rushed up to Harlem at night to sit around places thick with smoke and the smell of bad gin, where Negroes danced about with each other until the small hours of the morning."[45] Whites attended the parties of A'Lelia Walker and Clinton Moore, danced at the drag balls, and lauded Gladys Bentley to their friends. With its sexually tolerant population and its quasi-legal nightlife, Harlem offered an oasis to white homosexuals. For some, a trip to Harlem was part of a larger rebellion against the Prohibition Era's conservative moral and political climate. For Van Vechten, and for many other white lesbians and gay men, Harlem offered even deeper rewards. Blair Niles based her *Strange Brother* on her friend and confidant Leland Pettit, a young, white, gay man from Milwaukee and the organist at Grace Church. According to *Strange Brother*, Pettit frequented the homosexual underworld in Harlem because he found social acceptance, and because he identified with others who were also outcasts from American life. This identification and feeling of kinship, undoubtedly shared by other white lesbians and gay men, may have been the beginnings of homosexual "minority consciousness."[46]

There was considerable interaction between black and white homosexuals. Both Van Vechten and Pettit, for example, were frequent visitors to a small rooming house on 137th Street known as "Niggerati Manor," a center of New Negro creativity, where Thurman, Hughes, and Nugent rented rooms. Niggerati Manor developed a reputation for wild parties and bizarre behavior. According to theater critic Theophilus Lewis, "It was said that the inmates of [this] house spent wild nights in tuft hunting and the diversions of the cities of the plains and delirious days fleeing from pink elephants."[47] The chaotic life at Niggerati Manor would eventually be recounted by Thurman in his *Infants of the Spring*.

During the summer of 1926, the Niggerati Manor group organized, edited, and published the first (and only) issue of a little magazine entitled *Fire!*. Everyone contributed something. Aaron Douglas submitted a stunning red and black cover, Hughes and Cullen contributed poetry, Zora Hurston offered a short story, and Van Vechten provided money to get the project going. The magazine was intended to shock. To insure this, Thurman and his friends included Bruce Nugent's "Smoke, Lilies, and Jade" (published under the pseudonym "Richard Bruce" to avoid parental disapproval), a near-pornographic tale of homosexual self-discovery. A Harlem artist, clearly Nugent himself, falls in love with a stunning Latin Adonis, and after a night of passion discovers that

> He loved them both . . . there . . . he had thought it . . . actually dared to think it . . . one *can* love two [sexes] at the same time . . . one *can* . . . Beauty's hair was so black . . . and soft . . . was that why he loved Beauty . . . one *can* . . . or because his body was beautiful . . . and white and warm . . . or because his eyes . . . one *can* love . . . . [48]

Nugent's defence of homosexual love became the first published essay on homosexuality by an Afro-American. A good portion of Harlem found *Fire!* shocking. Locke, in apparent response to the overt homosexuality of "Smoke, Lilies, and Jade," suggested that "[Walt] Whitman would have been a better point of support than a left-wing pivoting on Wilde and Beardsley."[49] Nevertheless, the Niggerati were ostracized for no more than a few days.

Renaissance writers and artists continued to startle their readers by including black lesbian and gay experience in their work. Claude McKay's *Home to Harlem*, published in 1927, included discussion of Harlem lesbianism and featured a black gay male character. Bruce Nugent's poetry and art continued to draw on homosexual themes. *Passing*, Nella Larsen's 1929 novel of female friendship and racial discrimination, has recently been interpreted as an early lesbian novel.[50] Richmond Barthé's gay sensibility was evident throughout his work. Wallace Thurman's two books, *The Blacker the Berry* and *Infants of the Spring*, published in 1929 and 1932 respectively, both have significant lesbian and gay male content. Even Langston Hughes touched upon the topic in his beautifully spare depiction of a gay bar, "Cafe: 3 A.M."

The stock market crash of 1929 brought the glittering Harlem Renaissance to an abrupt halt. Without the money of the white pleasure-seekers, the buoyant spirit of Harlem gave way to the far more insistent reality of the worldwide Depression. The end of Prohibition took the lure out of Harlem's speakeasies; Jungle Alley went to seed. Many of the people most associated with the gay life in Jazz Age Harlem left the city or died. A'Lelia Walker died of a heart attack in 1931. Wallace Thurman died in 1934 of tuberculosis. Alexander Gumby also became seriously ill of tuberculosis, and was forced to close his Book Store and enter a sanitarium. Alberta Hunter and Jimmie Daniels left Harlem to cultivate

European careers. Gladys Bentley moved to Los Angeles. Ethel Waters travelled to Broadway, then went to Hollywood.

But despite these losses, the Harlem lesbian and gay community survived, although it became smaller, less "spectacular," and less racially integrated. Jeanne Flash Gray, who participated in Harlem gay life in the late 1930s and 1940s, remembers, "There were many places in Harlem run by and for Black Lesbians and Gay Men, when we were still Bull Daggers and Faggots and only whites were lesbians and homosexuals."[51] Caska Bonds and Clinton Moore continued with their apartment socials. Jackie Mabley and a chorus line of female impersonators were featured performers at a mafia-run nightclub on 133rd Street called The Ubangi Club. In the early 1940s, Lucky Roberts opened his bar Lucky's Rendezvous, of which an *Ebony* article would later comment: "Male couples are so commonplace . . . that no one looks twice at them."[52] Female impersonator Phil Black began throwing his annual Thanksgiving Day Funmaker's drag ball in 1945, a tradition that lasted within Manhattan's gay men's community for decades.[53] And Blind Charlie, who made his own beet wine in the bathtub and sold it at two pints for a dollar, ran a gay buffet flat on 110th Street near Central Park. Jeanne Flash Gray recalled, "We played, danced, got high, met and lost lovers in Blind Charlie's . . ."[54] The community built during the hope, optimism, and glitter of the Roaring Twenties was strong enough and resilient enough to weather the changing of the times.

PARIS LESBIANISM AND THE POLITICS OF REACTION, 1900–1940

◆

SHARI BENSTOCK

Early lesbian historians celebrated the sisterhood of lesbians they found in the famous coteries of early-twentieth-century Paris without considering the class privileges or political assumptions of these generally very wealthy women. In particular it has been difficult to acknowledge the painful internalization of misogyny, homophobia, and anti-Semitism that led many of these women to reactionary, even pro-Fascist beliefs. This essay forces us to deal with the complex links among artistic practices, political ideologies, and sexual preference. In particular, it suggests that Natalie Barney's strong identification with male power can be traced to both psychological and political roots that contrast sharply with those of the wealthy, anti-Fascist Bryher.

How can we describe the alignment of sexual choices and political ideologies among the artistic avant-garde in Paris during the opening decades of this century? In particular, what are the links between sexual choice and political practice among women of the Paris expatriate community? We cannot assume that artistic revolution against dominant bourgeois patterns necessarily develops from a liberal political commitment, nor can we assume that sexual choices resistant to patriarchy and heterosexuality are politically liberating. The Paris period offers striking evidence of the political and artistic effects of internalized patriarchal power structures that resulted in right-wing and pro-Fascist commitments among lesbians. While the politics of important members of the community are known and have often been commented on, scholarship about the Modernist cultural fabric has repressed the role sexuality played in constructing political choices. The important links between forms of economic and social privilege and psychosexual and political choices have been ignored in part because these interactions are complex in ways that resist generalization. An examination of the sexual and political commitments of Natalie Barney, Gertrude Stein, and Winifred Bryher in the context of expatriate experience demonstrates the contradictory, even idiosyncratic, nature of personal and cultural ideologies.[1]

A cursory examination of the political commitments of Paris women associated with the two major artistic salons of the period—Natalie Barney's at 20 rue Jacob and Gertrude Stein's shorter-lived salon at 27 rue de Fleurus—reveal deep political splits on questions of Fascism, anti-Semitism, and homophobia. Among those women who took positions on the political left, resisting the move toward totalitarian regimes in Europe following World War I, were Djuna Barnes, Sylvia Beach, Kay Boyle, Winifred Bryher, Colette, Nancy Cunard, Hilda Doolittle, Janet Flanner, Adrienne Monnier, and—from the distance of England—Virginia Woolf. Those with right-wing sympathies, who guardedly or openly supported Fascist causes, were Romaine Brooks, Elisabeth de Gramont, Radclyffe Hall, Lucie Delarue-Mardrus, Liane de Pougy, Alice Toklas, and Una Troubridge. In this latter group Gertrude Stein and Natalie Barney were the most outspoken, and the sexual-political dynamics of their lives suggest a good deal about the cultural unconscious of Paris Modernism.

Barney and Stein shared much by virtue of their American upbringing—financial security (in Barney's case, enormous wealth), love of art, literature, and music, generosity to younger writers and artists, the desire to find in Paris a life of intellectual and emotional fulfillment, and strong resistance against the socially determined pattern of women's lives leading to marriage and motherhood. They were, however, increasingly drawn to a politics of oppression, anti-Semitism, self-protectionism, and social and economic privilege that closed them off from any clear understanding of the political stakes between Fascism and Communism. The political commitments of both women changed markedly between the first and second World Wars. During World War I, Natalie Barney actively resisted the war on feminist grounds by organizing women of the Paris community in antiwar activities. Gertrude Stein and Alice Toklas returned from extended travels in Spain and Mallorca after the victory of Verdun in 1916 to begin work for the American Fund for French Wounded. The years following the war coincided with the rising fame of both Barney and Stein, and the 1930s marked crucial changes in their political attitudes. Although their politics differed markedly, they shared a sense of privileged and separate status in the Paris community that bound them to dominant rightist ideologies and to repressive political regimes. Such political attitudes were not unrelated to the ways in which they and other expatriate women lived their lesbianism or from their participation in the avant-garde culture of the time. Domestic politics and the more general arena of cultural politics were related: Participation in the Paris avant-garde as expatriates was determined by both sexual and artistic choices.[2]

The Sexual Politics of the Avant-Garde

For women who, like Barney and Stein, came to Paris early in the century, the city promised not only escape from American and English puritanism but also the possibility of artistic and sexual freedom beyond the boundaries of familial constraints and enforced domesticity. This proffered psychosexual liberation was elusive for almost all women of the expatriate community, however. The Paris cultural landscape of these years was a contradictory one in which repression and licentiousness served as reverse sides of the social/sexual code. Homosexual practices were accepted in certain pockets of the culture, in aristocratic salons and in secluded working-class bars, while *maisons closes* continued the traditional practice of providing same-sex love between women as titillation for male customers. Separated from home and family, expatriate lesbians could act upon their sexual preferences, no longer finding it necessary to submerge their sexuality in the late-nineteenth-century ideology of "ennobling commitment" to community service or self-discipline. Nonetheless, these women felt the tensions and contradictions of French attitudes toward female sexuality in general and homosexuality in particular. The laws of normative sexuality were very much in place in Paris, protected by both church and state, and "deviancy" was tolerated provided it was discreet.

While the status of "expatriate" and "artist" allowed women the right to privacy and idiosyncratic dress and behavior, it did not allow for complete circumvention of the cultural norms; that is, sexual practices that were thought to be deviant needed to be hidden in public. In both life and art, lesbian choices had to be disguised, usually by translating homoerotic desires into the discourse of heterosexuality or by masking desire altogether.[3] Women who chose not to mask non-traditional sexual identities and desires in their writings found themselves without an audience, without access to publishers, and outside the boundaries of the parent community. Openly lesbian writing was either privately printed and circulated (Djuna Barnes's *Ladies Almanack*) or self-suppressed (Hilda Doolittle's autobiographical fictions).

Both heterosexual and homosexual women discovered—some more painfully than others—that the artistic community transplanted patriarchal values to a new setting, leaving women severely disadvantaged. Both the expatriate avant-garde and the resident Paris artistic community were dominated by men who defined the functions of modern art, organized their friends as participants in its various movements, wrote manifestos (which women were rarely invited to sign), and published political tracts. The radicalized forms of avant-garde art masked the conservative attitudes of a masculine sexual economy that defined itself in predominantly phallic and heterosexual images. As Susan Suleiman has explained, this art was "based on the suppression of what is 'other' in female sexuality."[4] For example, the avant-garde continued to think of the female as a subject *for* art rather than a producer *of* art, and this founding principle accounts in part for the fact that women's contributions to Modernism have been consistently devalued or dismissed.[5] They gave new life to myths that linked sexuality and death, and portrayed women as toys of the male imagination. Following Anne-Marie Dardigna, we might argue that although the avant-garde politicized both art and sexuality in this century, the result was a further underwriting of patriarchy in its more reactionary forms:

> The twentieth century is characterized in literature by the total freedom of the subjective instance: the subject can finally tell all about its fantasies, its perversions, its hidden desires. That is well and good. . . . But what voices are heard then? Always those of men. And what do they say? Nothing new: that women are dangerous, that they must be dominated, that their "flesh" must be conquered by assimilating them to a male model or by putting them to death . . . in any case, that they must be suppressed.[6]

Dardigna claims that in the early years of the century art became a battleground in which the male artist staked his claims to the collaboration of sexuality and politics to repress dissident cultural elements. Women who chose to produce art *and* to live an alternative sexuality constituted a dissident element. Thus, we must question, as does Susan Suleiman, the extent to which "the 'high-cultural' productions of the avant-gardes of our century stand in a relation of complicity rather than in a relation of rupture vis-a-vis dominant ideologies." Misogyny was masked and homosexual fears were repressed through stylistic innovations. The Oedipal myth of human sexuality, compulsively reimagined by the avant-garde, served as the bedrock of Modernist "style."[7]

The link between Freudian notions of sexuality and avant-garde stylistic practices was later discovered by Jacques Lacan, who used Modernist texts to demonstrate the truth of his discovery that in psychosexual development the masculine position strives to represent phallic truth while the feminine position is subjected to that "truth."[8] In the Lacanian text—psychosexual and avant-garde at once—female homosexuality rests in a refusal to accept this subjection. Instead, it takes the masculine position. Under these conditions, lesbianism mimes the patriarchal law, registering its effects on and between women. Its sexual politics are not of "otherness," but rather of sameness with the masculine. The belief that homosexuality can only write resistance *against* the patriarchal Oedipal law through a reenactment *of* the law's repressive workings was culturally overdetermined in Europe between the wars.[9]

The complicity of right-wing ideologies and avant-garde cultural practices in this period enforced, rather than resisted, the power structures inherent in sexual choice. This reinforcement of dominant cultural values allowed lesbians with economic and class privileges to act on their sexuality in an atmosphere of relative freedom, protected from the economic and legal penalties that were placed on such actions among working-class women or immigrants in French society. The famous expatriate salons of these years—established by Edith Wharton, Barney, and Stein—differed enormously from each other and from their French models of the eighteenth and nineteenth centuries; but salon society had always protected its participants, including those who practiced "sexual deviancy." Devoted to preserving conservative class and cultural values, salons were symbols of aristocratic noblesse oblige. Expatriate salons that supported a subversive art movement, viewed as bohemian from the perspective of the French aristocracy, established for themselves a kind of exclusionary—and therefore exclusive—status, taking the privileges of this earlier tradition.

It is difficult, even dangerous, to generalize about the reasons for political alignments among women of the expatriate community. Right-wing and pro-Fascist sympathizers were not found among heterosexual women, and with the exception of Natalie Barney, lesbians with strong feminist commitments were also left-wing and anti-Fascist. The right-wing lesbianism fostered by this culture developed among the economically and socially privileged, who identified less with the values of totalitarian politics than with the underlying fears those values hoped to assuage. It replicated in many respects the ideology of the male avant-garde, for it was male-identified, misogynistic, and homophobic, and displaced onto Jews a fear of the "other." The sexual choice that should have placed these women in resistance against a culture that devalued them instead fostered an identification with the repressive masculinity of totalitarian political movements. In this context "sexuality" was not separate from political allegiances but symptomatic of them. The women who most wholeheartedly accepted the tenets of the Parisian male avant-garde were most unable to see totalitarianism as an exaggerated form of the patriarchy they had fled from in England and America.

Privilege and Political Choice

Significantly, certain rich women of the Paris community—Bryher and Cunard, for example—politically resisted the luxury their wealth and social standing could have provided for them. Bryher, Cunard, and H. D.

were involved in the Harlem Renaissance and in movements for black equality. Cunard served as a free-lance correspondent during the Spanish Civil War, raising monies for Spanish war relief, and later working for de Gaulle's Free French government in exile in London. Bryher secretly smuggled Resistance workers, Jews, and intellectuals (including Walter Benjamin and Arthur Koestler) out of Nazi-occupied territories; her location in Switzerland and her inherited fortune were crucial to this effort. Less-wealthy women of the Paris artistic community were also devoted to anti-Fascist causes, some staying on in Paris during the war to take up positions of resistance to Fascist claims, and working to provide safe passage for Jews and other refugees. Sylvia Beach and Adrienne Monnier helped Gisèle Freund, the literary photographer, to escape first from Germany and later from occupied France. Beach, captured as an enemy alien, spent six months in a concentration camp for women. Janet Flanner worked for the Allied effort in New York during the war. Flanner, who had written exhaustively on the rise of Fascism for *The New Yorker* during the 1930s, especially the events in Spain and the Nazi campaign of anti-Semitism in Austria, was certified as a war correspondent toward the end of the Second World War.

Other women also associated with the community—notably Barney, Brooks, de Gramont, Delarue-Mardrus, de Pougy, Hall, Stein, Toklas, and Troubridge—followed a line of least resistance, even a line of self-interest. These women, who tacitly or openly aligned themselves with Fascist programs founded on homophobia and anti-Semitism, carved out an internal exclusion for themselves under the terms of Fascism. They felt that economic privilege, social class, and in some cases religion (de Pougy was Catholic and Hall, Toklas, and Troubridge all converted to Catholicism) could offer them safe passage against an "enemy" whose power they admired but whose program of establishing German nationalism had disrupted their lives.[10] Although each of them believed the war to be apocalyptic, bringing about the end of European civilization as they had known it, all assumed that—were they spared death by deprivation during these years—they could reestablish their former lives under the terms of aristocratic and cultured entitlement that a Nazi government would provide. Writing in her private journals in 1934, de Pougy called for "a young king, a dictator, a president, someone devoted to his cause, loving his country as himself." During the bloody Fascist uprising of 7 February 1934 (described in horrifying detail in Janet Flanner's "Letter from Paris" in *The New Yorker*, 10 February 1934), de Pougy's sympathies were with the young French Fascists. On the day after the uprising, walking along the rue des Capucines, she wandered among them, enthralled with their order and discipline. Later she argued that a newspaper seller, who claimed that these were the same men who had burned the newspaper kiosks the night before, was incorrect, that such discipline could not give way to violence. Like Barney and Brooks, de Pougy was a great admirer of "the pure and strong" Mussolini. Claiming that "one can only admire [him]," she attested to his desire to do "good for beautiful Italy," and expressed the hope that Hitler would do the same for Germany, and prayed that France would "find a man as powerful, firm, feeling and pure enough to revive in it all its clarity and fire its force and mutilated grandeur."[11]

Natalie Barney shared many of Liane de Pougy's political views (although she did not share de Pougy's increasing commitment to the Catholicism of her Breton childhood). Like de Pougy and all the other women of this community who developed right-wing beliefs, Barney feared Communism, for she felt that France had become weakened under the *front populaire* and the Socialist politics of Léon Blum in the 1930s. An avowed feminist, Barney was nonetheless never able to see what a political thinker like Virginia Woolf so clearly articulated—the extension of patriarchy into Fascism and the need for Fascism both to hate women and to use them.[12] One-quarter Jew, Barney was also anti-Semitic and, like Stein, drawn to Fascist theories of economics. Barney fell under the sway of Ezra Pound's theory of usury (with its anti-Semitic base), convinced that both the First World War and its inevitable aftermath in the second war were efforts by Jews to "secure greater profits" in a commercialized world. Writing from her Italian villa during the Second World War, she asked: "Why all this mystery about financing the second act of this continuous war? Are not its bankers secured against loss either by the victory of the Allies or assured of revenge by getting their money's worth of Aryan flesh?"[13] Fleeing Paris for Italy in spring 1940, Barney castigated a French neighbor for hating the Nazis, claiming that the French would later be embarrassed to discover their own defeat and the "rightness" of the Nazi cause. She wrote in her unpublished memoirs "that Fascism and Nazism, while modernizing [Europe's] structures and improving the welfare of its populations, tried to safeguard all its traditional and local colours—and whether their joint efforts actually succeed or not—will remain to their everlasting honour."

Gertrude Stein's politics were far more complex than Barney's, and it would be a mistake to think that the two women were "right-wing" in the same ways. Nonetheless, Stein's anti-Semitism was a mark of her own self-hatred as a Jew: It allowed her to turn a blind eye to the fate of other Jews, and it blinded her to the gravity of her own situation during the Second World War. The measures of safety Stein took for herself and her possessions—particularly her manuscripts and the art collection in the rue Christine apartment in Paris—were born out of a fear of a Communist uprising in France, not of imminent war. In the mid-thirties, Toklas made copies of all Stein's unpublished manuscripts (a process that took several years), shipping them to Carl Van Vechten in New York. Fearful of war and aware of Stein's vulnerability should the Nazis invade France, Van Vechten pleaded with Stein and Toklas to take refuge in America. Stein was determined to stay on in France, however. Urged by the American consul in Lyon to leave after the fall of France to the Nazis, Stein said to Toklas, "Well, I don't know—it would be awfully uncomfortable and I am fussy about my food. Let's not leave."[14] A perhaps facetious remark, this statement nonetheless stresses the priorities of Stein's life.

Stein and Toklas took shelter in their summer house in southeast France, Stein's personal safety and the safekeeping of her art collection assured at the highest levels of the Vichy government—in no small measure due to the continued vigilance of Bernard Faÿ, director of the Bibliothèque Nationale under Pétain and later imprisoned for life for his collaboration with the Vichy government. Although Stein did not "collaborate" (as some have mistakenly thought), she did survive the war because friends in high places created an "internal exclusion" for her and Alice Toklas under the terms of the Nazi occupation. Stein was not openly a Nazi sympathizer, as was Barney, but like Barney, de Pougy, Hall, and Troubridge, she was afraid that the Allies would be defeated and the lifestyle that she found so comfortable and congenial would be destroyed. Stein was terrified of Communism: She had outspoken views on economics and was committed to a kind of free-market theory of exchange that masked economic protectionism.[15] Like several other women in this group, Stein not only survived the European conflict, but lived comparatively comfortably during these difficult years, aided by the economic security of inherited monies, the increasing value of her art collection, royalties on *The Autobiography of Alice B. Toklas*, friends in strategic government positions, and geographical location.

Contextualizing Culture

To understand something of the terms under which such women as Barney and Stein survived the Second World War, to comprehend their common dilemma as expatriate women living nontraditional lifestyles and to distinguish the differences of their backgrounds and political choices, it is necessary to look closely at their domestic lives. It was in the domestic arena, Virginia Woolf discovered, that Fascism prospered, especially as it capitalized on the hierarchy of attitudes toward gender that marriage supported, attitudes rooted in the economic advantage held by men over women.[16] If class status and economic privilege allowed women of the Paris community to act freely on nontraditional sexual choices, these privileges also bound women more closely to the institution of patriarchy—the central support of Fascism, according to *Three Guineas*. Cases in point are the couplings of Gertrude Stein (1874–1946) and Alice B. Toklas (1877–1967) and of Natalie Barney (1876–1972) and Renée Vivien (1877–1909).

When Stein and Toklas met in Paris in 1907 they both longed for a stable and secure domestic existence, a desire shared by many other women of the Left Bank community, including Sylvia Beach and Adrienne Monnier, Bryher and H. D., Janet Flanner and Solita Solano. Stein and Toklas wanted marriage, one that repeated bourgeois heterosexual relationships. As a couple, they followed the conventions of nineteenth-century Victorian domesticity, and their coupling reproduced an entire cast of family characters: Stein, who at first was "husband," also played "Baby" to Toklas's role as "Mama," while Carl Van Vechten—one of Stein's most steadfastly loyal supporters—played "Papa." Stein's writings created an extended family of characters, a farmyard full of animals, and a catalogue of the necessary elements of domesticity (houses, tables, food, beds, flowers, etc.) unparalleled among avant-garde writers.

Stein's creative enterprise was a rigorously philosophical and playfully literary examination of every facet of patriarchy—from domestic arrangements and family loyalties to grammatical rules. Her investigations revealed multiple contradictions of patriarchal laws (including the laws of sexual identity), contradictions that she herself embodied and nourished with a loving attention that drove her to discover their founding principles. This interrogation of cultural and linguistic structures was carried on from a position of household power (as "Baby" Stein was a male child, a "he," with all the charms and autocratic powers of the disruptive adored infant). Catharine R. Stimpson has commented:

> Despite her sexual preferences, Stein never ceased to believe in bourgeois heterosexuality: its decencies, norms, and families. This had at least two consequences. First, Stein equated the mind, especially that of genius, with masculinity. She was a frequent Tory about who should labor in laboratories. Next, she equated sexuality with heterosexuality. Necessarily, such an ideology tore at her ambitions and sexual desires. She was at odds with her own compulsions for work and for love.[17]

Stein never broke from the conventional patterns of the family life into which she was born, but a lesbian relationship allowed her to play many roles. She was the father whose word was law; she was the baby whose cries must be calmed; and as the responsible head of household, she often indulged in the infantile and irresponsible. Her forebears were rugged individualists, industrialists and businessmen who believed in progress and looked to the future. She took her place in a line of American literary and political founding fathers; she worked proudly, patriotically, and patriarchally, and she expected to be served.[18]

This family structure suggests that Stein upheld the law of Oedipal sexual identity. She represented the law, and thus was also freed to transgress it. By way of this law Stein participated in the patriarchal privilege that underwrote avant-garde art, and it was her art that was privileged before all else in the coupling. Alice, the "Mrs.," the wife, the "little Jew," occupied a position with respect to (and in respect of) this same law: her "husband" and "baby" may have been biologically female, but "he" acted as a male, leaving Alice to take the female role. She feminized this role intensely—from her choice of beaded jewelry and lace handkerchiefs, careful manicures, and love of perfumes, to her fondness for rich pastries and sweet desserts. Toklas paid an enormous price for the role she created for herself in Stein's life, and the suffering was made worse by the self-imposed law that prevented her from ever admitting— even to her closest friends—that Stein was often unkind to her, too demanding of her energies and loyalties, too certain of her need to serve and to be loved.

Stein trained Toklas to fear her, beginning with their second meeting at the rue de Fleurus apartment. Toklas was late for their appointment, having taken time to lunch in the Bois de Boulogne with her friend Harriet Levy—of whom Stein was probably jealous. Toklas writes that Stein "had not her smiling countenance of the day before. She was now a vengeful goddess and I was afraid. I did not know what had happened or what was going to happen. Nor is it possible for me to tell about it now."[19] Like any member of an oppressed group—like a wife—Toklas discovered over the years ways to secure her place with Stein and ways to make Stein bow to her will, and publicly she participated in the power and prestige of her mate, precisely to the degree that she played so well the demure and respectful wife. Toklas determined who might see Stein or establish terms of friendship with her; she saw to it that Stein's relationship with Hemingway, for instance, came to an end. Natalie Barney was among the Paris friends (including Winifred Bryher and Sylvia Beach) who watched with dismay the dynamics of this relationship, appalled at Toklas's suffering and servitude.

In Stein's thinking, gender identity and biological identity did not coincide. Catharine Stimpson has remarked that Stein was a "woman writer only partly freed from patriarchal ideologies of work and love, her rhetoric is that of the conventional male role in a love affair: desire; command; fear of rejection; gratification; and abandonment. Once again, like the falcon circling and returning to its trainer, she could not resist the lure of the alluring bait of gender."[20] This lure of the patriarchal ideology Stein so intensely interrogated in her writing had its political component. She could not break the psychological transfer of her female body to masculine gender: The female represented everything weak and subservient, powerless and victimized; the masculine represented power and authority, strength and leadership.

Nor could Stein give up the comforts of bourgeois life attended to by a loving spouse. She struggled every day of the Second World War to maintain on a diminished scale the life of the years that had preceded it; her letters to Carl Van Vechten detail her determination in this effort, as though to block out the reality of the war. Occupying herself "with the business of daily living," never missing a meal and rarely doing without butter and eggs,[21] Stein also relied on a technique that had helped her survive the long years of public ridicule of her work: She cultivated her self-importance, continuing to make an exception of herself. Gertrude Stein willed herself to believe that she would be spared deprivations, physical and mental suffering, the loss of a way of life on which her creative powers depended, simply because she was Gertrude Stein. She did not like the Nazis, but she respected and feared the strength of their enterprise. She loved the Americans, having romantic notions of patriotism and pride in their military power, and she cheered their victory as though the Second World War were a long afternoon of football. From the record of Stein's writings and conversations, however, it remains unclear whether she ever understood what was at stake in this war, what had led to it, or what her own position was in it.

Natalie Barney survived the war by similar means, suffering only the temporary discomfort of relocation in Italy. She took a villa near Florence so that Romaine Brooks, her companion since World War I, could continue painting. They left Paris in June 1940, returning in May 1946 after Barney's gouvernante, Berthe Cleyrergue, had made the house at 20 rue Jacob habitable again. In the intervening six years, Barney and Brooks lived comfortably in Italy, finding friendships in the new setting. In a telling gesture, they lowered chaises longues into a trench they had ordered prepared in the garden of the villa. From this below-ground vantage point, they sunned themselves in the afternoon, safe from the bombers overhead.[22]

Barney's letters to Berthe Cleyrergue, who stayed on in Paris to look after Barney's house, were a litany of domestic requests. Barney made the same requests of Cleyrergue as she did during her annual three-month holiday in the south of France, asking her gouvernante to mend and clean her clothes, polish the silverware, and care for her library, as well as regularly cash checks on her account at the Crédit Lyonnais bank. Barney's demands not only suggest the ways in which Berthe Cleyrergue had always served her and the degree to which Barney was a difficult and exacting employer but also the extent to which Barney was completely unaware of the war's effects on daily life in Paris. Shockingly, these letters show no regard for Cleyrergue's own needs and concerns, and Barney adds to wartime exertions the requirement that her faithful gouvernante provide pastries and cakes for the many friends Barney left behind in Paris. Cleyrergue comments on these requests: "We suffered a lot, those of us in Paris during the war. These letters were doubly painful for me. I said to myself, 'she has everything she needs there in Italy. Here, we are dying of hunger, and she always has something else to ask.' She waited a long time for my responses. Oh those letters! I read and reread them at least ten times. Henri [Cleyrergue's husband] couldn't bring himself to read them."[23] Cleyrergue's reward for these services came later, in substantial monetary gifts dispensed in classically patrician gestures.

Natalie Barney's feminism was blind to questions of class, outspoken in its anti-Semitism, and male-identified in its claims to sexual privileges. Barney was aristocratic in her efforts to create a privileged women's culture in Paris, committing herself only to women of breeding or of great artistic talent. While Gertrude Stein's "feminism" was characterized by a rugged individualism identified with the American West, displaying qualities of independence, outspokenness, courage, and strength, Natalie Barney's was a gift of lifelong friendship to women who met her cultural standards. If Stein and Toklas remained very much products of a late-nineteenth-century American puritanism that honored family values, worshipped domesticity, and practiced sexual discretion, Natalie Barney placed herself in an earlier, less custom-bound tradition. She played the role of an eighteenth-century aristocrat, enforcing a *droit de seigneur* that insured her privilege and sexual freedom. Bertha Harris has commented that Barney's wealth was at the root of her "commitment to the pursuit of the beautiful and the resurrection of attic ecstasy." As the leader of women who "escaped the American Gothic with huge hunks of papa's fortune stuffed in their pockets—fortunes made for the most part by the usual grinding-the-noses-of-the-poor and fortunes spent by these women solely on themselves and on each other,"[24] Barney was uninterested in developing a feminist politics that extended beyond class and culture. Nor was she able to see that her enthrallment to the privileges of her social and economic situations prevented a wider, less self-serving, political commitment.

The self-indulgence and narcissicism described by Harris as the common denominator of Paris lesbianism often masked early emotional losses—especially the deaths of parents—that affected adult behavior. Albert Barney's death at age fifty-two, when his daughter was twenty-six, provided her an inheritance with which to purchase a life of leisure and freedom in Paris. Barney was relieved at the death of her father, whose surreptitious sexual indiscretions educated her in the ways of the patriarchy and whose efforts to arrange a marriage of social and economic advantage further alienated her. John Tarn's premature death, when his daughter Pauline (Renée Vivien) was just nine years of age, left her at the mercy of a capricious and manipulative mother, who felt herself in competition with her daughters and who manipulated the terms of her husband's will to their financial disadvantage. Vivien, however, felt herself emotionally abandoned by her father's death, especially since her mother's lover was immediately installed in the family home, where he assumed parental privileges.

One might argue that Vivien's own early death was prefigured in the loss of her father. Her life and art were devoted to the cult of fatal love, one that lasts beyond the grave, each lover faithful to the ideal image embodied in the other. Like Barney, Vivien hated the patriarchy. While Barney turned patriarchal laws to her own advantage—assuming for herself their rights and privileges—Vivien lived and died according to the law that woman's sexuality leads to death. Suffering from consumption, anorexia, and drug abuse, she died in 1909, a few months after her thirty-second birthday. Natalie Barney was guilt-stricken by Vivien's death, perhaps realizing her own role in hastening its inevitability: She had refused to abide by the laws of bourgeois monogamy. Knowing that her lover's writing was dependent on the "desire to desire," Barney committed infidelities as if such trespasses might temporarily bring a halt to Vivien's enormous productivity. Instead, such behavior fueled Vivien's psychosexual pathology and her poetic gift. She produced over twenty volumes of poetry and prose, and her artistic genius rested in morbid desires for and fears of death. Among expatriate women, Vivien is the most extreme example of contradictory responses to early emotional losses: These losses were the source of her art, the impediment to long-term relationships, and a component factor in her addictive behavior and early death.

A significant number of expatriate women experienced parental deaths at crucial moments in their lives, however, and the effects of these deaths should not be overlooked in an effort to understand the sexual and political commitments of these women. Barney, Brooks, Bryher, Hall, Troubridge, and Vivien all lost their fathers, while during their teenage years Stein and Toklas lost their mothers to cancer (two years later Stein's father died, leaving Gertrude and Leo Stein in the care of their older brother, Michael).

In every case, these deaths resulted in changed family and financial situations and also psychosexual traumas that affected their later relationships with friends and lovers. Barney and Hall were made independently wealthy by their fathers' deaths (Hall's father had earlier abandoned the family, which left her psychologically scarred), while the death of Una Troubridge's father when she was in her mid-twenties left her family financially endangered and led directly to her marriage with Troubridge, a financially secure widower some twenty-five years older than she. The death of Stein's mother left Gertrude and Leo in the care of a demanding and cold father, whom they ignored. Daniel Stein's death then left Gertrude and Leo with a debilitating dependency on each other. Alice Toklas cared for her aging father in the family home until she met Gertrude Stein in 1907, when she abandoned her responsibilities as elder child to take up new familial responsibilities with Stein. While parental deaths often left daughters rich and free of family constraints, these deaths also confirmed losses that had already taken place within the family structure—fathers who were absent or unsupportive, mothers who were jealous, emotionally unstable, and victimized by patriarchy.

The distribution of monies from the family fortunes also affected the emotional lives of expatriate women. The cases of Albert Barney and John Ellerman are exemplary. Barney's fortune was divided among his wife and two daughters, arriving at the very moment Natalie Barney wanted to establish her Parisian life. She was at last responsible to no one. Although Alice Pike Barney, her mother, lived part of every year in Paris, she did not interfere in Natalie's life. Winifred Ellerman, however, knew for almost twenty years before her father's death that English law would prevent her from inheriting the bulk of his immense fortune. The loss of the money was of less interest to her than the loss of the shipping company, which in her youth she had dreamed of eventually directing. She showed enormous interest in and talent for the duties the directorship required, while her brother lacked both interest and talent, and under his directorship the company lost power and prestige. She had always wanted to be male and was angered that on biological grounds she should be denied her inheritance. Ironically perhaps, her feminist commitment apparently was strengthened through this knowledge of English legal sex-bias, and she used her fortune to help others establish independent lives and careers. She preferred helping individual women to survive, and was especially supportive of women such as Adrienne Monnier and Sylvia Beach, who were quietly courageous.

John Ellerman died in 1933, when his daughter was almost forty years old. In order to protect her financial interests over the years, and to avoid conflict with her family, she had been forced to mask her lesbianism. She arranged two marriages to ensure her independence, the first to Robert McAlmon in 1921 and the second to Kenneth Macpherson in 1927. Barney had been preserved from such subterfuges because her father died before having successfully arranged for his daughter's marriage. By the 1930s, however, Winifred Ellerman was deeply involved in political causes unknown to her family. Through Nancy Cunard she and H. D. had met members of the Harlem Renaissance and had begun supporting black avant-garde writing and filmmaking. Violently anti-Fascist, her refugee work was well underway by the early 1930s and continued throughout the war. In these years, H. D. was psychoanalyzed by Freud, and the commitment to psychoanalysis carried with it, in Susan Friedman's words, "a profound identification with Jews" and to other marginal groups in European society.[25] Winifred Ellerman's home became a way station on the escape route from Austria, Germany, and eastern Europe and a meeting place for intellectuals and artists who were endangered by European Fascism or victims of American racial and religious prejudice. It was her money that supported expatriate Paris women in these years following the American stock market collapse.

In these same years, Natalie Barney's salon continued as a meeting place for members of the French avant-garde and the few Americans still resident in Paris. The salon had always been strongly literary and artistic and thoroughly apolitical, and it was no less so in the 1930s. Janet

Flanner, whose political analyses in *The New Yorker* grew increasingly left-wing and militant in these years and who was in frequent attendance at the salon, apparently did not breach etiquette by politicizing Barney's Friday gatherings. (Berthe Cleyrergue, who shared Flanner's political opinions, admits that the two women gossiped together like schoolgirls.) Louis Ferdinand Céline, whose anti-Semitic writings had won him a wide reading audience, was the literary celebrity of the moment. Inflation and the devalued French franc were blamed on the *front populaire* and the economic policies of Leon Blum, the Jewish prime minister. Soviet Communism was feared; Fascist leaders were admired; the Spanish Civil War seemed removed precisely because Spain remained an outdated culture. Tea was poured, cakes were served, laughter echoed, and no one spoiled the party by commenting on the self-serving, reactionary political commitments of all but a few members of the Paris lesbian community.

Natalie Barney, still strongly pacifist in her beliefs, fled in terror as the Nazis rolled into Paris in 1940. Fearing Communism more than Fascism, doubting the hoped-for Allied victory, she threw in her lot with the side she thought would be victorious. When she returned to Paris in 1946, it was as though she were back from an extended vacation, irritated that her gouvernante had not been able to better preserve the rue Jacob house and its belongings, refusing to believe Berthe's stories of the war's atrocities. Within a short time, Barney reassembled the surviving members of the salon, and on Friday afternoons tea was again poured and cakes were again served.

RUSSIA'S GAY LITERATURE AND CULTURE: THE IMPACT OF THE OCTOBER REVOLUTION

◆

SIMON KARLINSKY

The widespread belief that the Bolsheviks liberated Russia's homosexuals has long been a point of pride for gay leftists and a confirmation of the worst fears of those on the right who see an intrinsic and subversive link between communism and homosexuality. In this essay, Simon Karlinsky reviews the experience of gay and lesbian Russian writers to challenge the assumptions about Bolshevik policies underlying both perspectives. He documents a brief flowering of gay literary culture between the revolutions of 1905 and February 1917, and then shows how it withered during the 1920s as the Bolsheviks, even as they decriminalized homosexuality, steadily restricted its expression in the arts. The denigration of gay literature was due in part to the class background and politics of several prominent gay authors, but it resulted as well from the Bolsheviks' general unease with sexuality and their belief that homosexuality was a mental illness. The Stalinist crackdown on homosexuals, although enormously worse, did not represent a total break with earlier Bolshevik policies, as previously thought. Karlinsky also briefly discusses the ways in which gay people survived the Stalinist years and the reemergence of an underground gay literature since the early 1970s.

FOR PETER, WITH LOVE

When the topic of repression and liberation in Russia is brought up, many people in the West tend to visualise it in simplistic and schematic terms. First, they believe that Tsarist Russia was an inflexible tyranny that had never changed since the time of Ivan the Terrible. Oscar Wilde's 1883 melodrama *Vera; or The Nihilists*, in the first scene of which the characters converse while an endless file of political prisoners in chains is slowly marched off to Siberia, is a good illustration of this view.[1] Then, according to the popular scheme, Lenin and Trotsky overthrew the tsar, freed the serfs, and liberated women and gays. Still later, Joseph Stalin supposedly reversed the gains of Lenin's liberating revolution and converted the Soviet Union into a police state.

To understand the history of human rights and freedoms in Russia, including the rights of gays and lesbians, we need to consider at least *six* revolutionary changes that the country has experienced during the past century and a quarter. They are: (1) the liberal reforms of Tsar Alexander II in the early 1860s (the "first revolution from above"); (2) the massive, nation-wide uprising known as the Revolution of 1905; (3) the peaceful overthrow of the monarchy by a coalition of moderate-democratic and libertarian-socialist parties in February 1917; (4) the October Revolution at the end of 1917, led by Lenin and Trotsky; (5) the collectivization of agriculture and the suppression of the remaining freedoms of speech and press, followed by Stalin's reign of terror begun in 1929 and, except for some relaxation during World War II, continued until his death in 1953; and finally (6) the "second revolution from above" currently waged by Mikhail Gorbachev, with his campaigns for an open society (*glasnost'*) and economic reconstruction (*perestroika*). The revolutions of 1905 and of February 1917, which brought unprecedented new freedom of expression for Russian gay and lesbian writers are all too often conflated in Western minds with the Bolshevik-led October Revolution, routinely credited with the sexual liberation achieved by the two earlier revolutions.[2]

There is a considerable body of evidence that prior to the Westernizing reforms of Peter the Great (at the very beginning of the eighteenth century) male homosexuality was widespread and tolerated in all strata of Russian society. This is attested by foreign travelers and also by the sermons and denunciations by Russian Orthodox churchmen of the sixteenth and seventeenth centuries, who repeatedly complained about the prevalence of homosexuality.[3]

Beneficial as the Westernization of the eighteenth century was for Russia, it also brought in its wake a previously uncommon abhorrence for the less usual forms of sexual expression. During the reign of Peter the Great, in 1706, his German military advisers drafted a new Military Legal Code, *Moskovitische Kriegsreglament*. Patterned after the military code that existed then in Sweden, this was the first legislation in Russian history that penalized consensual male homosexuality. The prescribed penalty for "sodomy between two men" was burning at the stake. However, the tsar, who was known to dabble in bisexuality on occasion, soon mitigated this penalty and there are no known instances when it was applied. The provisions of the 1706 legislation were incorporated and broadened in the Military Code of 1716, which called for corporal punishment for sodomy and for the death penalty or hard labor for life when rape or other use of violence was proven. The consensus of Russian historians is that the military regulations of 1706 and 1716 pertained only to soldiers on active duty and did not concern the rest of the population.[4]

Criminalization of male homosexual behavior for the whole of Russian society came with the promulgation of a new Legal Code drafted in 1832 during the reign of the most brutal of the Romanovs, Nicholas I. This code did not retain the military legislation of Peter the Great, but was instead patterned on the criminal codes that existed at the time in various German principalities, especially that of Würtemberg, which it copied. Following the example of these countries, the new code included Article 995, which prohibited *muzhelozhstvo*, a term that the courts interpreted as anal intercourse between men. An entry on homosexuality in the *Brockhaus-Efron Encyclopedia* (vol. 20, St. Petersburg, 1897) states that attempts to charge persons with homosexual practices other than anal under Article 995 were not recognized by Russian courts. There was also Article 996, which covered homosexual rape and seduction of male minors or mentally retarded men. The violators of Article 996 were to be deprived of all rights and sent to do hard labor in Siberia for ten to twenty years.

The penalty prescribed for violating Article 995 was deprivation of all rights and resettlement in Siberia for four to five years. Leo Tolstoy's novel *Resurrection* (1899) contains a vignette about a high government official who was convicted under the provisions of Article 995. The man arranges to be transferred, keeping the same rank, to one of the major Siberian cities, where because of his culture and musical talent he is received at the city's best homes. Tolstoy intended this episode, and another one in the same novel where a government-employed lawyer advocates equal rights for homosexuals, to illustrate the corruption and moral laxity of Tsarist Russia.

Article 995 could not have been enforced very stringently, for in the first half of the nineteenth century we find several prominent statesmen and writers whose homosexuality was a matter of general knowledge. One man who could not reconcile his homosexuality with his conservatism and his fundamentalist religiosity was the great writer Nikolai Gogol (1809–1852). This conflict caused Gogol to starve himself to death at the age of forty-three.[5] At the opposite social pole of nineteenth-century Russia there were male homosexuality and lesbianism among the peasant religious sects in the far north of Russia and in the religious dissident communities along the river Volga. Two of these sects, the Khlysty (the name is a distorted plural form of "Christ") and the Skoptsy (Castrates) had recognizable homosexual, bisexual, and sado-masochistic traits in their folklore and religious rituals. (There is a comprehensive bibliography on these sects' rituals cited in the notes to Boris Filippov's biography of the poet Nikolai Kliuev, to be discussed below.)

The Post-Reform Situation

The abolition of serfdom, the replacement of a corrupt judiciary system with trials by jury open to the press and the public, reduction of military draft from twenty-five years to five, and other liberal reforms initiated by Alexander II in 1861 did not make Russia a democracy. But they did free fifty-two million enslaved human beings, allow some autonomy in local self-government and relax the censorship of books and periodicals. The reforms also radicalized Russian universities, encouraged revolutionary ferment (unintentionally, of course), and brought in their wake a feminist movement, which eventually secured the access of women to higher education and their entry into numerous professions.[6]

In this new atmosphere homosexuality became far more visible in both Russian life and literature. One of the greatest Russian celebrities of the 1870s and 1880s, both nationally and internationally, was the explorer and naturalist Nikolai Przhevalsky (1839–1888). His books about his travels and adventures (such as his discovery of the undomesticated horse, *Equus przevalskii*), were translated into other languages and avidly read in England and America. A biography by Donald Rayfield shows that each of Przhevalsky's expeditions was planned to include a male lover-companion between the ages of sixteen and twenty-two. His renown was so great that he could represent each new lover to the authorities as an indispensable personal assistant needed for the planned expedition, whereupon the Russian government would pay for the education of the lover and commission the youth as a lieutenant in the army.[7] Przhevalsky's coeval, the bisexual novelist and literary critic Konstantin Leontiev (1831–1891), whose book on Tolstoy's novels remains to this day a recognized classic, was not as well known as the explorer. This was because his contemporaries and posterity felt uncomfortable with his virulently reactionary politics ("slightly to the right of the tsar," as a modern critic described his views) and also with the rhapsodic glorification of male beauty and the male body so often found in his stories and novels.[8]

Prominent on the Russian literary scene during the last two decades of the nineteenth century were two lesbian couples. Anna Yevreinova (1844–1919) held a degree in law from Leipzig University and was highly active in the feminist movement. She was the founder of the important literary journal *The Northern Herald*, which she edited jointly with her lover-companion Maria Feodorova. Polyxena Soloviova (1867–1924) was a Symbolist poet and the first translator of *Alice in Wonderland* into Russian. She shared her life with Natalia Manaseina, the wife of a well-known scholar who left her husband to become Soloviova's lover. In a fictional guise, the emergence of lesbians and gay men on the cultural scene of the 1890s was reflected in the novel *People of the 1890s* by the now-forgotten writer Alexander Amfiteatrov. Published in 1910, the novel had as two of its principal characters a powerful lesbian banker and a gay "decadent" poet, who appeared in public in garish makeup and jewelry, worn to show his gayness.

Among the notable and overt gay figures of that period were the popular poet Alexei Apukhtin (a classmate and one-time lover of Peter Tchaikovsky); Prince Vladimir Meshchersky, the conservative and notoriously gay novelist and publisher, frequently invited to the imperial palace by the last three tsars (when Meshchersky was caught on the palace grounds, performing a sexual act with a soldier of the guard, Tsar Alexander III ordered that the witnesses be silenced and the charges dropped); and of course the mostly gay coterie of "The World of Art" group, headed by Sergei Diaghilev, which in 1898 inaugurated the art journal of the same name that in a few years permanently changed the view Russians had of their cultural heritage. Diaghilev coedited the journal with his cousin and lover Dmitry Filosofov.[9] After the breakup of his long relationship with Filosofov, Diaghilev found a new lover in Vaslav Nijinsky. His subsequent involvement with ballet, which affected that art in every country, is too well-known to dwell on.

In the new introduction to a French edition of her biography of Tchaikovsky (first published in Russian in 1936, reissued in French in 1987), Nina Berberova cites several other circumstances that can confirm the visibility and impunity of male homosexuals in turn-of-the-century Russia.[10] There were at least seven gay Grand Dukes at the time (uncles, nephews, or cousins of the last two tsars). The most flamboyant of this group was the Grand Duke Sergei Alexandrovich, the uncle of Nicholas II. This uncle regularly went to the theater and other public functions with his current lover. Gay relatives were not restricted to royalty but seem to have turned up in many upper-class Russian families. Vladimir Nabokov's memoir about his Russian childhood, *Speak, Memory*, shows that each of his parents had a gay brother, as did Nabokov himself (his brother, Sergei Nabokov, who lived in Austria with his lover, perished in a Nazi gas chamber during World War II).

With regard to the lower classes (peasants and the urban proletariat), Peter Tchaikovsky's private diaries published by his brother Ippolit (*Dnevniki*, Moscow, 1923) are a good source. We read in them of a likable cab driver and hustler named Vanya whom Tchaikovsky saw when he came to Moscow from his home in the country (at times, the composer's schedule was so crowded that the diary entry reads "Vanya. Hands only"). A homosexual butler at the estate of a wealthy friend Tchaikovsky visited became the composer's sympathetic listener during a crisis in one of his love relationships. The diaries also describe the composer's visits to lowly Moscow taverns that were apparently gay hangouts. Mikhail Kuzmin's novel *Wings* and Nikolai Kliuev's poetry (both to be discussed below) mention, respectively, a Saint Petersburg gay bathhouse patronized by men of all classes, and gay farmers and farmhands whose love-making Kliuev immortalized in some of his poems.

Nina Berberova's wide research on the situation of Russian homosexuals at the time of Tchaikovsky's death yielded only one instance in the 1890s of a man who was charged under the provisions of Articles 995 or 996 of the penal code. This was the case of a man named Langovoy, who taught classical languages at an elegant private boarding school for boys. Parents of several of his students lodged a complaint that Langovoy had seduced their sons. The case got into the newspapers. Langovoy was tried and found guilty of having had sex with a boy of thirteen. The sentence was banishment to the provincial city of Saratov. After five years, Langovoy was amnestied and allowed to resume his teaching job. Given this cultural atmosphere, the recently revived canard about Tchaikovsky being forced to poison himself by a group of fellow alumni of the School of Jurisprudence supposedly hostile to his homosexuality can be seen as a web of fantasies.[11]

During the half-century that preceded the revolutions of 1917, one can find the presence of relatively well-adjusted Russian gays and lesbians in every stratum of society, including the peasantry, the merchant class, the army and the clergy. One area of Russian life where they were invisible was in the revolutionary movement. An enormously important aspect of Russian society from the 1860s on was the radicalization of the educated class, so vividly reflected in such literary classics as Turgenev's novels *Fathers and Sons* and *Virgin Soil*, Dostoevsky's *The Possessed* and Andrei Bely's *Petersburg*.

Whether their ideas were Populist or Marxist, whether their revolutionary programs came from Proudhon, Bakunin, or Plekhanov, Russian revolutionaries of the late nineteenth and early twentieth centuries subscribed to a Victorian, puritanical and patriarchal ethic devised in the 1860s by the utilitarian positivists of that period. The ascetic outlook of Russian radicals at the end of the nineteenth century has been ably analyzed and documented by the British historian Aileen Kelly in an essay where she summed up those revolutionaries' ideal as follows:

> The revolutionary was to turn himself into a flawless monolith by suppressing all private emotions, interests, and aspirations that stood in the way of the total and unhesitating subordination of his reason and

will to a doctrine of revolutionary change. Not only art, literature, and personal relations, but all intellectual enquiry, when not directly relevant to the cause, were prohibited as the futile pastimes of superfluous men.[12]

This was the tradition that formed the thinking of such key revolutionary figures as Lenin, Trotsky, and Stalin. The Russian anarchist Alexander Berkman, in an American jail for attempting to assassinate a man he saw as an "exploiter," discovered that working-class men could be gay and have homosexual desires. This struck Berkman as a shattering reversal of everything that the Russian revolutionary tradition had taught him. Berkman communicated what he had learned to the anarchist leader Emma Goldman (Berkman's former lover), who early on had made the rights of homosexuals a part of her political agenda. Berkman's book about his prison experiences, first published in New York in 1912,[13] had an impact on the thinking of a few revolutionary leaders in Russia, with the result that during the parliamentary period between the revolutions of 1905 and February 1917 at least two antimonarchist parties supported the repeal of the laws that prohibited any form of consensual, adult sexual expression: the Anarchists and the middle-of-the-road Constitutional Democrats. One of the founders of the Constitutional Democratic Party, also known as Kadets, was Vladimir Nabokov, Sr., the father of the novelist. He contributed a scholarly article on the legal status of Russian homosexuals (cited in Notes 4 and 5 below) to the homosexual emancipationist journal published by Magnus Hirschfeld in Berlin.

But the view that the state should not regulate private sexual relationships and that sexual preferences transcended class boundaries, espoused by Goldman, Berkman and Vladimir Nabokov, Sr., was not typical of Russian early-twentieth-century revolutionary leadership. A far more common attitude toward sex can be found in Lenin's correspondence of January 1915 with Inessa Armand, his close political ally. Armand sent Lenin her draft of a pamphlet, intended for dissemination among women factory workers, about the rights of women in the Socialist state of the future. Lenin disagreed violently with Armand's statement that in a society based on equality a woman should have as much right as any man to have casual affairs and to refuse to bear children if she didn't want them. Such rights, in Lenin's view, were of interest only to the women of the bourgeoisie. Proletarian women, Lenin assured Armand, would not want and should not be given such "bourgeois" rights. In the German Communist Clara Zetkin's book *Reminiscences of Lenin*, which records her conversations with him shortly before his death in 1924, we see that Lenin in power retained the same negative view of sexuality that he had earlier conveyed to Armand. In Zetkin's last chapter, "Women, Marriage and Sex," we read that Lenin regarded *any* kind of sexual liberation as antisocial and non-Marxist.[14]

Between the Revolutions of 1905 and 1917

The nation-wide uprising in the summer of 1905 forced Nicholas II to issue his October Manifesto, which authorized a parliamentary system and virtually abolished preliminary censorship of books and periodicals. After 1906, there appeared gay and lesbian poets, fiction writers, and artists who saw in the new freedom of expression a chance to depict their lifestyles in an honest and affirmative manner. Mikhail Kuzmin (1872–1936), the most outspoken, prolific, and well-known of Russia's gay writers, made his literary debut in 1906, when he published his autobiographical novel *Wings*, a story of a young man who slowly realizes that he is a homosexual. He learns through experience to value his orientation and to see its positive side. At the end of the book, he agrees to live with a sophisticated older man who loves him, a decision that makes him feel as if he has grown wings.

Between 1906 and 1923, Kuzmin wrote several other novels, numerous short stories, some plays, and a great deal of poetry, most of them depicting gay love and gay sex. His stories and poems appeared in the best literary journals of the time. His plays were performed in theaters and staged by amateur groups. *Wings* became the catechism of Russian gay men, and it was republished every few years. Its last publication in Kuzmin's lifetime occurred in 1923, when a publishing house owned by the Soviet government brought it out in Berlin. After that it was not published anywhere until the rediscovery of Kuzmin by Western scholars in the 1970s, when *Wings* was translated into most Western languages and found a new and enthusiastic reading audience.[15]

Among other important literary phenomena between about 1905 and 1910 was the appearance of the novel *Thirty-Three Freaks* and the collection of stories *The Tragic Zoo* by Lydia Zinovieva-Annibal. These two books did for Russian lesbians what Kuzmin's *Wings* had done for gay men: They showed the reading public that lesbian love could be serious, deep, and moving. Some of the writings of Zinovieva-Annibal (1866–1907) were published after her untimely death by her husband Viacheslav Ivanov, a major Symbolist poet and essayist. Ivanov was a bisexual, who included in his much-acclaimed verse collection *Cor Ardens* (1911) a section called "Eros" where he openly depicted his infatuation with another man.

Around 1910 there appeared in Russia a group of poets called peasant—not only because of their origin, but because the fate and survival of the peasant way of life in the twentieth century was their central theme. The undisputed leader of this group was Nikolai Kliuev (1887–1937). Born in a peasant family belonging to the Khlysty sect, Kliuev learned (and taught his followers) how to combine his native village folklore with the modernist style and versification developed by the Russian Symbolist poets. His two books of verse published in 1912, *The Chiming Pines* and *Brotherly*

Songs, created a sensation and made Kliuev a celebrity. Kliuev's unconcealed homosexuality did not prevent most poets and critics as well as many literate peasants from seeing him as the foremost literary spokesman for the whole of Russian peasantry.

Kliuev had affairs with many peasant intellectuals, but the greatest love of his life was Sergei Esenin (1895–1925), better known in the West because of his brief marriage to the American dancer Isadora Duncan. For about two years (1915–1917), Kliuev and Esenin lived together as lovers and wrote about this in their poetry. Esenin was a remarkable poet in his own right. Although married to three famous women (a celebrated actress, and Leo Tolstoy's granddaughter, in addition to Duncan), Esenin could write meaningful love poetry only when it was addressed to other men.[16]

The new freedom to depict homosexual relationships in prose and poetry did not go unchallenged. A number of writers and critics were outraged or disgusted. The conservative response was epitomized in G. P. Novopolin's indignant book *The Pornographic Element in Russian Literature* (1909). Taking an openly racist approach, Novopolin wrote that, to his knowledge, homosexuality had previously existed only among the "less-civilized" peoples: the mountaineer tribes in the Caucasus and the Arab countries. Introduction of such themes into Russian literature by Zinovieva-Annibal and Kuzmin were read by Novopolin as efforts to corrupt Russian young people. His book condemned these two writers as purveyors of filth.

At the other end of the political spectrum from Novopolin there was Maxim Gorky. A member of the Bolshevik Party since 1905 and a close personal friend of Lenin, Gorky was at that time the most popular revolutionary writer anywhere. Everything he wrote was translated into other languages, his books enjoyed enormous sales, and his earnings were one of the main sources of financial support for the Bolshevik Party. In the summer of 1907, Gorky wrote to the playwright Leonid Andreyev about the favorable depiction of homosexuality in the writings of Kuzmin and Viacheslav Ivanov: "They are old-fashioned slaves, people who *can't help* confusing freedom with homosexuality. For them, for example, 'personal liberation' is in some peculiar way confused with crawling from one cesspool into another and is at times reduced to freedom for the penis and nothing more." Another typical response from the political left can be found in a book of essays by the Socialist journalist Alexei Achkasov, published in 1908. Achkasov defended the scandalously successful novel *Sanin* by Mikhail Artsybashev (whose protagonist asserted the right of any good-looking man to take by force any woman he desired, because women, in his view, enjoy being raped by attractive males). Achkasov wrote that because Sanin's lust was stallion-like, it was closer to human nature and more normal than the "spider-like and snail-like lust which the priests of the upside-down Eros preach." The "mass pilgrimages to Sodom and Lesbos" in post-1906 Russian literature were undertaken to deflect young people from the "glorious struggle of three years ago" and to serve the interests of the enemies of "political and social change and renewal," Achkasov concluded.[17]

But the Symbolists and the Acmeists, groups that were then in the vanguard of Russian literary life, acclaimed the lesbian and gay writers as important new talents who had important new things to say.[18] Some of the other literary figures who wrote on lesbian and gay themes on the eve of World War I were Marina Tsvetaeva (1892–1941),[19] one of the greatest poets of this century (unlike Esenin, Tsvetaeva could write beautiful love lyrics addressed to either men or women); the short story writer Sergei Auslender; the poet Riurik Ivnev, whose obsessive theme was a dream of being burned or singed by a male lover;[20] Yevdokia Nagrodskaya, the author of trashy best-sellers, whose 1911 whodunit *At the Bronze Door* revolved around the question of which of the three male protagonists would turn out to be gay; the fine lesbian poet Sophia Parnok (1885–1933); and a few lesser writers one could name.

There were also gay artists on the scene, such as Konstantin Somov and Russia's foremost painter of male nudes Kuzma Petrov-Vodkin, to say nothing of gay musicians, scholars, actors, and stage directors. The overwhelmingly gay atmosphere around the various enterprises that Sergei Diaghilev undertook from 1898 on—whether an art journal, art exhibit, production of an opera, organization of concerts or of a ballet company—was only the most obvious example of the amazing tolerance of homosexuality which typified that period. Such figures as Diaghilev, Kliuev, and Kuzmin were national celebrities, much written about in the press. Their homosexuality was known to everyone and caused no problems in their social or professional lives.

The Post-Revolutionary Situation

The provisional government, formed by the Constitutional Democrats and Socialist Revolutionaries after the abdication of Nicholas II in February 1917, lasted for only eight months. Constantly sabotaged by the monarchists on the right and by Bolsheviks on the left, the regime managed to promote human rights and freedoms on a scale not experienced in Russia before or since. That was when women and minorities were given full civil and political rights, including the vote. Freedom of religion, speech, press, labor unions, and strikes became a reality, the prominent feminist Sophia Panina was given a cabinet-level post, and all vestiges of censorship were abolished. The seizure of power by Lenin and Trotsky in October 1917 was hailed by many then (and is still often regarded) as an enhancement of the rights gained by the revolutions of

1905 and February 1917. But as far as rights (including gay rights) and personal freedoms are concerned, the October Revolution was actually a reversal and a negation of the two earlier revolutions rather than their continuation.[21]

In the early 1920s, Christopher Isherwood visited the Hirschfeld Institute in Berlin. In *Christopher and His Kind*, he wrote that Magnus Hirschfeld, the leading figure in the German gay liberation of the period, "was being drawn into an alliance with the Communists"[. . .] "because the Soviet government, when it came to power in 1917, had declared that all forms of sexual intercourse between consenting adults are a private matter, outside the law."[22] This misreading of the Bolshevik leaders' position on gay liberation cropped up in Germany and England in the 1920s, and it gained wide currency in the West in the 1970s. It is usually backed by the claim that in December 1917 Lenin's government abolished all laws against homosexuality, as is asserted in John Lauritsen and David Thorstad's much-quoted 1974 book.[23]

There existed before the revolution only two laws in this area, the already mentioned Articles 995 and 996. What was abolished was the entire Criminal Code of the Russian Empire, of which these articles were only a small portion. Nina Berberova, who left the Soviet Union in 1922 and who had many gay friends both in the USSR and in emigration, when told of the American publications that state that homosexuality was legalized by the Soviet leaders in 1917, thought it too funny for words. "But in that case, the abolition of the old Code had also legalized murder, rape and incest," she said. "We had no laws on the books against *them* in 1917–22 either."[24]

The February Revolution was met by Russian writers and other intellectuals with almost universal support. But the October Revolution quickly split the literary community. With remarkable unanimity, all male gay and bisexual writers welcomed the October takeover. Nikolai Kliuev saw in Lenin a new peasant tsar who would protect village life from modernization and support the traditional ways of the peasantry. Esenin equated Russia giving birth to the worldwide revolution with nature yielding a harvest and the Virgin Mary giving birth to Christ. Mikhail Kuzmin, as his diaries and the poems and memoirs about him (cited in John Malmstad's biography) show, saw in the October Revolution a "long-awaited miracle" and characterized those who were opposed to it as "animals and scum."

When the civil war ended, a new Soviet Criminal Code was promulgated in 1922 and amended in 1926. In the sexual sphere, this code prohibited sex with minors under the age of sixteen, male and female prostitution, and pandering. It did not mention sexual contacts between consenting adults, which meant that adult male homosexuality was legal. The provisions of this code extended to the Central Russian and the Ukrainian Republics of the USSR. But, according to Valery Chalidze, an expert on Soviet criminal law, the previously widespread homosexual practices in the Caucasus (e.g., Georgia) and in the Moslem areas of Central Asia (the Azerbaijan, Turkmen, and Uzbek Soviet Socialist Republics) were persecuted and punished during the 1920s.[25]

In Central Russia, including Moscow and Leningrad, two forms of the Soviet government's negative attitude to homosexuality became evident after the end of the civil war: morbidizing it by regarding it as a mental disorder; and dismissing or ignoring its manifestations in literary works that appeared in the 1920s. If the nineteenth-century legislation considered homosexuality as a crime to be punished, the Soviet regime in the 1920s saw it as an illness to be cured. This view is clearly stated in the book *Sexual Life of Contemporary Youth*, published in Moscow in 1923 under the aegis of the People's Commissariat of Public Health and authored by Izrail Gel'man. The book was based on an anonymous questionnaire about sexual practices, circulated among young factory workers, farmers and university students. Two of the respondents were lesbians, aged twenty-three and twenty-eight, both of working-class background and both ardent Communists. The author's comments on these two cases reads: "Science has now established, with precision that excludes all doubt, [that homosexuality] is not ill will or crime, but sickness [. . .]. The world of a female or male homosexual is perverted, it is alien to the normal sexual attraction that exists in a normal person."[26]

The other prominent Soviet "expert" on homosexuality in the 1920s, Mark Sereisky, stressed that it should not be punished because it is a form of mental illness. He emphasized the pathology of the phenomenon by replacing the verb "to be" when writing of it with the verb "to suffer." Sereisky opened his entry on homosexuality in the Soviet Medical Encyclopedia (reprinted in the first edition of the Great Soviet Encyclopedia in 1930) by defining it as "sexual attraction, counter to nature, to persons of one's own sex." He then stated that some 2 percent of men "suffer from homosexuality" and that some outstanding figures, such as Socrates and Leonardo da Vinci, "were victims of homosexuality." Sereisky listed a number of emotional infirmities to which homosexuals are supposedly prone: They tend to be hysterical, infantile, and rude and to live in a world of their own fantasy. The entry in the medical encyclopedia ends with Sereisky's description of his experiments to cure male homosexuality by transplanting a heterosexual man's testicle(s) to a homosexual. He believed that this method could "cure" all homosexuals once the problem of the body's rejection of alien tissues was solved.[27]

If the medical view in the Soviet Union of the 1920s was that homosexuality was a curable illness, in the literary and intellectual spheres it was mentioned less and less, and was all but unmentionable by 1930. The right to publish literary works on gay and lesbian themes, won after the Revolution of 1905, still obtained till 1929. Established gay poets, such as

Kliuev, Kuzmin, and Parnok, were producing their best work during the 1920s, but their books were either not reviewed in the Soviet press or dismissed as something irrelevant to the new Socialist society.

The example of this self-imposed blindness to gay themes was set by Leon Trotsky's discussion of Nikolai Kliuev's long poem "The Fourth Rome" (1922). By that time, Kliuev had lost his illusion that the Soviet regime would protect the religious dissenter sects (the Bolsheviks persecuted them far worse than the tsars had), and he saw the urbanization and electrification campaign as a threat to the nature and wildlife of his native Olonets region. Kliuev was also disappointed that his ex-lover Esenin had given up his peasant ways, joined an urban poets' group, and announced in a poem that he would henceforth go about "in a top hat/ And in patent leather shoes."

The first section of "The Fourth Rome," addressed to Esenin, described in an "eat your heart out" tone Kliuev's newfound lover, the peasant-born novelist Nikolai Arkhipov, and the ecstasy of making love to him. In its explicit homoeroticism the poem has no precedent in Russian poetry. With densely crowded images, Kliuev depicted his five fingers, "five fellows both reckless and wild," reaching for his lover's genitalia "in red-haired woodland, near waterfall veins," and bringing him to orgasm. He sang the glories of Arkhipov's body, with its "shore of nipples, the torrid island of buttocks/The valley of the groin, the plateau of knees," and predicted that Arkhipov "shall be beloved by my people" because he comforted the poet in his hour of need.[28]

Here is how Trotsky paraphrased this opening section of "The Fourth Rome" in his influential book *Literature and Revolution*: "Recently, Kliuev embarked on a quarrel in verse with Esenin, who resolved to start wearing a frock coat and top hat and informed us of this in his poem. Kliuev saw in this a betrayal of peasant roots and he peevishly berated the younger poet, exactly like a wealthy peasant scolding his younger brother who decided to marry a hussy from the city and join the down-and-outs."[29] Trotsky ignored the powerful gay eroticism of the passage and discussed the conflict in class terms only: The poet Kliuev represented the wealthy peasantry (*kulaks*), incapable of understanding Socialism and doomed to extinction, while Esenin, a poor peasant, was still salvageable. (In actuality, Esenin came from a far more affluent family than Kliuev.)

It is important to note that Trotsky did not attack the poets for their homosexuality—indeed, he virtually heterosexualized them with his reference to the "city hussy"—but only for what he saw as their class origin. This became the standard approach of the Soviet press during the 1920s to all writers, whether gay or not, whose reputations dated from prerevolutionary times. Esenin, Kliuev, and Kuzmin were highly supportive of the October Revolution when it came, but this did not prevent

Trotsky and the Soviet press from seeing them as superfluous in postrevolutionary times. As John Malmstad's biography of Kuzmin and Boris Filippov's of Kliuev show, they were, after about 1922, more and more stereotyped in the Soviet press, Kuzmin as a bourgeois aesthete and Kliuev as a spokesman for the exploitative *kulaks*. But well-established non-gay poets such as Anna Akhmatova and Osip Mandelstam were also treated with scorn during the same period because their art, like Kuzmin's, had deep roots in Western culture. The poets and novelists of the peasant group, who before the revolution saw Kliuev as their leader, were berated during the 1920s for their idealization of traditional village ways. (In 1988, Soviet literary magazines began to publish massive documentation about the brutal persecution of various writers and other cultural figures by the Soviet government, from the early 1920s until the end of the Brezhnev period.)

The lesbian poet Sophia Parnok, on the other hand, was not reviled in the 1920s as either bourgeois or lesbian. She had not acquired a significant reputation before the revolution as Kuzmin and Kliuev had. When her two most important and mature books, *Music* (1926) and *In a Hushed Voice* (1928), appeared they were greeted by total silence in the press. No one, except for a few poets in the USSR, was aware of these two books' publication.[30] The gradual clampdown on gay authors may have had as much to do with their class backgrounds (as perceived by the regime) as with their homosexuality, but it still resulted in a steady decline in the visibility of gay literature and art in the course of the 1920s. We must also remember that among the numerous talented poets and prose writers who appeared on the literary scene after the October Revolution there was not a single lesbian or gay figure.

Though consensual homosexuality was nominally legal in the Soviet Union in the 1920s, most gay men who wanted a career in the arts or in government had to resort to a tactic practiced to this day—marriage to a woman—in order to deflect suspicions. This practice was unknown in Russia prior to the October Revolution. The painter Kuzma Petrov-Vodkin, noted for his male nudes, was married early in the 1920s, after which he specialized in scenes of farming and numerous portraits of his wife. The poet Pavel Antokolsky and the actor-director Yury Zavadsky were lovers in 1918 according to Marina Tsvetaeva's memoirs, and made no secret of their relationship. By the mid-1920s, they were married men. Riurik Ivnev, the bard of gay sado-masochism in prerevolutionary times, dropped gay themes, got married, and was allowed to join the Soviet diplomatic corps.

The Soviet authorities, in line with the medical views of the time, believed that a gay man could be easily cured by marriage or by medical treatment. A good example is the case of Chicherin. The diplomat Georgy Chicherin (1872–1936), a classmate of Kuzmin, had been quite comfortable with his orientation prior to 1917. After joining the Bolshevik Party in 1918, he broke all contact with Kuzmin and his other gay friends. Chicherin scored many diplomatic victories for the Soviet Union between 1918 and 1925. Then he was urged by the Soviet Government to commit himself to a series of psychiatric clinics in Germany. A memoir published much later by his cousin in the West revealed that the illness in question was his homosexuality. No cure was achieved, and in 1930 Chicherin was dismissed from his post, again "for reasons of health."[31]

Another major figure whom the Soviet authorities tried to keep in a lifelong closet was the great filmmaker Sergei Eisenstein. Eisenstein may have internalized the homophobia of the Russian and international Communist movements, as when he told the Soviet critic Sergei Tretiakov that if it were not for Marx, Lenin, and Freud, he would have ended up as "another Oscar Wilde."[32] But he did yield to his gay desires when visiting Berlin and Paris and even more so during his 1930–1932 stay in Mexico to make a film, where he became openly gay and almost caused an international scandal. The Soviet government blackmailed him into returning to Moscow by threatening to disclose his private life. Before he was allowed to make another film, he had to submit to that Soviet cure-all for homosexuality: marriage. His friend and assistant Pera Attasheva volunteered to go through the ceremony, though they never lived together.[33]

The Stalinist Period

The growing hostility of the Soviet government and press to homosexuality, observable during the 1920s, culminated in the new law, Article 154a (soon changed to 121) of the Soviet Penal Code. This law, announced on December 17, 1933, and made compulsory for all the republics of the Soviet Union on March 7, 1934, outlawed sexual relations between men and prescribed five years of hard labor for voluntary sexual acts and eight years for using force or threats and for sex with a consenting minor.[34] Maxim Gorky, true to form, hailed that decree on the pages of both *Pravda* and *Izvestiia* as a "triumph of proletarian humanitarianism" and wrote that legalization of homosexuality had been the main cause of Fascism.[35] Ironically, this was the same time the Nazis in Germany launched their persecution of German homosexuals, claiming in many cases that gays had a particular affinity for Communism.

As Wilhelm Reich pointed out in 1936 and Valery Chalidze in 1977, Article 121 did not merely make homosexuality a crime against public morality. It was now seen as a crime against the state. Reich wrote that homosexuality was placed in the same category as other crimes against society such as "banditism, counterrevolutionary activities, sabotage, espionage, etc." Chalidze noted that "the Soviet authorities apparently seriously believed that homosexuality was a political crime." Cases of this nature were often investigated not by the police "but by the agencies of state security." Reich testifies that in January 1934 there were mass arrests of homosexuals in Moscow, Leningrad, Kharkov, and Odessa, including many actors, musicians and other artists.[36]

From about 1930 on, the opinion that homosexuality equalled opposition to the Soviet system became entrenched in the minds of Soviet bureaucracy. In 1936, Commissar of Justice Nikolai Krylenko proclaimed that there was no reason for anyone to be homosexual after two decades of Socialism, and that those who persisted in remaining homosexual must be "remnants of the exploiting classes" and, as such, deserved five years of hard labor. No one from the working class could possibly be homosexual, so the people who hang out "in their vile secret dens are often engaged in another kind of work, the work of counterrevolution."[37]

Yet, during the Stalinist age, Soviet persecution of gay men was neither continuous nor total. In the case of well-known personalities, such as Eisenstein, the popular operatic tenor Sergei Lemeshev, the pianist Sviatoslav Richter, and numerous male ballet dancers, the authorities were willing to look the other way, provided the man was married and kept his homosexuality out of public view. During my own experiences as liaison officer and conference interpreter in the 1940s and 1950s (in the undivided and then divided postwar Germany), I met a considerable number of Soviet gay men who were in the Red Army or the diplomatic corps or were entertainers. Most of them managed to escape detection and found ways to express their gay sexuality.[38]

The Post-Stalinist Decades

During the decades that followed Stalin's death in 1953, foreign scholars and tourists were again able to come to the USSR for extended stays. Homosexuality was (and still is) a state crime. But foreign visitors were able to find clandestine gay communities in all major cities.[39] As they had done under Stalin, the Soviet political police still used homosexuals as informers and for recruiting foreign gay men for espionage.[40] Several memoirs published abroad and cited in Vladimir Kozlovsky's book describe instances where straight KGB agents were required to participate in gay sex for purposes of entrapment.[41]

Still, the post-Stalinist years *were* a time of slow social change. The decade of the 1970s witnessed the emergence of gay and lesbian writers, the first under the Soviet regime (writers who treated gay and lesbian themes in the 1920s had all come out before the October Revolution). Unable to publish their work, they had to resort to *samizdat* (literally, "self-publishing") or *tamizdat*, "publishing over there," that is, sending their writings abroad. Not much is known so far about Yevgeny Kharitonov, who worked as a teacher of pantomime, circulated his gay fiction in *samizdat* and died of heart failure in 1981 at the age of forty.[42] Far better documented is the case of poet Gennady Trifonov who served a hard-labor sentence in 1976–1980 for privately circulating his gay poems[43] and who since 1986 has been allowed to publish essays and reviews in Soviet periodicals, provided he makes no reference to gay topics. Two Soviet writers have come out as gay after emigrating from the USSR. They are David Dar (1910–1980), the widower of the noted novelist Vera Panova; and Edward Limonov, the bisexual author of the autobiographical novel *It's Me, Eddie*, which contains detailed descriptions of the narrator's intimate contacts with American black men.[44]

More light has been shed on the situation of lesbians in the Soviet Union in recent years in memoirs published abroad by women who had served time in gulag camps and were able to observe lesbian behavior there,[45] and in works of fiction by Soviet feminist writers expelled from the USSR.[46] It is now possible for Soviet writers in good standing with the authorities to mention homosexual topics in their work published in the West. Thus, the poet Viktor Sosnora described in his book of meditations, *The Flying Dutchman* (published in West Germany in 1979), the dismemberment of a famous and elderly actor by four drunken army officers in a Leningrad bar. Sosnora begged the barmaid to call the police but she laughed and urged the soldiers on. When he persisted, she replied that homosexuals are not human beings and that anyone who defended them had to be one himself.[47]

The current *glasnost'* campaign has made homosexuality a mentionable topic in the Soviet press, but it has not done anything for gay rights so far. The two most hopeful signs in this area go back fifteen years into the past. In 1973, there was published in Leningrad a *Textbook of Soviet Criminal Law* whose authors pointed out that no logical or scientific grounds had ever been stated in any Soviet juridical publication for criminalizing consensual sexual acts between males. The authors cited the example of other Socialist countries where antihomosexual laws have been rescinded without any demonstrable harm to society.[48] Also in 1973 came the publication abroad of Venedikt Erofeev's *Moscow to the End of the Line*.[49] A *samizdat* classic since 1968, the book is an odyssey of an alcoholic who manages to get drunk at every subway station in Moscow by consuming anything from champagne to furniture polish. This is accompanied by a stream of this man's consciousness about the dishonesty and secretiveness of Soviet society. A part of his interior monologue, used by Kozlovsky as an epigraph to his book, reads: "Allow me to point out that in our country homosexuality has been eradicated, finally but not totally. Or, more correctly, totally, but not entirely. Or, still more correctly, entirely and totally, but not fully. Because what is it that people have on their minds these days? Nothing but homosexuality." Should these two unrelated phenomena (the textbook and Erofeev's quip) find successors in the next decade or so and should they multiply, understanding of homosexuality in the Soviet Union at the end of the twentieth century might yet return to the levels observable in the century's first two decades.

SWASTIKA, PINK TRIANGLE, AND YELLOW STAR: THE DESTRUCTION OF SEXOLOGY AND THE PERSECUTION OF HOMOSEXUALS IN NAZI GERMANY

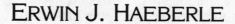

ERWIN J. HAEBERLE

Much early sexological research, indeed the very concept of sexology, was the work of German Jews. As Erwin Haeberle shows, Hitler's rise to power at first curtailed, then prevented, and finally destroyed all German sex research and a flourishing sex reform movement—the first stage in the systematic persecution of German homosexuals between 1933 and 1945. Haeberle traces the confluence of anti-Semitism, antifeminism, and homophobia in the sexual ideology of Nazism, and in so doing expands our understanding of the Holocaust.

Shortly before his death in exile, the great German sexologist Magnus Hirschfeld (1868–1935) wrote an autobiographical sketch in which he described his persecution by the Nazis:

> After the War, when the Nazi movement gripped Munich and spread in ever larger circles throughout Germany, Hirschfeld's name was placed on the proscription list. After delivering a popular scientific lecture

Note: Originally published, in somewhat different form, in *The Journal of Sex Research*, vol. 17, no. 3 (August 1981): 270–287.

in Munich, he was brutally attacked in the streets. Unconscious, he was taken to the Surgical Clinic, where his injury was diagnosed as a fracture of the skull. As the press carried a notice that the attack had proven fatal, Hirschfeld had an opportunity of reading his own obituary.[1]

What was behind this assault? How could a middle-aged physician and scholar, a lifelong advocate of peaceful persuasion, provoke such violence? Why was he singled out, when his colleagues remained unharmed? These questions are at least partially answered by Hirschfeld's friend and collaborator Max Hodann in another work written in exile:

The academic gates were closed to Hirschfeld, and even after the fall of the Hohenzollern Empire in 1918 the Weimar Republic had no chair anywhere for the tireless investigator. Hirschfeld's work was more unwelcome to the political reaction in Central Europe than even Sigmund Freud's. He was simply labelled as a "propagandist for homosexuality," and the anti-Semitism so strongly developed in Germany, even before Hitler's advent, was also an element in consolidating opposition to his work. Moreover, Hirschfeld's political sympathies were always definitely "Left," *i.e.* liberal and progressive, although he took no active part in politics . . .[2]

According to Hodann, Hirschfeld provoked the reactionary opposition by being a Jew, a leftist, and an advocate of homosexual rights. Indeed, similar reasons are given by Hirschfeld himself in the above-mentioned autobiographical sketch:

The Nazis persecuted Hirschfeld, not only on account of his "non-Aryan" extraction, but also because of his open acknowledgment of pacifistic and socialistic tendencies, and his work in sexual science.[3]

The difference between the two recollections is slight: Both mention Jewishness and leftist tendencies, but where Hodann lists propaganda for homosexuality, Hirschfeld merely speaks of sexual science in general as a sufficient cause for his persecution. Yet today we may ask whether either of them really told the whole story or, for that matter, even wanted it told. After all, some sources suggest that there was still another reason for the persistent, widespread hostility. Indeed, this reason, which is never mentioned either by Hirschfeld himself or by his friends, may very well have been decisive.

We get a hint at the truth in the work of Albert Moll, a fellow Jew and fellow sexologist, who, in 1926, organized the first Congress for Sex Research in Berlin without inviting Hirschfeld's participation. This struck many observers as odd, since the latter had not only convened the first Congress for Sexual Reform a few years before, but also founded the first

Institute for Sexology in the same city. Moreover, this Institute attracted visitors from all over the world quite apart from any special occasion. Under the circumstances, the deliberate snubbing of Hirschfeld was bound to attract attention, and thus Moll found himself forced to explain his action in print. His defense, while couched in academic language, is remarkably blunt:

> People complain that important researchers were not invited to the congress . . . for example . . . Magnus Hirschfeld . . . Therefore, a frank observation: He was not invited, because it had to be assumed that important personalities would not have attended the congress if Magnus Hirschfeld had received an invitation. The reason is . . . that many serious researchers do not consider him an objective seeker of truth, because . . . he confuses science with propaganda. However, an additional reason not to invite Magnus Hirschfeld was his problematic nature, about which I have a great deal of material, although I do not want to publish it at this time without being forced to do so.[4]

This statement leaves no doubt that Hirschfeld was unpopular not only with Nazis and anti-Semitic enemies of sexology. Indeed, it shows quite clearly that he had little support even among his own colleagues. Again, the charge of unscientific propaganda is made, a reference to his work on behalf of homosexual rights. After all, by the time of this particular controversy, he had already been openly active in this regard for nearly thirty years. His *Scientific Humanitarian Committee*, his *Yearbook for Sexual Intermediate Stages*, his book *Homosexuality*, and his ceaseless campaign for repeal of Paragraph 175, the German sodomy law, had made him a well-known, and as we see here, notorious public figure. However, as we also discover, such notoriety was anathema to Moll and many other sexologists who strove, above all, for social and academic acceptance. This overriding concern also explains their attitude toward Hirschfeld as a private individual: They were quite uncomfortable with his "problematic nature," i.e., his homosexuality.

The fact that Hirschfeld was a homosexual who both in his private and professional life associated with individuals considered sick by his conservative colleagues obviously damaged his reputation. Nevertheless, being financially independent, he made no apologies and persisted in his lifestyle. Furthermore, he never hesitated to use science in the service of sexual reform. His motto *Per scientiam ad justitiam* guided him as an organizer of the World League for Sexual Reform, whose presidency he shared with Auguste Forel and Havelock Ellis, and which held congresses in Copenhagen (1928), London (1929), Vienna (1930), and Brno (1932). In contrast, the congresses of Moll's International Society for Sex Research (Berlin, 1926; London, 1930) carefully avoided practical proposals or social and political resolutions, cultivating instead the ideal of a neutral, "disinterested" sexology. In fact, when pressured, Moll tended to side with the establishment. Always a militaristic super-patriot, he even found something good to say about the Nazis, once they had come to power.[5]

Not so Hirschfeld. When, in 1922, the German foreign minister Rathenau was murdered by the right, the signal was clear: The victim was not only a democrat, but also a Jew and a homosexual. For the growing fascist movement, chauvinism, anti-intellectualism, anti-Semitism, and homophobia, were part of the same program. When Hitler finally took over the government, all sexological work, progressive and conservative, suffered restrictions, because it was largely conducted by Jews. Thus, both Hirschfeld's congresses for reform and Moll's congresses for research came to an end. The sexological journals had to cease publication. However, at first the neutral, "respectable" sexologists remained physically unmolested. Again, it was only the notorious Hirschfeld who became the target of violence. As he recalls in his sketch:

> Although the Nazis themselves derived great profit from Hirschfeld's theories (and called on him personally for help) they continued his persecution relentlessly; they terrorized his meetings and closed his lecture halls, so that for the safety of his audiences and himself, Hirschfeld was no longer able to make a public appearance.
>
> Those were the conditions . . . when Hirschfeld left his fatherland. . . . (A)fter several years of absence, (he) again stepped on European soil; now he heard tales and warnings from Germany that his life was in danger if he returned. . . . It was in Switzerland that the news reached him that . . . the "Nazi Committee against the Un-German Spirit" had broken into his Institute. . . . Thereupon the Institute was officially closed. . . . A few days after the destruction of his Institute, Hirschfeld was in Paris; visiting a cinema, he saw with his own eyes, on the screen before him, the burning of his library.[6]

This act of official vandalism took place on May 6, 1933, a little more than three months after Hitler had become Chancellor. It was one of the very earliest acts of government terror, preceding by years the later Nazi excesses. As a matter of fact, the action seemed so precipitous, even to those who expected the worst, that many searched for some rational explanation. Thus, Ludwig L. Lenz, a gynecologist who worked at the Institute and who managed to escape with his life, later speculated in his *Memoirs* about the true motive by emphasizing the personal help Hirschfeld had given to Nazi officials:

> . . . our Institute was used by all classes of the population and members of every political party. . . . We thus had a great many Nazis under treatment at the Institute. There was, for instance, a lady from Potsdam who, in referring to Dr. Hirschfeld, invariably said "Dr. Kirschfeld." When I drew her attention to this mistake, she replied blushing and glancing at the swastika on her breast: "Oh, Doctor, if you don't mind I should rather say 'Dr. Kirschfeld,' it sounds more Aryan."

Why was it then, since we were completely non-party, that our purely scientific Institute was the first victim which fell to the new regime? "Fell" is, perhaps, an understatement for it was totally destroyed; the books from the big library, my irreplaceable documents, all the pictures and files, everything, in fact, that was not nailed down or a permanent fixture was dragged outside and burned. What explanation is there for the fact that the trades union buildings of the socialists, the communist clubs and the synagogues were only destroyed at a much later date and never so thoroughly as our pacific Institute? Whence this hatred, and, what was even more strange, this haste and thoroughness?

The answer to this is simple and straightforward enough—we knew too much.

It would be against medical principles to provide a list of the Nazi leaders and their perversions. One thing, however, is certain—not ten percent of those men who, in 1933, took the fate of Germany into their hands, were sexually normal. . . . Many of these personages were known to us directly through consultations; we heard about others from their comrades in the party who boasted of their exalted friends . . . ; and of others we saw the tragic results: I refer here especially to a young girl whose abdomen was covered with pin scratches caused through the sadism of an eminent Nuremberg Nazi; I refer also to a thirteen year old boy who suffered from a serious lesion of the anal muscle brought about by a senior party official in Breslau and to a youth from Berlin with severe rectal gonorrhea, etc. etc. . . . Our knowledge of such intimate secrets regarding members of the Nazi Party and our other documentary material—we possessed about forty thousand confessions and biographical letters—was the cause of the complete and utter destruction of the Institute for Sexology.[7]

Lenz's assertion certainly raises some interesting questions. For example, if the Institute did indeed keep tens of thousands of confessions and biographical letters, does it make sense to assume that they were all thrown into the fire? Is it not rather more likely that they were saved for use by the Gestapo? Indeed, is it not possible that the entire event was staged to deceive, and that the apparent destruction of the Institute was really a cover operation to retrieve Hirschfeld's case histories and other incriminating evidence against both prominent Nazis and their opponents? Was some of this evidence perhaps used one year later in the murder of Röhm and other SA leaders?

In all probability, such questions can no longer be answered. In any case, we know what happened in further political developments. Already, in the fall of 1933 the first homosexuals were sent to the first concentration camps, and in the following summer Hitler eliminated his closest friend Röhm and certain SA leaders as potential rivals. The strictly political motivation of this ruthless power play was initially too obvious to be entirely denied, but later it was conveniently obscured by charges of homosexual depravity. Still, one year later, in 1935, the infamous Paragraph 175, which had criminalized anal intercourse between males, was expanded to include all forms of male homosexual contact, and the courts subsequently broadened the application to a point where even a kiss or purely visual contact became punishable.

Hirschfeld did not survive long enough to learn of this strengthening of a law he had fought all his life. He died just a few weeks before this event in France. Neither did he learn of the subsequent enactment of another legal outrage, the so-called Nuremberg laws, which discriminated against Jews and made them, in fact, second-class citizens. Especially the "Law for the Protection of German Blood and German Honor" of September, 1935, which punished sexual intercourse between Jews and non-Jews as "race defilement," created an entirely new class of criminals who soon entered the ever expanding concentration camps.

Of course, the Nazis did not stop at the mere sexual repression of the Jews and their friends, but soon passed ever more repressive measures. In the same year, 1935, Jewish physicians were forced to leave public hospitals; Jewish teachers and students were removed from German schools, since they could not provide proper role models for the new Aryan generation. Soon the local and individual harassment of Jews also became more intense. It was only during the Olympic Games of 1936 in Berlin that Hitler stage-managed a brief, deceptive lull for the benefit of international observers. Still, at the same time the persecution of homosexuals was stepped up in massive bar raids, in order to present visiting athletes and journalists with a "morally clean" Germany. These raids greatly increased the number of homosexual concentration camp inmates. Curiously enough, there was also concern about possible diplomatic complications, and thus a special order was given by Himmler not to arrest homosexual foreigners.

Needless to say, once the Olympics were over, the anti-Semitic government policies were resumed with increasing force. In 1938, all Jewish physicians lost their license. Thus, even the heterosexual, conservative, "respectable" Albert Moll was finally silenced and deprived of his livelihood. Too late he discovered that, being a Jewish sexologist, his respectability could not save him, and that, for the Nazis, he was no better than Hirschfeld—a despised, inferior enemy of the people whose work was fit only to be burned.

Moll died the following year, thus being spared many later legal indignities and eventual transportation to one of the death camps. Yet his fate is perhaps even more tragic than Hirschfeld's, who, as a "leftist" and homosexual, had never been under any illusion about the true character of Germany's new régime. At any rate, by the beginning of the Second World War, this character was no longer obscure to anyone. The so-called Third Reich had no use for reason, compassion, or moderation:

Racism as well as political and sexual repression were loudly proclaimed and openly enacted programs.

Therefore, the once celebrated academic freedom of German universities quickly came to an end. By the same token, any scientific or scholarly investigation of sexual questions now appeared dangerous. Sexology and related critical efforts, such as psychoanalysis, were denounced as "Jewish science," an epithet which was meant to convey the idea of "degenerate" folly, but which, ironically and unintentionally, contained a kernel of truth. As a science, sexology was indeed Jewish in the sense that its pioneers had largely been German and Austrian Jews. This, in the eyes of the Nazis, tainted the whole enterprise and made its eradication all the more urgent. All sexologists, Jewish or not, came under attack. Thus, once their books had been burned, and once Hirschfeld, Hodann, and Lenz had been joined in exile by Wilhelm Reich, Max Marcuse, and Sigmund Freud, German sexology was effectively dead.

We have to remember that *Sexualwissenschaft*, or the science of sex, had, from its inception, served a critical function, i.e., its original impetus had been the critique of prevailing sexual attitudes and traditional assumptions about sex. After all, in the preceding century many other supposedly natural forces, such as the economy, political power, and social organization, had come under critical scrutiny by the new sciences of economics and sociology. These described what they studied as man-made phenomena—arbitrary, often unreasonable, but controllable and subject to modification. Indeed, whether they knew it or not, economists and sociologists soon provided the intellectual tools for change, perhaps even radical change. By the same token, sexology, according to its first proponents and organizers Bloch, Hirschfeld, Eulenburg, Krauss, Körber, and Rohleder, demystified the alleged unchangeable "natural" force of sex and tried to bring it under some sort of rational control.[8] Through their research, they hoped to provide the means for reforming the sexual life of their time. This, more than anything else, was the reason for the hostility they encountered. Yet there was no honest way of avoiding the clash. Even cautious, conservative sex researchers like Moll found themselves drawn to the cause of reform, however reluctantly. In fact, Moll, with all his personal distaste for Hirschfeld's perennial crusading, had no moral or intellectual choice but to support it in principle, and thus both of them, each in his own way, fought for homosexual rights. In short, sexology, as understood by its founders, was a new critical science with obvious social, legal, and political implications.

Any such science had to be more than unwelcome to Hitler and the Nazis. Through all the years of his struggle for power he had appealed to popular prejudices and resentments. Democratic government, labor unions, ethnic and religious tolerance, scrupulous legal procedure, the women's movement, modern art, sexual emancipation—these and many other progressive achievements had always provoked his fury. His contempt for all intellectuals was outspoken. In spite of his talent for using modern technology, his general world view was that of a half-educated nineteenth-century petty bourgeois. His sexual views in particular were rigid, narrow, and patriarchal. Thus, Nazi policies toward women were always openly reactionary. As Alfred Rosenberg, the chief ideologue of Nazism, had made clear even before 1933:

> The emancipation of women from the women's emancipation movement is the first demand of a female generation trying to rescue nation and race, the eternally unconscious, the foundation of all civilization, from decline. . . . A woman should have every opportunity to realize her potential, but one thing must be made clear: Only a man must be and remain judge, soldier and politician.[9]

And once power had been won, another Nazi propagandist became even more specific:

> In the ideology of National Socialism there is no room for the political woman. . . . (Our) movement places woman in her natural sphere of the family and stresses her duties as wife and mother. The political woman, that post-war creature, who rarely "cut a good figure" in parliamentary debates, represents the denigration of women. The German uprising is a male phenomenon.[10]

In accordance with this philosophy, the Nazi state embarked on a program of redefining the role of women along traditional lines. Massive propaganda efforts through Nazi organizations for women and teenage girls cultivated an ideal image of old-fashioned German womanhood. Mothers with many children received a government medal, the "German Mother's Cross of Honor," as a reward for their efforts on behalf of a rising birth rate. This policy reflected both a desire to outbreed the European "inferior races" and to provide soldiers for future Nazi conquests. The already mentioned law against "race defilement" served the same purpose of promoting "Aryan" superiority. Indeed, eventually "Aryan" maternity homes (*Lebensborn*, or Spring of Life) were set up, which welcomed both married and unmarried pregnant women, and a European kidnapping program collected "racially desirable" children from newly subjugated countries in the East.

The reverse side of this policy was, of course, the systematic murder of mental patients, the handicapped, and the elderly in hospitals and nursing homes, although, in this case, public resistance finally imposed some restraint. However, once the war had begun, the massive executions of "subhumans" in Poland and Russia and the so-called final solution of the Jewish problem could proceed without interference by anyone. All of this is so well known and well documented in so many widely accessible sources that it does not require additional comment here. Instead, as the present context suggests, it may be more useful to concentrate on another, and hitherto rather neglected, aspect of Nazi sexual policies—the persecution of homosexuals.

The attitude toward homosexual behavior often provides a reliable clue as to the rigidity of all other sexual attitudes in a particular society. Where the obsession with sexual deviance is strong, the conforming majority usually can be assumed to strain under its self-imposed sexual restrictions. The greater the need to persecute others, the greater the need to control oneself, to resist the temptations of sexual freedom. We have already mentioned how one such temptation, the rational study of sex, had been eliminated from the nation's life; now we may perhaps turn to a concrete example and discuss the fate of a specific group of people who were defined as sexually deviant. In other words, we may ask: What would have happened to Magnus Hirschfeld if, instead of remaining abroad, he had actually dared to return to Germany? Would he, as a Jew, like Moll, have been left alone before the "final solution"? Or would he, as a homosexual, have been killed even before the time of his natural death in 1935?

In order to answer these questions, it is necessary to know concrete details about the Nazi policies toward homosexuals, but this subject has long been grossly neglected by researchers. Immediately after the end of the Nazi regime, it was obvious even to those outside Germany that homosexuals had been a special category of inmates in the concentration camps. Indeed, the first great study of the camps, Eugen Kogon's *Der SS-Staat*, included a moving discussion of their fate in the total record of horror.[11] This book, written by a survivor and former political prisoner, soon became a classic. It was also translated into English, and thus became the major source of information for non-German students of the camps. However, Kogon's aim had been a general description, and thus the homosexual prisoners remained marginal figures. The precise information he gave about them was scanty. Nevertheless, apart from a few personal memoirs of German homosexuals which attracted no serious attention, nothing more was published on the matter for decades. Indeed, the whole subject proved distasteful to both the Germans and the Allies. After all, male homosexual behavior remained a crime in both East and West Germany as well as in Great Britain, the United States, and the Soviet Union. Thus, the homosexual inmates of Nazi concentration camps were not considered to have been unjustly imprisoned, and therefore they also remained uncompensated for their suffering. Not only that: For more than another twenty years they were subject to potential reimprisonment in their newly divided country. It was only in the late 1960s that the two Germanies reformed their old sodomy paragraph 175 and decriminalized all sexual contact between consenting male adults.

Soon thereafter, an emerging "gay rights" movement, especially in the U.S., discovered the Nazi persecution of homosexuals. Unfortunately, because of the paucity of information and the complete absence of solid research, misconceptions and exaggerations were common. "Underground papers" and "gay freedom rallies," even a Broadway play and then some of its reviews painted a lurid, and all too often inaccurate, historical picture.[12] Finally, and very appropriately, a team of German researchers shouldered the task of ascertaining some basic facts. Rüdiger Lautmann, a sociologist at the University of Bremen, together with some collaborators, examined original camp records and published the findings in a major study dealing with a whole variety of societal responses to homosexuality.[13] The following observations are based mainly on this recent study.

It is often assumed by casual students of Nazism that Hitler and many Nazi leaders were originally quite tolerant of homosexuality, that the entire SA leadership, for example, was homosexual, and that the intolerance set in only after the murder of Röhm and his friends in 1934. However, all these assumptions are false. While it is true that Röhm and some of his cronies were, in some situations, rather open about their homosexuality, the SA as such was by no means affected, even in most of its leadership. Furthermore, although Hitler protected Röhm as long as he needed him, he never approved of his sexual orientation which he considered a weakness. Most Nazi leaders themselves fought against "moral degeneracy," a concept which included homosexual conduct, and, long before their rise to power, actually went on record condemning it. When, during an early election campaign, a homosexual rights organization requested a formal statement on homosexuality from all political parties, Hitler's National Socialist Party gave the following official response:

Suprema lex salus populi!
Communal welfare before personal welfare!
Those who are considering love between men or between women are our enemies. Anything that emasculates our people and that makes us fair game for our enemies we reject, because we know that life is a struggle and that it is insanity to believe that all human beings will one day embrace each other as brothers. Natural history teaches us a different lesson. Might makes right. And the stronger will always prevail against the weaker. Today we are the weaker. Let us make sure that we will become the stronger again! This we can do only if we exercise moral restraint. Therefore we reject all immorality, especially love between men, because it deprives us of our last chance to free our people from the chains of slavery which are keeping it fettered today.[14]

Coincidentally, this declaration was issued on May 14, 1928, Magnus Hirschfeld's sixtieth birthday.

As the text shows, there could be no doubt about the Nazi position on homosexuality, even before 1933. Its association with weakness, the claim that it "emasculates" the people, and its equation with immorality show quite clearly that the Nazis catered to the sexual fears of the uninformed. Moreover, the proclamation that "might makes right" and that homosexuals are "enemies" accurately foreshadows the already contemplated later Nazi policies. In fact, the very first year of Hitler's rule saw the establishment of the first concentration camps and the imprisonment of the first homosexuals in them. Together with transvestites and pimps, they represented the "sexual degenerates" (later to be joined by the "race defilers") who remained a part of the inmate population as long as the camps existed.

This is not the place to give a history and description of Nazi concentration camps. They are easily accessible elsewhere.[15] In the present context it is sufficient to remember that being sent to these camps was called "Protective Custody," and that they stood outside the traditional legal system. Eventually, they came to be run entirely by Himmler's SS and, especially after the outbreak of the war, they expanded considerably, providing, among other things, slave labor for certain industries. In their final phase, some of them were used as extermination camps, i.e., places for mass executions, although, as in the case of Auschwitz-Birkenau, the two functions of extermination and slave labor were combined.

People became concentration camp inmates for a variety of reasons and in a variety of ways. As far as the homosexual inmates were concerned, they might simply be arrested and brought in by the Gestapo, especially if they were also politically suspect, or they might be sent in after having been convicted of homosexual conduct in an ordinary court. Eventually, the government even created a special office, the "Reichs-Center for the Fight against Homosexuality and Abortion" in the headquarters of the criminal police, a fact illustrating both the extent of Nazi homophobia and its connection with the ideology of reproduction at all costs.[16] However, the various persecuting bodies and agencies, whether they were legal, semi-legal, or illegal, often cooperated in such a way that many individuals found themselves in double jeopardy. On the other hand, by no means all men convicted of homosexual behavior in a regular court and sent to a regular prison also ended up in a concentration camp. Moreover, some homosexuals in prominent positions, certain artists and show business personalities, etc. remained altogether unmolested.[17]

All of this has to be kept in mind when one considers the fate of those who had the misfortune of finding themselves in the camps. Their total number has long been a subject of speculation, and occasionally some estimates have been offered that were very wide off the mark. Today, thanks to the research of Lautmann and his collaborators, we can assume that the actual figure lies somewhere between five thousand and fifteen thousand, with about ten thousand as the most defensible guess.[18] In any case, the horror lies not so much in the numbers as in the pattern of persecution which mirrored, in some nightmarish and exaggerated way, the "normal" harassment homosexuals had suffered before the Nazi régime, and which they still suffer in many countries today.

Except for outright murder on the spot, the most severe form of Nazi persecution was indeed imprisonment in a concentration camp. The study of Lautmann and his colleagues provides a great deal of insight into the details of this imprisonment, as far as the homosexuals are concerned. It is not necessary to repeat these details here, but the following conclusions can briefly be listed: The homosexuals were usually near the bottom of the prisoner hierarchy; they were often singled out for special tortures and dangerous work, and their mortality rate was very high.[19] The whole horrible story is a subject for special research, and in the present context it seems sufficient to make a few general points: (a) the SS soon developed special categories of camp inmates and gave them different external markings; (b) at the same time, care was taken to keep the different groups together inside the same camp, in order to degrade all of them, facilitate their control, and to pit them against each other; (c) inmates were used in various administrative and supervisory positions to assist in the actual running of the camps. This created a sort of prisoner class system with different privileges, opportunities, and chances of survival.

While individual cunning, initiative, or luck could make a difference in the life of some prisoners, their fate in general was determined by the category to which they had been assigned. In this respect, the homosexuals as a group fared very badly. At first, they had been marked with a yellow stripe or bar inscribed with the capital letter "A" (usually interpreted in camp jargon as "Arschficker," an obscene reference to anal intercourse), or with a big black dot and the number 175 painted on their uniforms (a reference to the paragraph number of the sodomy law). Eventually, however, the SS developed an elaborate color-coding system for their prisoners, and since it has often been a source of confusion for later discussions of the camps, a brief explanation may be in order.

The best and briefest summary is found in Kogon's classic study:

Who belonged in a concentration camp, according to the Gestapo? Above all, *four groups* of people: political adversaries, members of "inferior races" and "inferiors from the standpoint of race-biology," criminals, and "asocials." . . . All groups of prisoners in the concentration camp had to wear external markings which were sewn on their clothing, namely a number and a triangle of a certain color on the left side of the chest as well as the right trouser leg. *Red* was the color of the political prisoners. . . . The other colors and designations were as follows: *Green* for criminals . . . *violet* for Jehovah's witnesses, *black* for asocials, *pink* for homosexuals, at times *brown* for gypsies. . . . Jews wore an inverted yellow triangle underneath their red, green, black, or other markings, forming a star with six points. The so-called *race defilers*, Jews or non-Jews, . . . received an inverted black triangular outline over their yellow or green triangles . . .

In the case of *foreigners*, the first letter of their nationality was printed on the triangle: "T" for Tchech, "F" for French . . . and so on.

Members of penal companies had a black, dollar-sized dot between the lower point of the triangle and the number. Those suspected of escape attempts had red-and-white targets painted on both chest and back . . .

Colors, markings, and special designations—in this respect the whole concentration camp was a crazy farm. Occasionally, there were veritable rainbow constellations: For example, there once was a Jewish Jehovah's witness as a race defiler with penal colony dot and escape target!

It must be emphasized that the markings were no absolute guarantee that the prisoner truly belonged to the category. . . . Indeed, occasionally it happened that, rightly or wrongly, markings were changed.[20]

Of the various prisoner categories, only two were clearly based on sexual considerations: the homosexuals and the "race defilers." For them the markings became concrete, outwardly visible "stigmata of degeneration," and their treatment proceeded accordingly. They were usually despised even by their fellow inmates. As Kogon points out:

Inside the concentration camp, mere suspicion was enough to label a prisoner as homosexual and thus to expose him to denigration, general suspicion, and special dangers. On this occasion it must be stated that the homosexual practice was widespread in the camps. However, the prisoners only ostracized those who had been marked by the SS with a pink triangle.[21]

Thus, the antihomosexual prejudice, so carefully nurtured in Western civilization over so many centuries, proved its strength even among the condemned, and the hypocrisy, which is inevitably part of it, triumphed even in this modern, man-made hell.

In the case of the homosexuals, the color pink was, of course, meant to signal weakness and effeminacy in accordance with the Nazi perception of their character. On the other hand, there was also at least one attempt to alter this character "scientifically" by the administration of chemically distilled "maleness." As Kogon reports:

In the fall of 1944 . . . the Danish SS-Sturmbannführer *Dr. Vaernet* . . . appeared in the Buchenwald concentration camp. With permission by *Himmler* . . . Vaernet started a series of experiments aimed at the *elimination of homosexuality*. The implantation of synthetic hormones into the right lower abdomen was meant to lead to a sex drive reversal. Of the total of 15 test subjects (including two previously castrated males) . . . two died, undoubtedly as a result of the operation. . . .

The others died a few weeks later as a result of general weakness. The human guinea pigs in this experiment were not otherwise mistreated. However, there was no positive result either.[22]

The verbal denigration of homosexuals, their stigmatization, imprisonment, and finally, forced "cures" for their alleged medical condition—in all these respects the Nazis merely continued and intensified what had long been general practice and what, in various forms, still continues in many societies, including our own. In this sense, the fate of homosexuals under Nazism is not past history that can safely be left to historians. In fact, as already mentioned, the historians have, so far, failed in this area.* For historians, the persecution of homosexuals has, since Edward Gibbon's report on Justinian's antisodomy crusade, remained a subject they "touch with reluctance and despatch with impatience." Thus, it remains for sexologists to write the history of sexual oppression.[23] Indeed, before Hitler, it had been sexologists like Hirschfeld who had done most to illuminate this history for the benefit and enlightenment of their contemporaries. Unfortunately, in the end all of this work proved of little avail against the deliberate neo-barbarism of the Nazi regime.

Returning now to the earlier question of what would have happened to Hirschfeld, if he had dared to return to Germany, there can be no doubt that he would indeed have paid with his life. As a Jew, he might have been spared until the beginning of the war, but as a well-known homosexual and spokesman for homosexual causes, he would have been arrested in 1934 at the latest. He would have been sent to a concentration camp where, because of his age and poor health, he could not have survived more than a few days or weeks. Of course, Hirschfeld knew very well that he could no longer live in Germany, and thus he settled in France, where he was warmly received and even began to build another Institute, before he suddenly died on his sixty-seventh birthday.

If Hirschfeld had survived long enough to flee to America, however, he would eventually have experienced serious difficulties. He had visited the United States twice, in 1893 and 1931, and actually had a brother living there. However, as a homosexual, he would have found the climate of the so-called McCarthy era more than chilling. Indeed, if Hirschfeld had survived in Europe to the age of eighty-four, he would have no longer even been admitted to the United States or would have become subject to deportation. In 1952 the U.S. Congress passed a new law aimed at preventing homosexuals from entering the country, defining them as "afflicted with a psychopathic personality."[24] If they were found out after having entered, they were to be deported, a practice upheld by the U.S.

Ed. note: Since the original publication of this article, a number of studies have appeared, most notably Richard Plant's pioneering work: *The Pink Triangle: The Nazi War Against Homosexuality*, New York, 1986.

Supreme Court in 1967.[25] Undoubtedly, a man like Hirschfeld would have been an unavoidable target for the new law, especially since he was also known to have "leftist," i.e., socialist, leanings. Thus, it is clear that the Nazi persecution of homosexuals in general and Hirschfeld's fate in particular did not constitute isolated and otherwise incomprehensible events. Instead, when seen in the context of still-prevailing social attitudes and government policies in many countries, they are merely sobering examples of excess. Their underlying causes are still waiting to be removed.

WORLD WAR II
◆
AND THE
◆
POSTWAR ERA

MARCHING TO A DIFFERENT DRUMMER: LESBIAN AND GAY GIs IN WORLD WAR II

◆

ALLAN BÉRUBÉ

World War II has increasingly been recognized as a turning point in American life. Allan Bérubé's research reveals the war to have had a major impact on homosexual identity as well. This revised script from a 1980 slide show, which the author has presented to over one hundred audiences in North America, argues that World War II was a watershed that contributed to the emergence of a postwar gay political movement in the United States. The military's wartime adoption of a policy designed to manage homosexuality, together with the individual lesbian and gay soldier's strategies for coping with the resulting public stigma, made homosexuality of increasing concern to federal institutions and strengthened the homosexual component of the veteran's identity.

The U.S. military has a long tradition of purging homosexuals from its ranks. In January, 1982, the Pentagon released a directive that may be its strongest antigay policy to date. "Homosexuality is incompatible with military service," the directive explained, because it undermines military discipline, creates security risks, and gives the military a bad reputation. Even a member of the armed forces who "has stated that he or she is a homosexual" or "desires" to "engage in homosexual conduct" is considered a threat to the military under these rules.[1]

The massive mobilization of all Americans for World War II allowed

Note: Originally published, in somewhat different form, in the *Advocate*, October 15, 1981.

the U.S. military to adopt its first explicit antihomosexual policy, which included provisions for temporarily utilizing homosexual men and women in situations that served the war effort. As one Women's Army Corps (WAC) officer testified early in 1944, during a secret investigation into lesbian activity in the WAC, "The Surgeon General's Office in the latest circular letter, particularly for soldiers overseas, [stressed] that homosexual relationships should be tolerated" as long as they were private, consensual, and did not disrupt the unit.[2] The military, in spite of its contempt for homosexuals, was not above using lesbian and gay GIs when it needed them to win a war.

The implementation of this secret policy was just one of the radical social changes that made World War II a turning point in the lives of lesbian and gay Americans. The massive war mobilization forced many American women and men to discover their homosexuality for the first time, to end their isolation in small towns and find other people like themselves, and to strengthen their identity as a minority in American society. Their experiences in the military and on the assembly line, their discovery of gay nightlife in the cities, and their struggle to survive the postwar antigay crackdowns all helped to lay the groundwork for gay life as we know it today. World War II was as crucial to these women and men as the 1969 Stonewall Rebellion would be to a later generation, but its impact was lost in the tragedy of a world war, with no gay movement or gay press to record its history.

Most Americans, when they talk about World War II, begin by telling what they were doing on December 7, 1941, the day Pearl Harbor was attacked. Stuart Loomis, a gay man who was twenty-one and still living in Omaha, Nebraska, remembers "sitting upstairs in the balcony of Walgreen's drugstore late in the afternoon, listening to a rebroadcast of President Roosevelt's announcement to Congress and talking with my friends—my gay set—over malted milks and peanut butter sandwiches, about what *we* were going to do. What was going to happen to *us*?"[3]

Stuart Loomis's generation soon discovered that the war mobilization made them part of a massive migration of Americans. More than fifteen million civilians—mostly women—moved across state lines during the war, lured by the millions of new defense jobs, while nearly as many men were drafted into the military. Black workers moved to northern and West Coast cities where they found new jobs; servicemen and their families flocked to port cities; Japanese-Americans were "relocated" in internment camps while the government shipped Mexican farmworkers into California to replace the evacuated Japanese workers. This massive mobilization radically changed the character of American life during the war. Women, for example, found a new opportunity to leave male-run households and live in all-female worlds. As wage earners working in well-paying defense jobs, wearing men's clothes to do "men's work," and living, working, and relaxing with each other, many women for the first time fell in love with other women, socialized with lesbians, and explored the gay nightlife that flourished in the crowded cities.

Lisa Ben left a small northern California town and moved to Los Angeles to find secretarial work. "I got my own room," she recalled, "with kitchen privileges, and from there I met some gay girls. They lived on the floor above me, and one day we were all sunbathing on the garage roof, and they got to talking and I got to listening. . . . So when I heard these girls talk, I started talking, and finally they asked me, 'Do you like boys, or do you go out strictly with girls?' And I said, 'If I had my rathers, I'd go out strictly with girls,' and they said, 'Have you always felt this way?' and I said, 'Yes,' and they said, 'Well, then you're like we are,' and I said, 'You mean, you're like that?' Then they took me to a girls' softball game. . . . Then we went to the If Club, dancing, and ah! that was where I met lots of girls."[4] Lisa Ben's coming-out experience so radically changed her life that immediately after the war she began the first lesbian newsletter in the United States, which she called *Vice-Versa*.

Perhaps the most unusual experience for American women in World War II was the chance to enlist in the military, the largest women's branch being the Women's Army Corps, with nearly 150,000 women in the ranks. Unlike male branches of the military, however, which consisted primarily of draftees, the WAC was an all-volunteer corps. A nationwide campaign encouraged women to sign up with the WACS as well as with the Women Marines, the Women's Army Air Corps, the WAVEs, and the Coast Guard SPARS. The official rationale for recruiting women was that they were "releasing men to fight," but authorities later admitted that women also enlisted to overcome the restrictions of conventional women's roles, to learn new skills, and, for "a certain number of women," to "be with other women."[5] These women who chose to "be with other women" enlisted in great numbers, and lesbians seem to have made up a large percentage of the corps.

WAC officers faced a difficult dilemma when it came to formulating a policy on lesbian relationships within the corps. On the one hand, since the public had stigmatized the WAC as an army of lesbians and prostitutes, officers tried to prevent any disruptive witch hunts that might further discredit the corps and its recruiting program. On the other hand, while encouraging intimacy because it helped to unite the corps, officers tried to discourage any overt homosexual behavior. The official WAC policy on homosexuality was made clear in a secret lecture to officer candidates in 1943, which warned against "indulging in witch hunting or speculation." It was explained that, without men, women naturally formed "relationships in companionship and working together." The lecture even acknowledged the experience of coming out in the WAC: "Sometimes [a relationship] can become an intimacy that may eventually take some form of sexual expression. It may appear that, almost spontaneously, such a relationship has sprung up between two women, neither of whom is a confirmed active homosexual."[6]

The lecturer was right. Life in the military provided many opportunities for women to form lesbian relationships. "Sami," a lesbian veteran, described how she came out in the navy during the war: "I was sitting in the barracks in Florida, and this one woman that I admired greatly—she was a little older than I, very articulate, very up, and a lot of fun—I just adored her. We were sitting next to each other on the couch with our feet propped up on the table and she started stroking my leg, and I thought, 'Wow! What's all this!' And I just got terribly excited about it. I just was instantly enchanted with this woman and had a lot of sexual attraction toward her. Eventually we got in bed together. We never talked about it, but we had a mad, mad love affair. . . . She had said that she had never related to a woman before. We didn't talk about what we were doing, we just did it and felt good about it. I just thought, well, this is the way it's going to be forever."[7]

Women in every branch of the military had similar experiences during the war. WAC officers were instructed by their superiors that only women whom they could prove to be "addicted to the practice" were to be discharged. "Any officer," warned the lecturer, "bringing an unjust or unprovable charge against a woman in this regard will be severely reprimanded."[8]

Early in 1944 the policy against witch-hunting was put to a test. The mother of a WAC recruit wrote to Washington, complaining that Fort Oglethorpe, a WAC basic training camp in Georgia, was "full of homosexuals and sex-maniacs." The Inspector General's office sent an emergency team to investigate. Witnesses testified that "women having the appearance of perverts have been observed at Fort Oglethorpe; . . . these women affect mannish appearance by haircut, by the manner of wearing the clothing, by posture, by stride, by seeking 'to date' other girls such as a man would, and when with other girls pay all the bills. . . . These addicts have certain signals by which they recognize each other. . . . The signal is said to be a whistle of the 'Hawaiian War Chant.' . . . Expressions common between them are said to include, 'We're going to have a gay time tonight'; 'Are you in the mood?' and 'Messing around.' " In spite of this testimony, the investigative team concluded that they could not find any real homosexual "addicts" and concerned themselves rather with how to keep as many of these women in the WAC as possible. Clearly Washington needed lesbian WACs to do their part in winning the war. The report recommended that there be no further investigations for the duration of the war.[9]

Gay men, as well as women, discovered that the war mobilization also gave them new opportunities to come out, but for different reasons. The tension of living in the all-male world of the military, the comradeship that came with fighting a common enemy, and the loneliness of being away from home in strange cities looking for companionship all helped to create a kind of "gay ambiance," as one veteran put it. Servicemen openly cruised each other in the anonymity of crowded bus and train stations, city parks, restrooms, YMCAs, beaches, and streets. They doubled up in hotel beds, slept on the floor in movie theaters, and went home with strangers when there was no other place to sleep.

While this gay ambiance was attractive to many gay men, foremost in their minds after Pearl Harbor was an eagerness to participate in the war effort. Their patriotism was sometimes dampened, however, by rumors that the military was mistreating gay servicemen. Shortly before Pearl Harbor, both the army and navy made it their policy to keep all homosexuals out of the service. While men in World War I had been court-martialed for committing homosexual acts, never before had the U.S. military set out to identify and reject all homosexual recruits.

This impossible task created a dilemma for military authorities. How could they eliminate homosexuals from their ranks when they needed every warm body they could get? And how were they going to tell exactly who was genuinely homosexual? The military assigned the task of identifying homosexuals to draft board members and military doctors, who were supposed to become experts on homosexuality overnight. Standardized psychiatric testing, developed after World War I, made their job a little easier. Millions of men were asked at induction physicals if they had ever had homosexual feelings or experiences. For many, this was the first time that they had had to think of their lives in homosexual terms. This mass sexual questioning was just one of the ways that homosexuality became an issue during the war.

Gay men who wanted to serve in the military could easily get past this screening, however. "I walked into this office," recalls Bob Ruffing, who enlisted in the navy, "and here was this man who was a screaming belle—lots of gold braid but he was a queen if ever I saw one. And he asked me the standard questions, ending up with, 'Did you ever have any homosexual experiences?' Well, I looked him right in the eye and said, 'No.' And he looked right back and said, 'That's good.' Both of us lying through our teeth!"[10]

Most of these interviews lasted no more than three minutes. How could you identify a homosexual in three minutes? Easy, reported *Newsweek*. You could tell homosexuals by "their effeminate looks and behavior and by repeating certain words from the homosexual vocabulary and watching for signs of recognition." This screening, needless to say, identified only obviously effeminate men, many of whom were not gay. "Scores of these inverts," *Newsweek* complained, "managed to slip through induction centers." The military, in fact, accepted possibly a million or more gay men into the ranks during the war.[11]

Many gay soldiers, however, did not even know they were homosexual until after they were in the armed forces, where life in the barracks was especially charged with homosexual tension. A wartime psychiatric study of barracks life described what it called "homosexual buffoonery," a game that straight men played with each other. "In the barracks," the study observed, "usually when the men are getting undressed . . . various persons will 'kiddingly' assume the role of overt homosexual. One soldier, returning from the shower in the nude, will be greeted with catcalls, salacious whistling, comments like 'Hey Joe! You shouldn't go around like that—you don't know what that does to me!' Joe will respond by wriggling his hips in feminine fashion after coyly draping a towel around himself. . . . Others act the part of active solicitors for sexual favors. 'How much do you want for sleeping with me tonight?'; 'Come into my bed and I'll give you the time of your life.' "[12]

Young gay draftees had to grow up fast to survive being surrounded by all this joking about queers. While some gay men found safety in keeping to themselves, others sought out each other for support. "When I first got in the navy," recalled one man, "in the recreation hall, for instance, there'd be eye contact, and pretty soon you'd get to know one or two people and kept branching out. All of a sudden you had a vast network of friends, usually through this eye contact thing, sometimes through outright cruising. You could get away with it in that atmosphere."[13] These circles of gay friends were well known in military life. "You kind of migrated to other gays in the barracks," explained an army man, "and sometimes it would be referred to as the 'fruit corner' or the 'fruit salad.' But not with much violent intent. You were thought to be queer, but nobody could prove anything, unless you were caught."[14]

While the military generally tolerated gay men because of the manpower shortage, getting caught having sex with a man could be a serious crime. The brigs were notorious for guards who enjoyed beating up gay prisoners as well as prisoners of color. If a gay man was thrown in the brig, he found himself in a no man's land, where even his gay friends avoided him to protect themselves.

Some gay men could not take the harassment or isolation of life in the military and tried to get out. Army regulations clearly stated that homosexuality was an "undesirable habit or trait of character" and sufficient grounds for discharge. The catch-22 procedure for discharge, however, involved special board hearings, hospitalization in the psychiatric ward, the risk of a court-martial, and even a prison sentence. Discharges for homosexuality, often printed on blue paper, were sometimes called "blue discharges"; neither honorable nor dishonorable they labelled a gay man or lesbian as an "undesirable." Blue discharges could have "HS" or other codes for homosexual stamped on them, disqualifying a veteran from all GI rights and benefits and often preventing women as well as men from getting a civilian job. The thousands of men and women who received these discharges formed the first wave of gay veterans to seek refuge in New York, San Francisco, Los Angeles, and other cities during the war.

As a result of these discharge procedures, military psychiatric wards were often filled with gay patients, some trying to get out of the military, others being kicked out. Psychiatrists took advantage of these captive patients to develop new techniques for identifying homosexuals. One study of over two hundred gay patients in an army hospital in 1944 observed, "Homosexuals tend to group together and it is interesting to observe the speed and certainty with which they are able to recognize one another. Within a few hours after admission to the ward, the homosexual will have located others of his type and becomes one of the group. They tend to stay grouped together and rarely include heterosexuals in their activities. . . . It is wise to insist that these cases be hospitalized for observation."[15]

A study of fourteen hundred patients in another hospital made its purpose even clearer. Homosexuals, the study observed, did not show a "gag reflex" when a tongue depressor was put down their throat. This "Gag Reflex Test," the study concluded, "is a definite aid in screening candidates not only for the military services, but for positions where the sexual deviate must be eliminated."[16] This military identification of homosexuals set a precedent for the massive screenings and purges of homosexual women and men and their acquaintances from federal agencies following the war.

While the military discharged thousands of men for being homosexual during the war, few were sent to prison. Those who were, however, were segregated, often received brutal treatment, and were set up as examples for the rest of the troops. A black serviceman stationed at the racially segregated Tuskegee Army Air Field in Alabama describes how officers treated black soldiers charged with homosexuality: "The way they dealt with the black troops was that if you were identified as a 'punk' or you were caught or confessed, you were removed from your position and you were given a pair of blue fatigues. You were made to know that if you got in trouble there was nobody going to help you. 'Even Mrs. Roosevelt ain't gonna come down here.' They even pointed out a tree where several people had been lynched. And you learned that very early. They put them in the blue outfits, put them in a barracks by themselves, where the sissies, the punks, were. Each was assigned eight men to march them three times a day from the barracks to the mess hall, taking the catcalls and stuff. It was horrible. I remember one man—I went up to him one morning and I put my hand on him and said, 'It's terrible what's going on,' and he said, 'Stay away from me, or you'll be called one too.' "[17]

Most gay men stayed in the military and ultimately received honorable discharges. For these men, being gay in the military could have its special advantages, particularly for young draftees who had never left home. "You see," a twenty-year-old draftee wrote to a gay friend in 1945, "the army is an utterly simplified existence for me—I have no one to answer to as long as I behave during the week and stay out of the way of the MPs on weekends. If I go home, how can I stay out all night or promote any serious affair? My parents would simply consider me something perverted and keep me in the house."[18]

With weekend passes and furloughs, the military gave its personnel the freedom to explore the gay nightlife that flourished during the war. In large cities servicemen and women found gay bars like Bradley's in Hollywood, The Black Cat in San Francisco, Mary's Tavern in Denver, and a small number of lesbian bars, such as the If Club in Los Angeles and Mona's in San Francisco. These were among the first exclusively gay or lesbian bars in America. They branched out from, and sometimes replaced, the bohemian cafes, hotel bars, skid row taverns, night clubs, and cafeterias of the 1930s where "queers," "fairies," and "dykes" could blend in with other social outcasts. These few meeting places of the Depression could not handle the large number of homosexuals uprooted by the war. As a result, lesbians and gay customers moved from bar to bar looking for a place that would accept their business. Bar owners sometimes discovered that catering to a gay crowd could improve their business, at least until the police or military put the heat on. Lesbians and gay men took advantage of a more tolerant social climate during the war to stake out a new public turf in these bars. Later, in the 1950s and 1960s, the successors to these wartime bars, which lawmakers called "homosexual hangouts," became a major battleground in the fight for public meeting places free from harassment.[19]

While lesbians and gay men could meet each other in these bars, on military bases, and even in defense plants, it was difficult for anyone to maintain a lasting relationship during the war. Lovers were transferred to other bases; couples and circles of friends split up as troops, including women's units, were sent overseas. Sometimes lovers never came back. Countless lesbians and gay men during the war faced the deaths of their lovers silently and alone.

A black aircorpsman who was stationed in the South remembers how he faced the death of his boyfriend. "In those days we couldn't tell anybody who we were. But we liked to be together. I used to send him books, and I had lunch with him. We played the game of 'circling,' which is all you could do in those days. He came up to my office one morning and he said, 'I'd like to have lunch with you. Can you meet me at 12:00 at the PX?' I said that would be good. And at 11:45 I looked out the window and I could see this burst. His plane blew up in front of my face. He was killed. You never really get over something like that. And you know, something happened. I stopped living for a while. And I couldn't grieve, because I'd be a punk if I grieved, and be treated like those men in the blue outfits."[20]

Because of these separations, letters and photographs became absolute necessities of life. But lesbians and gay men writing letters to their lovers and friends faced the special problem of wartime censorship. Military censors, of course, cut out all information that might aid the enemy, but this surveillance made it necessary for gay and lesbian correspondents to be careful not to expose their homosexuality. To get around this, gay men befriended sympathetic censors or tricked others by using campy phrases, signing a woman's name (like Dixie or Daisy), or changing the gender of their friends. Sailors became WAVEs, boyfriends became WACs, Robert became Roberta. There must exist, hidden in closets and attics all over America, a huge literature of these World War II letters between lesbians and between gay men that would tell us even more about this important part of American history.

By the end of the war, in August 1945, most Americans were exhausted from years of casualties, rationing, long work hours, and separations from loved ones and were anxious to settle down to a normal life again. Unfortunately, "normal life" meant different things to different people. For black Americans, it meant losing wartime jobs and stepping up their fight against segregation and discrimination. For women, it meant a return to the home as wives and mothers. And for lesbians and gay men, it meant witch hunts, bar raids, arrests, and a retreat to the closet.

The tolerance that some homosexual men and women experienced during the war proved to be all too temporary. Many patriotic lesbians and gay men saw their wartime freedom disappear as the country they fought for began to turn against them with the advent of peace. Churches, the media, schools, and government agencies conducted a heavy-handed campaign to reconstruct the nuclear family, to force women back into their traditional roles, and to promote a conservative sexual morality. A tactic of this campaign was to isolate homosexual men and women and identify them, like Communists, as dangerous and invisible enemies. These attacks on nonconformists of all kinds soon replaced the live-and-let-live climate of the war years.

Throughout the war, to prepare for peacetime, the government, industry, and the media had carefully controlled the radical social changes that were necessary to win the war. Advertisements reminded women that even though their labor was desperately needed in heavy industry, their jobs were only temporary and ultimately belonged to men. White men in America were supposed to come first both in war and in peace, and their return as head of the household was one of the goals men and women were both supposed to be fighting for. By early 1945, as soon as the end of the war was in sight, the media began to prepare the nation's women and men for their reentry into "normal" life. "Rosie the Riveter," the media's symbol for women working in heavy industry during the war, disappeared from the magazine covers, replaced by the traditional symbol of American womanhood: the young mother and wife, whose fantasies were of babies, whose only joy was to please her husband and children and to buy new appliances for her kitchen. The media took the reality of postwar families struggling to reestablish their lives and transformed it into hard-hitting propaganda for the nuclear family. Lesbians and gay men, many of them unable or unwilling to conform to this narrow family ideal, stood out more and more as "queers" and "sex deviates" who endangered the fragile security of the postwar American family.

While the media tried to lure women back into the home, the government drove women out of industry and the military. Thousands of women working in shipyards, for example, were fired shortly after V-J Day. Anti-lesbian witch hunts in the military, generally avoided during the war, spread like an epidemic after the war. The extent of these witch hunts is still unknown, but we are beginning to realize that they affected hundreds of women. Many lesbian veterans remember them with horror and pain. "I was trained as an aviation machinist mate," remembers a woman stationed at a Florida naval base in 1945, "which is not a usual women's task. [My] first important love relationships with women were in the navy. And then—this was near the end of the war—the interrogation came about and I was terrified. I remember I was interrogated and was scared to death and just lied through my teeth. I stopped running around with the women I was running around with and felt very isolated. The other people that I had been really friendly with—the relationships just were cut off completely."[21] In the film *Word Is Out*, Pat Bond recalled what happened to her WAC unit stationed in occupied Japan after the war: "They started an incredible witch hunt in Tokyo. Unbelievable. Sending five hundred women home for dishonorable discharges. Every day there were courts-martial and trials—you were there testifying against your friends, or they were testifying against you . . . until you got afraid to look your neighbor in the eye. Afraid of everything."[22] These women had nowhere to turn. Gay and lesbian organizations did not yet exist, and liberal and radical organizations refused to help homosexuals who pleaded with them for support.[23]

According to some veterans, similar military purges affected gay men after the war at U.S. bases in Europe, Asia, and stateside. Thousands of men were put in detention barracks and shipped home with dishonorable discharges on special "queer" ships. On some bases, gay office workers were able to sabotage these purges by warning their friends just before the investigation teams arrived. Many of these discharged personnel could not return to their hometowns, so they remained in port cities, where they became a part of the rapidly growing urban gay population in the early 1950s.

The civilian world had its counterpart to the military witch hunts. The U.S. Senate and many state legislatures held unprecedented antihomosexual hearings, causing the firing of thousands of men and women from government jobs merely for being suspected of "homosexual perversion." The FBI began nationwide surveillance of gay and lesbian bars, compiling enormous lists of homosexuals and "associates of homosexuals." In addition, local antigay crusades swept through many American towns and cities, particularly where gay bars had become most visible and were continuing to multiply. Refugees from these crackdowns moved from city to city, looking for more tolerant surroundings. A San Francisco grand jury even held special hearings to curb what it called a postwar "invasion of sex deviates." States began to pass laws to close down the growing number of bars that catered to "sex perverts," both male and female. Massive bar raids and street arrests received prominent coverage in the press. Pulp magazines, exploiting the national paranoia, ran antigay articles in nearly every issue, with titles such as "Hidden Homos and How to Spot Them."

How did the postwar years affect the new generation of lesbians and gay men? Many returning veterans based their decisions for civilian life on their newly discovered homosexuality. "I can't change," wrote a gay GI in a letter shortly before his discharge in 1946. "I have no desire to change, because it took me a long, long time to figure out how to enjoy life. For you'll agree, I'm not going back to what I left."[24] Many veterans left their parents, abandoned small towns, and migrated to large cities they had seen for the first time during the war. There they created lesbian and gay neighborhoods, risked going to the growing number of lesbian and gay bars, and looked for work that would allow them to lead relatively open lives. Others, who had found lovers after the war, tried to settle down into quiet, private lives and even joined the exodus to the suburbs. Reuniting with wartime friends, they socialized with other gay couples in their homes and avoided the bars. With the heat on in public gay life, private homes were often the safest places to be gay.

While this backlash pushed many into the closet, it also forced others to realize the extent of their oppression, their identity as a minority, and the power of their numbers. Like the GI facing his discharge, many could not go back to what they left. Some even came out with a vengeance. It was thus no accident that the postwar years witnessed the birth of a small gay and lesbian movement in America, beginning with veterans' social groups, the Mattachine Society, and the Daughters of Bilitis. The taste of freedom during the war, the magnitude of the postwar crackdown, and the example of the growing black civil rights movement caused more and more lesbians and gay men to think of themselves as an unjustly persecuted minority. They increasingly realized that when they defended their new bars from attacks by queerbashers, when lesbians kicked straight men out of their bars, when bar owners challenged the cops and liquor control boards, and when lesbian and gay defendants began to plead "not guilty" in court, they were actually fighting to establish a public turf of their own, defending their right to gather in public places. After they returned home, the generation of World War II veterans began to lay the groundwork that made the Stonewall Rebellion and gay liberation possible.

"IMAGINE MY SURPRISE": WOMEN'S RELATIONSHIPS IN MID-TWENTIETH CENTURY AMERICA

◆

LEILA J. RUPP

The original version of this essay, written in 1980, was a response to the publication of two homophobic works, *The Life of Lorena Hickok* and *The Making of a Feminist: Early Journals and Letters of M. Carey Thomas*, which dismissed evidence of their subjects' erotic involvement with women. This revised version incorporates some of the developments in lesbian history since 1980 while still addressing the question of how to characterize women's relationships in the past. Using evidence drawn from the files of the American Woman's Party after women's suffrage had been achieved, Rupp discusses the emotional and erotic complexities of the relationships among women whose primary commitments were to women. Although they lived into the 1940s and 1950s, when a lesbian culture existed, these white, middle-class women did not identify themselves as lesbians. However difficult the endeavor, Rupp argues, historians need to be careful in describing women's relationships neither to deny their significance to the individuals involved nor to impose modern sexual categories on them.

When Carroll Smith-Rosenberg's article, "The Female World of Love and Ritual," appeared in the pages of *Signs* in 1975, it revolutionized the way in which women's historians look at nineteenth-century American society and even served notice on the historical profession at large that

Note: Originally published in *Frontiers, A Journal of Women Studies* 5, no. 3 (Fall 1980).

women's relationships would have to be taken into account in any consideration of Victorian society.[1] Since then we have learned more about relationships between women in the past, but we have not reached consensus on the issue of characterizing these relationships.

Debate within the women's movement has centered around the work of two writers. In 1980, Adrienne Rich published "Compulsory Heterosexuality and Lesbian Existence," in which she argued for the concept of a lesbian continuum based on solidarity among women and resistance to patriarchy rather than on identity or sexual behavior.[2] The next year, Lillian Faderman's *Surpassing the Love of Men*, which traced the history of women's relationships, suggested that the nineteenth-century phenomenon of romantic friendship involved a deep commitment and sensuality but not, ordinarily, genital sexuality.[3] As a result of the controversy that has swirled around these works, we have no simple answer to the question, asked of a variety of historical figures: Was she a lesbian?

Meanwhile, outside the feminist world, Smith-Rosenberg's work has increasingly been misused to deny the sexual aspect of relationships between prominent women in the past. In response, feminist scholars have reacted to such distortions by bestowing the label "lesbian" on women who would themselves not have used the term. The issue goes beyond labels, however, because the very nature of women's relationships is so complex. The problem of classification becomes particularly thorny in twentieth-century history with the establishment of a lesbian identity. I would like to consider here the issue of women's relationships in the twentieth century by reviewing the conflicting approaches to lesbian labelling, by tracing the continuity of romantic friendship into the mid-century, and, finally, by suggesting a conceptual approach that recognizes the complexity of women's relationships without denying the common bond shared by all women who have committed their lives to other women in the past.

Looking first at what Blanche Cook proclaimed "the historical denial of lesbianism," we find the most publicized and most egregious example in Doris Faber's *The Life of Lorena Hickok: E. R.'s Friend*, the story of the relationship of Eleanor Roosevelt and reporter Lorena Hickok.[4] Author Doris Faber presented page after page of evidence that delineated the growth and development of a love affair between the two women, yet she steadfastly maintained that a woman of Eleanor Roosevelt's "stature" could not have *acted* on the love that she expressed for Hickok. This attitude forced Faber to go to great lengths with the evidence before her. For example, she quoted a letter Roosevelt wrote to Hickok and asserted that it is "particularly susceptible to misinterpretation." Roosevelt's wish to "lie down beside you tonight and take you in my arms," Faber claimed, represented maternal—"albeit rather extravagantly" maternal—solicitude. For Faber, "there can be little doubt that the final sentence of the above letter does not mean what it appears to mean" (p. 176).

Faber's book received far more public attention than serious works of lesbian history because the idea of a famous and well-respected—even revered—woman engaging in lesbian acts was titillating. An article about the Hickok book was even carried in the *National Enquirer* which, for a change, probably presented the material more accurately, if more leeringly, than the respectable press.[5]

Faber's interpretation, unfortunately, is not an isolated one. She acknowledged an earlier book, *Miss Marks and Miss Woolley*, for reinforcing her own views "regarding the unfairness of using contemporary standards to characterize the behavior of women brought up under almost inconceivably different standards."[6] Anna Mary Wells, the author of the Marks and Woolley book, set out originally to write a biography of Mary Woolley, a president of Mount Holyoke, but almost abandoned the plan when she discovered the love letters of the two women. Ultimately Wells went ahead with a book about the relationship, but only after she decided, as she explained in the preface, that there was no physical relationship between them.

Another famous women's college president, M. Carey Thomas of Bryn Mawr, received the same sort of treatment in a book that appeared at the same time as the Hickok book, but to less fanfare.[7] The discovery of the Woolley-Marks letters sparked a mild panic among Mount Holyoke alumnae and no doubt created apprehension about what might lurk in Thomas's papers, which were about to be microfilmed and opened to the public.[8] But Marjorie Dobkin, editor of *The Making of a Feminist: Early Journals and Letters of M. Carey Thomas*, insisted that there was nothing to worry about. Thomas admittedly fell for women throughout her life. At fifteen, she wrote: "I think I must feel towards Anna for instance like a boy would, for I admire her so . . . and then I like to touch her and the other morning I woke up and she was sleep and I admired her hair so much that I kissed it. I never felt so much with anybody else." And at twenty: "One night we had stopped reading later than usual and obeying a sudden impulse I turned to her and asked, 'Do you love me?' She threw her arms around me and whispered, 'I love you passionately.' She did not go home that night and we talked and talked." At twenty-three, Thomas wrote to her mother: "If it were only possible for women to elect women as well as men for a 'life's love!' . . . It is possible but if families would only regard it in that light!" (pp. 72, 118, 229).

Thomas did in fact choose women for her "life's loves," but Dobkin, who found it "hard to understand why anyone should very much care" about personal and private behavior and considered the question of lesbianism "a relatively inconsequential matter," assured us that "physical contact" unquestionably played a part in Thomas's relationships with women, but, making a labored distinction, insisted that "sexuality" just as unquestionably did not (pp. 79, 86).

The authors of these three books were determined to give us an "acceptable" version of these prominent women's relationships in the past, and they seized gratefully on Smith-Rosenberg's work to do it. Likewise, Arthur Schlesinger, Jr., in *The New York Times Book Review*, found the question of whether Hickok and Roosevelt were "lovers in the physical sense" an "issue of stunning inconsequence," but cited Smith-Rosenberg's work to conclude that the two women were "children of the Victorian age" which accepted celibate love between women.[9]

As Blanche Cook pointed out in her review of Faber's book, however, it is absurd to pretend that the years 1932 to 1962 now belong to the nineteenth century.[10] Although it is vitally important not to impose modern concepts and standards on the past, we have gone entirely too far with the notion of an idyllic Victorian age in which chaste love between people of the same sex was possible and acceptable.

It is not surprising, in light of such denials of sexuality, that many feminist scholars have chosen to claim as lesbians all women who have loved women in the past. Blanche Cook has concluded firmly that "women who love women, who choose women to nurture and support and to create a living environment in which to work creatively and independently, are lesbians."[11] Cook named as lesbians Jane Addams, the founder of Hull House who lived for forty years with Mary Rozet Smith; Lillian Wald, also a settlement house pioneer, who left evidence of a series of intense relationships with women; and Jeannette Marks and Mary Woolley. All, Cook insisted, in the homophobic society in which we live, must be claimed as lesbians.

In the simplest terms, we are faced with a choice between labelling women lesbians who might have violently rejected the notion or glossing over the significance of women's relationships by considering them asexual and Victorian.[12] But what is problematic enough when we are dealing with a period in which the concept of lesbianism did not exist becomes even more troubling when we turn to the twentieth century.

What the research increasingly suggests is that two separate largely class-bound forms of relationships between women existed. We seem to have little trouble identifying the working-class phenomena—"crossing" women who dressed and worked as men and who married women, and lesbian communities that grew up around the bars and, eventually, in the military—as sexual and, therefore, lesbian. But what about the middle- and upper-class romantic friends? It is not a question of nineteenth-century romantic friends becoming lesbians in the twentieth century. Despite the sexualization of American society at the turn of the century and the concomitant "discovery of lesbianism," romantic friendship and "Boston marriage" continued to exist.[13] I would like to illustrate this continuity, and therefore the complexity of women's relationships in historical perspective, with examples from the American women's rights movement in the late 1940s and 1950s.

I have found evidence of a variety of relationships in collections of women's papers and in the records of women's organizations from this period. I do not have enough information about many of these relationships to characterize them in any definitive way, nor can I even offer much information about some of the women. But we cannot afford to overlook whatever evidence women have left us, however fragmentary. Since my research focuses on feminist activities, the women I discuss here are by no means a representative group of women. The women's rights movement in the period after the Second World War was composed primarily of white, privileged women who maintained a preexisting commitment to feminism by creating an isolated and homogeneous feminist community.[14]

Within the women's rights movement were two distinct phenomena—couple relationships and intense devotion to a charismatic leader—that help clarify the problems that face us if we attempt to define these relationships in any cut-and-dried fashion. None of the women who lived in couple relationships and belonged to the women's rights movement in the post-1945 period would, as far as can be determined, have identified themselves as lesbians. They did, however, often live together in long-term committed relationships, which were accepted in the movement, and they did sometimes build a community with other women like themselves. Descriptions of a few relationships that come down to us in the sources provide some insight into their nature.

Jeannette Marks and Mary Woolley, subjects of the biography mentioned earlier, met at Wellesley College in 1895 when Marks began her college education and Woolley arrived at the college as a history instructor. Less than five years later they made "a mutual declaration of ardent and exclusive love" and "exchanged tokens, a ring and a jeweled pin, with pledges of lifelong fidelity."[15] They spent the rest of their lives together, including the many years at Mount Holyoke where Woolley served as president and Marks taught English. Mary Woolley worked in the American Association of University Women and the Women's International League for Peace and Freedom. Jeannette Marks committed herself to suffrage and, later, through the National Woman's Party, to the Equal Rights Amendment. It is clear from Marks's correspondence with women in the movement that their relationship was accepted as a primary commitment. Few letters to Marks in the 1940s fail to inquire about Woolley, whose serious illness clouded Marks's life and work. One married woman, who found herself forced to withdraw from Woman's Party work because of her husband's health, acknowledged in a letter to Marks the centrality of Marks's and Woolley's commitment when she compared her own reason for "pulling out" to "those that have bound you to Westport," the town in which the two women lived.[16] Mary Woolley died in 1947, and

Jeannette Marks lived on until 1964, devoting herself to a biography of Woolley.

Lena Madesin Phillips, the founder of the International Federation of Business and Professional Women's Clubs, lived for some thirty years with Marjory Lacey-Baker, an actress whom she first met in 1919. In an unpublished autobiography included in Phillips's papers, she straightforwardly wrote about her lack of interest in men and marriage. As a young girl, she wrote that she "cared little for boys," and at the age of seven she wrote a composition for school that explained: "There are so many little girls in the school and the thing i [sic] like about it there are no boys in school. i [sic] like that about it."[17] She noted that she had never taken seriously the idea of getting married. "Only the first of the half dozen proposals of marriage which came my way had any sense of reality to me. They made no impression because I was wholly without desire or even interest in the matter." Phillips seemed unperturbed by possible Freudian and/or homophobic explanations of her attitudes and behavior. She explained unabashedly that she wanted to be a boy and suffered severe disappointment when she learned that, contrary to her father's stories, there was no factory in Indiana that made girls into boys. She mentioned in her autobiography the "crushes" she had on girls at the Jessamine Female Institute—nothing out of the ordinary for a young woman of her generation, but perhaps a surprising piece of information chosen for inclusion in the autobiography of a woman who continued to devote her emotional energies to women.

In 1919, Phillips attended a pageant in which Lacey-Baker performed and she inquired about the identity of the woman who had [t]he most beautiful voice I ever heard."[18] Phillips "lost her heart to the sound of that voice," and the two women moved in together in the 1920s. In 1924, according to Lacey-Baker's notes for a biography of Phillips, the two women went different places for Easter; recording this caused Lacey-Baker to quote from *The Prophet*: "Love knows not its own depth until the hour of separation."[19] Phillips described Lacey-Baker in her voluminous correspondence as "my best friend," or noted that she "shares a home with me."[20] Phillips's friends and acquaintances regularly mentioned Lacey-Baker. One male correspondent, for example, commented that Phillips's "lady-friend" was "so lovely, and so devoted to you and cares for you."[21] Phillips happily described the tranquillity of their life together to her many friends: "Marjory and I have had a lovely time, enjoying once more our home in summertime. . . . Marjory would join in the invitation of this letter and this loving greeting if she were around. Today she is busy with the cleaning woman, while I sit with the door closed working in my study."[22] "We have had a happy winter, with good health for both of us. We have a variety of interests and small obligations, but really enjoy most the quiet and comfort of Apple Acres."[23] "We read and talk and work."[24]

Madesin Phillips's papers suggest that she and Marjory Lacey-Baker lived in a world of politically active women friends. Phillips had devoted much of her energy to international work with women, and she kept in touch with European friends through her correspondence and through her regular trips to Europe accompanied by Lacey-Baker. Gordon Holmes, of the British Federation of Business and Professional Women, wrote regularly to "Madesin and Maggie." In a 1948 letter she teased Phillips by reporting that "two other of our oldest & closest Fed officers whom you know could get married but are refusing—as they are both more than middle-aged (never mind their looks) it suggests 50-60 is about the new dangerous age for women (look out for Maggie!)."[25] Phillips reported to Holmes on their social life: "With a new circle of friends around us here and a good many of our overseas members coming here for luncheon or tea with us the weeks slip by."[26] The integral relationship between Phillips's social life and her work in the movement is suggested by Lacey-Baker's analysis of Phillips's personal papers from the year 1924: "There is the usual crop of letters to LMP following the Convention [of the BPW] from newly-met members in hero-worshipping mood—most of whom went on to be her good friends over the years."[27] Lacey-Baker was a part of Phillips's movement world, and their relationship received acceptance and validation throughout the movement, both national and international.

The lifelong relationship between feminist biographer Alma Lutz and Marguerite Smith began when they roomed together at Vassar in the early years of the twentieth century. From 1918 until Smith's death in 1959, they shared a Boston apartment and a summer home, Highmeadow, in the Berkshires. Lutz and Smith, a librarian at the Protestant Zion Research Library in Brookline, Massachusetts, worked together in the National Woman's Party. Like Madesin Phillips, Lutz wrote to friends in the movement of their lives together: "We are very happy here in the country—each busy with her work and digging in the garden."[28] They traveled together, visiting Europe several times in the 1950s. Letters to one of them about feminist work invariably sent greetings or love to the other. When Smith died in 1959, Lutz struggled with her grief. She wrote to her acquaintance Florence Kitchelt, in response to condolences: "I am at Highmeadow trying to get my bearings. . . . You will understand how hard it is. . . . It has been a very difficult anxious time for me."[29] She thanked another friend for her note and added, "It's a hard adjustment to make, but one we all have to face in one way or another and I am remembering that I have much to be greatful for."[30] In December she wrote to one of her regular correspondents that she was carrying on but it was very lonely for her.[31]

The fact that Lutz and Smith seemed to have many friends who lived in couple relationships with other women suggests that they had built a community of women within the women's rights movement. Every year Mabel Vernon, a suffragist and worker for peace, and her friend and companion Consuelo Reyes, whom Vernon had met through her work with the Inter-American Commission of Women, spent the summer at Highmeadow. Vernon, one of Alice Paul's closest associates during the suffrage struggle, had met Reyes two weeks after her arrival in the United States from Costa Rica in 1942. They began to work together in Vernon's organization, People's Mandate, in 1943, and they shared a Washington apartment from 1951 until Vernon's death in 1975.[32] Reyes received recognition in Vernon's obituaries as her "devoted companion" or "nurse-companion."[33] Two other women who also maintained a life-long relationship, Alice Morgan Wright and Edith Goode, also kept in contact with Lutz, Smith, Vernon, and Reyes. Sometimes they visited Highmeadow in the summer.[34] Wright and Goode had met at Smith and were described as "always together" although they did not live together.[35] Like Lutz and Smith, they worked together in the National Woman's Party, where they had also presumably met Vernon. Both Wright and Goode devoted themselves to two causes, women's rights and humane treatment for animals. Wright described herself as having "fallen between two stools—animals and wimmin."[36] The two women traveled together and looked after each other as age began to take its toll.

These examples illustrate what the sources provide: the bare outlines of friendship networks made up of woman-committed women. Much of the evidence must be pieced together, and it is even scantier when the women did not live together. Alma Lutz's papers, for example, do not include any personal correspondence from the post-1945 period, so what we know about her relationship with Marguerite Smith comes from the papers of her correspondents. Sometimes a relationship surfaces only upon the death of one of the women. For example, Agnes Wells, chairman of the National Woman's Party in the late 1940s, explained to an acquaintance in the Party that her "friend of forty-one years and house-companion for twenty-eight years" had just died.[37] When Mabel Griswold, executive secretary of the Woman's Party, died in 1955, a family member suggested that the Party send the telegram of sympathy to Elsie Wood, the woman with whom Griswold had lived.[38] This kind of reference tells us little about the nature of the relationship involved, but we do get a sense of acceptance of couple relationships within the women's rights movement.

A second important phenomenon found in the women's rights movement—the charismatic leader who attracted intense devotion—also adds to our understanding of the complexity of women's relationships. Alice Paul, the founder and leading light of the National Woman's Party, inspired devotion that bordered on worship. One woman even addressed her as "My Beloved Deity."[39] But, contrary to both the ideal type of the charismatic leader and the portrait of Paul as it exists now in historical scholarship, Paul maintained close relationships with a number of women she had first met in the suffrage struggle.[40] Paul's correspondence in the

National Woman's Party papers does not reveal much about the nature of her relationships, but it does make it clear that her friendships provided love and support for her work.

It is true that many of the expressions of love, admiration, and devotion addressed to Paul seem to have been one-sided, from awe-struck followers, but this is not the only side of the story. Paul maintained close friendships with a number of women discussed earlier who lived in couple relationships with other women. She had met Mabel Vernon when they attended Swarthmore College together, and they maintained contact throughout the years, despite Vernon's departure from the Woman's Party in the 1930s.[41] Of Alice Morgan Wright, she said that, when they first met, they ". . . just became sisters right away."[42] Jeannette Marks regularly sent her love to "dear Alice" until a conflict in the Woman's Party ruptured their relationship.[43] Other women, too, enjoyed a closer relationship than the formal work-related one for which Paul is so well known.

Paul obviously cared deeply, for example, for her old friend Nina Allender, the cartoonist of the suffrage movement. Allender, who lived alone in Chicago, wrote to Paul in 1947 of her memories of their long association: "No words can tell you what that [first] visit grew to mean to me & to my life. . . . I feel now as I did then—only more intensely—I have never changed or doubted—but have grown more inspired as the years have gone by. . . . There is no use going into words. I believe them to be unnecessary between us."[44] Paul wrote that she thought of Allender often and sent her "devoted love."[45] She worried about Allender's loneliness and gently encouraged her to come to Washington to live at Belmont House, the Woman's Party headquarters, where she would be surrounded by loving friends who appreciated the work she had done for the women's movement.[46] Paul failed to persuade her to move, however. Two years later Paul responded to a request from Allender's niece for help with the cost of a nursing home with a hundred-dollar check and a promise to contact others who might be able to help.[47] But Allender died within a month at the age of eighty-five.

Paul does not seem to have formed an intimate relationship with any one woman, but she did live and work within a close-knit female world. When in Washington, she lived, at least some of the time, at Belmont House; when away she lived either alone or with her sister, Helen Paul, and later with her lifelong friend Elsie Hill. It is clear that Alice Paul's ties—whether to her sister or to close friends or to admirers—served as a bond that knit the Woman's Party together. That Paul and her network could also tear the movement asunder is obvious from the stormy history of the Woman's Party.[48]

Alice Paul is not the only example of a leader who inspired love and devotion among women in the movement. One senses from Marjory Lacey-Baker's comment, quoted above—that "newly met members in hero-worshipping mood" wrote to Lena Madesin Phillips after every BPW convention—that Phillips too had a charismatic aura. But the best and most thoroughly documented example of a charismatic leader is Anna Lord Strauss of the League of Women Voters, an organization that in the post-1945 years distanced itself from women's rights.

Strauss, the great-granddaughter of Lucretia Mott, came from an old and wealthy family; she was prominent and respected, a staunch liberal who rejected the label of "feminist." She never married and her papers leave no evidence of intimate relationships outside her family. Yet Strauss was the object of some very strong feelings on the part of the women with whom she worked. She, like Alice Paul and Madesin Phillips, received numerous hero-worshipping letters from awe-struck followers. But in her case we also have evidence that some of her coworkers fell deeply in love with her. It is hard to know how the women discussed here would have interpreted their relationship with Strauss. The two women who expressed their feelings explicitly were both married women, and in one case Strauss obviously had a cordial relationship with the woman's husband and children. Yet there can be no question that this League officer fell in love with Strauss. She found Strauss "the finest human being I had ever known" and knowing her "the most beautiful and profound experience I have ever had."[49] Loving Strauss—she asked permission to say it—made the earth move and "the whole landscape of human affairs and nature" take on a new appearance.[50] Being with Strauss made "the tone and fiber" of her day different; although she could live without her, she could see no reason for having to prove it all the time.[51] She tried to "ration and control" her thoughts of Strauss, but it was small satisfaction.[52] When Strauss was recovering from an operation, this woman wrote: "I love you! I can't imagine the world without you. . . . I love you. I need you."[53]

Although our picture of this relationship is completely one-sided—for Strauss did not keep copies of most of her letters—it is clear that Strauss did not respond to such declarations of love. This woman urged Strauss to accept her and what she had to say without "the slightest sense of needing to be considerate of me because I feel as I do." She understood the "unilateral character" of her feelings, and insisted that she had more than she deserved by simply knowing Strauss at all.[54] But her hurt, and her growing suspicion that Strauss shunned intimacy, escaped on occasion. She asked: "And how would it hurt you to let someone tell you sometime how beautiful—how wonderful you are? Did you ever let anyone have a decent chance to try?"[55] She realized that loving someone did not always make things easier—that sometimes, in fact, it made life more of a struggle—but she believed that to withdraw from love was to withdraw from life. In what appears to have been a hastily written note, she expressed her understanding—an understanding that obviously gave her both pain and comfort—that Strauss was not perfect after all: "Way back there in the crow's nest (or at some such time) you decided not to become embroiled in any intimate human relationship, except those you were, by birth, committed to. I wonder. . . . There is something you haven't mastered. Something you've been afraid of after all."[56]

This woman's perception that Strauss avoided intimacy is confirmed elsewhere in Strauss's papers. One old friend was struck, in 1968, by Strauss's ability to "get your feelings out and down on paper!" She continued: "I know you so well that I consider this great progress in your own inner state of mental health. It is far from easy for you to express your feelings. . . ."[57] This aspect of Strauss's personality fits with the ideal type of the charismatic leader. The other case of a woman falling in love with Strauss that emerges clearly from her papers reinforces this picture. This woman, also a League officer, wrote in circuitous fashion of her intense pleasure at receiving Strauss's picture. In what was certainly a reference to lesbianism, she wrote that she hoped Strauss would not think that she was "one of those who had never outgrown the emotional extravaganzas of the adolescent." Before she got down to League business, she added:

> But, Darling, as I softly close the door on all this—as I should and as I want to—and as I must since all our meetings are likely to be formal ones in a group—as I go back in the office correspondence to "Dear Miss Strauss" and "Sincerely Yours," . . . as I put myself as much as possible in the background at our March meeting in order to share you with the others who have not been with you as I have—as all these things happen, I want you to be very certain that what is merely under cover is still there—as it most surely will be—and that if all the hearts in the room could be exposed there'd be few, I'm certain, that would love you more than . . . [I].[58]

Apparently Strauss never responded to this letter, for a month later, this woman apologized for writing it: "I have had qualms, dear Anna, about that letter I wrote you. (You knew I would eventually of course!)." Continuing in a vein that reinforces the previously quoted perception of Strauss's inability to be intimate, she wrote of imagining the "recoil . . . embarrassment, self-consciousness and general discomfort" her letter must have provoked in such a "reserved person." She admitted that the kind of admiration she had expressed, "at least in certain classes of relationships (of which mine to you is one)—becomes a bit of moral wrong-doing."[59] She felt ashamed and asked forgiveness.

What is clear is that this was a momentous and significant relationship to at least one of the parties. Almost twenty years later, this woman wrote of her deep disappointment in missing Strauss's visit to her city. She had allowed herself to dream that she could persuade Strauss to stay with her awhile, even though she knew that others would have prior claims on Strauss's time. She wrote:

I have not seen you since that day in Atlantic City when you laid the gavel of the League of Women Voters down. . . . I do not look back on that moment of ending with any satisfaction for my own behavior, for I passed right by the platform on which you were still standing talking with one of the last persons left in the room and shyness at the thought of expressing my deep feeling about your going—and the fact that you were talking with someone else led me to pass on without even a glance in your direction as I remember though you made some move to speak to me! . . . But if I gave you a hurt it is now a very old one and forgotten, I'm sure—as well as understood.[60]

Whatever the interpretation these two women would have devised to explain their feelings for Strauss, it is clear that the widely shared devotion to this woman leader could sometimes grow into something more intense. Strauss's reserve and her inability to express her feelings may or may not have had anything to do with her own attitude toward intimate relationships between women. One tantalizing letter from a friend about to be married suggests that Strauss's decision not to marry had been made early: "I remember so well your answer when I pressed you, once, on why you had never married. . . . Well, it is very true, one does not marry unless one can see no other life."[61] A further fragment, consisting of entries in the diary of Doris Stevens—a leading suffragist who took a sharp swing to the right in the interwar period—suggests that at least some individuals suspected Strauss of lesbianism. Stevens, by this time a serious redbaiter and, from the evidence quoted here, a "queerbaiter" as well, apparently called a government official in 1953 to report that Strauss was "not a bit interested in men."[62] She seemed to be trying to discredit Strauss, far too liberal for her tastes, with a charge of "unorthodox morals."[63]

Stevens had her suspicions about other women as well. She recorded in her diary a conversation with a National Woman's Party member about Jeannette Marks and Mary Woolley, noting that the member, who had attended Wellesley with Marks, "Discreetly indicated there was 'talk.' "[64] At another point she reported a conversation with a different Woman's Party member who had grown disillusioned about Alice Paul. Stevens noted that her informant related "weird goings on at Wash. hedquts wherein it was clear she thought Paul a devotee of Lesbos & afflicted with Jeanne d'Arc identification."[65] Along the same lines, the daughter of a woman who had left the National Woman's Party complained that Alice Paul and another leader had sent her mother a telegram that "anybody with sense" would think "was from two people who were adolesant [sic] or from two who had imbied [sic] too much or else Lesbians to a Lesbian."[66]

Such comments suggest that the intensity of women's relationships and the existence and acceptance of couple relationships in women's organizations had the potential, particularly during the McCarthy years, to attract denunciation. Doris Stevens herself wrote to the viciously right-wing and anti-Semitic columnist Westbrook Pegler to "thank you for knowing I'm not a queerie" despite the fact that she considered herself a feminist.[67] Although the association between feminism and lesbianism was not new in the 1950s, the McCarthyite connection between political deviance and homosexuality seemed to fuel suspicion.[68] How real the threat was for women is suggested by two further incidents involving opposition to the appointment of women, both described in the memoirs of India Edwards, a top woman in the Truman administration.[69]

In 1948, opposition to tax court judge Marion Harron's reappointment to the bench arose from Harron's fellow judges, who cited her lack of judicial temperament and "unprovable charges of an ethical nature." Although Edwards did not specify the nature of the charges, we know from *The Life of Lorena Hickok* that Harron had written letters to "E. R.'s friend" that even Doris Faber had to admit were love letters. The other case that Edwards described left no doubt about what ethical and moral charges were involved. When Truman appointed Kathryn McHale, long-time executive director of the American Association of University Women, to the Subversive Activities Control Board, Senator Pat McCarran advised Truman to withdraw her name and threatened to hold public hearings during which "information would be brought out that she was a lesbian."

On the whole, though, the feminists who lived in couple relationships managed to do so respectably, despite the emergence of a lesbian culture and the occasional charges of lesbianism. This was because they worked independently or in professional jobs, had the money to buy homes together, and enjoyed enough status to be beyond reproach in the world in which they moved. Women who later identified as lesbians but did not attach an identity to their emotions and behaviors in the 1950s describe that period as one in which women might live together without raising any eyebrows, but it is important to remember that even the class privilege that protected couple relationships would not necessarily suffice if women sought to enter powerful male-dominated institutions.[70]

What exactly should we make of all this? In one way it is terribly frustrating to have such tantalizingly ambiguous glimpses into women's lives. In another way, it is exciting to find out so much about women's lives in the past. I think it is enormously important not to read into these relationships what we want to find, or what we think we should find. At the same time, we cannot dismiss what little evidence we have as insufficient when it is all we have; nor can we continue to contribute to the conspiracy of silence that urges us to ignore what is not perfectly straightforward. Thus, although it is tempting to try to speculate about the relationships I have described here in order to impose some analysis on them, I would rather simply lay them out, fragmentary as they are, in order to suggest a conceptual approach that recognizes the complexities of the issue.

It is clear, I think, that none of these relationships can be easily categorized. There were women who lived their entire adult lives in couple relationships with other women, and married women who fell in love with other women. Were they lesbians? Probably they would be shocked to be identified in that way. Alice Paul, for example, spoke scornfully of *Ms.* magazine as "all about homosexuality and so on."[71] Another woman who lived in a couple relationship distinguished between the (respectable) women involved in the ERA struggle in the old days and the "lesbians and bra-burners" of the contemporary movement.[72] Sasha Lewis, in *Sunday's Women*, reported an incident we would do well to remember here. One of her informants, a lesbian, went to Florida to work against Anita Bryant and stayed with an older cousin who had lived for years in a marriagelike relationship with another woman. When Lewis's informant saw the way the two women lived—sharing everything, including a bedroom—she remarked about the danger of Bryant's campaign for their lives. They were aghast that she would think them lesbians, since, they said, they did not do anything sexual together.[73] If even women who chose to share beds with other women would reject the label "lesbian," what about the married women, or the women who avoided intimate relationships?

What is critical here, I would argue, is that these women lived at a time during which some women *did* identify as lesbians. The formation of a lesbian identity, from both an individual and historical perspective, is enormously significant. So far, most of the historical debate over the use of the term "lesbian" has focused on earlier periods.[74] Passionate love between women has existed, but it has not always been named. Since it *has* been named in the twentieth century, and since there *was* such a thing as a lesbian culture, we need to distinguish between women who identify as lesbians and/or who are part of a lesbian culture, where one exists, and a broader category of women-committed women who would not identify as lesbians but whose primary commitment, in emotional and practical terms, was to other women. There is an important difference between, on the one hand, butch-fem couples in the 1950s who committed what Joan Nestle has aptly called an act of "sexual courage" by openly proclaiming the erotic aspect of their relationships, and, on the other, couples like Eleanor Roosevelt and Lorena Hickok or Alma Lutz and Marguerite Smith.[75]

We know that identity and sexual behavior are not the same thing.[76] There are lesbians who have never had a sexual relationship with another woman and there are women who have had sexual experiences with women but do not identify as lesbians. This is not to suggest that there is no difference between women who loved each other and lived together but did not make love (although even that can be difficult to define, since sensuality and sexuality, "physical contact" and "sexual contact" have no distinct boundaries) and those who did. But sexual behavior—something about which we rarely have historical evidence anyway—is only one of a number of relevant factors in a relationship. Blanche Cook has said everything that needs to be said about the inevitable question of evidence: "Genital 'proofs' to confirm lesbianism are never required to confirm the heterosexuality of men and women who live together for twenty, or fifty, years." Cook reminds us of the publicized relationship of General Eisenhower and Kay Summersby during the Second World War: They "were passionately involved with each other. . . . They were inseparable. But they never 'consummated' their love in the acceptable, traditional, sexual manner. Now does that fact render Kay Summersby and Dwight David Eisenhower somehow less in love? Were they not heterosexual?"[77]

At this point, I think, the best we can do as historians is to describe carefully and sensitively what we do know about a woman's relationships, keeping in mind both the historical development of a lesbian identity (Did such a thing as a lesbian identity exist? Was there a lesbian culture?) and the individual process that we now identify as "coming out" (Did a woman feel attachment to another woman or women? Did she act on this feeling in some positive way? Did she recognize the existence of other women with the same commitment? Did she express solidarity with those women?). Using this approach allows us to make distinctions among women's relationships in the past—intimate friendships, supportive relationships growing out of common political work, couple relationships—without denying their significance or drawing fixed boundaries. We can recognize the importance of friendships among a group of women who, like Alma Lutz, Marguerite Smith, Mabel Vernon, Consuelo Reyes, Alice Morgan Wright, and Edith Goode built a community of women but did not identify it as a lesbian community. We can do justice to both the woman-committed woman who would angrily reject any suggestion of lesbianism and the self-identified lesbian without distorting their common experiences.

This approach does not solve all the problems of dealing with women's relationships in the past, but it is a beginning. The greatest problem remains the weakness of sources. Not only have women who loved women in the past been wisely reluctant to leave evidence of their relationships for the prying eyes of a homophobic society, but what evidence they did leave was often suppressed or destroyed.[78] Furthermore, as the three books discussed at the beginning show, even the evidence saved and brought to light can be savagely misinterpreted.

How do we know if a woman felt attachment, acted on it, recognized the existence of other women like her, or expressed solidarity? There is no easy answer to this, but it is revealing, I think, that both Doris Faber and Anna Mary Wells are fairly certain that Lorena Hickok and Jeannette Marks, respectively, did have "homosexual tendencies" (although Faber insists that even Hickok cannot fairly be placed in the "contemporary gay category"), even if the admirable figures in each book, Eleanor Roosevelt and Mary Woolley, certainly did not. That is, both of these authors, as hard as they try to deny lesbianism, find evidence that forces them to discuss it, and both cope by pinning the "blame" on the women they paint as unpleasant—fat, ugly, pathetic Lorena Hickok and nasty, tortured, arrogant Jeannette Marks.

So we present what evidence we have, being careful to follow Linda Gordon's advice and "listen quietly and intently" to the women who speak to us from the sources.[79] In the case of twentieth-century history, we may also have the opportunity to listen to women speak in the flesh. We may privately believe that all the evidence suggests that a woman was a lesbian, but what do we do if she insisted, either explicitly or implicitly, that she was not? That is why the process of coming out is so important to us as historians. In a world in which some women claimed a lesbian identity and built lesbian communities, the choice to reject that identification has a meaning of its own. It is imperative that we not deny the reality of any woman's historical experience by blurring the distinctions among different kinds of choices. At the same time, recognition of the common bond of commitment to women shared by diverse women throughout history strengthens our struggle against those who attempt to divide and defeat us.

MIGRANCY AND MALE SEXUALITY ON THE SOUTH AFRICAN GOLD MINES

◆

T. DUNBAR MOODIE (WITH VIVIENNE NDATSHE AND BRITISH SIBUYI)

Virtually no work has appeared on the history of homosexuality anywhere in sub-Saharan Africa, let alone in South Africa, and some would claim that there is no history to be written. But the field of southern African history in general is burgeoning, resulting in a richly textured reconstruction of the cultures of black resistance to white exploitation on the mines and farms of that troubled land. Moodie makes an unprecedented contribution to that field as well as to gay history in this social history of homosexual relations on the mines.

Sometimes exploitative, often mutually rewarding, homosexual relations in the mining compounds were familiar to miners, company officials, and missionaries alike. They were also highly organized: "Mine marriages" were governed by strict conventions, whose terms were enforced by black and white mine officials alike, each recognizing ways in which they served their differing purposes. Moodie shows how some men used the system of mine marriages to supplement their incomes and resist the pressures toward urbanization and proletarianization; he suggests homosexuality has declined on the mines in recent years because of changes in the relationship between town and countryside and in the structure of family life. Moodie's subtle analysis of the social/political context and the power dynamics of mine relationships reminds us of the critical importance of such contextualization. His evidence also makes one wonder if some of the "men" in mine marriages stayed in the urban areas

411

precisely because the social conditions obtaining there—unlike those in the villages, where heterosexual marriage was the cornerstone of a man's economic status—made it possible for them to create and sustain such relationships.

This paper deals with the sexual conduct of black migrant workers on the South African gold mines. The argument is framed by Foucault's suggestion that our manner of defining the psychological character of individuals in terms of their sexual preferences is a recent phenomenon. Thus the psychoanalytic conception of "homosexuality" is an invention rather than a discovery. The paper also follows Foucault[1] in demonstrating the impossibility, at least in the case of black miners, of sensibly discussing sexuality outside the context of power relations.

The first part of the paper is a descriptive analysis, a phenomenology, of male sexual experience on the mines. It deals first with miners' sexual relationships with "boys," known as "the wives of the mine." The second part is more diachronic, depicting with a very broad brush the argument that for junior partners in certain of the men-boy relationships, sexual subordination was actually used as a resource in the long-standing resistance by migrant miners to proletarianization. Proletarianization, however, as it has eventually come to the gold mines, has had sexual implications which help to reinforce rejection of migrancy by contemporary black miners and their wives.

It is very important to stress the tentative nature of the conclusions reached herein. Discussion of "mine marriages," for instance, depends on material collected by Vivienne Ndatshe[2] in a remarkable series of life histories from old men in Pondoland and an interview with a single Tsonga individual by British Sibuyi.[3] These are recollections dating from the 1930s, 1940s, and 1950s. While rather scanty archival evidence confirms these accounts and thus enables us to generalize with some certainty, most such written material dates from an earlier period (1900–1920).

Thus, while the account offered here conforms to the evidence available to me, it is presented as an initial foray into a complex and sensitive area. It might well be modified and amplified by further enquiry, especially by more intensive interviewing. Meanwhile, this paper represents a tentative socio-historical analysis of a very delicate but often avoided aspect of the lives not only of black miners but of all men and women everywhere—that is the relationship of sexual desire and social and personal power.

Note: This essay was written for this volume, but was originally published, in somewhat different form, in *Journal of Southern African Studies* 14 (January 1988): Vol. 14, no. 2, 228–56. Used with permission.

"Wives of the Mine"

In February, 1987, in the Bushbuckridge area, British Sibuyi interviewed an old Tsonga man,[4] one Philemon, who had worked on the
mines from the late 1940s to the early 1960s. This man told him of what
he called *tinkonkana* or "wives [used interchangeably with "boys"] on
the mine." His account went as follows:

> On the mines there were compounds which consisted of houses, each
> of which had a *xibonda*[5] inside. Each of these *xibondas* would propose
> a boy for himself, not only for the sake of washing his dishes, because
> in the evening the boy would have to go and join the *xibonda* on his
> bed. In that way he had become a wife. He [the "husband"] would
> "double his join" [stay twelve months instead of the normal six] on the
> mines because of this boy. He would "make love" with him. The
> "husband" would penetrate his manhood between the boy's thighs.
> You would find a man buying a bicycle for his boy. He would buy him
> many pairs of trousers, shirts and many blankets.

In important particulars this story summarizes many other accounts
mentioned in interviews with Mpondo mine workers and scattered through
the archival records under the heading of "unnatural vice."[6] First, the
sexual activity itself hardly ever involves anal penetration but rather takes
place externally through "the satisfaction of sexual passions by action
between the thighs."[7] This is typical of a form of sexual play common
amongst adolescent Nguni boys and girls called *metsha* among Xhosa-
speakers and *hlobongo* by the Zulu. Moreover, these young "boys" of
the miners are not merely sexual partners, but are also "wives" in other
ways, providing domestic services for their "husbands" in exchange for
substantial remuneration. Second, "homosexual" relations on the mines
seem to take place almost exclusively between senior men (men with
power in the mine structure) and younger men. There is in fact an entire
set of rules, an *mteto*, governing this type of relationship, whose parameters are well known and enforced by black mine authorities.

My discussion of "mine marriages" will be structured around an expansion of these two points.

"Men" and "Boys"

Amongst the traditional Xhosa, *metsha* is the most common form of
erotic activity prior to marriage. According to the Mayers,[8] it is fundamental to peer group socialization. Premarital sexual play is expected and
indeed prescribed among young persons, but premarital pregnancy incurs
disabilities in the adult world and "instant complete exclusion from the
pleasures of the youth organization." The expectation is thus that tradi-

tional young unmarried Nguni couples will practice precisely that mode of external sexual activity that we found described by Philemon for "mine marriages." In 1907, H. M. Taberer, at that time in the Transvaal Native Affairs Department, investigated missionary charges of endemic "unnatural vice" in the compounds (in the wake of a furor about Chinese "catamites"). He reported that *metsha* sexual practices were very common among Mozambican mine workers but that "actual sodomy is very rare and is generally looked upon with disgust"[9] even by Mozambicans. In 1916 a Compound Manager told the Boksburg Native Inspector that he had recently seen heavily scented young Mozambicans at a dance "wearing imitation breasts." He noticed that they had greased themselves heavily in the crotch and asserted "that a great deal of what goes on is *hlobongo* [Zulu for *metsha*] and not the other."[10] When in 1928, the Transkeian Territories General Council moved that a delegation of senior councillors be sent to the Witwatersrand compounds to lecture Xhosa mine workers on the evils of "immoral practices obtaining among laborers working on the mines,"[11] the delegation was informed by the director of Native Labor, H. S. Cooke, that the immorality that did occur was in the form of *inkotshane*. He continued that "except that the subject was a male and not a female it took the form of what is known amongst Transkeian Natives as *ukemetsha* which, when girls were concerned, was to some extent condoned by Native Custom."[12]

One old Mpondo was indeed quite open with Vivienne Ndatshe about his affairs on the mines:

> There were boss boys who liked boys. I did that once myself. There were boys who looked like women—fat and attractive. My "girlfriend" was a Basuto young lad. I did not ill-treat him as other boss boys did. I was very nice to him.

He smiled while talking to Ms. Ndatshe about this matter and asked her not to tell others at his home. She promised not to and asked him why he got involved with the boy. He replied:

> First, miners were not allowed to go and visit women in the township.[13] Also I felt very lonely for all the long period without meeting a woman. Because of boredom I needed someone to be with me. I was not doing that in public—not in the room but in the old section underground where people no longer worked. I proposed love to him in the compound—called on him in our spare time. I did promise to give him some of my pay, but not all of it as others did. Then he agreed. I warned him that everything was our secret because I did not want my home boys to know that I was doing that as they might tell people at home or girlfriends in the country. I loved that boy very much.

Ms. Ndatshe asked whether the Sotho youngster didn't have feelings himself when they slept together. The response was revealing about the expectations of "men":

He had quick feelings, but he had to control himself as he was my girlfriend. I loved him because he was a very quiet person. Other miners didn't notice at all. They were proposing love to him in my presence. If they had known, they would never have done that because there would be trouble. We parted as we left for our homes. We didn't write to each other. It was only friendship on the mines.

Although these relationships for the Mpondo seldom extended beyond one contract and were never brought home[14] ("it was only friendship on the mines"), and although men preferred to conceal these liaisons from their home fellows, everyone knew that such affairs existed and joked with each other about them. Young men en route to the mines in 1976 were told jokingly that they would become "girlfriends of the Shangaans."[15] According to Ndatshe, old men, long since retired from the mines, sit around at beer drinks in Pondoland and talk of men who wanted to make love to them. They laugh because they know that "among us there were those who practiced it."

Similar feelings were expressed as early as the turn of the century by Junod of the Tsonga:[16] "The immense majority of the Natives themselves do not consider this sin as of any importance at all. They speak of it with laughter." At home in Pondoland, however, people do not admit openly to it, "because it was a disgrace." According to Philip Mayer, a similar ambivalence prevails among the traditional Xhosa about extramarital affairs with married women at home. Everyone knows it goes on, but one is expected to be discreet about it.[17] Even among the Tsonga, said Philemon, "the elders would not talk about it because it was taboo. It's just like now, son. If you had a wife, surely you would not tell me what you do with your wife behind doors."

Testimony is divided over the extent of public knowledge of these affairs on the mines themselves. One of the reasons it is difficult to pin down exactly how much is known is because young men are expected to serve their elders anyway and may do so without sexual exchanges. Also, people choose not to interfere in such matters. In 1976, an induna[18] explained:

What is public knowledge is that it goes on. Otherwise, the culprits keep it scrupulously discreet. One does notice unnatural closeness and attentiveness, for example one may walk into an otherwise empty room and discover a couple talking in undertones. I know this, myself. What I do is discreetly withdraw. It comes out into the open . . . when disaffection sets in. But we all know it takes place.

Indeed, the indunas enforce the monetary aspects of such agreements. Observers[19] in 1976 reported that "those who are engaged in this business know each other, give advice to each other and help each other pay the . . . boys in due time and accordingly." There is then a code of behavior with regard to "mine marriages," and despite different intensities of management opposition to these relationships in different periods, the code and its enforcement seem to have been little changed.

Certain rooms specialized in these relationships. One of the Sotho-speaking participant observers[20] found himself in such a room, where all but two of the inmates slept in pairs (one of the other two slept out), and they spoke of fellow miners as of women. There was much talk of "marriage" in the room, and when they got drunk men kissed each other openly. They were quite discreet outside the room, however. Even within the room, Philemon reported that "people would not make love when others were still conversing in the evening—they would wait for everybody to 'sleep.' "

"Mine marriage," then, implied more than casual sex underground or in the rooms. These relationships were supposed to be exclusive, and hence "men" might sometimes fight over attractive "boys." For instance, a certain Mpondo when he was senior enough, wanted to have his own "boy." This he did at Luipaardsvlei, where he was a boss boy. "He had a young Xhosa boy from Ciskei. He was paying him, but not all his money, without knowing that he had another man. He was nearly stabbed by the man." Another Mpondo said that as a "boy," he was not able to get a woman in town "because my man was very jealous." Whenever sexual infidelity by "boys" took place, not the "wife" but the older initiating seducer would be blamed and often assaulted.

The older men paid their "wives" generously for their services,[21] which often went well beyond the merely sexual. According to Taberer's report:[22]

> An *inkotshane*'s duty appears to be to fetch water, cook food and do any odd work or run messages for his master and at night time to be available as bedfellow. In return for these services the *inkotshane* is well fed and paid, presents and luxuries are lavished upon him. . . .

Philemon, the Tsonga informant, explained how "mine marriages" were built into the everyday social lives of at least "Shangaan" compound dwellers. On the weekends, for instance:

> People from different houses would bring money together and then buy things like tea and bread (which were considered to be luxuries) and eat together. "Husbands" would bring along their wives. Also, when somebody was leaving the mines forever, farewell parties would be made where workers from different houses would come together. . . . The boys would make the tea when the "husbands" were seated around the tables. . . .

As part of their normal duties, boys "would wash and iron their husbands' clothes and pack everything neatly. They did not wait to be told because it was their job." Philemon, who continues to work as a migrant but now has a room in town, was mildly nostalgic for the advantages of "mine marriage."

> It's unlike now when you spend all your money buying clothes and giving money to your wife with whom you are not even staying. That's somehow a loss of money. I mean who does not even wash your vest, while with those it was better because evenings were for "legs."

Indeed, mine "wives" took on the behavior of women or servants in their relations with their "spouses." Thus among the Tsonga "the boy [would] tell his 'hubby' if ever he was going away, say home or to the shops . . . and, if the 'hubby' had time, he would also come along." Furthermore, "he would not just stand up and say it. He had to say goodbye or any other thing when in a kneeling position." The boys would "gossip, just like women . . . perhaps discussing things like 'my husband bought me this' or 'my husband is good for this and that . . .' And if a husband was stingy he would also come under discussion." The Tsonga were less secretive than members of other groups.

> "Wives" were also expected to "look feminine" [according to Philemon]. They would get pieces of clothing material and they would sew it together so that it appeared like real breasts. They would then attach it to other strings that make it look almost like a bra so that at the evening dancing "she" would dance with the "husband." I mean it would appear very real. Don't forget that guys used to play guitars there . . . [Another] thing that a *nkonkana* had to do was either to cover his beard with a clothing material or had to cut it completely off. He was now so-and-so's wife. How would it sound if a "couple" looked identical! There had to be differences and for a *nkonkana* to stay clean shaven was one of them. Once the *nkonkana* became a "grown-up" he could then keep his beard to indicate his maturity, which would be demonstrated by him acquiring a boy.

In their sexual relations, too, the young men were expected to behave with womanly decorum. Consider the Sotho "wife" mentioned in the account given above, who might have wished to respond ardently to his Mpondo husband, but who, as the "husband" expressed it, "had to control himself because he was my girlfriend." The Tsonga informant expanded on such hints, saying, "Don't forget, the boy would never make a mistake of 'breathing out' into the 'hubby.' It was taboo. Only the 'hubby' could 'breathe out' into the boy's legs."

The implication is inescapable. Proper "wifely" sexual behavior was essentially passive, at least receptive rather than intrusive. Boys might "wish they were so-and-so's wife . . ., for the sake of security, for the acquisition of property . . ., and for the fun itself," but they were certainly subordinate, both socially and sexually. Although the relationships might end in "divorce" after a quarrel or upon returning home, there was also a "natural" point at which they could be terminated. As the boy became "old enough," he might "wish to start his own family" on the mine, becoming the senior partner. Nor could his partner refuse him that right, according to the Tsonga custom:

> As long as you are old enough there would be no problem. I mean that was the way of life. You would just have to explain that you are experiencing some biological problems at night. [It was not possible for the boy to penetrate the *sibonda*, only the *sibonda* could.] You would then have to wait for newcomers . . .

There was thus a "biological" period (somewhere in his middle twenties, it would seem, but also depending on the extent of one's mine experience), when a "boy" would become a man, unable to endure any longer his nonejaculatory sexual role. That would be the end of it for the "marriage." Thus men who were sexually active with senior men in their youth themselves took boys when they became "boss" boys themselves. If the dominant mores of white society decreed that all black men, even senior mine employees, were "boys," black workers themselves graduated from being "boys" for their fellow workers to being "men" with their own "boys" as they gained mine experience. Indeed, the entire system of "mine marriages" was thoroughly interwoven with the power structure of the mines themselves.

The Rules of "Mine Marriage" (Mteto ka Sokisi)

The parallels between the social organization of male sexuality on the mines and social formations at home are very striking. Bantu-speaking communities are not only patriarchal, but also gerontocratic, organized on principles of seniority. Without respect for elders the entire fabric of traditional Bantu-speaking societies would begin to unravel. In the words of the Mayers, "Respect for seniority is essentially the same as respect for law as against mere force."[23] Principles of seniority on the mines coincided to a considerable extent with age and status in the home societies, and they governed sexual relations in both locales. Junod[24] wrote in 1904, of how such affairs were part of compound authority structure:

> When a gang of new workers arrives in a Compound, the Native induna, who has the supervision of the Compound, and the Native policemen, who have their rooms at the entrance of the yard, come and *humutsha* i.e., make proposals to the younger ones, not only to little boys (there are only a few of these) but also to boys up to the age of twenty or more. If these lads consent to become their *bakontshana*, they will be treated with greater kindness than the others. Their husbands will give them ten shillings to woo them (*buta*) and will choose them easy occupations. . . .

Furthermore, Junod suggests that where the authority structure of the compound stops, the indigenous seniority principle takes over. Those who have not been propositioned by the mine police "will probably receive a similar proposal from their older companions in the mine," who will then aid them at work.

Amongst the Tsonga (Shangaans, Mozambicans), then, the practice of "mine marriage" was firmly entrenched in the authority structure *on the compound*. Transgressions against the rules governing such relationships were dealt with in the indunas' courts. For other language groups on the mines, although indunas would certainly hear cases connected with transgressions of what all called *mteto ka Sokisi*,[25] the black authority structure *underground* seems to have been more important in the establishment of these socio-sexual practices. Testimony is universal for all periods including the present that black Team Leaders (ironically called boss "boys" in the past) would come down especially hard on youngsters with whom they were "in love," letting up only when the boys succumbed to them. An old Mpondo described the situation in his youth as follows:

> On the first week he nearly ran away. It was very difficult to *layisha* (load) and the boss boy was really pushing him and told him, "you will agree." First he didn't understand what he was talking about and he asked another old man why the boss boy was so cruel to him. The old man laughed at him. He told him that the boss boy was after him as he was young and fat.

Since the mine compounds were "ethnically" segregated but work teams were always integrated, the work situation was the place where cross-ethnic sexual relationships would have been initiated. Indeed, because among groups other than Mozambicans, "homosexual" patterns were less well established, boss boys apparently sought out partners from other groups than their own. At any rate, blacks with authority in the work situation would have been the ones who spearheaded the spread of "mine marriages" across "ethnic" lines.

The parallels between the initiation of "mine marriages" and certain types of marriages at home, at least among some Nguni peoples, are too striking to leave unnoted. Philip Mayer[26] reports that among traditional Bomvana and Gcaleka Xhosa, the majority of marriages are *thwala* marriages, arranged by the father without consulting the woman or sometimes even her mother. Even as women who have been through *thwala* may comfort themselves with the reflection that their husbands are good to them and send money regularly so that they can build up the homestead, so also the young men who agreed to be "wives of the mine" could say they did so for the money or the gifts, adding wryly "why should we worry since we cannot get pregnant." One Mpondo man told Vivienne Ndatshe that when he started at Daggafontein Mine in 1940, his "boss boy, who was a Xhosa, treated [him] very nicely because he was in love with [him]." This man offered him all his wages. He agreed because he was "on business" at the mine. He "needed money desperately as [he] wanted to buy cattle and pay lobola for [his] wife and build [his] *umzi* [homestead]." Some boys reportedly had two or three lovers "which was very dangerous because these men might kill one another." They took chances because "they only did that for money."

So men became "wives" on the mines in order to become husbands and therefore full "men" more rapidly at home. Even as in *thwala* marriages among the Xhosa, attraction was necessarily on only one side in the beginning, although in both cases affectionate mutuality might grow. Also in both cases, at least amongst the Mpondo, the junior partner bore the indignity partly out of sheer physical necessity and partly out of interest in "building an *umzi*"—the true goal to which every traditionalist Xhosa-speaker aspired.[27]

Senior partners in the "mine marriage" system were presumably quite well established at home by the time they undertook the responsibility of having a "boy" of their own—or they were *tshipa*, men who had absconded from country ways and become creatures of the mines and townships. At any rate, becoming a "husband" on the mines was one of the accoutrements of seniority in the mine system, a perquisite of success in the mine world, making somewhat more comfortable the hardships of the migrant life. Certainly, that was the way the Tsonga saw it—and that seems also to have been the Mpondo point of view.

It is important to stress, however, that "wives of the mine" were not the only options for sexual relations open to black miners. Compounds on the gold mines were never closed, unlike the diamond mines, so men who wished to leave on afternoons or weekends could always do so with a simple "permission slip" from a clerk at the gate. Indeed old miners report traversing the Rand to visit friends from home working on other distant mines. Another important reason for leaving the mine was to visit women in town. These "town women"[28] often entered into fairly long-term liaisons with miners, serving them alcohol and providing sexual services in exchange for gifts, monetary or otherwise. One old Mpondo who had been a mine "wife" in his early years reported:

> I had an induna as my best friend who took me to the township. Again I had a boy, and the induna had one too. In the township we both had girlfriends. We left the boys in the compound when we went to town, but we never spent the night in the township. We just spent a few hours with our girlfriends and then returned to our boys. We loved them better.

It is important to remember that this man, when Ms. Ndatshe interviewed him, was married and living in an *umzi* in the country with his wife and family. Why did he prefer "boys" during his earlier years on the mines?

That being so, why did he seek a town girlfriend at all? What does he mean when he says that they "loved [their boys] better"?

On the basis of the statements of other migrants, part of the answer seems to lie in a deep-seated fear of "town women." Some of this is the simple and quite legitimate apprehension of being robbed. Several of the old men with town lovers asserted that they dared not go to sleep lest their pockets be picked. Others feared venereal disease. A deeper fear than any of these, I believe, was that of losing one's rural identity. The attractions of town women might seduce one into forgetting one's home, absconding, becoming *tshipa*, or in Sotho *lekholoa*, "the one who stays a long time on the mines." After all, in a society where rural marriage established an economic base for retirement the dangers of going *tshipa* were the subject of many a cautionary tale. "Mine wives," after all, would always eventually "grow up" and become men so that there was a natural limit to "mine marriage," a biological terminus, as it were. Furthermore, women might have children, with all the responsibilities implied in African society by that fact.

Also important was the stability of "mine marriage"—its integration into a well-ordered system. Part of the attraction of arrangements with "boys" was surely their reliability, their assuredness as opposed to the heady but risky attractions of "town women," who might seduce one away from *umzi*-building at home. Indeed, the "wives of the mine" were on hand with their services on an everyday basis, very important in a society where older men have a basic right to the benefits of domesticity. Is it any wonder that senior men on the mines would return to their "boys" because "we loved them better"? Indeed, such "love" might become a permanent preference. There is evidence that in the long term, "some men preferred boys." Next to alcohol and "town women," my informants listed "homosexuality" as a major reason for men to abscond from home, abandoning wife and *umzi* for the urban scene. Such men either became fixtures on the mines, often puppets of mine management, or they left the mines for urban employment or to join urban criminal gangs.[29]

What of the white mine administration? How did whites view the *mteto ka Sokisi*? The Tsonga informant, Philemon, reported that white miners themselves practiced *metsha* with their *picannins* (black underground personal aides). Whether or not this was typical, the white compound staff certainly knew of "mine marriages" and turned a blind eye to them. Philemon was quite clear on that, saying, "On all the mines it was the Law of Sokisi. The whole bureaucracy on the mines knew about it, and they did not oppose it anyway . . . They helped to solve problems pertaining to it, especially the Compound Managers."

Although gold mine compounds were never closed, several Mpondo informants reported that on arrival at a mine, new recruits would be told by the mine authorities to stay away from town because of danger of assaults and above all to avoid town women. "There are 'women' on the mine," they were informed. Because workers who drank in town on weekends might be good for little work on Mondays, it was in management's interest to keep them away from women and the alcohol they supplied. Besides securing steady productivity, management's condoning of "mine marriages" had a further motivation as well. It helped assure the co-optation of black supervisors into mine hegemony.[30] Thus sex of the "mine marriage" type served the interests of the industry, as Charles van Onselen claims for the Rhodesian mines.[31]

Moreover, compound managers had other reasons to tolerate the practice. In 1916, a Native Inspector who suggested measures to stamp out "unnatural vice" cautioned that compound managers would be reluctant to enforce them for fear of wildcat strikes led by irate boss boys and black surface authorities.[32] His recommendations were ignored, and a report survives of at least one wildcat strike of the sort that he had predicted. On October 20, 1941, the South African Police at Boksburg were called in to quiet a compound demonstration led by boss boys on East Geduld Gold Mine.[33] Apparently the Sotho compound police had brought to the attention of the compound manager that, in the words of the police report:

> The Basutos are in the habit of holding dances in the compound during the night and that at these dances the young natives are dressed as women and squeezing and kissing are resorted to. Such dances are foreign to native custom and the compound manager warned the Basutos that these dances must stop. However, the dances were continued and twelve of the ringleaders and organizers of these dances were dismissed and sent to Johannesburg. They all admitted that they continued the dances and disobeyed the instructions of the compound manager. When the shift came up from underground in the afternoon, they heard of the dismissal of the twelve men. They then gathered and demanded their return else the compound manager and all the Basuto police boys must leave. They became rowdy and would not listen to anything the compound manager said.

Notice the solidarity of workers on behalf of the *mteto ka Sokisi*. Note also that amongst the Sotho, the support was from underground rather than the black surface authorities. This confirms the foregoing account of the means by which "mine marriages" were spread among non-Tsonga groups. It is difficult to imagine Tsonga compound police objecting to dances involving mine "wives." Indeed, this is the only such report among the 120 in the archives from the 1940s. Generally "mine marriages" buttressed the self-esteem of black authority figures and afforded considerable personal comfort to both parties. They were thus rarely challenged collectively and openly by blacks or proscribed by the white authorities.

Mine Sexuality and Social Change

Sexual activity reinforces people's understanding of themselves and each other in terms of gender and power. Indeed, sexual activity, which may confirm our self-formation as "men" and "women," "intrusive" and "seductive," "powerful" and "weak," cuts across more general structures of power and meaning, sometimes affirming and sometimes denying them. Thus sexual activity may be part of the topography of resistance and co-optation not only in domestic struggles but also in more general struggles against oppression. Further, resistance at one point within a shifting structure of power may at the same time imply subordination at another point—and vice versa. Consider changes in the incidence of "mine marriage," for instance.

Inkontshane marriages fitted well into the *umzi* system, at least for the junior partners. The "homosexuality" that reinforced the seniority system on the mines and preserved for older miners the rights and privileges of their masculinity thus also served in more subtle ways to protect the seniority system back home. For Mpondo young men it reinforced their resistance to proletarianization by enabling them to earn the right to an *umzi* back home more quickly. Even today, Schlemmer and Moller have found that those most likely to resist urbanization were people with land in the country.[34] As land became more scarce and the homestead system became more fragile, South African workers were "freed," in the classical Marxist sense, to leave the mines for industry and to settle in town. The mines accommodated by extending their recruitment system farther and farther north.[35] Pondoland and certain conservative parts of the Transkei remained substantial sources of supply, as did Lesotho and Mozambique for somewhat different reasons, but much of the labor force after 1950 was recruited in the tropical north. I have no evidence that the black authorities on the compound and underground were able to talk or coerce youngsters from the far north into "marriage," but my guess is that they probably did—and the young men submitted for reasons similar to those of the Mpondo.

Since 1973, however, the rise in the price of gold enabled the mining houses to raise mine wages. The decision to do so was made as liberation movements were succeeding in traditional labor supply areas to the north. It was felt that higher wages would assure a more productive labor force drawn from South Africa itself or its puppet states and therefore less subject to political pressures from their country of origin. Indeed, the majority of mine workers now do come from Lesotho and the Xhosa-speaking areas. The impact on patterns of sexuality has been quite fascinating.

Apparently with the gradual collapse of the *umzi* system at home and shifts in recruiting patterns, more Xhosa miners began to seek women in town. For these men without firm roots in the countryside, the old "mine marriages" seem less satisfying. (Besides, management is now clamping down much more firmly on "homosexuality.") The wives of many miners have moved to set up domicile on farms or as illegal lodgers in townships near the mines because they are no longer able to support themselves on the land at home. Typically in the past such "squatter" families have permanently urbanized and formed the nucleus of the black working class. With the rise in mine wages since 1973, however, the men are less likely to move from mining to the urban workforce, and these more proletarianized mine families are starting to make redundant the entire system of migrant labor on the mines.[36]

Conclusion

What have the social changes described in the previous section to do with our central theme of sexuality? Whether we are dealing with traditional marriage, "mine marriage," "town women," or the recently emerging squatter marriages, the central expectation is that mature men with authority in their social and economic sphere are entitled to regular sexual activity. The gender of their partner seems of less import than the overriding right to sexual congress. Furthermore, sexuality involves more than the physical act. It also involves a range of personal services that more senior men are reluctant to be without. In this, "mine marriages" are clearly modelled on traditional rural marriage, with the gender of the partner representing a fairly minor inconvenience. There is, however, one very important respect in which "mine marriage" has differed from rural marriages. This is the fundamentally important factor of long-term reproduction, whether that be understood in its narrow sense as childbearing and child-rearing, or whether it encompass the entire process that is implied in the Xhosa notion of "building an *umzi*." The responsibilities for reproduction within the homestead structure were such, however, that the reproductive sterility of "mine marriages" were viewed as an advantage compared to liaisons with "town women." Even amongst the Tsonga, for whom *inkotshane* marriage was more closely integrated with the home system, these relationships were believed to have a biologically defined terminal point—at which point, like the Greeks for Foucault,[37] they came up against principles of male assertiveness firmly rooted in popular consciousness. "Boys" always became "men," whether they took a male or a female partner.

Because "mine marriages" were isomorphic, in relational terms, with marriages at home, they are breaking down as the home system collapses. Nuclear families, bonded by affection and reproduction in the narrow sense of procreation, more closely resemble miners' original relationships with town mistresses than "mine marriages" as such. The old arrangements represented accommodations to migration and at the same time resistances to proletarianization. Once proletarianization came to the mines, both through the underdevelopment of the sending areas and by the shift in management recruitment policies, "mine marriages" in their typical form and the entire system of migrant labor as it had existed heretofore were doomed.

There has thus been a central shift in the expression of male sexuality and its function in the proletarianization of black miners in South Africa. If the "wives of the mine" were in the past a facet of more general resistance to proletarianization, the contemporary turn to "town women" and squatter families represents accommodation to the exigencies of stable wage-earning. Male sexuality, far from retarding the proletarianization of both men and women, now has become one important reason for country wives to move to town. Where "homosexual" behavior on the mines had been both a source of rural resistance to the wage economy and also an accommodation to the migrant system, so now "heterosexual" behavior challenges the migrant system even as rural society breaks down and patriarchal authority is transformed and integrated into the nuclear family.

The generally acknowledged dropoff in the incidence of "homosexuality" on the mines is popularly attributed to management's determination to enforce its abolition and the appointment of social workers with therapeutic training as counselors on the mines. Such a conclusion presumes that same-sex sexual congress is a sign of personality disorder—or at least severe social deprivation. While there may be an element of the latter in the incidence of mine "homosexuality," I hope that the foregoing account will call into question such simplistic and ahistorical assumptions. Sexuality too has a social history. Sexual activity and sexual preferences among African miners in South Africa are as much social constructions as individual choices. "Homosexuality" as an individual "personality type" describes the triumph of the therapeutic in our own society rather than a universal and inevitable category.

ORAL HISTORY AND THE STUDY OF SEXUALITY IN THE LESBIAN COMMUNITY: BUFFALO, NEW YORK, 1940-1960

◆

MADELINE DAVIS AND ELIZABETH LAPOVSKY KENNEDY

The gay liberation movement of the 1970s attacked the tradition of highly defined masculine (butch) and feminine (femme) sex roles in the lesbian community as demeaning imitations of the heterosexual world. This essay pioneers in placing butch-femme relationships in their historical context, and argues that they were politically and personally important choices. The largely working-class lesbians described here fought to create a public space in which emotionally fulfilling sexual relations could develop. The creation of a lesbian bar community in Buffalo went hand in hand with the creation of a lesbian sexual identity. Oral history is critical to recovering the gay and lesbian past because so little unprejudiced written material survives; Davis and Kennedy discuss the methodological problems involved in exploring that crucial but problematic area of lesbian history: sexual mores and behavior.

Note: Originally published, in somewhat different form, in *Feminist Studies* 12, no. 1 (Spring 1986): 7–26. This article is a revision of a paper originally presented at the "International Conference on Women's History and Oral History," Columbia University, New York, 18 November 1983. We want to thank Michael Frisch, Ellen DuBois, and Bobbi Prebis for reading the original version and offering us helpful comments. We also want to thank Rayna Rapp and Ronald Grele for their patience throughout the revision process.

We began a study of the history of the Buffalo lesbian community, 1930–1960, to determine that community's contribution to the emergence of the gay liberation movement of the 1960s.[1] Because this community centered around bars and was highly role defined, its members often have been stereotyped as low-life societal discards and pathetic imitators of heterosexuality. We suspected instead that these women were heroines who had shaped the development of gay pride in the twentieth century by forging a culture for survival and resistance under prejudicial conditions and by passing this sense of community on to newcomers; in our minds, these are indications of a movement in its prepolitical stages.[2] Our original research plan assumed the conceptual division between the public (social life and politics) and the private (intimate life and sex), which is deeply rooted in modern consciousness and which feminism has only begun to question. Thus we began our study by looking at gay and lesbian bars—the public manifestations of gay life at the time—and relegated sex to a position of less importance, viewing it as only incidentally relevant. As our research progressed we came to question the accuracy of this division. This article records the transformation in our thinking and explores the role of sexuality in the cultural and political development of the Buffalo lesbian community.

At first, our use of the traditional framework that separates the public and private spheres was fruitful.[3] Because the women who patronized the lesbian and gay bars of the past were predominantly working class and left no written records, we chose oral history as our method of study. Through the life stories of over forty narrators, we found that there were more bars in Buffalo during the forties and fifties than there are in that city today. Lesbians living all over the city came to socialize in these bars, which were located primarily in the downtown area. Some of these women were born and raised in Buffalo; others had migrated there in search of their kind. In addition, women from nearby cities, Rochester and Toronto, came to Buffalo bars on weekends. Most of the women who frequented these bars had full-time jobs. Many were factory workers, taxi drivers, bartenders, clerical workers, hospital technicians; a few were teachers or women who owned their own businesses.[4]

Our narrators documented, beyond our greatest expectations, the truth of our original hypothesis that this public bar community was a formative predecessor to the modern gay liberation movement. These bars not only were essential meeting places with distinctive cultures and mores, but they were also the central arena for the lesbian confrontation with a hostile world. Participants in bar life were engaged in constant, often violent, struggle for public space. Their dress code announced them as lesbians to their neighbors, to strangers on the streets, and of course to all who entered the bars. Although confrontation with the straight world was a constant during this period, its nature changed over time. In the forties, women braved ridicule and verbal abuse, but rarely physical conflict. One narrator of the forties conveys the tone: "There was a great difference in looks between a lesbian and her girl. You had to take a streetcar—very few people had cars. And people would stare and such."[5] In the fifties, with the increased visibility of the established gay community, the concomitant postwar rigidification of sex roles, and the political repression of the McCarthy era, the street dyke emerged. She was a full-time "queer," who frequented the bars even on week nights and was ready at any time to fight for her space and dignity. Many of our fifties' narrators were both aware and proud that their fighting contributed to a safer, more comfortable environment for lesbians today.

> Things back then were horrible, and I think that because I fought like a man to survive I made it somehow easier for the kids coming out today. I did all their fighting for them. I'm not a rich person; I don't even have a lot of money; I don't even have a little money. I would have nothing to leave anybody in this world, but I have that that I can leave to the kids who are coming out now, who will come out into the future, that I left them a better place to come out into. And that's all I have to offer, to leave them. But I wouldn't deny it; even though I was getting my brains beaten up I would never stand up and say, "No, don't hit me, I'm not gay. I'm not gay." I wouldn't do that.

When we initially gathered this material on the growth and development of community life, we placed little emphasis on sexuality. In part we were swept away by the excitement of the material on bars, dress, and the creation of public space for lesbians. In addition, we were part of a lesbian feminist movement that opposed a definition of lesbianism based primarily on sex. Moreover, we were influenced by the popular assumption that sexuality is natural and unchanging and the related sexist assumption of women's sexual passivity—both of which imply that sexuality is not a valid subject for historical study. Only recently have historians turned their attention to sexuality, a topic that used to be of interest mainly to psychologists and the medical profession. Feminists have added impetus to this study by suggesting that women can desire and shape sexual experience. Finally, we were inhibited by the widespread social reluctance to converse frankly about sexual matters. Thus for various reasons, all stemming, at least indirectly, from modern society's powerful ideological division between the public and the private, we were indisposed to consider how important sexuality might have been to the women we were studying.

The strength of the oral history method is that it enables narrators to shape their history, even when their views contradict the assumptions of historians. As our work progressed, narrators volunteered information about their sexual and emotional lives, and often a shyly asked question would inspire lengthy, absorbing discourse. By proceeding in the direction in which these women steered us, we came to realize that sexuality and sexual identity were not incidental but were central to their lives and their community. Our narrators taught us that although securing public space was indeed important, it was strongly motivated by the need to provide a setting for the formation of intimate relationships. It is the nature of this community that it created public space for lesbians and gay men, while at the same time it organized sexuality and emotional relationships. Appreciation of this dynamic interconnection requires new ways of thinking about lesbian history.

What is an appropriate framework for studying the sexual component of a lesbian community's history and for revealing the role of sexuality in the evolution of twentieth-century lesbian and gay politics? So little research has been done in this area that our work is still exploratory and tentative. At present, we seek primarily to understand forms of lesbian sexual expression and to identify changes in sexual norms, experiences, and ideas during the 1940s and 1950s. We also look for the forces behind these changes in the evolving culture and politics of the lesbian community. Our goal has been to ascertain what part, if any, sexuality played in the developing politics of gay liberation. As an introduction to this discussion, we shall present our method of research because it has been crucial in our move to study sexuality, and so little has been written on the use of oral history for research on this topic.

Using Oral History to Construct the History of the Buffalo Lesbian Community

The memories of our narrators are colorful, illuminating, and very moving. Our purpose, however, was not only to collect individual life stories, but also to use these as a basis for constructing the history of the community. To create from individual memories a historically valid analysis of this community presented a difficult challenge. The method we developed was slow and painstaking.[6] We treated each oral history as a historical document, taking into account the particular social position of each narrator and how that might affect her memories. We also considered how our own point of view influenced the kind of information we received and the way in which we interpreted a narrator's story. We juxtaposed all interviews with one another to identify patterns and contradictions and checked our developing understanding with other sources, such as newspaper accounts, legal cases, and labor statistics.

As mentioned earlier, we first focused on understanding and documenting lesbian bar life. From the many vibrant and humorous stories about adventures in bars and from the mountains of seemingly unrelated detail about how people spent their time, we began to identify a chronology of bars and to recognize distinctive social mores and forms of lesbian consciousness that were associated with different time periods and even with different bars. We checked and supplemented our analysis by research into newspaper accounts of bar raids and closings and actions of the State Liquor Authority. Contradictions frequently emerged in our material on bars, but, as we pursued them, we found they were rarely due to idiosyncratic or faulty memory on the part of our narrators but to the complexity of bar life. Often the differences could be resolved by taking into account the different social positions of our narrators or the kinds of questions we had asked to elicit the information we received. If conflicting views persisted we tried to return to our narrators for clarification. Usually, we found that we had misunderstood our narrators or that contradictions indeed existed in the community at the time. For instance, narrators consistently told us about the wonderful times in bars as well as how terrible they were. We came to understand that both of these conditions were part of the real experience of bar life.

When we turned our attention to sexuality and romance in this community, we were at first concerned that our method would not be adequate. Using memories to trace the evolution of sexual norms and expression is, at least superficially, more problematic than using them to document social life in bars. There are no concrete public events or institutions to which the memories can be linked. Thus, when a narrator talks about butch-fem sexuality in the forties, we must bear in mind the likelihood that she has modified her view and her practice of butch-fem sexuality in the fifties, sixties, seventies, and eighties. In contrast, when a narrator tells about bars in the forties, even though social life in bars might have changed over the last forty years, she can tie her memories to a concrete place like Ralph Martin's bar, which existed during a specific time period. Although not enough is known about historical memory to fully evaluate data derived from either type of narrative, our guess is, that at least for lesbian communities, they are equally valid.[7] The vividness of our narrators' stories suggests that the potential of oral history to generate full and rich documents about women's sexuality might be especially rich in the lesbian community. Perhaps lesbian memories about sexual ideals and experiences are not separated from the rest of life because the building of public communities is closely connected with the pursuit of intimate relationships. In addition, during this period, when gay oppression marked most lesbians' lives with fear of punishment and lack of acceptance, sexuality was one of the few areas in which many lesbians found satisfaction and pleasure. This was reinforced by the fact that, for lesbians, sexuality was not directly linked with the pain and/or danger of women's responsibility for childbearing and women's economic dependence on men. Therefore, memories of sexual experience might be more positive and more easily shared. But these ideas are tentative. An understanding of the nature of memory about sexuality must await further research.

The difficulty of tying memories about sexual or emotional life to public events does present special problems. We cannot identify specific dates for changes in sexual and emotional life, such as when sex became a public topic of conversation or when role-appropriate sex became a community concern. We can talk only of trends within the framework of decades. In addition, we are unable to find supplementary material to verify and spark our narrators' memories. There are no government documents or newspaper reports on lesbian sexuality. The best one can find are memoirs or fiction written about or by residents in other cities, and even these don't exist for participants in working-class communities of the forties.[8] In general, we have not found these problems to require significant revision of our method.

Our experience indicates that the number of people interviewed is critical to the success of our method, whether we are concerned with analyzing the history of bar life or of emotional and sexual life. We feel that between five and ten narrators' stories need to be juxtaposed in order to develop an analysis that is not changed dramatically by each new story. At the present time, our analysis of the white lesbian community of the fifties is based on oral histories from over fifteen narrators. In contrast, we have only five narrators who participated in the white community of the forties, four for the black community of the fifties, and one from the black community of the forties. Therefore, we emphasize the fifties in this article and have the greatest confidence in our analysis of that decade. Our discussion of the forties must be viewed as only tentative. Our material on the black community is not yet sufficient for separate treatment and so black and white narrators' memories are interspersed throughout the article.

Sexuality as Part of the Cultural-Political Development of the Buffalo Lesbian Community

Three features of lesbian sexuality during the forties and fifties suggest its integral connection with the lesbian community's cultural-political development. First, butch-fem roles created an authentic lesbian sexuality appropriate to the flourishing of an independent lesbian culture. Second, lesbians actively pursued rich and fulfilling sexual lives at a time when sexual subjectivity was not the norm for women. This behavior was not only consistent with the creation of a separate lesbian culture, but it also represented the roots of a personal and political feminism that characterized the gay liberation movement of the sixties. Third, although butch-fem roles and the pursuit of sexual autonomy remained constant throughout this period, sexual mores changed in relation to the evolving forms of resistance to oppression.

Most commentators on lesbian bar life in the forties and fifties have noted the prominence of butch-fem roles.[9] Our research corroborates this; we found that roles constituted a powerful code of behavior that shaped the way individuals handled themselves in daily life, including sexual expression. In addition, roles were the primary organizer for the lesbian stance toward the straight world as well as for building love relationships and for making friends.[10] To understand butch-fem roles in their full complexity is a fundamental issue for students of lesbian history; the particular concern of this article is the intricate connection between roles and sexuality. Members of the community, when explaining how one recognized a person's role, regularly referred to two underlying determinants: image, including dress and mannerism, and sexuality.[11] Some people went so far as to say that one never really knew a woman's role identity until one went to bed with her. "You can't tell butch-fem by people's dress. You couldn't even really tell in the fifties. I knew women with long hair, fem clothes, and found out they were butches. Actually I even knew one who wore men's clothes, haircuts and ties, who was a fem."

Today, butch-fem roles often elicit deep emotional reactions from many heterosexuals and lesbians. The former are affronted by women assuming male prerogatives, the latter by lesbians adopting male-defined role models. The hostility is exemplified by the prevalent ugly stereotype of the butch-fem sexual dyad: the butch with her dildo or penis substitute, trying to imitate a man, and the simpering passive fem who is kept in her place by ignorance. This representation evokes pity for lesbians because women who so interact must certainly be sexually unfulfilled; one partner cannot achieve satisfaction because she lacks the "true" organ of pleasure, and the other is cheated because she is denied the complete experience of the "real thing." Our research counters the view that butch-fem roles are solely an imitation of sexist heterosexual society.

Inherent to butch-fem relationships was the presumption that the butch is the physically active partner and the leader in lovemaking. As one butch narrator explains, "I treat a woman as a woman, down to the basic fact it'd have to be my side doin' most of the doin'." Insofar as the butch was the doer and the fem was the desired one, butch-fem roles did indeed parallel the male/female roles in heterosexuality. Yet unlike the dynamics of many heterosexual relationships, the butch's foremost objective was to give sexual pleasure to a fem; it was in satisfying her fem that the butch received fulfillment. "If I could give her satisfaction to the highest, that's what gave me satisfaction." As for the fem, she not only knew what would give her physical pleasure, but she also knew that she was neither object of nor receptacle for someone else's gratification. The essence of this emotional/sexual dynamic is captured by the ideal of the "stone butch," or untouchable butch, that prevailed during this period. A "stone butch" does all the "doin' " and does not ever allow her lover to reciprocate in kind. To be untouchable meant to gain pleasure from giving pleasure. Thus, although these women did draw on models in heterosexual society, they transformed those models into an authentically lesbian interaction. Through role-playing they developed distinctive and fulfilling expressions of women's sexual love for women.

The archetypal lesbian couple of the 1940s and 1950s, the "stone butch" and the fem, poses one of the most tantalizing puzzles of lesbian history and possibly of the history of sexuality in general.[12] In a culture that viewed women as sexually passive, butches developed a position as sexual aggressor, a major component of which was untouchability. However, the active or "masculine" partner was associated with the giving of sexual pleasure, a service usually assumed to be "feminine." Conversely, the fem, although the more passive partner, demanded and received sexual pleasure and in this sense might be considered the more self-concerned or even more "selfish" partner. These attributes of butch-fem sexual identity remove sexuality from the realm of the "natural," challenging the notion that sexual performance is a function of biology and affirming the view that sexual gratification is socially constructed.

Within this framework of butch-fem roles, individual lesbians actively pursued sexual pleasure. On the one hand, butch-fem roles limited sexual expression by imposing a definite structure. On the other hand, this structure ordered and gave a determinant shape to lesbian desire, which allowed individuals to know and find what they wanted. The restrictions of butch-fem sexuality, as well as the pathways it provided for satisfaction, are best captured and explored by examining what it meant for both butch and fem that the butch was the doer; how much leeway was there before the butch became fem, or the fem became butch?

Although there was complete agreement in the community that the butch was the leader in lovemaking, there was a great deal of controversy over the feasibility or necessity of being a "stone butch." In the forties, most butches lived up to the *ideal* of "the untouchable." One fem, who was in a relationship with an untouchable butch at that time and tried to challenge her partner's behavior, met only with resistance. Her butch's whole group—those who hung around Ralph Martin's—were the same. "Because I asked her one time, I said, 'Do you think that you might be just the only one?' 'Oh no,' she said. 'I know I'm not, you know, that I've discussed with . . . different people.' [There were] no exceptions, which I thought was ODD, but, I thought, well, you know. This is how it is."

In the fifties, the "stone butch" became a publicly discussed model for appropriate sexual behavior, and it was a standard that young butches felt they had to achieve to be a "real" or "true" butch. In contrast to the forties, a fifties' fem, who was out in the community would not have had to ask her butch friend why she was untouchable, and if there were others like her. She would have known it was the expected behavior for butches. Today our narrators disagree over whether it was, in fact, possible to maintain the ideal and they are unclear about the degree of latitude allowed in the forties or fifties before a butch harmed her reputation. Some butches claim that they were absolutely untouchable; that was how they were, and that's how they enjoyed sex. When we confronted one of our narrators, who referred to herself as an "untouchable," with the opinion of another narrator, who maintained that "stone butches" had never really existed, she replied, "No, that's not true. I'm an 'untouchable.' I've tried to have my lover make love to me, but I just couldn't stand it. . . . I really think there's something physical about that." Like many of our butch narrators, this woman has always been spontaneously orgasmic; that is, her excitement level peaks to orgasm while making love to another woman. Another "stone butch" explains: "I wanted to satisfy them [women], and I wanted to make love—I love to make love. I still think that's the greatest thing in life. But I don't want them to touch me. I feel like that spoils the whole thing—I am the way I am. And I figure if a girl is attracted to me, she's attracted to me because of what I am."

Other butches who consider themselves, and had the reputation of being, untouchable claim that it is, as a general matter, impossible to be completely untouchable. One, when asked if she were really untouchable, replied, "Of course not. How would any woman stay with me if I was? It doesn't make any sense. . . . I don't believe there was ever such a class—other than what they told each other." This woman preferred not to be touched, but she did allow mutual lovemaking from time to time during her long-term relationships. A first time in bed, however:

> There's no way in hell that you would touch me . . . if you mean untouchable like that. But if I'm living with a woman, I'd have to be a liar if I said that she hadn't touched me. But I can say that I don't care for it to happen. And the only reason it does happen is because she wants it. It's not like something I desire or want. But there's no such thing as an untouchable butch—and I'm the finest in Buffalo and I'm telling you straight—and don't let them jive you around it—no way.

This narrator's distinction between her behavior on a first night and her behavior in long-term relationships appeared to be accepted practice. The fact that some—albeit little—mutuality was allowed over the period of a long relationship did not affect one's reputation as an untouchable butch, nor did it counter the presumption of the butch as the doer.

This standard of untouchability was so powerful in shaping the behavior of fifties' butches that many never experienced their fems making love to them. By the seventies, however, when we began our interviewing, norms had changed enough so that our butch narrators had had opportunities to experience various forms of sexual expression. Still, many of them—in fact all of those quoted above on "stone butches"—remained untouchable. It was their personal style long after community standards changed. Today these women offer explanations for their preference that provide valuable clues about both the personal importance and the social "rightness" of untouchability as a community norm in the forties and fifties. Some women, as indicated in one of the above quotes, continue to view their discomfort with being touched as physical or biological. Others feel that if a fem were allowed the physical liberties usually associated with the butch role, distinctions would blur and the relationship would become confusing. "I feel that if we're in bed and she does the same thing to me that I do to her, we're the same thing." Another narrator, reflecting on the fact that she always went to bed with her clothes on, suggests that "what it came to was being uncomfortable with the female body. You didn't want people you were with to realize the likeness between the two." Still other butches are hesitant about the vulnerability implicit in mutual lovemaking. "When the first girl wanted to make a mutual exchange sexually, . . . I didn't want to be in the position of being at somebody's disposal, or at their command that much—maybe that's still inside me. Maybe I never let loose enough."

But many untouchables of the fifties did try mutual lovemaking later on, and it came as a pleasant surprise when they found they enjoyed being touched. "For some reason . . . I used to get enough mental satisfaction by satisfying a woman . . . then it got to the point where this one woman said, 'Well, I'm just not gonna accept that,' and she started venturing, and at first I said, 'No, no,' and then I said, 'Well, why not?' and I got to enjoy it." This change was not easy for a woman who had spent many years as an "untouchable." At first she was very nervous and uncomfortable about mutual sex, but "after I started reaching physical climaxes instead of just mental, it went, that little restlessness about it. It just mellowed me right out, y'know." The social pressure of the times prevented some women from experiencing expanded forms of sexual expression they might have enjoyed, and it also put constraints upon some women who had learned mutual sex outside of a structured community. One of our narrators had begun her sex life with mutual relations and enjoyed it immensely, but in order to conform to the community standard for butches, adopted untouchability as her sexual posture. She acceded to this behavioral change willingly and saw it as a logical component of her role during this period.

How was a community able to monitor the sexual activities of its members, and how might people come to know if a butch "rolled over" —the community lingo for a butch who allowed fems to make love to her? The answer was simple: fems talked! A butch's reputation was based on her performance with fems.

Despite the fact that sexual performance could build or destroy a butch's reputation, some butches of the fifties completely ignored the standard of untouchability. Our narrators give two reasons for this. One reason is the opinion that a long-term relationship requires some degree of mutuality to survive. One butch, a respected leader of the community because of her principles, her affability, and her organizational skills, was not only "touchable" but also suspects that most of the butches she knew in the fifties were not "stone butches." "Once you get in bed or in your bedroom and the lights go out, when you get in between those sheets, I don't think there's any male or there's any female or butch or fem, and it's a fifty-fifty thing. And I think that any relationship . . . any true relationship that's gonna survive has got to be that way. You can't be a giver and can't be a taker. You've gotta both be givers and both gotta be takers." The second reason is the pleasure of being touched. Some women experienced this in the fifties and continued to follow the practice.

> When it came to sex [in the fifties] butches were untouchable, so to speak. They did all the lovemaking, but love was not made back to them. And after I found out how different it was, and how great it was, I said, "What was I missing?" I remember a friend of mine, that I had, who dressed like a man all her life . . . and I remember talking to [her] and saying to her, you know you've got to stop being an untouchable butch, and she just couldn't agree. And I remember one time reaching over and pinching her and I said, "Did you feel that?" and she said, "Yes," and I said, "It hurt, didn't it? Well, why aren't you willing to feel something that's good?"

Our information on fem sexuality is not as extensive as that on butch sexuality because we have been able to contact fewer fem narrators. Nevertheless, from the fems we have interviewed and from comments by butches who sought them out and loved them, we do have an indication that fems were not passive receivers of pleasure, but for the most part, knew what they wanted and pursued it.[13] Many butches attributed their knowledge of sex to fems, who educated them by their sexual responsiveness as well as by their explicit directions in lovemaking.

As implied by our discussion of butch sexuality, many fems had difficulty accepting "untouchability." One fem narrator of the forties had a ten-year relationship with an untouchable butch, and the sexual restrictions were a source of discomfort for her. "It was very one-sided, you know, and . . . you never really got a chance to express your love. And I think this kind of suppressed . . . your feelings, your emotions. And I don't know whether that's healthy. I don't think so." But at the same time the majority of these fems appreciated being the center of attention; they derived a strong sense of self-fulfillment from seeking their own satisfaction and giving pleasure—by responding to their butches. "I've had some that I couldn't touch no parts of their bodies. It was all about me. Course I didn't mind! But every once in a while I felt like, well, hey, let me do something to you. I could NEVER understand that. 'Cause I lived with a girl. I couldn't touch any part of her, no part. But boy, did she make me feel good, so I said . . . All right with me. . . . I don't mind laying down."

What emerges from our narrators' words is in fact a range of sexual desires that were built into the framework of role-defined sexuality. For butches of the period, we found those who preferred untouchability; those who learned it and liked it; those who learned it and adjusted to it for a time; those who preferred it, but sensed the need for some mutuality; and those who practiced mutuality regularly. For fems, we found those who accepted pleasure, thereby giving pleasure to their lovers; usually such women would aggressively seek what they wanted and instruct their lovers with both verbal and nonverbal cues. Some fems actively sought to make love to their butches and were successful. And finally, we found some women who were not consistent in their roles, changing according to their partners. In the varied sex lives of these role-identified women of the past, we can find the roots of "personal-political" feminism. Women's concern with the ultimate satisfaction of other women is part of a strong sense of female and potentially feminist agency and may be the wellspring for the confidence, the goals, and the needs that shaped the later gay and lesbian feminist movement. Thus, when we develop our understanding of this community as a predecessor to the gay liberation movement, our analysis must include sexuality. For these lesbians actively sought, expanded, and shaped their sexual experience, a radical undertaking for women in the 1940s and 1950s.

Although butch-fem roles were the consistent framework for sexual expression, sexual mores changed and developed throughout this period; two contradictory trends emerged. First, the community became more open to the acceptance of new sexual practices, the discussion of sexual matters, and the learning about sex from friends as well as lovers. Second, the rules of butch-fem sexuality became more rigid, in that community concern for role-appropriate behavior increased.

In the forties there were at least two social groups, focused in two prominent bars, Ralph Martin's and Winters. According to our narrators, the sexual mores of these two groups differed: The former group was somewhat conservative; the latter group was more experimental, presaging what were to become the accepted norms of the fifties. The lesbian patrons of Ralph Martin's did not discuss sex openly, and oral sex was disdained. "People didn't talk about sex. There was no intimate conversation. It was kind of hush, hush . . . I didn't know there were different ways." By way of contrast, this narrator recalls a visit to Winters, where other women were laughing about "sixty-nine." "I didn't get it. I went to [my partner] and said, 'Somebody says "sixty-nine" and everybody gets hysterical.' " Finally her partner learned what the laughter was all about. At that time our narrator would have mentioned such intimacies only with a lover. It wasn't until later that she got into bull sessions about such topics. Not surprisingly, this narrator does not recall having been taught about sex. She remembers being scared during her first lesbian experience, then found that she knew what to do "naturally." She had no early affairs with partners older than herself.

The Winters' patrons had a more open, experimental attitude toward sex; they discussed it unreservedly and accepted the practice of oral sex. These women threw parties in which women tried threesomes and daisy chains. "People would try it and see how it worked out. But nothing really happened. One person would always get angry and leave, and they would end up with two." Even if their sexual adventures did not always turn out as planned, these women were unquestionably innovative for their time. Our narrator from the Winters' crowd reminisced that it was always a contrast to go home to the serene life of her religious family. She also raved about two fems who were her instructors in sexual matters, adding, "I was an apt pupil."

During the fifties the picture changed, and the mores of the Ralph Martin's group virtually disappeared. Sex came to be a conversation topic among all social groups. Oral sex became an accepted form of lovemaking, so that an individual who did not practice it was acting on personal preference rather than on ignorance or social proscription. In addition, most of our fifties' butch narrators recall having been teachers or students of sex. As in the Winters' group in the forties, an important teacher for the butch was the fem. "I had one girl who had been around who told me. I guess I really frustrated the hell out of her. And she took a piece of paper and drew me a picture and she said, 'Now you get this spot right here.' I felt like a jerk. I was embarrassed that she had to tell me this." According to our narrator, the lesson helped, and she explains that, "I went on to greater and better things."

The fifties also saw the advent of a completely new practice—experienced butches teaching novice butches about sex. One narrator remembers that younger women frequently approached her with questions about sex: "There must be an X on my back. They just pick me out. . . ." She recalls one young butch who "had to know every single detail. She drove me crazy. Jesus Christ, y'know, just get down there and do it—y'get so aggravated." The woman who aggravated her gives the following account of learning about sex:

> And I finally talked to a butch buddy of mine. . . . She was a real tough one. I asked her "What do you do when you make love to a woman?" And we sat up for hours and hours at a time. . . . "I feel sexually aroused by this woman, but if I take her to bed, what am I gonna do?" And she says, "Well, what do you feel like doing?" and I says "Well, the only thing I can think of doing is . . . all I want to do is touch her, but what is the full thing of it . . . you know." So when [she] told me I says, "Really," well there was this one thing in there, uh . . . I don't know if you want me to state it. Maybe I can . . . well, I won't . . . I'll put it in terms that you can understand. Amongst other things, the oral gratification. Well, that kind of floored me because I never expected something like that and I thought, well, who knows, I might like it.

She later describes her first sexual experience in which she was so scared that her friend had to shove her into the bedroom where the girl was waiting.

At the same time that attitudes toward discussions of and teachings about sexuality relaxed, the fifties' lesbian community became stricter in enforcing role-appropriate sexuality. Those who deviated from the pattern in the forties might have identified themselves as "lavender butch" and might have been labeled by others as "comme ci, comme ça." Although their divergence from the social norm would have been noticed and discussed, such women were not stigmatized. But the community of the fifties left little room to deviate. Those who did not consistently follow one role in bed were considered "ki-ki" (neither-nor), or more infrequently "AC/DC," both pejorative terms imposed by the community. Such women were viewed as disruptive of the social order and not to be trusted. They not only elicited negative comments, but they also were often ostracized from social groups. From the perspective of the 1980s, in which mutuality in lovemaking is emphasized as a positive quality, it is important to clarify that "ki-ki" did not refer to an abandonment of role-defined sex but rather to a shifting of sexual posture depending upon one's bed partner. Therefore, it was grounded absolutely in role playing. One of our narrators in fact defined "ki-ki" as "double role playing."[14]

These contradictory trends in attitudes and norms of lesbian sexuality parallel changes in the heterosexual world. Movement toward open discussion of sex, the acceptance of oral sex, and the teaching about sex took place in the society at large, as exemplified by the publication of and the material contained in the Kinsey reports.[15] Similarly, the lesbian community's stringent enforcement of role-defined behavior in the fifties occurred in the context of straight society's postwar move toward a stricter sexual division of labor and the ideology that accompanied it.[16] These parallels indicate a close connection between the evolution of heterosexual and homosexual cultures, a topic that requires further research.[17] At this point, we wish to stress that drawing parallels with heterosexuality can only partially illuminate changes in lesbian sexual mores. As an integral part of lesbian life, lesbian sexuality undergoes transformations that correspond with changing forms of the community's resistance to oppression.

Two developments occurred in this prepolitical period that are fundamental for the later emergence of the lesbian and gay liberation movement of the sixties. The first development was the flourishing of a lesbian culture; the second was the evolving stance of public defiance. The community of the forties was just beginning to support places for public gatherings and socializing, and during this period lesbians were to be found in bars only on weekends. Narrators of the forties do not remember having role models or anyone willing to instruct them in the ways of gay life. The prevalent feeling was that gay life was hard, and if people wanted it, they had to find it for themselves. In the fifties, the number of lesbian bars increased, and lesbians could be found socializing there every night of the week. As bar culture became more elaborate and open, lesbians more freely exchanged information about all aspects of their social lives, including sexuality. Discussion of sex was one of many dimensions of an increasingly complex culture. The strengthening of lesbian culture and the concomitant repression of gays in the fifties led the community to take a more public stance. This shift toward public confrontation subsequently generated enough sense of pride to counter the acknowledged detriments of gay life so that members of the community were willing to instruct newcomers both socially and sexually. Almost all our narrators who came out in the fifties remember a butch who served as a role model or remember acting as role models themselves. Instruction about sexuality was part of a general education into community life that developed in the context of expanding community pride.

However, the community's growing public defiance was also related to its increased concern for enforcing role-appropriate behavior in the fifties. Butches were key in this process of fighting back. The butches alone, or the butch-fem couple, were always publicly visible as they walked down the street, announcing themselves to the world. To deal effectively with the hostility of the straight world, and to support one another in physical confrontations, the community developed, for butches in particular, rules of appropriate behavior and forms of organization and exerted pressure on butches to live up to these standards. Because roles organized intimate life, as well as the community's resistance to oppression, sexual performance was a vital part of these fifties' standards.

From the vantage point of the 1980s and twenty more years of lesbian and gay history, we know that just as evolving community politics created this tension between open discussion and teaching about sex and strict enforcement of role-appropriate sexual behavior, it also effected the resolution. Our research suggests that in the late sixties in Buffalo, with the development of the political activities of gay liberation, explicitly political organizations and tactics replaced butch-fem roles in leading the resistance to gay oppression. Because butch-fem roles were no longer the primary means for organizing the community's stance toward the straight world, the community no longer needed to enforce role-appropriate behavior.[18] This did not mean that butch-fem roles disappeared. As part of a long tradition of creating an authentic lesbian culture in an oppressive society, butch-fem roles remain, for many lesbians, an important code of personal behavior in matters of either appearance, sexuality, or both.

HOMOSEXUALITY, HOMOPHOBIA, AND REVOLUTION: NOTES TOWARD AN UNDERSTANDING OF THE CUBAN LESBIAN AND GAY MALE EXPERIENCE

◆

LOURDES ARGUELLES AND B. RUBY RICH

This essay argues that North Americans need to look beyond the Mariel exodus and the simplistic assumption that Castro's Cuba is repressive and homophobic to the more complicated reality under which Cuban homosexuals actually live. During the 1950s many male homosexuals were associated with servicing the tourist industry or upper-class Cubans, while lesbians were almost all closeted. The fundamental homophobia of Cuban society was encouraged by the puritanism of the postrevolutionary decade after 1959, and much of gay life was attacked as a remnant of Cuba's sexual exploitation by Americans. Since the 1970s, though, the conditions for homosexuals have improved, and lesbians in particular have benefitted from the fuller integration of women into Cuban society. Although they have not achieved full acceptance, Arguelles and Rich argue, many Cuban homosexuals prefer remaining in a revolutionary society to emigrating to societies where sexual encounters are so often commodified.

Thousands of homosexual men and women have migrated to the United States and to other capitalist nations since the start of the socialist revolution in Cuba in 1959.[1] This exodus has been interpreted as stemming

Note: Originally published, in somewhat different form, in *Signs, A Journal of Women in Culture and Society*, Summer 1984.

almost exclusively from the homophobic nature of the Castro regime and a set of repressive policies that have purportedly rendered gay and lesbian expression on the island virtually impossible.[2] At least, such has been the interpretation within North American gay academic and artistic circles and within segments of the Left.[3]

Conventionally accepted factors such as economic incentives and individual ambition, which migration theorists usually point to as powerful stimulators to individual departures, are seldom considered in evaluations of Cuban gays' migratory patterns since the revolution began. The more structuralist explanations for international population movements, which stress the role of capital and of capitalist states in organizing migratory flows from less developed to more developed economies, have yet to be invoked in the interpretation of gay migration from Cuba.[4]

Such reductive interpretation is consistent with the acritical nature of bourgeois thought and its well-known tendency to simplify motivations and homogenize differences among "lesser mortals": Third World peoples, ethnic minorities, the working class, and particularly the gay and female segments within them. It is also consistent with the easy way in which this style of thought validates suspect information; Cuban "refugee" testimony and subsequent conversations with the newly arrived Cubans, for example, becomes the main source for evaluation of Cuban gay life, despite knowledge of the pressures on émigrés to testify to political persecution in their country of origin in order to attain the legal and economic advantages of refugee status in their new country.[5]

The success of this interpretation has served anti-Cuban interests, most notably the American state, rather well. First, credibility of the story has neutralized badly needed support for the Cuban revolution among its natural allies (North American progressive lobbies) and legitimated the presence in traditionally liberal circles of some of the more reactionary elements within the Cuban émigré population. Second, it has obscured the changing realities and subtleties of everyday gay life on the island as part of the ongoing revolutionary process itself. Third, it has made the historical legacy of prerevolutionary political economy and homophobia seem immaterial to an understanding of contemporary Cuban gay and lesbian issues. Fourth, it has helped to conceal the oppressive and exploitative features of life for gay men and women in the émigré enclaves. Fifth, it has distanced gay activists in capitalist mainstream culture from minority gays involved in the liberation movements of their respective countries and national communities. Finally, the continual scapegoating of Cuban revolutionary homophobia has made the growing number of progressive gay émigrés who criticize but also support the revolution into living contradictions: invisible to gay liberation forces but easy targets for the homophobic anti-Castro army in exile.

This report is based on research on lesbian and gay male experience conducted between 1979 and 1984 in Cuba and in Cuban émigré enclaves in the United States, Puerto Rico, Mexico, and Spain. The object of the investigation was to begin apprehending the nature and dynamics of Cuban gay experience so as to provide an adequate context in which contemporary Cuban gay life, migration, and resettlement could be understood. The research was also intended as a preliminary contribution to two areas of inquiry that remain grossly underdeveloped: description of gay and lesbian everyday life in Third World countries and communities, and theory on the nature of the relationships between the structures of sexuality and the corresponding structures of socialist organization.[6] The data were obtained through diverse systems of inquiry (historical analysis, along with survey, field, and experiential methods) and interpreted within a theoretical framework drawn from lesbian-feminist and critical gay scholarship and the politicoeconomic and phenomenological study of Cuban social life.

We are aware of the risks incurred by disseminating this study: giving ammunition to anti-Cuban lobbies and to strongly homophobic cliques on the island and risking the enmity of those Cuban émigrés who have long capitalized on this unexamined issue as a condemnation of the revolutionary process. Despite such risks, we and most of the collaborators of the study (the dozens of Cuban gays and lesbians who willingly shared their lives and analyses throughout the investigation) strongly believe that the benefits of initiating an informed discourse on Cuban homosexuality will far outweigh the potential costs—that there is an urgent need for it because of both the ongoing debates regarding sexuality and repression within capitalist and socialist countries and the complexities of gay and lesbian existence in Cuba and abroad.

Prerevolutionary Cuba

With the exception of bourgeois homosexuals who spent extended periods of time abroad, most Cubans engaging in homosexual relations before the revolution (whatever their sexual identity) gravitated toward the capital city of Havana in search of work and a more liberated lifestyle. Job opportunities in the interior of the island were severely limited due to the country's sharply uneven development pattern.[7] Further, Cuba's Afro-Hispanic patriarchal culture, with its emphasis on compulsory heterosexuality, was strongest in rural areas.[8] Also, the very smallness of prerevolutionary villages and cities made life intimate; sexual policing was thus an easy task and an effective deterrent against deviance from the norm. The openly homosexual man or woman who remained in the interior was often ostracized or cast in the role of village queer—the homosexual version of the village idiot.[9]

Even in the Havana of the 1950s, everyday life was not easy for the working-class or petty-bourgeois homosexual. Unemployment was high and had been steadily increasing throughout the decade. The scarcity of productive occupations demanded a strictly closeted occupational life. For all women, and especially for lesbians, employment almost invariably entailed continual sexual harassment. Aida, a lesbian seamstress now living in Miami, remembers: "At work, you had to pretend to have a boyfriend all the time . . . make up stories . . . even get someone to accompany you to work once or twice. . . . If not, you were in trouble. Because they'd be after you every day, every hour, every minute, caressing you, showing off their genitals. It was hell."[10]

The only occupational sector showing substantial growth was that connected to tourism, drug distribution, gambling, and prostitution. This sector was mostly controlled by American organized crime and members of an indigenous bourgeoisie directly linked to Batista's political apparatus.[11] It employed more than two hundred thousand workers as petty traders, casino operators, entertainers, servants, and prostitutes.[12]

During this period of severe sexual repression in advanced capitalist nations, homosexual desire was often channeled into illegal and lucrative offshore markets like the Havana underworld. Not surprisingly, then, Cuban homosexuals had preferential hiring treatment in the Havana tourist sector in order to meet the demands of American visitors and servicemen for homoerotic experiences. Other buyers of homosexual desire were the fathers and sons of the Cuban bourgeoisie, who felt free to partake of homoerotic practices without being considered homosexual as long as they did not take the passive, so-called female role in sexual relations. Yet another common practice for Cuban heterosexual men was the procurement of a lesbian prostitute's favors for a night.[13]

Apart from employment realities, social pressures made thousands of prerevolutionary homosexuals part of this underworld. Even homosexuals such as students (who were differently placed) were integrated into this subculture through the bars that they frequented: the St. Michel, the Dirty Dick, El Gato Tuerto. Then (as is still today the case in the U.S.) most of these bars were owned and operated by organized crime. Given the sharply stratified nature of prerevolutionary Cuba, working-class heterosexual men in order to make a living were also drawn into this underworld or alternatively into a homosexual underground dominated by the Cuban homosexual bourgeoisie. The bourgeois male homosexual of this era tended out of guilt to avoid same-class liaisons with other homosexuals and was constantly on the lookout for the heterosexual macho from the lower strata of the population. Thus, in many ways prerevolutionary homosexual liaisons in themselves fostered sexual colonialism and exploitation.

The commodification of homosexual desire in the Havana underworld and in the bourgeois homosexual underground during the prerevolutionary era, however, did not produce a significant toleration of homosexual life-styles in the larger social arena. Attitudes in traditional workplaces and within the family involved a combination of ridicule and violence toward the *locas*, or queens, and shame toward the *maricones*, or faggots. *Tortilleras* (or dykes)—considerably less visible owing to the overall repression of female sexuality—were either ignored or made objects of ridicule. If legal sanctions and official harassment were rare, this tolerance was due less to social acceptance than to overriding considerations of profit and the economic interests of the underworld that dominated the Cuban political apparatus.[14]

The consumer structure of the Havana underworld never spawned a "gay culture" or "gay sensibility" even in strictly commercial terms, due to its isolation from the mainstream of social life and the degree of guilt and self-hatred afflicting its members. Homosexual expressions in literature and other arts were few and guarded when compared to the intellectual and artistic achievements of gays in other Latin American countries such as Brazil, Mexico, and Argentina. Even sympathetic observers of the homosexual scene frequently derided those engaged in same-sex relationships. When misogyny was added to homophobia, the reactions to lesbians in particular could be vitriolic. The following passage from Guillermo Cabrera Infante's more recent writings is typical of those of the period: "Margarita was under and on top of her . . . as if swimming, indecently rubbing her . . . trying to create for herself the instrument that nature had denied her."[15]

Homosexual challenges to the sexual order of everyday life and its rigid gender identities tended to be private and frequently were projected onto religious practices such as *Santeria*, an Afro-Cuban cult comprised of a syncretism of West African (primarily Yoruban) beliefs and rituals with those of Roman Catholicism. Because the *Santeria* gods "mount" either sex arbitrarily during ceremonies of possession, *Santeria* was and still is a favored form of gender transcendence for many Cuban homosexual men and lesbians.

Thus, in this prerevolutionary setting, discreet lesbian or gay male identities in the modern sense—identities that are based on self-definition and involve emotional as well as physical aspects of same-sex relations—were rare.[16] Erotic loyalty (and, in the case of women, subservience) to the opposite sex was assumed as normal even by homosexuals. Hence, for many Cubans of this era, homosexuality was a mere addendum to customary marital roles. Among others, it was just a profitable commodification of sexual fantasy. For the vast majority, homosexuality made life a shameful and guilt-ridden experience. Such was gay Havana in its fabled *avant la guerre* period.

The Revolutionary Era

The revolution of 1959 eradicated the Havana underworld and initiated the development of a productive economy. With the profit motive removed, the superficial tolerance of homosexuality by the strongly homophobic Cuban society quickly eroded. At the same time, the revolutionary leadership rallied against the evils of capitalist vice—which were often associated with homosexuality. The demands of a revolutionary puritanism left few heterosexual escape clauses and no homosexual leeway at all.

Emigration began immediately. The promoters and overlords of the Havana underworld along with large numbers of their displaced workers (many of them homosexuals) headed for Miami. Many lesbians who had liaisons with members of the bourgeoisie followed their male protectorate to Miami, as did gay men who had worked for U.S. firms or had done domestic work for the native bourgeoisie. Bourgeois homosexuals, many of whom had lived largely abroad anyway, now moved out permanently.

The exodus and resettlement of so many homosexuals was made possible by an unprecedented legal accommodation: The United States never invoked the Immigration and Naturalization Act of 1952, which authorized the barring and expulsion of "sexually deviant" aliens, against these 1959 immigrants. The Florida Legislative Investigation Committee continued this official blindness when its 1964 report on homosexuality in the state omitted any reference to the influx from Cuba.[17] Coming as it did at the end of a decade of McCarthyism, the Cuban gay immigration posed a difficult contradiction for the U.S. government, pitting its strong desire for a real advantage in the Cold War against its equally strong homophobia. Then, as now, anticommunism won out. Those fleeing the socialist revolution were welcomed despite their frequently open homosexuality.

Back in Cuba, life for homosexuals changed. Some veterans of the old underworld enclave joined counterrevolutionary activities or were pushed into them by the CIA. Other homosexuals, especially those from working-class backgrounds or students from petty-bourgeois families, worked to integrate themselves into the revolution. For the majority this meant going into a more guarded and, it was hoped, temporary closet. For these homosexuals, class and class interests were perceived as more elemental aspects of their identity than homosexual behavior. And the revolution spoke to these interests and this identity.

The limited social outlets still available for homosexuals, however, prolonged the relationship between the declining underworld and more progressive homosexuals, locking the two groups together for sheer companionship and sexual pleasure. Again, given the differences between male and female behavior and sexual rituals, this merging was much truer for homosexual men than for lesbians of the period. Not a few of the progressive homosexuals became implicated by default in counterrevolutionary activities and were even jailed. Young homosexuals seeking contact with "the community" in the bars and famous cruising areas of La Rampa were thus introduced to counterrevolutionary ideology and practice. One example of such a dynamic is the case of Rolando Cubela, a homosexual student leader who fought in the revolutionary army but was later enlisted by the CIA to assassinate Fidel Castro.[18]

At the same time, homosexual perspectives on the revolution could shift according to class interests. Petty-bourgeois homosexuals joined the remaining veterans of the underworld in opposing the revolution when their privileges were threatened by the laws of agrarian and urban reform. Pressures escalated. Propaganda campaigns directed by the CIA urging the Cuban people to emigrate were taking their toll on the island's population. The agency saw the potential migration of thousands of Cubans to the United States as an event that would discredit the Cuban revolution internationally, remove its much-needed technical personnel, and score an American Cold War victory. Therefore it used a number of campaigns tailored to appeal to different groups that felt threatened by the revolution.[19]

Meanwhile, the 1961 invasion of Giron (called the Bay of Pigs by the U.S.), systematic commando attacks from Florida bases, and internal CIA-sponsored subversion created in Cuba an increase in militarization, surveillance, and concern over national security. Realistic fears and objective dangers gave rise to paranoia, and (as in the McCarthy years here) anyone who was "different" fell under suspicion. Homosexual bars and La Rampa cruising areas were perceived, in some cases correctly, as centers of counterrevolutionary activities and began to be systematically treated as such.

In keeping with this narrowing of tolerance in the early 1960s, the Committees for the Defense of the Revolution (CDR), established just after the revolution, took on a new significance as watchdogs.[20] Created to meet the internal security needs of the island, the CDRs now expanded into social regulators, policing personal and public life in their neighborhoods with obviously negative implications for lesbians and male homosexuals. In this climate of postinvasion paranoia, private space was invaded as never before. Not surprisingly, deep suspicion came to dominate the everyday life of Cuban lesbians and male homosexuals—a feeling exacerbated by the fact that legal migration to the United States had been halted by new American immigration limitations and quotas. There was no longer any route out, except for risky escape on a small vessel or the long wait for legal migration through a third country (many of which formally or informally excluded homosexuals).

Major ideological changes also were taking place. The influential Popular Socialist Party (PSP) moved to fill an analytical vacuum on homosexuality by lending "scientific" credibility to the antihomosexual harangues of the revolutionary leadership and to the homophobia of the Cuban people. The leaders of the PSP, with an attitude resembling that of Soviet society in the thirties and forties, saw homosexuality as a product of bourgeois decadence. Further, the PSP leaders considered expression of sexuality not a private affair or a personal freedom but a fulfillment of obligation to society.[21]

The lesbian and homosexual male intelligentsia, now concentrated in the Cuban Writers' and Artists' Union (UNEAC), made no public countercritique on the issue of homosexuality. The homosexual resistance and survival strategies of the time were largely private, individual in nature, and lacked effective oppositional qualities. As a result, the silence permitted the PSP analysis to assume undisputed hegemony even in intellectual circles. Among many reasons for the absence of any such public gay countercritique and resistance in this period, three stand out. Foremost was the lack of a tradition of feminist discourse and, thus, of any liberatory and substantive base for discussions of sexual order and gender politics. Another reason lay in the contemporary conception of homosexuality: As a legacy of the prerevolutionary period, homosexuality was still seen, by both the Cuban gay and straight worlds, as something performed in the dark with little or no nonsexual implications. Self-interest dictated the third reason: Many closeted intellectuals who were bringing Cuba international recognition feared the loss of their personal privilege—especially the loss of their ability to travel abroad, which allowed so much latitude in their own sexual expression—if they spoke out against the official stand on homosexuality.

The sixties became increasingly difficult for homosexuals (particularly those at the vanguard of intellectual and artistic life). Their sexual practices began to be detailed in public and were invariably linked with bourgeois decadence or counterrevolutionary predispositions.[22] The growing crescendo of antihomosexual rhetoric culminated in 1965 in the establishment of UMAP camps (Military Units for the Aid of Production) aimed at safeguarding the revolution and guaranteeing the public good. Male homosexuals were among those drafted into the camps, while lesbians, due to their comparative invisibility and the sexism that mandated different treatment for women, were spared. After much international protest and internal denunciation, the camps were closed at the end of the sugar harvest in 1967. Described at length in other sources, the UMAP camps have become permanent symbols of Cuban homophobia. While short-lived and denounced extensively within and outside Cuba ever since their abolition, the camps remain a damnable episode in revolutionary history.[23]

The UMAP years had seen as well such forms of persecution as the forced disbanding of the El Puente Literary Group on the grounds that some of its members were homosexual. In the post-UMAP period, persecution continued in a less overt form. In the absence of a developed gay liberatory consciousness, some Cuban homosexuals retreated further into

Santeria and various forms of Eastern mysticism. Some migrated to the United States via a third country. Those who remained in Spain or in Mexico for years awaiting their American visa carved out small gay Cuban enclaves there. Homosexuals who chose to stay in Cuba became even more guarded, yet most continued to believe that the substantial material and emotional benefits they were deriving from the revolution outweighed the pain of repressing or concealing their sexuality.

It was only in the late sixties that a certain relaxation in the parameters of permissible sexual behavior in the international communist world began to filter into official circles in Cuba. In 1968, for instance, East Germany legalized homosexual acts between adults.[24] Cuba's need to relate to progressive political forces emerging in the United States and Western Europe also modified the official rhetoric, which began to describe homosexuals as sexual deviates (not criminals) to be cured (not condemned). While such changes in perspective were slowly occurring in official Cuban circles, everyday life for gays and lesbians began to improve.[25]

Three additional events marked the gradual but continual improvement in life conditions of gay men and lesbians in Cuba during the seventies: the First National Congress on Education and Culture, the promulgation of the Family Code, and the creation of a national group on sexual education. In 1971, the First National Congress delivered a mixed message to gays and the population at large. On the one hand, the customary denunciations of homosexuals as decadent were gone; homosexuality was no longer seen by the revolutionary leadership as a fundamental problem in Cuban society, but, rather, viewed as a form of sexual behavior requiring study. And for the first time in an official document, homosexuality was referred to in medical and psychological rather than criminal terms. On the other hand, declarations from the same congress called for the removal of homosexuals from the field of education, thus continuing the view of homosexuality as a contamination of the body politic.[26] Mayra, a lesbian photographer still living in Cuba, described these years: "You were not totally accepted by the revolution and there were positions you could not get if you were open about [being gay] unless you were in the arts. Still . . . there was no persecution unless you were involved in counterrevolutionary activities. Then you were in trouble, and usually it was blamed on the weakness of being a homosexual."[27]

Then in 1976, the celebrated Family Code began to make advances in eradicating sexism and, at least in principle, offered to Cubans for the first time a vision of more fluid gender definitions.[28] However, the code's focus on the nuclear family and its failure to address the compulsory nature of heterosexuality eventually made it less effective than anticipated in obtaining its goals and in reducing the popular homophobia of Cuban society.

In 1977 the Cuban National Group for Sexual Education was established, headed by a Cuban physician, Celestino Lajonchere, and an East

German sexologist, Monika Krause. Working primarily with those involved in health and education, the group helped publicize the latest findings on the nature of sexuality and made some progress, despite the resistance Krause credited to Cuba's "cultural heritage," in updating sexual attitudes, including those pertaining to homosexuality.[29] Because of the many gains in conditions for women during the seventies, life for lesbians improved markedly. Ada, a lesbian rural nurse, acknowledged that things were not "perfect" but stated nevertheless, "I remember how it was before [the revolution] and for the first time, I feel I'm a human being."[30]

Gains and setbacks merge throughout this period. The 1979 Penal Code, for example, was a disappointment to gays because it failed to legalize manifestations of homosexual behavior in the public sphere and left intact antigay laws dating to the Cuban Social Defense Code of 1939. By leaving in place legislation against "'public scandal" or "extravagance," the Penal Code continued to provide a rationale for gay paranoia.[31]

Throughout the late sixties and early seventies, Cuban gay men and lesbians continued to migrate in small numbers to the United States via a third country, as direct migration was still prohibited. Class interests and economic incentives were the main influences on their migration. In particular, the promise of unlimited consumption—the most effective propaganda of the capitalist society—remained as important an impetus for gays as for other emigrants. Family reunification was another shared goal. There was, however, a uniquely gay reason for leaving: the age-old, prerevolutionary tradition in which families encouraged gay offspring to emigrate in order to avoid family stigma. Since Havana no longer absorbed the sons and daughters into a homosexual occupational sector, emigration abroad took the place of the journey to the city.

The Mariel Exodus and Present Gay Life in Cuba

The year 1979 was an unsettled one. Even though living conditions were better than in any previous period and compared favorably with those in the rest of the Caribbean, there were serious problems. The economy still suffered from the U.S. blockade; suspicious epidemics afflicting the island's cash-crop harvests raised the specter of biological sabotage; and a productivity drive aimed at reducing *sociolismo* (slacking off) put workers under greater disciplinary pressure. Most critically, there was considerable frustration and unrest sparked by visits (the first since the revolution) of thousands of émigrés who brought gifts as well as tales of comfortable lives in the United States. These visits of "the American cousins" increased consumer envy and added to the effectiveness of counterrevolutionary propaganda.

Lesbians and gay men were particularly vulnerable. The CIA targeted the homosexual intelligentsia and worked to persuade its members to defect, promising generous academic grants and publishing contracts. The more cost-effective ploy of blackmail was also used, especially against those gays less willing to leave, in the hope that political anxiety would force victims into exile. Carlos Alberto Montaner, a Madrid-based anti-Castro writer, for example, published two full pages listing names of homosexuals inside Cuba in an attempt to discredit them and to encourage them to migrate.[32] Such cynical "assistance" in coming out continues to be a favored weapon against lesbians and gay men who are well integrated into the revolution.

The visits also provided a context in which Cuban lesbians and gay men could hear of the more open and affluent gay lifestyles available in the United States as a benefit of consumer capitalism. Other common reasons for wanting to emigrate included the lack of career mobility in a still underdeveloped economy and, for men, a traditional desire for the adventure of travel that had to focus on emigration since the United States and other capitalist nations deny tourist visas to Cubans. For some Cuban gays (especially for the men), emigration also provided wider sexual parameters than they felt could ever be possible in Cuba. Other Cuban lesbians and gay men, however, steadfastly refused to fulfill their gay identity at the cost of their national and political identities.

In the spring of 1980, through the instigation of the U.S. government, a series of events inside and outside of Cuba culminated in Fidel Castro's opening of the port of Mariel to allow a massive migration, thereby forcing the United States to accept an immigration far in excess of its own quotas. The boats leaving Mariel carried many who had waited years for a visa from the United States; many former political prisoners suffering social ostracism; young men bent on adventure, many with wives and children left behind; and gays, mostly male, opting for the comparatively more open gay life promised in the United States.[33]

Significantly, there were few lesbians in the Mariel exodus. Their small number by comparison with that of gay men points, again, to the fuller integration of women into Cuban society and the increased status and freedom enjoyed by lesbians, as women, under the revolution. For all the gay men and the few lesbians who left, there were many more who chose to stay. Their lives had been constantly improving. The revolution might not yet speak to the homosexual in them, but it continued to address other vital aspects of their being. They, in response, put the revolution—and Cuba—first, and put off sexual politics until later.

Today, life for lesbians and gay men in Cuba is similar, in some senses, to life for gay people in the United States pre-Stonewall, prior to the development of the gay liberation and lesbian-feminist movements and the modern identities they produced. In this, its style is not very different from that customary throughout most of Latin America and the Caribbean, where *se dice nada, se hace todo* (say nothing, do everything) is the rule. It is a closeted life but by no means a secret one. While the homosexuality of many men and women is a matter of common knowledge, it is never a matter of public record. Indeed, it is the complete absence of a public sphere that most clearly distinguishes the life of homosexuals in Cuba from any corresponding lifestyle in the United States or Western European urban centers.

Most commentary on homosexuality in revolutionary Cuba has concerned itself strictly with legal or occupational prohibitions. However, within the private sphere, there are a clear latitude and range of possibilities for lesbians and gay men that surprise the critical observer. The seeming contradictions in Cuba between homosexual expression and homosexual repression correspond quite clearly to the distinction made between private (expressive) and public (repressive) space. As delineated in a Latin American socialist setting, private space is far wider than in the United States, encompassing virtually all behavior outside the purview of official sanction or attention, while approved policy, published texts, and official stances compose the public sphere.

In the context of this dichotomy, there are two areas of particular concern to any critic of Cuban homophobia. One is the use of the laws governing public display to authorize "street sweeps" of obvious queens or lumpen gay males prior to major public events. Many informants explain that those arrested are gays engaged in black-market activities; others contend that they are engaged in sexual cruising or solicitation; yet others deny that the roundup of gays qua gays even occurs. Given the nature of the public sphere in Cuba, though, the actuality of these sweeps seems likely.[34]

A second area of concern is the effect of material conditions on the latitude of homosexual expression in the seemingly most private of private spheres: the bedroom. Havana's longstanding housing shortage reflects both the limited resources of an underdeveloped nation and the punitive effect of the U.S. blockade. An affliction to the entire urban population, the housing crisis has a special impact on Cuban homosexuals.

Due to the high divorce rate, Havana's housing shortage has forced many no-longer-married people into prolonged cohabitation or a return to the family home during the long wait for a new apartment. One temporary Cuban solution to the housing crisis has been the creation of a new institution, the *posada*—a legitimization of the well-known room-by-the-hour system formerly used by the commercial sex industry, now transformed into respectable rooms for hire for the couple in search of sexual privacy. By necessitating the transfer of the bedroom from the private into the public sphere, the housing crisis has created a situation particularly crippling to lesbian or gay male couples. By all accounts, lesbians and gay men do use the *posadas*. However, the homophobia of the society must make such an option more available to the couple with some special "in" or good connections than to the ordinary pair. The admission to *posadas*, like the ability to book hotel rooms and tables in the most select restaurants, rests on the individual manager's interpretation of official policy and thus frequently entails long waiting periods. The move, then, from private to public space is almost inevitably a movement from freer expression to greater repression for the Cuban homosexual.

Despite such restrictions and despite the fact that Party membership is an impossibility for known gays, homosexuals are nonetheless a visible feature of the Cuban social landscape. They appear at every level of the hierarchy in Cuban society, in government, and of course in the arts. They are no longer confined to an underworld economy or alienated from the mainstream of social life as they were in the prerevolutionary era. Particular individuals are well known and pointed to with pride as evidence of revolutionary nondiscrimination. They may not be "out" in the U.S. sense, in that prominent lesbians and gay men in the worlds of music, poetry, art, film, or literature never make their sexuality the subject of their work. Similarly, the absence of a gay public space means that there are no lesbian or gay bars; yet there is a flourishing homosexual social scene centered around private parties and particular homes. This rich "salon" society, a feature of Havana life in general, is particularly well suited to the expansive private sphere required by homosexuals. Beach resorts, where the zones of tolerance are much wider, offer other escapes from restriction.

While their sexuality may be an open secret inside Cuba, many lesbians and gay males who participate in cultural and academic exchanges with the United States become more guarded when abroad, fearful of how homosexual issues are utilized in the war against the Cuban revolution. But many still take the opportunity to visit lesbian and gay bars and bath houses in New York or San Francisco. Ironically, their own adjustment to a greater social integration in Cuba causes them increasingly to feel out of place in these sites, viewing their sexual consumerism as bizarre. Some, like Jorge, an artist, contend that, "for all the repression, there is more true sexuality for gays in Cuba."[35]

Conclusions

Lacking the necessary understanding or factual bases for their judgments, even progressive gay men and lesbians in the United States assist in perpetuating a dangerously misguided set of criteria by which Cuban homosexual issues—and the Cuban revolution, for that matter—are judged and found wanting. Similarly, inside Cuba the lives of homosexuals, in spite of some dramatic improvements, continue to be circumscribed by antiquated conceptions of homosexuality out of place in a modern and humane socialist society in transition.

The need for a distinctively Cuban socialist countercritique on behalf of homosexuality is increasingly evident. It must reconcile lesbian and gay male experiences with the island's realities and offer the international gay community critical insights into the immensely complex, rich, expressive, and problematic nature of those experiences. Until such a countercritique exists, the manipulation of the Cuban gay issue by anti-Cuban interests will remain largely unchallenged, and homosexual experience will continue to be marginalized within Cuban society.

It is obvious, however, that this countercritique is at present inhibited on at least three levels. First, the context today for any work on homosexuality in Cuba is inescapably that of a renewed Cold War, and few people—capable or not—are willing to undertake such a challenge, given the increasing manipulation from abroad to which Cuban gays can be exposed. Second, among gay men and lesbians in Cuba, the traumatic memories of the UMAP are a continued deterrent to public demand or support for such a countercritique. Third, the Cuban leadership has demonstrated a persistent reluctance to test the Cuban people's capacity for change on this subject. Other campaigns on unpopular topics—for example, the Family Code's professed mandate for equality between the sexes within the home—have been initiated, but no such effort has been directed against homophobia.

Recently, however, there are slight changes in official policy, intimations that progay elements inside and outside Cuba are putting moderate pressure on those in positions of influence on the island to consider the human and political costs of homophobia. For example, ICAIC (the Cuban Film Institute) opposed the screening of a gay documentary, *Word Is Out*, in a U.S. section of its 1983 international film festival. At the same festival, however, after an internal debate, ICAIC supported the presentation of a symposium paper—which was subsequently translated into Spanish and distributed to all festival delegates—detailing the politics and aesthetics of U.S. gay cinema.[36] Also significant were both the recent report in a major Cuban newspaper, *Juventud Rebelde*, urging tolerance for homosexuality, and the interested and nonantagonistic reception this article received from Cuban social researchers and university teachers at a conference held in Havana in the autumn of 1983.

Postscript

Since this article was originally published in 1984, changes have indeed occurred in Cuban society, both in directions anticipated by this article and in others particular to the late 1980s. Return visits to the island by the authors have permitted responses to the article (since published in Spanish in the Mexican paper, *La Jornada*) from Cuban lesbians and gay men. Overwhelmingly, they felt that progress was more marked than we suggested and that conditions of daily life had significantly improved during this decade. Many couples were living together, despite the housing crisis that had once made that a likelihood only for the married; some were open enough that they were able to joke about neighbors' reactions and adaptations.

On the other hand, the arrival of AIDS in Cuba is bound to affect the limits of tolerance for homosexuality there, as it has elsewhere. Thus far, Cuba is unusual in publicizing the disease, not as a gay disease, but rather as a sexually transmitted disease regardless of specific sexual practice. The number of cases has been extremely small (143 as of fall 1987).[37] The absence of an intravenous-drug-user population combined with the incidence of Cubans' service in Africa has created a different picture for the Cuban target group than the U.S. example. AIDS seems to be blamed on foreigners, foreign travel, and sexual contact with foreigners. While data on testing is not yet forthcoming, it would seem to be widespread, with the goal of testing the entire population. Partial quarantining (called "treatment") has already been initiated.

The current situation, then, is one on the brink of further change. Even as sexual construction in any society is a process, so in Cuba does this process continue. Our own efforts did not end with this article.[38] Nor can our research be considered either conclusive or concluded. Rather, it is one step in the development of a countercritique on Cuban homosexuality that will add to and in turn be enriched by that beginning to emerge from our gay male and lesbian compañeros in Cuba. To them, the *entendidos*,[39] this article is dedicated in solidarity.

GAY POLITICS AND COMMUNITY IN SAN FRANCISCO SINCE WORLD WAR II

◆

JOHN D'EMILIO

In the last two decades, social historians have increasingly turned to the writing of community histories of ethnic and racial groups, such as the blacks of Cleveland, the Italians of Chicago, and the Jews of New York. Historians of the gay and lesbian experience are beginning to do the same. In the following essay, John D'Emilio focuses attention on San Francisco, a city especially identified with the gay experience. He traces the relationship between community development and political mobilization since the Second World War, mapping the intricate ways in which community life and politics interact.

For gay men and for lesbians, San Francisco has become akin to what Rome is for Catholics: A lot of us live there and many more have made the pilgrimage. The gay male subculture in San Francisco is more visible and more complex than in any other city; lesbians in the Bay Area also sustain more institutions than their sisters elsewhere. San Francisco is one of the very few places where lesbians are residentially concentrated enough to be visible. For gay men and for lesbians, San Francisco is a special place.

The gay community in San Francisco and its politics have been a long time in the making. Surveying its history can tell us much not just about one city, but about the emergence of sexual minorities generally, about shifting forms of oppression, and changing political strategies.

Note: Originally published, in somewhat different form, in *Socialist Review* 55 (January, February 1981): 77-104.

The Historical Background

The distinction between behavior and identity is critical to an understanding of contemporary gay male and lesbian life. Jeffrey Weeks described it well in *Coming Out: Homosexual Politics in Britain*. "Homosexuality has existed throughout history," he wrote. "But what have varied enormously are the ways in which various societies have regarded homosexuality, the meanings they have attached to it, and how those who were engaged in homosexual activity viewed themselves. . . . As a starting point we have to distinguish between homosexual behavior, which is universal, and a homosexual identity, which is historically specific."[1]

In colonial America, in the family-centered household economy of the north, heterosexual relations and individual survival meshed, as production was based on the cooperative labor of husband, wife, and their children. Where forced labor predominated, white indentured servants and black slaves were deprived of the most basic control of their own bodies. In either setting, the presence of lesbians and gay men was literally inconceivable. Though evidence of homosexual activity in the colonial era survives (mainly through the court records that detailed its punishment), nothing indicates that men or women could make their erotic/emotional attraction for the same sex into a personal identity. The prevailing ideology reflected the facts of social existence. Homosexual behavior was labelled a sin and a crime, a discrete act for which the perpetrator received punishment, in this world and the next. In preindustrial America, heterosexuality remained undefined because it was truly the only way of life.[2]

The decisive shift in the nineteenth century to industrial capitalism provided the conditions for a homosexual and lesbian identity to emerge. As a free-labor system, capitalism pulled men and women out of the home and into the marketplace. Throughout the nineteenth and twentieth centuries, capital expanded its sway over more aspects of material life and began producing as commodities goods that were once made in the home. Free labor and the expansion of commodity production created the context in which an autonomous personal life could develop. Affection, personal relationships, and sexuality increasingly entered the realm of "choice," seemingly independent and disconnected from how one organized the production of goods necessary for survival. Under these conditions, men and women could fashion an identity and way of life out of their sexual and emotional attraction to members of the same sex. As industrial capitalism extended its hegemony, the potential for homosexual desire to coalesce into an identity grew. Not only had it become possible to be a lesbian or a homosexual: As time passed, more and more men and women could embody that potential.[3]

Beginning in the last third of the nineteenth century, evidence points to the appearance of men and women for whom same-sex erotic interests became an organizing principle for their personal life. Meeting places, rudimentary institutions, and friendship networks dotted the urban landscape. The medical profession "discovered" the homosexual, a new, exotic human type. The lead taken by the medical profession in reconceptualizing homosexuality as a condition that inheres in a person, rather than as a criminal, sinful act, was less a sign of scientific progress than an ideological response to a changing social reality: Some women and men were structuring their lives in a new way. During the first half of the twentieth century, the institutions and networks that constituted the subcultures of gay men and lesbians slowly grew, stabilized, and differentiated themselves. This process occurred in an oppressive context. Those who engaged in homosexual activity were severely punished if they were caught; the culture devalued homosexual expression in any form; and lesbians and gay men were denied information about the lives of their own kind and about their sexuality.[4]

Capitalist society differentiates and discriminates according to gender, class, and race. The evolution of gay life reflects those processes. For instance, in building upon its patriarchal origins, capitalism drew more men than women out of the home and into the paid labor force, and at higher wages. The potential for men to live outside the heterosexual family unit has been, consequently, proportionately greater and the difference is reflected in the contrasting incidence rates for homosexuality among men and women in the Kinsey studies. Also, because the public space of cities has traditionally been male space, it is not surprising that gay male life has been significantly more public than lesbian life.[5]

Postwar San Francisco

The slow, gradual evolution of a gay identity and of urban gay subcultures was immeasurably hastened by the intervention of World War II. The social disruption of the war years allowed the almost imperceptible changes of several generations to coalesce into a qualitatively new shape. World War II was something of a nationwide coming-out experience. It properly marks the beginning of the nation's, and San Francisco's, modern gay history.[6]

The war uprooted tens of millions of American men and women, plucking them from families, small towns, and the ethnic neighborhoods of large cities and depositing them in a variety of sex-segregated, nonfamilial environments. Most obvious among these were the armed services, but the home front also departed from the co-sexual, heterosexual norm of peacetime society with millions of women entering the labor force, often working and lodging in all-female space. Young men and women who, in normal times, might have moved directly from their parents' home into one with their spouse, experienced years of living away from kin, and away from the intimate company of the opposite sex. For a generation of Americans, World War II created a setting in which to experience same-sex love, affection, and sexuality, and to discover and participate in the group life of gay men and women. For some it simply confirmed a way of living and loving they had already chosen. For others, it gave meaning to little-understood desires, introduced them to men and women with similar feelings, and thus allowed them to "come out." For still others, the sexual underside of the war years provided experiences they otherwise would not have had and that they left behind when the war ended.[7]

If the war years allowed large numbers of lesbians and gay men to discover their sexuality and each other, repression in the postwar decade heightened consciousness of belonging to a group. One component of Cold War politics was the drive to reconstruct traditional gender roles and patterns of sexual behavior. Women experienced intense pressure to leave the labor force and return home to the role of wife and mother. Homosexuals and lesbians found themselves under virulent attack: purges from the armed forces; congressional investigations into government employment of "perverts"; disbarment from federal jobs; widespread FBI surveillance; state sexual psychopath laws; stepped-up harassment from urban police forces; and inflammatory headlines warning readers of the sex "deviates" in their midst. The tightening web of oppression in McCarthy's America helped to create the minority it was meant to isolate.[8]

These events also decisively shaped the gay history of San Francisco, initiating a process that has made it a unique place for lesbians and gay men. As a major port of departure and return for servicemen and women destined for the Pacific theater (and, later, for the postwar occupation of Japan and the fighting in Korea), and as an important center of war industry, the Bay Area's charm and physical beauty were exposed to large numbers of young, mobile Americans. Many stayed after demobilization; others later returned. Between 1940 and 1950 the population of San Francisco, which had declined during the 1930s, grew by over 125,000.

The growth included a disproportionate number of lesbians and gay men. The sporadic, unpredictable purges from the armed forces in the Pacific deposited lesbians and homosexuals, sometimes hundreds at a time, in San Francisco with dishonorable discharges. Unable or unwilling to return home in disgrace to family and friends, they stayed to carve out a new gay life. California, moreover, was the one state whose courts upheld the right of homosexuals to congregate in bars and other public establishments. Though the police found ways around the decision and continued to harass gay bars, the ruling gave to bars in San Francisco a tiny measure of security lacking elsewhere. By the late 1950s about thirty gay male and lesbian bars existed in the city. Such small advantages were significant, and over the years created a qualitative difference in the shape of gay life. Census statistics hint at the degree to which San

Francisco was attracting a gay populace. From 1950 to 1960 the number of single-person households doubled, accounting for 38 percent of the city's residence units.[9]

Under the combined impact of the war, the publication of the Kinsey studies, the persecutions of the McCarthy era, and the wide currency that a growing civil rights movement was giving to the concept of minority group status, some gay men and lesbians began building a political movement of their own. In 1950, a small group of male homosexuals who were members of the Communist Party or fellow-travelers formed the Mattachine Society in Los Angeles. Initially a secret underground organization, it developed a radical analysis of homosexuals as an oppressed minority and sought to build a mass movement of homosexuals working for their own emancipation. Though the founders were eventually purged and the philosophy and goals of the group transformed, the Mattachine did, at least, survive. In 1953 a branch was formed in San Francisco. Three years later, the organization's national office moved there and its monthly magazine, *Mattachine Review*, was published out of San Francisco. In 1955 in San Francisco, several lesbians founded the Daughters of Bilitis, a lesbian political group. DOB also published a monthly magazine, *The Ladder*, and tried, with limited success, to set up chapters in other cities.[10]

Throughout the 1950s, the "homophile" movement remained small and fragile. The combined membership of DOB and Mattachine in San Francisco probably never exceeded two hundred, yet no other American city reached even that number. Hostile as the social climate of the 1950s was to a gay movement, and notwithstanding the personal courage that involvement required, the feeble size of the movement stemmed in no small part from the political choices made by homophile leaders. Mattachine and DOB reflected (after its radical founders were purged) the accommodationist, conformist spirit of the Eisenhower era. They assiduously cultivated an image of middle-class respectability and denied that they were organizations of homosexuals, instead claiming that they were concerned with the problem of the "variant." They expected social change to come through the good offices of professionals. They saw their task primarily as one of educating the professionals who influenced public opinion and only secondarily as one of organizing lesbians and gay men. Moreover, in defining prejudice and misinformation as the problem, both DOB and Mattachine often found themselves blaming the victim. DOB regularly counseled lesbians to grow their hair long and wear dresses, and Mattachine firmly dissociated itself from the stereotypical promiscuous sexuality of male homosexuals, in one instance even applauding police for rounding up gay men who cruised a railroad terminal. Neither organization had kind words for the milieu of the gay bars, though they would have done well to consider why the bars were packed while their membership rolls remained tiny.[11]

Despite these limitations, one cannot dismiss the work of DOB and

Mattachine in making San Francisco what it is today. More copies of *The Ladder* and *Mattachine Review* were distributed in San Francisco than elsewhere. The city had more women and men doing gay "political" work than any other. They made contact with a significant number of professionals and initiated a dialogue that was a crucial step in changing antigay attitudes. As the national headquarters of both organizations, San Francisco attracted gay men and lesbians.

Though a militant, grass-roots nationwide liberation movement of lesbians and gay men did not emerge until the end of the 1960s, San Francisco alone witnessed the beginnings of militancy and a mass politics several years earlier. San Francisco was the first city to see the barrier between the movement and the gay subculture break down. The impetus for this pre-Stonewall wave of gay politics emerged not from homophile leaders but from the bar subculture, and resulted from a set of circumstances unique to San Francisco.[12]

San Francisco in the 1940s and 1950s was the setting for an underground literary movement of poets and writers who dissented from the dominant ethos of Cold War America, and who expressed through verse their opposition to the conformity and consumerism of the postwar era. By the mid-1950s, the bohemian literary scene in North Beach began attracting beat writers like Allen Ginsberg. Word of what was happening spread, and the San Francisco poets slowly reached a wider audience.

After 1957, however, what began as a small, underground movement was suddenly transmuted by the media into a nationwide generational rebellion against everything that America held sacred. The summer of 1958 witnessed the trial of Lawrence Ferlinghetti, the owner of City Lights bookstore, on charges of selling obscene literature (Ginsberg's *Howl*). Simultaneously, Kerouac's *On the Road* was published. Over the next two years the media turned a spotlight on the beat rebellion and on North Beach, the setting of the most visible, concentrated beat subculture. The sensationalistic portrayal of them quickly overshadowed the reality. As writers and as a social movement, they received almost universal condemnation. *Look* accused the beats of turning "the average American's value scale . . . inside out." The local press descended on North Beach, with the *Examiner* and the *Chronicle* running lurid series that exposed the boozing, drug-crazed, orgiastic, and sexually perverse life of San Francisco's beatniks. In a way that tended to become self-fulfilling, North Beach was labelled the "international headquarters" of the beat generation.[13]

The visibility of the beat subculture in North Beach had a major impact upon gay consciousness in San Francisco. Many of the central figures of the literary renaissance in San Francisco were, in fact, gay men—Robert Duncan, Jack Spicer, Robin Blaser, and, of course, Ginsberg—and through their work they carved out a male homosexual cultural space. Ginsberg's *Howl*, a local best-seller, openly acknowledged male homosexuality. In

describing gay male sex as joyous, delightful, and even holy, Ginsberg did
in fact turn American values inside out. The geography of the two
subcultures, moreover, overlapped considerably. Most importantly, the
philosophy behind the beat protest resonated with the experience of gays
in the 1950s. The beats were rebelling against the "straight" ethos of Cold
War society—career, home and family, suburban life—an ethos that
excluded lesbians and gay men. The beats provided a different lens
through which homosexuals and lesbians could view their lives—as a form
of protest against a stultifying lifestyle and set of values.

While the beats exerted their subtle influence upon the self-image of
the city's gay population, two homosexual-related scandals rocked the
city. In the midst of the 1959 mayoral campaign, one of the candidates
accused the incumbent mayor and his chief of police of allowing San
Francisco to become "the national headquarters of the organized homosexuals in the United States." The charges, based on the fact that
Mattachine and DOB were located in San Francisco, made front-page
headlines for several days. Political figures and the local press vigorously
denied the charges but the affair made the entire city aware of the
homophile organizations in its midst.[14]

The following spring, the city was treated to another extensive discussion of the gay presence in San Francisco when a "gayola" scandal hit the
police department. Several gay bar owners reported to the district attorney a long history of extortion by the police. One detective and state
liquor department investigator were caught with marked money and
pleaded guilty. Several other indicted officers opted for a jury trial that
dragged on throughout the summer. All of them were acquitted, but the
scandal seriously embarrassed the police department and the city
administration.[15]

Taken together, the beat phenomenon and the homosexual scandals
were giving San Francisco an unwelcome reputation as the home for the
nation's "deviates" and "rebels." By 1959, the police had increased their
patrols in North Beach and were systematically harassing beat gathering
places and individuals. The following year, immediately after the conclusion of the gayola trials, the police, with the support and encouragement
of the mayor, shifted their attention to the city's gay population. Felony
convictions of gay men, which stood at zero in the first half of 1960, rose
to twenty-nine in the next six months and jumped to seventy-six in the
first six months of 1961. Misdemeanor charges against gay women and
men stemming from sweeps of the bars ran at an estimated forty to sixty
per week during 1961. By October the state alcoholic beverage control
department had revoked the licenses of twelve of the city's thirty gay bars
and had initiated proceedings against another fifteen. Every one of the
bars that testified against the police department during the gayola inquiry
was shut down. The police, backed by the city's press, also intensified
surveillance of gay male cruising areas. Vice squad officers raided the-

aters showing male homosexual porn films and confiscated thousands of volumes of gay male and lesbian pulp fiction.[16]

Police harassment of gay bars was not new. In the 1950s, it was endemic to the gay male and lesbian subculture of American cities. What was novel about the San Francisco police crackdown was the social context in which it took place. The scandals of 1959 and 1960 led to an unprecedented degree of public discussion of homosexuality. Just as important, the stepped-up harassment followed upon the growing awareness of the beat rebellion and its subtle impact on gay consciousness in San Francisco. Thus, the conditions were present to encourage a political response to the antigay campaign.

Both DOB and Mattachine were too enmeshed in the accommodationist politics of the 1950s to resist attacks on aspects of gay life that both organizations deplored as unseemly. Instead, the first wave of rebellion emerged directly out of the bar subculture and out of the one bar, the Black Cat, where gay men, bohemian nonconformity, and police harassment most clearly converged. Located on Montgomery Street a few blocks from the center of North Beach, the Black Cat had a long history as a bohemian meeting place. In the 1940s the character of the bar began to change and it became more clearly a gay male bar. But it retained a special flavor. Allen Ginsberg described it as "the greatest gay bar in America . . . totally open, bohemian. . . . All the gay screaming queens would come, the heterosexual gray flannel suit types, longshoremen. All the poets went there." For over fifteen years, beginning in the late 1940s, its owner Sol Stoumen steadfastly engaged in a court fight against the state liquor board to stay open, spending over thirty-eight thousand dollars to finance his protracted court battle.[17]

During the 1950s, the Black Cat had a drag entertainer, José Sarria, who staged satirical operas on Sunday afternoons that drew an overflow crowd. Sarria took a traditional, sometimes self-deprecating, form of gay male humor—camp and drag—and transformed it into political theater. Outrageously dressed in female attire, he would perform Carmen, but Carmen as a homosexual hiding in the bushes trying to avoid capture by the vice squad. For years, Sarria ended his show without satire. As George Mendenhall, a pre-Stonewall activist, recalled it, "José would make these political comments about our rights as homosexuals and at the end . . . of every concert, he would have everybody in the room stand, and we would put our arms around each other and sing, 'God Save Us Nelly Queens.' It sounds silly, but if you lived at that time and had the oppression coming down from the police department and from society, . . . to be able to put your arms around other gay men and sing 'God Save Us Nelly Queens' . . . We were not really saying 'God Save Us Nelly Queens.' We were saying, 'We have our rights too.' "[18]

In 1961, at the height of the police crackdown, Sarria decided to run for city supervisor. He had no chance of winning, but victory wasn't his goal. "I was trying to prove to my gay audience," he recalled, "that I had the right, being as notorious and gay as I was, to run for public office, because people in those days didn't believe you had rights." Sarria's operas made him the best-known gay man in San Francisco; his reputation extended to the entire bar-going population. Though he collected only six thousand votes, his candidacy was the hot topic in the bars that fall, forcing patrons to think about their lives and their sexual orientation in political terms.[19]

Sarria's candidacy set in motion developments that fed lesbian and gay political activity in San Francisco throughout the 1960s. During his campaign, a group of gay men began publishing a biweekly newspaper that they distributed in the bars. Financed by advertising from gay tavern owners, the League for Civil Education *News* used a muckraking style to expose gay oppression. Headlines such as "SFPD ATTACKS HOMOS" and "WE MUST FIGHT NOW!" fueled an ongoing discussion of police abuses among bar patrons. LCE *News* encouraged gays to vote as a bloc and sponsored registration drives. By 1963 candidates for public office were taking ads in the paper. In 1962 several gay bar owners formed the Tavern Guild as a defense organization to resist attacks from the state. In 1964 some members of the Tavern Guild and a few other friends founded the Society for Individual Rights. SIR was virtually alone among pre-Stonewall gay male homophile organizations in legitimating the social needs of homosexuals. In addition to voter registration, candidates' nights during election time, public picketing, and other "political" activity, SIR sponsored dances, bridge clubs, and picnics, provided VD testing, and opened a community center. Its meetings often attracted more than two hundred people, and by 1968 it had a membership of almost a thousand, making it far and away the largest male homophile organization in the country.

By the mid-1960s, lesbians and gay men in San Francisco were breaking out of the isolation that oppression had imposed upon them. In 1964, Glide Memorial Methodist Church, whose social-action ministry in the Tenderloin forced it to confront the situation of young male hustlers, opened a dialogue with the city's homophile organizations. Out of it came the Council on Religion and the Homosexual. The ministers witnessed a vivid display of gay oppression when they sponsored a New Year's Eve Dance for San Francisco's gay community. The SFPD was there to photograph people as they entered California Hall and to arrest several "chaperones" for "obstructing" police officers. The police came under heavy attack from the press, the ACLU took the case, and a municipal judge dismissed all charges and reprimanded the police. Thereafter, a segment of the city's Protestant clergy spoke out for gay rights and initiated discussions of homosexuality within their denominations. Phyllis Lyon of DOB was hired to run CRH's educational program. In 1965, Del Martin of DOB helped organize Citizens Alert, a twenty-four-hour hotline to respond to incidents of police brutality. In 1966, DOB planned ten days of public forums at which city officials addressed themselves to gay concerns. Homophile groups cooperatively sponsored candidates' nights each year and local politicians began to court the gay vote. Some, like state legislator Willie Brown, enthusiastically took up gay concerns.[20]

Unlike the Stonewall Riot of 1969, the impact of Sarria's symbolic candidacy remained confined to San Francisco. The city's situation was too unique, gay men and lesbians in the rest of the country still too isolated and invisible, for it to have anything more than a local effect. At the end of the 1960s, news of a gay riot in New York could spread rapidly through the networks of communication created by the mass movements of the decade. In 1961, with the exception of the southern civil rights movement, those movements and those channels for disseminating information did not exist. And the absence of a nationwide gay movement placed limits in turn on how far gay politics in San Francisco could develop.

However, there were additional reasons why, on a local level, the discontent within the bars was channeled into reform politics. SIR and the Tavern Guild maintained a close working relationship (the two had an overlapping leadership) and SIR relied on the Guild for much of its funds and for publicity. Bar owners wanted police harassment of their businesses to end; once that goal had been achieved, as it largely had by about 1966, their interest in politics waned and their needs increasingly diverged from patrons who faced job discrimination and police harassment in other urban spaces. The dependence on gay entrepreneurs encouraged SIR's leaders not to rock the boat. Those gay men for whom the beats' cultural protest and glorification of nonconformity had originally struck a responsive chord found little in SIR to claim their allegiance. Instead, the heirs of the beats—the burgeoning hippie movement and counterculture in the Bay Area—offered them a more hospitable home. By the late 1960s gay politics in San Francisco had lost its dynamism.

Homophile politics in San Francisco remained within the limits of reformism during the 1960s and actively involved only a small fraction of its potential constituency. At most, two thousand men and women had organizational affiliation and of these only a few dozen could be considered hard-core activists. Yet the movement had achieved a level of visibility unmatched elsewhere. By the late 1960s mass magazines were referring to San Francisco as the gay capital of the United States. When the Stonewall Riot sparked a gay liberation movement, San Francisco's lesbian and gay male community could assume a leading role.

The Growth of the Gay Liberation Movement

The Stonewall Riot in New York in June 1969 was able to inspire a nationwide grass-roots liberation movement because of the mass radical movements that preceded it. Black militants provided a model of an oppressed minority that transformed their "stigma" into a source of pride and strength. The new left, antiwar, and student movements popularized a critique of American society and a confrontational style of political action. The counterculture encouraged the rejection of the values and lifestyle of the middle class, especially its sexual mores. Above all, the women's liberation movement provided a political analysis of sex roles and sexism.

Stonewall initiated a qualitatively different phase of gay and lesbian politics. Two aspects deserve emphasis. One is the notion of "coming out," which served both as a goal and a strategy. Coming out became a profoundly political step that an individual could take. It promised an immediate improvement in one's life, a huge step forward in shedding the self-hatred and internalized oppression imposed by a homophobic society. Coming out also became the key strategy for building a mass movement. Gay women and men who came out crossed a critical dividing line. They relinquished invisibility, made themselves vulnerable to attack, and became invested in the success of the movement. Visible lesbians and gay men, moreover, served as magnets that drew others to them.

Coming out quickly captured the imagination of tens of thousands, perhaps hundreds of thousands, of lesbians and gay men. A mass movement was born almost overnight. On the eve of Stonewall, after almost twenty years of homophile politics, fewer than fifty organizations existed. By 1973, there were more than eight hundred lesbian and gay male groups scattered across the country. The largest pre-Stonewall homophile demonstrations attracted only a few dozen people. In June 1970 five thousand women and men marched in New York to commemorate the Stonewall Rebellion. By the mid-1970s, the yearly marches in several cities were larger than any other political demonstrations since the decline of the civil rights and antiwar movements. Lesbians and gay men created publications and independent presses, record companies, coffeehouses, community centers, counseling services, health clinics, and professional associations.[21]

A second critical feature of the post-Stonewall era was the emergence of a lesbian movement. Lesbians were but a small fraction of the tiny homophile movement. The almost simultaneous birth of women's liberation and gay liberation propelled large numbers of lesbians into liberation politics. Lesbians were active both in early gay liberation groups and in feminist organizations. By 1970 the experience of sexism in gay liberation and of heterosexism in women's liberation inspired many lesbians to form organizations of their own, such as Radicalesbians in New York, the Furies Collective in Washington, D.C., and Gay Women's Liberation in San Francisco. Lesbian-feminism pushed the analysis of sexism and heterosexism beyond where either the women's or gay movement ventured and so cogently related the two systems of oppression that sectors of the women's movement and gay movement had to incorporate lesbian-feminist analysis into their political practice.[22]

Though gay liberation and women's liberation each played an important role in the emergence of a lesbian-feminist movement, in certain ways the latter exerted a special influence. The feminist movement provided the physical and psychic space for growing numbers of women to come out. As women explored their oppression together, it became easier to acknowledge their love for other women and to embrace "woman-identification." Many lesbians were already living independent, autonomous lives: Unencumbered by primary sexual and emotional attachments to men, lesbians had the freedom to explore the farthest reaches of a feminist future. They also had the inclination and need to build and sustain a network of institutions—coffeehouses, clinics, shelters, record companies, presses, schools, and communes—that continually nourished the growth of a lesbian-feminist politics. As opponents of feminism were quick to realize, the women's movement was, in fact, a "breeding ground" for lesbians.

Only a minority of lesbians and gay men joined organizations, but that minority decisively affected the lives of a much larger number. Through coming out and its example of gay pride, through the vastly increased flow of information that an activist minority stimulated, and especially through the inhibitions on police harassment that militancy imposed, lesbian and gay liberation transformed the self-image of many and offered the hope of a better life even to those who had never attended a meeting or participated in a demonstration.

In concrete terms a better life often translated into a decision to move to one of the handful of large cities known to have a well-developed gay subculture. America in the 1970s saw a massive sexual migration set in motion by the lesbian and gay movements. Here, San Francisco had a running start on every other city. Homophile groups were already getting attention from liberal politicians and had already limited police harassment of bars. Magazines played up San Francisco's reputation as a city that tolerated gays. The 1960s, moreover, established the Bay Area as an enclave of radical and lifestyle politics. The women's movement in the Bay Area, though not free of gay-straight conflict, was noticeably more hospitable to lesbians than elsewhere. While New York NOW, for instance, was purging lesbians from its ranks, San Francisco NOW was pushing for a lesbian rights resolution at the organization's 1971 national convention.

By the mid–1970s San Francisco had become, in comparison to the rest of the country, a liberated zone for lesbians and gay men. It had the largest number and widest variety of organizations and institutions. An enormous in-migration had created a new social phenomenon, residential areas that were visibly gay in composition: Duboce Triangle, Noe Valley, and the Upper Mission for lesbians; the Haight, Folsom, and above all the Castro for gay men. Geographic concentration offered the opportunity for local political power that invisibility precluded.

The explosive growth of the gay community and its political activism also made internal differences visible. For some gay men liberation meant freedom from harassment; for radicalesbians it meant overthrowing the patriarchy. Bay Area Gay Liberation participated in anti-imperialist coalitions while members of the Alice B. Toklas Democratic Club sought to climb within the Democratic party hierarchy. The interests of gay entrepreneurs in the Castro clashed with those of their gay employees. Gay male real-estate speculators displayed little concern for "brothers" who could not pay the skyrocketing rents. Gay men and women of color found themselves displaced by more privileged members of the community as gentrification spread to more and more neighborhoods. Sexual orientation created a kind of unity, but other aspects of identity brought to the surface conflicting needs and interests.

Community and Power in an Age of Adversity

The second half of the 1970s witnessed a rapid coming of age of gays as a political force in San Francisco. In 1975 George Moscone, a liberal state senator with a progay voting record, was elected mayor by a narrow margin of three thousand votes. Moscone credited gays with providing his margin of victory and included gays among the constituencies to be courted with political appointments. In November 1976 gay residential areas voted heavily for Proposition T, which mandated district elections for city supervisors. The following year Harvey Milk, a political outsider with few ties to the gay Democratic "establishment," won election from District 5, which included the Castro, Noe Valley, and the Haight. In June 1976 San Francisco surpassed New York in the size of its Gay Freedom Day march. The turnout of over ninety thousand alerted politicians to the potential significance of the gay vote.[23]

The antigay backlash of the New Right provided the stimulus that seemed to transform that potential into a force with real power. The repeal of gay rights ordinances in Dade County, Florida, and in Saint Paul, Wichita, and Eugene, Oregon, in 1977 and 1978, fueled a repressive legislative initiative in California. John Briggs, an ultraconservative state senator from Orange County with aspirations for higher office, announced plans to introduce legislation to prohibit gays from teaching in the public schools. When it became obvious that the legislation had no chance of passage, Briggs shifted tactics and mounted a campaign to have his proposal placed on the ballot as a statewide initiative. California voters would have to decide whether lesbians and gay men, as well as anyone who publicly or privately advocated or encouraged homosexual conduct, should be dismissed from jobs in the public school system.

The Briggs initiative ("Proposition 6" on the ballot) stimulated the most far-reaching and sustained gay organizing campaign in history. A bewildering array of organizations came into existence in every part of the state, with a wide range of political perspectives. Unlike the previous campaigns in other cities—low-key, respectable, "human rights" in emphasis—many in the anti-Briggs effort decided to confront issues of homophobia and sexuality directly, to link the antigay initiative with Proposition 7, a measure to reinstitute the death penalty, and to discuss the Briggs initiative as one part of a New Right strategy to attack racial minorities, women, and workers. The San Francisco lesbian and gay communities were in the forefront of the more radical approach to the anti-Briggs campaign.[24]

The mobilization of San Francisco's lesbians and gay men against Briggs secured other important gains and provided further evidence of growing gay power. The Prop 6 campaign forced most of the city's politicians to take a progay stand, however tenuous and opportunistic. In March 1978, after years of effort, a comprehensive gay rights ordinance was passed by the Board of Supervisors. The city allocated public funds for Gay Freedom Day activities; three hundred thousand people assembled for the rally at civic center. San Francisco's police chief, Charles Gain, announced a drive to recruit lesbians and gay men for the police force and urged gays already in the department to come out.

The anti-Briggs campaign also had a profound effect on the political career and image of Harvey Milk, San Francisco's gay supervisor. Milk was not the "leader" of the "No on 6" effort. But as the state's only openly gay elected official Milk was uniquely visible. This gave him a degree of political leverage that most local politicians only dream of attaining. He matured as a political leader, became more than a gay spokesperson, and began moving beyond liberalism. He worked hard to cement a coalition among gays, racial minorities, and the elderly. He became a strong advocate of rent control, opposed the redevelopment plans being pushed by downtown corporate interests, and introduced a resolution to have the South African consulate in San Francisco closed. During 1978 he helped to push Moscone away from mainstream liberalism and toward a populist-style coalition politics. By the time of the November election, Milk had become one of the most popular politicians in San Francisco and had achieved wide voter recognition throughout the state.

The November balloting brought a decisive victory to California's lesbians and gay men. Almost sixty percent of the electorate voted no on

Proposition 6. In San Francisco the figure was seventy-five percent, with only a handful of the city's nine hundred precincts supporting the measure. The California victory was enormously significant in checking the mood of gloom and despair that was infecting the lesbian and gay movement throughout the country. Locally, it stimulated celebrations and fueled a sense of growing, almost unstoppable, power. Then, less than three weeks later, Milk and Moscone were assassinated by former city supervisor Dan White.

The day after the murders, the *Chronicle* called them "politically motivated." The truth of that charge was apparent. White, a veteran, former cop and firefighter, was the most conservative member of the Board of Supervisors and notoriously antigay. His 1977 campaign included rhetorical attacks on "social deviates." The only supervisor to vote against the gay rights ordinance, he also supported the Briggs initiative. White and Milk stood at opposite ends of the political spectrum represented on the Board of Supervisors. The assassination of Milk and Moscone effected a political coup in San Francisco. There were no progressive Democrats of comparable stature to replace them. Dianne Feinstein, closely allied to downtown business interests and a mentor of Dan White, became mayor.

The assassination made clear that gay power in San Francisco, though real, was also fragile. The political momentum generated among lesbians and gay men in San Francisco by the antigay backlash, and the gains made in the city during 1977–1978, had tended to obscure the extent of homophobia in San Francisco. When Sheriff Hongisto campaigned for gays in Miami, for instance, the deputy sheriffs' association sent a telegram of support to Anita Bryant. Police chief Charles Gain's drive to recruit lesbian and gay cops aroused the ire of the rank and file. A few days after the massive 1977 Gay Freedom Day march, five gay businesses on Castro Street were bombed. While the Board of Supervisors debated the gay rights ordinance, arsonists were setting fires to gay-owned stores in the south-of-Market Folsom area. Throughout 1977 and 1978, street violence against lesbians and gay men was a pervasive problem. A few days after becoming mayor, Feinstein warned the gay community that it was a minority in a heterosexual society and had to respect the sensibilities and standards of the majority.

For a time it seemed as if gay men and lesbians were about to lose the ground they had gained. In December 1978, an antiporn bill introduced by Feinstein became law and the district attorney's office began an investigation and crackdown against gay male bookstores and theaters. In January, police officers assaulted and arrested two women as they left Amelia's, a lesbian bar in the Upper Mission. In March, a group of drunk off-duty cops burst into Peg's Place, a lesbian bar in the Richmond, and indiscriminately attacked patrons. The police began harassing gay male leather bars in the Folsom area and hassling young gays on Polk Street. The plan of these attacks was clear: Leave the Castro, the heavily gay male area, alone, but attack the "periphery" of the gay subculture—lesbian rather than gay male bars, gay youth rather than adults, sado-masochists rather than ordinary gays, porn stores and theaters rather than "good gay" meeting places.

Then came the Dan White murder trial: an all-white, all-straight jury; a prosecutor who never mentioned the political antagonisms between White and Milk and therefore could not prove premeditation; a taped confession, taken by White's former softball coach, that made jurors weep in sympathy for the defendant; and prosecution witnesses, like Mayor Feinstein, who praised the moral character of the killer. Throughout the trial the local press was unusually sympathetic toward the assassin of the city's mayor and gay supervisor. Cops were reported to be wearing "Free Dan White" t-shirts; a local reporter told me that when the manslaughter verdict (the lightest possible conviction) was announced, "Oh Danny Boy" was played on the police radio.[25]

The manslaughter verdict of May 21, 1979, sparked a riot, but did not cause the riot. The actions of the five to ten thousand gay men and women at City Hall that night were caused by six months of accumulating anger over police harassment and violence, street attacks, and an increasingly hostile city administration. The riot was the response of a community that had worked hard for its victories and then, after its greatest triumph, watched its dreams shattered by bullets from an assassin who represented everything that lesbians and gay men were fighting against.

Gay men and women at city hall attacked property; later that night, after the rioting was over, the police smashed heads. Rank-and-file police, packed into squad cars and vans, and encouraged by their officers, arrived on Castro Street and produced a terrifying display of indiscriminate violence. They charged into the Elephant Walk, a popular bar, smashing windows and upsetting tables. Screaming "dirty cocksuckers" and "sick faggots," and "we lost the battle of city hall; we won't lose this one," they attacked the bar's patrons. Others went marauding through the street, bloodying the faces of passersby. For two hours Castro Street was a virtual war zone, with the police on the offensive.

The anger that the Dan White verdict unleashed made it clear that the gay community in San Francisco was not about to relinquish its political power. By the end of the 1970s, the web of institutions in the community was too dense to be sundered by an assassin's bullet. Indeed, over the next few years gay men and lesbians were incorporated into the political life of the city as never before. Many elected officials, particularly liberal Democrats, routinely hired liaisons to the community, while others made use of gay political leadership on their staffs. Some lesbians and gay men were elected to minor posts in the city; many more were appointed to municipal regulatory boards.

The strength of the community became apparent during the 1980s when it was hit by the AIDS crisis. The lethal syndrome first came to light in

1981. The virus that seemed to cause the breakdown of the immune system was spread by blood and semen. The network of sexual meeting places that fostered recreational sex among gay men provided a hospitable environment for the rapid spread of the virus, and the AIDS caseload grew exponentially. By 1987 there were over forty-five thousand cases in the nation and over forty-four hundred in San Francisco. The overwhelming majority of the San Francisco cases were among gay men. Death became endemic, with survivors wondering if they would be next. A community that was bound together by an exuberant sexuality was forced to engage in serious soul-searching and to question what kind of future beckoned.[26]

Although AIDS was an unparalleled tragedy for the gay community around the nation, it also fostered a heightened level of political organizing. Wherever cases appeared in significant numbers, new organizations sprang to life to deal with the suffering. By the mid–1980s, AIDS was pushing gay issues toward the center of public debate. Groups that formed to provide social services soon found it necessary to plunge into the political arena to demand more funding for research and support services, to lobby for protection against discrimination, and to ward off the Orwellian proposals of right-wing pressure groups. The March on Washington in October 1987, in which six hundred thousand gay men, lesbians, and their allies converged on the nation's capital, testified to the depth of anger and political militancy that the AIDS crisis had generated.

As with so many other areas, the San Francisco community emerged as a leader in the response to AIDS. The city government, prodded by its highly visible gay constituency, provided proportionately more money more quickly than any other municipality. Support services proliferated, both on the part of government agencies and within the gay community itself. San Franciscans were saturated with educational materials and campaigns about safer sex; the incidence of diseases such as syphilis and gonorrhea plummeted as gay men altered their sexual habits to protect themselves. And a gay political leader in San Francisco, Cleve Jones, conceived and organized the "Names Project," a memorial quilt to those who died from AIDS that captured the attention and the sympathy of the nation.

But it would be wrong to overstate the political strength of lesbians and gay men in the city in the mid–1980s. For one, the San Francisco community existed in a larger social and political environment in which homophobia remained entrenched. The Reagan administration and the New Right continued to shape the national agenda to which gay activists had to react; in California, a conservative Republican governor, George Deukmejian, stymied progress at the state level. Within San Francisco itself, the community remained divided by political persuasion as well as identity. The progressive Harvey Milk Democratic Club and Stonewall Democratic Club engaged in rivalry with the more moderate Alice B.

Toklas Club. Gender, class, and racial identities shaped sometimes conflicting priorities among the gay population. Antigay violence, stimulated by AIDS, persisted as a problem, and the police were still not reliable defenders of the gay community.

Still, the previous few decades had witnessed a profound and lasting change in San Francisco (and in the nation at large). What was once a secret, despised identity had become the basis for an urban community, sharing many of the characteristics of more traditional ethnic groupings. And the community had, in turn, spawned a vigorous politics that gave it unusual national influence and served as a beacon of hope for others.

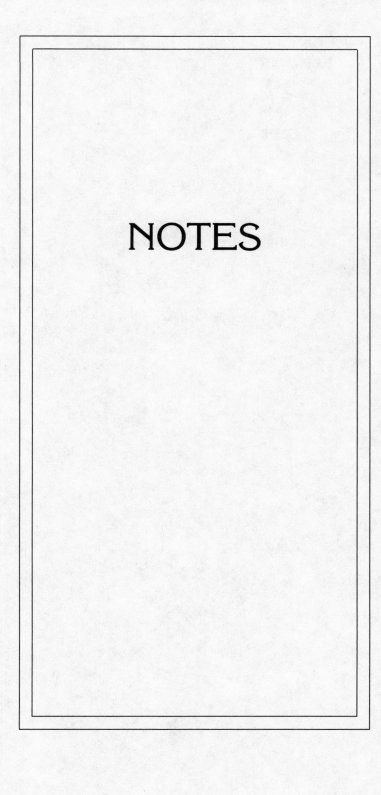

NOTES

Introduction

1. "The Female World of Love and Ritual: Relations Between Women in Nineteenth-Century America," *Signs: A Journal of Women in Culture and Society* 1 (Autumn 1975): 1–29.

2. Blanche Wiesen Cook, "Female Support Networks and Political Activism: Lillian Wald, Crystal Eastman, Emma Goldman," in *A Heritage of Her Own*, ed. Nancy Cott and Elizabeth Pleck (New York, 1979), 412–44; Andrew Hodges, *Alan Turing: The Enigma* (New York, 1983).

3. Richard Plant, *The Pink Triangle: The Nazi War Against Homosexuals* (New York, 1986); James D. Steakley, *The Homosexual Emancipation Movement in Germany* (New York, 1975); Manfred Herzer, "Hinweise auf das schwule Berlin in der Nazizeit," in *Eldorado: Homosexuelle Frauen und Maenner in Berlin, 1850–1950: Geschichte, Alltag und Kultur* (Berlin, 1984); Erwin Haeberle, "Swastika, Pink Triangle and Yellow Star: The Destruction of Sexology and the Persecution of Homosexuals in Nazi Germany," in this volume.

4. John D'Emilio, *Sexual Politics, Sexual Communities: The Making of a Homosexual Minority in the United States, 1940–1970* (Chicago, 1983); Toby Marotta, *The Politics of Homosexuality* (Boston, 1981); Salvatore J. Licata, "The Homosexual Rights Movement in the United States: A Traditionally Overlooked Area of American History," in *Historical Perspectives on Homosexuality*, ed. Salvatore J. Licata and Robert P. Peterson (New York, 1981).

5. Carole Vance, "Social Construction Theory: Problems in the History of Sexuality," in *Homosexuality, Which Homosexuality?*, ed. Theo van der Meer and Anja van Kooten Niekerk (London, 1989).

6. "Compulsory Heterosexuality and Lesbian Existence," *Signs* 5 (1980): 631–60.

7. *Heresies* 12 (1981): 21.

8. Randolph Trumbach, "London's Sodomites: Homosexual Behavior and Western Culture in the Eighteenth Century," *Journal of Social History* 11 (1977): 1–33; Alan Bray, *Homosexuality in Renaissance England* (London, 1982); Jeffrey Weeks, *Coming Out: Homosexual Politics in Britain from the Nineteenth Century to the Present* (London, 1977); Lillian Faderman, *Surpassing the Love of Men* (New York, 1981); John D'Emilio, "Capitalism and Gay Identity," in *Powers of Desire: The Politics of Sexuality*, ed. Ann Snitow, Christine Stansell, and Sharon Thompson (New York, 1983); idem., "Gay Politics and Community in San Francisco Since World War Two," in this volume.

9. Gilbert H. Herdt, *Guardians of the Flutes: Idioms of Masculinity* (New York, 1981), *Rituals of Manhood: Male Initiation in Papua New Guinea* (Berkeley, 1982), and *Ritualized Homosexuality in Melanesia* (1984).

Boswell, "Revolutions, Universals, and Sexual Categories"

1. For particularly articulate examples of "nominalist" history, see Robert A. Padgug, "Sexual Matters: On Conceptualizing Sexuality in History," *Radical History Review* 20 (1979): 3–33, reprinted in this volume; and Jeffrey Weeks, *Coming Out: Homosexual Politics in Britain from the Nineteenth Century to the Present* (London, 1977). Most older studies of homosexuality in the past are essentially realist; see bibliography in John Boswell, *Christianity, Social Tolerance and Homosexuality* (Chicago, 1980), p. 4, n. 3.

2. It is of substantial import to several moral traditions, e.g., whether or not homosexuality is a "condition"—an essentially "realist" position—or a "lifestyle"—basically a "nominalist" point of view. For a summary of shifting attitudes on these points within the Christian tradition, see Peter Coleman, *Christian Attitudes to Homosexuality* (London, 1980), or Edward Batchelor, *Homosexuality and Ethics* (New York, 1980).

3. Note that at this level the debate is to some extent concerned with the degree of convention that can be sustained without loss of accuracy. It is conventional, for instance, to include in a history of the United States treatment of the period before the inauguration of the system of government that bears that title, and even to speak of the "colonial U.S.," although while they were colonies they were not the United States. A history of Greece would likewise, by convention, concern itself with all the states that would someday constitute what is today called "Greece," although those states may have recognized no connection with each other (or even have been at war) at various points in the past. It is difficult to see why such conventions should not be allowed in the case of minority histories, so long as sufficient indication is provided as to the actual relationship of earlier forms to later ones.

4. Padgug, "Sexual Matters," p. 59.

5. For the variety of etiological explanations to date see the brief bibliography in Boswell, *Christianity*, p. 9, n. 9. To this list should now be added (in addition to many articles) three studies: Alan Bell and M.S. Weinberg, *Homosexualities: A Study of Diversity Among Men and Women* (New York, 1978); idem, *Sexual Preference: Its Development in Men and Women* (Bloomington, Indiana, 1981); and James Weinrich, *Sexual Landscapes* (New York, 1987). An ingenious and highly revealing approach to the development of modern medical literature on the subject of homosexuality is proposed by George Chauncey Jr., "From Sexual Inversion to Homosexuality: Medicine and the Changing Conceptualization of Female Deviance," *Salmagundi*, no. 58–59 (Fall 1982–Winter 1983): 114–46.

6. Moralia 767: *Amatorius*, trans. W. C. Helmhold (Cambridge, Mass., 1961), p. 415.

7. Boswell, *Christianity*, Part I *passim*, esp. pp. 50–59.

8. See Boswell, *Christianity*, pp. 125–27.

9. *Greek Anthology*, trans. W. R. Paton (Cambridge, Mass., 1918) 1.65.

10. Daphnis and Chloe, 4.11. The term *paiderastēs* here can not be understood as a reference to what is now called paedophilia, since Daphnis—the object of Gnatho's interest—is full grown and on the point of marriage. It is obviously a conventional term for "homosexual."

11. For Plato and Pollianus, see Boswell, *Christianity*, p. 30, n. 56; Athenaeus uses *philomeirax* of Sophocles and *philogynēs* of Euripides, apparently intending to indicate that the former was predominantly (if not exclusively) interested in males and the latter in females. Cf. *Scriptores physiognomici*, ed. R. Foerster (Leipzig, 1893), 1:29, p. 36, where the word *philogynaioi*, "woman lover," occurs.

12. Casina, V.4.957.

13. Epigrams 2.47.

14. Capitolinus, 11.7.

15. Boswell, *Christianity*, p. 127.

16. 2.4: Hostis si quis erit nobis, amet ille puellas:
        gaudeat in puero si quis amicus erit.

17. Saadia Gaon, *Kitāb al-'Amanāt wa'l-I ᶜ tikhadāt*, ed. S. Landauer (Leyden, 1880), 10.7, pp. 294–97 (English translation by S. Rosenblatt in *Yale Judaica Series*, vol. 1: *The Book of Beliefs and Opinions*).

18. *Kitāb*, p. 295.

19. Ibid.

20. *Kitāb mufākharāt al-jawārī wa'l-ghilmān*, ed. Charles Pellat (Beirut, 1957).

21. See discussion in Boswell, *Christianity*, pp. 257–8.

22. "Le Livre des caractères de Qostâ ibn Loûqâ," ed. and trans. Paul Sbath, *Bulletin de l'Institut d'Egypte* 23 (1940–41): 103–39. Sbath's translation is loose and misleading, and must be read with caution.

23. Ibid., p. 112.

24. ". . . waminhim man yamīlu īlā ghairihinna mini 'lghilmāni . . . ," ibid. A treatment of the fascinating term *ghulām* (pl. *ghilmān*), whose meanings range from "son" to "sexual partner," is beyond the scope of this essay.

25. Qustā discusses this at some length, pp. 133–36. Cf. F. Rosenthal, "ar-Râzî on the Hidden Illness," *Bulletin of the History of Medicine* 52, no.1 (1978): 45–60, and the authorities cited there. Treating "passive sexual behavior" (i.e., the reception of semen in anal intercourse) in men as a hereditary condition generally implies a conflation of Types A and C taxonomies in which the role of insertor with either men or women is thought "normal," but the position of the "insertee" is regarded as bizarre or even pathological. Attitudes toward *ubnah* should be taken as a special aspect of Muslim sexual taxonomy rather than as indicative of attitudes toward "homosexuality." A comparable case is that of Caelius Aurelianus: see Boswell, *Christianity*, p. 53; cf. remarks on Roman sexual taboos, below.

26. Weeks, *Coming Out*, p. 12.

27. See Boswell, *Christianity*, pp. 159–61.

28. *Aelfric's Lives of Saints*, ed. and trans. W. W. Skeat (London, 1881), p. 33.

29. Discussed in Boswell, *Christianity*, pp. 316ff.

30. "Sodomia" and "sodomita" are used so often and in so many competing senses in the High Middle Ages that a separate study would be required to present even a summary of this material. Note that in the modern West the term still has overlapping senses, even in law: In some American states "sodomy" applies to any inherently nonprocreative sex act (fellatio between husband and wife, e.g.), in others to all homosexual behavior, and in still others only to anal intercourse. Several "sodomy" statutes have in fact been overturned on grounds of unconstitutional vagueness. See, in addition to the material cited in Boswell, *Christianity*, pp. 52, 183–84; Giraldus Cambrensis, *Descriptio Cambriae*, 2.7; J. J. Tierney, "The Celtic Ethnogra-

phy of Posidonius," *Proceedings of the Royal Irish Academy* 60 (1960): 252; and *Carmina Burana: Die Lieder der Benediktbeurer Handschrift. Zweisprachige Ausgabe* (Munich, 1979), 95.4, p. 334 ("Pura semper ab hac infamia/nostra fuit minor Britannia"; the ms. has *Bricciavia*).

31. Walter Map, *De nugis curialium* 1.23, trans. John Mundy, *Europe in the High Middle Ages, 1150–1309* (New York, 1973), p. 302. Cf. discussion of this theme in Boswell, *Christianity*, chapter 8.

32. Prologue, 669ss. Of several works on this issue now in print see especially Monica McAlpine, "The Pardoner's Homosexuality and How it Matters," *PMLA*, January 1980, pp. 8–22; and Edward Schweitzer, "Chaucer's Pardoner and the Hare," *English Language Notes* 4, no. 4 (1967): 247–250 (not cited by McAlpine).

33. See Boswell, *Christianity*, p. 233.

34. 8565ss; cf. *Roman de la Rose* 2169–74, and Gerald Herman, "The 'Sin Against Nature' and its Echoes in Medieval French Literature," *Annuale Mediaevale* 17 (1976): 70–87.

35. "Altercatio Ganimedis et Helene: Kritische Edition mit Kommentar," ed. Rolf Lenzen, *Mittellateinisches Jahrbuch* 7 (1972): 161–86; English translation in Boswell, *Christianity*, pp. 381–89.

36. Boswell, *Christianity*, pp. 392–98.

37. *The Anglo-Latin Satirical Poets and Epigrammatists*, ed. Thomas Wright (London, 1872), 2:463.

38. The relationship between the words "propriety" and "property" is not coincidental, and in this connection is highly revealing. Although social attitudes toward sexual propriety in pre-Christian Europe are often touted as more humane and liberal than those which followed upon the triumph of the Christian religion, it is often overlooked that the comparative sexual freedom of adult free males in the ancient world stemmed largely from the fact that all the members of their household were either legally or effectively their *property*, and hence could be used by them as they saw fit. For other members of society what has seemed to some in the modern West to have been sexual "freedom" might be more aptly viewed as "abuse" or "exploitation," although it is of course silly to assume that the ability to coerce necessarily results in coercion.

39. Lesbianism is often regarded as peculiar or even pathological in cultures which accept male homosexuality with equanimity. In the largely gay romance *Affairs of the Heart* (see Boswell, *Christianity*, pp. 126–27) lesbianism is characterized as "the tribadic disease" [tēs tribakēs aselgeias] (s.28). A detailed analysis of the relationship of attitudes toward male and female homosexuality will comprise a portion of a study I am preparing on the phenomenology of homosexual behavior in ancient and medieval Europe.

40. Cf. n.5, above.

41. Since the publication of my remarks on this issue in *Christianity*, pp. 28–30, several detailed studies of Greek homosexuality have appeared, most notably those of Félix Buffière, *Eros adolescent: la pédérastie dans la Grèce antique* (Paris, 1980); and K. J. Dover, *Greek Homosexuality* (Cambridge, Mass., 1978). Neither work has persuaded me to revise my estimate of the degree to which Greek fascination with "youth" was more than a romantic convention. A detailed assessment of both works and their relation to my own findings will appear in the study mentioned above, no. 39.

42. Artemidorus Daldianus, *Onirocriticon libri quinque*, ed. R. Park (Leipzig, 1963) 1.78, pp. 88–89. (An English translation of this work is available: *The Interpretation of Dreams*, trans. R. J. White [Park Ridge, N.J., 1975]).

43. "Non est pedico maritus:/ quae faciat duo sunt: irrumat aut futuit" Martial 2:47 (cf. n. 14, above: *pedico* is apparently Martial's own coinage).

44. *Ceveo* is, that is, to *futuo* or *pedico* what *fello* is to *irrumo:* It describes the activity of the party being entered. The vulgar English "put out" may be the closest equivalent, but nothing in English captures the actual meaning of the Latin.

45. *Futuo/pedico* and *ceveo* are likewise both active.

46. Hunayn ibn Ishāq, trans., *Kitāb Taᶜbīr ar-Ru'yā*, ed. Toufic Fahd (Damascus, 1964), pp. 175–76.

47. For an overview of this literature since the material cited in note 1, see most recently Steven Epstein, "Gay Politics, Ethnic Identity: The Limits of Social Constructionism," *Socialist Review* 93/94 (1987): 9–54; also John D'Emilio, *Sexual Politics, Sexual Communities: The Making of a Homosexual Minority in the United States, 1940–1970* (Chicago, 1983); and the essays in Kenneth Plummer, ed., *The Making of the Modern Homosexual* (London, 1981). See also note 48.

48. Three recent writers on the controversy (Steven Murray, "Homosexual Categorization in Cross-Cultural Perspective," in Murray, *Social Theory, Homosexual Realities* [Gai Saber Monograph, 3] [New York, 1984]; Epstein, "Gay Politics"; and David Halperin, "Sex before Sexuality: Pederasty, Politics, and Power in Classical Athens" [in this collection] identify among them a dozen or more "constructionist" historians, but Murray and Halperin adduce only a single historian (me) as an example of modern "essentialist" historiography; Epstein, the most sophisticated of the three, can add to this only Adrienne Rich, not usually thought of as a historian. As to whether my views are actually "essentialist" or not, see further.

49. See, for example, Halperin, "Sex before Sexuality." Much of the controversy is conducted through scholarly papers: at a conference on "Homosexuality in History and Culture" held at Brown University in February 1987, of six presentations four were explicitly constructionist; two of these were by classicists. On the other hand, the standard volume on Attic homosexuality, K. J. Dover, *Greek Homosexuality* (New York, 1985), defies easy classification, but falls closer to an "essentialist" point of view than a "constructionist" one, and Keith DeVries's *Homosexuality and Athenian Society,* when it appears, will be a nonconstructionist survey of great subtlety and sophistication. See also David Cohen, "Law, Society and Homosexuality in Classical Athens," *Past and Present* 117 (1987): 3–21. For the (relatively few) recent studies of periods between Athens and the late nineteenth century, see Saara Lilja, *Homosexuality in Republican and Augustan Rome* (Helsinki, 1983) (Societas Scientiarum Fennica, Commentationes Humanarum Litterarum, 74); Alan Bray, *Homosexuality in Renaissance England* (London, 1982); James Saslow, *Ganymede in the Renaissance: Homosexuality in Art and Society* (New Haven, 1986); Guido Ruggiero, *The Boundaries of Eros: Sex, Crime and Sexuality in Renaissance Venice* (New York, 1985); Claude Courouve, *Vocabulaire de l'homosexualité masculine* (Paris, 1985).

50. An expression I use to include both women and men.

51. Of course, if a constructionist position holds that "gay person" refers only to one particular modern identity, it is then, tautologically, not applicable to the past.

Halperin, "Sex Before Sexuality"

An earlier version of this paper, taking the form of an extended book review of Harald Patzer's *Die griechische Knabenliebe* (Wiesbaden, 1982), appeared under the title "One Hundred Years of Homosexuality" in *The Mêtis of the Greeks,* ed. Milad Doueihi = *Diacritics,* 16, no. 2 (Summer 1986): 34–45. The present essay is closely based on this earlier work; it was first recast for delivery at a conference on "Homosexuality in History and Culture, and the University Curriculum," held at Brown University on 20–21 February 1987, and was later given as a public lecture at Duke University on 20 April 1987. For these more recent occasions I have eliminated the review format (and, hence, omitted consideration of Patzer's monograph), removed some of the documentation, supplemented the discussion of ancient sources, and translated into English citations from works in modern foreign languages. The most complete version of the essay will be found in my collection, *One Hundred Years of Homosexuality and Other Essays on Greek Love* (New York: Routledge, 1989).

The writing and revising of this paper have been generously supported by two fellowships, both funded by the Andrew W. Mellon Foundation, from the National Humanities Center and the Stanford Humanities Center, respectively. I am very grateful to Martha Nussbaum, for having invited me to speak at Brown, and to Peter Burian, for having invited me to speak at Duke, as well as to the audiences at both universities, for their sympathetic but rigorous scrutiny. I also wish to thank Barry D. Adam, Judith M. Bennett, Mary T. Boatwright, Elizabeth A. Clark, Kostas Demelis, Judith Ferster, Ernestine Friedl, Maud W. Gleason, Madelyn Gutwirth, Jean H. Hagstrum, Glenn W. Most, Cynthia B. Patterson, Daniel A. Pollock, Marilyn B. Skinner, Emery J. Snyder, Gregory Vlastos, and John J. Winkler for much friendly help and advice.

1. Wrongly, no doubt: The same entry in the *OED* records the use of the word by J. A. Symonds in a letter of the same year, and so it is most unlikely that Chaddock alone is responsible for its English coinage. See R. W. Burchfield, ed., *A Supplement to the Oxford English Dictionary* (Oxford, 1976), 2:136, s.v. homosexuality.

2. The terms "homosexual" and "homosexuality" appeared in print for the first time in 1869 in two anonymous pamphlets published in Leipzig and composed, apparently, by Karl Maria Kertbeny. Kertbeny (né Benkert) was an Austro-Hungarian translator and *littérateur* of Bavarian extraction, not a physician (as Magnus Hirschfeld and Havelock Ellis—misled by false clues planted in those pamphlets by Kertbeny himself—maintained); he wrote in German under his acquired Hungarian surname and claimed (rather unconvincingly) in the second of the two tracts under discussion not to share the sexual tastes denominated by his own ingenious neologism. For the most reliable accounts of Kertbeny and his invention, see Manfred Herzer, "Kertbeny and the Nameless Love," *Journal of Homosexuality*, 12.1 (1985): 1–26, and, now, Hubert Kennedy, *Ulrichs: The Life and Works of Karl Henrich Ulrichs, Pioneer of the Modern Gay Movement* (Boston, 1988). pp. 149–56. See also John Lauritsen and David Thorstad, *The Early Homosexual Rights Movement (1864–1935)* (New York: Times Change Press, 1974), pp. 6–8; Jean-Claude Féray, "Une histoire critique du mot homosexualité," *Arcadie* 28, nos. 325–328 (1981): 11–21, 115–24, 171–81, 246–58; Wayne Dynes, *Homolexis:*

A Historical and Cultural Lexicon of Homosexuality, Gai Saber Monograph No. 4 (New York: Gay Academic Union, 1985), p. 67, who notes that Kertbeny's term "might have gone unnoticed had not [Kertbeny's friend] Gustav Jaeger popularized it in the second edition of his *Entdeckung der Seele* (1880)." The earlier of Kertbeny's two pamphlets is reprinted in the *Jahrbuch für sexuelle Zwischenstufen* 7 (1905): 1–66.

3. George Chauncey, Jr., "From Sexual Inversion to Homosexuality: Medicine and the Changing Conceptualization of Female Deviance," in *Homosexuality: Sacrilege, Vision, Politics*, ed. Robert Boyers and George Steiner = *Salmagundi* 58–59 (1982–83): 114–46 (quotation on p. 116). Cf. Michel Foucault, *The History of Sexuality, Volume I: An Introduction*, trans. Robert Hurley (New York, 1978), pp. 37–38; Féray "Une histoire," esp. pp. 16–17, 246–56; Jeffrey Weeks, "Discourse, Desire and Sexual Deviance: Some Problems in a History of Homosexuality," in *The Making of the Modern Homosexual*, ed. Kenneth Plummer (London: Hutchinson, 1981), pp. 76–111, esp. 82ff.; John Marshall, "Pansies, Perverts and Macho Men: Changing Conceptions of Male Homosexuality," in *The Making of the Modern Homosexual*, pp. 133–54; Arnold I. Davidson, "Closing Up the Corpses: Diseases of Sexuality and the Emergence of the Psychiatric Style of Reasoning," in *Reason, Language and Method: Essays in Honour of Hilary Putnam*, ed. George Boolos (Cambridge, forthcoming). To be sure, the formal introduction of "inversion" as a clinical term (by Arrigo Tamassia, "Sull' inversione dell' istinto sessuale," *Rivista sperimentale di freniatria e di medicina legale* 4 [1878]: 97–117: the earliest published use of "inversion" that Havelock Ellis, *Sexual Inversion = Studies in the Psychology of Sex*, vol. 2, 3d ed. [Philadelphia, 1922]: 3, was able to discover) occurred a decade *after* Kertbeny's coinage of "homosexuality," but Ellis suspected the word of being considerably older: It seems to have been well established by the 1870s, at any rate, and it was certainly a common designation throughout the 1880s. "Homosexuality," by contrast, did not begin to achieve currency in Europe until the Eulenburg affair of 1907–1908 (see Féray, "Une histoire," pp. 116–22), and even thereafter it was slow in gaining ascendancy. The main point, in any case, is that "inversion," defined as it is by reference to gender deviance, represents an age-old outlook, whereas "homosexuality" marks a sharp break with traditional ways of thinking.

4. Chauncey, "From Sexual Inversion to Homosexuality," esp. pp. 117–22, citing W. C. Rivers, "A New Male Homosexual Trait (?)," *Alienist and Neurologist* 41 (1920): 22–27; the persistence of this outlook in the United States, along with some of its practical (military, legal, and ecclesiastical) applications, has now been documented by Chauncey, "Christian Brotherhood or Sexual Perversion? Homosexual Identities and the Construction of Sexual Boundaries in the World War One Era," *Journal of Social History* 19 (1985): 189–211 (reprinted in this volume), in a study of the role-specific morality that once governed sexual attitudes and practices among members of the United States Navy. For even more recent expressions of the traditional outlook in Great Britain, see the citations discussed by Marshall, "Pansies, Perverts, and Macho Men," pp. 149–52. Cf., also, Albert J. Reiss, Jr., "The Social Integration of Queers and Peers," *Social Problems* 9 (1961/62): 102–20, with references to earlier work; John H. Gagnon and William Simon, *Sexual Conduct: The Social Sources of Human Sexuality* (Chicago, 1973), 240–51; and, esp., Jack H. Abbott, "On 'Women,' " *New York Review of Books*, 28, no. 10 (June 11, 1981): 17. The classic statement of the "inversion" thesis is the opening chapter of Proust's *Sodom and Gomorrah*: see Marcel Proust, *À la recherche du temps perdu*, ed. Pierre Clarac and André Ferré (Paris,

1954), 2: 601–32, esp. 614–15, 620–22; *Remembrance of Things Past*, trans. C. K. Scott Moncrieff and Terence Kilmartin (New York, 1981), 2: 623–56, esp. 637–38, 643–45.

5. See Chauncey, "From Sexual Inversion to Homosexuality," pp. 122–25; Marshall, "Pansies, Perverts and Macho Men," pp. 137–53; Arnold I. Davidson, "How to Do the History of Psychoanalysis: A Reading of Freud's *Three Essays on the Theory of Sexuality*," in *The Trial(s) of Psychoanalysis*, ed. Françoise Meltzer, *Critical Inquiry* 13 (1986/87): 252–77, esp. 258–71; Jerome Neu, "Freud and Perversion," in *Sexuality and Medicine*, ed. Earl E. Shelp, Philosophy and Medicine, 22–23 (D. Reidel: Dordrecht, 1987), 1:153–84, esp. 153ff. For the modern distinction between "inversion" (i.e., sex-role reversal) and "homosexuality," see C. A. Tripp, *The Homosexual Matrix* (New York, 1975), 22–35.

6. For the lack of congruence between traditional and modern sexual categories, cf. Gilbert H. Herdt, ed., *Ritualized Homosexuality in Melanesia* (Berkeley, 1984), pp. viii–x; Gianni De Martino and Arno Schmitt, *Kleine Schriften zu zwischenmännlicher Sexualität und Erotik in der muslimischen Gesellschaft* (Berlin: author, 1985), esp. pp. 3–10. The new scientific conceptualization of homosexuality reflects, to be sure, a much older habit of mind, distinctive to northern and northwestern Europe since the Renaissance, whereby sexual acts are categorized not according to the modality of sexual or social roles assumed by the sexual partners but rather according to the anatomical sex of the persons engaged in them: see Randolph Trumbach, "London's Sodomites: Homosexual Behavior and Western Culture in the 18th Century," *Journal of Social History* 11 (1977): 1–33, esp. 2–9, with notes. This habit of mind seems to have been shaped, in its turn, by the same aggregate of cultural factors responsible for the much older division, accentuated during the Renaissance, between European and Mediterranean marriage-patterns; northern and northwestern Europe typically exhibits a pattern of marriage between mature coevals, a bilateral kinship system, neolocal marriage, and a mobile labor force, whereas Mediterranean societies are characterized by late male and early female marriage, patrilineal kinship organization, patrivirilocal marriage, and inhibited circulation of labor: see R. M. Smith, " 'The People of Tuscany and their Families in the Fifteenth Century: Medieval or Mediterranean?' " *Journal of Family History* 6 (1981): 107–28; recent work has produced evidence for the antiquity of the Mediterranean marriage-pattern: see M. K. Hopkins, "The Age of Roman Girls at Marriage," *Population Studies* 18 (1964/65): 309–27; Richard P. Saller, "Men's Age at Marriage and Its Consequences in the Roman Family," *Classical Philology* 82 (1987): 21–34, esp. 30; Martha T. Roth, "Age at Marriage and the Household: A Study of Neo-Babylonian and Neo-Assyrian Forms," *Comparative Studies in Society and History* 29 (1987): 715–47.

7. E.g., K. Freund, "A Laboratory Method for Diagnosing Predominance of Homo- or Hetero-Erotic Interest in the Male," *Behavior Research and Therapy* 1 (1963–64): 85–93; N. McConaghy, "Penile Volume Change to Moving Pictures of Male and Female Nudes in Heterosexual and Homosexual Males," *Behavior Research and Therapy* 5 (1967): 43–48. For a partial, and critical, review of the literature on testing procedures, see Bernard F. Riess, "Psychological Tests in Homosexuality," in *Homosexual Behavior: A Modern Reappraisal*, ed. Judd Marmor (New York, 1981), pp. 296–311. Compare the parallel tendency in the same period to determine the "true sex" of hermaphrodites: see Michel Foucault's introduction to *Herculine Barbin, Being the Recently Discovered Memoirs of a Nineteenth-Century French Hermaphrodite*, trans. Richard McDougall (New York, 1980), esp. pp. vii–xi.

8. See Foucault, *The Archaeology of Knowledge and the Discourse on Language*, trans. A. M. Sheridan Smith (New York, 1972), p. 190, for the introduction of this concept; for its application to the history of sexual categories, see Arnold I. Davidson, "Sex and the Emergence of Sexuality," *Critical Inquiry* 14 (1987/88): 16–48, esp. 48.

9. On the emergence of the concept of homosexuality, see Jeffrey Weeks, " 'Sins and Diseases': Some Notes on Homosexuality in the Nineteenth Century," *History Workshop* 1 (1976): 211–19, and *Sex, Politics and Society: The Regulation of Sexuality since 1800* (London, 1981), esp. pp. 96–121; also, Marshall, "Pansies, Perverts and Macho Men." For a lucid discussion of the sociological implications, see Mary McIntosh, "The Homosexual Role," *Social Problems* 16 (1968/69): 182–92, who also examines some of the quasi-theological refinements ("bisexuality," "latent homosexuality," "pseudo-homosexuality") that have been added to this intellectual structure in order to buttress its central concept.

10. *A Problem in Modern Ethics*, quoted by Jeffrey Weeks, *Coming Out: Homosexual Politics in Britain, from the Nineteenth Century to the Present* (London, 1977), p. 1.

11. While condemning "homosexuality" as "a bastard term compounded of Greek and Latin elements" (p. 2), Ellis acknowledged that its classical etymology facilitated its diffusion throughout the European languages; moreover, by consenting to employ it himself, Ellis helped further to popularize it. On the philological advantages and disadvantages of "homosexuality," see Féray, "Une histoire," pp. 174–76.

12. This passage, along with others in a similar vein, has been well discussed by Marshall.

13. Marshall, "Pansies, Perverts and Macho Men," p. 148, who goes on to quote the following passage from the preface to a recent survey by D. J. West, *Homosexuality Reassessed* (London, 1977), p. vii: "A generation ago the word homosexuality was best avoided in polite conversation, or referred to in muted terms appropriate to a dreaded and scarcely mentionable disease. Even some well-educated people were hazy about exactly what it meant." Note, however, that Edward Westermarck, writing for a scholarly audience in *The Origin and Development of the Moral Ideas*, could allude to "what is nowadays commonly called homosexual love" (2:456) as early as 1908. Westermarck's testimony has escaped the *OED* Supplement, which simply records that in 1914 George Bernard Shaw felt free to use the word "homosexual" adjectivally in the *New Statesman* without further explanations and that the adjective reappears in *Blackwood's Magazine* in 1921 as well as in Robert Graves's *Good-bye to All That* in 1929. The French version of "homosexuality," by contrast, showed up in the *Larousse mensuel illustré* as early as December 1907 (according to Féray, "Une histoire," p. 172).

14. The earliest literary occurrence of the German loan-word "homosexualist," of which the *OED* is similarly ignorant, took place only in 1925, to the best of my knowledge, and it illustrates the novelty that evidently still attached to the term: In Aldous Huxley's *Those Barren Leaves* we find the following exchange between a thoroughly modern aunt and her up-to-date niece, who are discussing a mutual acquaintance.

"I sometimes doubt," [Aunt Lilian] said, "whether he takes any interest in women at all. Fundamentally, unconsciously, I believe he's a homosexualist."

"Perhaps," said Irene gravely. She knew her Havelock Ellis [Part III, Chapter 11].

(The earliest occurrence of "homosexualist" cited in the *OED* Supplement dates from 1931.)

15. According, once again, to the dubious testimony of the *OED*'s 1976 Supplement, 2:85, s.v. heterosexuality. (Note that Kertbeny, the coiner of the term "homosexual," opposed it not to "heterosexual" but to *normalsexual:* Féray "Une histoire," p. 171.) On the dependence of "heterosexuality" on "homosexuality," see ibid., pp. 171–72; Harold Beaver, "Homosexual Signs (*In Memory of Roland Barthes*)," *Critical Inquiry* 8 (1981/82): 99–119, esp. 115–16.

16. Some doubts about the applicability of the modern concept of homosexuality to ancient varieties of sexual experience have been voiced by George Devereux, "Greek Pseudo-Homosexuality and the 'Greek Miracle,' " *Symbolae Osloenses* 42 (1968): 69–92, esp. 71–76; W. Thomas MacCary, *Childlike Achilles: Ontogeny and Phylogeny in the ILIAD* (New York, 1982), pp. 178–85; Bernard Sergent, *Homosexuality in Greek Myth*, trans. Arthur Goldhammer (Boston, 1986), pp. 46–47.

17. John Boswell, "Revolutions, Universals and Sexual Categories," *Salmagundi* 58–59 (1982–83): 89–113. esp. 20 (as reprinted in this volume). Boswell himself, however, argues for the contrary position, which has been most baldly stated by Vern L. Bullough, *Homosexuality: A History* (New York, 1979), pp. 2, 62: "Homosexuality has always been with us; it has been a constant in history, and its presence is clear." Opponents of the view advocated by Boswell and Bullough can be found in Guy Hocquenghem, *Homosexual Desire*, trans. Daniella Dangoor (London, 1978), esp. pp. 36–37; Paul Veyne, "La famille et l'amour sous le Haut-Empire romain," *Annales (E.S.C.)* 33 (1978): 35–63, esp. 52; Robert A. Padgug, "Sexual Matters: On Conceptualizing Sexuality in History," *Radical History Review* 20 (1979): 3–23 (reprinted in this volume); Weeks, *Sex, Politics and Society*, esp. pp. 96–121; Alan Bray, *Homosexuality in Renaissance England* (London: Gay Men's Press, 1982), esp. pp. 8–9, 13–32; Gayle Rubin, "Thinking Sex: Notes for a Radical Theory of the Politics of Sexuality," in *Pleasure and Danger: Exploring Female Sexuality*, ed. Carole S. Vance (Boston, 1984), pp. 267–319, esp. 285–86; De Martino and Schmitt, *Kleine Schriften;* Davidson, "Sex and the Emergence of Sexuality"; and, most pertinently, the essays collected in Plummer, ed., *The Making of the Modern Homosexual*. Additional fuel for the fires of historicism can be found in the writings of those who attempt to relate the rise of homosexuality to the rise of capitalism: see Hocquenghem; Jeffrey Weeks, "Capitalism and the Organisation of Sex," in *Homosexuality: Power & Politics*, ed. Gay Left Collective (London, 1980), pp. 11–20; Dennis Altman, *The Homosexualization of America* (New York, 1982), esp. pp. 79–107; John D'Emilio, "Capitalism and Gay Identity," in *Powers of Desire: The Politics of Sexuality*, ed. Ann Snitow, Christine Stansell, and Sharon Thompson (New York, 1983), pp. 100–13; Barry D. Adam, "Structural Foundations of the Gay World," *Comparative Studies in Society and History* 27 (1985): 658–71.

18. See Foucault, *The History of Sexuality,* pp. 68–69, and *The Use of Pleasure*, The History of Sexuality, vol. 2., trans. Robert Hurley (New York, 1985), pp. 35–52; Weeks, "Capitalism and the Organisation of Sex," p. 13 (paraphrasing Foucault:) "Our culture has developed a notion of sexuality linked to reproduction and genitality and to 'deviations' from these. . . ."; Féray, "Une histoire," pp. 247–51; Davidson, "How to Do the History of Psychoanalysis," pp. 258–62; Thomas Laqueur, "Orgasm, Generation, and the Politics of Reproductive Biology," in *Sexuality and the Social Body in the Nineteenth Century*, ed. Catherine Gallagher and Thomas Laqueur, *Repre-*

sentations 14 (Spring 1986): 1–41. The biological conceptualization of "sexuality" as an instinct is neatly disposed of by Tripp, *The Homosexual Matrix,* pp. 10–21.

19. See Foucault, *The History of Sexuality,* p. 43: "As defined by the ancient civil or canonical codes, sodomy was a category of forbidden acts; their perpetrator was nothing more than the juridical subject of them. The nineteenth-century homosexual became a personage, a past, a case history, and a childhood, in addition to being a type of life, a life form, and a morphology, with an indiscreet anatomy and possibly a mysterious physiology. Nothing that went into his total composition was unaffected by his sexuality. It was everywhere present in him: at the root of all his actions because it was their insidious and indefinitely active principle; written immodestly on his face and body because it was a secret that always gave itself away. It was consubstantial with him, less as a habitual sin than as a singular nature." Cf. Trumbach, "London's Sodomites," p. 9; Weeks, *Coming Out,* p. 12; Richard Sennett, *The Fall of Public Man* (New York, 1977), pp. 6–8; Padgug, "Sexual Matters," pp. 59–60; Féray, "Une histoire," pp. 246–47; Alain Schnapp, "Une autre image de l'homosexualité en Grèce ancienne," *Le Débat* 10 (March 1981): 107–17, esp. 116 (speaking of Attic vase-paintings): "One does not paint acts that characterize persons so much as behaviors that distinguish groups"; Pierre J. Payer, *Sex and the Penitentials: The Development of a Sexual Code 550–1150* (Toronto, 1984), pp. 40–44, esp. 40–41: "There is no word in general usage in the penitentials for homosexuality as a category. . . . Furthermore, the distinction between homosexual acts and people who might be called homosexuals does not seem to be operative in these manuals. . . ."

20. For ancient expressions by males of a sexual preference for males, see, e.g., Theognis, 1367–68; Euripides, *Cyclops* 583–84; Xenophon, *Anabasis* 7.4.7–8; Aeschines, *Against Timarchus* 41, 195; the fragment of Seleucus quoted by Athenaeus, 15.697de (= J. U. Powell, ed., *Collectanea Alexandrina* [Oxford, 1925], p. 176); an anonymous dramatic fragment cited by Plutarch, *Amatorius* 766f–767a (= August Nauck, ed., *Tragicorum Graecorum Fragmenta,* 2d ed. [Leipzig, 1926], p. 906, #355 [also in Kock, *Com. Att. Fr.,* 3:467, #360]); Athenaeus, 12.540e, 13.601e and ff.; Achilles Tatius, 2.35.2–3; pseudo-Lucian *Erôtes* 9–10; Firmicus Maternus, *Mathesis* 7.15.1–2; and a number of epigrams by various hands contained in the *Palatine Anthology:* V, 19, 65, 116, 208, 277, 278; XI, 216; XII 7, 17, 87, 145, 192, 198, and *passim.* See, generally, K. J. Dover, *Greek Homosexuality* (London, 1978), pp. 62–63; Boswell, "Revolutions, Universals, and Sexual Categories," pp. 98–101; John J. Winkler, "Unnatural Acts: Erotic Protocols in Artemidorus' Dream Analysis," in *The Constraints of Desire: The Anthropology of Sex and Gender in Ancient Greece* (New York, 1989).

21. Foucault, *The Use of Pleasure,* pp. 51–52, remarks that it would be interesting to determine exactly when in the evolving course of Western cultural history sex became more morally problematic than eating; he seems to think that sex won out only at the turn of the eighteenth century, after a long period of relative equilibrium during the middle ages: see, also, *The Use of Pleasure,* p. 10; "On the Genealogy of Ethics: An Overview of Work in Progress," in Hubert L. Dreyfus and Paul Rabinow, *Michel Foucault: Beyond Structuralism and Hermeneutics,* 2d ed. (Chicago, 1983), pp. 229–52, esp. 229; *The Care of the Self,* The History of Sexuality, vol. 3, trans. Robert Hurley (New York, 1986), p. 143. For a discussion of Foucault's approach to "the history of sexuality," see my review of the original French edition of *The Use of Pleasure:* "Sexual Ethics and Technologies of the Self in Classical

Greece," *American Journal of Philology* 107 (1986): 274–86, where I observe that the evidence newly assembled by Caroline Walker Bynum, *Holy Feast and Holy Fast: The Religious Significance of Food to Medieval Women* (Berkeley, 1987), suggests that moral evolution may not have been quite such a continuously linear affair as Foucault appears to imagine. (See, also, note 22.)

22. See, however, Stephen Nissenbaum, *Sex, Diet, and Debility in Jacksonian America: Sylvester Graham and Health Reform*, Contributions in Medical History, vol. 4 (Westport, Conn.: 1980), for an example from relatively recent history of the possible linkage between sexual and dietary morality. Hilary Putnam, *Reason, Truth and History* (Cambridge, 1981), pp. 150–55, in the course of analyzing the various criteria by which we judge matters of taste to be "subjective," argues that we are right to consider sexual preferences more thoroughly constitutive of the human personality than dietary preferences, but his argument remains circumscribed, as Putnam himself emphasizes, by highly culture-specific assumptions about sex, food, and personhood.

23. Boswell, "Revolutions, Universals, and Sexual Categories," pp. 21–27. Bullough, *Homosexuality*, p. 3, similarly appeals to Aristophanes's myth as "one of the earliest explanations" of homosexuality.

24. Boswell, "Revolutions, Universals, and Sexual Categories," p. 25; cf. Auguste Valensin, "Platon et la théorie de l'amour," *Études* 281 (1954): 32–45, esp. 37.

25. Something like this point is implicit in Luc Brisson, "Bisexualité et médiation en Grèce ancienne," *Nouvelle revue de psychanalyse* 7 (1973): 27–48, esp. 42–43; see also Neu, "Freud and Perversions," p. 177, n. 1. My own (somewhat different) reading of Aristophanes' speech is set forth in greater detail in "Platonic *Erôs* and What Men Call Love," *Ancient Philosophy* 5 (1985): 161–204, esp. 167–70; I have reproduced some of my earlier formulations here.

26. To be sure, a certain symmetry does obtain between the groups composed, respectively, of those making a homosexual and those making a heterosexual object-choice: Each of them is constituted by Aristophanes in such a way as to contain both males and females in their dual capacities as subjects and objects of erotic desire. Aristophanes does nothing to highlight this symmetry, however, and it may be doubted whether it should figure in our interpretation of the passage.

27. The term "boy" (*pais* in Greek) refers by convention to the junior partner in a pederastic relationship, or to one who plays that role, regardless of his actual age; youths are customarily supposed to be desirable between the onset of puberty and the arrival of the beard: see Dover, *Greek Homosexuality*, pp. 16, 85–87; Félix Buffière, *Eros adolescent: la pédérastie dans la Grèce antique* (Paris, 1980), pp. 605–14; N. M. Kay, *Martial Book XI: A Commentary* (London, 1985), pp. 120–21.

28. On the meaning of the term "philerast," see Elaine Fantham, "*Zêlotypia*: A Brief Excursion into Sex, Violence, and Literary History," *Phoenix* 40 (1986): 45–57, esp. 48, n. 10.

29. For an explication of what is meant by "a certain (nonsexual) pleasure in physical contact with men," see note 33.

30. See Dover, *Greek Homosexuality*, esp. pp. 73–109; a general survey of this issue together with the scholarship on it can be found in my essay, "Plato and Erotic Reciprocity," *Classical Antiquity* 5 (1986): 60–80.

31. Nor does Aristophanes make any allowance in his myth for what was perhaps the most widely shared sexual taste among his fellow Athenian

citizens—namely, an undifferentiated liking for good-looking women and boys (that is, a sexual preference not defined by an exclusively gender-specific sexual object-choice). Such a lacuna should warn us not to treat Aristophanes' myth as a simple description or reflection of contemporary experience.

32. Public lecture delivered at Brown University, 21 February 1987.

33. In "Plato and Erotic Reciprocity," I have argued that—in this one respect, at least—the picture drawn by Plato's Aristophanes, *if* taken to represent *the moral conventions* governing sexual behavior in classical Athens rather than the reality of sexual behavior itself—is historically accurate. To be sure, the pederastic ethos of classical Athens did not prohibit a willing boy from responding enthusiastically to his lover's physical attentions: Aristophanes himself maintains that a philerast both "enjoys" and "welcomes" (*khairein, aspazesthai:* 191e–192b) his lover's embraces. But that ethos did stipulate that whatever enthusiasm a boy exhibited for sexual contact with his lover sprang from sources other than sexual desire. The distinction between "welcoming" and "desiring" a lover's caresses, as it applies to the motives for a boy's willingness, spelled the difference between decency and degeneracy; that distinction is worth emphasizing here because the failure of modern interpreters to observe it has led to considerable misunderstanding (as when historians of sexuality, for example, misreading the frequent depictions on Attic black-figure pottery of a boy leaping into his lover's arms, take those paintings to be evidence for the strength of the junior partner's sexual desire). A very few Greek documents seem truly ambiguous on this point, and I have reviewed their testimony in some detail in the notes to "Plato and Erotic Reciprocity": see, esp. p. 64, nn. 10 and 11; p. 66, n. 14.

34. The notable exceptions are Bullough, *Homosexuality*, pp. 3–5, who cites it as evidence for the supposed universality of homosexuality in human history, and John Boswell, *Christianity, Social Tolerance, and Homosexuality: Gay People in Western Europe from the Beginning of the Christian Era to the Fourteenth Century* (Chicago, 1980), pp. 53n, 75n.

35. See P. H. Schrijvers, *Eine medizinische Erklärung der männlichen Homosexualität aus der Antike (Caelius Aurelianus DE MORBIS CHRONICIS IV 9)* (Amsterdam: B. R. Grüner, 1985), p. 11.

36. I have borrowed this entire argument from Schrijvers, pp. 7–8; the same point had been made earlier by Boswell, p. 53, n. 33.

37. Translation, with emphasis added, by I. E. Drabkin, ed. and trans., *Caelius Aurelianus: ON ACUTE DISEASES and ON CHRONIC DISEASES* (Chicago, 1950), p. 413.

38. As the chapter title, "De mollibus *sive subactis*," implies.

39. See, esp., the pseudo-Aristotelian *Problemata* 4.26, well discussed by Dover, *Greek Homosexuality*, pp. 168–70; by Boswell, *Christianity*, p. 53; and by Winkler, "Unnatural Acts"; generally, Foucault, *The Use of Pleasure*, pp. 204–14.

40. Compare Aeschines, *Against Timarchus* 185: Timarchus is "a man who is male in body but has committed a woman's transgressions" and has thereby "outraged himself contrary to nature" (discussed by Dover, *Greek Homosexuality*, pp. 60–68). On the ancient figure of the *kinaidos*, or *cinaedus*, the man who actively desires to submit himself passively to the sexual uses of other men, see the essays by John J. Winkler and by Maud W. Gleason in *Before Sexuality: The Construction of Erotic Experience in the Ancient Greek World*, ed. Halperin, Winkler, and Froma I. Zeitlin (Princeton, 1989). Davidson, "Sex and the Emergence of Sexuality," p. 22, is therefore quite wrong to claim that "Before the second half of the nineteenth century

persons of a determinate anatomical sex could not be thought to be really, that is, psychologically, of the opposite sex."

41. The Latin phrase *quod utranque Venerem exerceant* is so interpreted by Drabkin, *Caelius Aurelianus*, p. 901n., and by Schrijvers, *Eine medizinische Erklärung*, 32–33, who secures this reading by citing Ovid, *Metamorphoses* 3.323, where Teiresias, who had been both a man and a woman, is described as being learned in the field of *Venus utraque*. Compare Petronius, *Satyricon* 43.8: *omnis minervae homo*.

42. I follow, once again, the insightful commentary by Schrijvers, p. 15.

43. I quote from the translation by Drabkin, p. 905, which is based on his plausible, but nonetheless speculative, reconstruction (accepted by Schrijvers, p. 50) of a desperately corrupt text.

44. Anon., *De physiognomonia* 85 (vol. ii, p. 114.5–14 Förster); Vettius Valens, 2.16 (p. 76.3–8 Kroll); Clement of Alexandria, *Paedagogus* 3.21.3; Firmicus Maternus, *Mathesis* 6.30.15–16 and 7.25.3–23 (esp. 7.25.5).

45. Thus, Boswell, "Revolutions, Universals, and Sexual Categories," argues that the term "pederast," at least as it is applied to Gnathon by Longus in *Daphnis and Chloe* 4.11, is "obviously a conventional term for 'homosexual' " (p. 478n.10) and he would presumably place a similar construction on *paiderastês* and *philerastês* in the myth of Plato's Aristophanes, dismissing my interpretation as a terminological quibble or as a misguided attempt to reify lexical entities into categories of experience.

46. For a philosophical defense and qualification of this claim (and of other, similarly "constructionist," claims), see Ian Hacking, "Making Up People," in *Reconstructing Individualism: Autonomy, Individuality, and the Self in Western Thought*, ed. Thomas C. Heller, Morton Sosna, and David E. Wellbery, with Arnold I. Davidson, Ann Swidler, and Ian Watt (Stanford, 1986), pp. 222–36, 347–48.

47. On the characteristic failure of "culturally dominant ideologies" actually to dominate all sectors of a society, and for a demonstration of their greater pertinence to the dominant than to the dominated classes, see Nicholas Abercrombie, Stephen Hill, and Bryan S. Turner, *The Dominant Ideology Thesis* (London, 1980), esp. pp. 70–127.

48. See Winkler, "Unnatural Acts."

49. Artemidorus, *Oneirocritica* 1.2 (pp. 8.21–9.4 Pack).

50. Winkler, "Unnatural Acts."

51. I say "phallus" rather than "penis" because (1) what qualifies as a phallus in this discursive system does not always turn out to be a penis (see note 62) and (2) even when phallus and penis have the same extension, or reference, they still do not have the same intention, or meaning: "Phallus" betokens not a specific item of the male anatomy *simpliciter* but that same item *taken under the description* of a cultural signifier; (3) hence, the meaning of "phallus" is ultimately determined by its function in the larger socio-sexual discourse: i.e., it is that which penetrates, that which enables its possessor to play an "active" sexual role, and so forth: see Gayle Rubin, "The Traffic in Women: Notes on the 'Political Economy' of Sex," in *Toward an Anthropology of Women*, ed. Rayna R. Reiter (New York, 1975), pp. 157–210, esp. 190–92.

52. Foucault, *The Use of Pleasure*, p. 215.

53. In order to avoid misunderstanding, I should emphasize that by calling all persons belonging to these four groups "statutory minors," I do not wish either to suggest that they enjoyed the *same* status as one another or to obscure the many differences in status that could obtain between members of a single group—e.g., between a wife and a courtesan—differences that may

not have been perfectly isomorphic with the legitimate modes of their sexual use. Nonetheless, what is striking about Athenian social usage is the tendency to collapse such distinctions as did indeed obtain between different categories of social subordinates and to create a single opposition between them all, *en masse*, and the class of adult male citizens. On this point, see Mark Golden, "*Pais*, 'Child' and 'Slave,' " *L'Antiquité classique* 54 (1985): 91–104, esp. 101 and 102, n. 38.

54. Veyne, "La famille et l'amour," p. 55, and "Homosexuality in Ancient Rome," in *Western Sexuality: Practice and Precept in Past and Present Times,* ed. Philippe Ariès and André Béjin, trans. Anthony Forster (Oxford, 1985), pp. 26–35. Cf. Alan Dundes, Jerry W. Leach, and Bora Özkök, "The Strategy of Turkish Boys' Verbal Dueling Rhymes," *Journal of American Folklore* 83 (1970): 325–49, supplemented and qualified by Mark Glazer, "On Verbal Dueling Among Turkish Boys," *Journal of American Folklore* 89 (1976): 87–89; J. M. Carrier, "Mexican Male Bisexuality," in *Bisexualities: Theory and Research*, ed. Fritz Klein and Timothy J. Wolf = *Journal of Homosexuality* 11.1–2 (1985): 75–85; De Martino and Schmitt, *Kleine Schriften,* esp. pp. 3–22; Michael Herzfeld, *The Poetics of Manhood: Contest and Identity in a Cretan Mountain Village* (Princeton, 1985).

55. I have borrowed this analogy from Arno Schmitt, who uses it to convey what the modern sexual categories would look like from a traditional Islamic perspective: see De Martino and Schmitt, *Kleine Schriften*, p. 19.

56. Maurice Godelier, "The Origins of Male Domination," *New Left Review* 127 (May–June 1981): 3–17 (quotation on p. 17); see, also, Godelier, "Le sexe comme fondement ultime de l'ordre social et cosmique chez les Baruya de Nouvelle-Guinée. Mythe et réalité," in *Sexualité et pouvoir*, ed. Armando Verdiglione (Paris, 1976), pp. 268–306, esp. 295–96.

57. The same point is made, in the course of an otherwise unenlightening (from the specialist's point of view) survey of Greek social relations, by Bernard I. Murstein, *Love, Sex, and Marriage through the Ages* (New York, 1974), p. 58.

58. Cf. Padgug, "Sexual Matters," p. 3.

59. See Dover, *Greek Homosexuality*, pp. 63–67, for an extensive, but partial, list.

60. "Une bisexualité de sabrage": Veyne, "La famille et l'amour," pp. 50–55; cf. the critique by Ramsay MacMullen, "Roman Attitudes to Greek Love," *Historia* 32 (1983): 484–502. Other scholars who describe the ancient behavioral phenomenon as "bisexuality" include Brisson, "Bisexualité"; Schnapp, "Une autre image," esp. pp. 116–17; Hans Kelsen, "Platonic Love," trans. George B. Wilbur, *American Imago* 3 (1942): 3–110, esp. 40–41; Lawrence Stone, "Sex in the West," *The New Republic*, July 8, 1985, pp. 25–37, esp. 30–32 (with doubts). *Contra*, Padgug, "Sexual Matters," p. 59: "to speak, as is common, of the Greeks as 'bisexual' is illegitimate as well, since that merely adds a new, intermediate category, whereas it was precisely the categories themselves which had no meaning in antiquity."

61. Cf. T. M. Robinson, review of Dover, *Greek Homosexuality*, in *Phoenix* 35 (1981): 160–63, esp. 162: "The reason why a heterosexual majority might have looked with a tolerant eye on 'active' homosexual practice among the minority, and even in some measure within their own group [!], . . . is predictably a sexist one: to the heterosexual majority, to whom (in a man's universe) the 'good' woman is *kata physin* [i.e., naturally] passive, obedient, and submissive, the 'role' of the 'active' homosexual will be tolerable precisely because his goings-on can, without too much difficulty, be equated with the 'role' of the male *hetero*sexual, i.e., to dominate and

subdue; what the two have in common is greater than what divides them."
But this seems to me to beg the very question that the distinction between
heterosexuality and homosexuality is supposedly designed to solve.

62. By "phallus" I mean a culturally constructed signifier of social power:
for the terminology, see note 51. I call Greek sexuality phallic because (1)
sexual contacts are polarized around phallic action—i.e., they are defined by
who has the phallus and by what is done with it; (2) sexual pleasures other
than phallic pleasures do not count in categorizing sexual contacts; (3) in
order for a contact to qualify as sexual, one—and no more than one—of the
two partners is required to have a phallus (boys are treated in pederastic
contexts as essentially un-phallused [see Martial, 11.22; but cf. *Palatine
Anthology* XII: 3, 7, 197, 207, 216, 222, 242] and tend to be assimilated to
women; in the case of sex between women, one partner—the "tribad"—is
assumed to possess a phallus-equivalent [an over-developed clitoris] and to
penetrate the other: Sources for the ancient conceptualization of the tribad—
no complete modern study of this fascinating and long-lived fictional type,
which survived into the early decades of the twentieth century, is known to
me—have been assembled by Friedrich Karl Forberg, *Manual of Classical
Erotology*, trans. Julian Smithson [Manchester, 1884; repr. New York, 1966],
2:108–67; Gaston Vorberg, *Glossarium eroticum* [Hanau, 1965] pp. 654–55;
Werner A. Krenkel, "Masturbation in der Antike," *Wissenschaftliche Zeitschrift
der Wilhelm-Pieck-Universität Rostock* 28 [1979]: 159–78, esp. 171; see, now,
Judith P. Hallett, "Female Homoeroticism and the Denial of Roman Reality
in Latin Literature," *Yale Journal of Criticism*, 3.1 [1989], forthcoming).

63. Foucault, *The Care of the Self*, pp. 3–36, esp. 26–34; S. R. F. Price,
"The Future of Dreams: From Freud to Artemidorus," *Past and Present* 113
(November, 1986): 3–37, abridged in *Before Sexuality*.

64. See Waud H. Kracke, "Dreaming in Kagwahiv: Dream Beliefs and
Their Psychic Uses in an Amazonian Indian Culture," *The Psychoanalytic
Study of Society* 8 (1979): 119–71, esp. 130–32, 163 (on the predictive value of
dreams) and 130–31, 142–45, 163–64, 168 (on the reversal of the Freudian
direction of signification—which Kracke takes to be a culturally constituted
defense mechanism and which he accordingly undervalues); Thomas Gregor,
" 'Far, Far Away My Shadow Wandered . . .': The Dream Symbolism and
Dream Theories of the Mehinaku Indians of Brazil," *American Ethnologist* 8
(1981): 709–20, esp. 712–13 (on predictive value) and 714 (on the reversal of
signification), largely recapitulated in Thomas Gregor, *Anxious Pleasures: The
Sexual Lives of an Amazonian People* (Chicago, 1985), pp. 152–61, esp. 153.

65. Cf. Davidson, "Sex and the Emergence of Sexuality," p. 16.

66. Cf. Padgug, "Sexual Matters," p. 55: "In any approach that takes as
predetermined and universal the categories of sexuality, real history disappears."

67. My conclusion coincides exactly with that of Jeffrey Weeks, "Discourse, Desire and Sexual Deviance," p. 111: "Social processes construct
subjectivities not just as 'categories' but at the level of individual desires. This
perception . . . should be the starting point for future social and historical
studies of 'homosexuality' and indeed of 'sexuality' in general." Stephen
Greenblatt, "Fiction and Friction," in *Reconstructing Individualism*, ed. Heller,
Sosna, and Wellbury, pp. 30–52, 329–32, esp. 34, makes a similar point;
arguing that "a culture's sexual discourse plays a critical role in shaping
individuality," he goes on to say, "it does so by helping to implant in each
person an internalized set of dispositions and orientations that governs individual improvisations."

68. "Translations" (1972), lines 32–33, in Adrienne Rich, *Diving into the
Wreck: Poems 1971–1972* (New York, 1973), pp. 40–41 (quotation on p. 41).

Padgug, "Sexual Matters"

This essay represents a condensed and reworked version of the introduction to a much longer work on the nature of sexuality in history. The author would like to thank Betsy Blackmar, Edwin Burrows, Victoria de Grazia, Elizabeth Fee, Joseph Interrante, Michael Merrill, David Varas, and Michael Wallace for their invaluable comments on earlier drafts. He dedicates the essay to David Varas, without whose help and encouragement it would been impossible to write it.

1. Michel Foucault, *The History of Sexuality*, vol. 1 (New York, 1978), pt. 1.
2. As reported in Athenaeus, *Deipnosophistae* 12.450 d-f (= F. Jacoby, *Fragmente der Griech. Historiker* no. 539, fragment no. 2).
3. Cf. for other examples, Lucian, "The Ship" (Loeb Classical Library edition of Lucian, vol. VI, 481), or the "Love Stories," attributed to Plutarch (*Moralia* 771E–775E), which provide pairs of similar love tales, each consisting of one involving heterosexual love and one involving homosexual love.
4. Cf. Linda Gordon and Allen Hunter, "Sex, Family and the New Right," *Radical America* 11, no. 6/12 no. 1 (November 1977–February 1978): 9–26.
5. *New York Review of Books*, November 23, 1978, p. 51.
6. On biology as a realm of the necessary, cf. S. Timpanaro, *On Materialism* (London, 1978).
7. Cf. Helen H. Lambert, "Biology and Equality," *Signs* 4 (1978): pp. 97–11, esp. 104.
8. L. Malson, *Wolf Children* (New York, 1972), p. 9.
9. Cf. *ibid.*, p. 10.
10. Cf. *ibid.*, p. 48.
11. Mary Douglas, *Natural Symbols* (New York, 1973), p. 93.
12. George Bataille, *Death and Sensuality* (New York, 1962).
13. Cf. the important analysis of this and similar points in Denis de Rougement, *Love in the Western World* (New York, 1956), pp. 159ff.
14. Cf. Adolfo Sanchez Vazquez, *The Philosophy of Praxis* (London, 1977).
15. *Grundrisse*, p. 265.
16. Cf. the work of the so-called "symbolic interactionalists," best exemplified by Kenneth Plummer, *Sexual Stigma* (London, 1975). Their work, although not Marxist and too focused on individuals *per se*, does represent a major step forward in our understanding of sexuality as interpersonal.
17. K. Marx, F. Engels, *Collected Works* (New York, 1976), 5:4.
18. Mary McIntosh, "The Homosexual Role," *Social Problems* 16 (1968): 182–91, the pioneer work in this field, suggests the seventeenth century for the emergence of the first homosexual subculture. Randolph Trumbach, "London's Sodomites: Homosexual Behavior and Western Culture in the Eighteenth Century," *Journal of Social History* 11 (1977/78): 1–33, argues for the eighteenth century. Jeffrey Weeks, in two important works, "Sins and Disease," *History Workshop* 1 (1976): 211–219, and *Coming Out* (London, 1977), argues, correctly, I believe, that the full emergence of homosexual role and subculture occurs only in the second half of the nineteenth century. All of these works deal with England, but there is little reason to suspect that the general phenomenon, at least, varies very considerably in other bourgeois countries.

19. Weeks, *Coming Out*, p. 12.

20. The best work available on Greek homosexual behavior is K. J. Dover, *Greek Homosexuality* (London, 1978), which contains further bibliography.

21. Cf. Foucault, *History of Sexuality*, vol. 1, pts. 4–5, as well as Guy Hocquenghem, *Homosexual Desire* (London, 1978).

22. On the conceptualization of family, kinship, and household, see the important collective work by Rayna Rapp, Ellen Ross, and Renate Bridenthal, "Examining Family History," *Feminist Studies* 5 (1979): 174–200, as well as Rayna Rapp, "Family and Class in Contemporary America," *Science and Society* 42 (1978): 278–300. Cf. Mark Poster, *Critical Theory of the Family* (New York, 1978), and the critique of it by Ellen Ross in this issue.

23. This appears to be true even of such relatively unorthodox thinkers as Louis Althusser (*Lenin and Philosophy* [New York, 1971], pp. 127–86); E. Balibar (*Reading Capital* [New York, 1970], pt. 3); P. Hindess and B. Hirst (*Pre-Capitalist Modes of Production* [London, 1975], esp. ch. 1); and Claude Meillassoux (*Femmes Greniers et Capitaux* [Paris, 1975], pt. 1).

24. Cf. Raymond Williams, *Marxism and Literature* (New York, 1977), esp. pt. 2.

25. Rubin, "The Traffic in Women," in R. Reiter, ed., *Towards an Anthropology of Women* (New York, 1975), pp. 157–210, at 167. For other views similar to those of Rubin, on this point at least, cf. R. Bridenthal, "The Dialectics of Production and Reproduction in History," *Radical America* 10, no. 2 (1976): 3–11; Nancy Chodorow, "Mothering, Male Dominance and Capitalism," in Z. Eisenstein, ed., *Capitalist Patriarchy and the Case for Socialist Feminism* (New York, 1979), pp. 83–106; and Juliet Mitchell, *Women's Estate* (London, 1975).

26. Among recent works which come to this conclusion, and whose bibliographies and notes are useful for further study, see Joan Kelly, "The Doubled Vision of Feminist Theory," *Feminist Studies* 5 (1979): 216–27; Lise Vogel, "Questions on the Woman Question," *Monthly Review*, June 1979, pp. 39–60; Renate Bridenthal, "Family and Reproduction," the third part of Rapp, Ross, and Bridenthal, "Examining Family History"; Eli Zaretsky, *Capitalism and Personal Life* (New York, 1976), pp. 24ff.; and Ann Forman, *Femininity as Alienation* (London, 1977).

27. On the Greek *oikos* and related institutions, see W. K. Lacey, *The Family in Classical Greece* (London, 1968).

28. Cf. Foucault, *History of Sexuality*, vol. 1, and Zaretsky, *Capitalism and Personal Life*, for attempts to conceptualize the emergence of these categories. On the nonemergence of a separate sphere of the economy in noncapitalist societies, cf. Georg Lukacs, *History and Class Consciousness* (London, 1968), pp. 55–59, 223–55, and Samir Ámin, "In Praise of Socialism," in *Imperialism and Unequal Development* (New York, 1977), pp. 73–85.

29. For works which begin this process, cf. those cited in notes 25 and 26 above, plus the articles collected in Z. Eisenstein, *Capitalist Patriarchy*.

30. For a full discussion of this need and what it involves, see Lucien Sève. *Marxisme et theorie de personnalité* (3rd ed., Paris, 1972). Sève is best on the social conditioning of individual psychology and weakest on individual psychic processes themselves.

31. "Marx and Freud," pt. 1, *Socialist Review* no. 30 (1976): 3–56. This article, along with its two successors in *Socialist Review* no. 33 (1977): 59–84, and no. 36 (1977) 37–78, form a good introduction to the study of the relationship between Marx and Freud, arguing for their incompatibility.

32. An important recent attempt to demonstrate the social underpinnings of Freud's thought is Juliet Mitchell, *Psychoanalysis and Feminism*

(New York, 1974). Zaretsky, "Male Supremacy and the Unconscious," *Socialist Review* no. 21/22 (1975): 7–55, demonstrates several defects in Freud's understanding of socio-historical reality, but suggests that they are remediable.

33. Freud, "The Resistance to Psycho-Analysis," *Standard Edition* 19:218.

34. Cf. Freud, "Instincts and their Vicissitudes," *Standard Edition* 14:105–140.

35. Eisenstein, *Capitalist Patriarchy*, 3.

36. G. Deleuze and F. Guattari, *Anti-Oedipus* (New York, 1977). Cf. also the work of Herbert Marcuse, especially *Eros and Civilization* (Boston, 1955), and Norman O. Brown, *Life Against Death* (Middletown, Conn., 1959).

37. L. S. Vygotsky, *Mind in Society* (Cambridge, Mass., 1977); cf. Stephen Toulmin's essay on Vygotsky, "The Mozart of Psychology," *New York Review of Books*, September 28, 1978, pp. 51–57.

38. Lucien Sève, *Man in Marxist Theory and The Psychology of Personality* (Humanities Press, 1978).

Brown, "Lesbian Sexuality in Medieval and Early Modern Europe"

1. Ian Maclean summarizes the sources for contemporary attitudes in *The Renaissance Notion of Woman: A Study in the Fortunes of Scholasticism and Medical Science in European Intellectual Life* (Cambridge, 1980).

2. Women's lust allegedly led them to adultery and fornication with the devil as well as with men. Heinrich Kramer and Jakob Sprenger, *The Malleus Maleficarum*, Part 2, Q. 1, ch. 2. Published ca. 1486, the book became the most influential treatise on witchcraft. See also H. E. Midelfort, *Witch-hunting in Southwestern Germany, 1562–1684* (Stanford, 1972), pp. 105–6.

3. The notion that this charge was generally ignored is supported by the dearth of such cases found in extensive researches in the European criminal and inquisitorial archives. For Germany there are two trials, one in 1477 and one in 1721. For France, the jurist Jean Papon writes of one case brought before the *parlement* of Toulouse in 1533. Henri Estienne cites another case for 1535. And Michel Montaigne, in his *Diary of a Journey to Italy*, briefly describes the story of a young woman hanged in 1580 for engaging in a lesbian affair. For Spain, Antonio Gomez reports that two nuns were accused of "using material instruments," for which they were burned at the stake; and Cristobal de Chaves observes that in prison some women "made themselves into roosters" by fashioning penises which they tied to themselves. For Switzerland there is only one case, which came to trial in 1568; and for Italy there is also one case, which became the subject of Judith C. Brown's, *Immodest Acts: The Life of a Lesbian Nun in Renaissance Italy* (New York, 1986). The remaining cases are cited by Louis Crompton to argue that lesbian sexuality was as serious a concern as male homosexuality and that it was punished just as severely—a view I do not share. L. Crompton, "The Myth of Lesbian Impunity: Capital Laws from 1270 to 1791," *Journal of Homosexuality* 6 (Fall/Winter 1980/81): 17; see also E. W. Monter, "La sodomie à l'epoque moderne en Suisse romande," *Annales, E.S.C.* 29 (July/August 1974): 1029–30; Mary Elizabeth Perry, *Crime and Society in Early Modern Seville* (Hanover, 1982); and L.S.A.M. von Romer, "Der Uranismus in den Niederlanden bis zum 19. Jahrhundert, mit besonderer Berucksichtigung der

grossen Uranierverfolgung in Jahre 1730," *Jahrbuch für sexuelle Zwischenstufen* 8 (1906): 365–512.

4. St. Ambrose, *Commentarii in omnes Pauli epistolas*, cited in Crompton, "Lesbian Impunity," p. 14. Many sources mentioned in the following pages have also been cited in four earlier surveys: Derrick S. Bailey, *Homosexuality and the Western Christian Tradition* (London, 1955; reprinted Hamden, Conn. 1975); Michael Goodich, "Sodomy in Medieval Secular Law," *Journal of Homosexuality* 1, no. 3 (1976): 295–302; John Boswell, *Christianity, Social Tolerance, and Homosexuality: Gay People in Western Europe from the Beginning of the Christian Era to the Fourteenth Century* (Chicago, 1980), and L. Crompton, "Lesbian Impunity."

5. St. John Chrysostom, *In Epistolam ad Romanos;* the full text of the fourth homily is translated in Boswell, *Christianity*, pp. 359–62.

6. Crompton, "Lesbian Impunity," p. 14. Peter Abelard, *Commentarium super S. Pauli epistolam ad Romanos libri quinque*, in J.-P. Migne, ed. *Patrologiae cursus completus: Serie Latinae, 178*, p. 806.

7. Penitential of Theodore of Tarsus, in John McNeill and Helena M. Gammer, eds. *Medieval Handbooks of Penance* (New York, 1938), p. 185; Venerable Bede, "De Remediis peccatorum," in Migne, *Patrologiae Latinae* 94, pp. 569–70. Penitential of Pope Gregory III, J. D. Mansi, *Sacrorum conciliorum nova et amplissima collectio* (Graz, 1960), 12:293, 295. Hrabanus Maurus, "Paenitentiale ad Heribaldum," canon 25, in Migne, *Patrologiae Latinae*, 110, p. 490. A complete list of early medieval penitentials which cite lesbian sexuality and a thorough discussion of sexual issues may be found in Pierre J. Payer, *Sex and the Penitentials: The Development of a Sexual Code, 550–1150* (Toronto, 1984).

8. St. Thomas Aquinas, *Summa theologiae*, II.ii.154:11–12.

9. See the rubric *luxuria* in Sylvester Prierias Mazzolini, *Summa summarum, que Sylvestrina dicitur* (Bologna, 1515); Jean Gerson, "De septem vitiis capitalibus," in L. E. Du Pin, *Opera omnia* (Antwerp, 1706), 1: 345–46.

10. St. Antoninus, *Somma dello arcivescovo Antonio omnis mortalium cura;* St. Charles Borromeo, "Poenitentiale Mediolanense," in F. W. H. Wasserschleben, *Die Bussordnungen der abendlandischen Kirche* (Graz, 1958), pp. 722–23.

11. Letter 211, in St. Augustine, *Letters*, The Fathers of the Church Ser., vol. 32 (New York, 1956).

12. Possibly the only example of medieval lesbian literature, the poem was prompted by the temporary absence of one of the lovers. It is addressed "To G., her singular rose, from A.—." The poet writes, "When I recall the kisses you gave me, And how with tender words you caressed my little breasts, I want to die Because I cannot see you. . . . Come home, sweet love! Prolong your trip no longer; Know that I can bear your absence no longer. Farewell. Remember me." Boswell, *Christianity*, pp. 220–21. The provisions of the councils of Paris and Rouen are discussed in Bailey, *Homosexuality*, p. 132.

13. Crompton, "Lesbian Impunity," pp. 15–16.

14. Ibid., p. 18.

15. Cited in Boswell, *Christianity*, p. 158.

16. In his brilliant but controversial book, Boswell argues that the major turning point in Western attitudes toward homosexuality took place in the thirteenth century, when the treatment of homosexuals became considerably harsher. References to homosexuality therefore increased in the late medieval period. Most of the sources cited by Boswell, however, do not mention women.

17. St. Peter Damian, *Liber Gomorrhianus*, in Migne, *Patrologiae latinae,* vol. 145.

18. St. Bernardino of Siena (1380–1444), whose fulminations against male sodomites were legend, occasionally also preached against the sodomitical practices of women, but what he had in mind is not clear. San Bernardino of Siena, *Le prediche volgari*, P. Bargellini, ed. (Milan, 1936), pp. 402, 902; *Le prediche volgari*, C. Cannarozzi, ed., Sienese sermons, 1425: 2 vols. (Florence, 1958).

19. Writing in the twelfth century about the virtues and vices of French society, Etienne remarked: "The ladies there have discovered a sport / Where two little sows make a single one/ . . . Not all the ladies play the *molle;/* The one stretches back and the other squirms / The one acts the cock and the other the hen / And each plays her role." In *Le Livre des Manieres,* ed. R. Anthony Lodge (Geneva, 1979), lines 1104–1136.

20. Dante Alighieri, *The Divine Comedy: Inferno*, Canto 15, transl. John Ciardi (New York, 1982), p. 139.

21. Ludovico Ariosto, *Orlando Furioso*, canto 25, verse 36.

22. Agnolo Firenzuola, *I ragionamenti amorosi*, in *Opere*, ed. Delmo Maestro (Turin, 1977), p. 97.

23. It is obvious from Brantôme's tone that he was a scandal monger who did not really believe sexual relations between women had become fashionable. Nonetheless, his reasons for condemning or condoning lesbian practices can be taken to reflect not just personal opinion, but what his audience wanted to believe. Pierre de Bourdeille, Seigneur de Brantôme, *Les Vies des dames galantes* (orig. 17th c., Paris, 1962), pp. 122, 126.

24. Ibid., p. 123.

25. Ibid., p. 126.

26. Ibid., p. 121.

27. St. Augustine, *Contra mendacium*, cited in Boswell, *Christianity*, p. 157. Similarly, St. Jerome linked well-developed Greek and Judaic notions when he wrote that "as long as woman is for birth and children, she is different from man as body is from soul. But when she wishes to serve Christ more than the world, then she ceases to be a woman and will be called a man." *Commentarius in Epistolam ad Ephesios*, cited in Vern L. Bullough, "Transvestism in the Middle Ages," Vern L. Bullough and James Brundage, eds. *Sexual Practices and the Medieval Church* (Buffalo, 1982), p. 45.

28. Notions of female anatomy and the biological role in procreation may be found in Maclean, *Notions of Woman*, pp. 35–38. Also see Steven Greenblatt, "Fiction and Friction," in T. Heller, M. Sosna, and D. Wellberry, eds., *Reconstructing Individualism: Individuality and the Self in Western Thought* (Stanford, 1986), pp. 30–52.

29. Penitential of Theodore, p. 185.

30. J. D. Mansi, *Sacrorum conciliorum*, 12: 293–295, sec. 30.

31. Borromeo, however, gave men only ten to thirty days' penance for self-pollution. *Poenitentiale Mediolanense*, pp. 722–23.

32. Scholars have interpreted this law in different ways, ranging from loss of testicles, castration, and burning; to castration, loss of a limb and burning; to loss of a limb and burning. For female sodomites interpretations have included clitorectomies as a possible punishment. Bailey, *Homosexuality*, p. 106; Boswell, *Christianity*, p. 290; and Crompton, "Lesbian Impunity," p. 13.

33. Crompton, "Lesbian Impunity," p. 16.

34. The link between heresy and homosexuality may have stemmed from the negative attitudes toward procreation held by certain heretical

groups such as the Albigensians. Orthodox Christians attributed this horror of insemination to their preference for sodomitical practices. See Arlo Karlen, "The Homosexual Heresy," *Chaucer Review* 6, no. 1 (1971): 44–63; Vern L. Bullough, "Heresy, Witchcraft, and Sexuality," in Bullough and Brundage, *Sexual Practices*, pp. 206–17.

35. In Geneva there was a clear correlation between sodomy prosecutions and increased religious fervor in 1560–1610. William Monter, *Ritual, Myth and Magic in Early Modern Europe* (Thetford, Norfolk, 1983), pp. 116–17. Elsewhere there were also other influences at work. For Spain, Perry cites the authorities' desire to consolidate a newly formed political order. *Crime and Society in Seville*, p. 72. Possibly similar pressures were at work in England.

36. Cited in Crompton, "Lesbian Impunity," p. 18.

37. Ibid.

38. *Las siete partidas del sabio rey Don Alonso el Nono, nuevamente glosadas por el licenciado Gregorio Lopez* (Salamanca 1829–31; reprint of 1565 ed.), vol. 3, p. 178.

39. Antonio Gomez, *Ad leges Tauri*, L. 80, n. 34; reproduced in *Miss Marianne Woods and Miss Jane Pirie Against Dame Cumming Gordon* (New York, 1975), "Authorities," p. 5.

40. Prospero Farinacci, *De delictis carnis*, Q. 148, T. 16; *Miss Marianne Woods*, "Authorities," p. 4.

41. Several Venetian laws reveal the concern with dress as an expression of gender relations. In the late fifteenth and sixteenth centuries, the authorities prohibited fashions which blurred gender lines because they were "a kind of sodomy." Particularly prone to dressing in a masculine way were prostitutes who adopted manly attire in an effort to compete for male clients with male homosexuals. Patricia Labalme, "Sodomy and Venetian Justice in the Renaissance," *Tijdschrift voor Rechtsgeschiedens* 52, no. 3 (1984): 247–51.

42. It is, of course, difficult to make firm generalizations based on a small number of cases. In seventeenth-century Leiden, for instance, the only two cases of lesbian sexuality that have come to light involved transvestism, but the accused women were flogged and banished rather than executed; Dirk Jaap Noordam, "Homosocial Relations in Leiden (1533–1811)," in *Among Men, Among Women: Sociological and Historical Recognition of Homosocial Arrangements* (Amsterdam, 1983), pp. 218–23. On the other hand, the two French executions both involved transvestism, and in each case only the "male" in the relationship was killed. Similarly, in eighteenth-century Germany, execution was recommended only for the transvestite partner in a relationship; Brigitte Eriksson, "A Lesbian Execution in Germany, 1721: The Trial Records," *Journal of Homosexuality* 6, nos. 1/2 (1980/81): 27–40. In Spain, according to Gomez, only those who used material instruments were executed; the others were whipped and sent to the galleys.

The need to resolve issues of gender unambiguously severely tested the authorities when they occasionally confronted cases of hermaphroditism. Physicians and jurists usually agreed that the individual determine once and for all which gender to adopt. After this, it was a capital offense to adopt the dress or behavior of the other sex. Steven Greenblatt, "Loudon and London," *Critical Inquiry* 12, no. 2 (Winter 1986): 326–46.

Two episodes reveal the importance of transvestism. The first is the trial of Joan of Arc, whose worst offense was not her lack of sexual purity, which she had demonstrated beyond a doubt, but her dressing in male garments. Although she might point out that in the early church several female saints had also passed themselves off as men, the context for such actions had changed and so had the tolerance of the authorities. Indeed, the very hierarchy of values, which associated virtue, courage, and the pursuit of holiness with the male sex and held that a woman became a man when she served Christ, made it inevitable both that women would transgress dress codes and other gender rules and that society would punish them harshly for doing so. Marina Warner, *Joan of Arc: The Image of Female Heroism* (New York, 1980); Vern L. Bullough, "Transvestism in the Middle Ages," in Bullough and Brundage, *Sexual Practices*, pp. 43–54; John Anson, "Female Monks: The Transvestite Motif in Early Christian Literature," *Viator* 5 (1974): 1–32.

A second episode involves a French girl accused of transvestism almost two centuries later. After abandoning her home town, Marie discarded her female dress, became a weaver, and took a wife. When the authorities discovered her true sex, she was tried and sentenced to be hanged, which, according to Montaigne, "she said she would rather endure than to return to the state of a girl." Implicit in Marie's statement is the likelihood that she was offered a lighter sentence if she agreed to return to her proper station in life. As suggested both by her statement and by the fact that her "wife" did not share her fate, the authorities were more concerned about her violation of gender relations than about her sexual crime. Michel Montaigne, *Diary of a Journey to Italy in 1580 and 1581* in *The Complete Works* (Stanford, 1948), pp. 869–70.

43. *De bono conjugali*, in St. Augustine, *Treatises on Marriage and Other Subjects*, The Fathers of the Church Ser., 27: 9–51. St. Augustine, Letter 211.

44. Penitential of Theodore, p. 185. Rubric 21 of Gregory's penitential, entitled "On Sodomists," deals with homosexuality among clerics and boys. Rubric 30, "On Diverse and Minor Sins," deals with coitus between women (probably mutual masturbation), anal intercourse, and nonsexual transgressions. Mansi, *Sacrorum conciliorum*, 12:293, 295. For a different interpretation, see Boswell, *Christianity*, p. 180. Albertus Magnus, *Summa Theologiae*, cited in Boswell, *Christianity*, pp. 316–18. Thomas Aquinas, *Summa*, II.ii.93 and 94.

45. Vincente Filliuccio, *Moralium quaestionum*, in Lodovico Maria Sinistrari, *De sodomia*, item. 8.

46. I have used the term "lesbian sexuality" as a convenient way to describe acts and persons called "lesbian" in our own time. We must be aware, however, of the limitations of these terms and of the fact that for many reasons, they were not and could not have been used before the late nineteenth century, when new ways of thinking about women and women's sexuality emerged. (See George Chauncey, Jr., "From Sexual Inversion to Homosexuality: Medicine and the Changing Conceptualization of Female Deviance," *Salmagundi* 58–59 (Fall 1982–Winter 1983): 114–46.)

In applying sexual labels, we must remember that sexual experience, labelling, and self-identification are immensely varied and operate within socially defined categories that influence identity and behavior. Before the nineteenth century, women who engaged in sexual relations with other women were incapable of perceiving themselves as a distinct sexual and social group, and were not seen as such by others. The relegation of women to the private sphere precluded such perceptions because it prevented the formation of homosexual subcultures of the sort that were open to men. Except in convents or brothels women's lives and sexual identities were circumscribed by their families and the walls of their household.

Because of the complexity of the problem and its links to issues of sexual definition in the present, there has been much debate about applying the term "lesbian" to the premodern era. Adrienne Rich, for instance, has posited a lesbian continuum, in which lesbian identity is not tied to a self-conscious identity or even to sexual relations or attractions, but to emotional bonds that emerge between women in a patriarchal society. Thus all women in the past who even once chafed under the limits imposed on them by men and who felt solidarity or kinship with other women might be called lesbian ("Compulsory Heterosexuality and Lesbian Existence," *Signs: Journal of Women in Culture and Society* 5, no. 4 (Summer 1980): 631–60. The problem with this position is that it is fundamentally ahistorical in its inclusiveness. It makes it impossible to distinguish different historical epochs and leaves virtually no woman out of the label. A different stance is taken by Anne Ferguson, who argues that while some women can be described as sexually deviant in that they departed from the norm, the term "lesbian" should not be applied to women who lived before its emergence as a cultural category in the late nineteenth century ("Patriarchy, Sexual Identity, and the Sexual Revolution," *Signs*, 7, no. 1 (Autumn 1981): 158–66). While I agree with the substance of this argument, I have not subscribed to its conclusion because we have no other *shorthand* vocabulary to discuss the actions and perceptions of women who engaged in same-gender sexual relations.

47. The rediscovery of Sappho's poetry in mid-sixteenth century did not lead to the immediate adoption of the term "lesbian." Indeed, since contemporaries could not accept the sexual preferences of such a distinguished poet, sporadic efforts were made to give them a heterosexual interpretation. Francois Rigolot, "Louise Labe et la redécouverte de Sappho," *Nouvelle revue du 16ᵉ siècle* 1 (1983): 19–31. Marie-Jo Bonnet, *Un choix sans equivoque: Recherches historiques sur les relations amoureuses entre les femmes, XVI-XXᵉ siècle* (Paris, 1981), pp. 21–67.

48. Sinistrari, *De sodomia*, items 13, 15–17, 21–22. Reasoning backward, Sinistrari used the allegedly common Middle Eastern practice of performing clitorectomies as evidence of physiological differences between Western and non-Western women.

49. Ibid., items 29, 50.

50. Ibid., item 23.

51. Lopez, *Las siete partidas;* Jean Gerson, *Confessional ou Directoire des confesseurs*, no date, late fifteenth century. P. Glorieux questions the authorship of the text, but for our purposes what matters is that Renaissance readers attributed it to Gerson. See Jean Gerson, *Opera omnia*, ed. P. Glorieux (Paris, 1960), 1:85.

52. Monter, "La Sodomie," p. 1029.

53. As late as the nineteenth century, legal authorities, for quite different reasons, refused to believe that women could engage in sexual relations with each other. See Lillian Faderman, *Scotch Verdict* (New York, 1983).

Even in our own century, the subject of lesbian sexuality has not received adequate attention. Books on the history of sexuality have tended to ignore lesbians. Michel Foucault, for instance, makes almost no reference to them, and his argument that certain forms of sexuality only began to be denied by Western society in the seventeenth century can only be sustained by disregarding denial of lesbian sexuality in the medieval and early modern period.

Vivien Ng, "Homosexuality and the State in Late Imperial China"

1. This covers the late Ming (ca. 16th to mid–17th centuries) and Qing (1644–1912) periods.
2. See M. J. Meier, "Homosexual Offenses in Ch'ing Law," *T'oung Pao* 71 (1985), pp. 109–133; Vivien W. Ng, "Ideology and Sexuality: Rape Laws in Qing China," *Journal of Asian Studies* 46 (February 1987), pp. 57–70.
3. Robert H. van Gulik, *Sexual Life in Ancient China* (Leiden: E. J. Brill, 1974), p. 28.
4. *Duan xiu pian* (Shanghai, 1909–1911), p. 1b.
5. Gulik, *Sexual Life in Ancient China*, p. 63.
6. Robert E. Hegel, *The Novel in Seventeenth Century China* (New York: Columbia University Press, 1981), pp. 22–23.
7. Wu Han, "Wan Ming shi guan jiaji di shenghuo [Lifestyle of the scholar-official class in late Ming]," *Dagong bao* (April 19, 1934), p. 3.
8. Ibid.
9. Albert Chan, *The Glory and Fall of the Ming Dynasty* (Norman, Okla. University of Oklahoma Press, 1982), p. 314.
10. Shen Defu, *Wanli ye huo pian* [Wanli miscellanea], reprint ed. (Beijing, 1979), p. 621.
11. Wm. Theodore de Bary, "Individualism and Humanitarianism in Late Ming Thought," in *Self and Society in Ming Thought*, ed. Wm. Theodore de Bary (New York: Columbia University Press), p. 151.
12. Ibid., p. 182.
13. Patrick Hanan, *The Chinese Vernacular Story* (Cambridge: Harvard University Press, 1981), p. 10.
14. Ibid., p. 167.
15. The mother of the ancient philosopher Mencius was regarded by Confucian moralists as a paragon of motherhood.
16. Li Yu, "Silent Opera Number 6," in *Li Yu chuanji* [Collected Works of Li Yu], reprint ed. (Taipei: Cheng-wen Publishing Co.), pp. 5406–5407.
17. Li Yu, *Twelve Towers Number 6*, reprint ed. (Hong Kong: Guangwen Bookstore, n.d.).
18. See also Fang-fu Ruan and Yung-mei Tsai, "Male Homosexuality in Traditional Chinese Literature," *Journal of Homosexuality* 14 (1987), pp. 21–33.
19. I am grateful to Keith McMahon, University of Kansas, for the translation.
20. Shen Fu, *Six Records of a Floating Life* (New York: Penguin Books, 1983), p. 51.
21. Jottings are collections of anecdotes, supernatural tales, biographies, travel impressions, and records of unusual happenings. This literary genre experienced a boom in the late Ming/early Qing period. The compilers of these collections were mostly members of the literati class.
22. Shen Defu, *Wanli miscellenea*, p. 903.
23. Ibid., p. 896.
24. *Guobao wenjian lu* [Anthology of Retributive Tales], in *Biji xiaoshuo daguan* [Anthology of Scholarly Jottings], 3d series (Taipei, 1974), p. 6606.
25. In the aftermath of the collapse of the Ming dynasty, many Chinese conservatives blamed the loss of China to the alien Manchus on the hedonistic tendencies fostered by the Wang Yangming School of Neo-Confucianism.

They therefore assigned themselves the responsibility of restoring to China the more puritanical values of orthodox Confucianism, believing that such an effort could redeem China from its troubles.

References: Ng, "Homosexuality and the State in Late Imperial China"

Bian er chai (Hairpins Beneath His Cap). Late-Ming ed. (Gest Library, Princeton University).

Chan, Albert. 1982. *The Glory and Fall of the Ming Dynasty*. Norman, Okla.: University of Oklahoma Press.

Chan, Wing-tsit. 1973. *A Sourcebook in Chinese Philosophy*. Princeton: Princeton University Press.

de Bary, William Theodore. 1970. *Self and Society in Ming Thought*. New York: Columbia University Press.

Duan xiu pian (Chronicles of Cut Sleeve). 1909–1911. In *Xiangyen zongshu* (Anthology of Fragrant and Beautiful Things). Shanghai.

Gulik, Robert H. van. 1974. *Sexual Life in Ancient China*. Leiden: E. J. Brill.

Guobao wenjian lu. 1974. In *Biji xiaoshuo daguan*, 3d series. Taipei reprint ed.

Hanan, Patrick. 1981. *The Chinese Vernacular Story*. Cambridge: Harvard University Press.

Hegel, Robert E. 1981. *The Novel in Seventeenth-Century China*. New York: Columbia University Press.

Hsiao, Kung-chuan. 1960. *Rural China: Imperial Control in the Nineteenth Century*. Seattle: University of Washington Press.

Ji Yun. n.d. *Yue wei zao tang biji* (Jottings of Yue wei zao tang). Shanghai.

Li Yu. 1970. *Li Yu chuanji* (Complete Works of Li Yu). Taipei: Ch'eng-wen Publishing.

———. "The Antique Shop." In *Li Yu chuanji*.

———. "Male Mother of Mencius." In *Li Yu chuanji*.

———. "Pitying Fragrant Companion." In *Li Yu chuanji*.

———. *Rou putuan* (Carnal Prayer Mat). Meiji period Japanese edition.

Liang Chaoren. 1975. *Liang ban qiu yu an xu bi* (Jottings of Liang ban qiu yu an). Taipei: Wen Hai reprint ed.

Meijer, M. J. 1985. "Homosexual Offences in Ch'ing Law." *T'oung Pao*, 71: 109–33.

Ng, Vivien W. 1987. "Ideology and Sexuality: Rape Laws in Qing China." *Journal of Asian Studies* 46, no. 1:57–70.

Ruan, Fang-fu and Yung-mei Tsai. 1987. "Male Homosexuality in Traditional Chinese Literature." *Journal of Homosexuality* 14:21–33.

Sankar, Andrea Patrice. 1978. "The Evolution of the Sisterhood in Traditional Chinese Society: From Village Girls' Houses to Chai T'angs in Hong Kong." University of Michigan dissertation.

Shen Defu. 1979. *Wanli ye huo pian* (Wanli miscellanea). Beijing reprint ed.

Shen Fu. 1983. *Six Records of a Floating Life*. New York: Penguin Books.

Topley, Marjorie. 1975. "Marriage Resistance in Rural Kwangtung." In Margery Wolf and Roxanne Witke, eds. *Women in Chinese Society*. Stanford: Stanford University Press. pp. 111–142.

Wu Han. 1934. "Wan Ming shi guan jiaji di shenghuo" (Lifestyle of the scholar-official class in late Ming). *Dagong bao* (April 19 ed.).

Saslow, "Homosexuality in the Renaissance: Behavior, Identity, and Artistic Expression"

1. General surveys dealing with these issues include Vern R. Bullough, *Sexual Variance in Society and History* (Chicago and London: University of Chicago Press, 1976); A. L. Rowse, *Homosexuals in History* (New York: Macmillan, 1977); Marc Daniel and A. Baudry, *Les Homosexuels* (Paris: Casterman, 1975).

2. Principal documentary studies of individual European societies include Alan Bray, *Homosexuality in Renaissance England* (London: Gay Men's Press, 1982); Guido Ruggiero, *The Boundaries of Eros: Sex Crime and Sexuality in Renaissance Venice* (New York and Oxford: Oxford University Press, 1985); James M. Saslow, *Ganymede in the Renaissance: Homosexuality in Art and Society* (New Haven and London: Yale University Press, 1986); and essays by E. William Monter and Louis Crompton in Salvatore Licata and Robert Petersen, eds., *Historical Perspectives on Homosexuality (Journal of Homosexuality* 6, no.1/2, 1980/81). On the French court see Gilbert Robin, *L'Enigme sexuelle d'Henri III* (Paris: Westmael, 1964), with reference to primary sources. Concise though sometimes overstated biographies of numerous Renaissance figures, citing secondary sources, are found in Noel Garde, *Jonathan to Gide: The Homosexual in History* (New York: Vantage, 1964). An essential anthology that appeared as the present essay was going to press is *The Pursuit of Sodomy: Male Homosexuality in Renaissance and Enlightenment Europe,* eds. Kent Gerard, Gert Hekma (New York: Harrington Park Press, 1989); simultaneously published as *Journal of Homosexuality,* vol. 16 (1988).

3. Bullough, *Sexual Variance*, pp. 478ff.; Bray, *Homosexuality*, pp. 29ff.; Saslow, *Ganymede*, chaps. 2, 3.

4. Bullough, *Sexual Variance*, pp. 450, 478; Bray, *Homosexuality*, pp. 49–55, 65–74; Ruggiero, *Boundaries of Eros*, pp. 121–29. The comment on de Volonne, from the letters of Orléans's wife (see note 10), is quoted in Cecile Beurdeley, *L'Amour bleu* (New York: Rizzoli, 1978), a useful compendium of excerpts from original sources, though its analysis is superficial.

5. Christopher Hibbert, *The Rise and Fall of the House of Medici* (Harmondsworth: Penguin, 1974), 223; Benvenuto Cellini, *Autobiography,* tr. George Bull (Harmondsworth: Penguin, 1956), p. 64; Saslow, *Ganymede,* pp. 29–32. Jonathan Spence, *The Memory Palace of Matteo Ricci* (New York: Viking, 1984), discusses clerical homosexuality in Rome, esp. pp. 221–26.

6. Bray, *Homosexuality*, pp. 51ff.; Ruggiero, *Boundaries of Eros*, pp. 116, 142; cf. Baldassare Castiglione, *The Book of the Courtier*, 1524, tr. George Bull (Harmondsworth: Penguin, 1967), p. 171. I am grateful to Prof. Richard Sherr, Smith College, for permission to draw from his unpublished paper on dalla Balla, "Canons, Choirboys, and Homosexuality in Late 16th-Century Italy."

7. Bullough, *Sexual Variance*, chap. 15; Bray, *Homosexuality*, pp. 43–51; Ruggiero, *Boundaries of Eros*, pp. 115–34; Monter, in Licata and Petersen. On Sodoma see Giorgio Vasari, *Le Vite . . .* , 1568, ed. Gaetano Milanesi (Florence, 1865–79), 6:379–86.

8. Ruggiero, *Boundaries of Eros*, p. 142; Bray, *Homosexuality*, p. 14; Jonathan Katz, *Gay American History* (New York: Avon, 1976), p. 31.

9. Katz, *Gay History*, pp. 26–31.

10. On Philippe see *A Woman's Life at the Court of the Sun King:*

Letters of Liselotte von der Pfalz (Elisabeth Charlotte, Duchesse d'Orléans), tr. Elborg Forster (Baltimore: Johns Hopkins University Press, 1985). Other royal witnesses include Louis XIII's Anne of Austria and several Florentine Grand Duchesses: see Hibbert, *The Rise and Fall of the House of Medici*, pp. 287–320.

11. *Letters of King James VI and I*, ed. G. P. Akrigg (Berkeley and Los Angeles: University of California Press, 1984), e.g. no. 218; Cellini, *Vita*, 31, 39; Ruggiero, 115. The Portuguese material was discussed by Luiz Mott of University of Bahia in a paper at the International Gay History Conference, Toronto, 1985; see now Gerard and Hekma (as in note 2).

12. Monter in Licata and Petersen, p. 42; Bray, *Homosexuality*, pp. 14, 53–55; Ruggiero, *Boundaries of Eros*, pp. 113–15, 135–41; Spence, *Memory Palace*, pp. 226–33, citing Michel de Montaigne, *Journal de voyage en Italie*. For the question of subcultures in medieval France, see John Boswell, *Christianity, Social Tolerance, and Homosexuality* (Chicago: University of Chicago Press, 1980); Emmanuel Le Roy Ladurie, *Montaillou: The Promised Land of Error* (New York: Braziller, 1978), pp. 144–49. The problem in later centuries is discussed by Stephen Murray and Kent Gerard, "Renaissance Sodomitical Subcultures?" in *Among Men, Among Women: Sociological and historical recognition of homosocial arrangements* (Amsterdam: Universiteit, 1983); Gregory Sprague, "Male Homosexuality in Western Culture: The Dilemma of Identity and Subculture in Historical Research," *Journal of Homosexuality* 10 (1984):29–43.

13. The principal study of lesbianism in this period is Lillian Faderman, *Surpassing the Love of Men* (New York: Morrow, 1981), pp. 15–74. Broader than its title is Judith Brown, *Immodest Acts: The Life of a Lesbian Nun in Renaissance Italy* (New York and Oxford: Oxford University Press, 1986), a case study of Carlini that also surveys the available bibliography. The difficulties of determining the degree of genital sexuality in women's relationships were introduced by Carroll Smith-Rosenberg, "The Female World of Love and Ritual," in her *Disorderly Conduct: Visions of Gender* (New York and London: Oxford University Press, 1985). See also Bullough, *Sexual Variance*, chap. 15; Katz, *Gay History*, p. 36; Monter and Crompton, essays in Licata and Petersen (as in n. 2).

14. On this debate see esp. Bray, *Homosexuality*; Jeffrey Weeks, *Coming Out: Homosexual Politics in Britain from the Nineteenth Century to the Present* (London: Quartet Books, 1977); essays by Weeks, Bert Hansen, and Robert Padgug in "Sexuality in History," *Radical History Review* 20 (1979); Randolph Trumbach, "Sodomitical Subcultures, Sodomitical Roles, and the Gender Revolution of the Eighteenth Century," *Eighteenth-Century Life* 9 (1985):109–21; Jonathan Goldberg, "Renaissance Hom[m]osexuality," *Gay Studies Newsletter* 13, no. 2 (July 1986):9–12. Their approach is critiqued from an essentialist viewpoint by John Boswell, "Revolutions, Universals, Categories," *Salmagundi* 58/59 (1982/83):89–113.

15. Ruggiero, *Boundaries of Eros*, pp. 110–13, 141–44; Faderman, *Surpassing*, pp. 26, 35, 68–70; Bray, *Homosexuality*, 16–26. On the development of Christian attitudes in the Middle Ages see most recently Boswell, *Christianity*.

16. Marsilio Ficino, *Commentarium in Convivio Platonis*, 1474, ed. Sears R. Jayne (Columbia: University of Missouri Press, 1943), p. 207. Montaigne, Erasmus, and Bacon each wrote an essay "On Friendship." On Florentine circles see André Chastel, *Art et humanisme à Florence au temps de Laurent le Magnifique* (Paris: Presses universitaires de France, 1959), pp. 289–99.

17. Bray, *Homosexuality*, pp. 60–68; Joseph Pequigney, *Such Is My Love* (Chicago: University of Chicago Press, 1985); Equicola, *Libro di natura*

d'Amore (Venice, 1525), 112r; Ariosto, *Satires*, tr. and ed. Peter DeSa Wiggins (Athens: University of Ohio Press, 1976), Satire 6:15–22; Sherr, "Canons and Choirboys," *passim*.

18. Castiglione, *The Courtier*, Book 3; see further Saslow, *Ganymede*, chaps. 2, 3 (on Bandello, p. 74), and John DeCecco and Michael Shively, "From Sexual Identity to Sexual Relationships: A contextual shift," *Journal of Homosexuality* 9, nos. 2/3 (1983/84):1–26. The Florentine archives were discussed in a paper by Michael Rocke at the American Historical Association, Chicago, 1986, drawn from his forthcoming dissertation (State University of New York, Binghamton). On Brantôme, see Faderman, *Surpassing*, pp. 23–25; Bullough, *Sexual Variance*, p. 485; on passive/active roles, Ruggiero, *Boundaries of Eros*, pp. 117–22; Bray, *Homosexuality*, p. 13.

19. Seymour Kleinberg, "*The Merchant of Venice:* The Homosexual as Anti-Semite in Nascent Capitalism," in Stuart Kellogg, ed., *Essays on Gay Literature* (New York: Harrington Park Press, 1985).

20. Leonardo, *Codex atlanticus*, 252r.; Carlo Pedretti, *Leonardo da Vinci: A Study in Chronology and Style* (Berkeley and Los Angeles: University of California Press, 1973), pp. 161–62; *Lettere sull'arte di Pietro Aretino*, ed. Fidenzio Pertile and Ettore Camesasca, 3 vols. (Milan: del Milione, 1957–60), no. CCCLXIV, 3:177 (1545); Vasari, 6:379–86 (*Vita* of Sodoma).

21. Cellini, *Vita*, tr. Bull, pp. 335–38; Rowse, *Homosexuals in History*, p. 31; Beurdeley, *L'amour bleu*, pp. 117–18; Katz, *Gay History*, pp. 34–35.

22. Poliziano, *Stanze per la giostra, Orfeo, Rime*, ed. Bruno Maier (Novara: de Agostini, 1968), lines 331–56; Bullough, *Sexual Variance*, p. 447.

23. Saslow, *Ganymede*, chaps. 1,4; Cellini, *Vita*, tr. Bull, 335–38.

24. Sigmund Freud, *Leonardo da Vinci and a Memory of His Childhood*, tr. Alan Tyson (Harmondsworth: Penguin, 1963); Kurt Eissler, *Leonardo da Vinci: Psychoanalytic Notes on the Enigma* (New York: International Universities Press, 1961); Robert Liebert, *Michelangelo: A Psychoanalytic Study of His Life and Images* (New Haven and London: Yale University Press, 1983); Charles Kligerman, "Notes on Benvenuto Cellini," *Annual of Psychoanalysis* 3 (1975):409–21.

25. Laurie Schneider, "Donatello and Caravaggio: The iconography of decapitation," *American Imago* 33 (1976):76–91. On homosexual artists see Rudolf and Margot Wittkower, *Born Under Saturn* (London: Weidenfeld and Nicolson, 1962), with reference to original sources; Saslow, *Ganymede, passim*.

26. Donald Posner, "Caravaggio's Homo-erotic Early Works," *Art Quarterly* 34 (1971):301–24; Howard Hibbard, *Caravaggio* (New York: Harper and Row, 1983), pp. 30–35, 155–60.

27. See "Images of Sexual Vice in Quattrocento Art," unpublished paper by Joseph Manca (Seton Hall University). Spence, *Memory Palace*, details Christian disapproval or suppression of homosexuality in China, also touching on the Philippines, Japan, and India.

28. On Sappho and male perceptions of lesbianism, see Faderman, *Surpassing*, pp. 25–32.

29. The Zurich illustration appears in James Steakley, *The Homosexual Emancipation Movement in Germany* (Salem, N.H.: Ayer, 1982), p. 11. For de Bry's engraving, see Walter Williams, *The Spirit and the Flesh: Sexual Diversity in American Indian Culture* (Boston: Beacon Press, 1986), pp. 135–37, 297. On similar persecutions in Asia, see Spence, *Memory Palace*, pp. 221–28.

30. Bullough, *Sexual Variance*, pp. 441ff.; Peter Webb, *The Erotic Arts* (Boston: New York Graphic Society, 1975), pp. 103–36, 345–55; Williams, *Spirit and Flesh*, p. 297.

31. Thomas Carew, *Poems*, 1640 (facsimile repr. Menston: Scholar Press,

1969), pp. 217–19; Saslow, *Ganymede*, chap. 5. The French poet Théophile de Viau was condemned to death for erotic/heretical poems in 1623.

32. Bullough, *Sexual Variance*, chaps. 15, 16; Bray, *Homosexuality*, pp. 106–10. See, on the general issue, Jean Howard, "The New Historicism in Renaissance Studies," *English Literary Renaissance* 16 (1986): 13–43.

Gunn Allen, "Lesbians in American Indian Cultures"

1. I have read accounts that mention American Indian lesbians taken from a variety of sources, but those are all in publications that focus on gays and/or lesbians rather than on Native Americans.

2. Frederick Manfred, *The Manly-Hearted Woman* (New York: Bantam, 1978).

3. Natalie Curtis, *The Indians' Book* (New York: Dover, 1950), p. 4.

4. Bronislaw Malinowski, *Sex, Culture, and Myth* (New York: Harcourt, Brace & World, 1962), p. 12.

5. See John Bierhorst, ed., *Four Masterworks of American Indian Literature: Quetzalcoatl/The Ritual of Concolence/Cuceb/The Night Chant* (New York: Farrar, Straus and Giroux, 1974). Fr. Bernard Haile's work is included in Leland C. Wyman, ed., *Beautyway: A Navajo Ceremonial*, Bollingen Series, 53 (New York: Pantheon, 1975).

6. As it is accurately put by Jane Fishburne Collier in "Women in Politics," in *Women, Culture and Society*, ed. Michelle Zimbalist Rosaldo and Louise Lamphere (Stanford: Stanford University Press, 1974), p. 90.

7. John (Fire) Lame Deer and Richard Erdoes, *Lame Deer, Seeker of Visions: The Life of a Sioux Medicine Man* (New York: Simon and Schuster, 1972), p. 150.

8. Joan Bamburger, "The Myths of Matriarchy: Why Men Rule in Primitive Society," in Rosaldo and Lamphere, *Women, Culture and Society*, pp. 260–271.

Schalow, "Male Love in Early Modern Japan"

1. A partial translation can be found in E. Powys Mathers, trans., *Comrade Loves of the Samurai* (Tokyo: Charles E. Tuttle Co., 1972). A complete translation appears in Paul Gordon Schalow, "The Great Mirror of Male Love by Ihara Saikaku," 2 vols. (unpublished Ph.D. dissertation: Harvard University, 1985). Quotations from individual narratives in *The Great Mirror of Male Love* are identified in the text of the article by the name of the story and section: narrative number (IV:2—section four: narrative two) and can be found in vol. 1 of the dissertation.

2. For a general introduction to Ihara Saikaku, see Howard Hibbett, *The Floating World in Japanese Fiction* (London: Oxford University Press, 1959), chapter 3; Donald Keene, *World Within Walls* (London: Secker & Warburg, 1976), chapter 8.

3. See Margaret H. Childs, "Chigo Monogatari: Love Stories or Buddhist Sermons?" *Monumenta Nipponica*, 35, no. 2 (1980): 127–51.

4. See Teruoka Yasutaka, ed., *Nanshoku ōkagami*, In Gendaigoyaku Saikaku zenshū, vol. 3 (Tokyo: Shogakkan, 1976). Teruoka argues that

Saikaku's motive in writing *The Great Mirror of Male Love* was to make a national reputation by writing a work that would appeal to the Edo audience.

5. *Wakashudō* is frequently abbreviated to *shudō* or *jakudō* in *The Great Mirror of Male love*.

6. There were no equivalent terms for a similar choice available to women.

7. The evidence in literature for the bisexual norm is convincing, but it has not been discussed by Japanese or Western scholars because it is implicitly assumed. Saikaku's first work of fiction, *The Man Who Loved Love* (*Kōshoku ichidai otoko*, 1682) depicts a hero whose sexual experiences with women and men, and later youths, number in the hundreds. Similar heroes in Tokugawa literature are too numerous to mention, and there are innumerable historical cases to corroborate the literary impression that bisexuality was the social norm.

8. It is not clear whether the term "woman-hater" was coined by the bisexual majority or by the exclusively homosexual minority, but *The Great Mirror of Male Love* shows that it was used by the minority to identify itself. For a more detailed discussion of exclusive male homosexuality and its relation to the bisexual norm, see Paul Gordon Schalow, "Woman-Hater as Homosexual: Literary Evidence from 17th-Century Japan," in *Proceedings,* "Homosexuality, Which Homosexuality Conference" (Amsterdam: Free University, 1987).

9. The person who was (or acted the part of) the adult male was always the active partner in anal intercourse with the one who was (or acted as) the youth.

10. See, for example, Kronhausen, *The Complete Book of Erotic Art*, 2 vols. (New York: Bell, 1978). 1:265, plate 308; p. 281, plate 342.

11. The stages toward adulthood are outlined in Teruoka Yasutaka, ed. *Nanshoku ōkagami*, vol. 3 in Gendaigoyaku Saikaku zenshū (Tokyo: Shogakkan, 1976). The *Shin'yūki* (1643) divides the period one is a youth into three three-year intervals: ages 11–13; ages 14–16; and ages 17–19.

12. This step was also called *hangembuku*, "half coming-of-age."

13. "Love Letter Sent In a Sea Bass" (1:4) begins with a metaphorical description of the stages towards adulthood: "It is said that 'Cherry blossoms forever bloom the same, but people change with every passing year.' This is especially true of a boy in the bloom of youth. It is as if he were hit by a rain squall when the sleeve vents on his robe are sewn shut. He shudders under a rising wind when his temples are shaved. When at last he comes of age, his blossom of youth falls cruelly to the ground. All told, loving a boy can be likened to a dream that we are never given time to have."

14. Tokugawa Ieyasu achieved hegemony over Japan in 1603. The bakufu (military government) he established in Edo ruled Japan for over 250 years until 1868. Tokugawa rule was based on neo-Confucian ideals which emphasized hierarchy and rigid class stratification. The classes were, in descending order: the samurai, whose function in the course of the Tokugawa period changed from that of warriors to government administrators; farmers; small manufacturers and laborers; and merchants. The latter two classes were frequently lumped into a single group and called *chōnin*, or "townsmen," who were concentrated in the large urban centers of Kyoto, Osaka, and Edo. The relatively high status of farmers resulted from the fact that they were the only ones whose labor was deemed productive, for they produced rice, the staple of the Japanese diet and the economic foundation of the state. Merchants and manufacturers manipulated wealth and did not create it, so they ranked lower on the social scale. Merchants in particular were despised

because they dealt with cash, taking profits on the sale of goods and charging interest on loans.

15. An early-seventeenth-century manuscript, the *Seisuisho* (1623) tells the story of a woman who, apparently motivated by anger at her husband's neglect, offers to relinquish her position as wife to the youth her husband has taken in as his lover. The story ends with a Confucian exhortation that men must observe their duties to their wives, since insuring the continuation of one's lineage was a primary expression of filial piety, one of the central virtues of Confucian ethical morality.

16. "Two Old Cherry Trees Still in Bloom" (IV:4) states, "Sometimes, a daimyō will love one of his pages deeply and, even after the boy has grown up and established a family, will be unable to forget his youthful charms. This is praiseworthy." The fact that Saikaku calls this praiseworthy must be understood as a humorous appeal to his readership's exclusive orientation towards male love, since continuation of the youth's role into adulthood was normally a violation of social convention.

17. Narratives I:3, I:4, II:2, III:4, III:5, IV:2, and IV:3 deal with love triangles that cross status boundaries. Except for I:3 and I:4, all end tragically for the participants. For more on the conflict between obligation (*giri*) and human feeling (*ninjō*) in Tokugawa literature, see Donald Keene, *World Within Walls* (London: Secker & Warburg, 1976), pp. 260–261, 269.

18. There is one exception: "Drowned in Love With Winecups of Pearly Nautilus" (IV:1) describes the intense love of a certain man for his wife; when she dies, he remarries to please his family but finds that his new wife cannot replace the dead woman in his affections. The narrative concludes, "He found it impossible to abstain completely from sex, however, and since he was utterly bored with women he kept a boy at his side from then on. This apparently served as a perfectly satisfactory replacement." This final line is the only time male love is mentioned in the entire story.

19. *Shin'yūki* (1643) was the first manuscript to establish *nasake* as the primary criteria by which a youth's worthiness would be judged.

20. The term *ji-wakashu* does not actually appear in *The Great Mirror of Male Love*, but it appears in Teruoka Yasutaka, ed. *Nanshoku ōkagami*, vol. 3 in Gendaigoyaku Saikaku zenshū (Tokyo: Shogakkan, 1976). There, Teruoka distinguishes the two types of *wakashu* as "professional" (*shokugyō-teki*) and "non-professional" (*hishokugyō-teki*).

21. Narratives V:1, V:3, VI:1, VI:3, and VII:2 develop the subtheme of kabuki youths abandoning prostitution due to the love of a samurai. V:4 and VII:1 also depict kabuki youths abandoning prostitution for the sake of love, but without samurai influence.

22. This samurai custom was sometimes imitated by courtesans in the licensed quarter and actors in the kabuki theater to prove the sincerity of their love for a special patron.

23. There is one other case in *The Great Mirror of Male Love* in "The ABC's of Boy Love" (I:2) where a priest makes a vow of love with two youths simultaneously, but this is obviously not the norm.

24. The banning of "Grand Kabuki," later known as *wakashu* kabuki, occurred in two steps, first in Edo in 1651 and then in Kyoto and Osaka in 1652. It was part of the Tokugawa government's effort to control boy prostitution, motivated particularly by their desire to halt the frequently bloody samurai rivalries for the affections of boy actors. The name "kabuki" was temporarily abandoned in favor of "mime and dance stage show" to make explicit the break with the past. In Teruoka Yasutaka *Saikaku shinron* (Tokyo: Chuo Koronsha, 1982), Teruoka associates this clampdown on ka-

buki with the death in 1651 of the third shōgun Tokugawa Iemitsu, a well-known aficionado of kabuki who frequently invited actors to the shōgun's castle for performances and entertainment. This of course scandalized the stricter Confucianists, who could not abide such mingling of high and low.

25. This celebration took place in 1659 and was the three hundredth anniversary of Kanzan's death, not the three hundred and fiftieth as Saikaku wrote. Kanzan established the main temple of the Rinzai sect, Myōshin-ji, in Kyoto. The priests of the Rinzai sect were well-known for their wealth.

26. The Shogakkan edition of *Nanshoku ōkagami* (Nihon koten bungaku zenshū) contains an appendix of short biographies for all of the identifiable kabuki actors appearing in Saikaku's narrative.

27. For contemporary descriptions of kabuki actors, see the translations from actor evaluation books in Donald H. Shively, "Bakufu Versus Kabuki" in Hall and Jansen, eds., *Studies in the Institutional History of Early Modern Japan* (Princeton; Princeton University Press, 1968) pp. 231–61.

28. "Love: The Contest Between Two Forces" (I:1) is an introductory chapter and does not contain a storylike narrative.

29. The grafted tree and pair of one-winged birds are images frequently applied to married couples to show the depth of love between them.

30. See note 24.

31. After this point, even young kabuki actors were called *yarō*.

32. The artistic benefits to kabuki of government regulation are discussed in Shively, "Bakufu Versus Kabuki," pp. 259–61.

Trumbach, "The Birth of the Queen"

1. The summary statements of the introduction are more fully documented in Randolph Trumbach, "London's Sodomites: Homosexual Behavior and Western Culture in the Eighteenth Century," *Journal of Social History* 11 (1977): 1–33; "Sodomitical Subcultures, Sodomitical Roles and the Gender Revolution of the Eighteenth Century: The Recent Historiography," *Eighteenth-Century Life* 9 (1985): 109–121, reprinted in *'Tis Nature's Fault: Unauthorized Sexuality during the Enlightenment*, ed. R. P. Maccubin (New York, 1987).

2. *The Wandering Whore* (London, 1660–1663), 6 parts, part 3, p. 9; ed. Randolph Trumbach (reprint ed., New York: Garland, 1986).

3. *The Diary of Samuel Pepys*, ed. Robert Latham and William Matthews (London, 1971), 4: 209–210.

4. David M. Vieth, *The Complete Poems of John Wilmot, Earl of Rochester* (New Haven, 1978), pp. 117, 51, 53; Jeremy Treglown, *The Letters of John Wilmot, Earl of Rochester* (Chicago, 1980), pp. 230, 243, 160, 25–6.

5. Angeline Goreau, *Reconstructing Aphra* (New York, 1980), pp. 189–206; George Woodcock, *The Incomparable Aphra* (London, 1948), pp. 105–116.

6. *The Tryal and Condemnation of Mervin, Lord Audley, Earl of Castlehaven* (London, 1699), pp. 14–19, in *Sodomy Trials*, ed. Trumbach (reprint ed., New York, 1986). A more detailed narrative: Caroline Bingham, "Seventeenth-Century Attitudes Toward Deviant Sex," *Journal of Interdisciplinary History* 1 (1971):446–68.

7. D. C. Clark, "The Restoration Rake in Life and Comedy" (Ph.D. thesis, Florida State University, 1963); R. D. Hume, *The Development of English Drama in the Late Seventeenth Century* (Oxford, 1976), and *The Rakish Stage* (Carbondale, Ill., 1983).

8. Aphra Behn, "The Amorous Prince," in *Works*, ed. Montague Summers, 6 vols. (reprint ed., New York, 1967), 4: 186, 196–7, 210–11; Thomas Otway, "The Souldiers Fortune," in *Works*, ed. J. C. Ghosh, 2 vols. (reprint ed., Oxford, 1968), 2: 103–7; Nathaniel Lee, "The Princess of Cleve," in *Works*, ed. T. B. Strong and A. L. Cooke, 2 vols. (reprint ed., Metuchen N.J., 1968), 2: 157, 177–8.

9. *The Wandering Whore* (1660), part 4, p. 5; A. P. Hall and M. B. Hall, eds., *Correspondence of Henry Oldenburg* (Madison, Wis., 1973), 9: 298–302; Pierre Darmon, *Trial by Impotence* (London, 1985), pp. 40–51; J. M. Saslow, *Ganymede in the Renaissance* (New Haven, 1986), pp. 75–90, 220 n. 29, 222 n. 44.

10. Susan Staves, "A Few Kind Words for the Fop," *SEL*, 22 (1982): 413–428.

11. Alan Bray, *Homosexuality in Renaissance England* (London, 1981), pp. 130–1 n. 77.

12. [Nathaniel Lancaster?], *The Pretty Gentleman* (London, 1747), p. 6, quoted in Staves, "Kind Words," p. 419.

13. Staves, "Kind Words," pp. 421–8 (which I have modified); Tobias Smollet, *The Adventures of Roderick Random* (1748), ed. P.-G. Boucé (New York, 1981), pp. 194–9; Boucé, *The Novels of Tobias Smollet* (London, 1976), pp. 267–8.

14. *Satan's Harvest Home* (London, 1749), pp. 50–54; ed. Trumbach (reprint ed., New York, 1985); *Proceedings at . . . Old Bailey*, 22–25 February 1727: Richard Skekos; Louis Crompton, *Byron and Greek Love* (Berkeley, 1985), pp. 295–6 n. 26.

15. L. D. Potter, "The Fop and Related Figures in Drama from Johnson to Cibber" (Ph.D. thesis, Cambridge University, 1965), pp. 159–61.

16. *A Compleat Collection of Remarkable Tryals . . . in the Old Bailey*, 2 vols. (London, 1718), 1: 236–42; Bray, *Homosexuality*, pp. 98, 139; A. G. Craig, "The Movement for the Reformation of Manners, 1688–1715" (Ph.D. thesis, University of Edinburgh, 1980), pp. 168–75; John Dunton, *Athenianism*, 2 vols. (London, 1710), 2: 94.

17. *Tryal of Castlehaven*, preface; Greater London R.O.: MJ/SR/2028, Recog. 9.

18. *The Tryal and Conviction of several reputed Sodomites . . . 20th day of October 1707* (British Library: 515, 1. 2 (205)); Greater London R.O.: MJ/SP/Sept. 1707; *The Women-Hater's Lamentation* (London, 1707), in *Sodomy Trials*, ed. Trumbach; Hertfordshire Record Office: D/EP/F32, vol. 4, 10 October 1707.

19. *A full and true account of the discovery and apprehending a notorious gang of sodomites in St. James's* (London, 1709) (British Library: 515 1. 2 (209)); Edward Ward, *The Secret History of Clubs* (London, 1709), pp. 284–300, *recte* 290; Oxford English Dictionary, molly; Wayne Dynes, *Homolexis* (New York, 1985), *passim;* for faggot as early-nineteenth-century West Country for prostitute: Polly Morris, "Sexual reputation in Somerset, 1733–1850" (Ph.D. thesis, University of Warwick, 1985); *Hell Upon Earth* (London, 1729), p. 43; ed. Trumbach (reprint ed., New York, 1985): This is preceded by an account of fops and beaus, who are presented as silly, but interested in women (pp. 32–41); Dunton, *Athenianism*, pp. 94–99; [Jonathan Wild], *An Answer to a Late Insolent Libel* (London, 1718), p. 30.

20. Ward, *History of Clubs*; Wild, *Answer*, pp. 30–32, reprinted in F. S. Lyons, *Jonathan Wild* (London, 1936), pp. 278–81, and on which see Gerald Howson, *Thief-Taker General* (New York, 1970), pp. 60–5, *et passim; Select Trials at . . . the Old Bailey*, 4 vols. (London, 1742), 2: 362–72; ed. Trumbach,

(reprint ed. New York, 1985), 4 vols., in 2; James Dalton, *A Genuine Narrative . . . since October Last* (London, 1728), pp. 31–43.

21. Greater London R.O.: MJ/SR/2459: Newgate Calendar, #57, 60, MJ/SR/2461: New Prison List; *The London Journal*, 23, April 1726, 17 December 1726.

22. *St. James Evening Post*, 3–5 Oct. 1727; *Proceedings . . . Old Bailey* (1732), no. 6, pp. 166–170.

23. A. N. Gilbert, "Buggery and the British Navy, 1700–1861," *Journal of Social History* 10 (1976–7): 72–98, at p. 75.

24. Trumbach, "London's Sodomites," p. 18; "Sodomitical Assaults, Gender Role, and Sexual Development in Eighteenth-Century London," *Journal of Homosexuality* 16 (1988): 407–29.

25. Trumbach, "London's sodomites," p. 13; "Modern Prostitution and Gender in *Fanny Hill*," *Sexual Underworlds of the Enlightenment*, ed. G. S. Rousseau and Roy Porter (Manchester, 1987); J. H. Wilson, *All the King's Ladies* (Chicago, 1958), pp. 67–86; Pat Rogers, "The Breeches Part," in *Sexuality in Eighteenth-Century Britain* (Manchester, 1982), ed. P. G. Boucé, pp. 244–58; Charlotte Charke, *A Narrative of the Life* (London, 1755), reprint ed. L. R. N. Ashley (Gainesville, 1969); Lois Potter, "Colley Cibber: The Fop as Hero," *Augustan Worlds*, ed. J. C. Hilton et al. (New York, 1978), pp. 153–164; and see Lynne Friedl, "Passing women," in *Underworlds*, ed. Porter and Rousseau.

26. W. L. Williams, *The Spirit and the Flesh* (Boston, 1986); R. I. Levy, "The Community Function of Tahitian Male Transvestism," *Anthropological Quarterly* 44 (1971):12–21; Unni Wikan, *Behind the Veil in Arabia* (Baltimore, 1982), chap. 9; R. L. Munroe, J. W. M. Whiting, D. J. Hally, "Institutionalized Male Transvestism and Sex Distinctions," *American Anthropologist* 71 (1969):87–90. There are further useful studies of male transvestite groups in Evelyn Blackwood, ed., *The Many Faces of Homosexuality* (New York, 1986), especially by Charles Callender and L. M. Kochems, who deny that gay men are a third gender in modern Western culture, because they do not assume a consistent effeminate role. Some of the theoretical issues are discussed in S. O. Murray, *Social Theory, Homosexual Realities* (New York, 1984).

27. Lawrence Stone, *The Family, Sex and Marriage in England, 1500–1800* (New York, 1977); Randolph Trumbach, *The Rise of the Egalitarian Family* (New York, 1978).

Huussen, "Sodomy in the Dutch Republic"

1. L. F. Groenendijk, *De nadere reformatie van het gezin [Puritanism and the Family]* (Dordrecht: J. P. van den Tol, 1984); A. Th. van Deursen, *Het kopergeld van de Gouden Eeuta [Coppers of the Golden Age]*, vol. 3: *Volk en overheid [People and Government]* (Assen: Van Gorcum, 1979).

2. Heinz Schilling, "Religion und Gesellschaft in der calvinistischen Republik der Vereinigten Niederlande. 'Öffentlichkeitskirche' und Säkularisation: Ehe und Hebammenwesen; Presbyterien und politische Partizipation," in Franz Petri, ed., *Kirche und Gesellschaftlicher Wandel in deutschen und niederländischen Städten der werdenden Neuzeit* (Cologne and Vienna: Böhlau, 1980), pp. 197–250; Steven Ozment, *When Fathers Ruled: Family Life in Reformation Europe* (Cambridge: Harvard University Press, 1983).

3. Gisela Bleibtreu-Ehrenberg, *Tabu Homosexualität: Die Geschichte eines*

Vorurteils (Frankfurt: Fischer, 1978), is silent on the topics of the Reformation, Luther, Calvin, etc.

4. Willem Frijhoff, "Prophétie et société dans les Provinces-Unies aux XVIIe et XVIIIe siècles," in Marie-Sylvie Dupont-Bouchat, Willem Frijhoff, and Robert Muchembled, *Prophètes et sorciers dans les Pays-Bas XVIe-XVIIIe siècle* (Paris: Hachette, 1978), pp. 263–362; Van Deursen, *Kopergeld*, vol. 4: *Hel en hemel* [Hell and Heaven] (Assen: Van Gorcum, 1980).

5. John H. Langbein, *Prosecuting Crime in the Renaissance: England, Germany, France* (Cambridge: Harvard University Press, 1974), pp. 165ff.

6. Peter Pappus van Tratzberg, *Articul-brief, waer bij eenige annotatien gevoeght zijn [Articles on Military Law, with Addition of Annotations]* 6th ed. (Groningen, 1681), pp. 9, 48; Gerh. Feltman, *Aanmerkingen over den Articulbrief ofte Ordonnantie op de discipline militaire [Commentaries on the Articles or Ordinances on the Military Discipline]* 3rd ed. (The Hague, 1716), pp. 17–18, 63–65.

7. Joos de Damhouder, *Praxis rerum criminalium* (1554; Antwerp, 1601; rep. Aalen: Scientia, 1978), cap. 98, "De peccato contra naturam"; Antonius Matthaeus, *De criminibus ad Lib. XLVII et XLVIII Digestorum commentarius* (Utrecht, 1644), pp. 460–61. On Matthaeus see Felix Schlüter, *Antonius Matthäus II. aus Herborn, der Kriminalist des 17. Jahrhunderts, der Rechtslehrer Utrechts* (Breslau, 1929), pp. 92–93.

8. Herman Diederiks, "Patterns of Criminality and Law Enforcement During the Ancien Régime: The Dutch Case," in *Criminal Justice History: An International Annual* (New York, 1980), pp. 157–74.

9. Robert F. Oaks, " 'Things Fearful to Name': Sodomy and Buggery in Seventeenth-Century New England," *Journal of Social History* 12 (1978–79): 268–81.

10. G. R. Elton, "Crime and the Historians," in J. S. Cockburn, ed., *Crime in England 1550–1800* (London: Methuen, 1977), pp. 1–14.

11. On Leiden: D. J. Noordam. "Homosexualiteit en sodomie in Leiden, 1533–1811" ["Homosexuality and Sodomy at Leiden. 1533–1811"], *Leids Jaarboekje* 75 (1983): 72–105; and "Homosocial relations in Leiden (1533–1811)," in *Among Men, Among Women: Sociological and Historical Recognition of Homosocial Arrangements* (Gay Studies and Women's Studies Conference, University of Amsterdam [22–26 June 1983]); collected papers, Amsterdam Sociological Institute, University of Amsterdam (1983), pp. 218–23.

12. L. J. Boon, "De grote sodomietenvervolging in het gewest Holland, 1730–1731," ["The Great Persecution of Sodomites in the Province of Holland, 1730–31"], *Holland, regionaal-historisch tijdschrift* 8 (1976): 140–52; and "Utrechtenaren: de sodomieprocessen in Utrecht, 1730–1732" ["Utrechters: Trials against Sodomites in Utrecht, 1730–32"], *Spiegel Historiael, maandblad voor geschiedenis en archeologie* 17 (1982): 553–58; D. J. Noordam, "Homoseksuele relaties in Holland in 1776" ["Homosexual relations in Holland, 1776"], *Holland, regionaal-historisch tijdschrift* 16 (1984): 3–34.

13. A. N. Gilbert, "Buggery and the British Navy, 1700–1861," *Journal of Social History* 10 (1976–77): 72–98; R. Trumbach, "London's Sodomites: Homosexual Behaviour and Western Culture in the Eighteenth Century," *Journal of Social History* 11 (1977–78): 1–33.

14. Theo van der Meer, *De wesentlijke sonde van sodomie en andere vuyligheeden. Sodomieten-vervolgingen in Amsterdam, 1730–1811 [The Real Sin of Sodomy and other Lewdness. Persecutions of Sodomites in Amsterdam, 1730–1811]* (Amsterdam: Tabula, 1984), cases on pp. 86, 100, and—perhaps—178.

15. Noordam, "Homosexualiteit"; Van der Meer, *Der wesentlijke*, pp.

137–47; Rudolf Dekker and Lotte van de Pol, *Daar was laatst een meisje loos: Nederlandse vrouwen als matrozen en soldaten. Een historisch onderzoek [Dutch Women as Sailors and Soldiers. An Historical Study]* (Baarn: Ambo, 1982).

16. Pieter Loens, *Regtelyke aanmerkingen omtrent eenige poincten, concernerende de execrable sonde tegens de natuur [Legal Commentary Concerning Some Points in the Case of the Abominable Sin against Nature]* (Rotterdam, 1760).

17. [Abraham Perrenot], *Bedenkingen over het straffen van zekere schandelijke misdaad [Considerations on the Punishment of Certain Infamous Crimes]* (Amsterdam, 1777). On Perrenot and Beccaria see Noordam, "Homoseksuele," pp. 24–27.

18. A. D. Harvey, "Prosecutions for Sodomy in England at the Beginning of the Nineteenth Century," *Historical Journal* 21 (1978): 939–48.

19. Nocrdam, "Homosexualiteit,": 96; J. de Jong, L. Kooijmans, and H. F. de Wit, "Schuld en boete in de Nederlandse Verlichting" ["Guilt and Punishment during the Dutch Enlightenment"], *Kleio* 19 (1978): 237–44; Paul Kapteyn, *Taboe, ontwikkelingen in macht en moraal speciaal in Nederland [Taboo: Developments in Power and Morals, Especially in The Netherlands]* (Amsterdam: De Arbeiderspers, 1980); L. J. Boon, "Those Damned Sodomites: Public Images of Sodomy in the 18th Century Netherlands," in *Among Men, Among Women*, supp. 1, pp. 19–22. On the struggle against disorder in France, see Michel Rey, "Police et sodomie à Paris au XVIIIe siècle, du péché au désordre," *Revue d'Histoire Moderne et Contemporaine* 29 (1982): 113–24, and his contribution to *Among Men, Among Women*, pp. 197–206.

20. See, for example, Stephen Murray and Kent Gerard, "Renaissance Sodomite Subcultures?," in *Among Men, Among Women*, pp. 183–96; Jeffrey Weeks, "Discourse, Desire and Sexual Deviance: Some Problems in a History of the Modern Homosexuality," in Kenneth Plumner, ed., *The Making of the Modern Homosexual* (London: Hutchinson, 1981) pp. 76–111; Philippe Ariès, "Réflexions sur l'histoire de l'homosexualité," *Communications: Ecole des Hautes Etudes en Sciences sociale, Centre d'Etudes Transdisciplinaires (Sociologie, Anthropologie, Sémiologie)* 35 (1982): 56–67.

Duberman, "Writhing Bedfellows"

1. Thomas J. Withers to James H. Hammond, September 24, 1826, Hammond Papers, South Caroliniana Library, Columbia, S.C. The preceding quotations and paraphrases are from portions of his two letters not printed in this article.

2. Most of what is known about Withers can be found in two studies: William H. Freehling, *Prelude to Civil War: The Nullification Controversy in South Carolina, 1816–1836* (New York: Harper & Row. 1965); and Charles Robert Lee, Jr., *The Confederate Constitutions* (Chapel Hill: University of North Carolina Press, 1963).

3. Lee, *Confederate Constitutions*, pp. 28, 71, 75, 135.

4. See, for example, Clement Eaton, *The Mind of the Old South* (Louisiana State University Press: 1964), p. 21.

5. For those interested, the following studies (along with those by Freehling and Eaton, already cited) are the most authoritative. For Hammond's political career: Charles S. Sydnor, *The Development of Southern Sectionalism* (Louisiana State University Press, 1948); Allan Nevins, *The Ordeal of the*

Union and *The Emergence of Lincoln* (Scribners, 1947; 1950); Avery Craven, *The Growth of Southern Nationalism* (Louisiana State University Press, 1953); Holman Hamilton, *Prologue to Conflict* (University Press of Kentucky, 1964); and Steven A. Channing, *Crisis of Fear* (Simon & Schuster, 1970). For Hammond's economic views: David Bertelson, *The Lazy South* (Oxford, 1967); Robert S. Starobin, *Industrial Slavery in the Old South* (Oxford, 1970); Richard C. Wade, *Slavery in the Cities* (Oxford, 1964); R. R. Russel, *Economic Aspects of Southern Sectionalism* (University of Illinois Press, 1924); and Eugene Genovese, *The Political Economy of Slavery* (Pantheon, 1965). For Hammond's theories on slavery (and his treatment of his own slaves): William S. Jenkins, *Pro-Slavery Thought in the Old South* (University of North Carolina Press, 1935); William Stanton, *The Leopard's Spots* (University of Chicago Press, 1960); Eugene Genovese, *The World the Slaveowners Made* and *Roll, Jordan, Roll* (Pantheon, 1969; 1974); Kenneth Stampp, *The Peculiar Institution* (Knopf, 1956); William Taylor, *Cavalier and Yankee* (Braziller, 1957); John Hope Franklin, *The Militant South* (Beacon, 1956); and Herbert G. Gutman, *The Black Family in Slavery and Freedom* (Pantheon, 1976).

6. For reasons explained in the article, I've excerpted and published here only the erotic portions of the two letters. The remaining material is at any rate of little historical interest, dealing as it does with various mundane matters—news of friends, complaints about the Boredom of Life, youthful pontifications on public events.

7. If Hammond's letter is extant, its whereabouts is unknown.

8. A leading figure in politics in the antebellum period.

9. Freehling contains the best description of South Carolina in this period and the lifestyle of its ruling elite (see *Prelude*, especially pp. 11–24). Eaton is most helpful for biographical detail on Hammond himself. I've relied heavily on both books for the factual material in this section.

10. For additional details on Hammond's severity as a slaveowner, see Gutman, *Black Family,* pp. 221–2; Freehling, *Prelude*, pp. 68–71; and Genovese, *Roll*, p, 455, 561. For more on Hammond's skills as a planter, see Nevins, *Ordeal*, pp. 482–3.

11. Wade, *Slavery*, p. 122; Gutman, *Black Family*, pp. 62, 572.

12. Eaton's account (*Mind*, pp. 30 ff.), or perhaps the secret diary itself, is blurred on the central question of whether (and in what manner) Hammond's seduction proceeded. In a book published after the appearance of this essay, Drew Faust has argued that the seduction consisted of Hammond repeatedly fondling his four teenage nieces in their "most secret and sacred regions" over a two-year period, until one of his nieces finally told her father, Wade Hampton, about it (Drew Faust, *James Henry Hammond and the Old South: A Design for Mastery*, Baton Rouge: 1982).

13. Eaton, *Mind*, pp. 31–32.

14. The importance of regional variations in sexual mores is marginally confirmed in the linkage Walt Whitman made (in a letter to John Addington Symonds, August 19, 1890): My life, young manhood, mid-age, *times South* [italics mine], etc., have been jolly bodily. . . ."

15. Orlando Paterson (in his review of Bertram Wyatt Brown, *Southern Honor: Ethics and Behavior in the Old South*, in *Reviews in American History*, March 1984), makes this provocative comment: "There is not a single reference to homosexuality in the work. I draw attention to this not out of intellectual fashion, but simply because anyone acquainted with the comparative ethnohistory of honorific cultures will be immediately struck by it. Homosexuality is pronounced in such systems, both ancient and modern.

Southern domestic life most closely resembles that of the Mediterranean in precisely those areas which are most highly conducive to homosexuality. Does the author's silence imply its absence in the pronounced male bonding of the Old South?"

16. This seems the appropriate point to thank several other people whose advice or expertise proved of critical importance: Jesse Lemisch, Joan Warnow, Jonathan Weiss, Eric Foner, Martin Garbus, and Ann Morgan Campbell. To prevent any one of them being held accountable for actions and decisions for which I alone am ultimately responsible, I deliberately refrain from specifying which individual gave what advice or recommended which line of strategy.

Martin, "Knights-Errant and Gothic Seducers"

1. Carroll Smith-Rosenberg, "The Female World of Love and Ritual: Relations Between Women in Nineteenth-Century America," *Signs* 1 (1975), reprinted in Smith-Rosenberg, *Disorderly Conduct: Visions of Gender in Victorian America* (New York: Knopf, 1985), p. 75.

2. In the first volume of his history of sexuality, Michel Foucault, *La volonté de savoir* (Paris: Gallimard, 1976), chap. 2, pp. 23–67.

3. Taylor received major government appointments, serving as secretary of legation in imperial Russia in 1862, and as minister to Germany at the time of his death in 1878. His works were extraordinarily popular and frequently reprinted. His friend Boker similarly received diplomatic positions, as minister to Turkey (1871–1875) and Russia (1875–1879).

4. A fascinating contribution to the project of recuperation, focusing on a slightly later period, is John W. Crowley, "Howells, Stoddard, and Male Homosocial Attachment in Victorian America," in Harry Brod, ed., *The Making of Masculinities: The New Men's Studies* (Boston: Allen & Unwin, 1987), pp. 301–324. Crowley traces interesting connections between "gender identity and authorship" (p. 302), and shows the range of male friendships within Howells's life.

5. On the role of travel literature, see my "Cruising the Exotic," a review of Paul Fussell's *Abroad*, in *Gay Studies Newsletter* 10 (July 1983): 13. For some of the various forms this motif could take, see also my "Two days in Sodom, or, How Anglo-Canadian writers Invent Their Own Quebecs," *The Body Politic*, no. 35 (July/August 1977), pp. 28–30, where I argue that Quebec becomes Canada's "South." Melville's *Typee* is discussed as travel literature in my *Hero, Captain, and Stranger: Male Friendship, Social Critique, and Literary Form in the Sea Novels of Herman Melville* (Chapel Hill: University of North Carolina Press, 1986), pp. 18–19.

6. Martin, *Hero, Captain, and Stranger*, pp. 78–79, 84–85.

7. John Brent was apparently based on a real Captain Brent whom Winthrop had known in the West, and the story as a whole may have large autobiographical elements.

8. It would be another hundred years before Leslie Fiedler would return to this theme, in *Love and Death in the American Novel*. His description of the "archetypal relationship" that "haunts the American psyche" is very close to the situation of *John Brent:* "two lonely men, one dark-skinned, one white, bend together over a carefully guarded fire in the virgin heart of the American wilderness; they have forsaken all others for the sake of the austere, almost inarticulate, but unquestioned love which binds them

to each other and to the world of nature which they have preferred to civilization" (p. 187).

9. On Byron and Greece, see Louis Crompton, *Byron and Greek Love: Homophobia in 19th-Century England* (Berkeley and Los Angeles: University of California Press, 1985), esp. pp. 141–2. For Winthrop's contemporary Francis Parkman there was a similar response to the eroticism of the male Indian, and a similar sense of psychic threat. See Harold Beaver, "Parkman's Crack-Up: A Bostonian on the Oregon Trail," *NEQ* 48:84–103. I am grateful to Chris Looby for suggesting this connection.

10. See Hans Licht, *Sexual Life in Ancient Greece*, trans. J. H. Freese (London: Abbey, 1932), pp. 442–43. Aside from the classical sources, the concept was well known in nineteenth-century America, as Whitman's use of it in *Calamus* 28 suggests.

11. My understanding of these connections owes a great deal to Eve Kosofsky Sedgwick, *Between Men: English Literature and Male Homosocial Desire* (New York: Columbia University Press, 1985).

12. At almost exactly the same time that Winthrop's novels were being published, Karl Heinrich Ulrichs was establishing the first body of theoretical work on homosexuality, including the idea that the male homosexual had "the soul of a woman enclosed in a male body" (see John Lauritsen and David Thorstad, *The Early Homosexual Rights Movement (1864–1935)* [New York: Times Change Press, 1974], pp. 46–7).

13. Although the term is employed in *Between Men*, it is developed further in Sedgwick's essay, "The Beast in the Closet: James and the Writing of Homosexual Panic," in Ruth Bernard Yeazell, ed., *Sex, Politics, and Science in the Nineteenth-Century Novel*, Selected Papers from the English Institute, 1983–84 (Baltimore: Johns Hopkins University Press, 1986), pp. 148–86.

14. The first complete translation of *The Symposium* into English was published in 1850. Winthrop could also have read it in the original Greek.

15. It was even employed by Walt Whitman, otherwise devoted to creating a "new" homosexual identity, in poems such as "When I Peruse the Conquer'd Fame," from *Calamus* (1860) (see note 10). It would also lie behind E. M. Forster's evocation of such famous male couples in *The Longest Journey*. Greek friendships provided both a way of signalling one's sexuality to an alert readership and a way of justifying it, through an appeal to authority, for a wider audience.

16. Leslie Fiedler discusses the dynamics of American inter-racial relationships and homosexuality in *Love and Death in the American Novel*. He comments on the joining of fear of slave rebellion and lust, p. 377.

In directly colonial societies of the period, the African *was* in some sense the land that was to be possessed, and was clearly both desired and feared. There is a large body of study on the relationship between colonialism and sexuality. See, for instance, Sander L. Gilman, "Black Bodies, White Bodies: Toward an Iconography of Female Sexuality in Late Nineteenth-Century Art, Medicine, and Literature," *Critical Inquiry* 12 (Autumn 1985): 204–42; Gilman argues that "[b]y the eighteenth century, the sexuality of the black, both male and female, becomes an icon for deviant sexuality in general" (p. 209). As Dominique Mannoni argued some time ago, it is not so much that Europeans observe African sexuality as that they "project upon the colonial peoples the obscurities of their own unconscious—obscurities they would rather not penetrate" (*Prospero and Caliban: The Psychology of Colonization*, trans. Pamela Powesland [New York: Praeger, 1956], p. 19).

17. Edward Said remarks at the beginning of his fascinating study that the Orient is "one of [the West's] deepest and most recurring images of the Other" (*Orientalism*, [New York: Pantheon, 1978], p. 1). He gives too little attention to a study of the place that sexuality, and particularly male homosexuality, played in the creation and perpetuation of the figure of the Orient, although Gerome's naked snake charmer reproduced on the cover suggests one place to begin.

18. In English literature the concept had particular resonance because of its use in the Renaissance, notably in Shakespeare's sonnets, such as 144, "Two loves I have," or in Michelangelo's sonnets (translated by John Addington Symonds in the 1870s). It would of course find a notorious climax in Alfred Douglas's "Two Loves," cited at Wilde's trial in 1895. I discuss the importance of Platonic ideas of a higher love in 19th century American literature in my *The Homosexual Tradition in American Poetry* (Austin: University of Texas Press, 1979), pp. 85, 95–97, 110–13. In England, Plato was rediscovered in the late 18th century, and became "an inspiration and a passion" for Shelley and others; he came to dominate English academic culture by mid-century (see Richard Jenkyns, *The Victorians and Ancient Greece* [Cambridge: Harvard University Press, 1980], p. 228).

19. For a brief outline of Higginson and Hurlbut, see Jonathan Katz, *Gay American History, Lesbians and Gay Men in the U.S.A.* (New York: Crowell, 1976), p. 642 n.7.

20. Martin Duberman has argued, on the basis of a diary kept by F. S. Ryman in the 1880s, that "some 19th-century men were . . . remarkably full and unselfconscious in physically expressing affection for each other" (see his "Intimacy Without Orgasm," in *About Time: Exploring the Gay Past* [New York: Gay Presses of New York, 1986], pp. 41–48).

21. Taylor is discussed at greater length in my essay, "Bayard Taylor's Valley of Bliss: Pastoral and the Search for Form," *Markham Review* 9 (Fall 1979): 13–17.

Works Cited

Richard Croom Beatty. *Bayard Taylor: Laureate of the Gilded Age*. Norman: University of Oklahoma Press, 1936.

George William Curtis. *The Howadji in Syria*. 1856; reprint ed., New York: Harper, 1867.

Richard Henry Dana. *Two Years Before the Mast*. 1840; reprint ed., Garden City, N.Y.: Doubleday, n.d.

Mary Thacher Higginson. *Thomas Wentworth Higginson: The Story of His Life*. 1914; reprint ed., Port Washington, N.Y.: Kennikat, 1971.

Thomas Wentworth Higginson. *Cheerful Yesterdays*. Boston: Houghton Mifflin, 1898.

———. "Unmanly Manhood." *Woman's Journal*, February 4, 1882, p. 1.

Bayard Taylor. *Joseph and His Friend. A Story of Pennsylvania*. New York: Putnam, 1870.

———. *Poetical Works*. Household Edition. Boston, 1883.

Horace Traubel. *With Walt Whitman in Camden*. New York, 1908. Vol. II.

Theodore Winthrop. *Cecil Dreeme*. Boston: Ticknor and Fields, 1862.

———. *John Brent*. Ed. H. Dean Propst. New Haven: College and University Press, 1970.

"She Even Chewed Tobacco" Sources

Bérubé, Allan, "Lesbian Masquerade," *Gay Community News* 7 (November 17, 1979), 8–9.

Bérubé Allan, Clippings file, newspaper articles on passing women, San Francisco, Ca.

Davis, Madeline and Kennedy, Elizabeth Lapovsky, "Oral History and the Study of Sexuality in the Lesbian Community: Buffalo, New York, 1940–1960." *Feminist Studies* 12 (Spring, 1986), 7–26.

D'Emilio, John and Freedman, Estelle, *Intimate Matters: A History of Sexuality in America.* New York: Harper and Row, 1988.

Garber, Eric, " 'T'Aint Nobody's Bizness': Homosexuality in 1920s Harlem." In *Black Men/White Men*, ed. Michael J. Smith. San Francisco: Gay Sunshine Press, 1983.

Katz, Jonathan, ed., *Gay American History: Lesbians and Gay Men in the U.S.A.* New York: Thomas Crowell, 1976.

Katz, Jonathan Ned, ed., *Gay/Lesbian Almanac: A New Documentary.* New York: Harper & Row, 1983.

Roberts, JR, "In America They Call Us Dykes: Notes on the Etymology and Usage of 'Dyke.' " *Sinister Wisdom* 9 (Spring, 1979), 2–11.

Roberts, JR, "Lesbian Hoboes: Their Lives and Times." *Dyke* (Fall, 1977), 36–49.

Thompson, C.J.S., *The Mysteries of Sex: Women Who Posed as Men and Men Who Impersonated Women.* New York: Causeway Books, 1974.

Weeks, "Inverts, Perverts, and Mary-Annes"

1. F. Carlier, *Rapport d'un Officier de la Police Municipale de Paris* (Paris: 1864) and *Les Deux Prostitutions* (Paris: 1887). For a comment on Carlier's work see Vern L. Bullough, *Sexual Variance in Society and History* (New York: John Wiley & Sons, 1976), p. 638.

2. Xavier Mayne, *The Intersexes: A History of Similisexualism as a Problem in Social Life* (privately printed, 1908); Alfred C. Kinsey, Wardell B. Pomeroy, and Clyde E. Martin, *Sexual Behaviour in the Human Male* (Philadelphia and London: W. B. Saunders Co., 1948), p. 596; D. J. West, *Homosexuality* (Harmondsworth, England: Penguin Books, 1968), p. 127.

3. For example, see Simon Raven, "Boys Will Be Boys: The Male Prostitute in London," in H.M. Ruitenbeek, *The Problem of Homosexuality in Modern Society* (New York: E.P. Dutton, 1963).

4. Michael Craft, "Boy Prostitutes and Their Fate," *British Journal of Psychiatry* 12 (1966): 111.

5. Iwan Bloch, *The Sexual Life of Our Time* (London: William Heinemann, 1909), p. 313.

6. See for example Mary McIntosh, "The Homosexual Role," *Social Problems* 16, no. 2 (1968): 182–92; Kenneth Plummer, *Sexual Stigma: An Interactionist Account* (London: Routledge & Kegan Paul, 1975); Jeffrey Weeks, *Coming Out: Homosexual Politics in Britain from the Nineteenth Century to the Present* (London: Quartet, 1977).

7. For a useful summary of cross-cultural evidence see Randolph Trumbach, "London's Sodomites: Homosexual Behavior and Western Culture in the 18th Century," *Journal of Social History* 2, no. 1 (Fall 1977): 1–33.

McIntosh's "The Homosexual Role" is the classic statement on the construction of homosexual roles.

8. See, for example, F. L. Whitham, "The Homosexual Role: A Reconsideration," *The Journal of Sex Research* 13, no. 1 (February 1977): 1–11. It is also implied in Trumbach, "London's Sodomites."

9. A. J. Reiss, "The Social Integration of Queers and Peers," in Ruitenbeek.

10. H. Montgomery Hyde, *The Trials of Oscar Wilde* (Harmondsworth, England: Penguin Books, 1962), p. 172.

11. For discussions of subcultural formations see Trumbach, "London's Sodomites," and McIntosh.

12. On France see Carlier, *Les Deux Prostitutions* (Paris, 1887); Abraham Flexner, *Prostitution in Europe* (New York: 1914), p. 30, comments on the German situation; Mayne has a survey of the European legal situation relating to homosexuality.

13. See, for example, Carlier, *Les Deux Prostitutions*, p. 454; Jacobus X, *Crossways of Sex: A Study in Eroto-Pathology*, 2 vols. (Paris: Charles Carrington, 1904), 2:195; Werner Picton, "Male Prostitution in Berlin," *Howard Journal* 3, no. 2 (1931).

14. The transcripts of the trial in 1871 are preserved in London in the Public Record Office: DPP 4/6. This section is based on these transcripts.

15. Public Record Office: DPP 4/6, transcript for Day 1, p. 193.

16. Ibid., transcript for Day 2, p. 256.

17. Alfred Swaine Taylor, *Medical Jurisprudence* (London: 1861), p. 657.

18. Public Record Office: DPP 4/6, transcript for Day 1, p. 21.

19. Ibid., transcript for Day 2, p. 276. The work of A. Tardieu is referred to in Arno Karlen, *Sexuality and Homosexuality* (London: Macdonald, 1971), pp. 185, 217.

20. DPP 4/6, transcript for Day 1, p. 82.

21. Ibid., transcript for Day 3, p. 299.

22. On the legal situation see H. Montgomery Hyde, *The Other Love* (London: Mayflower Books, 1972), p. 17; Edward J. Bristow, *Vice and Vigilance: Purity Movements in Britain Since 1700* (Dublin: Gill and Macmillan, 1977), p. 29; Weeks, *Coming Out*, chapter 1.

23. See Henry Labouchère's parliamentary statement, quoted in *The Times*, 1 March 1890. For discussion of Labouchère's motives see F. B. Smith, "Labouchère's Amendment to the Criminal Law Amendment Bill," *Historical Studies* 17, no. 67 (October 1976).

24. Shaw is quoted in Ian Gibson, *The English Vice: Beating, Sex and Shame in Victorian England and After* (London: Duckworth, 1978), p. 164; see also p. 160. George C. Ives, *The Continued Extension of the Criminal Law* (London: 1922) gives a useful description of the legal developments.

25. Report of the Royal Commission on the Duties of the Metropolitan Police, Cmnd. 4156, 1908, 1, p. 119.

26. For a comment on this recommendation see *Howard Journal* 2, no. 4 (1929): 334.

27. For a discussion of the social and political conjunctures in which these enactments took place see Deborah Gorham, "The 'Maiden Tribute of Modern Babylon' Reexamined: Child Prostitution and the Idea of Childhood in Late-Victorian England," *Victorian Studies* 21, no. 3 (Spring 1978); Bristow, *Vice and Vigilance*, chapters 4 and 5; Weeks, *Coming Out*, chapter 1.

28. Abraham A. Sion, *Prostitution and the Law* (London: Faber & Faber, 1977), p. 33; Bristow, p. 54.

29. Cf. Judith R. Walkowitz and Daniel J. Walkowitz, " 'We are not beasts of the field': Prostitution and the Poor in Plymouth and Southampton under the Contagious Diseases Acts," *Feminist Studies*, 1, nos. 3–4 (1973); Judith R. Walkowitz, "The Making of an Outcast Group: Prostitutes and Working Women" in Martha Vicinus, ed., *The Widening Sphere* (Bloomington: Indiana University Press, 1977).

30. *Report of the Committee on Homosexual Offences and Prostitution*, Cmnd. 247 (London: HMSO, 1957), p. 39.

31. Cf. Havelock Ellis, *The Task of Social Hygiene* (London: Constable, 1912), p. 272.

32. Director of Public Prosecutions to Metropolitan Police Commissioner, 20 July 1889; Director of Public Prosecutions to Attorney General, 14 September 1889; Public Record Office: DPP 1/95/1.

33. Michael Schofield, *Sociological Aspects of Homosexuality* (London: Longman, Green & Co., 1965), p. 200.

34. Casement Diaries, 17 April 1903. Public Record Office: HO 161/2.

35. Ibid.

36. Cf. H. Montgomery Hyde, *The Trial of Sir Roger Casement* (London: William Hodge, 1964), p. clv.

37. "Walter," *My Secret Life*, 11 vols. (Amsterdam; privately printed, 1877), 1:14.

38. Plummer, *Sexual Stigma*, p. 147.

39. Cf. Trumbach, "London Sodomites."

40. Evelyn Hooker, "The Homosexual Community" in J. H. Gagnon and W. Simon, *Sexual Deviance* (London: Harper & Row, 1967), p. 174.

41. Public Record Office: DPP 4/6 transcript for Day 6, p. 243, Hurt to Boulton.

42. Cf. J. R. Ackerley, *My Father and Myself* (London: Bodley Head, 1966); Tom Driberg, *Ruling Passions: The Autobiography of Tom Driberg* (London: Jonathan Cape, 1977).

43. As revealed, for instance, in the volumes of *My Secret Life*. See also Leonore Davidoff, "Class and Gender in Victorian England: The Diaries of Arthur J. Munby and Hannah Cullwick," *Feminist Studies* 1, no. 5 (1979).

44. As described in Phyllis Grosskurth, *John Addington Symonds: A Biography* (London: Longmans, 1964).

45. This is from one of a series of interviews conducted with homosexual men over sixty, which formed part of a Social Science Research Council funded project on the organization of the homosexual subculture in England. The researchers were Mary McIntosh and Jeffrey Weeks. The research was carried out between April 1978 and July 1979. All unreferenced quotations come from these interviews.

46. E. M. Forster, *The Life to Come and Other Stories* (Harmondsworth, England: Penguin Books, 1975), p. 16; Edward Carpenter quoted in Timothy d'Arch Smith, *Love in Earnest* (London; Routledge & Kegan Paul, 1970), p. 192; Ackerley, *My Father and Myself*, p. 218; see also Anomaly, *The Invert, and His Social Adjustment*, 2nd ed. (London: Bailliere, Tindall & Cox, 1948), p. 179.

47. H. M. Scheuller and R. L. Peters, eds., *The Letters of John Addington Symonds* (Detroit: Wayne State University Press, 1969), 3:808.

48. See, for example, the views of Havelock Ellis, *Sexual Inversion* (New York: F. A. Davies, 1936), p. 22; Havelock Ellis and John Addington Symonds, *Sexual Inversion* (London: Wilson & Macmillan, 1897), p. 9.

49. Ackerley, *My Father and Myself*, p. 135.

50. Mayne, *The Intersexes*, p. 220.

51. On the worship of youth see d'Arch Smith, *Love in Earnest;* Brian Taylor, "Motives for Guilt-free Pederasty: Some Literary Considerations," *Sociological Review* 24, no. 1 (February 1976); George C. Ives, *Obstacles to Human Progress* (London: George Allen & Unwin, 1939), p. 200; Michael Davidson, *The World, the Flesh and Myself* (London: Mayflower-Dell, 1966), p. 88.

52. Cf. Paul Gebhard's comments, quoted in Robin Lloyd, *Playland: A Study of Boy Prostitution* (London: Blond & Brigg, 1977), p. 195:

> In female prostitution the prostitute rarely or never reaches orgasm and the client almost invariably does; in male prostitution the prostitute almost invariably reaches orgasm, but the client frequently does not.
> . . . The homosexual male ideally seeks a masculine-appearing heterosexual male, and the prostitute attempts to fit the image. Consequently the prostitute can do little or nothing for or to a homosexual client lest he betray a homosexual inclination of his own and ruin the illusion.
> This cannot be taken as a general statement of the situation but it does undoubtedly express one type of experience.

53. See Edward Carpenter's "Memoir" of George Merrill, Edward Carpenter Collection, Sheffield City Library, Sheffield, England.

54. Ackerley, *My Father and Myself*, p. 215.

55. Ibid., p. 136.

56. Interview with Gregory, January 1979.

57. L. Thoinot and A. W. Weysse, *Medico Legal Aspects of Moral Offences* (Philadelphia: F. A. Davis, 1911), p. 346.

58. Quoted in L. Chester, D. Leitch, and C. Simpson, *The Cleveland Street Affair* (London: Weidenfeld & Nicolson, 1977), p. 73.

59. H. Montgomery Hyde, *The Cleveland Street Scandal* (London: Weidenfeld & Nicolson, 1976), p. 28.

60. See *Reynolds Newspaper*, 12 January 1890; *The Referee*, 24 November 1889, for comments on the involvement of working-class boys in the Cleveland Street Scandal; and Peter Wildblood, *Against the Law* (Harmondsworth, England: Penguin Books, 1957), p. 80 for a similar view in the 1950s.

61. See, for examples, the contents of Carlier, *Les Deux Prostitutions*, p. 323.

62. Werner Picton, p. 90.

63. Ibid., p. 91.

64. Nanette J. Davis, "The Prostitute: Developing a Deviant Identity," in James M. Henslin, *Studies in the Sociology of Sex* (New York: Appleton-Century-Crofts, 1971), p. 297.

65. Public Record Office: DPP1/95/3, File 5.

66. Quoted in Hyde, *The Trials of Oscar Wilde*, p. 170.

67. See Ackerley, *My Father and Myself*, p. 135; Raven, "Boys Will Be Boys," p. 280.

68. *The Sins of the Cities of the Plain, or the Recollections of a Mary-Anne*, 2 vols. (London, 1881).

69. Saul's deposition, Public Record Office: DPP1/95/4, File 2.

70. See the report in the *Star*, 15 January 1890.

71. *Sins of the Cities of the Plain* 2: 109.

72. Mayne, *The Intersexes*, p. 430.

73. Quoted in Chester et al., *The Cleveland Street Affair*, pp. 46–47.

74. *Truth*, 21 December 1889, p. 49.

75. Public Record Office: DPP 1/95/3, File 4, transcript of trial, p. 6.

76. Public Record Office: DPP 1/95/4, Saul's deposition.

77. Ibid.
78. Ibid.
79. *Sins of the Cities of the Plain* vol. 2, quoted in Chester et al., *The Cleveland Street Affair*, p. 57.
80. F. Carlier, *Les Deux Prostitutions*, p. 317.
81. Hyde, *The Trials of Oscar Wilde*, pp. 60, 125, 162.
82. Rupert Croft-Cooke, *The Unrecorded Life of Oscar Wilde* (London and New York: W.H. Allen, 1972), p. 141.
83. For a colorful example of a male prostitute arrested in female clothes see the reference in Mayne, *The Intersexes*, p. 443. See also Quentin Crisp, *The Naked Civil Servant* (Harmondsworth, England: Penguin Books, 1977), p. 26.
84. Werner Picton, p. 90.
85. L. Chester et al., *The Cleveland Street Affair*, p. 225.
86. Saul's deposition, Public Record Office: DPP 1/95/4, File 2.
87. Cf. Michel Foucault, *The History of Sexuality*, vol. 1: *Introduction* (London: Allen Lane, 1979), p. 43; see also Weeks, *Coming Out*, p. 14.
88. Raven, "Boys Will Be Boys," p. 280.
89. Reiss, "Social Integration," pp. 264–71.

Vicinus, "Distance and Desire"

An earlier version of this essay was presented at the "Among Men, Among Women" Conference, University of Amsterdam, June 22–26, 1983. I am indebted to the participants of this conference for many helpful suggestions; the enthusiastic sharing of work and information made this international conference an especially happy and memorable experience. I am grateful to Estelle Freedman, Bea Nergaard, and Ann Scott for their comments and criticisms. Research for this essay was made possible by a grant from the American Council of Learned Societies and the John Simon Guggenheim Foundation; I wish to thank them for their timely assistance.

1. For a discussion of lesbian historiography in the context of the history of sexuality, see my review essay, "Sexuality and Power: A Review of Current Work in the History of Sexuality," *Feminist Studies* 8 (Spring 1982); 147–51; see also Estelle Freedman, "Sexuality in Nineteenth-Century America: Behavior, Ideology and Politics," *Reviews in American History* 10, no. 4 (1982): 196–215.
2. See George Chauncey, Jr., "From Sexual Inversion to Homosexuality: Medicine and the Changing Conceptualization of Female Deviance," *Salmagundi* 58/59 (Fall 1982–Winter 1983); 114–46.
3. Jeffrey Weeks, *Coming Out: Homosexual Politics in Britain from the Nineteenth Century to the Present* (London: Quartet Books, 1977), pp. 101–11; Gayle Rubin's introduction to Renée Vivien's *A Woman Appeared to Me*, trans. Jeannette Foster (Reno, Nev.: Naiad Press, 1976).
4. See Lillian Faderman, "The Morbidification of Love between Women by 19th-Century Sexologists," *Journal of Homosexuality* 4, no. 1 (1978): 73–90, and *Surpassing the Love of Men: Romantic Friendship and Love between Women from the Renaissance to the Present* (New York: William Morrow & Co., 1981), which generally values romantic friendships over the lesbian "underworld" and minimizes the issue of sexuality in romantic friendships. Using rather limited evidence, Nancy Sahli argues that after 1875 "smashing" (same-sex crushes) became suspect: "Smashing: Women's Relationships before

the Fall," *Chrysalis* 8 (Summer 1979): 17–27. Sahli has been used uncritically by Marjorie Houspian Dobkin in her edition of the early journals and letters of M. Carey Thomas, *The Making of a Feminist* (Kent, Ohio: Kent State University Press, 1979); and by Adrienne Rich, "Compulsory Heterosexuality and Lesbian Existence," *Signs: Journal of Women in Culture and Society* 5, no. 4 (Summer 1980): 631–60. For a more subtle analysis of the impact of the sexologists, see Carroll Smith-Rosenberg, "The Body Politic: Abortion, Deviance and the Sexualization of Language," in *Disorderly Conduct: Visions of Gender in Victorian America* (New York: Alfred A. Knopf, 1989).

5. Faderman, *Surpassing the Love of Men*, pp. 85–102, discusses the various psychological and social reasons why romantic friendships were accepted and flourished during the eighteenth century; she deals only indirectly with economic factors, but see pp. 184–89. See also Carroll Smith-Rosenberg, "The Female World of Love and Ritual: Relations between Women in Nineteenth-Century America," *Signs* 1, no. 1 (Autumn 1975): 19–27; William R. Taylor and Christopher Lasch, "Two 'Kindred Spirits': Sorority and Family in New England, 1839–1846," *New England Quarterly*, 36, no. 1 (1963): 23–41.

6. Matilda Pullan, *Maternal Counsels to a Daughter* (London: Darton & Co., 1855), p. 192, quoted in Deborah Gorham, *The Victorian Girl and the Feminine Ideal* (Bloomington: Indiana University Press, 1982), p.113.

7. Elizabeth M. Sewell, *Principles of Education, Drawn from Nature & Revelation, & Applied to Female Education in the Upper Classes* (New York: Appleton, 1871), p. 335.

8. See my book, *Independent Women: Work and Community for Single Women in England, 1850–1920* (Chicago: University of Chicago Press, 1985), ch. 5. See also Joyce Senders Pedersen, "Schoolmistresses and Headmistresses; Elites and Education in Nineteenth-Century England," *Journal of British Studies* 15, no. 1 (1975): 135–62, and "The Reform of Women's Secondary and Higher Education: Institutional Changes and Social Values in Mid and Late Victorian England," *History of Education Quarterly* 19, no. 1 (1979): 61–91.

9. I am indebted to my colleague John Kucich, who shared his own work and discussed the ideas in this paragraph with me.

10. Autobiography of Constance Maynard, Westfield College Archives, London, sec. 44 [1882], pp. 19–20. Maynard copied large sections of her diary directly into her autobiography.

11. L. H. M. Soulsby, "Friendship and Love," in *Stray Thoughts for Girls* (London: Longmans, Green, 1910), pp. 172, 176.

12. Theodora Benson, "Hot-Water Bottle Love," in *The Old School*, ed. Graham Greene (London: Jonathan Cape, 1934), p. 40.

13. See Dorothy Eva deZouche, *Roedean School, 1885–1955* (Brighton, 1955), p. 37; Rachel Davis, *Four Miss Pinkertons* (London: Williams & Moorgate, 1936), p. 71.

14. Benson, "Hot Water Bottle Love," p. 40.

15. Olivia [Dorothy Strachey Bussy], *Olivia* (London: Hogarth Press, 1949), pp. 56–60. Bussy wrote *Olivia* in 1933 at the age of sixty-four but did not actively seek a publisher until after World War II. The events described occurred in the early 1880s, at "Les Ruches," Marie Souvestre's school outside Paris. See Michael Holroyd, *Lytton Strachey: A Critical Biography* (New York: Holt, Rinehart & Winston, 1967), 1: 34–41.

16. Olivia, *Olivia*, p. 82.

17. Davis, *Four Miss Pinkertons*, p. 62.

18. Anne Ridler, *Olive Willis and Downe House: An Adventure in Education* (London: John Murray, 1967), p. 32.

19. The most famous example of the importance of the good-night kiss is in the film *Mädchen in Uniform* (1931), where the girls all eagerly wait each night for their favorite teacher, Fräulein von Bernbourg, to come and kiss them good-night. For an analysis of the anti-Nazi lesbianism of the film, see B. Ruby Rich's "*Maedchen in Uniform:* From Repressive Tolerance to Erotic Liberation," *Jump Cut* 24/25 (March 1981): 44–50.

20. Davis, *Four Miss Pinkertons*, p. 68.

21. A similar pattern of spiritual leadership and homoerotic emotions can be found in accounts of the boys' public schools, although there was also much greater concern about masturbation. See David Newsome, *Godliness and Good Learning: Four Studies on a Victorian Ideal* (London: John Murray, 1961), pp. 79–91; J. R. de S. Honey, *Tom Brown's Universe: The Development of the English Public School in the Nineteenth Century* (New York: Quadrangle, 1977), pp. 167–96; Jonathan Gathorne-Hardy, *The Public School Phenomenon, 597–1977* (London: Hodder & Stoughton, 1977), pp. 156–80.

22. Dobkin, ed., *The Making of a Feminist*, p. 92.

23. Helena Deneke, *Grace Hadow* (London: Oxford University Press, 1946), pp. 18–21.

24. See, e.g., Eleanor Roosevelt's grateful appreciation of Mlle. Souvestre, who took her on tour through Europe when she was sixteen (Roosevelt was a student at Allenswood and had classes with both Mlle. Souvestre and Dorothy Strachey [Bussy]); see *The Autobiography of Eleanor Roosevelt* (New York: Harper & Bros., 1958), pp. 29–32.

25. Diary of Constance Maynard, July 14, 1878, Westfield College Archives, London.

26. Quoted by Maynard, ibid., February 9, 1879.

27. Ibid., April 12, 1879.

28. Ibid.

29. See my article, " 'One Life to Stand beside Me': Emotional Conflicts of First-Generation College Women in England," *Feminist Studies* 8, no. 3 (Fall 1982): 602–28.

30. I am indebted to Laurence Senelick for reminding me of this crucial element in all teacher-student relationships, erotic or otherwise.

31. A similar pattern is described for male homosexual love in a boys' public school by T. C. Worsley in *Flannelled Fool: A Slice of Life in the Thirties* (London: Alan Ross, 1967), pp. 122–24.

32. In her autobiography Maynard, at seventy-seven, evaluated her life's work for women's education and commented, "The whole was spoiled & devastated by love, by what psycho-analysts call by highly disagreeable names, such as 'the thwarted sex instinct,' " and later, "It is all very well to call [my] loneliness 'sex feeling,' but I can honestly say my thoughts never strayed to a man" (sec. 44 [1882], p. 3; sec. 50 [1887], p. 172). Maynard appears never to have linked her passionate love of women with sex, which she defined narrowly as heterosexuality.

33. Ibid., sec. 44 [1883] pp. 23–24.

34. Olivia, *Olivia*, p. 102.

35. Ibid., p. 9.

36. Sara Burstall, *English High Schools for Girls* (London: Longmans, 1907), pp. 160–61.

37. Lilian Faithfull, *You and I: Saturday Talks at Cheltenham* (London: Chatto & Windus, 1928), p. 121.

38. Ridler, *Olive Willis and Downe House*, pp. 97–98.

39. See Gathorne-Hardy, *Public School Phenomenon*, pp. 79–93, 144–56.

40. I am obviously ignoring here an important but entirely separate discourse, that of the so-called sexual underworld, which would include women who cross-dressed as well as the libertine and the prostitute. This world is just now beginning to be investigated through police records and scandal sheets; the problems of interpretation and identification are obvious. For an initial exploration of cross-dressing among women, see the San Francisco Lesbian and Gay History Project, *"She Even Chewed Tobacco": Passing Women in Nineteenth-Century America* (1983, also in this volume), slide-tape distributed by Women Make Movies, 225 Lafayette Street, New York, N.Y. 10012; Jonathan Katz, *Gay American History: Lesbians and Gay Men in the U.S.A.* (New York: Thomas Y. Crowell, 1976), pp. 209–79.

41. Ethel Colquhoun, "Modern Feminism and Sex-Antagonism," *Quarterly Review* 219 (1913): 155.

42. Havelock Ellis's first edition of *Sexual Inversion* (London: Wilson & McMillan, 1897), e.g., was impounded by the English police as pornography after the sale of the third copy; they were particularly anxious to bring his bookseller to trial because of his anarchist connections. Distribution of the book was extremely limited in Great Britain; his multivolume *Studies in the Psychology of Sex* (New York: F. A. Davis, 1901) has never been published there to this day. See Phyllis Grosskurth, *Havelock Ellis: A Biography* (New York: Knopf, 1980), pp. 180–204.

43. Havelock Ellis, "Appendix B: The School-Friendships of Girls," in *Studies in the Psychology of Sex* (New York: Random House, 1936), 1:375.

44. Gillian Freeman, *The Schoolgirl Ethic: The Life and Work of Angela Brazil* (London: Allen Lane, 1976); Mary Cadogan and Patricia Craig, *You're a Brick, Angela! A New Look at Girls' Fiction from 1839 to 1975* (London: Victor Gollancz, 1976).

45. See, e.g., Colette's *Claudine* series, Rosamond Lehman's *Dusty Answer*, Josephine Tey's *Miss Pym Disposes*, Antonia White's *Frost in May*, not to mention numerous novels without settings in schools or colleges, such as Virginia Woolf's *Orlando*.

46. On American women's organizations, see Leila J. Rupp, " 'Imagine My Surprise': Women's Relationships in Historical Perspective," *Frontiers* 5, no. 3 (Fall 1980): 61–70, and also in this volume.

47. See Holroyd, *Lytton Strachey*; Quentin Bell, *Virginia Woolf: A Biography*, 2 vols. (London: Hogarth Press, 1972); Robert Skidelsky, *John Maynard Keynes: Hopes Betrayed, 1883–1920* (London: Macmillan Co., 1983). See also Winifred Ashton [Clemence Dane], *Regiment of Women* (London: William Heinemann, 1917). For attacks on the militant suffrage movement, see Sir Almroth Wright, *The Unexpurgated Case against Women's Suffrage* (London: Constable, 1913); Walter Heape, *Sex Antagonism* (London: Constable, 1913): Herbert J. Claiborne, "Hypertrichosis [excessive hair growth] in Women: Its Relation to Bisexuality (Hermaphroditism): With Remarks on Bisexuality in Animals, Especially Man," *New York Medical Journal* 99 (1914): 1178–84 (I am indebted to George Chauncey, Jr., for this citation).

48. Jeffrey Weeks, *Sex, Politics and Society: The Regulation of Sexuality since 1800* (London: Longman, 1981), p. 105. See also pp. 114–17 and 164–67, and Weeks, *Coming Out*, pp. 87–111, for an outline of the changes in attitudes toward sexuality during these crucial years.

49. Chauncey, "Sexual Inversion to Homosexuality," warns against

attributing "inordinate power to [medical] ideology as an autonomous social force" (p. 115).

50. Olivia, *Olivia*, p. 31.

Steakley, "Iconography of a Scandal"

1. A lengthier version of this article, containing forty-one illustrations, appeared in *Studies in Visual Communication* 9, no. 2 (Spring 1983): 20–51. I wish to thank Larry Gross for facilitating its publication.

2. In a speech on November 28, 1907, by Chancellor Bülow; *Stenographische Berichte über die Verhandlungen des Reichstags*, vol. 229, col. 1880.

3. Harden never fully disclosed the evidence he could bring to bear to force "a change of imperial personnel," but in a letter to Friedrich von Holstein dated November 15, 1908, he broadly hinted that his "trump" was Jakob Ernst, who later figured so prominently in the Eulenburg perjury trial: see *The Holstein Papers*, vol. 4; *Correspondence, 1897–1909*, ed. by Norman Rich and H. M. Fisher (Cambridge: Cambridge University Press, 1963), no. 1151. In a part of this letter notably omitted by the editors, Harden also linked the Kaiser with Eulenburg's private secretary and masseur, Karl Kistler; this passage appears in Isabel V. Hull, *The Entourage of Kaiser Wilhelm II, 1888–1918* (Cambridge: Cambridge University Press, 1982), p. 141. This evidence has been summarized and discussed by John C. G. Röhl, "The Emperor's New Clothes: A Character Sketch of Wilhelm II," in *Kaiser Wilhelm II: New Interpretations*, ed. by J. C. G. Röhl and Nicolaus Sombart (Cambridge: Cambridge University Press, 1982), p. 48.

4. Michael Balfour, *The Kaiser and His Times* (Boston: Houghton Mifflin, 1964), p. 290.

5. Ottokar Czernin von und zu Chudenitz, *In the World War* (London and New York: Cassell, 1919), p. 54.

6. *The Holstein Papers* 4, no. 1151.

7. Cf. I. V. Hull, *The Entourage of Kaiser Wilhelm II, 1888–1918*; Maurice Baumont, *L'Affaire Eulenburg et les origines de la Guerre Mondiale* (Paris: Payot, 1933; 2nd rev. ed., Geneva: Edito-Service, 1973); and the "Einleitung" to *Philipp Eulenburgs politische Korrespondenz*, vol. 1 (Boppard am Rhein: Harald Boldt, 1976), pp. 35–53, by the editor, J. C. G. Röhl, a British historian. Röhl also discusses the scandal in his monograph *Kaiser, Hof und Staat: Wilhelm II und die deutsche Politik* (Munich: C. H. Beck, 1987), pp. 60–71.

8. M. Hirschfeld, "Vor fünfundzwanzig Jahren," *Die Freundschaft* (Berlin), 15, no. 2 (February 1933): 2.

9. In a letter dated September 8, 1927, to Fritz-Wend Prince zu Eulenburg, quoted in Röhl, "Einleitung," p. 76.

10. See Jeffrey Weeks, "Discourse, Desire and Sexual Deviance: Some Problems in a History of Homosexuality," in *The Making of the Modern Homosexual*, ed. by Kenneth Plummer (London: Hutchinson, 1981), p. 106.

11. Particular importance attaches to these ephemera because of the enormous gaps in the documentary record. Eulenburg and others implicated in the scandal assiduously burned personal correspondence that might be subpoenaed, and according to Röhl ("Einleitung," p. 35) all of the evidentiary material collected during the course of his perjury trial was mysteriously destroyed by the Prussian Ministry of Justice in 1932.

12. This remark was attributed to Wilhelm von Liebenau by Herbert von Bismarck in a letter dated October 5, 1888, to his father, Chancellor Otto von Bismarck; *Staatssekretär Herbert von Bismarck: Aus seiner politischen Privatkorrespondenz*, ed. by Walter Bussmann and Klaus-Peter Hoepke (Göttingen: Vandenhoeck & Ruprecht, 1964), p. 523.

13. This epithet ("Busenfreund") is attributed to Wilhelm II himself, in a conversation on 1 January 1889 with his tutor, Georg Ernst Hinzpeter; it is quoted by I. V. Hull, "Kaiser Wilhelm II and the Liebenberg Circle," in *Kaiser Wilhelm II: New Interpretations*, p. 202.

14. *Staatssekretär Herbert von Bismarck: Aus seiner politischen Privatkorrespondenz*, p. 525.

15. Bismarck's comments are reconstructed by Maximilan Harden in "Fürst Eulenburg," in *Köpfe*, vol. 3: *Prozesse* (Berlin: Erich Reiss, 1913), p. 173. For other comments on homosexuality by the Iron Chancellor, see Otto von Bismarck, *Reflections and Reminiscences*, ed. by Theodore S. Hamerow (New York: Harper & Row, 1968), pp. 19–20.

16. This remark is attributed to the English diplomat Martin Gosselin in 1895: Röhl, "The Emperor's New Clothes: A Character Sketch of Wilhelm II," p. 37.

17. Hirschfeld, "Vor fünfundzwanzig Jahren," p. 2.

18. This remark was attributed to Edgard Count von Wedel, Chamberlain of Wilhelm II, in a diary entry dated June 17, 1907, by Hans von Tresckow, head of the Berlin vice squad. See H. von Tresckow, *Von Fürsten und anderen Sterblichen: Erinnerungen eines Kriminalkommissars* (Berlin: F. Fontane, 1922), p. 183. Wedel's homosexuality is discussed on pp. 142–43 of the same work.

19. On the role of Jews in German journalism, see Peter G. Pulzer, *The Rise of Political Anti-Semitism in Germany and Austria* (New York: John Wiley, 1964), p. 13. On Harden's use of the term "effectiveness," see Harry F. Young, *Maximilian Harden: Censor Germaniae* (The Hague: Martinus Nijhoff, 1959), p. 104.

20. Bismarck's comment is quoted in B. Uwe Weller, *Maximilian Harden und die "Zukunft"* (Bremen: Carl Schünemann, 1970), p. 39. See also Young, *Maximilian Harden*, p. 43.

21. Harden, "Praeludium," *Die Zukunft* 57 (1906): 266.

22. One instance of the word "sweet" denoting homosexuality is the very title of a contemporary novel by Karl Friedrich Linden, *Die Süssen: Ein Berliner Roman* (Budapest: G. Grimm, 1909). Note also that when Harden was convicted of libel in his second trial against Moltke, the court's decision was based in part on his use of the epithet "der Süsse" for Moltke. Taken together with his use of the word "warm," this term was interpreted by the court as synonymous with "homosexual": *Prozesse* (see note 28), p. 189.

23. Harden, "Dies irae," *Die Zukunft* 57 (1906): 291. The dialogue is cast in the form of a travesty of the "Night—Open Field" scene of Goethe's *Faust*.

24. Adolf Brand, "Paragraph 175" (originally published as a newspaper article in 1907, reprinted as a pamphlet in 1914), in *Documents of the Homosexual Rights Movement in Germany*, ed. by J. D. Steakley (New York: Arno, 1975), p. [2].

25. Harden, "Roulette," *Die Zukunft* 59 (1907): 118.

26. Wilhelm, *Memoirs of the Crown Prince of Germany* (New York: Charles Scribner's Sons, 1922), pp. 14–15. On the events leading up to the selection of the crown prince to inform the kaiser, see Hirschfeld, "Die Hofaffäre," *Monatsbericht des wissenschaftlich-humanitären Komitees* 6, no. 7 (July 1, 1907): 126–27.

27. On the list of homosexuals kept by the Berlin police, see von Tresckow, *Von Fürsten und anderen Sterblichen*, pp. 164–65.

28. A transcript of the testimony was published as vol. 11 of Hugo Friedländer's series *Interessante Kriminal-Prozesse von kulturhistorischer Bedeutung* (Berlin-Grunewald: Berliner Buchversand, 1920). References to this volume appear under the abridged title *Prozesse*.

29. Hirschfeld, "Zur Klärung," *Monatsbericht des wissenschaftlich-humanitären Komitees* 6, no. 12 (December 1, 1907): 232.

30. On sales of *Die Zukunft*, see von Tresckow, *Von Fürsten und anderen Sterblichen*, pp. 184–85.

31. Hirschfeld, "Wessen Schuld? Allgemeinere Betrachtungen zum Prozess Moltke-Harden," *Der Roland von Berlin* 5 (November 7, 1907), 1519.

32. *Vossische Zeitung*, November 6, 1907, evening ed., no. 522, pp. 2–4, and November 7, 1907, morning ed., no. 523, 5th Beilage, p. 1. Years after he had served his libel sentence, Brand bitterly maintained the truth of his original allegations and moreover added the charge that Bülow had more recently had a sexual affair with the pianist Karl Tausig; see Brand's review of Bülow's memoirs, "Tante Reichskanzler," *Eros* 2 (1930): 49–52.

33. *Vossische Zeitung*, 6 November 1907, evening ed., no. 522, p. 3.

34. Since the assertion that Hirschfeld may have perjured himself is a serious charge, an aside is in order. Brand testified that he had learned of Bülow's homosexuality from (among others) Joachim Gehlsen, editor of the anti-Semitic journal *Die Reichsglocke*, who in turn testified that his source was Hirschfeld. Hirschfeld argued that while he had indeed informed Gehlsen of various cases of homosexual blackmail—as he would inform any journalist—the question of Bülow's sexual orientation had never come up. A few weeks later, however, Hirschfeld pressed charges of slander and blackmail against Gehlsen. The case never came to trial because of Gehlsen's unexpected and premature death. It seems likely that Gehlsen sought to blackmail Hirschfeld by threatening to expose his perjury. For Hirschfeld's side of the dispute, see his "Zur Klärung," pp. 232–37, as well as his *Sexualpsychologie und Volkspsychologie: Eine epikritische Studie zum Harden-Prozess* (Leipzig; Georg H. Wigand, 1908), pp. 17–20, and "Paragraph 175," *Pan* 2 (1913): 863–64.

35. The kaiser's state of mind is discussed by Balfour, *The Kaiser and His Times*, p. 276, while Hirschfeld discusses the illness of the others in "Jahresbericht 1906/8," *Jahrbuch für sexuelle Zwischenstufen* 9 (1908): 651.

36. Since the perjury trial of Eulenburg was never concluded, this verdict may seem unduly harsh. It is indeed possible that Eulenburg never violated Paragraph 175, as he claimed. Since the law penalized "unnatural vice" and this vague phrase was generally construed by the courts to apply solely to anal intercourse, Eulenburg may have been technically innocent of violating the law by virtue of having engaged only in other sexual practices. (Indeed, this is apparently why Hohenau was acquitted in his court-martial.) But Eulenburg blundered by testifying that he had never engaged in any "filth" whatsoever, for this word was interpreted by the state prosecutor to include the full range of homosexual practices. Newspapers avoided going into detail on this aspect of Eulenburg's perjury trial, although it occupied the lawyers for days. A singularly explicit treatment of these issues was offered by J. L. Caspar in *Das Treiben der Homosexuellen: Volle Aufklärung zum Verständnis der Andeutungen und "halben Worte" im Moltke-Harden Prozess* (Leipzig: Leipziger Verlag, 1907).

37. Harden, "Fürst Eulenburg," pp. 252–53.

38. This suggestion was made by Axel von Varnbüler; see Röhl, "Einleitung," p. 42.

39. *Vossische Zeitung*, July 7, 1908, evening ed., no. 314, p. 3.

40. On the keyhole incident, see *Vossische Zeitung*, July 11, 1908, morning ed., no. 321, 1st Beilage, p. 2.

41. This is in an unpublished letter dated April 5, 1909, to Albert Ballin, quoted by Röhl, "Einleitung," p. 44.

42. See Weller, *Maximilian Harden und die "Zukunft,"* p. 161.

43. *Vossische Zeitung*, 27 October 1907, morning ed., no. 505, p. 1.

44. Ernst Bassermann, delegate of the National Liberal party, on November 28, 1907, in *Stenographische Berichte über die Verhandlungen des Reichstags*, vol. 229, col. 1889.

45. von Tresckow, *Von Fürsten und anderen Sterblichen*, p. 168.

46. Harden, "Fürst Eulenburg," p. 183. See also Rudolf Blümner, "L'Amour à l'allemande," *Der Sturm* 10 (1910): 179–80.

47. See Robert A. Nye, "Degeneration and the Medical Model of Cultural Crisis in the French Belle Époque," in *Political Symbolism in Modern Europe: Essays in Honor of George L. Mosse* (New Brunswick, N.J.: Transaction, 1982), pp. 19–41, and his "Degeneration, Neurasthenia and the Culture of Sport in Belle Époque France," *Journal of Contemporary History* 17 (1982): 51–68.

48. See especially Baumont, *L'Affaire Eulenburg et les origines de la Guerre Mondiale*; Henri Weindel and E. P. Fischer, *L'Homosexualité en Allemagne* (Paris: Juven, 1908); and John Grand-Carteret, *Derriere "Lui"* (Paris: E. Bernard, 1908).

49. See Michael Kettle, *Salome's Last Veil: The Libel Case of the Century* (London: Granada, 1977), pp. *n*–12; cf. also Samuel Igra, *Germany's National Vice* (London: Quality, 1945).

50. See the French and Italian cartoons reproduced by Hirschfeld, *Sittengeschichte des Weltkrieges* (Leipzig and Vienna: Verlag für Sexualwissenschaft Schneider, 1930) 1: 275, 279, 299.

51. This parallel is shown with remarkable clarity in two Social Democratic cartoons—one from 1907, the other from 1931—reproduced by Wilfried U. Eissler, *Arbeiterparteien und Homosexuellenfrage: Zur Sexualpolitik von SPD und KPD in der Weimarer Republik* (West Berlin: Verlag rosa Winkel, 1980), pp. 45 and 109. On Hitler's awareness of the parallel, see Otto Wagener, *Hitler aus nächster Nähe*, ed. by H. A. Turner (Frankfurt am Main: Ullstein, 1978), p. 200. For Hirschfeld's standpoint, see his "Röhm und Genossen, eine sexualkritische Studie," *Das Volk* (Olten, Switzerland), July 17, 1934, no. 164, Beilage, p. 1.

52. Harden, "Fürst Eulenburg," p. 248.

53. For a summary of the discussion of Goethe in volumes two through nine of the *Jahrbuch für sexuelle Zwischenstufen*, which Hirschfeld edited, see Max Birnbaum, "Notizen aus Goethes Werken über Homosexualität," *Zeitschrift für Sexualwissenschaft*, vol. 1 (1908), pp. 179–81; see also Max Katte (i.e., Karl Friedrich Jordan), "Schillers 'Malteser'—ein homosexuelles Dramenfragment," *Zeitschrift für Sexualwissenschaft* 1 (1908): 445–47.

54. See George L. Mosse, *Nationalism and Sexuality: Respectability and Abnormal Sexuality in Modern Europe* (New York: Howard Fertig, 1985), pp. 229–30, and Wolfgang Schivelbusch, *The Railroad Journey: Trains and Travel in the Nineteenth Century*, trans. by Anselm Hollo (New York: Urizen, 1979), pp. 118–21.

55. Hirschfeld, "Wessen Schuld? Allgemeinere Betrachtungen zum Prozess Moltke-Harden," p. 1522.

56. See, for example, the Reichstag speech on November 28, 1907, by Wilhelm August Otto Varenhorst of the Deutsche Reichspartei in *Steno-*

graphische Berichte über die Verhandlungen des Reichstags, vol. 229, col. 1889.

57. See, for example, von Tresckow, *Von Fürsten und anderen Sterblichen*, pp. 111–12.

58. See, for example, Otto Glagau's remarks in *Die Gartenlaube* in 1876, as quoted by Pulzer, *The Rise of Political Anti-Semitism in Germany and Austria*, p. 89.

59. Hirschfeld thus paraphrases an editorial entitled "Rattenkönig" from the July 3, 1908, issue of *März* in "Aus der Zeit," *Zeitschrift für Sexualwissenschaft* 1 (1908): 512.

60. Stöcker's March 3, 1906, speech appears in *Stenographische Berichte über die Verhandlungen des Reichstags*, vol. [215], col. 1712.

61. Cf. I. V. Hull, *The Entourage of Kaiser Wilhelm II, 1888–1918*, p. 297. For some early documentation on uniform fetishism, see John Addington Symonds, "Soldatenliebe und Verwandtes," in *Das konträre Geschlechtsgefühl*, by Havelock Ellis and J. A. Symonds, trans. by Hans Kurella (Leipzig: Georg H. Wigand, 1896), pp. 285–304, an excursus that was omitted from all subsequent English editions of *Sexual Inversion*. See also three works by Karl Heinrich Ulrichs first published in 1864: *Inclusa* (Leipzig: Max Spohr, 1898), p. 48; *Formatrix* (Leipzig: Max Spohr, 1898), pp. 47–48; and *Ara spei* (Leipzig: Max Spohr, 1898), pp. 101–03.

62. Cf. Michel Foucault, *Power/Knowledge*, ed. by Colin Gordon (New York: Pantheon, 1980), p. 17.

63. See, for example, Lt. Fritz Oswald Bilse, *Life in a Garrison Town* (New York and London: John Lane, The Bodley Head, 1904; originally published in 1903); Otto Erich Hartleben, *Rosenmontag: Offizierstragödie in fünf Akten* (Berlin: S. Fischer, 1900); and Franz Adam Beyerlein, *"Jena" or "Sedan"?* (New York: George H. Doran, 1914; originally published in 1903) as well as Beyerlein's *Taps*, trans. by Charles Swickard (Boston: John W. Luce, 1915; originally published in 1903).

64. His speech of November 19, 1907, appears in *Stenographische Berichte über die Verhandlungen des Reichstags*, vol. 229, cols. 1913–1916.

65. Hirschfeld, *Sexualpsychologie und Volkspsychologie*, p. 20.

66. See Mosse, "Nationalism and Respectability: Normal and Abnormal Sexuality in the Nineteenth Century," *Journal of Contemporary History* 17 (1982): 221–46, as well as Hull, "The Bourgeoisie and Its Discontents: Reflections on 'Nationalism and Respectability'," *Journal of Contemporary History* (1982): 247–68. On the "prehistory" of the modern homosexual, see Steakley, "Sodomy in Enlightenment Prussia: From Execution to Suicide," in *The Pursuit of Sodomy: Male Homosexuality in Renaissance and Enlightenment Europe*, ed. by Kent Gerard and Gert Hekma (New York: Haworth, 1989), pp. 163–75.

67. *Vossische Zeitung*, October 27, 1907, evening ed., no. 504, p. 3.

68. Hirschfeld, *Sexualpsychologie und Volkspsychologie*, pp. 1–3.

69. Cf. Hull, *The Entourage of Kaiser Wilhelm II, 1888–1918*, pp. 133–136, 145, 296–297.

70. In a letter to Nathaniel Rothschild dated September 17, 1904, quoted by Röhl, "Einleitung," p. 37.

71. In a letter by Axel von Varnbüler dated April 15, 1898, quoted *ibid.*, p. 40.

72. Eulenburg to Moltke, July 10, 1907, quoted by Hull, "Kaiser Wilhelm II and the 'Liebenberg Circle,' " p. 199.

73. *Vossische Zeitung*, November 6, 1907, evening ed., no. 522, p. 3.

74. *Vossische Zeitung*, December 31, 1907, morning ed., no. 609, 1st Beilage, p. 2.

75. Eulenburg's testimony is quoted by Hirschfeld, "Zur Klärung," p. 24.

76. Harden, "Fürst Eulenburg," p. 258.

77. Foucault, *The History of Sexuality*, vol. 1: *An Introduction*, trans. by Robert Hurley (New York: Pantheon, 1978), p. 124.

78. Dr. Siegfried Heckscher, a Reichstag delegate of the Freisinnige Vereinigung, made these points in an article in the *Hamburger Fremdenblatt*, October 31, 1907. The article is reprinted in its entirety as "Paragraph 175" in the more accessible *Sexualreform* 2 (1907): 362–64.

79. Harden, "Fürst Eulenburg," pp. 182–83, 244, 248, 278.

80. Harden, "Kommerzienrath Israel," *Die Zukunft* 53 (1905): 314.

81. Hirschfeld, *Sexualpsychologie und Volkspsychologie*, pp. 5–6.

82. Hirschfeld, "Zur Klärung," p. 242, and "Einleitung und Situations-Bericht," *Jahrbuch für sexuelle Zwischenstufen* 10 (1909): 20.

83. Wilhelm Hentschel, "Die Ursachen der Gleichgeschlechtlichkeit," *Politisch-anthropologische Revue* 8 (1909): 93.

84. The number of convictions under the same-sex provisions of Paragraph 175 (for the law also penalized bestiality) increased nearly fifty percent in the wake of the Eulenburg scandal. In the five-year span 1903–1907, the annual average was 363 convictions; the average rose to 542 in the years 1909–1913. In 1908, the number dropped to 282, a decrease which Magnus Hirschfeld may have accounted for when he noted that homosexuals were probably especially cautious during the height of the scandal; see his "Materialien," *Zeitschrift für Sexualwissenschaft*: (1908) 53. The statistics are extracted from Rudolf Klare, *Homosexualität und Strafrecht* (Hamburg: Hanseatische Verlagsanstalt, 1937), pp. 144–145.

85. See Ilse Kokula, *Weibliche Homosexualität um 1900 in zeitgenössischen Dokumenten* (Munich: Frauenoffensive, 1981), pp. 30–31, 248ff.

86. Hirschfeld, "Zur Klärung," p. 231.

87. See Richard J. Evans, *The Feminist Movement in Germany, 1894–1933* (London and Beverly Hills: Sage, 1976), p. 156.

88. See note 82.

89. *Vossische Zeitung*, November 6, 1907, evening ed., no. 522, p. 3.

90. *Vossische Zeitung*, December 24, 1907, morning ed., no. 601, 1st Beilage, p. 3.

91. On Eulenburg and the occult, see Röhl, *Kaiser, Hof und Staat*, pp. 71–76.

92. This point was first made by J. Grand-Carteret, *Derrière "Lui,"* p. 59. There were earlier images of homosexuals, but these high art images were highly restricted in circulation; for a representative collection, see Cecile Beurdeley, *L'Amour bleu*, trans. by Michael Taylor (New York: Rizzoli, 1978). Other early images, such as the broadsides on executions of sodomites, were more widely distributed but generally lacked any specifically homosexual quality; see, for example, the images in Alan Bray, *Homosexuality in Renaissance England* (London: Gay Men's Press, 1982), pp. 15, 94–95.

93. *Vossische Zeitung*, October 27, 1907, morning ed., no. 505, p. 1.

94. *Stenographische Berichte über die Verhandlungen des Reichstags*, vol. [208], *Anlageband*, cols. 2308–2309.

95. The complaint was voiced by National Liberal delegate Ernst Bassermann in a speech on November 28, 1907, reported in *Stenographische Berichte über die Verhandlungen des Reichstags*, vol. 229, col. 1890. The editorial suggestion appeared in the *Vossische Zeitung*, October 27, 1907, morning ed., no. 505, p. 1.

96. Hirschfeld, *Sexualpsychologie und Volkspsychologie*, pp. 22–23.

97. The concern about military service was voiced by Center Party delegate Peter Spahn in a Reichstag speech on November 18, 1907; *Stenographische Berichte über die Verhandlungen des Reichstags*, vol. 229, col. 1875.

98. In a Reichstag speech on February 20, 1908, by W. A. O. Varenhorst, reported in *Stenographische Berichte über die Verhandlungen des Reichstags*, vol. 230, col. 3299.

99. Foucault, *Power/Knowledge*, p. 125.

Smith-Rosenberg, "Discourses of Sexuality and Subjectivity"

1. An expanded version of this essay appeared as the final chapter of my book, *Disorderly Conduct: Visions of Gender in Victorian America* (New York: Knopf, 1985). For a full history of the development of the earlier, longer version, see my note to the essay in *Disorderly Conduct*; I remain deeply indebted to Esther Newton for her insights into the "New Woman." This version includes a new interpretation of the discordant sexual discourses adopted by the successive generations of New Women, an interpretation which I developed as a member of the Gender Seminar, the School of Social Sciences, Institute for Advanced Study, Princeton. I am indebted to Joan Scott, Istvan Hont, and the other members of the seminar for a year of fruitful suggestions and advice. This version has specifically benefited from the editing skills of Martha Vicinus. As always, Alvia Golden's fine literary and critical hand has greatly improved its argument and style.

2. Numerous histories of specific institutions of higher education for women have been written; the following general studies are especially useful for surveying the beginning years of these colleges: Mabel Newcomer, *A Century of Higher Education for American Women* (New York: Harper and Row, 1959), Thomas Woody's encyclopedic *Education in the United States*, 2 vols. (New York: Science Press, 1929).

3. For some of the New Women's discussions of what college education meant to them, see Vida Scudder, *On Journey* (New York: E. P. Dutton, 1937); Mary Kinsbury Simkhovitch, *Neighborhood: My Story of Greenwich House* (New York: W. W. Norton, 1938); for Florence Kelley, Josephine Goldmark, *Impatient Crusader* (Urbana: University of Illinois Press, 1953); for Alice and Edith Hamilton, Madeleine P. Grant, *Alice Hamilton: Pioneer Doctor in Industrial Medicine* (New York: Abelard-Schuman, 1967): for M. Carey Thomas, Marjorie Housepian Dobkin, *The Making of a Feminist: Early Journals and Letters of M. Carey Thomas* (Kent, Ohio: Kent State University Press, 1979).

4. Victor Turner, *Ritual Process* (Chicago: Aldine, 1969), chaps. 3 and 4. For a detailed folkloric study of rituals in women's colleges, see Virginia Wolf Briscoe, "Bryn Mawr College Traditions: Women's Rituals as Expressive Behavior" (Ph.D. thesis, University of Pennsylvania, 1981), vols. 1 and 2.

5. Grant, *Alice Hamilton*; Goldmark, *Impatient Crusader*; Mari Jo Buhle, *Women and American Socialism, 1870–1920* (Urbana: University of Illinois Press), chaps. 2 and 3; Allen F. Davis, *Spearheads of Reform: Social Settlements and the Progressive Movement, 1890–1914* (New York: Oxford University Press, 1967), passim; Ellen Lagemann, *A Generation of Women* (Cambridge, Mass.: Harvard University Press, 1979).

6. Anna Mary Wells, *Miss Marks and Miss Woolley* (Boston: Houghton Mifflin, 1978). Vida Scudder dedicates her autobiography (as she did her first book) to Florence Converse, "Comrade and Companion." See Nan Bauer Moglen's fine article concerning Scudder and Converse,"Vida to Florence, Comrade and Companion," *Frontiers* 4 (1979): 13–20. For Scudder's more general comments on friendships between women, see *On Journey*, pp. 104–15. Blanche Wiesen Cook presents a detailed study of this pattern in her excellent *Women and Support Networks* (New York: Out and Out Books, 1978); see also Leila Rupp's sophisticated analysis of this phenomenon in her essay "Imagine My Surprise," reprinted in this volume.

7. See Carroll Smith-Rosenberg, "The Female World of Love and Ritual" in *Disorderly Conduct*, pp. 53–76.

8. For its most famous male explication, see Edward Clarke, *Sex in Education; or, A Fair Chance for the Girls* (Boston: J. R. Osgood, 1873). See also the women's response in Julia Ward Howe, *Sex and Education: A Reply to Dr. E. H. Clarke's "Sex in Education"* (New York: Arno Press, 1972 [1874]). All the American doyens of gynecology in the late nineteenth century shared the conviction that higher education might interfere with a woman's maternal functions. See Thomas Addis Emmett, *The Principles and Practice of Gynecology* (Philadelphia: H. C. Lea, 1879), p. 21; Thomas Smith Clouson, *Female Education from a Medical Point of View* (Edinburgh: Macniven and Wallace, 1882), p. 20; S. Weir Mitchell, *Fat and Blood* (Philadelphia: J. B. Lippincott, 1885), and *Doctor and Patient* (Philadelphia: J. B. Lippincott, 1888), passim; William Goodell, *Lessons in Gynecology* (Philadelphia: D. G. Brinton, 1879), p. 9; William Edgar Darnall, "The Pubescent Schoolgirl," *American Gynecological and Obstetrical Journal* 18 (June 1901): 490; Board of Regents, University of Wisconsin, *Annual Report for the Year Ending September 30, 1877* (Madison, 1877), p. 45.

9. For the bourgeois feminist refutation of the doctors, see Howe, *Sex and Education*, passim. See also Sarah H. Stevenson, *The Physiology of Woman, Embracing Girlhood, Maternity and Mature Age*, 2nd ed. (Chicago: Cushing, Thomas, 1881), pp. 68, 77; Alice Stockman, *Tokology: A Book for Every Woman*, rev. ed. (Chicago: Sanitary Publishing Co., 1887), p. 257. Health reformers were often sympathetic to women's claims that not too much but too little mental stimulation was the cause of their ills. See Martin Luther Holbrook, *Hygiene of the Brain and Nerves and the Cure of Nervousness* (New York: U.S. Book Co., 1878); James C. Jackson, *American Womanhood: Its Peculiarities and Necessities* (Dansville, N.Y.: Austin, Jackson, 1870).

10. Lillian Faderman, *Surpassing the Love of Men* (New York: William Morrow, 1981); Nancy Sahli, "Smashing: Women's Relations Before the Fall," *Chrysalis* 8 (1979): 17–22; Smith-Rosenberg, "The Female World of Love and Ritual," *Disorderly Conduct*; George Chauncey, Jr., "From Sexual Inversion to Homosexuality: Medicine and the Changing Conceptualization of Female Deviance," *Salmagundi* 58/59 (Fall 1982/Winter 1983): 114–46.

11. Samuel Gregory, *Facts and Important Information for Young Women on the Subject of Masturbation* (Boston: George Gregory, 1857); Gross and Co., *Hygieana: A Non-Medical Analysis of the Complaints Incidental to Females* (London: G. Booth, 1829), see especially pp. 64 and 66.

12. In the various collections of women's personal papers read for "The Female World of Love and Ritual," I found no reference to women reading any of these French novels—even, or perhaps especially, among those women who seemed most sensually involved with other women.

13. For three excellent analyses of the sexologists' attitudes toward

homosexuality, see Chauncey, "From Sexual Inversion to Homosexuality"; Jane Caplan, "Sexuality and Homosexuality," in *Women in Society*, ed. Cambridge Women's Studies Group (London: Virago, 1980), pp. 149–67; Sheila Rowbotham and Jeffrey Weeks, *Socialism and the New Life: the Personal and Sexual Politics of Edward Carpenter and Havelock Ellis* (London: Pluto, 1977).

14. Richard von Krafft-Ebing, *Psychopathia Sexualis with Especial Reference to the Antipathetic Sexual Instinct*, trans. F. J. Rebman (Brooklyn: Physicians and Surgeons Book Co., 1908), pp. 333–36. Originally published in Stuttgart in 1886.

15. Ibid., pp. 334–35, 351, 355.

16. Ibid.

17. Sigmund Freud, "Contribution I, the Sexual Aberrations," in *Three Contributions to the Theory of Sex* (New York: E. P. Dutton, 1962 [1905]), pp. 1, 6. See also Kaplan, "Sexuality and Homosexuality," pp. 153, 155–57; Weeks, "Havelock Ellis and the Politics of Sex Reform," in Rowbotham and Weeks, *Socialism and the New Life*, pp. 151–55, 160, 163, 172, 178; David Kennedy, *Birth Control in America: The Career of Margaret Sanger* (New Haven, Conn.: Yale University Press, 1970), pp. 29–35. Jonathan Katz cites Emma Goldman's letter to Magnus Hirschfeld praising Ellis's work on behalf of male homosexuals. Ellis also wrote an introduction to Radclyffe Hall's *Well of Loneliness*. See Katz, *Gay American History: Lesbians and Gay Men in the U.S.A., A Documentary* (New York: Thomas Crowell, 1976), pp. 379, 403.

18. Ellis, "Sexual Inversion in Women," *Alienist and Neurologist* 16 (1895): 147–48, states that women who are attracted to true inverts, and who, in turn, attract them are "the pick of the women whom the average man would pass by." See also pp. 145–46.

19. Ibid., pp. 146–48, 152–53, 155–57. For Ellis's distinction between "homosexuality" and "inversion," see his "Sexual Inversion with an Analysis of Thirty-three New Cases," *Medico-Legal Journal* 13 (1895–96): 262–64. To compare Ellis's attitudes toward male homosexuals and lesbians, see his *Sexual Inversion* (Philadelphia: F. A. Davis, 1901), p. 283. For an early article attacking European sodomy laws, see Ellis, "Sexual Inversion in Relation to Society and the Law," *Medico-Legal Journal* 14 (1896–97): 279–88. Caplan offers an insightful analysis of Ellis's thoughts on male homosexuality in "Sexuality and Homosexuality," pp. 156–67. See also Weeks's analysis of Ellis and male homosexuality, "Havelock Ellis," in Rowbotham and Weeks, *Socialism and the New Life*, pp. 153–55, 160–61. Weeks presents a forceful case for Ellis's essentially conservative attitude toward women, pp. 169–80. For Ellis on the biological and social polarity of women and men, see his *Men and Women* (London: Walter Scott, 1894).

20. Ellis, "Sexual Inversion in Women," pp. 155–56. For a series of case studies detailing these characteristics among educated and intelligent women, see pp. 148–53.

21. R. W. Shufeldt, "Dr. Havelock Ellis on Sexual Inversion," *Pacific Medical Journal* 65 (1902): 199–207.

22. William Lee Howard, "Effeminate Men and Masculine Women," *New York Medical Journal* 71 (1900): 687.

23. See Sahli, "Smashing." For contemporary comment, see Margaret Otis, "A Perversion Not Commonly Noted," *Journal of Abnormal Psychology* (1913); Kate Richards O'Hare, "Prison Lesbianism" (191–20) and Charles A. Ford, "Homosexual Practices of Psychology" (1929); all are cited and abstracted in Katz's invaluable *Gay American History*.

24. William S. Barker, "Two Cases of Sexual Contrariety," *St. Louis Courier of Medicine* 28 (1903): 269–71.

25. The list of companionate-marriage advocates and sex reformers is vast, but see Christina Simmons's path-breaking article, "Companionate Marriage and the Lesbian Threat," *Frontiers* 4 (1979): 54–59. For specific attacks on women who were hostile or indifferent to heterosexual relations, see Floyd Dell, "Sex in Adolescents," in *Sex Education: Facts and Attitudes* (New York: Child Study Association of America, 1934), p. 49; Dorothy Dunbar Bromley and Florence Haxton Britten, *Youth and Sex: A Study of 1300 College Students* (New York: Harper and Row, 1938), p. 129; John F. W. Meagher, "Homosexuality: Its Psychopathological Significance," *The Urologic and Cutaneous Review* 33 (1929): 508, 512; Edward Podolsky, " 'Homosexual Love' in Women," *Popular Medicine* 1 (February 1935): 375; Ralph Hay, "Mannish Women or Old Maids?" *Know Thyself* 1 (July 1938); and Floyd Dell, *Love in the Machine Age: A Psychological Study of the Transition from Patriarchal Society* (New York: Farrar, 1930).

26. For a further discussion of these ideas, see the longer version of this essay in Smith-Rosenberg, *Disorderly Conduct*, pp. 245–96; see especially pp. 283–87.

27. Buhle, *Women and American Socialism*, chap. 4; Elaine Showalter, "Introduction," *These Modern Women* (Old Westbury, N.Y.: Feminist Press, 1978), pp. 3–29; Luhan, quoted in Judith Schwartz, *Radical Feminists of Heterodoxy: Greenwich Village, 1912–40* (Lebanon, N.H.: Victoria Publishers, 1982), p. 1. See also Gertrude Stein's attacks on M. Carey Thomas for being a single-minded feminist and sexually forbidding in *Fernhurst*, in *Fernhurst, QED and Other Early Writings* (New York: Liveright, 1971 [written 1904?]).

28. Millay, "First Fig," in *The Norton Anthology of Modern Poetry*, ed. Richard Ellman and Robert O'Clair (New York: W. W. Norton, 1973), p. 492. See also Millay's poem "Love Is Not All: It Is Not Meat Nor Drink" for a summation of this generation's view of the centrality of sexuality and love in their life aims.

29. Frances Wilder to Edward Carpenter, reprinted by Ruth F. Claus, "Confronting Homosexuality: A Letter from Frances Wilder," *Signs* 2 (1977): 928–33.

30. For a classic analysis of Republican political discourse see J. G. A. Pocock, *The Machiavellian Moment. Florentine Political Thought and the Atlantic Republican Tradition* (Princeton: Princeton University Press, 1975). While Pocock does not draw explicit attention to the sexual nature of political rhetoric, the sexuality of its imagery is apparent throughout his presentation of it. See as well, Gordon Wood, *The Creation of the American Republic, 1776–1787* (Chapel Hill: University of North Carolina Press, 1969). I am particularly indebted to Istvan Hont of the Political Science Department, Columbia University, for his suggestive comments about the sexualization of seventeenth- and eighteenth-century political and economic rhetoric. For a discussion of the role gender played in the sexualization of the political subject, see Carroll Smith-Rosenberg, "Domesticating Virtue," in *Literature and the Body*, ed. Elaine Scarry (Baltimore: Johns Hopkins Press, 1988).

31. See, for example, Nancy F. Cott, "Passionlessness: An Interpretation of Victorian Sexual Ideology, 1790–1850," *Signs* 4 (1978): 219–36; and Martha Vicinus, *Independent Women: Work and Community for Single Women, 1850–1920* (Chicago: University of Chicago Press, 1985).

32. Virginia Woolf, *Orlando: A Biography* (New York: Harcourt Brace Jovanovich, 1956 [1928]); Djuna Barnes, *Nightwood* (New York: New Direc-

tions, 1961 [1937]); Radclyffe Hall, *The Well of Loneliness* (New York: Coucici-Friede, 1934 [1928]). For suggestive analyses of these novels, see Catherine Stimpson, "Zero Degree Deviance: The Lesbian Novel in English," *Critical Inquiry* 8 (Winter 1981): 363–79 and Kenneth Burke, "Version, Con-, Per-, In- (Thoughts on Djuna Barnes's Novel *Nightwood*)," in *Language as Symbolic Action* (Berkeley: University of California Press, 1966), pp. 240–53.

33. Sandra Gilbert, "Costumes of the Mind: Transvestism as Metaphor in Modern Literature," *Critical Inquiry* 7 (Winter 1980): 391–417.

34. Susan Gubar, "Blessings in Disguise: Cross-Dressing as Re-Dressing for Female Modernists," *Massachusetts Review* (Autumn 1981): 477–508.

35. Gilbert, "Costumes," pp. 404–7, proposes this vision of Orlando. I am indebted to Lucienne Frappier-Mazur for bringing the European male literary tradition of the novel of initiation to my attention. Frappier-Mazur has explored George Sand's *The Countess of Rudolstadt* as a feminist inversion of this form. See her article in the special issue on psycho-poetics in *Poetics* (Spring/Summer 1984), "Desire, Writing and Identity in the Romantic Mystical Novel: Notes for a Definition of the Feminine."

36. See Newton's interpretation of *The Well of Loneliness:* "The Mythic Mannish Lesbian," in this volume; Barnes, *Nightwood*, pp. 1–7.

37. For a superb analysis of the Trickster, see Barbara Babcock-Abrahams, " 'A Tolerated Margin of Mess': The Trickster and His Tales Reconsidered," *Journal of the Folklore Institute* 11 (1975): 147–86.

38. For a detailed (and somewhat psychoanalytic) interpretation of the Winnebago Trickster, see Paul Radin, *The Trickster: A Study in American Indian Mythology* (New York: Philosophical Library, 1956).

39. Babcock-Abrahams, " 'Tolerated Margin of Mess,' " pp. 153–60. See also Laura Makarius, "Ritual Clowns and Symbolic Behavior," *Diogenes* 69 (1970): 44–73, especially p. 66; Katherine Luomala, *Maui-of-a-Thousand-Tricks* (Bernice Bishop Museum Bulletin 198 [1949]), cited by Babcock-Abrahams.

40. For Barnes's presentation of Frau Mann and her fellow circus characters, see *Nightwood*, pp. 11–13, 113.

41. For a superb anthology on the subject of symbolic inversion, see *The Reversible World: Symbolic Inversion in Art and Society*, ed. Barbara A. Babcock (Ithaca, N.Y.: Cornell University Press, 1978), and especially Babcock's "Introduction," pp. 13–36, and David Kunzle's "World Upside Down: The Iconography of a European Broadsheet Type," pp. 39–94.

42. See, for example, Barnes, *Nightwood*, p. 135.

Newton, "The Mythic Mannish Lesbian"

This essay is a revision of one which first appeared in *Signs: Journal of Women in Culture and Society*, 9, no. 4 (Summer 1984): 557–575. That in turn emerged from a very different earlier paper entitled "The Mythic Lesbian and the New Woman: Power, Sexuality and Legitimacy," written with Carroll Smith-Rosenberg and presented by us at the Berkshire Conference on the History of Women, Vassar College, June 16, 1981. A revised version of that paper has appeared in French under the title "Le Myth de la lesbienne et la femme nouvelle," in *Strategies des femmes* (Paris: Editions Tierce, 1984). Smith-Rosenberg's further use of this material has appeared as "The New Woman as Androgyne: Social Disorder and Gender Crisis, 1870–1936," in

Disorderly Conduct (New York: Knopf, 1985). Developing the Radclyffe Hall material independently, I drew conclusions that do not represent Smith-Rosenberg's thinking and for which she is not responsible. But we worked jointly for two years, and I am in her debt for all I learned from her as a historian and as a friend. I am also indebted to the editorial board of The Lesbian issue of *Signs*, especially Susan Johnson and an anonymous peer reviewer; the members of the Purchase women's studies seminar, particularly Mary Edwards, Suzanne Kessler, and Louise Yellin, who read drafts and made helpful suggestions, as did David M. Schneider, Carole Vance, Wendy McKenna and especially Amber Hollibaugh. I thank the Lesbian Herstory Archives in New York, where I did early research, and Jan Boney for technical help. And for another kind of insight and support, without which this paper might never have been written, I thank the women of the B. group.

1. Two key texts are Radicalesbians, "The Woman Identified Woman," reprinted in *Radical Feminism*, ed. Anne Koedt, Ellen Levine, and Anita Rapone (New York: Quadrangle, 1973), pp. 240–45; and Adrienne Rich, "Compulsory Heterosexuality and Lesbian Existence," *Signs: Journal of Women in Culture and Society* 5, no. 4 (Summer 1980): 631–60. The best analysis of how these ideas have evolved and of their negative consequences for the feminist movement is Alice Echols, "The New Feminism of Yin and Yang," in *Powers of Desire*, ed. Ann Snitow, Christine Stansell, and Sharon Thompson (New York: Monthly Review Press, 1983), pp. 439–59.

2. Sasha Gregory Lewis, *Sunday's Women* (Boston: Beacon Press, 1979), p. 42.

3. Andrea Dworkin, *Pornography and Silence: Culture's Revenge against Nature* (New York: Harper & Row, 1981), p. 219.

4. On passing women, see San Francisco Lesbian and Gay History Project, "She Even Chewed Tobacco": Passing Women in Nineteenth-Century America (1983), slide-tape distributed by Women Make Movies, 225 Lafayette Street, New York, N.Y. 10012; Jonathan Katz, *Gay American History: Lesbians and Gay Men in the U.S.A.* (New York: Thomas Y. Crowell, 1976), pp. 209–80.

5. Since I wrote this essay, a useful biography of Radclyffe Hall has appeared, *Our Three Selves: The Life of Radclyffe Hall* by Michael Baker (New York: William Morrow, 1985), along with a biography of Hall's lover, *Una Troubridge: The Friend of Radclyffe Hall* by Richard Ormrod (New York: Carroll & Graf, 1985). Although these works contain fascinating material I had not seen before, they did not impel me to modify the ideas expressed here. See my review, ". . . Sick to Death of Ambiguities," in *The Women's Review of Books*, January 1986.

6. "Most of us lesbians in the 1950s grew up knowing nothing about lesbianism except Stephen Gordon's swagger," admits Blanche Wiesen Cook, herself a critic of Hall; see Cook's " 'Women Alone Stir My Imagination': Lesbianism and the Cultural Tradition," *Signs* 4, no. 4 (Summer 1979): 719–20. Despite Stephen Gordon's aristocratic trappings, her appeal transcended geographic and class barriers. We know that *The Well* was read early on by American lesbians of all classes (personal communication with Liz Kennedy from the Buffalo Oral History Project [1982]; and see Vern Bullough and Bonnie Bullough, "Lesbianism in the 1920s and 1930s: A Newfound Study," *Signs* 2, no. 4 [Summer 1977]: 895–904, esp. 897). *The Well* has been translated into numerous languages. According to Una Troubridge, in the 1960s it was still steadily selling over a hundred thousand copies a year in America alone; Troubridge was still receiving letters of appreciation ad-

dressed to Hall almost twenty years after Hall's death (Una Troubridge, *The Life and Death of Radclyffe Hall* [London: Hammond, Hammond & Co., 1961]). Even today, it sells as much as or more than any other lesbian novel, in straight and women's bookstores (personal communication with Amber Hollibaugh [1983], who has worked at Modern Times Bookstore [San Francisco], Djuna Books, and Womanbooks [New York City]).

7. Hall deserves censure for her possible fascist sympathies, but this is not the focus of feminist attacks on her. In any case, such sympathies developed after she wrote *The Well*; see Troubridge, pp. 118–24.

8. For the anti-*Well* approach, see Cook; Lillian Faderman and Ann Williams, "Radclyffe Hall and the Lesbian Image." *Conditions* 1, no. 1 (April 1977): 31–41; Catharine R. Stimpson, "Zero Degree Deviancy: The Lesbian Novel in English," in *Writing and Sexual Difference*, ed. Elizabeth Abel (Chicago: University of Chicago Press, 1982), pp. 243–60; Lillian Faderman, *Surpassing the Love of Men* (New York: William Morrow & Co., 1981), pp. 322–23; Vivian Gornick, "The Whole Radclyffe Hall: A Pioneer Left Behind," *Village Voice* (June 10–16, 1981). Only Inez Martinez, whose approach is quite different from mine, defends Hall: see "The Lesbian Hero Bound: Radclyffe Hall's Portrait of Sapphic Daughters and Their Mothers," *Journal of Homosexuality* 8, nos. 3/4 (Spring/Summer 1983): 127–37.

9. Many lesbians' connection to the mannish lesbian was and is painful. The relation of any stigmatized group to the figure that functions as its symbol and stereotype is necessarily ambiguous. Even before lesbian feminism, many lesbians hastened to assure themselves and others that they were not "like that." Lesbians who could pass for straight (because they were married or appeared feminine) often shunned their butch sisters. I have dealt with these concepts at length in *Mother Camp: Female Impersonators in America* (Chicago: University of Chicago Press, 1979).

10. See esp. Faderman, *Surpassing the Love of Men*. The pro-romantic friendship, anti-Radclyffe Hall line of thought has recently led to its logical absurdity in the encyclopedic *Women of the Left Bank* (Austin: University of Texas Press, 1986). Shari Benstock arguing, correctly, that Natalie Barney's vision of lesbianism was different from Hall's, concludes that Barney and Vivien were almost a difference species from Hall and a long list of other women who formed a "later generation, one that had been liberated to dress, talk, smoke, and act like men" (p. 307). Unfortunately for this hypothesis, Barney and Vivien were only four and two years older than Hall; Una Troubridge, supposedly one of the mannish ones, hardly ever dressed or acted like a man, despite Romaine Brooks's famous portrait. Benstock continues, "Barney was democratic enough to encourage the participation of both types of women [in her salon], just as she invited men . . ." (p. 307). Since Barney had affairs with many of the mannish women Benstock mentions, I wonder how "democratic" her motives were.

11. See Carroll Smith-Rosenberg, "The Female World of Love and Ritual," *Signs* 1, no. 1 (Autumn 1975): 1–30; and Faderman, *Surpassing the Love of Men*. On the contradictions within the romantic friendship system, see Martha Vicinus, " 'One Life to Stand Beside Me': Emotional Conflicts of First-Generation College Women in England," *Feminist Studies* 8, no. 3 (Fall 1982): 602–28.

12. George Chauncey, Jr., "From Sexual Inversion to Homosexuality: Medicine and the Changing Conceptualization of Female Deviance," *Salmagundi*, nos. 58/59 (Fall 1982/Winter 1983), pp. 114–45, esp. 117. Chauncey argues that even if some doctors began to assert a female sexual subjectivity

in the last third of the nineteenth century, this remained a minority opinion until the twentieth, see p. 118 fn. 6. He has reached the same conclusion I have regarding the "necessary" masculinity of the early lesbian persona.

13. For a related approach, see Carolyn Burke, "Gertrude Stein, the Cone Sisters, and the Puzzle of Female Friendship," in Abel, ed., *Writing and Sexual Difference*, pp. 221–42. Gertrude Stein shared the second generation's frustrations with "daughters spending a lifetime in freeing themselves from family fixations" (p. 223).

14. *The Unlit Lamp* (New York: Dial Press, 1981) p. 284.

15. Among many examples, the heterosexual misery of Jean Rhys's heroines; Emma Goldman's love problems as documented in Alice Wexler's recent biography *Emma Goldman in America* (Boston: Beacon Press, 1984); the female suffering documented by Ellen Kay Trimberger among Greenwich Village sex radical women, "Feminism, Men, and Modern Love: Greenwich Village, 1900–1925," in *Powers of Desire*.

16. See Paul Robinson, *The Modernization of Sex* (New York: Harper & Row, 1976), pp. 2, 3, and chap. 1.

17. Christina Simmons, "Companionate Marriage and the Lesbian Threat," *Frontiers* 4, no. 3 (Fall 1979): 54–59.

18. Ruth F. Claus, "Confronting Homosexuality: A Letter from Frances Wilder," *Signs* 2, no. 4 (Summer 1977): 928–33.

19. Ibid., p. 931.

20. Sandra Gilbert has developed this idea in the context of modernist literature in "Costumes of the Mind: Transvestism as Metaphor in Modern Literature," in Abel, ed., *Writing and Sexual Difference*, pp. 193–220.

21. Chauncey argues that medical opinion began to shift from an exclusive focus on "inversion" as gender reversal to "homosexuality" as deviant sexual orientation in the 1930s. The change has had only limited effect on popular ideology.

22. I am most indebted here to Carroll Smith-Rosenberg, who developed the prototype of this section on the sexologists. See "The New Woman as Androgyne" in *Disorderly Conduct*.

23. Richard von Krafft-Ebing, *Psychopathia Sexualis*, trans. Franklin S. Klaf (1886; New York: Bell Publishing Co., 1965), pp. 262–64.

24. Ibid., p. 264.

25. Ibid., pp. 278–79.

26. Havelock Ellis, "Sexual Inversion in Women," *Alienist and Neurologist* 16 (1895): 141–58.

27. See Robinson, *Modernization of Sex*, for a balanced appraisal of Ellis's radicalism in sexual issues vs. his misogyny.

28. Ellis, "Sexual Inversion," pp. 147–48.

29. Ibid., p. 152.

30. Ibid., p. 148.

31. Ibid., p. 153.

32. Freud's analysis was by far the most sophisticated. He rejected the trapped-soul paradigm and distinguished between "choice of object" and "sexual characteristics and sexual attitude of the subject." However, his insights were distorted by his antifeminism and his acceptance of a biological base for gender. See esp. "The Psychogenesis of a Case of Homosexuality in a Woman," in *Freud: Sexuality and the Psychology of Love*, ed. Philip Rieff (New York: Collier Books, 1963), pp. 133–59.

33. All page numbers cited in the text are from Radclyffe Hall, *The Well of Loneliness* (New York: Pocket Books, 1950).

34. Gilbert, "Costumes," p. 206.

35. My use of Freud's concepts indicates my conviction that it does begin to explain sexual desire, at least as it operates in our culture. Hall rejected or ignored Freud, presumably because of the implication, which so many drew from his work, that homosexuality could be "cured" (see Faderman and Williams "Radclyffe Hall," p. 41 n. 11).

36. Ruth-Jean Eisenbud asserts that "primary lesbian choice" occurs at about age three, resulting from the little girl's "precocious eroticism" directed toward a mother who is excluding her ("Early and Later Determinates of Lesbian Choice," *Psychoanalytic Review* 69, no. 1 [Spring 1982]: 85–109, esp. 99), Martinez, "Lesbian Hero Bound," whose theme is the mother/daughter relationship in Hall's two novels, ignores the concept of mother/daughter eroticism, rejecting any relevance of the psychoanalytic model.

37. See especially the extraordinary passage beginning, "The mother and daughter found very little to say to each other . . .", p. 75.

38. Vera Brittain, *Radclyffe Hall: A Case of Obscenity?* (New York: A. S. Barnes, 1969), p. 92.

39. The sexologists' discourse, itself hostile to women, "also made possible the formation of a 'reverse' discourse: homosexuality began to speak in its own behalf, to demand that its legitimacy or 'naturality' be acknowledged, often in the same vocabulary, using the same categories by which it was medically disqualified" (Michel Foucault, *The History of Sexuality*, vol. 1, *An Introduction* [New York: Vintage Books, 1980], p. 102).

40. Superficially, cultural feminism reunites lesbians and straight women under the banner of "female values." As Echols points out, hostility still surfaces "as it did at the 1979 Women Against Pornography conference where a lesbian separatist called Susan Brownmiller a 'cocksucker.' Brownmiller retaliated by pointing out that her critic 'even dresses like a man' " (Echols, "New Feminism," p. 41).

41. Sexologists often use the concept of "gender dysphoria syndrome" synonymously with "transsexualism" to describe the "pathology" of people who apply for gender reassignment surgery. Of course the effort to describe and treat transsexualism medically has been awkward since gender is a cultural construct, not a biological entity. My broader use of "gender dysphoria" is in agreement with some sexologists who limit the word "transsexual" to people who actually have had surgery to alter their bodies. Gender dysphoria, then, refers to a variety of difficulties in establishing conventional (the doctors say "adequate" or "normal") gender identification; intense pain and conflict over masculinity and femininity is not limited to people who request reassignment surgery. See Jon K. Meyer and John Hoopes, "The Gender Dysphoria Syndromes," *Plastic and Reconstructive Surgery* 54 (October 1974): 447. Female-to-male transsexuals appear to share many similarities with lesbian butches. The most impressive difference is the rejection or acceptance of homosexual identity. Compare *The Well* to the lives described in Ira B. Pauly, "Adult Manifestations of Female Transsexualism," in *Transsexualism and Sex Reassignment*, ed. Richard Green and John Money (Baltimore: Johns Hopkins University Press, 1969), pp. 59–87. Gender dysphoria could very fruitfully be compared with anorexia nervosa, a more socially acceptable and increasingly common female body-image problem. As feminists, we need a much more sophisticated vocabulary to talk about gender. Sexologists are often appallingly conservative, but they also deal with and try to explain important data. See e.g., John Money and Anke A. Ehrhardt, *Man & Woman, Boy & Girl* (Baltimore: Johns Hopkins University Press, 1972). For a radical scholarly approach, see Suzanne J. Kessler and Wendy McKenna, *Gender: An Ethnomethodological Approach* (University of Chi-

cago Press, 1985). One of the best recent pieces on gender reversal is Pat Califia, "Gender-Bending: Playing with Roles and Reversals," *Advocate* (September 15, 1983).

42. See Money and Ehrhardt, *Man & Woman*, pp. 18–20.

43. There is a long and complicated debate within anthropology about this. See Harriet Whitehead, "The Bow and the Burden Strap: A New Look at Institutionalized Homosexuality in Native North America," in *Sexual Meanings: The Cultural Construction of Gender and Sexuality*, ed. Sherry B. Ortner and Harriet Whitehead (Cambridge: Cambridge University Press, 1981), pp. 80–115; Walter Williams, *The Spirit and the Flesh* (Boston: Beacon Press, 1986); several articles in *Anthropology and Sexual Behavior*, ed. Evelyn Blackwood (New York: The Haworth Press, 1985); and Paula Gunn Allen's essay in this volume.

44. Two impressive beginnings are Joan Nestle, "Butch-Fem Relationships," and Amber Hollibaugh and Cherríe Moraga, "What We're Rollin' Around in Bed With," both in *Heresies 12* 3, no. 4 (1981): 21–24, 58–62. The latter has been reprinted in Snitow, Stansell, and Thompson, eds., *Powers of Desire*, pp. 394–405.

Chauncey, "Christian Brotherhood or Sexual Perversion?"

1. This is a revised version of a paper originally presented at the conference "Among Men, Among Women: Sociological and Historical Recognition of Homosocial Arrangements," held at the University of Amsterdam, June 22–26, 1983. I am grateful to Allan Bérubé, John Boswell, Nancy Cott, Steven Dubin, James Schultz, Anthony Stellato, James Taylor, and my colleagues at the Amsterdam conference for their comments on earlier versions.

2. The Newport investigation was brought to the attention of historians by Frank Freidel, *Franklin D. Roosevelt: The Ordeal* (Boston, 1954), pp. 41, 46–47, 96–97, and Jonathan Katz, *Gay American History: A Documentary* (New York, 1976), p. 579n. Katz reprinted the Senate report in *Government Versus Homosexuals* (New York, 1975), a volume in the Arno Press series on homosexuality he edited. A useful narrative account of the naval investigation is provided by Lawrence R. Murphy, "Cleaning Up Newport: The U.S. Navy's Prosecution of Homosexuals After World War I," *Journal of American Culture* 7 (Fall, 1984): 57–64.

3. Murphy J. Foster presided over the first Court of Inquiry which began its work in Newport on March 13, 1919 and heard 406 pages of testimony in the course of 23 days (its records are hereafter cited as *Foster Testimony*). The second court of inquiry, convened in 1920 "to inquire into the methods employed . . . in the investigation of moral and other conditions existing in the Naval Service; [and] to ascertain and inquire into the scope of and authority for said investigation," was presided over by Rear Admiral Herbert O. Dunn and heard 2500 pages of testimony in the course of eighty-six days (hereinafter cited as *Dunn Testimony*). The second trial of Rev. Kent, *U.S. v. Samuel Neal Kent*, heard in Rhode Island District Court in Providence beginning January 20, 1920, heard 532 pages of evidence (hereinafter cited as *Kent Trial*). The records are held at the National Archives, Modern Military Field Branch, Suitland, Maryland, R.G. 125.

4. I have used "gay" in this essay to refer to men who identified themselves as sexually different from other men—and who labelled them-

selves and were labelled by others as "queer"—because of their assumption of "feminine" sexual and other social roles. As I explain below, not all men who were homosexually active labelled themselves in this manner, including men, known as "husbands," who were involved in long-term homosexual relationships but nonetheless maintained a masculine identity.

5. *Foster Testimony*, Ervin Arnold, 5; F.T. Brittain, 12, Thomas Brunelle, 21; *Dunn Testimony*, Albert Viehl, 307; Dudley Marriott, 1737.

6. Frederick Hoage, using a somewhat different construction than most, referred to them as "the inverted gang" (*Foster Testimony*, 255).

7. *Foster Testimony*, Arnold, 5: *Dunn Testimony*, Clyde Rudy, 1783. For a few of the many other comments by "straight" sailors on the presence of gay men at the Y.M.C.A., see *Dunn Testimony*, Claude McQuillin, 1759, and Preston Paul, 1836.

8. A man named Temple, for instance, had a room at the Y where he frequently took pickups (*Foster Testimony*, Brunelle, 207–8); on the role of the elevator operators, see William McCoy, 20, and Samuel Rogers, 61.

9. *Foster Testimony*, Arnold, 27; Frederick Hoage, 271; Harrison Rideout, 292.

10. Ibid., Hoage, 267; Rogers, 50; Brunelle, 185.

11. Ibid., Gregory A. Cunningham, 30; Arnold, 6; *Dunn Testimony*, John S. Tobin, 720–21.

12. For an elaboration of the conceptual distinction between "inversion" and "homosexuality" in the contemporary medical literature, see my article, "From Sexual Inversion to Homosexuality," Medicine and the Changing Conceptualization of Female Deviance," *Salmagundi* 58/59 (Fall 1982/Winter 1983): 114–46.

13. *Foster Testimony*, Rogers, 50–51.

14. E.g., an article which included the following caption beneath a photograph of Hughes dressed in women's clothes: "This is Billy Hughes, Yeo. 2c. It's a shame to break the news like that, but enough of the men who saw 'Pinafore' fell in love with Bill, without adding to their number. 'Little Highesy,' as he is affectionately known, dances like a Ziegfeld chorus girl . . ." (" 'We Sail the Ocean Blue': 'H.M.S. Pinafore' as Produced by the Navy," *Newport Recruit* 6 [August 1918]: 9). See also, e.g., "Mayor Will Greet Navy Show Troupe: Official Welcome Arranged for 'Jack and Bean-stalk' Boys," which quoted an admiral saying, " 'It is a corker. I have never in my life seen a prettier "girl" [a man] than "Princess Mary." She is the daintiest little thing I ever laid eyes on' " (*Providence Journal* [26 May 1919]: 9). I am grateful to Lawrence Murphy for supplying me with copies of these articles.

15. *Dunn Testimony*, John S. Tobin, 716; *Foster Testimony*, Charles Zipf, 377; confirmed by Hoage, 289, and Arnold (*Dunn Testimony*, 1405). The man who received the women's clothes was the Billy Hughes mentioned in the newspaper article cited in the previous note. I am grateful to Allan Bérubé for informing me of the regularity with which female impersonators appeared in navy shows during and immediately following World War I.

16. Ibid., Hoage called it a "faggot party" and "a general congregation of inverts" (267); Brunelle, who claimed to have attended the party for only 15 minutes, noted the presence of the sailors and fighters; he also said only one person was in drag, but mentioned at least two (194, 206); John E. McCormick observed the lovers (332).

17. For the straight sailors' nicknames, see *Foster Testimony*, William Nelson Gorham, 349. On the ubiquity of nicknames and the origins of some of them, see Hoage, 253, 271; Whitney Delmore Rosenszweig, 397.

18. *Dunn Testimony*, Hudson, 1663.

19. *Foster Testimony*, Rideout, 76–77.

20. Ibid., Cunningham, 29. For other examples, see Wade Stuart Harvey, 366; and *Dunn Testimony*, Tobin, 715.

21. *Foster Testimony*, George Richard, 143; Hoage, 298.

22. Ibid., Rideout, 69; see also Rogers, 63; Viehl, 175; Arnold, 3; and *passim*.

23. An investigator told the navy that one gay man had declined to make a date with him because "he did not like to 'play with fire' . . . [and] was afraid Chief Brugs would beat him up" (*Foster Testimony*, Arnold, 36); the same gay man told the court he had travelled to Providence with Brugs two weekends in a row and gone to shows with him (Rogers, 53–54). Speaking of another couple, Hoage admitted he had heard "that Hughes has travelled with Brunelle separately for two months or so" and that "they were lovers." He added that "of course that does not indicate anything but friendship," but that "naturally I would suspect that something else was taking place" (Hoage, 268).

24. Ibid., Hoage, 313.

25. Ibid., Arnold, 5.

26. Ibid., Viehl, 175; Brunelle, 235; Rideout, 93. Hoage, when cross-examined by Rosenszweig, denied another witness's charge that he, Hoage, had *boasted* of browning Rosenszweig, but he did not deny the act itself—nor did Rosenszweig ask him to do so (396).

27. Ibid., Hoage, 271; Rogers, 131–136.

28. Ibid., Rogers, 39–40; other evidence tends to confirm Rogers' contention that he had not known openly gay men or women before joining the navy. For other examples of the role of the war in introducing men to gays, see Brunelle 211; and in the *Dunn Testimony*, Rudy, 1764. For extended discussions of the similar impact of military mobilization on many people's lives during World War II, see Allan Bérubé, "Marching to a Different drummer: Lesbian and Gay GIs in World War II," in this volume; and John D'Emilio, *Sexual Politics, Sexual Communities: The Making of a Homosexual Minority in the United States, 1940–1970* (Chicago, 1983), 23–39.

29. *Foster Testimony*, Rideout, 78.

30. *Dunn Testimony*, E. M. Hudson questioning Bishop James De Wolf Perry, 609 (my emphasis).

31. Ibid., Jeremiah Mahoney, 698.

32. Ibid., Tobin, 717.

33. Witnesses who encountered gay men at the hospital or commented on the presence of homosexuals there included Gregory Cunningham, *Foster Testimony*, 29; Brunelle, 210; John McCormick, *Dunn Testimony*, 1780; and Paul, 1841. Paul also described some of the open homosexual joking engaged in by patients, *Foster Testimony*, 393–94.

34. *Foster Testimony*, Hervey, 366; Johnson, 153, 155, 165, 167; Smith, 221.

35. Ibid., Johnson, 153; Smith, 169.

36. Ibid., Smith, 171.

37. Ibid., Hoage, 272. Hoage added that "[t]rade is a word that is only used among people temperamental [i.e., gay]," although this does not appear to have been entirely the case.

38. Ibid., Hoage, 269, 314; Rudy, 14. The decoy further noted that, despite the fairy's pleas, "I insisted that he do his work below my chest."

39. Frederick Hoage provided an example of this pattern when he de-

scribed how a gay civilian had taken him to a show and dinner, let him stay in his room, and then "attempted to do what they call 'browning.' " But he devoted much of his testimony to *denying* that *his* "tak[ing] boys to dinner and to a show," offering to share his bed with sailors who had nowhere else to stay, and giving them small gifts and loans had the sexual implications that the court obviously suspected (*Foster Testimony*, Hoage, 261, 256, 262, 281–82). For other examples of solicitation patterns, see Maurice Kreisberg, 12; Arnold, 26; *Dunn Testimony*, Paul, 1843. Edward Stevenson described the "trade" involved in military prostitution in *The Intersexes: A History of Semisexualism* (privately printed, 1908), 214. For an early sociological description of "trade," see Albert Reiss, Jr., "The Social Integration of Queers and Peers," *Social Problems* 9 (1961): 102–20.

40. *Foster Testimony*, Rudy, 13.

41. *Dunn Testimony*, Paul, 1836; see also, e.g., Mayor Mahoney's comments, 703.

42. *Foster Testimony*, James Daniel Chase, 119 (my emphasis); Zipf, 375.

43. Ibid., Walter F. Smith, 169.

44. See, e.g., the accounts of Hoage, *Foster Testimony*, 271–72, and Rideout, 87.

45. *Foster Testimony*, Smith, 169.

46. Alfred Kinsey, Wardell Pomeroy, and Clyde Martin, *Sexual Behavior in the Human Male* (Philadelphia, 1948), 650–51.

47. *Foster Testimony*, Arnold, 6; *Dunn Testimony*, Arnold, 1495.

48. *Kent Trial*, 21.

49. Ibid., defense attorney's interrogation of Charles McKinney, 66–67. See also, e.g., the examination of Zipf, esp. pp. 27–28.

50. Ibid., Zipf, 2113, 2131 (the court repeatedly turned to the subject). The "manly" decoy was Clyde Rudy, 1793.

51. The ministers' efforts are reviewed and their charges affirmed in the Senate report, 67th Congress, 1st session, Committee on Naval Affairs, *Alleged Immoral Conditions of Newport (R.I.) Naval Training Station* (Washington, D.C., 1921), and in the testimony of Bishop Perry and Reverend Hughes before the Dunn Inquiry.

52. *Dunn Testimony*, Rev. Deming, 30; Rev. Forster, 303.

53. Hudson quoted in the Senate report, *Alleged Immoral Conditions* 8; see also *Dunn Testimony*, Tobin, 723, cf. Arnold, 1712. For the ministers' criticism, see. e.g., Bishop Perry, 529, 607.

54. *Foster Testimony*, Hoage, 319.

55. Ibid., Brunelle, 216. He says the same of Kent on p. 217.

56. *Kent Trial*, cross-examination of Howard Rider, 296.

57. Ibid., Malcolm C. Crawford, 220–23; Dostalik, 57–71.

58. *Foster Testimony*, interrogation of Hoage, 315, 318.

59. *Dunn Testimony*, Deming, 43.

60. *Kent Trial*, Kent, 396, 419, 403.

61. Ibid., Herbert Walker, 318–20; Bishop Philip Rhinelander, 261–62; Judge Darius Baker, 277; see also Rev. Henry Motett, 145–49, 151.

62. Ibid., interrogation of C.B. Zipf, 37–38.

63. *Dunn Testimony*, Rev. Deming, 42; Bishop Perry, 507.

64. Ibid., Perry, 678.

65. Jonathan Katz argues that such a perspective was central to Puritan concepts of homosexuality. "The Age of Sodomitical Sin, 1607–1740," in his *Gay/Lesbian Almanac: A New Documentary* (New York, 1983), pp. 23–65. But see also John Boswell, "Revolutions, Universals and Sexual Categories," *Salmagundi* 58/59 (Fall 1982/Winter 1983): 89–113 (reprinted in this volume).

66. This argument was first introduced by Mary McIntosh, "The Homosexual Role," *Social Problems* 16 (1968): 182–92, and has been developed and modified by Jeffrey Weeks. *Coming Out: Homosexual Politics in Britain from the Nineteenth Century to the Present* (London, 1977); Michel Foucault, *The History of Sexuality: An Introduction*, transl. by Robert Hurley (New York, 1978); Lillian Faderman, *Surpassing the Love of Men: Romantic Friendships and Love Between Women From the Renaissance to the Present* (New York, 1981); Kenneth Plummer, ed., *The Making of the Modern Homosexual* (London, 1981); and Katz, *Gay/Lesbian Almanac*. Although these historians and sociologists subscribe to the same general model, they disagree over the timing and details of the emergence of a homosexual role, and McIntosh's original essay did not attribute a key role in that process to medical discourse.

67. The situation had changed considerably by World War II, when psychiatrists occupied a more influential position in the military, which used them to help select and manage the more than 15 million men and women it mobilized for the war. See, for instance, the role of psychiatrists in the records of courts-martial conducted from 1941–43 held at the National Archives (Army A.G. 250.1) and the 1944 investigation of lesbianism at the Third WAC Training Center, Fort Oglethorpe, Georgia (National Archives, Modern Military Field Branch, Suitland, Maryland, R.G. 159, Entry 26F). Allan Bérubé's important forthcoming study, *Coming Out Under Fire*, will discuss at length the role of psychiatrists in the development and implementation of WWII-era military policies.

68. *Dunn Testimony*, Hudson, 1630.

69. *Foster Testimony*, 300. The transcript does not identify the speaker, but the context strongly suggests it was Hudson.

70. *Dunn Testimony*, 1628, 1514.

71. George Frank Lydston, "Sexual Perversion, Satyriasis, and Nymphomania," *Medical and Surgical Reporter* 61 (1889): 254. See also Chauncey, "From Sexual Inversion to Homosexuality," 142–43.

72. John D'Emilio has provided the most sophisticated analysis of this process in *Sexual Politics, Sexual Communities: The Making of a Homosexual Minority in the United States, 1940–1970* (Chicago, 1983). See also Toby Moratta, *The Politics of Homosexuality* (Boston, 1981), and the pioneering studies by Jeffrey Weeks and Lillian Faderman cited in note 66.

73. One would also hesitate to assert that a single definition of homosexuality obtains in our own culture. Jonathan Katz has made a similar argument about the need to specify the meaning of homosexual behavior and identity in his *Gay/Lesbian Almanac*, although our analyses differ in a number of respects (see my review in *The Body Politic*, no. 97 (1983): 33–34).

74. Lillian Faderman, in "The Mordification of Love Between Women by 19th-Century Sexologists," *Journal of Homosexuality* 4 (1978): 73–90, and *Surpassing the Love of Men*, is the major proponent of the argument that the medical discourse stigmatized romantic friendships. Alternative analyses of the role of the medical literature and of the timing and nature of the process of stigmatization having been proposed by Martha Vicinus, "Distance and Desire: English Boarding-School Friendships," *Signs: Journal of Women in Culture and Society* 9 (1984): 600–22; Carroll Smith-Rosenberg, "The New Woman as Androgyne: Social Disorder and Gender Crisis, 1870–1936," in *Disorderly Conduct: Visions of Gender in Victorian America* (New York, 1985), 245–96; and Chauncey, "From Sexual Inversion to Homosexuality." On the apparent ubiquity of the early twentieth-century public image of the lesbian as a "mannish woman," see Esther Newton, "The Mythic Mannish Lesbian: Radclyffe Hall and the New Woman," *Signs* 9 (1984): 557–575.

Nineteenth-century medical articles and newspaper accounts of lesbian couples stigmatized only the partner who played "the man's part" by dressing like a man and seeking male employment, but found the "womanly" partner unremarkable, as if it did not matter that her "husband" was another female so long as she played the conventionally wifely role (see Chauncey, 125ff). The medical reconceptualization of female deviance as homosexual object choice rather than gender role inversion was underway by the 1920s, but it is difficult to date any such transition in popular images, in part because they remained so inconsistent.

Garber, "A Spectacle in Color"

Many people have contributed to my research over the years. I am particularly grateful to George Chauncey, Jr., Angela Y. Davis, Bruce Kellner, the American Studies Department, San Francisco State University, and the members of the San Francisco Lesbian and Gay History Project for their encouragement and critical suggestions. I am also grateful for the friendship and support of the late Richard Bruce Nugent, who helped start me on my exploration of gay Harlem in the Jazz Age.

1. See: Jervis Anderson, *This Was Harlem* (New York: Farrar, Straus, Giroux, 1982); Nathan Irvin Huggins, *Harlem Renaissance* (New York: Oxford University Press, 1971); Bruce Kellner, *The Harlem Renaissance: A Historical Dictionary of the Era* (Westport: Greenwood, 1984); and David Levering Lewis, *When Harlem Was in Vogue* (New York: Knopf, 1981).

2. Bessie Smith, "Foolish Man Blues," *The Empress*, Columbia CG 30818. For a discussion of the role of effeminacy in 1920s gay male culture, generally, see George Chauncey, Jr., "Gay Male Society in the Jazz Age," *Village Voice* (1 July 1986): 29–34.

3. Quoted in Sandra Lieb, *Mother of the Blues: A Study of Ma Rainey* (Amherst: University of Massachusetts Press, 1981), pp. 122–23.

4. Bessie Jackson (pseud. of Lucille Bogan), "B.D. Woman's Blues," *AC/DC Blues: Gay Jazz Reissues*, Stash ST–106.

5. George Hanna, "Boy in the Boat," *AC/DC Blues: Gay Jazz Reissues*, Stash ST–106.

6. Pinewood Tom, "Sissy Man," *Straight and Gay*, Stash ST–188.

7. Paul Oliver, *Blues Fell This Morning: The Meaning of the Blues* (New York: Horizon, 1961), p. 112.

8. Joan Nestle, "Lesbians and Prostitutes: An Historical Sisterhood," *A Restricted Country* (Ithaca: Firebrand Books, 1987), p. 169.

9. Kellner, *The Harlem Renaissance*, pp. 100–01.

10. Jonathan Katz, *Gay American History* (New York: Crowell, 1976), pp. 167–69.

11. Interview with Mabel Hampton by Joan Nestle, 21 May 1981. Used with the kind permission of Joan Nestle.

12. Quoted in Ira De A. Reid, "Mrs. Bailey Pays the Rent," *Ebony and Topaz: A Collectanea*, ed. Charles S. Johnson (New York: National Urban League, 1927), pp. 147–48.

13. Wallace Thurman, *Infants of the Spring* (New York: Macaulay, 1932), p. 184.

14. Alexander Gumby collection, Columbia University; Samuel Steward, personal interview, 1981.

15. Marjorie Worthington, *The Strange World of Willie Seabrook* (New

York: Harcourt, Brace & World, 1966), p. 64.; see also: Osbert Sitwell, "New York in the Twenties," *The Atlantic* (February 1962): 41; Carl Van Vechten, "A'Lelia Walker," *"Keep A-Inching Along": Selected Writings of Carl Van Vechten about Black Art and Letters* (Westport: Greenwood, 1979), pp. 152–54; and Langston Hughes, *The Big Sea* (New York: Knopf, 1940), pp. 244–47.

16. Bricktop, *Bricktop* (New York: Atheneum, 1983), p. 57.

17. Interview of Ruby Smith by Chris Albertson, 1971. Reproduced on *AC/DC Blues: Gay Jazz Reissues*, Stash ST–106.

18. Ed Kirkeby, *Ain't Misbehavin': The Story of Fats Waller* (New York: Dodd, Mead, 1966), pp. 99–100.

19. David Fontaine, personal interview, 1984.

20. Edouard Roditi, interview with Ray Gerard Koskovich, 30 May 1983. Used with the kind permission of Ray Gerard Koskovich.

21. Helen Lawrenson, *Stranger at the Party: A Memoir* (New York: Random House, 1975), pp. 169–70.

22. Richard Bruce Nugent, personal interview, 1981.

23. On Edmond's: Ethel Waters, *His Eye is on the Sparrow* (Garden City: Doubleday, 1951), pp. 149–50; on Lulu Belle's: Richard Bruce Nugent, personal interview, 1981; on the Hot Cha: Jimmy Daniels, personal interview, 1984.

24. Eric Garber, "Gladys Bentley: The Bulldagger who Sang the Blues," *Outlook* 1 (1988), pp. 52–61.

25. Hughes, *The Big Sea*, p. 226.

26. Eslanda Robeson to Fania Van Vechten, Carl Van Vechten papers, New York Public Library. Many thanks to Martin Bauml Duberman for bringing this reference to my attention.

27. Quoted in Lewis, *When Harlem Was in Vogue*, p. 242.

28. Blair Niles. *Strange Brother* (New York: Harris, 1949), pp. 38–64.

29. Hughes, *The Big Sea*, p. 273.

30. Taylor Gordon, *Born to Be* (Seattle: University of Washington Press, 1975), p. 228.

31. Charles Henri Ford and Parker Tyler, *The Young and Evil* (New York: Arno, 1975), p. 151.

32. On Porter Grainger see: Chris Alberston, *Bessie* (New York: Stein and Day, 1972), pp. 140–41; on Phil Black see: Phil Black, "I Live in Two Worlds," *Our World* 8 (October 1953): 12–15; on Frankie "Half Pint" Jaxon see: Sheldon Harris, *Blues Who's Who* (New Rochelle, N.Y.: Arlington House, 1979) pp. 273–74.

33. For information on Smith: Albertson, *Bessie*; on Rainey: Lieb, *Mother of the Blues*; on Hunter and Waters: Frank C. Taylor, *Alberta Hunter: A Celebration in Blues* (New York: McGraw-Hill, 1987); On Waters: Waters, *His Eye is on the Sparrow*; on Baker: Lynn Haney, *Naked at the Feast: A Biography of Josephine Baker* (New York: Dodd, Mead, 1981).

34. Quoted in Lieb, *Mother of the Blues*, p. 125.

35. Two divergent views of Hughes's sexuality are offered by: Faith Berry, *Langston Hughes: Before and Beyond Harlem* (Westport: Lawrence Hill, 1983); and Arnold Rampersad, *Life of Langston Hughes*, vol. 1: *I, Too, Sing America* (New York: Oxford, 1986).

36. Hughes, *The Big Sea*, p. 238.

37. Arna Bontemps, "The Awakening: A Memoir," *Harlem Renaissance Remembered* (New York: Dodd, Mead, 1972), p. 12; see also Lewis, *When Harlem Was in Vogue*, pp. 75–77.

38. On McKay: Wayne F. Cooper, *Claude McKay: Rebel Sojourner in*

the Harlem Renaissance (Baton Rouge: Louisiana State University Press, 1987); on Barthé, personal interview, 1982; on Nugent: Eric Garber, "Richard Bruce Nugent," *Afro-American Writers from the Harlem Renaissance to 1940: Dictionary of Literary Biography*, vol. 51 (Detroit: Gale Research, 1987), pp. 213–21.

39. Quoted in John A. Williams, "Afterword," to Wallace Thurman, *Infants of the Spring* (Carbondale: Southern Illinois University Press, 1979), p. 289.

40. Quoted in Anderson, *This Was Harlem*, p. 201.

41. Lewis, *When Harlem Was in Vogue*, pp. 87–88.

42. Bruce Kellner, *Carl Van Vechten and the Irreverent Decades* (Norman: University of Oklahoma Press, 1968); and Kellner, "Carl Van Vechten," *Afro-American Writers from the Harlem Renaissance to 1940: Dictionary of Literary Biography*, vol. 51 (Detroit: Gale Research, 1987), pp. 322–327.

43. Hughes, *The Big Sea*, p. 223.

44. Rain James, *All About New York: An Intimate Guide* (New York: John Day, 1931). p. 249.

45. Mercedes de Acosta, *Here Lies the Heart: A Tale of My Life* (New York: Reynal, 1960), p. 128.

46. Blair Niles, *Strange Brother* (New York: Harris, 1949), pp. 151–56; on Pettit: Richard Bruce Nugent, personal interview, 1981, and letter from Edyth McKitrick, Archivist, Grace Church, to the author, dated 28 February 1983.

47. Theophilus Lewis, Wallace Thurman obituary, undated, in Gumby Scrapbooks, Columbia University.

48. Richard Bruce Nugent, "Smoke, Lilies and Jade," *Fire!* 1 (1926), pp. 33–39.

49. Alain Locke, *The Survey* (August 15–September 15, 1927): 563.

50. Deborah E. McDowell, "Introduction," *Quicksand and Passing* (New Brunswick: Rutgers University Press, 1986).

51. Jeanne Flash Gray, "Memories," *The Other Black Woman* 1 (n.d.): 3.

52. "Harlem's Strangest Nightclub," *Ebony* 7 (December 1951): 82–83.

53. Black, "I Live in Two Worlds," p. 13.

54. Gray, "Memories," p. 3.

Benstock, "Paris Lesbianism"

1. The links between economic/social privilege and psychosexual/political choice for women of this period have been overlooked or repressed for several reasons. First, women's contributions to avant-garde art have never been taken seriously, nor has their lived experience in Paris been distinguished from that of their male counterparts. The major texts that address the politics of the expatriate avant-garde are grounded in misogyny. See, for example, Malcolm Cowley, *Exile's Return: A Literary Odyssey of the 1920's* (New York: Viking, 1951), Frederick, J. Hoffman, *The Twenties: American Writing in the Postwar Decade* (New York: Collier, 1962), and Hugh Kenner, *The Pound Era* (Berkeley: University of California Press, 1971). Second, it is painful for feminists to discuss the coincidence of right-wing lesbianism. Discussions of the Paris lesbian community and its individual members have usually avoided direct comment on the political commitments of this community or the political implications of economic and social privilege of its

members. Bertha Harris avoids these issues; see "The More Profound Nationality of Their Lesbianism: Lesbian Society in the 1920s" in *Amazon Expedition: A Lesbian Feminist Anthology*, ed. Phyllis Birkby et al. (New York: Times Change, 1973). Blanche Wiesen Cook is exceptional in her direct address of these questions; see " 'Women Alone Stir My Imagination': Lesbianism and the Cultural Tradition" in *Signs* 4 (1979) pp. 718–39.

2. I have written about this subject before in *Women of the Left Bank: Paris 1900–1940* (Austin: University of Texas Press, 1986). A fuller examination of the lives and works of members of the Paris art community is provided there, including bibliographies of primary and secondary works, and works on sexual and cultural politics of the period. Important additions to this bibliography are Jean-Paul Goujon's biography of Renée Vivien, *Tes blessures sont plus douces que leurs caresses: Vie de Renée Vivien* (Paris: Deforges, 1986) and his edition of her writings, *Oeuvre Poétique complete de Renée Vivien*, ed. Jean-Paul Goujon (Paris: Deforges, 1986), and Edward Burns, ed., *The Letters of Gertrude Stein and Carl Van Vechten*, 2 vols. (New York: Columbia University Press, 1986). These latter works incorporate important information on the sexual politics of Natalie Barney and Gertrude Stein.

3. Gertrude Stein discovered a mass reading public only with the publication of *The Autobiography of Alice B. Toklas* (New York: Harcourt and Brace, 1933; London: Bodley Head, 1933), a text she hoped Hollywood would film so that she could replenish her dwindling finances at the end of the 1930s. Stein stayed on in France during the second war in part because she did not have the money to live elsewhere—or to live in the comfortable style to which she had accustomed herself.

Barney and Vivien both found reading audiences in France that at first assumed their love poetry followed the traditional forms of male address to a female beloved (and the two women exploited this form in part to create such an effect). Vivien began publishing as R. Vivien and later as Paule Riverdale. She did not want to be recognized as the author of her own works, afraid of the interest in her private life and possible hostility that public knowledge of her identity might bring about. She changed her name from Pauline Tarn to Renée Vivien in part to disguise her writing identity from members of her bourgeois family. When her identity became public, she experienced some unpleasant encounters and accusations of moral degeneracy, corruption of young girls, etc. Djuna Barnes did not publish *Ladies Almanack* (Paris: Privately Printed, 1928; New York: Harper and Row, 1972) under her own name, although many members of the Left Bank community knew her to be the author of it; she signed herself a "Lady of Fashion," not so much as protection against the subject matter of the text but because she claimed it was not serious, a form of joke.

4. Susan Rubin Suleiman, "Pornography, Transgression, and the Avant-Garde: Bataille's Study of the Eye" in *The Poetics of Gender*, ed. Nancy K. Miller (New York: Columbia University Press, 1986), p. 129.

5. It is true that these women were more important in the Paris context than they have been in literary histories of the period. However, their "importance" in that context was often because they were seen as essential handmaidens to Modernism, serving as book sellers, publishers, translators, editors, patrons, *saloniéres*, and supporters. Their own writings were, with rare exceptions, overlooked by their contemporaries.

6. Anne-Marie Dardigna, *Les chateaux d'Eros ou l'infortune du sexe des femmes* (Paris: Maspero, 1981.) Quoted in Suleiman, p. 129.

7. Suleiman, p. 128. She comments that "from the Surrealists to the *Tel Quel* group and to some of the so-called 'postmodernists' in American writ-

ing, twentieth-century avant-gardes have proclaimed, and in a sense lived on (or off) their adversary, subversive relation to the dominant culture. But insofar as the dominant culture has been not only bourgeois but also patriarchal, the productions of the avant-garde appear anything but subversive" (p. 129). The implications of this assertion have not been thoroughly examined in terms of women Modernists, the most important of whom were lesbian, nor have its implications been studied for those women writers whose work was not *on the surface*, in terms of "style," avant-garde. Of particular interest are the writings of Natalie Barney and Renée Vivien, both of whom purposely adopted outmoded and highly stylized French poetic forms. See Benstock, *Women of the Left Bank*, pp. 277–304.

8. Both Freud and Lacan articulated their understanding of human sexuality through myth and literature. Importantly for our concerns, Lacan turned to Modernist texts to verify his theories. The life and works of James Joyce were particularly symptomatic for him, as were the works of Georges Bataille, whose pornographic narrative Susan Suleiman discusses. Bataille was the first husband of Lacan's wife, Sylvia, who left Bataille when she discovered herself pregnant with Lacan's child. Bataille and Lacan remained close friends. See Elisabeth Roudinesco, *La Bataille de cent ans: L'histoire de psychanalyse en France* (Paris: Flammarion, 1985), vol. 2 passim.

For cogent readings of Lacan's interpretation of female sexuality, see Juliet Mitchell and Jacqueline Rose, ed., *Feminine Sexuality: Jacques Lacan and the école freudienne* (New York: Pantheon, 1982); Ellie Ragland-Sullivan, *Jacques Lacan and the Philosophy of Psychoanalysis* (Urbana: University of Illinois Press, 1986); and Jane Gallop, *The Daughter's Seduction: Feminism and Psychoanalysis* (Ithaca: Cornell University Press, 1982) and *Reading Lacan* (Ithaca: Cornell University Press, 1985). This theory is problematic in every way, especially on questions of lesbianism; indeed, the Freudian/ Lacanian myth of human sexuality seems to have taken root and assumed power as a cultural script precisely to the degree that female sexuality—separate from male perceptions of and fantasies about that sexuality—stands outside its story.

9. Certainly for the period under discussion here, the dominant theories of sexuality—including those of Havelock Ellis, Richard von Krafft-Ebing, Karl Heinrich Ulrichs, as well as Freud—suggested that the phallic-patriarchal law was inescapable, and homosexuality described itself in terms of an inversion of the Oedipal law. See Benstock, *Women of the Left Bank*, pp. 50–60, Esther Newton, "The Mythic Mannish Lesbian: Radclyffe Hall and the New Woman," and Martha Vicinus, "Distance and Desire: English Boarding-School Friendships" in this volume.

10. Elisabeth de Gramont and Lucie Delarue-Mardrus were Catholic, members of the French aristocracy and upper classes. De Pougy, born of middle-class Breton parents, was convent educated. Despite her career as one of the best known *grandes horizontales* of the *belle époque*, an actress and dancer at the Moulin Rouge, de Pougy never left the church, and as she aged was drawn back to its teachings. During World War II she took refuge in a Dominican convent in Switzerland and was later transferred to a clinic run by French nuns, where she eventually died. In these years de Pougy tried desperately to reconcile her present piety with her personal past, seeking assurance that she had been forgiven for aspects of her sinful behavior. According to Paul Bernard, her "Breton faith . . . remained sentimental and infantile." See Jean Chalon and Paul Bernard, ed., *Lettres a Liane de Pougy de Max Jacob et Salomon Reinach* (Paris: Plon, 1980), p. 161 (my translation).

Renée Vivien converted to Catholicism in the last months of her life, thus accepting as she approached death the church that had previously represented for her an instrument of sexual repression and the enforcement of patriarchal codes. The link between Vivien's sexual politics, her religious conversion, and the larger arena of cultural politics is difficult to trace because her premature death exempted her from necessary political decision in the face of the first and second world wars.

Alice Toklas converted to Catholicism after Gertrude Stein's death, in part to assure herself that she and Stein could be together beyond the grave. Born into a culturally Jewish but nonreligious family, Stein died outside the bounds of any formal religion and received a protestant burial in Père Lachaise cemetery in Paris. A Paris priest later promised Alice that if she would convert the two women would be together among God's chosen for eternity, despite Gertrude's separate beliefs.

Radclyffe Hall and Una Troubridge were both converts to Catholicism, Hall's the more determined faith. They too were concerned to share immortality together. Their early work with the Society for Psychical Research in London was an effort to make contact with Mabel Batten, Hall's earlier lover, to expiate the guilt they felt in allowing her to die alone while they were away together on a secret tryst.

The move toward a powerfully hierarchical religion by all of these women suggests another line of investigation between sexual and political choice and cultural identity. Natalie Barney remained resolutely outside the gates of any religion; it is ironic, however, that she lost both de Pougy and Vivien to Catholicism. She tried unsuccessfully to save de Pougy from her life as a courtesan (a change eventually effected by Prince Ghika, who could support de Pougy in the style to which her work had accustomed her). She tried, through friendship, to save Vivien from death. This effort was unsuccessful, probably because Barney could not maintain the sexual fidelity Vivien claimed was necessary. However, Vivien's death wish was allied to her need to be betrayed, a condition Barney probably understood. See *Aventures de l'esprit* (Paris: Emile-Paul, 1929, rpt. Paris: Editions Persona, 1982).

11. Liane de Pougy, *Mes Cahiers bleus*, ed. R. P. Rzewuski (Paris: Plon, 1977), p. 284.

12. Woolf's views are outlined in *Three Guineas*, where she reads cultural politics through a variety of institutions—education, law, religion, the military, marriage, and patriarchy. Woolf was excoriated in the British press for arguing that feminism opposed Fascism and that patriarchal domestic politics were repressive in ways essential to Fascism. The domestic politics of right-wing lesbianism support Woolf's claims. See Shari Benstock, *Textualizing the Feminine: Essays on the Limits of Genre* (Norman: University of Oklahoma Project for Discourse and Theory, 1989), especially Chapter 4, "Figuring Feminism in *Three Guineas*."

13. Natalie Barney, "Memoirs of a European American," unpublished manuscript (Paris: Fonds Jacques Doucet, University of Paris).

14. Gertrude Stein, "The Winner Loses: A Picture of Occupied France," in *Selected Writings of Gertrude Stein*, ed. Carl Van Vechten (New York: Vintage, 1972), p. 632.

15. For Stein's writings on economics, see her five pieces about money in *The Saturday Evening Post*: "Money" (June 13, 1930), 208, p. 50; "More About Money" (July 11, 1936), 209, p.2; "Still More About Money" (July 25, 1936), 209, p. 4; "All About Money" (August 22, 1936), 209, 8 (p. 54); "My Last About Money" (October 1936), 209, 15, p. 78. No detailed work on Stein's economic beliefs has yet been done, but her monetary philosophy offers an important resource for understanding her political choices. For an

analysis of Barney's economic beliefs, see Natalie Barney, "Memoirs of a European American" and Benstock, *Women of the Left Bank*, pp. 413–18.

16. Virginia Woolf, *Three Guineas* (New York: Harcourt Brace Jovanovich, 1938), pp. 53–57.

17. Catharine R. Stimpson, "Gertrude Stein and the Transposition of Gender" in Nancy K. Miller, *The Poetics of Gender* (New York: Columbia University Press, 1986), p. 4.

18. I have quite purposely emphasized only one side of Stimpson's argument, Stein's repetition of the patriarchal position, although Stimpson's work outlines possible revisions of the masculine/feminine hierarchies in Stein's life and work. See also Catharine R. Stimpson, "The Mind, the Body, and Gertrude Stein," *Critical Inquiry* 3 (1977), pp. 491–506, and "Gertrice/Altrude" in *Mothering the Mind: Twelve Studies of Writers and Their Silent Partners*, ed. Ruth Perry and Martine Watson Brownley (New York and London: Holmes and Meier, 1984), pp. 123–39.

19. Alice B. Toklas, *What Is Remembered* (New York: Holt, Rinehart, 1963; rpt. San Francisco: North Point Press, 1985).

20. Stimpson, "Gertrude Stein," p. 8.

21. Stein, "A Picture of Occupied France," p. 637.

22. Barney, "Memoirs."

23. Michele Causse, ed., *Berthe ou un demi-siècle auprès de l'Amazone* (Paris: Editions Tierce, 1980), p. 145.

24. Harris, pp. 79–80.

25. Susan Stanford Friedman, "Modernism of the 'Scattered Remnant': Race and Politics in H.D.'s Development," in *Feminist Issues in Literary Scholarship*, ed. Shari Benstock (Bloomington: Indiana University Press, 1987), p. 227. See also Barbara Guest, *Herself Defined: The Poet H.D. and Her World* (New York: Doubleday, 1984).

Karlinsky, "Russia's Gay Literature and Culture: The Impact of the October Revolution"

1. The persistence of this misinformed view among many intelligent, well-read people can be exemplified by John Cheever's essay on Anton Chekhov, "The Melancholy of Distance," in James McConkey ed., *Chekhov and Our Age* (Ithaca, N.Y.: Cornell University, 1985). In it, Cheever claimed that Chekhov wrote fiction and plays because that "was all one could write without being sent to Siberia" (pp. 133–34). In reality, Chekhov published his powerful indictment of the conditions at the penal colony at Sakhalin, *The Island of Sakhalin*, in 1894, *without* securing the approval of the government censors and with no repercussions. Tolstoy's novel *Resurrection*, with its derogatory description of the tsarist system and its sympathetic portrayal of revolutionaries, was cleared for publication by the censors in 1899. These are only two out of hundreds of examples one could cite to show the absurdity of Wilde's and Cheever's perceptions of turn-of-the-century Russia.

2. Wilhelm Reich, in the second half of his *The Sexual Revolution*, examines sexual liberation in the Soviet Union, which Reich visited in 1929. (The book was first published in German as *Die Sexualität im Kulturkampf* in 1930. An expanded German version, with much new material on the Soviet situation, came in 1936. A translation into English, with the new title, *The*

Sexual Revolution, appeared in 1945. I've used a revised version of this translation, New York: Farrar, Straus and Giroux, 1969.)

Though critical of many measures adopted under Lenin and Stalin, Reich assumes throughout that no sexual rights existed in Russia prior to the October Revolution. Nor is the book particularly reliable on the situation of Russian homosexuals in 1917–1929. But Reich is highly informed about the period that followed 1929, after he had studied the conditions in the Soviet Union in person.

3. On the situation of male homosexuals in the Kievan (eleventh to thirteen centuries A.D.), the Muscovite (fourteenth to seventeenth centuries) and the modern periods of Russian history, see my survey "Russia's Gay Literature and History (11th–20th centuries)," *Gay Sunshine*, no. 29/30 (Summer/Fall 1976) (referred to hereafter as GS 76). Polemics about this piece and correction of errors, *Gay Sunshine*, no. 31 (Winter 1977). Updated translation into Italian: *Sodoma* no. 3, 1986.

In that 1976 survey I cited the book *Rerum moscovitarum commentarii* by Sigmund von Herberstein, who served as the ambassador of the Holy Roman Empire to Moscow early in the sixteenth century; and the poem "To Dancie" by the English poet George Turberville, who visited Moscow in 1568. Both of these authors reported, with shock and amazement, the prevalence of male homosexuality in all social classes in Russia at that time. GS 76 also quoted complaints about the impunity of homosexuality by such churchmen as the Metropolitan Daniel (his Sermon no. 12, dating from the 1530s) and the Archpriest Avvakum (in his *Autobiography*, 1673). Numerous other instances of testimony by foreign visitors and denunciations by Russian clergymen about the undisguised practice of "the sin of Sodom" in Muscovite Russia could be cited.

The Croatian Catholic priest Juraj Krizhanitch, who stayed in Russia from 1659 to 1677, described the Muscovite gay mores in his book *The Russian State in the Middle of the 17th Century* (cited from the Russian translation, *Russkoe gosudarstvo v polovine XVII veka*, Moscow, 1860. Chapter 2, pp. 17–18): "Here in Russia, this repulsive crime is treated simply as a joke. Nothing is more frequently discussed in humorous public conversations. One man brags of having committed this sin, another man reproaches someone about it, while a third man invites you to sin. The only thing lacking is for them to commit this crime in public." Summarizing the available testimony, Sergei Soloviov, the most authoritative Russian historian of the nineteenth century, concluded: "Nowhere, either in the Orient or in the West, was this vile, unnatural sin taken as lightly as in Russia" (S.M. Soloviov, *Istoriia Rossii*, 3rd ed. Saint Petersburg, 1910, p. 750). I am grateful to Alexander Poznansky for suggesting these last two examples and for additional information on legislation concerning homosexuality in Russia, cited in the following notes.

4. On the military regulation of 1706, see M. P. Rosenheim (or Rozengeim), *Ocherk istorii voenno-sudnykh uchrezhdenii v Rossii do konchiny Petra Velikogo* (Historical Survey of Institutions of Military Justice Up to the Demise of Peter the Great), Saint Petersburg, 1878, p. 299. On the military code of 1716, Vladimir Nabokoff, "Die Homosexualität in Russischen Strafgesetzbuch," *Jahrbuch für sexuelle Zwischenstufen*, Berlin, no. 5, 1903, p. 1160. On the applicability of these laws to military men only, S. I. Viktorsky, *Istoriia smertnoi kazni v Rossii i sovremennoe ee sostoianie* (A History of the Death Penalty in Russia and Its Present Status), Moscow, 1912, p. 145.

5. On Gogol's homosexuality, see my book *The Sexual Labyrinth of*

Nikolai Gogol (Cambridge, Mass.: Harvard University Press, 1976). The book also surveys the situation of Russian male homosexuals of the educated class during the first half of the nineteenth century. On the rarity and difficulty of enforcing Article 995 in the nineteenth century, see the article by Nabokoff (i.e., Vladimir Nabokov, Sr., the father of the novelist), cited in note 4 above.

6. On liberalization in the areas of free speech and press after the reforms of the 1860s and the Revolution of 1905, see Jacob Walkin, *The Rise of Democracy in Pre-Revolutionary Russia: Political and Social Institutions Under the Last Three Tsars* (New York: Frederick A. Prager, 1962). On the progress of women's rights in pre-revolutionary decades and on women's situation during the Soviet period, the most informed and least prejudiced book is Gail Warshovsky Lapidus, *Women in Soviet Society. Equality, Development, and Social Change* (Berkeley and Los Angeles: University of California Press, 1978). The first sentence of chapter 1 reads: "No discussion of the problem of sexual equality in Soviet society can take the Bolshevik revolution of 1917 as its starting point." Yet this has been the starting point for most Western studies of the sexual politics in the Soviet Union from the 1920s to our time.

7. On Nikolai Przhevalsky, see Donald Rayfield, *The Dream of Lhasa: The Life of Nikolai Przhevalsky, Explorer of Central Asia* (Ohio University Press, 1977). Also my reviews of this book, "Przhevalsky: The Russian Livingstone," *University Publishing*, no. 5 (Summer 1978); and "Gay Life Before the Soviets: Revisionism Revised," *The Advocate*, no. 339, April 1, 1982.

8. Konstantin Leontiev's novel *The Egyptian Dove* was published in a rather lame translation by George Reavey (Weybright and Talley, 1969). The publication of this novel in English brought forth two important essays on Leontiev: Clarence Brown, "Slightly to the Right of the Czar," *The New Republic*, April 17, 1969; and W. H. Auden, "A Russian Aesthete," *The New Yorker*, April 1970. In Russian, there is a full-scale critical biography: Yury Ivask, *Konstantin Leont'ev. Zhizn' i tvorchestvo* (Bern, Switzerland: Herbert Lang & Co., 1974).

9. On the relationship between Diaghilev and Filosofov and their role in the whole of Russian turn-of-the-century culture, see Vladimir Zlobin, *A Difficult Soul: Zinaida Gippius* (Berkeley and Los Angeles: University of California Press, 1980); also my essays "Sergei Diaghilev, Public and Private," *Christopher Street*, March 1980 (reprinted in *The Christopher Street Reader*, [New York: Coward-McCann, 1983]; "A Cultural Educator of Genius," in Nancy Van Norman Baer, ed., *The Art of Enchantment, Diaghilev's Ballets Russes, 1909–1929*, published by the M.H. de Young Memorial Museum in conjunction with their Diaghilev exhibit, 1988–89, San Francisco, pp. 14–25; and "Diaghilev," *International Encyclopedia of Dance*, Selma Jeanne Cohen, et al., eds. (Berkeley and Los Angeles: University of California Press, forthcoming).

10. Nina Berberova's account of Russian homosexuals in the 1890s is in "Préface à l'édition de 1987" to her book *Tchaïkovski* (Paris: Actes Sud, 1987).

11. For refutation of the renewed rumors about Tchaikovsky's forced suicide see Nina Berberova, Malcolm H. Brown, and Simon Karlinsky, "Tchaikovsky's Death Was *Not* a Suicide," *High Fidelity*, August 1981; and the same three authors' "Doubts About Tchaikovsky," *New York Times*, August 9, 1981. The most devastating critique of the suicide version is Alan M. Kriegsman, "The Great Suicide Debate," *Washington Post*, March 28,

1982. Nina Berberova's new introduction, cited above, the authoritative essay by the historian Alexander Poznansky, "Tchaikovsky's Suicide: Myth and Reality," in *19th Century Music*, volume 11, no. 3, Spring 1988 and Poznansky's forthcoming book on Tchaikovsky and the homosexuals of his time should lay to rest for good the untenable claims of the suicide theory proponents, including those of Tchaikovsky's biographer David Brown.

12. Aileen Kelly, "Self-Censorship and Russian Intelligentsia, 1905–1914," *Slavic Review*, 46, no. 2 (Summer 1987). The author does not restrict her purview to the period mentioned in the title, but traces and documents the negative attitudes toward all forms of sexuality among Russian radicals beginning with the 1860s.

13. On the negative view of homosexuality in the Russian revolutionary tradition at the end of the nineteenth and beginning of the twentieth centuries, see Alexander Berkman, *Prison Memoirs of an Anarchist* (reissued New York: Schocken Books, 1970).

14. V. I. Lenin, *Polnoe sobranie sochinenii* [Complete Collected Writings] (Moscow, 1958), 49, pp. 50–57, contains the cited correspondence with Inessa Armand. Lenin on sexual liberation: Clara Zetkin, *Reminiscences of Lenin* (New York: International Publishers 1934); the book was written ten years earlier.

15. For a biography of Mikhail Kuzmin, see John E. Malmstad, "Mixail Kuzmin: A Chronicle of His Life and Times" (in English) in vol. 3 of Kuzmin's collected poetry, *Sobranie stikhotvorenii* (in Russian), edited by Malmstad and Vladimir Markov (Munich: Wilhelm Fink Verlag, 1977). See also my review article on this collection, "Death and Resurrection of Mikhail Kuzmin," *Slavic Review*, 38, no. 1 (March 1978) and the section on Kuzmin in GS 76. A selection of Kuzmin's fiction, plays and poetry in English translation by Michael Green, *Selected Prose and Poetry*, was published by Ardis in 1980. An edition in Russian of Kuzmin's complete collected prose writings is being currently brought out by Berkeley Slavic Specialties, Berkeley, California, under the editorship of Valdimir Markov et al. Seven volumes have appeared so far.

16. The relationship between Nikolai Kliuev and Sergei Esenin is discussed in greater detail in GS 76. A volume of Kliuev's poetry in English, translated and with a preface by John Glad (Nikolai Klyuev, *Poems*) was published by Ardis in 1977. Of the recent biographies of Esenin in English, only Gordon McVay, *Isadora & Esenin*, Ardis, 1980, deals with this poet's bisexuality in detail, if a bit reluctantly. See also my review of Gordon McVay's earlier book, *Esenin, A Life* (Ardis, 1976), in *The New York Times Book Review*, May 9, 1976. A two-volume edition of Kliuev's writings, *Sochineniia* [Works], Gleb Struve and Boris Filippov, eds., was published by A. Neimanis, Munich, 1969. Of particular interest are Boris Filippov's biographical essay, which cites a number of publications on homosexual and bisexual practices in the religious rituals of such sects as the Khlysty, whose folklore Kliuev had incorporated into his poetry; and the British Esenin specialist Gordon McVay's selection of letters and other documents, obtained from secret Soviet archives, which illustrate Kliuev's love affairs with Esenin and other men. Filippov's and McVay's contributions are both in volume 1.

17. Maxim Gorky and Leonid Andreyev, *Neizdannaia perepiska* [Unpublished Correspondence], in the series *Literaturnoe nasled stvo* [Literary Heritage] (Moscow, 1965), 72; 288. I am grateful to Vladimir Kozlovsky for pointing out this correspondence in his book (see note 34). Alexei Achkasov, *Artsybashevskii Sanin: Okolo polovogo voprosa* [Artsybashev's *Sanin*: Concerning the Sexual Question] (Moscow: 1908) pp. 5–7 and 16–18.

18. A sympathetic account by a visiting foreigner of the reception in the Russian intellectual community of Kuzmin's, Zinovieva-Annibal's and Viacheslav Ivanov's books can be found in Werner Daya, "Die sexuelle Bewegung in Russland" [The Sexual Movement in Russia], *Zeitschrift für Sexualwissenschaft*, no. 1, Leipzig, 1908. I thank Siegfried Tornow of West Berlin for sending me his unpublished lecture "Homosexuality and Politics in Soviet Russia," from which I learned of Daya's article.

19. On Marina Tsvetaeva's life, writings and lesbianism, see my book *Marina Tsvetaeva, The Woman, Her World and Her Poetry* (Cambridge: Cambridge University Press, 1985). Her relationships with women are more fully documented in the second printing, 1987.

20. On Riurik Ivnev's gay pyro-masochism, see Gordon McVay, "Black and Gold: the Poetry of Riurik Ivnev," *Oxford Slavonic Papers*, New Series, vol. IV (Oxford: Clarendon Press, 1971).

21. The most complete and reliable account of human rights in Russia before, during and after the February and October revolutions is Mikhail Heller and Alexander Nekrich, *Utopia in Power: The History of the Soviet Union From 1917 to the Present* (New York: Simon & Schuster, Summit Books, 1986).

22. Christopher Isherwood, *Christopher and His Kind*, Farrar, Straus & Giroux, 1976, pp. 17–18.

23. John Lauritsen and David Thorstad, *The Early Homosexual Rights Movement (1864–1935)* (New York: Times Change Press, 1974). The book is a good source on the early homosexual movements in Germany and England. But the section on Russia (pp. 62–70) is deplorably biased and uninformed. The authors follow Wilhelm Reich in the assumption that no liberation of any kind was possible in Russia prior to the October Revolution. They cite Mikhail Kuzmin's 1920 volume of gay verse, *Veiled Pictures*, as something that became possible only under the Bolshevik rule. They quote five lines from Mark Sereisky's article on homosexuality in the 1930 edition of the Great Soviet Encyclopedia about the impunity of male homosexuality in the Soviet Union, but do not note that the context surrounding these lines describes the condition as a serious mental illness in urgent need of a cure.

The main exhibit in their case for the Bolsheviks' enlightened views of homosexuality is a rather mysterious brochure by Dr. Grigory Batkis, *Die Sexualrevolution in Russland*, published in Berlin in 1925. It is claimed in the German edition that the work was first published in the USSR in Russian in 1923. But while the German edition is available at some libraries, no researcher has been able to find a copy in Russian, either in the Soviet Union or abroad. As Wayne R. Dynes points out in his *Homosexuality. A Research Guide* (New York: Garland, 1987), p. 141, the Batkis brochure was printed "for foreign consumption" and never appeared in the USSR.

24. Professor Berberova said this when I visited her at her home in Princeton in 1977. I showed her Isherwood's statement as well as John Lauritsen's and David Thorstad's book and their rebuttal to my 1976 survey article (GS 76).

25. Valery Chalidze, *Criminal Russia. Essays on Crime in the Soviet Union*, translated from the Russian by P. S. Falla (New York: Random House, 1977), pp. 143–144.

26. I. Gel'man, *Polovaia zhizn' sovremennoi molodezhi. Opyt sotsial'no-biologicheskogo obsledovaniia* [Sexual Life of Contemporary Youth. An Essay in Sociological and Biological Investigation] (Moscow and Petrograd: State Publishing House, 1923).

27. M. Sereisky, "Gomoseksualizm," in *Bol'shaia meditsinskaia entsik-*

lopediia [The Great Medical Encyclopedia], P.A. Semashko, ed. (Moscow, 1929), vol. 77, 1929, columns 668–72. This article was reprinted in an abridged form in the first edition of *The Great Soviet Encyclopedia*, 1930.

28. Nikolai Kliuev, "Chetvertyi Rim" [The Fourth Rome], *Sochineniia* 2: 229–303. For an English translation of the beginning of this poem (with some vexing misprints) see GS 76.

29. Lev (Leon) Trotsky, *Literatura i revoliutsiia* [Literature and Revolution] (Moscow: Glavlit, 1923), p. 47. The passage on Kliuev and Esenin is cited in my own translation from the original Russian edition, rather than from the available English translation (Ann Arbor: University of Michigan Press, 1960), where this passage is on p. 65.

30. Only in the 1970s, when the Soviet scholar Sophia Poliakova prepared the complete collection of Parnok's poetry, wrote her biography and sent them to be published in the West, did this major lesbian poet achieve posthumously the acclaim that was her due. See Sophia Parnok, *Sobranie stikhotvorenii* [Collected Poems], S. Poliakova, ed. (Ann Arbor: Ardis, 1979). The introductory essay by Poliakova is a biography of Parnok and a study of her poetry. Poliakova has also published a book about the love affair between Parnok and Marina Tsvetaeva in 1914–1916 and its reflection in their writings, *Zakatnye ony dni* [The Sunset Days of Yore] (Ann Arbor: Ardis, 1983). The affair of Tsvetaeva with Parnok is described in chapter 3, "Two Rival Suns," in Karlinsky, *Marina Tsvetaeva*. See also Rima Shore, "Remembering Sophia Parnok (1885–1933)," *Conditions: Six*, 1980.

31. On Georgy Chicherin's homosexuality, see Malmstad, "Mixail Kuzmin," pp. 24–25 and notes 28 and 29 to chapter 1. The biographies of Chicherin in the various editions of *The Great Soviet Encyclopedia* always mention his sojourn in Germany in search of a cure for an unspecified illness. A note to Alexander Meyendorff's memoir "My Cousin, Foreign Commissar Chicherin," *Russian Review*, April 1971, explains that references to Chicherin's poor health or health problems were euphemisms for his homosexuality.

32. Marie Seton, *Sergei M. Eisenstein*, revised ed. (London: Dennis Dobson, 1978), p. 119. (Originally published in 1952 by The Bodley Head.) Other passages in Seton's book that deal with Eisenstein's homosexuality are on pp. 30, 48–49, 73, 133–34, 139, 231–32, 279, and 426 ff.

33. Some of the other sources on Sergei Eisenstein's homosexuality are Stan Brakhage, *Film Biographies* (Berkeley: Turtle Island, 1977), pp. 98–99, where Kenneth Rexroth reports a conversation with Eisenstein in which the director admitted that he was forced to return to the Soviet Union by a threat to expose his sex life; Thomas Waugh, "A Fag-Spotter's Guide to Eisenstein," *Body Politic*, no. 35, July/August 1977, an excellent demonstration of homoerotic imagery in Eisenstein's films (I thank Tom Waugh for providing me with the texts of the last two items); and Jerry Heil, *The Russian Literary Avant-Garde (1920s and 1930s)* (doctoral dissertation, University of California, Berkeley, 1984), pp. 130–31 and 168–69. On the role of the American pro-Communist writer Upton Sinclair in cutting off the funds for Eisenstein's Mexican film project and denouncing him to Stalin when Sinclair found out about the director's sex life, see Edmund Wilson, "Eisenstein in Hollywood," in Wilson, *The American Earthquake* (New York: Doubleday, 1958) pp. 367–413.

34. The text of Article 121 is cited on p. 155 of Vladimir Kozlovsky, *Argo russkoi gomoseksual'noi subkul'tury* [The Slang of Russian Homosexual Subculture] (Benson, Vt.: Chalidze Publications, 1986). The book is a cornucopia of information about the situation of lesbians and gay men in Russian and Soviet culture.

35. Maxim Gorky, *Sobranie sochinenii v 30 tomakh* [Collected Writings in 30 volumes] (Moscow: 1953), 27: 238. This essay appeared in both *Pravda* and *Izvestiia* on May 23, 1934.

36. Reich, *The Sexual Revolution*, pp. 209–210; Chalidze, *Ugolovnaia Rossiia* (the Russian edition of his *Criminal Russia*) (New York, 1977), pp. 227–28, cites instances of homosexual activities viewed as political crimes by the Soviet judiciary authorities. This attitude is confirmed by the speech of Nikolai Krylenko (see note 37).

Other sources on the wave of arrests of Soviet homosexuals in 1934 are Philip Jason, "Progress to Barbarism," *Mattachine Review*, August 1957 (an interview with a witness of those events); and Boris Nikolaevsky, *Power and Soviet Elite*, Janet D. Zagoria, ed. (New York, 1965), p. 31.

37. A transcript of Krylenko's speech was published in *Sovietskaia iustitsiia* [Soviet Law] (Moscow, 1936), no. 7. It is cited in Kozlovsky, *Argo russkoi*, p. 154.

38. My own contacts with Soviet gay men in Germany are described in "Gay Life in the Age of Two Josephs: McCarthy and Stalin" (a review of John D'Emilio's book *Sexual Politics, Sexual Communities*, couched in the form of a personal memoir), *The Advocate*, no. 366, April 28, 1983.

39. "G." (pen name of an American scholar and critic), "The Secret Life of Moscow," *Christopher Street*, June 1980.

40. George Schuvaloff (pen name of a Soviet writer who recently died in New York), "Gay Life in Russia," *Christopher Street*, September 1976.

41. Kozlovsky, *Argo russkoi*, pp. 156–59, cites three instances from memoirs published in the West in 1975, 1979, and 1982 where heterosexual KGB agents were compelled by their superiors to engage in gay sex in order to entrap foreign visitors for purposes of espionage.

42. On Kharitonov, see Kozlovsky, *Argo russkoi*, pp. 185–186. On pp. 193–95, Kozlovsky reproduces Kharitonov's prose fragment "A Leaflet" (Listovka), a sort of manifesto for gay rights and an examination of Soviet society's hostility to homosexuals.

43. See my article "The Soviet Union vs. Gennady Trifonov," *The Advocate*, August 19, 1986. Since some of his work is now publishable, Trifonov has given up his fight for an exit visa (a fight in which he was engaged during the last two decades) and chosen to stay in the Soviet Union.

44. Limonov's *It's Me, Eddie* was published in Russian by Index Publishers, New York, 1979. The English translation by S. I. Campbell was brought out by Random House, New York, 1983. On Limonov's subsequent novels, see Edward J. Brown, "Eddie-Baby on the Town," *The Nation*, September 26, 1987.

45. Lesbians in gulag camps are mentioned in the second volume of Eugenia Ginsburg's memoirs, published in English as a separate book, *Within the Whirlwind*, trans. Ian Boland (New York: Harcourt Brace Jovanovich, 1981). Kozlovsky cites extensive passages from *Moi vospominaniia* [My Memoirs] by E. Olitskaya, vol. 2 (Frankfurt, 1971), about lesbian customs in the Soviet labor camps as well as several other authors of memoirs and fiction on this theme on pp. 111–17 of his book.

46. On lesbian themes and experience described by Soviet feminist writers see Tatiana Mamonova, ed., *Women and Russia: Feminist Writings from the Soviet Union* (Boston: Beacon Press, 1984); and Julia Voznesenskaya, *The Women's Decameron*, translated by W. B. Linton (Boston: Atlantic Monthly Press, 1986).

47. Viktor Sosnora, *Letuchii gollandets* [The Flying Dutchman], (Frankfurt/Main; Posev, 1979), pp. 211–213.

48. Mikhail Shargorodsky and Pavel Osipov, *Kurs sovetskogo ugolovnogo prava* [Textbook of Soviet Criminal Law], vol. 3, (Leningrad, 1973). Quoted in Kozlovsky, *Argo russkoi*, pp. 163–64 and Tornow, "Homosexuality and Politics."

49. Venedikt Erofeev (pen name), *Moskva-Petushki*, Ami (Israel), no.3, 1973. English translation as *Moscow to the End of the Line*, 1980. Cited in Kozlovsky, *Argo russkoi*, p. 6.

Haeberle, "Swastika, Pink Triangle, and Yellow Star"

Note: All quotes, except those from Hirschfeld, Hodann, and Lenz, were translated from the German for this essay by the author.

1. Magnus Hirschfeld, "Autobiographical Sketch," *Encyclopaedia Sexualis*, ed. Victor Robinson (New York, 1936), pp. 317–21.

2. Max Hodann, *History of Modern Morals* (London, 1937), pp. 49 f.

3. Hirschfeld, "Autobiographical Sketch."

4. Albert Moll, "Der 'reaktionäre' Kongress für Sexualforschung" in *Zeitschrift für Sexualwissenschaft* 13, no. 10 (January 1927): 322 f.

5. Moll published these comments in his *Reminiscences* of 1936. See John Money and Herman Musaph, eds. *Handbook of Sexology* (New York, 1977), pp. 24–27.

6. Hirschfeld, "Autobiographical Sketch."

7. Ludwig, L. Lenz, *The Memoirs of a Sexologist* (New York, 1954), pp. 429 ff.

8. Iwan Bloch first proposed the concept of *Sexualwissenschaft* or sexology in his book *The Sexual Life of Our Time* (1907). Hirschfeld, Rohleder, and Krauss edited the first sexological journal, the *Zeitschrift für Sexualwissenschaft* (1908). Hirschfeld, Bloch, Eulenburg, and Körber founded the first sexological society, the *Ärztliche Gesellschaft für Sexualwissenschaft* (1913).

9. Alfred Rosenberg, *Der Mythos des XX. Jahrhunderts* (München, 1930), p. 512.

10. Engelbert Huber, *Das ist Nationalsozialismus* (Stuttgart, 1933), pp. 121 f.

11. Eugen Kogon, *Der SS-Staat* (Frankfurt/Main, 1946). Engl. transl. *The Theory and Practice of Hell* (New York, 1950).

12. Martin Sherman, *Bent* (New York, 1979). First performance at O'Neill Theater Center, Waterford, Conn. 1977.

13. Rüdiger Lautmann, ed. *Seminar: Gesellschaft und Homosexualität* (Frankfurt/Main, 1977).

14. Reprinted in Rudolf Klare, *Homosexualität und Strafrecht* (Hamburg, 1937), p. 149.

15. See for example Kogon, *Der SS-Staat*, Martin Broszat, "Nationalsozialistische Konzentrationslager 1933–1945" in Buchheim Hans et al., *Anatomie des SS-Staates* (Olten, 1965), vol.2.

16. The records of this agency, which was established on October 10, 1936, are now in the German Democratic Republic (East Germany) and, so far, have not been available to researchers.

17. On October 29, 1937, Himmler gave a special order not to bother homosexual artists and actors, unless caught *in flagranti*. Otherwise special permission for an arrest was required. See also Lautmann, *Seminar*, p. 330.

18. Ibid., p. 333.

19. See Kogon, *Der SS-Staat*, p. 50 and Lautmann, *Seminar*, pp. 325–65.
20. Kogon, *op. cit.* p. 46 and pp. 50 f.
21. Kogon, *op. cit.* p. 263.
22. Kogon, *op. cit.* p. 264.
23. Another important exception is the work of the historian Vern L. Bullough, *Sexual Variance in Society and History* (New York: 1976).
24. *Immigration and Nationality Act of 1952*, par. 212 (a) (4), 8 U.S.C., par. 1182 (a) (4), 1964; popularly known as the McCarran Act.
25. *Boutilier v. Immigration and Naturalization Service*, 387 U.S. 118, 1967. Boutilier, a Canadian national, who had lived in the United States for twelve years, and whose mother, stepfather, and three sisters also lived in the United States, was denied citizenship and deported solely because of his homosexuality, although he had never been convicted of illegal homosexual behavior.

Bérubé, "Marching to a Different Drummer"

This article was originally published in the *Advocate*, October 15, 1981, and is based on the script of the author's slide/lecture, "Marching to a Different Drummer." The author wishes to thank the following people for their assistance and support in developing the script for this slide/lecture: Jonathan Katz, John D'Emilio, JoAnn Castillo, and others doing lesbian and gay history research; the members of the San Francisco Lesbian and Gay History Project; the women and men who agreed to be interviewed about their World War II experiences; the women and men who sponsored showings of the presentation in their homes to raise funds for initial research expenses; and many others whose names cannot be included here.

1. Department of Defense Directive 1332.14 (Encl. 3), Enlisted Administrative Separations, January 28, 1982, Section H, pp. 1–9 to 1–13.
2. Report, "Investigations of Conditions in the 3d WAC Training Center, Fort Oglethorpe, Georgia," July 19, 1944, p. 25, File 333.9, Record Group No. 159, National Archives.
3. Author's interview with Stuart Loomis, March 25, 1980, San Francisco.
4. "An Interview With Lisa Ben," Leland Moss, *Gaysweek*, January 23, 1978, pp. 14–16.
5. William C. Menninger, *Psychiatry in a Troubled World* (New York: Macmillan, 1948), p. 106.
6. "Sex Hygiene Course, Officers and Officer Candidates, Women's Army Auxiliary Corps," May 27, 1943, War Department Pamphlet No. 35–1, "Lecture I: Introduction," pp. 3–4, and "Lecture V: Homosexuality," pp. 24–29.
7. Interview with "Sami" (a pseudonym) by JoAnn Castillo, San Francisco Lesbian and Gay History Project.
8. WAAC "Sex Hygiene Course," pp. 28–29.
9. Report, Fort Oglethorpe investigation, pp. 1, 29–30. For a comparison between World War II and postwar military policies toward lesbians, see Allan Bérubé and John D'Emilio, "The Military and Lesbians during the McCarthy Years," *Signs: Journal of Women in Culture and Society* 9, no. 4 (Summer 1984): 759–75; reprinted in *The Lesbian Issue: Essays from Signs*, edited by Estelle B. Freedman, Barbara C. Gelpi, Susan L. Johnson, and Kathleen M. Weston (Chicago, University of Chicago Press, 1985), pp. 279–95.

10. Author's interview with Bob Ruffing, May 14, 1980, San Francisco.

11. "Homosexuals in Uniform," *Newsweek*, June 9, 1947, p. 54. The estimate of one million gay servicemen equals 6.25 percent of the sixteen million men who served in World War II. Alfred Kinsey's study, which was in part conducted during the war, concluded that 4 percent of white males in the United States were exclusively homosexual after adolescence and that 8 percent were exclusively homosexual for at least three years between the ages of sixteen and fifty-five. Alfred C. Kinsey, Wardell B. Pomeroy, Clyde E. Martin, *Sexual Behavior in the Human Male* (Philadelphia: W. B. Saunders, 1948), pp. 650–51.

12. Irving L. Janis, "Psychodynamic Aspects of Adjustment to Army Life," *Psychiatry* 8 (May 1945): 170–71.

13. Author's interview with Bob Ruffing.

14. Author's interview with Ben Small, July 22, 1980, San Francisco.

15. Lewis H. Loeser, "The Sexual Psychopath in the Military Service," *American Journal of Psychiatry* 102 (July 1945): 92–101.

16. Nicolai Gioscia, "The Gag Reflex and Fellatio," *American Journal of Psychiatry* 107 (November 1950): 380.

17. Author's interview with [anonymous], May 28, 1980, San Francisco.

18. Letters from "Marty" to "Howard" (pseudonyms), January 30 and 31, 1945, in collection of the author.

19. On the local and state campaigns against lesbian and gay bars in the San Francisco Bay Area during the 1950s and 1960s, see " 'Resorts for Sex Perverts,' " a slide/lecture by Allan Bérubé.

20. Author's interview with [anonymous], May 28, 1980, San Francisco.

21. Interview with "Sami" by JoAnn Castillo.

22. *Word Is Out: Stories of Some of Our Lives*, edited by Nancy Adair and Casey Adair (San Francisco: New Glide Publications/A Delta Special, 1978), pp. 60–61.

23. See, for example, 1951 correspondence between lesbian WAAFs and the American Civil Liberties Union in Bérubé and D'Emilio, "The Military and Lesbians During the McCarthy Years."

24. Letter from "Dan" to "Howard" (pseudonyms), December 17, 1945, in collection of author.

Rupp, "Imagine My Surprise"

Holly Near's song, "Imagine My Surprise," celebrates the discovery of women's relationships in the past. The song is recorded on the album, *Imagine My Surprise*, Redwood Records. I am grateful to Holly Near and Redwood Records for their permission to use the title here.

This is a revised version of an article originally published in *Frontiers: A Journal of Women Studies* 5 (Fall 1980). The original research was made possible by a fellowship from the Radcliffe Research Scholars Program. Additional research, funded by the National Endowment for the Humanities, was undertaken jointly with Verta Taylor for our book, *Survival in the Doldrums: The American Women's Rights Movement* (1987).

1. Carroll Smith-Rosenberg, "The Female World of Love and Ritual: Relations between Women in Nineteenth Century America," *Signs* 1 (1975): 1–29.

2. Adrienne Rich, "Compulsory Heterosexuality and Lesbian Existence," *Signs* 5 (1980): 631–60. See also Ann Ferguson, Jacquelyn N. Zita, and

Kathryn Pyne Addelson, "On Compulsory Heterosexuality and Lesbian Existence: Defining the Issues," *Signs* 7 (1981): 158–99.

3. Lillian Faderman, *Surpassing the Love of Men: Romantic Friendship and Love between Women from the Renaissance to the Present* (New York: William Morrow, 1981). See also Faderman's *Scotch Verdict* (New York: Quill, 1983), a compelling re-creation of the trial of two Edinburgh schoolteachers accused of having sex together (the model for Lillian Hellman's *The Children's Hour*). Faderman argues against a sexual component in the two women's relationship, suggesting that "for many women, what *ought* to be, in fact *was*" (p. 126).

For examples of reviews that discussed the controversial nature of Faderman's argument, see the Muriel Haynes's review of *Surpassing the Love of Men* in *Ms.* 9 (June 1981): 36; and reviews of *Scotch Verdict* by Karla Jay in *Women's Review of Books* 1 (December 1983): 9–10 and by Terry Castle in *Signs* 9 (1984): 717–20.

4. Blanche Wiesen Cook, "The Historical Denial of Lesbianism," *Radical History Review* 20 (1979): 60–65; Doris Faber, *The Life of Lorena Hickok: E. R.'s Friend* (New York: William Morrow, 1980).

5. Edward Sigall, "Eleanor Roosevelt's Secret Romance—the Untold Story," *National Enquirer*, November 13, 1979, pp. 20–21.

6. Anna Mary Wells, *Miss Marks and Miss Woolley* (Boston: Houghton Mifflin, 1978); Faber, *Lorena Hickok*, p. 354. Cook, "Historical Denial," is a review of the Wells book.

7. Marjorie Housepian Dobkin, *The Making of a Feminist: Early Journals and Letters of M. Carey Thomas* (Kent, Ohio: Kent State University Press, 1980).

8. *The New York Times*, August 21, 1976, p. 22.

9. Arthur Schlesinger, Jr., "Interesting Women," *The New York Times Book Review*, February 17, 1980, p. 31.

10. Cook, review of *The Life of Lorena Hickok*, *Feminist Studies* 6 (1980): 511–16.

11. Cook, "Female Support Networks and Political Activism: Lillian Wald, Crystal Eastman and Emma Goldman," *Chrysalis* 3 (1977): 48.

12. In a review of books on Frances Willard, Alice Paul, and Carrie Chapman Catt, Gerda Lerner criticized the denial of sexuality in relationships in which women shared their lives "in the manner of married couples." In an attempt to bridge the two approaches, Lerner suggested that perhaps Paul, Willard, Catt, along with Susan B. Anthony, Anna Dickinson, and Jane Addams, were "simply what Victorian 'lesbians' looked like." Gerda Lerner, "Where Biographers Fear to Tread," *Women's Review of Books* 11 (September 1987): 11–12.

13. On the significance of class, see Myriam Everard, "Lesbian History: A History of Change and Disparity," *Journal of Homosexuality* 12 (1986): 123–37 and "Lesbianism and Medical Practice in the Netherlands, 1897–1930," paper presented at the Berkshire Conference of Women Historians, Wellesley, Massachusetts, 1987. Not all the lesbian communities we know of prior to the 1950s were working class, however. There were middle- and upper-class communities in Europe and, to a lesser extent, among American bohemians at the turn of the century. On "crossing" women, see Jonathan Katz, *Gay American History* (New York: Thomas Y. Crowell, 1976), and *Gay/Lesbian Almanac* (New York: Harper and Row, 1983). On the emergence of a lesbian community, see Madeline Davis and Elizabeth Lapovsky Kennedy, "Oral History and the Study of Sexuality in the Lesbian Community: Buffalo, New York, 1940–1960," in this volume; Joan Nestle, "Butch-

Fem Relationships: Sexual Courage in the 1950's," *Heresies: The Sex Issue* 12 (1981): 21–24; Allan Bérubé, "Coming Out Under Fire," *Mother Jones* (February/March 1983): 23–45; and John D'Emilio, *Sexual Politics, Sexual Communities: The Making of a Homosexual Minority in the U.S. 1940–1970* (Chicago: University of Chicago Press, 1983).

On the "discovery of lesbianism," see Nancy Sahli, "Smashing: Women's Relationships Before the Fall," *Chrysalis* 8 (1979): 17–27; George Chauncey, Jr., "From Sexual Inversion to Homosexuality: Medicine and the Changing Conceptualization of Female Deviance," *Salmagundi* 58/59 (Fall 1982/Winter 1983): 114–46; Christina Simmons, "Women's Sexual Consciousness and Lesbian Identity, 1900–1940" (paper presented at the Berkshire Conference of Women Historians, Northhampton, Massachusetts, 1984); Esther Newton, "The Mythic Mannish Lesbian: Radclyffe Hall and the New Woman," in this volume.

14. See Leila J. Rupp and Verta Taylor, *Survival in the Doldrums: The American Women's Rights Movement, 1945 to the 1960s* (New York: Oxford University Press, 1987).

15. Wells, *Miss Marks and Miss Woolley*, p. 56.

16. Caroline Babcock to Jeannette Marks, February 12, 1947, Babcock papers, box 8 (105), Schlesinger Library, Radcliffe College, Cambridge, Massachusetts. I am grateful to the Schlesinger Library for permission to use the material quoted here.

17. "The Unfinished Autobiography of Lena Madesin Phillips," Phillips papers, Schlesinger Library.

18. "Chronological Records of Events and Activities for the Biography of Lena Madesin Phillips, 1881–1955," Phillips papers, Schlesinger Library.

19. "Chronological Records of Events and Activities for the Biography of Lena Madesin Phillips, 1881–1955," Phillips papers, Schlesinger Library.

20. Lena Madesin Phillips to Audrey Turner, January 21, 1948, Phillips papers, Schlesinger Library; Phillips to Olivia Rossetti Agresti, April 26, 1948, Phillips papers, Schlesinger Library.

21. Robert Heller to Phillips, September 26, 1948, Phillips papers, Schlesinger Library.

22. Phillips to Mary C. Kennedy, August 20, 1948, Phillips papers, Schlesinger Library.

23. Phillips to Gordon Holmes, March 28, 1949, Phillips papers, Schlesinger Library.

24. Phillips to [Ida Spitz], November 13, 1950, Phillips papers, Schlesinger Library.

25. Holmes to Madesin & Maggie, December 15, 1948, Phillips papers, Schlesinger Library.

26. Phillips to Holmes, March 28, 1949, Phillips papers, Schlesinger Library.

27. "Chronological Record of Events and Activities for the Biography of Lena Madesin Phillips, 1881–1955," Phillips papers, Schlesinger Library.

28. Alma Lutz to Florence Kitchelt, July 1, 1948, Kitchelt papers, box 6 (177), Schlesinger Library.

29. Lutz to Kitchelt, July 29, 1959, Kitchelt papers, box 7 (178), Schlesinger Library.

30. Lutz to Florence Armstrong, August 26, 1959, Armstrong papers, box 1 (17), Schlesinger Library.

31. Lutz to Rose Arnold Powell, December 14, 1959, Powell papers, box 3 (43), Schlesinger Library.

32. Mabel Vernon, "Speaker for Suffrage and Petitioner for Peace," an

oral history conducted in 1972 and 1973 by Amelia R. Fry, Regional Oral History Office, University of California, 1976. Courtesy, the Bancroft Library.

33. Press release from Mabel Vernon Memorial Committee, Vernon, "Speaker for Suffrage"; obituary in the *Wilmington Morning News*, September 3, 1975, Vernon, "Speaker for Suffrage."

34. Alice Morgan Wright to Anita Pollitzer, July 9, 1946, National Woman's Party papers, reel 89. The National Woman's Party papers have been microfilmed and are distributed by the Microfilming Corporation of America. I am grateful to the National Woman's Party for permission to quote the material used here.

35. Alice Paul, "Conversations with Alice Paul: Woman Suffrage and the Equal Rights Amendment," an oral history conducted in 1972 and 1973 by Amelia R. Fry, Regional Oral History Office, University of California, 1976, p. 614. Courtesy, the Bancroft Library. Nora Stanton Barney to Alice Paul, n.d. [received May 10, 1945], National Woman's Party papers, reel 86.

36. Wright to Pollitzer, n.d. [July 1946], National Woman's Party papers, reel 89.

37. Agnes Wells to Pollitzer, August 24, 1946, National Woman's Party papers, reel 89.

38. Paul to Dorothy Griswold, February 2, 1955, National Woman's Party papers, reel 101.

39. Lavinia Dock to Paul, May 9, 1945, National Woman's Party papers, reel 86.

40. See, for example, Susan D. Becker, *The Origins of the Equal Rights Amendment: American Feminism Between the Wars* (Westport, Conn.: Greenwood Press, 1981), and Christine A. Lunardini, *From Equal Suffrage to Equal Rights: Alice Paul and the National Woman's Party, 1910–1928* (New York: New York University Press, 1986).

41. Vernon, "Speaker for Suffrage."

42. Paul, "Conversations," p. 197.

43. Jeannette Marks to Paul, March 25, 1945, National Woman's Party papers, reel 85; Marks to Paul, March 30, 1945, National Woman's Party papers, reel 85; Marks to Paul, April 27, 1945, National Woman's Party papers, reel 85.

44. Nina Allender to Paul, January 5, 1947, National Woman's Party papers, reel 90.

45. Paul to Allender, March 9, 1950, National Woman's Party papers, reel 96.

46. Paul to Allender, November 20, 1954, National Woman's Party papers, reel 100; Kay Boyle to Paul, December 5, 1954, National Woman's Party papers, reel 100; Paul to Nina, December 6, 1954, National Woman's Party papers, reel 100.

47. Boyle to Paul, February 13, 1957, National Woman's Party papers, reel 103; Paul to Boyle, March 5, 1957, National Woman's Party papers, reel 103.

48. See Leila J. Rupp, "The Women's Community in the National Woman's Party, 1945 to the 1960s," *Signs* 10 (1985): 715–40.

49. Letter to Anna Lord Strauss, December 22, 1945, Strauss papers, box 6 (118), Schlesinger Library. Because of the possibly sensitive nature of the material reported here, I am not using the names of the women involved.

50. Letter to Strauss, September 19, 1946, Strauss papers, box 6 (119), Schlesinger Library.

51. Letter to Strauss, May 9, 1947, Strauss papers, box 6 (121), Schlesinger Library.

52. Letter to Strauss, June 28, 1948, Strauss papers, box 6 (124), Schlesinger Library.

53. Letter to Strauss, February 26, 1951, Strauss papers, box 1 (15), Schlesinger Library.

54. Letter to Strauss, December 22, 1945, Strauss papers, box 6 (118), Schlesinger Library.

55. Letter to Strauss, May 9, 1947, Strauss papers, box 6 (121), Schlesinger Library.

56. "Stream of consciousness," March 10, 1948, Strauss papers, box 6 (124), Schlesinger Library.

57. Augusta Street to Strauss, n.d. [1968], Strauss papers, box 7 (135), Schlesinger Library.

58. Letter to Strauss, February 11, 1949, Strauss papers, box 6 (125), Schlesinger Library.

59. Letter to Strauss, March 3, 1949, Strauss papers, box 6 (125), Schlesinger Library.

60. Letter to Strauss, March 8, 1968, Strauss papers, box 7 (135), Schlesinger Library.

61. Lilian Lyndon to Strauss, April 23, 1950, Strauss papers, box 1 (14), Schlesinger Library.

62. Diary entries, August 30, 1953 and September 1, 1953, Doris Stevens papers, Schlesinger Library.

63. Diary entry, August 24, 1953, Doris Stevens papers, Schlesinger Library.

64. Diary entry, February 4, 1946, Doris Stevens papers, Schlesinger Library.

65. Diary entry, December 1, 1945, Doris Stevens papers, Schlesinger Library.

66. Katharine Callery to Stevens, Aug. 17, 1944, Stevens papers, Schlesinger Library.

67. Stevens to Westbrook Pegler, May 3, 1946, Stevens papers, Schlesinger Library.

68. See Margaret Jackson, "Sexual Liberation or Social Control? Some Aspects of the Relationship between Feminism and the Social Construction of Sexual Knowledge in the Early Twentieth Century," *Women's Studies International Forum* 6 (1983): 1–17; Carroll Smith-Rosenberg, "Discourses of Sexuality and Subjectivity: The New Woman, 1870–1936," in this volume; and John D'Emilio, "The Homosexual Menace: The Politics of Sexuality in Cold War America," unpublished paper presented at the Organization of American Historians Conference, Philadelphia, 1982.

69. India Edwards, *Pulling No Punches* (New York: Putnam's 1977), pp. 189–90.

70. Interviews by Leila J. Rupp and Verta Taylor; see Rupp and Taylor, *Survival in the Doldrums*.

71. Paul, "Conversations," pp. 195–96.

72. Interview conducted by Taylor and Rupp, December 10, 1979.

73. Sasha Gregory Lewis, *Sunday's Women: A Report on Lesbian Life Today* (Boston: Beacon Press, 1979), p. 94.

74. See, for example, the discussion in Judith C. Brown, *Immodest Acts: The Life of a Lesbian Nun in Renaissance Italy* (New York: Oxford University Press, 1986), pp. 171–73.

75.. Nestle, "Butch-Fem Relationships."

76. Much of the literature on lesbianism emphasizes this crucial distinction between identity and experience. See, for example, Barbara Ponse,

Identities in the Lesbian World: The Social Construction of Self (Westport, Conn.: Greenwood Press, 1978); and E. M. Ettore, *Lesbians, Women and Society* (London: Routledge & Kegan Paul, 1980).

77. Cook, "Historical Denial," p. 64.

78. The Mount Holyoke administration closed the Marks-Woolley papers when Wells discovered the love letters, and the papers are only open to researchers now because an American Historical Association committee, which included Blanche Cook as one of its members, applied pressure to keep the papers open after Wells, to her credit, contacted them. Faber describes her unsuccessful attempts to persuade the archivists at the FDR Library to close the Lorena Hickok papers.

79. Linda Gordon, "What Should Women's Historians Do: Politics, Social Theory, and Women's History," *Marxist Perspectives* 3 (1978), 128–36.

Moodie, "Migrancy and Male Sexuality"

For support for the research upon which this paper is based I must thank primarily Hobart and William Smith Colleges. Besides the theological students of the AIM projects and participant observers in the 1976 Mine Study and 1983 Thabong Study, three persons were crucial in bringing me to this topic: George Chauncey, Jr., who had questions I could not answer while at the Yale-Wesleyan Southern African Research Program in 1979–1980; Meredith Aldrich, my wife, who kept those questions alive for me; and Vivienne Ndatshe, who went out into Pondoland to find some answers with remarkable results. Finally, Patrick Harries' generosity made possible the inclusion of British Sibuyi's extraordinary interview with Philemon. Earlier versions of this paper were presented at the Yale-Wesleyan Southern African Research Program, the Wits History Workshop, and Queen Elizabeth House in Oxford, where I benefitted from helpful discussion.

1. Michel Foucault, *The History of Sexuality* (New York, 1978), vol. 1.

2. Vivienne Ndatshe was trained as a research assistant by my wife, Meredith Aldrich, for her work in Grahamstown. Ms. Ndatshe is an ex-teacher now working as a domestic servant in Durban. She grew up in the Lusikisiki district of the Transkei whence her father migrated to work on the mines, and she offered to collect life histories for me at her home. Her interviews with Mpondo ex-miners in August 1982 turned up much of the material that made this paper possible. Copies of her field notes on the Mpondo interviews are housed at the African Studies Institute at the University of the Witwatersrand. In October 1984, I visited Pondoland with her to conduct follow-up interviews on aspects of the life histories that dealt with collective resistance on the mines. Tapes of those interviews are also at the African Studies Institute but they contain little of relevance to this paper. I did, however, meet several of the men cited herein.

3. British Sibuyi is a student in history at the University of Cape Town. I was kindly sent a transcript of his interview by Patrick Harries.

4. While members of most of the southern African tribal groups have migrated to work on the gold mines, workers from Southern Mozambique have a history of migration that predates gold mining. These Mozambicans have mostly but not exclusively been Tsonga-speaking and are known on the mines as "Shangaans." The general location of the Tsonga group straddles the border between Mozambique so that "Shangaans" may also come from

the northeastern Transvaal. Other important mine migrants have included Xhosa-speakers from Transkei and Ciskei, including Mpondo from the northern Transkei, Sotho-speakers from Lesotho, and "Tropicals" from central Africa.

5. For understanding this paper, it will help the reader to know that there are two lines of black authority on the mines. The first, which deals with domestic life and recreation in the compounds, is headed by the white compound manager. The senior black compound officials were called *indunas* (usually one for each ethnic group). They control the mine "police boys" (now called "tribal representatives"). *Isibondas* are elected from representatives (one or two to a room). The second line of black supervision operates underground. Here the senior black worker is the "boss-boy" (now called "team leader"). In the past the team was largely made up of shovellers ("*layisha* boys"). Historically "machine-boys" or "drillers" were somewhat independent of the control of the boss-boy, although this has changed in the past fifteen years. The boss-boy falls under the formal authority of the white miner, the lowest level white underground worker. This man is traditionally assisted by a black personal assistant underground called a *picannin*. For an account of the authority structure on a gold mine in the seventies, see T. D. Moodie, "Formal and Informal Power Structures on a South African Gold Mine," *Human Relations* (August 1980), vol. 33, no. 8.

6. It is significant that official enquiries into "unnatural vice" took place at the insistence of missionaries working on and around the compounds and not at the request of management who turned a blind eye to such affairs.

7. Taberer Report, 1907, Chamber of Mines, 1899–1910, N series, N35. I am indebted to Charles van Onselen for a copy of this document.

8. Philip and Iona Mayer, "Socialization by Peers: The Youth Organization of the Red Xhosa" in Philip Mayer, ed., *Socialization* (London, 1970).

9. Taberer Report, 1907.

10. Transvaal Archives, files of the Government Native Labour Bureau (henceforth NLB), 229, 583/15/145, 16/2/16, Replies to Circular from Director of Native Labor on Unnatural Vice.

11. NLB 374, 110/28/110, TTGC 1928 Session, 4/5/28.

12. Transvaal Archives, files of the Department of Native Affairs (henceforth NTS), 2091, 213/280, 30/11/28.

13. Many workers mentioned this as a fact, although several later described relationships with town women. Apparently the truth of the matter was that management discouraged forays into town but could not actually legally forbid them. As a result, novices tended to obey the informal advice given them at initiation whereas more experienced men were liable to ignore it.

14. According to Philemon, amongst the Tsonga (Shangaans, Mozambicans) "mine marriages" were accepted, indeed taken for granted by women (including wives) and elders at home, and relationships might extend beyond a single contract ("when the time to go back arrived, one partner would inform the other through a letter so that they could [meet] at a stipulated place . . . on the mines").

15. The evidence here is from the reports of theological students who kept journals while working on the mines under the auspices of the Agency for Industrial Mission (henceforth AIM) in the winter of 1976. Copies of these materials are housed with SALDRU at the University of Cape Town.

16. H. A. Junod, *The Life of a South African Tribe* (New York, 1966) 1: 294.

17. See Philip Mayer, *Wives of Migrant Miners*, vol. 3 of *Migrant*

Labor: Some Perspectives from Anthropology (Grahamstown, 1978), pp. 116–26; also, Monica Hunter, *Reaction to Conquest* (London, 1961), pp. 203–10.

18. 1976 Welkom mine study, Induna interview, 27/7/76; copies of this material are in my possession; originals are held by Anglo-American Corporation.

19. AIM, 1976 Theologians Group Report; Mines No. 1.

20. 1976 Welkom Mine Study, Tsebe statement, 6/7/76.

21. According to the Tsonga informant, young men were paid very generously in kind. The Mpondo reported payments in cash. There are other differences between the information from members of the two groups which probably reflect genuine differences in practices.

22. Taberer Report, 1907, p. 2.

23. Mayer, "Socialization by Peers," p. 16.

24. Junod, *Life of a South African Tribe*, pp. 492–93.

25. For a tentative discussion of the origins of this name see Charles van Onselen, *Studies in the Social and Economic History of the Witwatersrand, vol. 2: New Nineveh* (London, 1982), pp. 179–89.

26. Mayer, *Wives of Migrant Workers*, pp. 27–31; see also Monica Hunter, *Reaction to Conquest*, pp. 186–90 and 531, where it is reported that in Pondoland *thwala* marriages were arranged with the woman's consent. Both Sean Redding and Malusi Mpumlwana have pointed out to me that the latter pattern may be more typical in the Transkei also, although Mpumlwana knows from personal experience of cases similar to those described by Mayer.

27. For an account of the importance of homestead agriculture for Tswana traditionalists, see Hoyt Alverson, *Mind in the Heart of Darkness* (New Haven, 1980).

28. For an account of "town women" and their relationships with migrant miners see the more complete article in from which this is excerpted.

29. For a graphic account of such urban gangs with a strong "homosexual" component in the early years on the Rand, see van Onselen, *New Nineveh*, chapter 4; William Beinart's biographical essay on "M'" touches on both mine and gang "homosexuality" during the 1930s (in Shula Marks and Stanley Trapido, *The Politics of Race, Class and Nationalism* [London, 1987]).

30. For a discussion of management hegemony and worker resistance on the gold mines in a specific historical context see Moodie, "The Moral Economy of the Black Miners' Strike of 1946," *JSAS*, October 1985.

31. van Onselen, *Chibaro* (Johannesburg, 1980), pp. 174–82.

32. NLB 229, 585/15/145, 16/2/16.

33. NTS 7675, 102/332, 20/10/41.

34. Hermann Giliomee and Lawrence Schlemmer, *Up Against the Fences* (New York, 1985), chaps. 10–12.

35. See Alan Jeeves and David Yudelman, "New Labor Frontiers for Old: Black Migrants to the South African Gold Mines, 1920–85," *JSAS* 13 (1986).

36. The reader should be warned that the historical argument here is an oversimplified sketch of complicated processes still under way in South Africa. More detail may be found in the original article, which is itself rather tentative about these sweeping generalizations.

37. See Foucault, *The Use of Pleasure*, vol. 2, part IV.

Davis and Kennedy, "Oral History and the Study of Sexuality in the Lesbian Community"

1. This research is part of the work of the Buffalo Women's Oral History Project, which was founded in 1978 with three goals: (1) to produce a comprehensive, written history of the lesbian community in Buffalo, New York, using as the major source oral histories of lesbians who came out prior to 1970; (2) to create and index an archive of oral history tapes, written interviews, and relevant supplementary materials; and (3) to give this history back to the community from which it derives. Madeline Davis and Elizabeth (Liz) Kennedy are the directors of the project. Avra Michelson was an active member from 1978 to 1981 and had a very important influence on the development of the project. Wanda Edwards has been an active member of the project since 1981, particularly in regard to research on the black lesbian community and on racism in the white lesbian community.

2. This hypothesis was shaped by our personal contact with Buffalo lesbians who came out in the 1940s and 1950s, and by discussion with grass-roots gay and lesbian history projects around the country, in particular, the San Francisco Lesbian and Gay History Project, the Boston Area Gay and Lesbian History Project, and the Lesbian Herstory Archives. Our approach is close to and has been influenced by the social constructionist tendency of lesbian and gay history. See in particular, Jonathan Katz, *Gay American History, Lesbians and Gay Men in the U.S.A.* (New York: Thomas Y. Crowell, 1976); Gayle Rubin, Introduction to *A Woman Appeared to Me* by Renée Vivien (Reno, Nevada: Naiad Press, 1976), iii–xxxvii; Jeffrey Weeks, *Coming Out: Homosexual Politics in Britain from the Nineteenth Century to the Present* (London: Quartet Books, 1977). We want to thank all these sources which have been inspirational to our work.

3. The Buffalo Women's Oral History Project has written two papers on bar life, both by Madeline Davis, Elizabeth (Liz) Kennedy, and Avra Michelson: "Buffalo Lesbian Bars in the Fifties," presented at the National Women's Studies Association, Bloomington, Indiana, May 1980, and "Buffalo Lesbian Bars: 1930–1960," presented at the Fifth Berkshire Conference on the History of Women, Vassar College, Poughkeepsie, N.Y., June 1981. Both papers are on file at the Lesbian Herstory Archives, P.O. Box 1258, New York, New York 10116.

4. We think that this community could accurately be designated as a working-class lesbian community, but this is not a concept many members of this community would use; therefore, we have decided to call it a public bar community.

5. All quotes are taken from the interviews conducted for this project between 1978 and 1984. The use of the phrase "lesbian and her girl" in this quote reflects some of our butch narrators' belief that the butch member of a couple was the lesbian and the fem member's identity was less clear.

6. A variety of sources were helpful for learning about issues and problems of oral history research. They include the Special Issue on Women's Oral History, *Frontiers 2* (Summer 1977); Willa K. Baum, *Oral History for the Local Historical Society* (Nashville, Tenn.: American Association for State and Local History, 1974); Michael Frisch, "Oral History and *Hard Times:* A Review Essay," *Oral History Review* (1979): 70–80; Ronald Grele, ed., *Envelopes of Sound: Six Practitioners Discuss the Method, Theory, and Practice of Oral History and Oral Tradition* (Chicago: Precedent Publishing,

1975); Ronald Grele, "Can Anyone over Thirty Be Trusted: A Friendly Critique of Oral History," *Oral History Review* (1978): 36–44; "Generations: Women in the South," *Southern Exposure* 4 (Winter 1977); "No More Moanin'," *Southern Exposure* 1 (Winter 1974); Peter Friedlander, *The Emergence of a UAW Local, 1936–1939* (Pittsburgh: University of Pittsburgh Press, 1975); William Lynwood Montell, *The Saga of Coe Ridge: A Study in Oral History* (Knoxville: University of Tennessee Press, 1970); Studs Terkel, *Hard Times: An Oral History of the Great Depression* (New York: Pantheon Books, 1970); Martin B. Duberman, *Black Mountain: An Exploration in Community* (Garden City, N.Y.: Doubleday, 1972); Sherna Gluck, ed., *From Parlor to Prison: Five American Suffragists Talk about Their Lives* (New York: Vintage, 1976); and Kathy Kahn, *Hillbilly Women* (New York: Doubleday, 1972).

7. For a helpful discussion of memory, see John A. Neuenschwander, "Remembrance of Things Past: Oral Historians and Long-Term Memory," *Oral History Review* (1978): 46–53; many sources cited in the previous note also have relevant discussions of memory; in particular, see Frisch, "Oral History and *Hard Times*," Grele, *Envelopes of Sound*; Friedlander, *Emergence of a Local*, and Montell, *Saga of Coe Ridge*.

8. See for instance, Joan Nestle, "Esther's Story: 1960," *Common Lives/Lesbian Lives* 1 (Fall 1981): 5–9; Nestle, "Butch-Fem Relationships, Sexual Courage in the 1950s," *Heresies* 12 (1981): 21–24; Audre Lorde, "Tar Beach," *Conditions*, no. 5 (1979): 34–47; and Lorde, "The Beginning," in *Lesbian Fiction*, ed. Elly Bulkin (Watertown, Mass.: Persephone Press, 1981), 255–74. Lesbian pulp fiction can also provide insight into the emotional and sexual life of this period; see for instance, Ann Bannon's *I Am a Woman* (Greenwich, Conn.: Fawcett Publications, 1959) and *Beebo Brinker* (Greenwich, Conn.: Fawcett Publications, 1962).

9. See, for instance, Nestle, "Butch-Fem Relationships"; Lorde, "Tar Beach"; Del Martin and Phyllis Lyon, *Lesbian/Woman* (New York: Bantam Books, 1972): John D'Emilio, *Sexual Politics, Sexual Communities: The Making of a Homosexual Minority in the United States, 1940–1970* (Chicago: University of Chicago Press, 1983).

10. For a full discussion of our research on butch-fem roles, see Madeline Davis and Elizabeth (Liz) Kennedy, "Butch-Fem Roles in the Buffalo Lesbian Community, 1940–1960" (paper presented at the Gay Academic Union Conference, Chicago, October 1982). This paper is on file at the Lesbian Herstory Archives.

11. These two main determinants of roles are quite different from what would usually be considered as indicators of sex roles in straight society; they do not include the sexual division of labor.

12. The origins of the "stone butch" and fem couple are beyond the scope of this paper. For an article that begins to approach these issues, see Esther Newton, "The Mythic Mannish Lesbian: Radclyffe Hall and the New Woman," *Signs* 9 (Summer 1984): 557–75, reprinted in this volume.

13. Our understanding of the fem role has been enhanced by the following: Nestle's "Butch-Fem Relationships" and "Esther's Story"; Amber Hollibaugh and Cherrie Moraga, "What We're Rolling Around in Bed With: Sexual Silences in Feminism: A Conversation Toward Ending Them," *Heresies* 12 (1981): 58–62.

14. For indications that "ki-ki" was used nationally in the lesbian subculture, see Jonathan Katz, *Gay/Lesbian Almanac, A New Documentary* (New York: Harper & Row, 1983), pp. 15, 626.

15. Alfred C. Kinsey, Wardell B. Pomeroy, and Clyde E. Martin, *Sexual Behavior in the Human Male* (Philadelphia: W. B. Saunders, 1948);

and Alfred Kinsey et al., *Sexual Behavior in the Human Female* (Philadelphia: W. B. Saunders, 1953). Numerous sources document this trend; see, for instance, Ann Snitow, Christine Stansell, and Sharon Thompson, eds., *Powers of Desire: The Politics of Sexuality* (New York: Monthly Review Press, 1983), in particular, Introduction, sec. 2, "Sexual Revolutions," and sec. 3. "The Institution of Heterosexuality," pp. 9–47, 115–71, 173–275; and Katz, *Gay/Lesbian Almanac*.

16. See Mary P. Ryan, *Womanhood in America: From Colonial Times to the Present* (New York: Franklin Watts, 1975).

17. A logical result of the social constructionist school of gay history is to consider that heterosexuality is also a social construction. Katz, in *Gay/Lesbian Almanac*, begins to explore this idea.

18. Although national homophile organizations began in the fifties, no such organizations developed in Buffalo until the formation of the Mattachine Society of the Niagara Frontier in 1969. But we do not think that the lack of early homophile organizations in this city made the bar community's use of roles as an organizer of its stance toward the straight world different from that of cities where homophile organizations existed. In general, these organizations, whether mixed or all women, did not draw from or affect bar communities. Martin and Lyon in chap. 8, "Lesbians United," *Lesbian/Woman* [237–79], present Daughters of Bilitis [DOB] as an alternative for those dissatisfied with bar life, not as an organization to coalesce the forces and strengths of the bar community. Gay liberation combined the political organization of DOB and the defiance and pride of bar life and therefore affected and involved both communities.

Arguelles and Rich, "Homosexuality, Homophobia, and Revolution"

1. Note that the term "homosexual" and not "gay" is used when describing prerevolutionary Cuban society. Both words are used, along with "lesbian," in the discussion of Cuba after 1959. Whether the term "gay" should be applied at all to the style of homosexuality and homosexual identities common in Cuba is arguable, while the term "lesbian" seems less politically specific and hence applicable to different historical periods. But differentiation among these terms is necessarily imprecise, due to the lack of theoretical work on cross-cultural usage.

2. See, e.g., stories on the "gay" Mariel migration in the *Washington Post*, July 7, 1980; *Oakland Tribune*, August 3, 1980; and the *Advocate* August 21, 1980.

3. See, e.g., Allen Young, *Gays under the Cuban Revolution* (San Francisco: Grey Fox Press, 1981); Dennis Altman, *The Homosexualization of America, the Americanization of the Homosexual* (New York: St. Martin's Press, 1982).

4. See articles on Cuban gay migration in the *Boston Gay Community News*, October 25, 1980; and the *Advocate*, August 21, 1980.

5. For a discussion on the problems of bourgeois interpretations of "refugee" testimony, see Geoffrey Fox, *Working Class Emigrés from Cuba* (Palo Alto, Calif.: R & E Associates, 1970), pp. 11–21.

6. For more information on research method, see Lourdes Arguelles, "The Gay Issue in Cuban and Cuban-American Studies" (paper presented at the Cuban American Studies Conference, Massachusetts Institute of Technology, Cambridge, May 27, 1984).

7. Juan y Verena Martinez Alier, *Cuba: Economia y sociedad* (Paris: Ruedo Iberico, 1972), esp. pp. 26–57.

8. See Fernando Ortiz, *Los Negros Esclavos* (Havana: Revista Bimestre Cubana, 1916); Wyatt MacGaffey and Clifford R. Barnett, *Twentieth-Century Cuba: The Background of the Castro Revolution* (New York: Doubleday, 1965), p. 62.

9. For an analysis of the role of honor and shame in small villages, see J. G. Peristany, "Introduction," in *Honour and Shame: The Values of Mediterranean Society*, ed. J. G. Peristany (London: Penguin Books, 1965). See also M. T. Mulhare, "Sexual Ideology in Pre-Castro Cuba" (Ph.D. dissertation, University of Pittsburgh, 1969).

10. Personal interview, Miami, June 23, 1982.

11. Fulgencio Batista was the Cuban dictator who assumed power officially for the second time through a military coup on March 10, 1952, and ruled until his overthrow in 1959.

12. The best portraits of fifties Havana are found in the less inhibited guidebooks. See A. Roberts, *Havana: Portrait of a City* (New York: Coward-McCann, 1953).

13. Key informant interviews, Havana and Miami, 1982. See also articles in *Bohemia* and *Carteles* magazines, 1957–1959.

14. Key informant interviews, Havana, November 14, 1981. For details on the 1939 Cuban Penal Code's specifying of prison sentences for homosexual behavior, see José A. Martinez, *Codigo de defensa social* (Havana: Jesus Montero, 1939), esp. articles 384–85.

15. Guillermo Cabrera Infante, *La Habana para un infante difunto* (Barcelona: Seix Barral, 1981), p. 621; our translation.

16. On modern gay identities, see John D'Emilio, "Capitalism and Gay Identity," in *Powers of Desire: The Politics of Sexuality*, ed. Ann Snitow, Christine Stansell, and Sharon Thompson (New York: Monthly Review Press, 1983), esp. p. 104.

17. Florida Legislative Investigation Committee, *Homosexuality and Citizenship in Florida* (Tallahassee: Florida State Legislature, 1964).

18. See Anthony Summers, *Conspiracy* (Paris: Gallancz, 1980), esp. pp. 349–52; Warren Hinckle and William Turner, *The Fish Is Red: The Story of the Secret War against Castro* (New York: Harper & Row, 1981), esp. pp. 191–92. Cubela was apparently distraught because he felt that his homosexuality had precluded his receiving a high-level post in the revolutionary government; his thoughts of this period were obtained through interviews with his friends, Madrid, August 1980.

19. For a historical chronology of CIA anti-Cuba campaigns, see Lourdes Arguelles, "The U.S. National Security State: The CIA and Cuban Emigré Terrorism," *Race and Class* 23, no. 4 (Spring 1982): 287–304.

20. See Richard Fagen, "Mass Mobilization in Cuba: The Symbolism of the Struggle," *Journal of International Affairs*, 20, no. 2 (1966): 254–71. By 1963, there were already 102,500 Committees for the Defense of the Revolution, with a membership of 1.5 million; it was later calculated that one out of every two adults in Cuba actively participated in a CDR.

21. See, e.g., Carlos Rafael Rodriguez, *La revolucion rusa y sus consecuencias* (Havana: Fundamentos, 1955), and *Lo que es esencial en las diferencias entre capitalismo y comunismo* (Havana: Fundamentos, 1956).

22. Key informant interviews, Havana, July 1982. See Lisandro Otero, "Para una definicion mejor de Jose Lezama Lima," *Boletin del Circulo de cultura Cubana* (New York; August 9, 1983).

23. For a thorough discussion of the camps, the critical literature on

them, and persecution of homosexuals in this period, see Jorge Dominguez, *Cuba: Order and Revolution* (Cambridge, Mass.: Belknap Press, 1978), esp. pp. 357, 393.

24. Armando Fluvia, "La represion legal," in *El Homosexual ante la sociedad enferma*, ed. Jose R. Enriquez (Barcelona: Tusquets, 1978), pp. 72–93.

25. For an account of lesbian life in this period, see Barbara Coro, "A Cuban Lesbian's Story," *Chicago Gay Life* (March 13, 1981), pp. 17–19.

26. Proceedings of the First National Congress on Education and Culture (Havana, 1972). For documents on the conference, the aftermath, and the relevance of the well-known Heberto Padilla case to issues of homosexuality and intellectual formalism, see Lourdes Casal, *El caso Padilla—literatura y revolucion en Cuba: Documentos* (New York: Ediciones Nueva Atlantida, 1971), and "Homosexuality in Cuba," *Jump Cut: A Review of Contemporary Cinema* 19 (December 1978): 38–39.

27. Personal interview, Havana, August 16, 1981.

28. See *Granma Review*, English ed. (March 3, 1975), pp. 3–5; also Margaret Randall, "La mujer cubana en 1974," *Casa* 15 (March–April 1975); 67–75.

29. Personal interview with Monika Krause, Havana, October 13, 1983.

30. Personal interview, Pinar del Rio, Cuba, July 1, 1982.

31. Codigo Penal de la Republica de Cuba, Havana, March 1, 1979, esp. articles 354, 359, 367.

32. Carlos Alberto Montaner, *Informes secretas sobre la revolucion cubana* (Madrid: Playor, 1978).

33. See "The Refugee Dilemma," a special issue of *In These Times*, vol. 4, no. 28 (June 18–July 1, 1980), esp. Lee Aitken and Pat Aufderheide, "The Anti-Castro Welcome Wagon," pp. 6–8.

34. Key informant interviews, Miami-Havana, June 1982. Denials taken from a personal interview with Dr. J. Vega Vega, vice-president of the Cuban National Association of Jurists, Havana, October 13, 1983.

35. Personal interview, New York, 1983.

36. See B. Ruby Rich, "The Aesthetics of Self-Determination" (paper presented at the Fifth International Film Festival of Latin American Cinema, ICAIC, Havana, 1983). Information drawn from author's meetings with ICAIC, August and December, 1983.

37. See the report in *Cuba Update* 8, nos. 5–6 (Winter 1987): 10. Published by the Center for Cuban Studies, New York City.

38. This was the first of a two-part article. Part 2 appeared in *Signs: Journal of Women in Culture and Society* 11, no. 1 (1985): 120–36. Part 2 focuses on gay and lesbian life in the Cuban enclaves of the United States and on the ways in which the American state and anti-Castro groups have used the Cuban gay issue to manipulate sentiment, often in contradictory directions. Readers interested in pursuing our discussion here are referred to this continuation.

39. *Entendido* is the Cuban subcultural term for "gay."

D'Emilio, "Gay Politics and Community in San Francisco"

1. Jeffrey Weeks, *Coming Out: Homosexual Politics in Britain from the Nineteenth Century to the Present* (London, 1977), pp. 2–3.

2. The best treatment of colonial America is Jonathan Ned Katz, *Gay/Lesbian Almanac* (New York, 1983), pp. 23–133.

3. See D'Emilio, "Capitalism and Gay Identity," in Ann Snitow, Christine Stansell, and Sharon Thompson, eds., *Powers of Desire: The Politics of Sexuality* (New York, 1983), pp. 100–13; and Eli Zaretsky, *Capitalism, the Family and Personal Life* (New York, 1976).

4. On the medical model and the changing social expression of homosexuality see Katz, *Gay/Lesbian Almanac*, pp. 173–74, and *Gay American History* (New York, 1976), pp. 129–207; George Chauncey, Jr., "From Sexual Inversion to Homosexuality: Medicine and the Changing Conceptualization of Female Deviance," *Salmagundi*, no. 58/59 (Fall 1982/Winter 1983): 114–146; and Lillian Faderman, *Surpassing the Love of Men* (New York, 1981).

5. For a sense of the varieties of gay and lesbian experience see Eric Garber, "A Spectacle in Color: The Lesbian and Gay Subculture of Jazz Age Harlem" (in this volume); George Chauncey, Jr., "Christian Brotherhood or Sexual Perversion?: Homosexual Identities and the Construction of Sexual Boundaries in the World War I Era" (in this volume); and Faderman, *Surpassing the Love of Men*.

6. Much of the evidence and the argument about postwar San Francisco's gay community and its politics is taken from D'Emilio, *Sexual Politics, Sexual Communities: The Making of a Homosexual Minority in the United States, 1940–1970* (Chicago, 1983).

7. *Ibid.*, pp. 23–29; Allan Bérubé, "Marching to a Different Drummer: Lesbian and Gay GIs in World War II" (in this volume); and "Coming Out Under Fire," *Mother Jones*, February–March 1983, pp. 23–29, 45.

8. D'Emilio, *Sexual Politics, Sexual Communities*, pp. 40–53; Allan Bérubé and John D'Emilio, "The Military and Lesbians During the McCarthy Years," *Signs* 9 (1986); 759–75; D'Emilio, "The Homosexual Menace: The Politics of Sexuality in Cold War America," in Kathy Peiss and Christina Simmons, eds., *Passion and Power* (Philadelphia, 1989); Katz, *Gay American History*, pp. 91–108.

9. See the interview with Pat Bond in Nancy and Casey Adair, *Word Is Out* (San Francisco, 1978), pp. 55–65; D'Emilio, *Sexual Politics, Sexual Communities*, pp. 182–85.

10. D'Emilio, *Sexual Politics, Sexual Communities*, pp. 57–107; Del Martin and Phyllis Lyon, *Lesbian/Woman* (San Francisco, 1972).

11. D'Emilio, *Sexual Politics, Sexual Communities*, pp. 108–125. The political perspective of the homophile movement in the 1950s can be gleaned from a reading of its three periodicals: *Mattachine Review*, *The Ladder*, and *ONE*.

12. The discussion of events in San Francisco in the 1960s is drawn from D'Emilio, *Sexual Politics, Sexual Communities*, pp. 176–95.

13. *Look*, August 19, 1958, pp. 64ff. On the Beats see Bruce Cook, *The Beat Generation* (New York, 1971); John Tytell, *Naked Angels* (New York, 1976); and Dennis McNally, *Desolate Angel: Jack Kerouac, the Beat Generation, and America* (New York, 1979).

14. On the election controversy, see the San Francisco *Progress*, October 7, 1959, where the original charges were made, and the *News-Call-Bulletin*, the *Examiner*, and the *Chronicle*, October 9, 1959, and the days following.

15. The gayola scandal received extensive coverage in San Francisco's newspapers from May through August 1960.

16. D'Emilio, *Sexual Politics, Sexual Communities*, pp. 183–85.

17. *Allen Ginsberg: Gay Sunshine Interview with Allen Young* (Bolinas, Ca., 1974), pp. 11–12; *Stoumen* v. *Reilly*, 234 P. 2d 969.

18. Nancy and Casey Adair, *Word Is Out*, pp. 73–74.

19. "Gay Life in the 1950s: Interview with José Sarria," KPFA-FM, Berkeley, Ca., March 14, 1979.

20. D'Emilio, *Sexual Politics, Sexual Communities*, pp. 188–95.

21. On gay liberation see Dennis Altman, *Homosexual Oppression and Liberation* (New York, 1972); Toby Marotta, *The Politics of Homosexuality* (Boston, 1981); Donn Teal, *The Gay Militants* (New York, 1971); Karla Jay and Allen Young, eds., *Out of the Closets: Voices of Gay Liberation* (New York, 1972); and Laud Humphreys, *Out of the Closets* (Englewood Cliffs, N.J., 1972).

22. On lesbian-feminism see Jay and Young, *Out of the Closets*, especially pp. 172–203; Sidney Abbott and Barbara Love, *Sappho Was a Right-On Woman* (New York, 1972); Nancy Myron and Charlotte Bunch, eds., *Lesbianism and the Women's Movement* (Baltimore, 1975); and Jill Johnston, *Lesbian Nation* (New York, 1973).

23. On San Francisco in the 1970s see, especially, Randy Shilts, *The Mayor of Castro Street* (New York, 1982); and Frances FitzGerald, *Cities on a Hill* (New York, 1987).

24. See Shilts, *The Mayor of Castro Street*; and Amber Hollibaugh, "Sexuality and the State," *Socialist Review*, no. 45 (May-June 1979): 55–72.

25. The discussion of events surrounding the trial and the verdict is taken from personal observation, conversations, and a reading of San Francisco papers during a long stay in San Francisco in 1979.

26. The literature on AIDS is already immense but see, especially, Dennis Altman, *AIDS in the Mind of America* (Garden City, N.Y., 1986); Cindy Patton, *Sex and Germs* (Boston, 1985); and Randy Shilts, *And the Band Played On* (New York, 1987).

NOTES ON CONTRIBUTORS

◆

Paula Gunn Allen (Laguna Pueblo-Sioux-Scottish-American and Lebanese-American) is Professor of Ethnic Studies/Native American Studies at the University of California, Berkeley. She has held fellowships from the National Research Council, Ford Foundation, the Institute of American Cultures at U.C.L.A., and the National Endowment for the Arts. She is the author of six books of poetry, a novel, *The Woman Who Owned the Shadows* (Spinsters Ink, 1983), and a collection of essays, *The Sacred Hoop: Recovering the Feminine in Native American Traditions* (1986), and the editor of *Studies in American Indian Literature* (1983). She currently lives in the Bay Area with her son.

Lourdes Arguelles was born in Cuba and educated in the United States and Europe, receiving her Ph.D. from New York University. She is currently Senior Lecturer in Human Development and Crosscultural Women's Studies at the School of Social Welfare at the University of California, Los Angeles, as well as a psychotherapist in private practice. She is also active as a research and training consultant in AIDS prevention education in Southern California. Her work has appeared in major academic and popular journals around the world.

Shari Benstock is Professor of English at the University of Miami. She is author of *Women of the Left Bank: Paris 1900–1940*, a feminist literary history of women's contributions to Modernism, and co-author of the forthcoming two-volume study, *Modernism Made Manifest*, which examines the role of journals, reviews, and little magazines in establishing Modernist political ideologies in America, England, and France between 1890 and 1940. She is also editor of *Feminist Issues in Literary Scholarship* and *The Private Self: Theory and Practice in Women's Autobiographical Writings*.

Allan Bérubé is a founding member of the San Francisco Lesbian and Gay History Project. He is the author of *Coming Out Under Fire: Lesbian and Gay Americans and the Military During World War II* (Free Press, 1989).

John Boswell is Professor of History at Yale University. He is best known for his book *Christianity, Social Tolerance and Homosexuality: Gay People in Western Europe from the Beginning of the Christian Era to the Fourteenth Century* (University of Chicago Press, 1980); his most recent book is *The Kindness of Strangers: The Abandonment of Children in Western Europe from Late Antiquity to the Renaissance* (Pantheon, 1989).

Judith C. Brown is Associate Professor of History at Stanford University. She is the author of *Immodest Acts: The Life of a Lesbian Nun in Renaissance Italy* (Oxford University Press, 1986) and "A Woman's Place

576

Was in the Home: Women's Work in Renaissance Tuscany," in *The Discourses of Sexual Difference in Early Modern Europe*, M. Ferguson et al., eds. (University of Chicago Press, 1986).

George Chauncey, Jr., did his graduate work at Yale University and is now a post-doctoral fellow at the Center for Historical Analysis at Rutgers University. His articles on the history of gender and sexuality have appeared in *Salmagundi*, the *Journal of Social History*, the *Village Voice*, and several anthologies. He is currently finishing a book, *Gay New York: A Social and Cultural History of Male Homosexuality in New York City, 1890–1970*, to be published by Pantheon.

Madeline Davis is the chief conservator for the Buffalo and Erie County Public Library System and a cofounder of the Buffalo Women's Oral History Project. Since 1970 she has been active in the gay liberation and lesbian feminist movements. She is also a singer/songwriter and has produced a tape of lesbian feminist music, *Daughter of All Women* (1982). She is currently working on a book, *Boots of Leather, Slippers of Gold: The History of a Lesbian Community*, with Elizabeth Kennedy.

John D'Emilio is Associate Professor of History at the University of North Carolina at Greensboro. He is the author of *Sexual Politics, Sexual Communities: The Making of a Homosexual Minority in the United States* (1983) and, with Estelle Freedman, *Intimate Matters: A History of Sexuality in America* (1988).

Martin Bauml Duberman is Distinguished Professor of History at Lehman College, The City University of New York. He is the author of eleven books and the recipient of The Bancroft Prize (*Charles Francis Adams, 1807–1886*), the Vernon Rice/Drama Desk Award (*In White America*), a special prize from the National Academy of Arts and Letters for his "contributions to literature," was a Finalist for the National Book Award (*James Russell Lowell*), and in 1988 won the Manhattan Borough President's Gold Medal in Literature. His latest book is a biography of Paul Robeson (Knopf, 1989). Duberman was one of the founders of the Gay Academic Union and the newly inaugurated Center for Lesbian and Gay Studies at CUNY, and was on the originating Boards of the National Gay Task Force and Lambda Legal Defense.

Eric Garber is a founding member of the San Francisco Lesbian and Gay History Project. He is the co-author of *Uranian Worlds: A Reader's Guide to Alternative Sexuality in Science Fiction and Fantasy* (1983), the co-editor of *Worlds Apart: An Anthology of Lesbian and Gay Science Fiction and Fantasy* (1986), and has written for *The Advocate, Outlook*, and the *Dictionary of Literary Biography*. He has presented his slide show about gay life in Jazz Age Harlem, "T'Ain't Nobody's Bizness," to audiences across the country and is currently working on a book-length study of the subject.

Erwin J. Haeberle, Ph.D., Ed.D., is Director of the Department of Information and Dokumentation at the AIDS-Zentrum, Federal Health Office, Berlin (West), Director of Historical Research at the Institute for Advanced Study of Human Sexuality, San Francisco, President of the German Society for Social Scientific Research, Head of the AIDS Task Force of the World Association of Sexology, and a member of the International Academy of Sex Research. He has been a research fellow at Yale University, the University of California, Berkeley, and the Kinsey Institute. He is author of *The Sex Atlas* (New York, 1978) and of an exhibition (with accompanying booklet), *The Birth of Sexology, 1908–1933*, shown in Washington, D.C., Hamburg, Copenhagen, and several other European cities.

David M. Halperin is Professor of Literature at the Massachusetts Institute of Technology and has been a Fellow of the American Academy in Rome, the National Humanities Center, and the Stanford Humanities Center. He has written articles on Greek and Latin poetry, on Greek philosophy, and on Soviet literature; he is also the author of *Before Pastoral: Theocritus and the Ancient Tradition of Bucolic Poetry* (Yale University Press, 1983) and the co-editor (with John J. Winkler and Froma I. Zeitlin) of *Before Sexuality: The Construction of Erotic Experience in the Ancient Greek World* (Princeton University Press, 1989). He is currently preparing *One Hundred Years of Homosexuality and Other Essays on Greek Love* for Routledge and *The Metaphysics of Desire: Plato and the Origins of Erotic Theory in the West* for Yale University Press.

Arend H. Huussen, Jr., is Professor of History at the Rijksuniversiteit, Groningen, The Netherlands.

Simon Karlinsky teaches Russian literature and drama at the University of California, Berkeley. In earlier incarnations he was a musician, soldier, and conference interpreter. His books include *The Sexual Labyrinth of Nikolai Gogol, Russian Drama from Its Beginnings to the Age of Pushkin*, and *Marina Tsvetaeva: The Woman, Her World, and Her Poetry*.

Elizabeth (Liz) Kennedy is Associate Professor of American Studies/ Women's Studies at the State University of New York at Buffalo and a cofounder of the Buffalo Women's Oral History Project. She is an anthropologist by training, but since 1970 has actively worked to build a women's studies B.A. and M.A. program at SUNY/Buffalo and to further the field of women's studies. She is coauthor of *Feminist Scholarship: Kindling in the Groves of Academe* with Ellen DuBois et al. and is currently working on a book, *Boots of Leather, Slippers of Gold: The History of a Lesbian Community*, with Madeline Davis.

Robert K. Martin is Professor of English at Concordia University in Montreal. He is the author of *The Homosexual Tradition in American Poetry* and *Hero, Captain, and Stranger: Male Friendship, Social Critique, and Literary Form in the Sea Novels of Herman Melville*.

Dunbar Moodie is Professor of Sociology at Hobart and William Smith Colleges. His book, *The Rise of Afrikanerdom*, deals with the ideological origins of Afrikaner nationalism, and he is currently at work on a study of domination and resistance on the South African gold mines.

Esther Newton teaches women's studies and anthropology at the State University of New York, Purchase. She is the author of *Mother Camp: Female Impersonators in America* and is currently at work on a history of the Cherry Grove community on Fire Island.

Vivien W. Ng is Assistant Professor of History and Women's Studies at the University of Oklahoma. Her published works include "Ch'ing Laws Concerning the Insane: An Historical Survey" and "Ideology and Sexuality: Rape Laws in Qing China." She is currently working on a book-length study of sexuality in late imperial China.

Robert A. Padgug received his doctorate in classical history. He has been researching the history of sexuality, in particular in Greek antiquity, for a number of years. Currently employed in the health insurance industry, his recent interests have focused on social and economic aspects of the AIDS crisis.

B. Ruby Rich is a feminist critic who has written widely on issues of film and sexuality, with a special interest in Latin America. A frequent contributor to the *Village Voice*, she has also published in *Feminist Studies, Signs, American Film*, and other journals. She serves as Director of the Film Program at the New York State Council on the Arts.

Leila J. Rupp teaches women's history at Ohio State University. She is the author of *Mobilizing Women for War: German and American Propaganda, 1939–1945* and, with Verta Taylor, *Survival in the Doldrums: The American Women's Rights Movement, 1945 to the 1960s.* She is a member of the Board of Directors of central Ohio's Stonewall Union.

The San Francisco Lesbian and Gay History Project was formed in 1979 and produced the slide show from which the article in this volume is drawn. Allan Bérubé, Honey Lee Cottrell, Estelle Freedman, Amber Hollibaugh, and Liz Stevens contributed to the production.

James M. Saslow teaches art history at Queens College, City University of New York, and is Contributing Editor for Art of *The Advocate.* He is the author of *Ganymede in the Renaissance: Homosexuality in Art and Society* and a contributor to the anthology *Lavender Culture.*

Paul Gordon Schalow received his Ph.D. in Japanese literature from Harvard University in 1985 and presently teaches Japanese language and literature at Rutgers University. He is the translator of *The Great Mirror of Male Love* by Ihara Saikaku (Stanford University Press, 1989).

Carroll Smith-Rosenberg is a Professor in the Department of History and the Department of Psychiatry at the University of Pennsylvania. She is the author of *Religion and the Rise of the American City* (1971) and *Disorderly Conduct: Visions of Gender in Victorian America* (1985), as well as numerous essays and reviews on nineteenth-century women and sexuality, including the classic "The Female World of Love and Ritual."

James D. Steakley is Associate Professor of German at the University of Wisconsin, Madison. Author of *The Homosexual Emancipation Movement in Germany* (1975), he has conducted extensive research and taught on gay culture in everyday life in Berlin from 1700 to the present, with special attention to the Nazi era and the contemporary division into East and West. He is currently at work on an intellectual biography of Dr. Magnus Hirschfeld, the German-Jewish sexologist, psychiatrist, and homosexual emancipationist.

Randolph Trumbach was trained at Johns Hopkins and is Professor of History, Baruch College, City University of New York. He is the author of *The Rise of the Egalitarian Family: Aristocratic Kinship and Domestic Relations in Eighteenth-Century England.* Since 1976 he has been at work on a new book, *Sex and the Gender Revolution: Reputation and Variance in Eighteenth-Century London;* the essay in this volume, and a number of others, are preliminary studies.

Martha Vicinus is Professor of English and Women's Studies at the University of Michigan, Ann Arbor. She is the author of *The Industrial Muse* (1974), *Independent Women: Work and Community for Single Women, 1850–1920* (1985), and essays on Victorian popular culture and nineteenth-century sexuality, as well as the editor of two anthologies on Victorian women. She was Editor of *Victorian Studies* (1969–81) and is currently an Editor of *Feminist Studies.*

Jeffrey Weeks has been preoccupied with the history, social organization, and politics of sexuality since the mid-1970s. He is the author of a number of books, including *Coming Out* (1977), *Sex, Politics, and Society* (1981), and *Sexuality and Its Discontents* (1985). He currently works as an academic administrator in London and is a visiting research fellow at the University of Southampton, England. He is also an Editor of *History Workshop Journal.*